Graphic Reproduction

Graphic
Reproduction

Dr. William P. Spence, Dean
School of Technology and Applied Science
Pittsburg State University
Pittsburg, Kansas

Dr. David G. Vequist, Chairman
Department of Printing
Pittsburg State University
Pittsburg, Kansas

Chas. A. Bennett Co., Inc.

Peoria, Illinois 61615

Copyright © 1980

**By William P. Spence and
David G. Vequist**

80 81 82 83 84   RM   5 4 3 2 1

ISBN 87002-285-7

Library of Congress Catalog Number 78-67627

Printed in the United States of America

PREFACE

This book has been designed to serve as a class text and reference book in graphic reproduction. It covers the basic processes currently in use in the industry. Emphasis has been placed on the new, evolving technology. The simple, basic techniques have also been included so that the book can be used for a beginning class. It contains sufficient technical depth and breadth that it can serve also as a text for advanced classes in graphic reproduction.

An important feature is the stress placed on how to perform the various tasks in the industry. These are described and fully illustrated. The supporting technical information is provided in as simple a manner as possible. For example, the theory of photography is explained. The explanation is supplemented with detailed instructions in line and halftone photography and developing film.

The principles behind the various types of offset plates are given. The steps to produce these plates are recorded. Detailed information on how to operate offset and letterpress equipment is included. Along with this are technical considerations which must be known for successful press operation. Since color printing is increasingly important, a great deal of material in this area is included.

Composition procedures are changing rapidly. The text carries the reader through from the simple hand-set type to the current technology of computers and scanners in composition.

The text thoroughly covers letterpress and offset printing and all the areas involved in each. In addition it includes planning, careers, and proofreading. Graphic design is covered, including the basic design techniques in common use.

Realizing that the bindery operations should be a first consideration in any printed job, the authors have included a chapter on bindery. It is sufficient to permit the reader to see the more common aspects of the bindery area.

Of concern to all segments of the printing industry is a knowledge of papers and inks. These have been covered in detail. A separate chapter is devoted to each.

Considerable effort has been expended to illustrate the text so that it is clear and easy to use. The use of a second color helps focus attention on important parts of an illustration. Some illustrations are in full color.

Special acknowledgment is made of the contributions of the following persons who helped with technical advice, did some of the writing, and were a constant resource as content for the book was developed.

Mr. Ray Boyer—Proofreading
Mr. David Butler—Screen Process Printing
Mr. Richard Jacques—Lithography
Mr. Dean Powell—Presswork
Mr. Robert Roberts—Composition
Mr. Paul Ryson—Composition, Platemaking, Copy Preparation, Color Separation

In addition, special thanks are given to the hundreds of firms that supply tools, materials, and services to the industry. Without their constant support, it would have been impossible to bring together the vast scope of technical material available in this text.

David G. Vequist
William P. Spence

TABLE OF CONTENTS

The Printing Industry

Graphic reproduction is the production of a visual message using words, illustrations, and photographs. The message could be anything from a set of blueprints for building a house to advertising materials. This book is a means of presenting a message. Whenever it is necessary to communicate an idea, graphic methods are very effective. A drawing or picture shows more than could be said with hundreds of words. Words and pictures combined can present an even clearer message.

Visual communication is one of the most widely used methods of relaying information. The graphic reproduction industry is one of the largest business activities in the world. There are very few commercial activities today that do not use graphic communication.

There are many methods of reproducing images. The methods can be grouped into two types—copying and printing. In *copying methods* the original material is exposed to photosensitive material. In this way one copy is made for each exposure. The major copying methods are by photography, stabilization process, microfilm, blueprints, diazo process, electrostatic duplication, and various office copying machines.

Printing methods reproduce copy by a mechanical system of transferring ink or dye to paper and other materials. The printing is not done directly from the original material as it is in copying methods. Printing requires the preparation of special image carriers from which the image is reproduced. The major printing processes are spirit duplication, mimeograph, offset, letterpress, gravure, and screen.

COPYING METHODS

Photography is a process that uses a light-sensitive film to record the image of some object. The film, a silver halide material, is exposed in a camera. The developed film becomes a negative copy of the object. The negative is used to produce positive copies, which are made by exposing the negative to photographic paper. This paper is developed, fixed, washed, and dried. Photographic copies of almost anything can be made. They can be enlarged or reduced, made in black and white or color.

How a photograph is made is shown in Fig. 1-1. The object to be photographed is a drinking glass. The lens of the camera focuses an image of the drinking glass onto the film. The film has a coating that reacts to light. When the light from the drinking glass passes through the lens and hits the film, a chemical change occurs that puts the image on the film. The film is developed to produce a *negative*. On the negative, the whites of the original object are black. The black areas are transparent (clear). Positive prints are made by directing a light through the negative onto a sheet of photo-

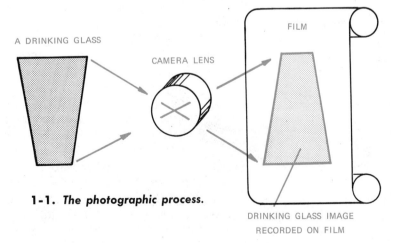

1-1. The photographic process.

A DRINKING GLASS

CAMERA LENS

FILM

DRINKING GLASS IMAGE
RECORDED ON FILM

11

graphic paper. The paper is developed, producing a black and white photograph.

Photography produces an image of high quality, but it is a slow process if many copies are needed. Therefore, it is not a good process to use for large volume production. Also, the cost per reproduction is high compared with other methods.

The *stabilization process* is a photographic process. The exposure of the stabilization paper is the same as in photography. After the exposure is made, the stabilization process has two steps—developing and fixing. These two steps take place in about ten seconds. Produced are stable-line, halftone or continuous-tone prints.

The machine for developing the image is shown in Fig. 1-2. All chemicals necessary for the development of the image are on the surface of the special stabilization paper. After exposure, the paper is run through the machine. An activator solution is applied to the surface of the paper. The silver halides on the paper are converted to metallic silver. The machine then applies a stabilizer solution. It dissolves the undeveloped halides, stops the development of the paper,

ITEK Corp.

1-3. *This is a microfilm reader-printer. The screen on the left shows an enlargement of the drawing that is on microfilm. If a copy is wanted, the machine on the right produces an enlarged image on paper.*

Fotorite, Inc.

1-2. *This machine develops the photographic image in the stabilization process.*

and fixes the print. These procedures are all carried out automatically in the stabilization processor.

Microfilm images are related to the photographic process. Microfilm is a negative image of graphic matter, such as a drawing, that has been greatly reduced. The film, exposed in a camera, is a light-sensitive silver halide material. The negative produced, called a microfilm, can be used to make multiple copies of the image. A microfilm reader-printer serves this purpose. Fig. 1-3. When the micro-

film is placed in the machine, it appears greatly enlarged on the screen. The machine can also make a paper copy of the image enlarged to the original size.

A *microfiche* is a 4″ × 6″ microfilm negative that can contain up to sixty 8 1/2″ × 11″ pages. Fig. 1-4. Each microfiche also contains information to identify its contents.

A microfiche is inexpensive to make and easy to store. Since each microfiche can contain up to sixty pages, thousands of pages of material can be stored in a small file drawer.

ED 037 543 REVIEW AND SYNTHESIS OF RESEARCH ON THE PLACEMENT AND FOLLOW-UP OF VOCATIONAL ED. STUDENTS. LITTLE, J. KENNETH. OHIO ST. UNIV., COLUMBUS. CTR. FOR VOC. AND TECH. ED. FEB. 70. 54P.

I OF I
ED
037543

END
DEPT OF HEALTH
EDUCATION AND
WELFARE
U.S. OFFICE OF
EDUCATION
ERIC
DATE FILMED
7 2 70

1-4. A microfiche. Each rectangle on the card is one 8 1/2″ × 11″ page of printed material.

Essential to the use of microfiche is a means of enlarging it so it can be read and copies can be printed. One such machine is shown in Fig. 1-5. This machine serves as a reader and printer. Small portable units are available for reading purposes.

Blueprints are used mainly to reproduce copies of engineering drawings. The original drawing is made on translucent paper in pencil or ink. It is placed on a sheet of blueprint paper and exposed to a light source. Fig. 1-6. Blueprint paper is coated with an iron salt and a developer. Exposure to light reduces the salts to a ferrous state, and when washed in water, they turn the paper blue. The areas under the lines of the drawing are not exposed to the light. When the paper is washed, the salts under the lines wash away. The white paper shows wherever a line appeared on the drawing. The blueprint is dried. The copy pro-

3M Company
1-5. A microfiche reader-printer. The unit produces an 8 1/2″ × 11″ black and white paper copy in 30 seconds. Heat is used to process the prints.

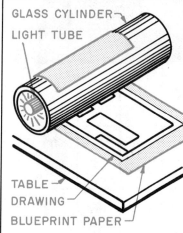

GLASS CYLINDER
LIGHT TUBE

TABLE
DRAWING
BLUEPRINT PAPER

STEP I
THE BLUEPRINT PAPER IS
EXPOSED WITH THE DRAW-
ING TO A LIGHT.

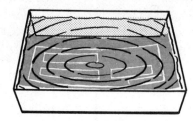

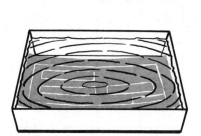

STEP 3
THE BLUEPRINT IS BATHED
IN A POTASSIUM BICHRO-
MATE SOLUTION.

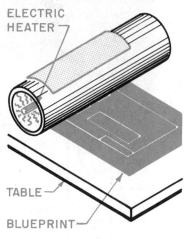

ELECTRIC
HEATER

TABLE
BLUEPRINT

STEP 5
THE BLUEPRINT IS DRIED.

STEP 4
THE BLUEPRINT IS RINSED
IN WATER.

1-6. How a blueprint is made.

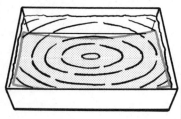

STEP 2
THE BLUEPRINT IS WASHED
IN WATER.

duced is the same size as the original drawing.

Blueprint machines perform all these operations automatically. Fig. 1-7. This process is finding less use because of the development of the diazo process.

The *diazo* process is much like the blueprint process. It uses an original copy on translucent paper. The original is placed on top of the diazo-coated sheet. Together they are exposed to a light source. Fig. 1-8. The diazo coating not protected from the light by the lines on the drawing is destroyed by the light. After the light exposure, the sheet is exposed to heated ammonia vapors. This causes the diazo coating that remains under the lines of the original drawing to turn blue. The finished copy has blue lines on a white background. The copy is the same size as the original. The entire copying process

1-7. A blueprint machine.

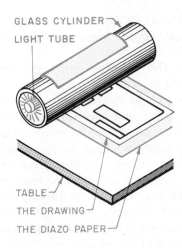

GLASS CYLINDER
LIGHT TUBE

TABLE
THE DRAWING
THE DIAZO PAPER

STEP 1
THE DIAZO PAPER IS EXPOSED
WITH THE DRAWING TO THE
LIGHT.

THE AMMONIA IS EVAPORATED
BY THE HEATER. VAPORS
GO THROUGH THE HOLES AND
DEVELOP THE PRINT.

THE DIAZO PRINT
PASSES OVER HOLES.

ELECTRIC
HEATER

AMMONIA RUNS IN PAN

STEP 2
THE PRINT IS DEVELOPED
WITH AMMONIA VAPORS.

1-8. How a dry diazo whiteprint is made.

1-9. A whiteprint machine.

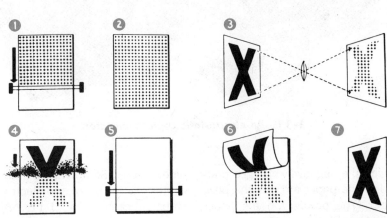

Xerox Corp.

1-10. How Xerography works. 1. Surface of selenium-coated plate is electrically charged as it passes under wires. 2. The coated plate is charged with positive electricity. 3. The sheet to be copied ("X") is projected through a lens. The plate is exposed to a light. The image projected remains on the plate as a positive electrical charge. The positive charge in the other areas is drained away by the light. The positive charge is shown by the "X" on the plate. The white area is where the positive charge has been drained away. 4. A negatively charged powder, called toner, is spread over the selenium-coated plate. It sticks to the positively charged image. 5. A sheet of paper placed over the plate receives a positive electrical charge. 6. The positively charged paper attracts the negatively charged powder on the plate, forming a direct positive image. 7. The paper is heated for a few seconds, fusing the powder to the paper. This forms a permanent print on the paper.

takes place in one machine. Fig. 1-9.

Diazo compounds are coated on paper, cloth, metal, and foil.

Electrostatic duplicating is a dry printing process. It uses no ink or pressure. It operates on elecrostatic principles. The steps in Xerography, shown in Fig. 1-10, are as follows:

A plate made of an electrically conductive material is used. It is coated with a photoconductive material. The plate is sprayed with electrons. It has a positive electrical charge. This plate is exposed to the material to be printed by a projection lens, much the same as exposing a standard photograph. Wherever the light hits the plate, the posi-tive electrostatic charge is lost. The material to be copied prevents the light from hitting the plate. This area remains charged. A powder is applied to the plate. It has a negative charge; therefore, it sticks to the positively charged area. The powder falls away from the area that lost the electrical charge.

The image on the plate is now transferred to the paper. The paper is given a positive charge. When it is placed over the plate

Xerox Corp.

1-11. *An electrostatic copier-duplicator.*

sheets are exposed to a source of light, producing a negative copy of the original.

The negative copy is next placed with the sensitive emulsion side next to the sensitive surface of a special copy paper. Copy paper has an emulsion of gelatin and silver sulfide or colloidal silver. Together they are developed. A chemical reaction takes place between the negative and the copy paper. This produces a black and white positive copy of the original material on the copy paper.

with the negatively charged powder, the paper attracts the powder. The powder on the paper forms a positive image. The paper is heated for a few seconds. This fuses the powder to the paper and gives a permanent copy. Some copiers use pressure to attach the image to the paper.

Office copy machines are used to make copies directly from an original. The material is usually typewritten. Some office machines use the diazo and electrostatic processes. Fig. 1-11. Another process in use is diffusion-transfer reversal, which operates as follows:

The original material to be copied is placed on top of a sheet of negative paper. The surface of the negative paper has a sensitive emulsion of gelatin and grains of silver salts. The two

PRINTING METHODS

The most commonly used printing methods have four stages of production. Fig. 1-12. First, an original image must be developed. An *original image* is the artwork, illustrations, photographs, and/or copy of the words to be reproduced. How the original image is developed will vary somewhat with the reproduction process to be used.

Second, the original image must be converted to printing-image carriers. A *printing-image carrier* is used to make a copy of the original image that can be inked and used to print the image. The kinds of carriers used vary with the process. For example, a letterpress can use the metal type as the carrier. The words are printed directly from the type. An offset press will use a metal plate with the image on it as a carrier.

Third, the printing image is inked. This forms an *ink image* on the face of the printing-image carrier. This ink image is transferred to the material upon which it is to be reproduced. This is the fourth stage and produces the

1-12. *The four stages of printing.*

THE ORIGINAL IMAGE

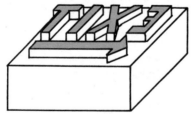

THE INK IMAGE

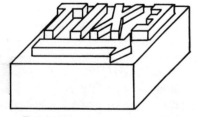

THE PRINTING-IMAGE CARRIER

THE PRINTED IMAGE

1-13. *A spirit duplicator.*

final product, the *printed image* on some kind of material—a sheet of paper, plastic, cloth, or some other material.

Spirit duplication is a printing method that requires a special master. The master is a heavy paper with a dye-carbon sheet placed face-up behind it. This master is the image carrier.

The original image is typed or drawn on the heavy paper. The dye carbon sticks to the back of the paper. The master is placed on a spirit duplicating machine with the dye carbon image facing the paper to be printed. Fig. 1-13. A special fluid dissolves the dye (the ink image) so it prints (the printed image) on each sheet of paper run through the machine. A master will print about 300 copies before the dye-carbon coating is gone.

Mimeograph is a printing system that has been in use a long time. The image to be printed is typed or drawn (the original image) on a porous, fibrous paper (the image carrier) coated on both sides with a waxy material. It is called a stencil. The image is cut through the surface of the stencil. The stencil is mounted on the cylinder of the mimeograph machine. Ink (the ink image) is forced through the

lines cut into the stencil. It prints (the printed image) on the paper sheets that feed through the machine. Stencils will run from 5,000 to 15,000 copies before they begin to fail. Fig. 1-14.

THE OFFSET PROCESS

In the offset process the image (the original image) to be printed is developed on the suface of a thin, flat metal sheet (the image carrier). This process is similar to developing a photograph. The sheet is called an *offset plate*. This plate is mounted on the offset press. As the press operates, the image on the plate receives a coat of ink (the ink image). This ink image is transferred (offset) to a cylinder covered with a rubber blanket. The rubber-covered cylinder prints the image on the paper (the printed image). Fig. 1-15.

The offset process differs from other printing processes in two ways. First, the process uses the principle that grease and water do not mix. Second, the image to be printed is offset on a rubber roller, which then prints the image on the paper. The printing is not done directly from the offset plate.

The offset press has five basic parts: The dampening system, inking system, printing unit, feeding system, and delivery system. Fig. 1-15.

The *dampening system* has several rollers. The fountain roller deposits a water solution onto the other rollers. They carry the water solution onto the plate cylinder. This solution coats the plate except in the areas containing the image. These image areas have a grease base and repel water.

1-14. *A mimeograph machine.*

The *inking system* is made up of an inking fountain and several rollers. The inking fountain holds the ink and distributes it to the rollers. The rollers break down the ink so it is deposited on the plate cylinder in a uniform layer. The oil-based ink coats the image because it has a grease base. Ink does not stick to the rest of the cylinder because that part has a water solution coating.

The *printing unit* has three main cylinders. These are the plate, blanket, and impression cylinders. The *plate cylinder* holds the offset plate. The inking and dampening rollers touch this cylinder. As it revolves, the plate receives a layer of water solution, and the image gets a layer of ink. This is offset on the *blanket cylinder*. The press has many adjustments that make allowances for the plate thickness, paper thickness, and the pressure between cylinders. When properly adjusted, a uniform ink image

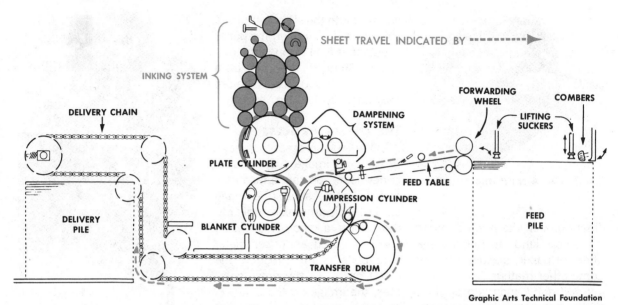

SHEET TRAVEL INDICATED BY ------------►

INKING SYSTEM

DELIVERY CHAIN

DAMPENING SYSTEM

FORWARDING WHEEL

COMBERS

LIFTING SUCKERS

PLATE CYLINDER

FEED TABLE

IMPRESSION CYLINDER

DELIVERY PILE

BLANKET CYLINDER

FEED PILE

TRANSFER DRUM

1-15. *The offset process. Paper is delivered from the feed pile on the right. Ink is delivered through the inking system. The printing plate is on the plate cylinder. The inking system inks the plate. The ink image is offset on the blanket cylinder. The paper runs between the impression cylinder and the blanket cylinder. Here the ink image is transferred to the paper. It flows to the delivery pile.*

will be offset on the blanket cylinder. The paper is fed between the blanket cylinder and the *impression cylinder*. The impression cylinder is very smooth. It provides the backing for the paper as the blanket cylinder transfers the ink image to the paper.

The *feeding system* is an automatic device that gets the paper to the printing unit. On high-speed machines suckers are used to feed the paper into the press. A sucker is a tube with a vacuum. The vacuum lifts a sheet of paper and moves it forward toward the printing unit.

The *delivery system* carries the printed sheets away from the

1-16. *An offset press.*

printing unit and stacks them in a pile. This system usually consists of two endless chains having gripper bars spaced to receive one sheet for each revolution of the blanket cylinder.

A typical offset press is shown in Fig. 1-16. Detailed information on offset presses is presented in Chapters 15 and 16.

THE LETTERPRESS PROCESS

The letterpress process of printing uses raised letters on type. Drawings and illustrations also have raised surfaces. A simple example of letterpress printing is shown by a rubber stamp. The raised letters are inked and pressed on a paper to print the image. Fig. 1-17. In the letterpress process, letter and illustration surfaces receive a layer of ink. This inked surface is pressed against a piece of paper. The ink is transferred from the face of the type to the paper. This is often called *relief printing.*

The letters on the type and the illustrations are made in reverse so that they read correctly when printed. Fig. 1-18.

1-18. *Hand-set type. Notice that the image is in reverse.*

Letterpress printing is done with flat and curved forms. The type and illustrations are assembled and fastened together in units called forms. The type, set in a flat manner, can be inserted in some presses. The job is printed directly from the flat type. Or, flat metal plates can be made from the type. These are placed on the press instead of the original type. Detailed information on letterpress plates is found in Chapter 19.

Several types of presses are used in letterpress printing: the platen press, flatbed cylinder press, and the rotary press.

On a platen press the type is held in an upright position. The paper is pressed against the type with a metal platen. Fig. 1-19. A typical platen press is shown in Fig. 1-20. Detailed information on the platen press is found in Chapter 21.

The type is held in a horizontal position on the *flatbed cylinder press.* The type is locked in a flat form. The paper is held to a cyl-

1-17. *A rubber stamp illustrates the letterpress process. The raised letters are inked and pressed against a piece of paper, forming an image of the letters.*

1-19. *How an automatic platen press operates.*

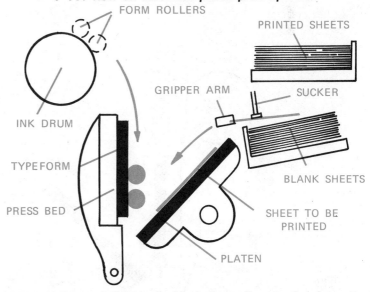

FORM ROLLERS

PRINTED SHEETS

GRIPPER ARM

SUCKER

INK DRUM

BLANK SHEETS

TYPEFORM

SHEET TO BE PRINTED

PRESS BED

PLATEN

1-19A. *A sheet is fed from the blank sheet pile onto the platen. To do this, the sucker lifts the sheet off the paper pile. A gripper arm grasps the sheet and moves it to the platen. The form rollers move from the ink drum down over the typeform. This puts a coating of ink on the form.*

("How an automatic platen press operates" continued on next page.)

("*How an automatic platen press operates*" continued.)

FORM ROLLERS MOVE
TO INK DRUM

SHEET BEING
PRINTED

GRIPPER ARM RETURNS
TO PICK UP ANOTHER
SHEET

1-19B. *The platen closes against the typeform. The inked form prints on the sheet. The form rollers move up to the ink drum. Here they receive a fresh coating of ink while the form is printing. The gripper arm returns to the blank sheet pile to pick up another sheet.*

inder and is rolled over the type. The ink impression on the type prints on the paper. Fig. 1-21. Other varieties of flatbed cylinder presses print two colors on one side of the sheet with one pass through the press. Another kind prints one color on both sides of the sheet with one pass through the press.

The *vertical-bed cylinder press*, Fig. 1-22, operates much the same as the flatbed cylinder press.

Detailed information on cylinder presses is found in Chapter 22.

The *rotary press* uses curved metal relief plates. They are cast from the original type. The plate is fastened to a cylinder. The paper is fed between the plate cylinder and an impression cyl-

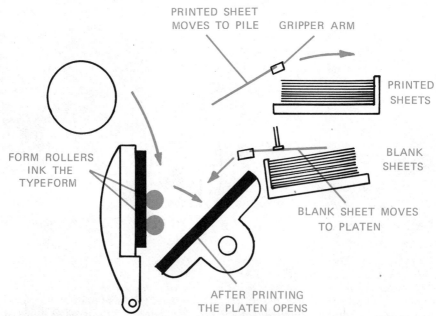

PRINTED SHEET
MOVES TO PILE   GRIPPER ARM

PRINTED
SHEETS

FORM ROLLERS
INK THE
TYPEFORM

BLANK
SHEETS

BLANK SHEET MOVES
TO PLATEN

AFTER PRINTING
THE PLATEN OPENS

1-19C. *After the sheet is printed, the platen opens. A gripper arm moves the printed sheet to the printed sheet pile. At the same time the form rollers move down over the typeform again. Another sheet from the blank sheet pile is moved to the platen. The press is ready to close and print another sheet.*

Heidelberg

1-20. *An automatic platen press.*

1-21. *How a flatbed cylinder press works.*

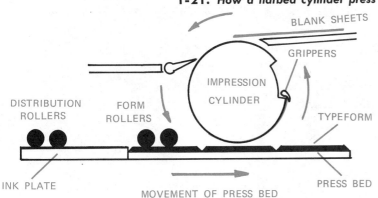

BLANK SHEETS

GRIPPERS

IMPRESSION CYLINDER

DISTRIBUTION ROLLERS

FORM ROLLERS

TYPEFORM

INK PLATE

MOVEMENT OF PRESS BED

PRESS BED

1-21A. *The typeform is locked to the press bed. It takes two revolutions of the cylinder to print one sheet. On the first revolution the blank sheets of paper are fed into the press. They make contact with the impression cylinder. They are held on the cylinder with grippers. The impression cylinder makes one rotation pressing the paper against the typeform. The press bed moves under the cylinder as the cylinder rotates. The image is printed.*

1-21B. *As the printing cycle is completed, the form rollers move over the ink plate and receive a new coating of ink.*

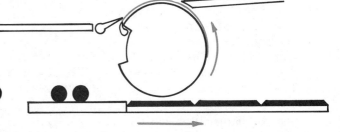

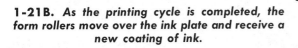

("How a flatbed cylinder press works" continued on next page.)

("How a flatbed cylinder press works" continued.)

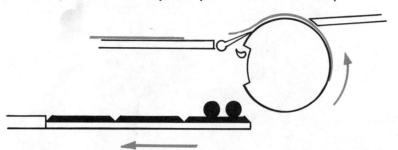

1-21C. *On the second revolution of the impression cylinder the printed paper is released. At the same time the typeform moves under the form rollers. The form is inked. As the impression cylinder starts the next rotation, the form moves back under the cylinder. Another sheet of paper is fed into the press and the process is repeated.*

natural or synthetic rubber formed over a matrix. A matrix is a mold with the image to be reproduced raised above the surface. The rubber is cured on the matrix. When it is removed, it has taken the form of the image in the mold. The image carrier is mounted on the press cylinder.

Flexographic printing is done on rotary-type presses. There are two major types in use. One is the stack-type. Fig. 1-24. This press can print from several plates at one time. It can pro-

inder. The ink image is printed on the paper as it is squeezed between these two cylinders. Fig. 1-23.

There are other varieties of the rotary press. Some have several plate cylinders. Each plate prints a different color. It is possible to print four to six colors on one pass through the press.

Flexographic printing is a form of letterpress printing. The primary differences are the kind of inks used and the image carriers.

The major use for flexography is for printing in the packaging industry. Materials such as paper bags and boxes, plastic foils, cellophane, and metal foils can be printed. It is sometimes used in high-speed book printing and business forms reproduction.

The image carrier is either

1-22. *How a vertical automatic cylinder press operates.*

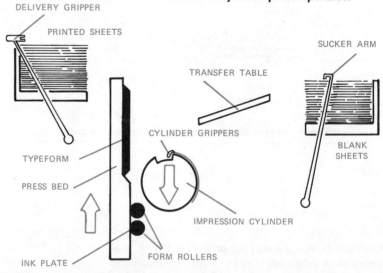

1-22A. *The typeform is locked to the vertical press bed. The press bed and the impression cylinder move up and down. When the bed moves up, the cylinder moves down. The press moves through two cycles to print a single sheet. The press is shown here with the bed up and the cylinder down. In this position the form rollers receive a coating of ink. The blank sheet on the cylinder is ready to be printed.*

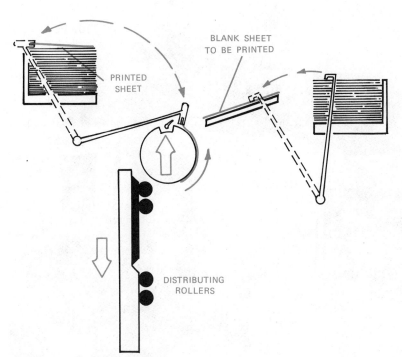

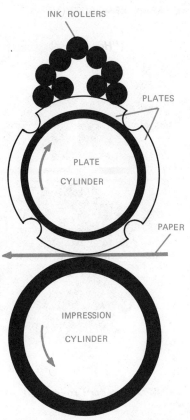

1-22B. *In the second cycle the impression cylinder rotates and moves up. The press bed moves down. The form rollers ink the form for the next impression. The blank sheet is rotated by the impression cylinder against the moving typeform. When the impression cylinder reaches its top position, the cylinder grippers open. The delivery gripper removes the sheet and places it on the delivery pile. While this is underway, the sucker arm moves a sheet of blank paper to the transfer table. The sheet is moved along the transfer table to the impression cylinder. The cylinder grippers grasp the blank sheet. Now the impression cylinder moves down to its lowest position. It does not rotate during this move. The press bed moves to its highest position. The form rollers ink the form. It is now in the position shown in Fig. 1-22A. The printing cycle is ready to begin again.*

1-23. *How a rotary letterpress operates. The plates used to print the image are fastened to the plate cylinder. They are inked as they rotate against the inking rollers. The impression cylinder presses the blank paper against the inked plate cylinder. One sheet is printed for every revolution of the plate cylinder.*

duce duplicate printings or print several different jobs at the same time. A second type of press is the single-impression, cylinder flexography press.

Both of these presses print off a web. A *web* is a large roll of paper which is fed into the press.

THE GRAVURE PROCESS

The gravure process is one in which the ink image is printed on paper from ink-filled cavities on a metal surface. The material to be printed is etched in the metal and sunk below the surface. The depressions are very tiny and

shallow. There are thousands of small depressions per square inch.

The major uses of gravure printing are gravure newspapers, magazines, packages, wood-grain, and floor coverings.

In the printing process, ink is

Wolverine Flexographic Mfg. Co.

1-24. *A standard roll-to-roll, four-color flexographic printing press.*

spread over the metal surface. Excess ink is removed with a blade called the doctor blade. The metal surface is free of ink, while the thousands of depressions are full of ink. Each little hole acts as an inkwell. When paper is pressed against the metal surface, the ink transfers to it much the same as a blotter picks up ink. The ink dots printed on the paper surface form the image. It would take about ten such inkwells to print the period at the end of this sentence.

Gravure can be printed from flat plates or a cylinder. If a cylinder is used, it is called rotogravure. The process is shown in Fig. 1-25. The paper is fed to the press from a web. The paper flows between the gravure cylinder and the impression cylinder.

The gravure cylinder is the printing cylinder. The impression cylinder presses the paper against the gravure cylinder. The ink in the inkwells is deposited on the paper. The gravure cylinder revolves into the ink fountain and refills the inkwells. It continues around and prints another image. This is a rapid, continuous process.

The first step in gravure printing is the preparation of the copy—the material to be printed. The text (words) to be printed is set in type by the usual methods. A proof is printed off this type. (A proof is a single copy.) The proof is glued in position on the page to be printed. Space is left for photographs. They are made the exact size of the space and pasted in place.

Next, two photos are made of

the page. One is called a *line* shot. Only material with solid lines, such as type proofs or ink drawings, is photographed.

The other photo is called a *tone* shot. It includes photos and drawings which have various shades or tones.

A layout person puts together the line shots and tone shots into the final page arrangement, referred to as the layout. A single positive copy is made of the two shots combined. The positive is made on a sheet of clear acetate plastic.

Next, the positive is photographically transferred to rotofilm. *Rotofilm* is made up of three layers. The first layer is clear acetate 0.007″ thick. It supports the photographic emulsion layer. The emulsion layer takes the photographic image.

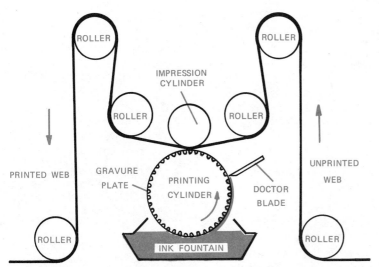

1-25. *How the gravure process works. The web of paper passes between the impression cylinder and the printing cylinder. A heavy layer of ink from the ink fountain fills the cavities in the cylinder. The doctor blade scrapes the ink off the surface, but the ink remains in the cavities. This ink is transferred to the paper as it runs against the impression cylinder.*

The emulsion that was exposed to light hardens during developing. The more light to strike the emulsion, the harder it becomes.

The rotofilm is then applied to a steel cylinder with a copper surface. This is the cylinder into which the inkwells will be etched. A common-sized cylinder would be 80″ long and 13.697″ in diameter. It weighs about 2,000 pounds. The cylinder is prepared by electroplating a thin copper shell on the surface. Fig. 1-26. A copper shell 0.00625″ thick is deposited on the cylinder. It is polished with a fine stone until it has a thickness of 0.006″. The slightest variation in the diameter of 13.697″ will cause serious problems. Fig. 1-27.

The rotofilm emulsion, now developed, is placed on the cylinder. Fig. 1-28. The emulsion is now called *resist*. It will resist the action of acids that will be used to etch the cylinder. Each row of

This layer is thinner than the cellophane wrapper on a cigarette package. Between the layers is a waterproof membrane.

The rotofilm process begins by placing a line screen on the rotofilm. It is then exposed to the film with a yellow light. A *line*

screen is a plastic sheet that has a series of lines running at right angles to each other. It looks much like window screen. Screens are identified by the number of lines per inch. A 200-line screen has 200 lines per inch. The line screen is used to divide up the printing surface into inkwells. If a 200-line screen is used, there are 40,000 inkwells per square inch. This first exposure locates the inkwells on the rotofilm.

Next, the positive is placed over the screen and rotofilm. It too is exposed with yellow light. This exposure controls the size of the inkwells to be etched in the metal plate.

Next, the line screen is removed. The positive remains on the rotofilm. It is exposed with ultraviolet light. This exposure controls the depth of the inkwells to be etched in the metal plate.

The rotofilm is now developed.

1-26. *The electroplating process puts a copper shell on the cylinder.*
The Denver Post

1-27. *The copper shell is 0.00625″ thick. The cylinder is polished with a fine stone until the shell thickness is 0.006″.*
The Denver Post

25

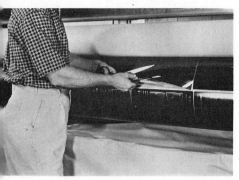

1-28. *The rotofilm emulsion is set in place on the cylinder.*

1-29. *Once the rotofilm is bonded to the cylinder, the acetate base is pulled away and discarded. Now only the gelatin, or resist, remains on the cylinder.*

1-30. *The cylinder is moved over a trough and rotated while diacetone alcohol removes the waterproof membrane. Hot water then washes away the unhardened portions of the gelatin.*

resist is placed in the order the pages will appear when printed.

The resist is bonded to the cylinder by pressing it with a roller. This roller applies 1,300 pounds pressure on the resist. Next, the thin acetate layer is removed from the surface of the resist. Fig. 1-29. Only two layers of the rotofilm remain. These are the waterproof membrane and the emulsion. The cylinder is now rotated in a solution of diacetone alcohol, which dissolves the waterproof membrane. The cylinder is then washed with hot water. Fig. 1-30. The hot water softens the parts of the resist that were not hit by light. Remember, the parts of the resist hit by light during exposure hardened. Left on the cylinder are thousands of tiny dots of emulsion. The thicker dots resist the acid etch and will, therefore, have shallower inkwells. These will print lighter since they hold less ink.

The cylinder is now etched with concentrated iron chloride. This process takes 9 to 10 minutes. Fig. 1-31. Then a thinner solution is used for 12 to 14 minutes. The cylinder is now washed. Before it is placed on the press, every square inch of the cylinder is carefully examined with a 12-power glass. Fig. 1-32. Each inkwell is examined to see that it is the proper depth, width, and shape. If the cylinder is perfect, it is sent to the pressroom.

A rotogravure press is shown in Fig. 1-33. Such a press can print up to 96 pages at one time and up to 48,000 copies an hour.

If a job is to be printed in one color, such as black, one cylinder is needed. If it is to be in several colors, a separate cylinder must

1-31. *The cylinder revolves in a bath of concentrated iron chloride. The person doing the etching must wear heavy rubber gloves to protect the hands from the acid.*

be etched for each color. Color work is very difficult because each color has to be printed in exactly the correct place or the work will appear blurred.

1-32. *When the etching process is finished, every square inch of the cylinder is examined with a magnifying glass. Areas that need special attention are etched by hand.*

1-33. A four-color rotogravure press. Each unit prints a different color and operates as shown in Fig. 1-25. This is a precision machine, weighing many tons. The paper is fed from webs.

Fig. 1-34 shows the operation of a five-unit rotogravure press. It is set to print black on one side of a sheet and four colors on the other. All of this happens with one pass through the press. Unit A will print black on one side. Units B, C, D, and E will print the four colors on the other side.

The Screen Process

The screen process is very different from the letterpress and gravure processes. The printing unit is a finely woven cloth or metal screen that is stretched tightly over a frame. The image (the original image) to be printed is cut into a stencil. The stencil is fastened to the screen (the image carrier). The screen is placed against the object on which it is to print. Ink (the ink image) is forced through the stencil and screen onto the

object. The screen is lifted, leaving behind the printed image. See Fig. 1-35.

There are two commercial techniques for making stencils: the hand-cut film method and the photographic method.

The hand-cut film method uses original art in pencil, paint, or ink. The outlines of the design are necessary, but the line quality of the art is not important.

The film used is made up of two layers. It has a transparent layer covered with a lacquer layer. The film is taped over the art. The lacquer side of the film is up. Since the film is transparent, the design shows through.

The design is cut into the lacquer layer with a sharp blade. The areas to be printed are lifted off, leaving the transparent layer untouched. The lacquer layer of the film is fastened to the screen. The transparent layer is peeled away, leaving the openings cut in the lacquer exposed.

The ink is forced through the screen in these open areas, printing the image.

There are many different processes used to make *photographic stencils*. The photographic stencil method requires perfect, finished artwork. This artwork is photographed, producing a negative. The black opaque parts of the negative do not permit light to pass through. Light does pass through the clear areas on the negative.

One way of making a photographic stencil is the transfer method. The negative is placed over a sheet of transfer photo film. The film is made of two thin tissues. The top side is a gelatin. The lower side is a transparent backing sheet. The film and negative are exposed to a light source. The gelatin area exposed to light washes away. The other gelatin areas harden. The film is then stuck to the screen with the gelatin layer next to the screen.

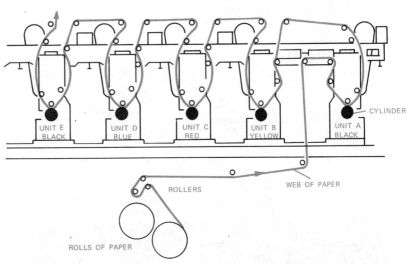

1-34. The sheet is first fed into Unit A. Here one side is printed in black. As it goes to Unit B, notice the web is flipped over. The next four units print yellow, red, blue, and black on the back of the sheet. This means that four-color printing can be done on one side of the web. One color is on the other side.

1-35. Screen process printing. A. The image to be printed is cut into the stencil, either by hand or photographically. B. The stencil is applied to the screen. The areas of the screen around the stencil that are not to print are lacquered out so the ink does not go through. The screen is placed on the object to be printed. C. Ink is forced through the stencil and screen onto the object. D. The frame is lifted, leaving the printed image.

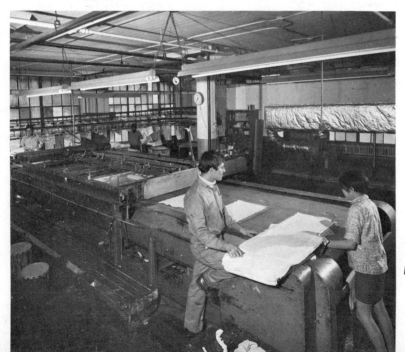

The transparent back is peeled off leaving the hardened gelatin layer on the screen. The screen is now ready to print.

If a job has several colors, a stencil is made of each color. After the first color has been printed and dried, the second color is printed.

Screen printing is widely used in industry. Common applica-

Precision Screen Machines, Inc.

1-36. A mechanical screen process press. It is printing designs on fabric.

tions are printing on glass, metal, paper, cardboard, textiles, and plastic surfaces. The surfaces can be curved. A mechanical screen process machine printing on fabric is shown in Fig. 1-36. Detailed information on screen process printing is presented in Chapter 24.

REVIEW QUESTIONS

1. The methods for reproducing images can be grouped into two types. Name them.
2. Photography produces images of high quality. Why, then, is it not a good process for high volume production?
3. The most common printing methods have four stages of production. Name them.
4. What are the six major printing processes?
5. In the offset process, the printing is done directly from an offset plate. True or False?
6. The letterpress process uses raised surfaces as image carriers. True or False?
7. Flexographic printing is a form of letterpress printing. True or False?
8. In the gravure process the ink image is printed from ink-filled cavities on a metal surface. True or False?
9. In the screen process the image is transferred to a screen from a rubber roller. True or False?

Chapter 2

Careers in Graphic Reproduction

One of the most important decisions you have to make is the choice of a career. Much of what happens during your lifetime is related to your career. It influences the atmosphere in which you will spend the major portion of your time. The type of people you associate with depends to a large extent upon your career. Where you live and how much you earn are influenced by your career choice.

It is essential that a career be one in which you enjoy the activities. It must offer you the oppportunity to find fulfillment and satisfy your need to achieve success.

The graphic reproduction industry is in a period of rapid growth and technological change. Many of the processes, materials, and machines now in use were not in existence a few years ago. It appears that this period of change and growth is just starting, and that the future is one of challenge.

As you study in the field of graphic reproduction, observe carefully the duties required in the various areas. Be alert to raising career questions such as: What does a camera operator need to know? What operations does a press operator perform? Do I enjoy some activities more than others?

A CAREER DEPENDS UPON EDUCATION

The career you can have in the graphic reproduction industry depends a great deal upon your education. There are some jobs which require very little special preparation. These are called unskilled jobs, and they can be learned at work. For example, the operation of some machines in a bindery requires little preparation. The person who sets up the machines, makes the adjustments, and decides how a job is to be done requires more education. This level, often called the craft level, generally takes years to learn. The most common methods of learning a skilled trade in graphic reproduction are by serving an apprenticeship, or attending a vocational-technical school, community college, or four-year college technical program.

Management, supervisory, and administrative positions in the industry are usually filled by college graduates. The best preparation is found at colleges offering majors in printing technology and printing management. These combine printing, management, and business administration courses over the four years of academic study.

Some vocational schools and colleges offer the opportunity of acquiring job experience through a cooperative education program. In this program students spend part of their time in school and part on the job. Such programs enable students to finish their formal education and receive technical preparation on industrial equipment. If a cooperative program is not available, an alert student can often find a part-time job after school or on Saturdays, and gain trade experience in this manner. However, for advancement in the printing industry, there is no substitute for completion of high school. It is a minimum requirement, with additional post–high school education needed for the better paying technical jobs.

WHERE ARE THE JOBS?

The largest number of people working in the graphic reproduction field are employed in the *printing and publishing* of newspapers, magazines, and books. The second largest number are employed in *job and commercial printing,* an area that produces a wide variety of work, such as advertising material, letterheads, catalogs, maps, and calendars.

There are many *specialty printers.* These firms produce a limited range of products, such as business forms or yearbooks.

A *bindery* may be a part of a large commercial printing company, or a separate company which does no printing but assembles materials printed by others. A typical example is a company which binds books.

Many large corporations, such as one manufacturing an extensive line of electrical products, have their own printing departments. These are organized and operated like any printing concern except all their production is devoted to the printing needs of that company, such as brochures, forms, and service manuals.

There are companies that produce items needed by commercial printing firms. For example, platemaking companies specialize in the manufacture of electrotypes and stereotypes for companies that do the actual printing. Some companies specialize in composition services, while others make film separations for process color printings.

Related industries which employ many workers include those manufacturing printing equipment, paper, inks, solvents, film, chemicals, plates, and rollers.

The companies utilizing the various printing processes extend far beyond those which reproduce images on paper. The textile industry prints on fabrics. Other industries print on metal, glass, plastics, and other materials. All utilize the materials and techniques of graphic reproduction.

JOB CLASSIFICATIONS

The graphic reproduction in- dustry is in reality made up of many industries; each one is involved with a phase of graphic reproduction. The industry produces a vast array of products using different processes, materials, and techniques. Some of the industries that make up the total graphic reproduction industry are:

* Printing and publishing
* Packaging
* Paper and paper products
* Printing machinery manufacturing and service
* Coatings
* Printing ink
* General printing supplies
* Bindery
* Newspaper publishing
* Magazine publishing
* Book publishing
* Photography
* Advertising

While these industries are diverse but related, the jobs within them can be roughly classified into several major categories. These include creative workers, specialized technicians, the technologist, the skilled craftsperson, sales and marketing staff, and management personnel.

The *creative workers* include those who write and edit newspapers, books, and magazines; artists and commercial illustrators, graphic designers; and advertising staff. They create the message and images to be communicated.

The *specialized technicians* are those who are involved in the technical aspects of production, where knowledge is of greater significance than manipulative skill. Jobs in this area include computer staff, data processing employees, estimators, process control and quality control staff positions.

The scientifically prepared college graduate works to develop new processes and new materials. This could be an engineer working to develop a new platemaking machine or a chemist developing inks to print on new materials, such as plastics. Generally these people are employed by the companies who supply the industry with the machines and materials needed for printing production.

About one-third of the workers are in the fourth category—the *skilled printing crafts*. These workers are directly involved with the printing production process. Typical jobs include those of the press operator, compositor, platemaker, bookbinder, stripper, and proofreader. (These jobs are described later in this chapter.) They also include the workers who maintain the printing plant, such as machinists and electricians.

Another category of jobs in the graphic reproduction industry is *sales and marketing*. The functions of sales and marketing personnel are discussed in Chapter 3, "Planning, Copyfitting, and Measurement."

The *management* staff is responsible for setting the operating policies of the industry, and must make the decisions necessary for its operation and financial success. This includes company presidents, vice-presidents, comptrollers, treasurers, and plant superintendents. They generally have completed four years of college and have experience in several phases of graphic reproduction.

CAREERS IN THE SKILLED CRAFTS

The printing industry provides employment for more than one million workers. Approximately one-third of these jobs are in the skilled crafts. The other jobs are in related areas: estimator, mailer, computer programmer, computer typist, administrator, clerical worker, maintenance, and sales personnel.

More than half of the nation's printing employees are located in New York, Illinois, California, Pennsylvania, and Ohio. A majority of the jobs are near large manufacturing, commercial, or financial areas. The leading centers of printing employment are New York City, Chicago, Los Angeles, Philadelphia, San Francisco-Oakland, Cincinnati, Cleveland, Boston, Detroit, Minneapolis-St. Paul, Washington, D.C., St. Louis, and Baltimore.

COMPOSING ROOM OCCUPATIONS

The composing room is where the copy is set, checked for errors, and assembled into final printing form. Composition varies with the printing process to be used. Compositors working in letterpress printing will be working with metal type and photoengravings. See Chapter 7, "Relief Composition—Hand," and Chapter 8, "Relief Composition—Machine." Those working in an offset printing plant will produce the words and other images on film. See Chapter 6, "Cold Composition."

METAL TYPE COMPOSITION OCCUPATIONS

Hand compositors (typeset-ters) set type by hand. They assemble one letter at a time in a tool called a composing stick. See Chapter 7. Hand setting of type is seldom done today except for larger type sizes or a very small job, such as printing calling cards.

Typesetting machine operators use semiautomatic machines which set type rapidly. The most frequently used hot metal composition machine is the Linotype. The machine has a keyboard somewhat like a typewriter. See Chapter 8.

The operator sets the words and spaces them by striking the proper keys. The machine casts a line of metal type. Another metal typecasting machine is the Monotype. The Monotype has two parts, a keyboard and a caster. The operator strikes the keys on the keyboard. This produces a punched tape. The tape is fed into the mechanism of the casting machine which casts the metal type.

Bank workers assemble the metal type on trays called galleys. They then print trial copies of the type. These copies are called galley proofs. *Proofreaders* check the galley proofs with the original copy and mark the errors. *Make-up persons* assemble the metal type and photoengravings of illustrations as they will appear as pages. These page forms are arranged in proper sequence by a stoneman. See Chapter 20, "Imposition and Lockup."

Composing room workers will generally start by learning hand composition, page makeup, lockup, lineup, and proofreading. After some experience they may operate metal typesetting ma-chines and photocomposition machines.

Compositors frequently learn their job by serving an apprenticeship. (During an apprenticeship a person works on the job with an experienced worker and learns by watching and helping.) Frequently apprentices attend evening classes to increase their skills and technical knowledge. Many compositors learn their skills in vocational schools, where they get both theory and shop experience.

COMPOSITION OCCUPATIONS IN OFFSET PRINTING

Phototypesetting machine operators use a machine that has a keyboard somewhat like a typewriter. The most common types produce a punched paper tape or record on a magnetic tape. The tape is fed into a phototypesetting machine which reads the material on the tape and photographs each individual character indicated by it. The paper on which this is photographed is developed, and the words appear as positive images on paper. Phototypesetters must understand basic darkroom practices because they frequently are required to develop the positives on which the image was photographed. See Chapter 6.

Computers are finding increased use in composing operations. The input to the computer is either punched paper or magnetic tape. Punched tape is often used because it has been commonly used to operate conventional typesetting equipment. The tape is punched on Teletypesetter machinery or a tape-punching machine that utilizes a typewriter keyboard. The operator types in the instruction codes, such as the line length and spacing, and then proceeds to type the manuscript without regard to line length and hyphenation. The punched tape is ready for computer processing. The computer performs all the necessary typesetting functions, including justification and hyphenation, and produces a finished tape. This tape is used to operate both hot metal typecasting and photographic typesetting machines.

Tape-perforating machine operators must be expert typists, understand the English language, and be expert at spelling.

PHOTOENGRAVERS

Photoengravers operate machines that make metal plates of illustrations and pictures. The finished plate has a printing surface that stands out in relief; that is, it is raised above the surface of the plate. Photoengravings are combined with metal type for use in the letterpress process. See Chapter 19, "Plates for Letterpress Printing." In small shops all the steps in making a photoengraving may be performed by one person. In larger shops each worker performs a particular operation. The photoengraving process includes camera operators, printers, etchers, finishers, routers, blockers, and proofers.

The camera operator photographs the material to be printed. These can be line drawings or photographs. The camera operator develops the negative. A *printer* produces the image on a metal plate. The plate is coated with a light-sensitive solution, and the negative is placed over it. This is then exposed to arc lights.

The areas of the plate forming the image are protected by the light-sensitive solution. After exposure the plate is given to an *etcher,* who places it in an acid bath. The nonimage areas are etched away, leaving the image areas in relief. The *finisher* inspects the etched plate and touches up parts that were not etched properly by cutting into the plate with hand tools. The *router* then cuts away metal from the nonprinting part of the plate so it does not touch the ink rollers during printing. The *blocker* mounts the metal plate on a base and adjusts it so it is type-high. A proof of the finished plate is made by the *proofer.*

Most photoengravers are employed in companies whose main purpose is to produce plates for printing concerns. They usually do no printing. The most common way to become a photoengraver is to serve an apprenticeship.

ELECTROTYPERS AND STEREOTYPERS

Electrotypers and *stereotypers* make duplicate press plates of the typeforms assembled by the compositor. These duplicates can be made from metal, rubber, or plastic. Electrotypes are used mainly for book and magazine printing. Stereotypes, which are less durable, are used primarily in newspaper work.

Duplicate plates are necessary for long-run printing jobs because the original form would wear out. It is preserved, and the printing is done by duplicates (or copies). See Chapter 19.

Nearly all electrotypers and stereotypers learn the trade through an apprenticeship.

These are separate crafts, and usually a person learns one or the other.

PRESS OPERATORS

The actual printing of a job is performed in the pressroom. The persons operating the presses are called *press operators.* They install the printing forms or plates on the press; make all adjustments, such as ink flow; and set the guides so that the paper feeds properly and the impression is printed in the exact place desired. The smaller presses are usually operated by one press operator. Larger presses require a press operator and several helpers, called *press assistants.*

Press operators usually are trained to operate either letterpress or offset press equipment. The manner of operation is quite different, and special training is needed for each. See Chapter 21, "Platen Press Operation;" Chapter 22, "Cylinder Press Operation;" and Chapter 16, "Operation and Adjustment of the Offset Press."

Press operators are trained through an apprenticeship or in vocational schools. A press operator should have high mechanical aptitude and ability to visualize color. Some presses require heavy lifting and the stamina to stand for long periods.

Offset printing is the fastest growing method of printing. Many new developments in this method have caused the letterpress method to be less important. This should be considered as career choices are made.

LITHOGRAPHIC OCCUPATIONS

Lithographic occupations are

those in which printing is done from a plane surface, rather than printing by relief as in letterpress printing. In this rapidly expanding area specialized workers perform various parts of the total process. The camera operator makes negatives of the copy. In larger companies the operator may specialize as a line or halftone photographer or as a color-separation photographer.

The negatives are retouched by *lithographic artists*. They lighten or darken parts of the negative to improve the results. They also are expected to sharpen or even reshape images on the negatives. This is a delicate, highly skilled job, performed using chemicals, dyes, and special tools. Often the lithographic artist specializes in one phase of work, such as dot etching, retouching, or lettering.

The negatives are arranged in a layout on paper, glass, or film. The person doing this work is a *stripper*. A stripper arranges and tapes the film, blocks of type, pictures, and other artwork on layout sheets, called flats. These are photographed by the platemaker for use in making offset plates. See Chapter 13.

The *platemaker* exposes the offset plate material and the photographic flats made by the stripper to the proper light source. The platemaker then develops the plate to bring out the image. See Chapter 14, "Offset Platemaking."

Automatic plate processing equipment is speeding production, increasing quality, and requiring different training for those who operate it. There is less personal, hands-on involve-

ment expected of the platemaker in an up-to-date printing establishment. He or she must learn to operate new equipment that was not commonly found in a platemaking department a few years ago.

A well-rounded lithographic technician usually serves an apprenticeship. Many areas of the craft are taught in vocational schools.

BINDERY OCCUPATIONS

Many printed items need finishing after they are printed. They may require cutting, folding, stapling, sewing, or other finishing operations. This work is performed by bindery workers. Many bookbinders employed in commercial binderies only perform bindery operations for other printing concerns. Many printing companies will have their own bindery departments to perform the most frequently needed operations. See Chapter 23, "Bindery and Finishing."

There are several types of binderies. Edition binderies bind books, magazines, and pamphlets that are printed in large quantities. Trade or job binderies do contract work for printers and publishers. Blank-book or loose-leaf binderies bind blank books, such as ledgers.

Bindery operations require the ability to plan work carefully. Well-prepared bindery workers understand the total printing production process. They also know how to operate many complex, high-speed machines, such as programmed cutters, folders, and collators. In large binderies many of the operations are broken down into small steps, and

relatively unskilled employees can be quickly taught to do that single operation.

Preparation for a bindery position is usually through an apprenticeship.

THE FUTURE OF THE SKILLED CRAFTS

The relative importance of the various skilled printing trades is changing with technological changes in the industry. A comparison of these trades with projections for the future is shown in Fig. 2-1.

In the bookbinding area there will be a slight decrease in the number of workers needed, though the area still presents employment opportunities through retirements and normal staff turnover.

In the composition area the amount of work to be done will increase in the future. However, slightly fewer workers will be needed because of technological changes in typesetting equipment which permit each worker to produce more work.

The total number of workers in the areas of electrotype and stereotype production is expected to decline moderately due to technological changes, such as automatic platecasting machines and the development of rubber and plastic plates, which can be cast outside of electrotype and stereotype companies' plants.

The number of lithographic workers is expected to increase in the next few years. This will come about with an increased use of photos, drawings, and the widespread use of color. While the volume of work will increase

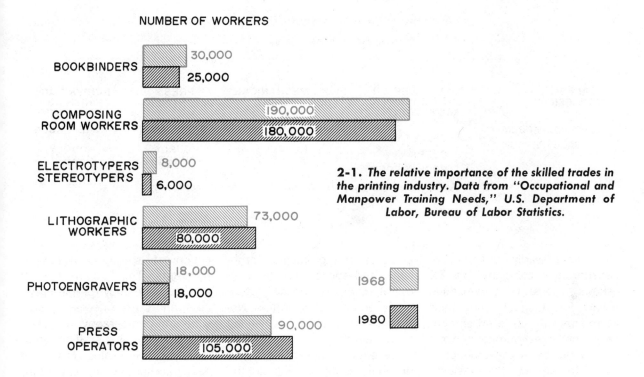

NUMBER OF WORKERS

BOOKBINDERS 30,000 / 25,000

COMPOSING ROOM WORKERS 190,000 / 180,000

ELECTROTYPERS STEREOTYPERS 8,000 / 6,000

LITHOGRAPHIC WORKERS 73,000 / 80,000

PHOTOENGRAVERS 18,000 / 18,000

PRESS OPERATORS 90,000 / 105,000

1968   1980

2-1. *The relative importance of the skilled trades in the printing industry. Data from "Occupational and Manpower Training Needs," U.S. Department of Labor, Bureau of Labor Statistics.*

a great deal, technological advances will enable each worker to produce more work, thus reducing the number of new workers needed.

The steady switch from letterpress to offset printing will cause a steady decline in the number of photoengravers needed in the future.

It is anticipated that the number of press operators and assistants will increase in the future. Improved press equipment may slow this growth, but the demand for printing in the future is estimated to be so great that more press operators will be needed.

The rapid technological changes in the printing industry are creating new jobs that differ from the traditional "job" production trades. Some of these, such as computer use in composition and automatic plate processing, have been mentioned. One other trend to observe is a move toward inline production. Inline production refers to the joining of areas, such as press and bindery, which transforms typical job production into continuous production. Workers are involved with the total production process rather than with one phase. This could likely be the most far-reaching change of all in the years ahead.

MANAGEMENT CAREERS

Printing management refers to those positions which are in-

volved in the day-to-day operation of the printing business. These include the top management staff, sales, accounting, estimating, production scheduling, and purchasing.

The term *top management* is often used when referring to the president, members of the board of directors, executive staff members, and the plant general manager. This top-level group is responsible for establishing the policies used to operate the business.

In a small company the president is often the person who started the company. This person could be sole owner, though financial pressures may make it necessary to sell part interest in the company. These co-owners

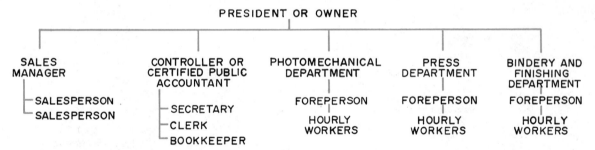

A TYPICAL SMALL LITHOGRAPHIC COMPANY

PRESIDENT OR OWNER

SALES MANAGER	CONTROLLER OR CERTIFIED PUBLIC ACCOUNTANT	PHOTOMECHANICAL DEPARTMENT	PRESS DEPARTMENT	BINDERY AND FINISHING DEPARTMENT
SALESPERSON SALESPERSON	SECRETARY CLERK BOOKKEEPER	FOREPERSON HOURLY WORKERS	FOREPERSON HOURLY WORKERS	FOREPERSON HOURLY WORKERS

2-2. *An organization chart for a small lithographic company.*

do not necessarily become active in running a company. Fig. 2-2 shows a possible organization chart for a small lithographic company with 25 to 40 employees. The largest number of workers would be in the production area. In this case the president works directly with the forepersons of the various production, sales, and business areas. The president is directly involved in the details of the total operation.

If the company grew over the years, it would be impossible for the president to have time to tend to all these details. Fig. 2-3 shows a possible organization for the company if it grew to have 100 or more employees. Notice that a top management position, *plant superintendent,* was added to relieve the president of direct responsibility for production. The plant superintendent works directly with the department forepersons. The sales area was assigned to an executive with sales ability. This person could be given the position of *vice-president.* The business operation was taken over by *treasurer* or *comptroller.* As the company grew, the president got farther away from the day-to-day sales,

business and production problems, and spent more time on overall company policy, future plans, and overall operation. Notice that the company is headed by a board of directors, which represents the stockholders. The president is responsible to the board for the total operation of the company.

The *sales staff* of a printing company is concerned with selling the services of the concern. This could be printed material, such as a brochure or advertising space in a newspaper. The staff must understand the total printing operation, the fundamentals of design, and the principles of advertising. They must work constantly on customer relations. They serve as technical representatives to potential customers and advise them about their printing needs. The functions of the sales staff are discussed further in Chapter 3.

The advertising aspects of sales are generally headed by an *advertising manager.* In a large company both the sales manager and advertising manager might report to a vice-president. Fig. 2-3. The advertising manager oversees the planning and exe-

cution of specific advertising programs. This person has a staff to write copy, prepare layouts, and do the necessary artwork and photography. It is also necessary for this staff to work closely with the sales staff.

The accounting department in a large firm is usually headed by a comptroller or a treasurer. This person has the responsibility to protect the total assets of the company. Positions in the accounting area are those of auditor, general accountant, cost accountant, credit manager, and a variety of clerks, such as those keeping the payroll and customer billings.

The production area in a large concern is headed by a *plant superintendent.* (This title can vary.) This person is responsible for the operation of all phases of production in all departments. The superintendent must work with the purchasing department to see that supplies and paper are ordered. The responsibility for employee work records, pay rates, and state and federal wage and hour laws are included. The superintendent is also responsible for maintaining the flow of work, job planning, and scheduling workers and equipment for maximum effectiveness and safety.

The various production departments will generally be headed by a foreperson, responsible to the plant superintendent for the efficient operation of production in a certain area. The foreperson does the production scheduling and assigns the workload to the hourly employees. Included is responsibility for the technical and mechanical phases of production and utilization of them for maximum efficiency and quality. In the typical plant illustrated in Fig. 2-3 there are forepersons for the following departments: photomechanical, press, bindery and finishing, and production scheduling. The production scheduling department is usually headed by the *production manager*. This manager is responsible for scheduling all production operations. The production manager's office maintains a production board showing where each job is within the plant. The manager receives all estimates and production details for each job, checks and approves them, and sees that production begins. Often the duties include the purchase of paper. The *chief estimator* is part of the production scheduling staff. The duties include training the estimator-production personnel and responsibility for the accuracy of all estimates. *Estimator-production* personnel do the actual estimating and establish production details. They work with the sales staff to set costs on jobs to be bid. They receive the orders for items or services sold from the sales department, along with artwork and copy; they turn over

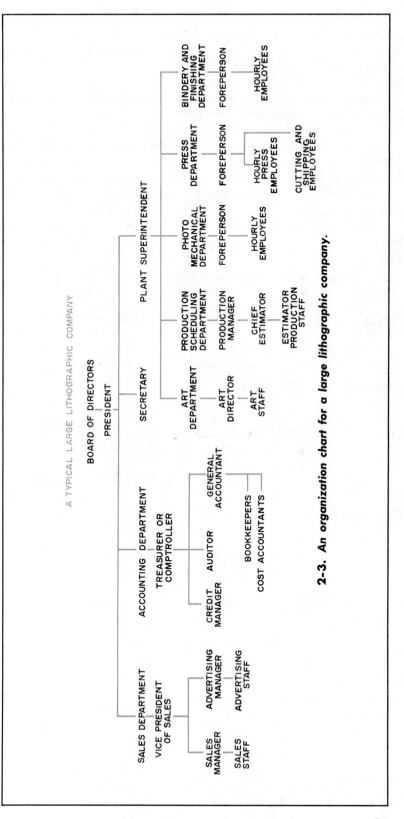

2-3. An organization chart for a large lithographic company.

the complete details to the production manager for processing. This means that the estimator-production personnel assemble all items needed for the job, such as samples of color, amount and kind of paper, and delivery date.

After approval by the production manager, the job is turned over to the art director as the first step in production. It is the responsibility of the estimator-production personnel to keep track of the job while it is in pro-

duction and see that it is delivered on time. They check all proofs and see that corrections are made.

The functions of the estimator are discussed further in Chapter 3.

The *art director* is responsible for the total operation of the art department. This includes the technical processes, quality of work, and job schedules. The director must be aware of costs and operate so that a profit can

be made. Duties include hiring and training art employees.

The art department employees perform a variety of tasks. In small departments they have a wider range of tasks than in larger departments which permit specialization. Duties usually include graphic design, making line drawings, airbrush work, preparing artwork for photography, and lettering.

REVIEW QUESTIONS

1. The largest number of people working in the graphic reproduction field are employed in the printing and publishing of advertising material. True or False?
2. Is a bindery always part of a printing company?
3. Workers in the skilled printing crafts are directly involved with printing production. Name four typical skilled crafts in the printing industry.
4. Copy is set in the composing room. True or False?
5. Most photoengravers work for companies which produce plates for printing concerns. True or False?
6. Electrotypers and stereotypers work on typesetting machines. True or False?
7. What are the press operator's helpers called?
8. What is the fastest growing method of printing?

THE STEPS IN PRINTING PRODUCTION

A very generalized summary of printing production is detailed in Figs. 3-1 and 3-2, found on pages 40 and 41. This brief report mentions areas that are covered by various chapters of the text. Before a job can be planned, there must be an understanding of the processes in each phase of printing.

ART AND COPY PREPARATION

The first stage of producing a job is the preparation of the art and copy for reproduction. Figs. 3-1 and 3-2. This work is often performed by the art department of the company selling the job. The customer has a great deal to say about this stage of production, since he or she must be satisfied with the end results. The art staff must give careful consideration as to how the job is to be printed. They must consult with the production staff whenever it is not clear which processes are to be used. Sometimes the production staff receives the artwork and the copy already converted into the proper image form for reproduction, such as a photograph. Sometimes the production staff has to generate the text into image carriers.

The art staff produces the finished art. It is called "camera ready." This means that all images, type, and pictures are ready to be photographed. The art staff gives complete instructions, such as how to crop photographs, and how all parts of the job are to be positioned. The layout of the total job, called a dummy, which was approved by the customer, is part of the material given to the printing staff.

Considerable detail on copy design and art preparation can be found in Chapter 5, "Graphic Design," and Chapter 9, "Preparing Copy for the Camera."

JOB ANALYSIS, PLANNING, SCHEDULING

It is the purpose of those responsible for job planning to decide exactly how a job will go through the printing plant. The job to be printed is carefully analyzed, and a production schedule is made. Often it is necessary to consult with those in charge of the various departments so that everything is coordinated. The main purpose of planning production is to anticipate difficulties that may occur when doing a job and to make provisions for handling them before they occur.

The job planner must know which processes can be performed in the plant and which

must be sent away to some other plant. For example, some plants have all their typesetting done by a typesetting company. Others may send away transparencies to have color separations made. All of these out-of-house processes must be scheduled and completed before the job can be printed.

The planners must also be aware of the job load of each department as they make the production schedule. They also must keep the delivery date in mind. The bid price is an important consideration, or else the planners might develop a production plan that would increase the cost beyond the acceptable limit and lose money on the job.

The purchasing agent should be informed as to the necessary materials and services. A job cannot be printed until the materials are in the shop.

The production schedule must include the time the job is to be on each machine. If the estimate is carefully done, it is frequently used by the production manager in planning overall printing schedules. If the estimating is generally poor, the planner will want to reconsider the time allotments.

Points at which the job is checked for accuracy and quality must be established. Other areas

PHASES OF OFFSET PRINTING

Phases	Workers Involved	Work Performed	For Details Read
1. Copy and art preparation	Copywriters; advertising, sales staff; commercial artists; photographers; book designers	Write text material, make original drawings, take photos, decide on layout and design of job, select materials, copyfit, imposition	Chapter 3, "Planning, Copyfitting, and Measurement" Chapter 5, "Graphic Design" Chapter 20, "Imposition and Lockup"
2. Text composition	Punched-tape machine operators, photocomposition machine operators, darkroom staff, typists for direct-image production, proofreaders	Film negatives and positives, paper positives or negatives, typewritten copy on paper, or direct-image plates	Chapter 6, "Cold Composition" Chapter 9, "Preparing Copy for the Camera"
3. Art and photo conversion	Camera operators, color separation, color correction, darkroom workers	Produce photographic positives, negatives, or transparencies on film for photomechanical making of image carriers	Chapter 10, "Line Photography" Chapter 11, "Halftone Photography"
4. Stripping	Layout workers, strippers	Assemble photographic negatives and positives into a flat, as indicated by the job layout, so they may be exposed as a unit to an image carrier	Chapter 13, "Laying Out and Stripping the Flat"
5. Producing the image carrier	Platemaker	Expose the flat to the image carrier desired; develop and finish it for use on the press	Chapter 14, "Offset Platemaking"
6. Printing the job	Press operators, assistant press operators, helpers, production supervisors, quality control staff	Print the job	Chapter 15, "Offset Press Systems" Chapter 16, "Operation and Adjustment of the Offset Press"
7. Bindery and completion of the job	Operators of the following machines: collators, folders, gatherers, cutters, inserters, serving, casing-in, adhesive and plastic binding, drilling, case making	Assemble and bind the printed sheets into their final size and form	Chapter 23, "Bindery and Finishing"

3-1. *The phases of offset printing production.*

that must be notified of schedules are the receiving and shipping departments. The receiving department must dispatch materials received to the proper place at the time they are needed. Shipping instructions and the delivery schedule must be carefully observed.

PHASES OF LETTERPRESS PRINTING

Phases	Workers Involved	Work Performed	For Details Read
1. Copy and art preparation	Copywriters; advertising, sales staff; commercial artists; photographers; book designers	Write text material, make original drawings, take photos, decide on layout and design of job, select materials, copyfit, imposition	Chapter 3, "Planning, Copyfitting, and Measurement" Chapter 5, "Graphic Design" Chapter 20, "Imposition and Lockup"
2. Text composition	Linotype, Monotype, Ludlow, hand compositors; Intertype operators; layout and lockup workers; proofreaders	Set hot metal type, assemble into desired units, pull proofs, proofread	Chapter 7, "Relief Composition—Hand" Chapter 8, "Relief Composition—Machine" Chapter 4, "Proofreading"
3. Converting picture images to relief carriers	Electroplater, engraving machine operators, platemakers, photoengravers, strippers	Produce relief plates	Chapter 19, "Plates for Letterpress Printing"
4. Assembling relief image carriers	Lockup workers, press operator, stonemen	Assemble hot type and picture relief images into forms for printing	Chapter 13, "Laying Out and Stripping the Flat"
5. Making duplicate plates if needed	Electrotypers, stereotypers, molders of rubber and plastic plates	Produce flat or curved electrotypes and stereotypes, or flat rubber and plastic plates	Chapter 19, "Plates for Letterpress Printing"
6. Printing the job	Press operators, assistant press operators, helpers, production supervisors, take-off workers, quality control staff	Print the job	Chapter 21, "Platen Press Operation" Chapter 22, "Cylinder Press Operation" Chapter 26, "Ink" Chapter 25, "Paper"
7. Bindery and completion of the job	Operators of the following machines: collators, folders, gatherers, cutters, inserters, serving, casing-in, adhesive and plastic binding, drilling, case making	Assemble and bind the printed sheets into their final size and form	Chapter 23, "Bindery and Finishing"

3-2. *The phases of letterpress printing production.*

Job analysis, planning, and scheduling involve the entire supervisory force of a plant. Communication and coordination are essential to the proper functioning of a plant and the earning of a fair profit.

PRODUCTION OF IMAGE CARRIERS

Image carriers are the devices which contain the image to be printed; they are used in the actual printing process. These include all of the processes mentioned in Chapter 1, "The Printing Industry." The common carriers include offset plates, letterpress plates, metal typeforms, gravure cylinders, and process screens. Figs. 3-1 and 3-2.

The quality of the art and copy

preparation is critical to the production of quality image carriers, which, in turn, are essential to quality reproduction in the pressroom. Careful inspection of the image carrier is necessary before it is sent to the pressroom for the actual printing process.

THE ACTUAL PRINTING PROCESS

The more commonly used printing processes are explained in Chapter 1, "The Printing Industry." Figs. 3-1 and 3-2. The press operators receive the image carriers and mount them on the press. They make all the preparatory press adjustments needed to produce quality work. In this process the press operators must continue to observe the job specifications developed originally as the job was sold and estimated. The specifications tell everything they need to know: the kind of paper, color of ink, and how the job is to be bound or finished. In addition, they have the production analysis schedule to follow.

A mistake or poor work at this point is extremely expensive. All mistakes are expensive, but if a press operator runs a job that is rejected, the loss is most damaging.

BINDERY AND FINISHING

After a job is printed, it usually requires some binding or finishing operation. Figs. 3-1 and 3-2. Some companies have their own binderies, and the job is scheduled in as part of the production plan. Others ship the job to commercial binders for the finishing operations. The binding and finishing operations convert the printed job into its final form so

that it is ready to perform the purpose for which it was designed.

Coordination between the press and bindery operations is essential. The bindery staff needs to understand the job and have the job dummy available. They need information on trims, bleeds, die cuts, folds, assembly information, and other bindery and finishing operations required. The bindery packages the completed job, and the shipping department arranges delivery to the customer.

MEASUREMENT IN PRINTING

Accurate measurement is vital to all phases of the printing process. Through the years printers in many countries developed systems of measurement to be applied to printing. The current system evolved from those which became accepted and found increasing use. Across the world there is a movement to the metric system as the basis for all measurement. The movement has found wide acceptance and is gradually influencing measurements in the printing industry. Some of the changes underway include graphic arts

film, the lines on halftone screens, the measures of volume for mixing ink, newspaper layouts, and sizes of envelopes and business forms, paper sizes, printing plates, and book sizes. The emergence of computer-assisted phototypesetting has provided increased drive for metric conversion. This will perhaps speed the phasing out of hot metal typesetting, since it would be difficult to convert to metric from the printers' point system.

Segments of the industry are advocating international standards of measurement for the printing industry. The advantages of standard sizes the world over are tremendous.

THE METRIC SYSTEM

The existing metric system of measurement was formalized at the 11th General Conference of Weights and Measures held in 1960. The name given the system was Système International d'Unités. English-speaking countries refer to it as the International System of Units and abbreviate it "SI".

The base SI units are shown in Fig. 3-3. These are the metre, second, kilogram, kelvin, am-

SI BASE UNITS

Quantity	Unit	Symbol
Length	metre	m
Time	second	s
Mass	kilogram	kg
Temperature	kelvin	K
Electric current	ampere	A
Luminous intensity	candela	cd
Amount of substance	mole	mol

3-3. *The seven base units of the SI metric system.*

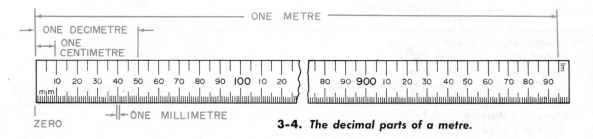

3-4. *The decimal parts of a metre.*

3-5. *U.S. customary and metric measures of length.*

pere, candela, and mole. The metre (m) is the base unit of length. It is divided into 10 parts called decimetres (dm). The decimetre (dm) is divided into 10 parts called centimetres (cm). The centimetre (cm) is divided into 10 parts called millimetres (mm). Fig. 3-4.

Notice that these are decimal parts of the metre. There are 10 decimetres in a metre; thus, one decimetre equals 0.1 metre. There are 10 centimetres in a decimetre and 10 decimetres in a metre. Therefore there are 10 × 10, or 100, centimetres in a metre. One centimetre is 0.01 metre. There are 1000 millimetres in a metre. Therefore, one millimetre is 0.001 metre. Fig. 3-5.

Surface measure is found in the same manner as when using the U.S. customary system. The difference is the unit of measure. The volume of solids is stated in terms of the unit of length used, cubed. For example, a square box one metre on each side has a volume of one cubic metre (1 m³). Fig. 3-6.

When measuring liquids and the capacity of containers, the litre and millilitre are used. A millilitre is 1/1000 of a litre. A

MEASURES OF LENGTH

Customary
    12 inches (in.) = 1 foot (ft.)
    3 feet (ft.) = 1 yard (yd.)
Metric
    Base unit 1 metre (m)
    1 decimetre (dm) = 1/10 metre or 0.1 m
    1 centimetre (cm) = 1/100 metre or 0.01 m
    1 millimetre (mm) = 1/1000 metre or 0.001 m
Conversions
    Customary to Metric
    1 inch = 25.4 millimetres
    1 inch = 2.54 centimetres
    1 foot = 30.48 centimetres
    1 foot = 0.3048 metre
    1 yard = 91.44 centimetres
    1 yard = 0.9144 metre
    Metric to Customary
    1 millimetre = 0.039 37 inch
    1 centimetre = 0.3937 inch
    1 metre = 39.37 inches
    1 metre = 3.2808 feet
    1 metre = 1.0936 yards

SURFACE MEASURE

Customary
    1 square foot (ft.²) = 144 square inches (in.²)
    1 square yard (yd.²) = 9 square feet (ft.²)
Metric
    1 square centimetre (cm²) = 100 square millimetres (mm²)
    1 square decimetre (dm²) = 100 square centimetres (cm²)
Conversion
    1 square inch (in.²) = 6.45 square centimetres (cm²)
    1 square centimetre (cm²) = 0.155 square inches (in.²)
    1 square foot (ft.²) = 0.093 square metre (m²)
    1 square metre (m²) = 10.763 square feet (ft.²)
    1 square yard (yd.²) = 0.8361 square metre (m²)
    1 square metre (m²) = 1.196 square yards (yd.²)

3-6. *U.S. customary and metric surface measure.*

MEASURES OF VOLUME OR CAPACITY

Customary—Liquid Measure
    1 pint (pt.) = 16 ounces (oz.)
    1 quart (qt.) or 32 ounces (oz.) = 2 pints (pt.)
    1 gallon (gal.) or 128 ounces (oz.) = 4 quarts (qt.)
    1 gallon (gal.) = 231 cubic inches (cu. in.)

Metric—Liquid Measure
    Base unit 1 cubic metre (m^3)
    1 cubic metre (m^3) = 1000 litres (L) or 1000 cubic decimetres (dm^3)
    1 litre (L) = 1 cubic decimetre (dm^3)
    1 litre (L) = 1000 millilitres (mL)
    1 kilolitre (kL) = 1000 litres (L)

Conversions
    1 quart = 0.946 litre
    1 litre = 1.056 quarts
    1 gallon = 3.785 litres
    1 litre = 0.264 gallons
    1 cubic metre = 33.814 fluid ounces (liquid)

3-7. *U.S. customary and metric measures of volume or capacity.*

MEASURES OF MASS (WEIGHT)

Customary (Avoirdupois)
    1 pound (lb.) = 16 ounces (oz.)

Metric
    Base unit 1 kilogram (kg)
    1 kilogram (kg) = 1000 grams (g)
    1 gram (g) = 1000 milligrams (mg)

Conversion
    1 ounce = 28.350 grams
    1 gram = 0.035 ounces
    1 pound = 0.454 kilograms
    1 kilogram = 2.205 pounds

3-8. *U.S. customary and metric measures of mass.*

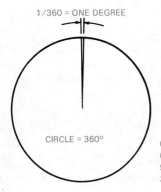

1/360 = ONE DEGREE

CIRCLE = 360°

3-9. *Angular measure.*

60 SECONDS (60″) = 1 MINUTE (1′)
60 MINUTES (60′) = 1 DEGREE (1°)
90 DEGREES (90°) = A RIGHT ANGLE
360 DEGREES (360°) = A COMPLETE CIRCLE

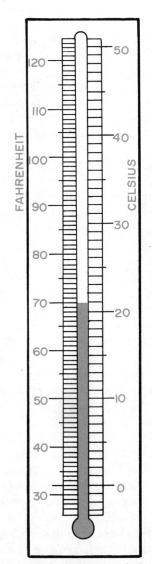

FAHRENHEIT

CELSIUS

3-10. *A comparison of degrees Fahrenheit and Celsius.*

COMMON MEASURES

Centimetres	× 0.3937	= Inches
Centimetres	× 10	= Millimetres
Degrees (of an angle)	× 60	= Minutes
Gallons	× 3.785	= Litres
Gallons	× 8	= Pints
Gallons	× 4	= Quarts
Gallons	× 128	= Ounces (liquid)
Gallons	× 3785	= Cubic centimetres
Grams	× 0.03527	= Ounces (avoirdupois)
Grams	× 15.432	= Grains
Inches	× 2.540	= Centimetres
Litres	× 0.2642	= Gallons
Litres	× 1.057	= Quarts
Litres	× 2.113	= Pints
Millimetres	× 0.1	= Centimetres
Millimetres	× 0.03937	= Inches
Ounces (avoirdupois)	× 0.0625	= Pounds
Ounces (avoirdupois)	× 28.35	= Grams
Ounces (liquid)	× 0.02957	= Litres
Pounds	× 16	= Ounces (avoirdupois)
Pounds	× 256	= Drams
Pounds	× 7000	= Grains

To convert degrees Celsius to degrees Fahrenheit, multiply by 9/5 and add 32.

To convert degrees Fahrenheit to degrees Celsius, subtract 32 and multiply by 5/9.

3-11. A comparison of common U.S. customary and metric measures.

litre is a little more than a quart. Fig. 3-7.

Mass is the amount of matter in an object. It is the term used to refer to what we commonly call weight, except that the influence of gravity, which varies in different places, is not present in determining mass. The basic unit of mass is the kilogram. Fig. 3-8. It equals about 2 1/2 pounds under the avoirdupois system. (Avoirdupois weight is a system of weights and measures used in English-speaking countries. It is based on a pound that contains 16 ounces and is equal to 453.59 grams.)

The metric unit of time is the second. The minute (min) and second (s) will continue in use even though they are not based on multiples of 10 and therefore not decimal. For the present, 60 seconds will equal one minute and 60 minutes will equal one hour, just as in the U.S. customary system.

Even though the radian is the metric unit for a plane angle, the degree (°) will continue to maintain its present meaning. A circle equals 360 degrees. Fig. 3-9.

The metric base unit of temperature is the kelvin (K). It has its zero point at absolute zero. This equals −273.15 °C. However, the kelvin will be used only for thermodynamic applications. All other temperature measurements will be in degrees Celsius (°C). On the Celsius scale, 100 °C is the boiling point of water, and 0 °C is the freezing point of water. Fig. 3-10.

The metric unit of luminous intensity is the candela (cd). The SI unit of light flux is the lumen (lm). Light flux is the amount of light passing through an area per second. A 100-watt incandescent bulb emits about 1700 lumens.

In Fig. 3-11 are comparisons of common U.S. customary and metric measures. These can be used when converting a measure from one system to the other.

Since it will be some years before the change to the metric system is complete, printers will

MILLIMETRES TO DECIMAL INCHES

mm	in.	mm	in.	mm	in.	mm	in.	mm	in.
1	0.0394	21	0.8268	41	1.6142	61	2.4016	81	3.1890
2	0.0787	22	0.8662	42	1.6536	62	2.4410	82	3.2284
3	0.1181	23	0.9055	43	1.6929	63	2.4804	83	3.2678
4	0.1575	24	0.9449	44	1.7323	64	2.5197	84	3.3071
5	0.1969	25	0.9843	45	1.7717	65	2.5591	85	3.3465
6	0.2362	26	1.0236	46	1.8111	66	2.5985	86	3.3859
7	0.2756	27	1.0630	47	1.8504	67	2.6378	87	3.4253
8	0.3150	28	1.1024	48	1.8898	68	2.6772	88	3.4646
9	0.3543	29	1.1418	49	1.9292	69	2.7166	89	3.5040
10	0.3937	30	1.1811	50	1.9685	70	2.7560	90	3.5434
11	0.4331	31	1.2205	51	2.0079	71	2.7953	91	3.5827
12	0.4724	32	1.2599	52	2.0473	72	2.8247	92	3.6221
13	0.5118	33	1.2992	53	2.0867	73	2.8741	93	3.6615
14	0.5512	34	1.3386	54	2.1260	74	2.9134	94	3.7009
15	0.5906	35	1.3780	55	2.1654	75	2.9528	95	3.7402
16	0.6299	36	1.4173	56	2.2048	76	2.9922	96	3.7796
17	0.6693	37	1.4567	57	2.2441	77	3.0316	97	3.8190
18	0.7087	38	1.4961	58	2.2835	78	3.0709	98	3.8583
19	0.7480	39	1.5355	59	2.3229	79	3.1103	99	3.8977
20	0.7874	40	1.5748	60	2.3622	80	3.1497	100	3.9371

3-12. *Table for converting milli-metres to decimal inches.*

FRACTIONAL INCHES TO MILLIMETRES

in.	mm	in.	mm	in.	mm	in.	mm
1/64	0.397	17/64	6.747	33/64	13.097	49/64	19.447
1/32	0.794	9/32	7.144	17/32	13.494	25/32	19.844
3/64	1.191	19/64	7.541	35/64	13.890	51/64	20.240
1/16	1.587	5/16	7.937	9/16	14.287	13/16	20.637
5/64	1.984	21/64	8.334	37/64	14.684	53/64	21.034
3/32	2.381	11/32	8.731	19/32	15.081	27/32	21.431
7/64	2.778	23/64	9.128	39/64	15.478	55/64	21.828
1/8	3.175	3/8	9.525	5/8	15.875	7/8	22.225
9/64	3.572	25/64	9.922	41/64	16.272	57/64	22.622
5/32	3.969	13/32	10.319	21/32	16.669	29/32	23.019
11/64	4.366	27/64	10.716	43/64	17.065	59/64	23.415
3/16	4.762	7/16	11.113	11/16	17.462	15/16	23.812
13/64	5.159	29/64	11.509	45/64	17.859	61/64	24.209
7/32	5.556	15/32	11.906	23/32	18.256	31/32	24.606
15/64	5.953	31/64	12.303	47/64	18.653	63/64	25.003
1/4	6.350	1/2	12.700	3/4	19.050	1	25.400

3-13. *Table for converting frac-tional inches to millimetres.*

have to change decimal fractions and common fractions to metric measure or vice versa. Tables to help with this are found in Figs. 3-12 through 3-15.

THE PRINTING POINT SYSTEM OF MEASUREMENT

The measurements used in the printing industry must be very accurate. Some of the mate-rial used is quite thin. The sys-tem of measurement developed for use in printing is based on a unit called a *pica*. A pica is 0.166 of an inch, or about 1/6 of an

DECIMAL INCHES TO MILLIMETRES

in.	mm	in.	mm	in.	mm
0.001	0.0254	0.01	0.254	0.1	2.54
0.002	0.0508	0.02	0.508	0.2	5.08
0.003	0.0762	0.03	0.762	0.3	7.62
0.004	0.1016	0.04	1.016	0.4	10.16
0.005	0.1270	0.05	1.270	0.5	12.70
0.006	0.1524	0.06	1.524	0.6	15.24
0.007	0.1778	0.07	1.778	0.7	17.78
0.008	0.2032	0.08	2.032	0.8	20.32
0.009	0.2286	0.09	2.286	0.9	22.86

3-14. *Table for converting decimal inches to millimetres.*

INCHES TO MILLIMETRES

in.	mm	in.	mm	in.	mm	in.	mm
1	25.4	26	660.4	51	1295.4	76	1930.4
2	50.8	27	685.8	52	1320.8	77	1955.8
3	76.2	28	711.2	53	1346.2	78	1981.2
4	101.6	29	736.6	54	1371.1	79	2006.8
5	127.0	30	762.0	55	1397.0	80	2032.0
6	152.4	31	787.4	56	1422.4	81	2057.4
7	177.8	32	812.8	57	1447.8	82	2082.8
8	203.2	33	838.2	58	1473.2	83	2108.2
9	228.6	34	863.6	59	1498.6	84	2133.6
10	254.0	35	889.0	60	1524.0	85	2159.0
11	279.4	36	914.4	61	1549.4	86	2184.4
12	304.8	37	939.8	62	1574.8	87	2209.8
13	330.2	38	956.2	63	1600.2	88	2235.2
14	355.6	39	990.6	64	1625.6	89	2260.6
15	381.0	40	1016.0	65	1651.0	90	2286.0
16	406.4	41	1041.4	66	1676.4	91	2311.4
17	431.8	42	1066.8	67	1701.8	92	2336.8
18	457.2	43	1092.2	68	1727.2	93	2362.2
19	482.6	44	1117.6	69	1752.6	94	2387.6
20	508.0	45	1143.0	70	1778.0	95	2413.0
21	533.4	46	1168.4	71	1803.4	96	2438.4
22	558.8	47	1193.8	72	1828.8	97	2463.8
23	584.2	48	1219.2	73	1854.2	98	2489.2
24	609.6	49	1244.6	74	1879.6	99	2514.6
25	635.0	50	1270.0	75	1905.0	100	2540.0

3-15. *Table for converting inches to millimetres.*

3-16. *The printers' system of measurement.*

inch. Six picas are only 0.004 less than an inch. Therefore, it is commonly said that six picas equal one inch. Fig. 3-16.

Center for Metric Education
Western Michigan University

3-17. *Customary and metric equivalents of printers' units of measure.*

Each pica is divided into *points*. A point is 0.0138 of an inch. It takes 12 points to equal one pica (0.166 inches).

The point system used in printing is compared with the customary system in Fig. 3-17. Notice the slight difference between the approximate fractional size and the actual size. Customary and metric equivalents of the printers' units of measure are also shown in Fig. 3-17. The customary and printers' unit equivalents of metric measure are shown in Fig. 3-18.

PRINTERS' UNITS CONVERSIONS

PRINTERS' UNITS		CUSTOMARY MEASURE			METRIC
Picas	Points	Approximate Fractional Inches	Decimal Inches		Millimetres
	1	1/64	0.014		0.35
	2	1/32	0.028		0.70
	3	3/64	0.042		1.05
	4	7/128	0.055		1.40
	5	1/16	0.069		1.75
	6	5/64	0.083		2.10
	7	3/32	0.097		2.45
	8	7/64	0.111		2.80
	9	1/8	0.125		3.15
	10	9/64	0.138		3.50
1	12	21/128	0.166		4.20
	14	25/128	0.194		4.90
	18	1/4	0.249		6.30
2	24	21/64	0.332		8.40
	30	53/128	0.414		10.50
3	36	1/2	0.498		12.60
	42	37/64	0.581		14.70
4	48	85/128	0.664		16.80
5	60	53/64	0.828		21.00
6	72	1	0.996		25.20

METRIC UNITS CONVERSIONS

METRIC	PRINTERS' UNITS		CUSTOMARY
Millimetres	Points	Approximate Picas and Points	Decimal Inches
1	2.86		0.039
2	5.71		0.079
3	8.57		0.118
4	11.43		0.157
5	14.29	1 + 2¼	0.197
6	17.14	1 + 5	0.236
7	20.00	1 + 8	0.276
8	22.86	1 + 10¾	0.315
9	25.71	2 + 1½	0.354
10	28.57	2 + 4½	0.394
15	42.86	3 + 6¾	0.591
20	57.14	4 + 9	0.787
25	71.43	5 + 11	0.984
30	85.71	7 + 1¼	1.181
35	100.00	8 + 3½	1.378
40	114.28	9 + 5¾	1.575
45	128.57	10 + 4	1.772
50	142.85	11 + 6¼	1.969
75	214.28	17 + 5¼	2.953
100	285.71	23 + 8½	3.937

MEASURING TOOLS

The tool used for measuring is the line or type gauge. Fig. 3-19. It has picas laid off on one edge. Each pica is further divided into a size called nonpareil, which has 6 points. The other edge of the line gauge is divided into inches the same as an ordinary ruler. Line gauges are usually made of steel or brass. The scales are usually etched into the metal.

A variety of scales are used in the various printing areas. Some of these are shown in Fig. 3-20. Notice the scales that are available include inches, picas, points,

Center for Metric Education
Western Michigan University

3-18. *Printers' and customary equivalents of millimetres.*

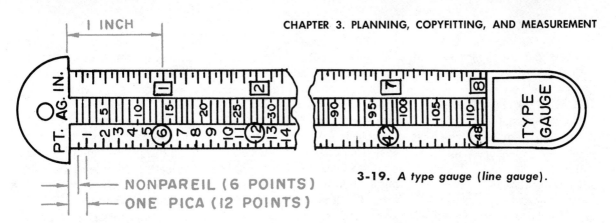

NONPAREIL (6 POINTS)
ONE PICA (12 POINTS)

3-19. *A type gauge* (*line gauge*).

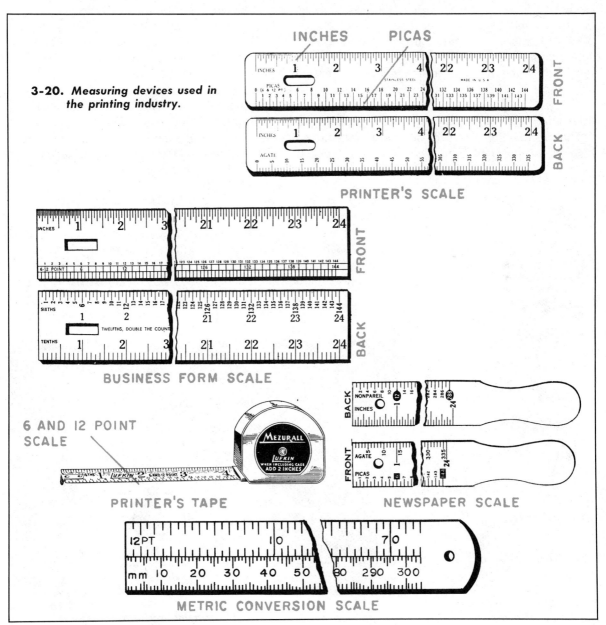

3-20. *Measuring devices used in the printing industry.*

INCHES   PICAS

PRINTER'S SCALE

BUSINESS FORM SCALE

6 AND 12 POINT SCALE

PRINTER'S TAPE

NEWSPAPER SCALE

METRIC CONVERSION SCALE

an agate (5 1/2 point) scale, and metric scales.

THE MICROMETER CALIPER

Many thin materials are used in printing. Items such as offset plates are measured in thousandths of an inch. To make such measurements, a precision measuring tool called a micrometer caliper is used. Some micrometers have a vernier scale on the thimble, which makes it possible to measure in ten-thousandths of an inch. The important parts of the micrometer are shown in Fig. 3-21.

Measuring with a Micrometer

The micrometer is used by holding it in the right hand. The frame can rest on the palm of the hand. The adjustments are made by turning the thimble, which is held between the thumb and index finger. Fig. 3-22. The thimble is rotated counterclockwise until the space between the anvil and the spindle is slightly larger than the part to be measured. Slip the part between the anvil and spindle. Rotate the thimble clockwise until the spindle gently touches the part being measured. Do not force the spindle tight. Just make a gentle contact. Then turn the ratchet stop. It will slip when the proper pressure is reached. This makes it possible to get the same pressure every time. The size of the part being measured can now be read on the sleeve and thimble.

Reading the Micrometer in Thousandths

The spaces marked on the sleeve each equal 25 thousandths (0.025) of an inch. The measurements on the thimble each equal one thousandth of an inch. Study Fig. 3-23. Notice that seven marks are visible on the sleeve. This equals 0.025″ × 7 or 175 thousandths (0.175) of an inch. Added to this is the number of thousandths on the thimble. Notice the thimble reads 3 thousandths (0.003) of an inch. Fig. 3-23. The thickness of the part being measured is 0.175 + 0.003, or 0.178 inch.

Each time the thimble makes one complete revolution, it moves out the sleeve 0.025″. This is one mark on the sleeve.

If very thin material of less than 0.025″ is to be measured, the reading will be found only on the thimble. All thicknesses from 0.001″ to 0.024″ are read on the thimble.

READING THE METRIC MICROMETER

The metric micrometer is used in the same manner as just described for one graduated in the U.S. customary decimal system.

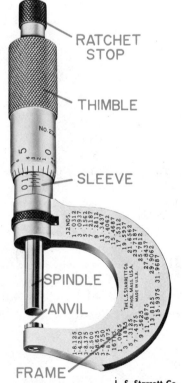

RATCHET STOP

THIMBLE

SLEEVE

SPINDLE

ANVIL

FRAME

L. S. Starrett Co.

3-21. The parts of a micrometer caliper.

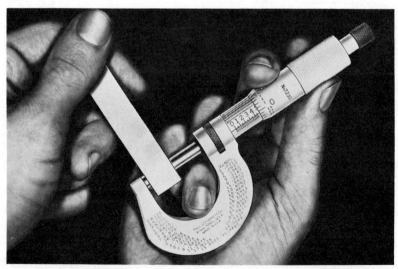

L. S. Starrett Co.

3-22. How to hold an outside micrometer caliper.

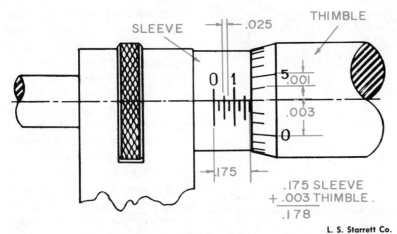

SLEEVE · .025 · THIMBLE

.175 SLEEVE
+ .003 THIMBLE
.178

L. S. Starrett Co.

3-23. *How to read a micrometer caliper graduated in thousandths of an inch.*

sions. Each graduation on the bevel is equal to 0.01 mm.

To read a metric micrometer, add the total reading (in millimetres) visible on the sleeve to the reading (in hundredths of a millimetre) indicated on the thimble that coincides with the longitudinal line on the sleeve.

In the example shown in Fig. 3-25, notice that five marks are visible on the sleeve. This equals 5 mm. Beyond this on the sleeve is one 0.5-mm line visible; so the distance on the sleeve is 5.5 mm. To this is added the

The graduations on the metric micrometer are in hundredths of a millimetre. Fig. 3-24. One complete revolution of the thimble advances the spindle away from or toward the anvil 0.5 millimetre.

The longitudinal line on the sleeve is graduated in millimetres from 0 to 25 mm and each millimetre is subdivided into 0.5 mm. It requires *two* revolutions of the thimble to move the spindle a distance of 1 millimetre.

The beveled edge of the thimble is graduated into 50 divi-

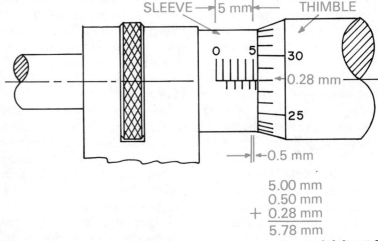

SLEEVE — 5 mm — THIMBLE

0.28 mm

0.5 mm

5.00 mm
0.50 mm
+ 0.28 mm
5.78 mm

L. S. Starrett Co.

3-25. *How to read a metric micrometer caliper graduated in hundredths of a millimetre.*

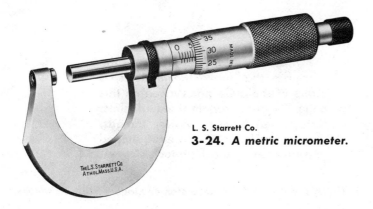

L. S. Starrett Co.
3-24. *A metric micrometer.*

measurement on the thimble. The line 28 matches with the longitudinal line on the sleeve. This equals 0.28 mm. The total distance is therefore 5 mm + 0.5 mm + 0.28 mm, which equals 5.78 mm.

PAPER AND PLATE GAUGES

Another measuring device is a *paper gauge micrometer.* Fig.

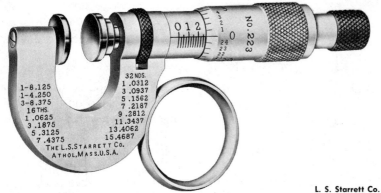

3-26. *A paper gauge micrometer graduated in thousandths of an inch.*

3-26. It is used to measure the thickness of paper and paper-board in increments of 0.0001''. It operates exactly like the micrometer caliper. More information about using this tool can be found in Chapter 25, "Paper."

A plate *type-high gauge* is another measuring tool found in printing shops. It is used to measure accurately the thickness of metal plates. Fig. 3-27.

COPYFITTING

Copyfitting is the process of finding out how much space is needed to print the words in a job. If more copy is provided than available space will accept, the copy must be edited to shorten

it. Sometimes the layout must be changed to provide more space. This must be decided before the job is sent to be printed. If changes are made after composition is started, the cost is increased.

TYPED COPY

The copy for text matter should be typewritten so that a word and character count can be made. It should be double spaced on 8 1/2 × 11 inch paper. The left and top page margins should be 1 1/2 inches. This provides space for the proofreader to mark corrections.

It greatly helps the copyfitting process if the manuscript is

typed with an established line width, so all lines have an equal number of characters. A convenient spacing is 60 characters per line if a pica (12-point) typewriter is used and 72 per line for an elite (10-point) typewriter. The pica typewriter produces 10 characters per inch, and the elite has 12 characters per inch.

The manuscript given to the printer should be as accurate as possible. Changes should be made on the typewritten copy before it is set. After the copy is set, it is expensive to make changes. The proofreading of copy after the type is set is done to catch errors made in composition.

Fig. 3-28 shows a proof of a paragraph that has been set and sent to a customer for approval. Notice the changes made on the proof copy by the customer. All of these changes are editorial. The customer made changes in the wording of the sentences. What problems does this cause the printer? To change one word or letter, the entire line must be reset. Some of the changes require a long word to be inserted for a short one. This forces a word onto the next line. The paragraph will have to be entirely

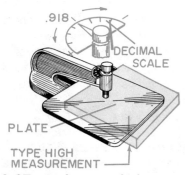

3-27. *A plate type-high gauge.*

bicycle   *compose.*

A bike, like all other products or the machines that make the products, is made of the piece parts given on this page. They have certain standard forms: flat planes, curves, angles, threads, *shown* grooves and holes. They are cut, shaped and finished by machine tools.

These forms

3-28. *A proof on which the customer made editorial changes.*

reset. This greatly increases the cost of composition. All editorial alterations are billed to the customer. Errors which are the fault of the printer are corrected at no charge.

CALCULATING THE AREA NEEDED FOR COPY

Two ways of calculating the area needed for the copy are the square inch and the character count methods.

Square Inch Method of Copyfitting

Copyfitting tables have been developed for various type sizes. These tables give the average number of words per square inch for each type size. Fig. 3-29.

This method can be used to find how many square inches are needed to set a job in a certain type size. The following steps show how this is done:

1. Examine the typed copy. Estimate the total *number of words* in the copy.

2. Select the *type size* to be used in setting the job.

3. Divide the *word count per square inch* for this type size (from the table) into the *total words* to be set.

4. This will tell how many *square inches* of space are needed for the copy in the job.

Another use of the tables is to find the size of type to use when the space available and the number of words are known. This is done by dividing the *number of words* by the *square inches* of space available. This gives the maximum number of *words per square inch* that can be used. Refer to the table, Fig. 3-29, to see which type size will set this amount.

WORDS PER SQUARE INCH FOR VARIOUS TYPE SIZES

Point Size Of Type	Words Per Square Inch	
	Type Set Solid	Type Leaded 2 Points
6	45	33
7	37	26
8	30	22
9	26	20
10	20	15
11	16	13
12	13	11

3-29. *Words per square inch of copy by point size of type.*

The square inch method is useful for preliminary planning of printed copy. It is simple to use and gives a reasonably accurate estimate.

Character Count Method of Copyfitting

There are many kinds of typefaces available for hot metal and cold photographic composition. The actual width of these faces varies a great deal. This means that the same copy set in different faces will occupy different amounts of space. The character count method is an accurate way to figure space requirements because it takes into account the size differences of the various typefaces.

1. Count the number of characters in the typewritten copy.

To find the number of characters per line, examine the typewritten copy. Each letter on a typewriter requires the same space. The typewritten copy is often typed to a specified width. For example, the typed line length used could be 60 charac-

ters. This includes spaces, letters, and punctuation.

The number of characters in the copy is found by multiplying the number of characters in one line by the number of typewritten lines. For example, assume a typewriter is set to type a line 60 characters long. The typed copy has 25 lines to a page. Five pages are typed in this manner. Partial lines are counted as complete lines. The number of characters is 60 characters per line × 25 lines per page × 5 pages = 7,500 characters.

If the typewritten copy is not typed with a uniform number of characters per line, the count is made as follows:

A. Draw a line at the end of the shortest line. Fig. 3-30.

B. Count the characters in this line. Every letter, space, and punctuation mark counts as a character.

C. Multiply the number of characters in one line by the number of *full* lines.

D. Count the characters to the right of the line and those in the

|←——————— 53 CHARACTERS ———————→|

The term copyfitting describes the process by which we
determine whether the manuscript copy when set in type
will make more lines, fewer lines, or the same number of
lines as the copy. +18

Our unit of measurement for copyfitting is characters
per line for both manuscript-copy lines and typeset lines.
Each letter, numeral, punctuation mark, and space between
words counts as a character. + 28

Since practically all manuscript copy is typewritten we
begin by learning to measure the number of characters in
a typewritten line, paragraph, or page. +39

—11

In standard typewriter faces all ~~characters~~ characters
are of the same width. That is, a capital M, for example,
occupies the same width as a lowercase i. +41

+25
CHARACTERS

```
   53 CHARACTERS PER LINE
  X10 FULL LINES
  530
 +151 (18+28+39+41+25)
  681
  —11 MISTAKE
  670 TOTAL CHARACTER COUNT
```

3-30. *The character count method of copyfitting.*

partial lines. Subtract any words or characters that may have been struck as unwanted.

E. Add these together for a total character count.

2. Select the typeface, size of typeface, and the pica length of the line to be set.

3. Find the alphabet length of the typeface selected. The alphabet length is the length of a complete set of lowercase letters in one typeface. Fig 3-31 gives alphabet lengths for a few typefaces. This measurement is in points. Both hot and cold typefaces available are specified by their alphabet length. For example, the alphabet length of 10-point Garamond No. 3 with italic is 118 points. Fig. 3-31.

4. Next refer to the *Characters by Picas* table. Fig. 3-32 (pages 56 and 57). Find the alphabet length of the typeface to be used in the left column. Find the pica size of the length of the line to be set across the top. Notice that the 118-point alphabet length that is set 30 picas long gives 86 characters per line. If the exact alphabet length is not available, use the next highest length.

5. Divide the number of characters in the copy to be set by the characters per line from Step 4. This gives the number of lines that will be needed. If the job has 7,500 characters as in Step 1, and it is set in 10-point Garamond No. 3 with lines 30 picas long, it will take 88 lines of type to do the job. This is found by dividing the 7,500 characters to be set by 86 characters of type per line.

6. Find the length of the total copy. Multiply the type size by the number of lines. If the type is 10-point and there are 88 lines, the length of the copy will be $88 \times 10 = 880$ points.

If the type is leaded, this factor must be added to each line. Leading is the addition of extra space between the lines of type. For example, if the type is leaded two points, the 10-point face is on a 12-point body. Each line is therefore 12 points wide. The lines will be 88×12, giving copy 1,056 points long.

COPYFITTING DISPLAY TYPE

Display type, such as headlines and titles, must be copyfitted using the unit count method. The *unit count method* assigns each character a width. The length of the line is the sum of these widths. It is assumed that all letters fall into one of four sizes. These are thin, normal, wide, and extra wide. The thin is 1/2 unit; normal, 1 unit; wide, 1 1/2 units; and extra wide, 2 units. Fig. 3-33 found on page 58 shows the unit sizes for various letters.

LOWER-CASE ALPHABET LENGTHS
(IN POINTS)

Typeface	Type Size in Points														
	5	5½	6	7	7½	8	9	10	11	12	14	18	24	30	36
Antique No. 1 w Italic	···	···	97	···	···	122	132	141	···	165	190	···	···	···	···
Baskerville w Italic & s.c.	···	···	90	95	···	106	116	129	139	149	170	···	···	···	···
Bodoni Book	···	···	···	···	···	···	···	···	···	···	···	187	233	298	···
Bodoni	···	···	···	···	···	···	···	···	···	···	···	208	267	317	385
Bookman w Italic & s.c.	···	···	92	101	···	110	119	132	144	156	186	···	···	···	···
Caledonia w Italic & s.c.	···	···	91	101	···	109	119	130	140	151	171	230	288	···	···
Caslon No. 3	···	···	···	···	···	···	···	···	···	···	···	265	347	421	···
Caslon No. 3 Italic	···	···	···	···	···	···	···	···	···	···	···	268	350	411	···
Century Bold w Italic	···	···	···	···	···	116	···	146	···	168	201	228	305	···	···
Century Bold	···	···	···	···	···	···	···	···	···	···	···	222	305	366	422
Cheltenham	···	···	···	···	···	···	···	···	···	···	···	···	239	288	345
Cheltenham Italic	···	···	···	···	···	···	···	···	···	···	···	···	···	300	···
Electra w Electra Bold	···	···	···	···	···	104	117	125	135	142	159	···	···	···	···
Franklin Gothic	···	···	···	···	···	···	···	···	···	···	···	277	340	···	···
Garamond No. 3 w Italic & s.c.	···	···	87	95	···	103	111	118	125	133	150	198	254	···	···
Gothic No. 13	···	···	···	···	···	···	···	···	···	136	161	180	224	235	316
Gothic No. 16	···	···	···	···	···	···	164	···	···	180	216	234	303	373	424
Helvetica w Italic	···	···	···	···	···	111	···	138	···	165	···	···	···	···	···
Helvetica w Bold	···	···	···	···	···	···	···	138	···	165	···	···	···	···	···
Ionic No. 5 w Italic & s.c.	84	94	104	114	121	127	139	146	···	163	···	···	···	···	···
Memphis Light w Italic & s.c.	···	···	97	···	···	104	···	134	···	166	195	···	···	···	···
Memphis Light	···	···	···	···	···	···	···	···	···	···	···	226	311	360	421
Metrolite No. 2 w Italic	···	···	94	···	···	108	···	135	···	160	187	232	303	···	···
Old Style No. 1 w Italic & s.c.	83	···	91	101	···	109	118	126	135	150	178	···	···	···	···
Paragon w Italic & s.c.	···	···	108	120	124	129	136	145	···	···	···	···	···	···	···
Spartan Light w Medium	···	···	89	···	···	93	104	117	···	138	158	217	271	···	···
Spartan Book w Italic & s.c.	···	···	89	···	···	98	113	128	139	148	165	218	271	···	···
Times Roman w Italic & s.c.	···	84	90	100	···	109	118	125	135	148	162	···	···	···	···
Times Roman w Bold	···	84	90	100	···	109	118	125	135	148	162	···	···	···	···
Trade Gothic w Bold	···	···	98	104	···	111	122	133	140	149	180	212	276	···	···
Typeface	5	5½	6	7	7½	8	9	10	11	12	14	18	24	30	36

Mergenthaler Linotype Co.

3-31. *Alphabet lengths for selected typefaces.*

Study the headlines in Fig. 3-34 which appears on page 58. The upper one is made of capital and lowercase letters. The lower headline is made of all capital letters. Notice the difference in the unit count of each example.

Usually the space available for display type is decided before the copy is written. The display copy written must fit this space. The unit count shown for display type in printing type-specimen books can be used as line maximums. Newspapers establish maximum unit counts for various typefaces they use.

LEGAL RESTRICTIONS ON PRINTED MATERIALS

There are legal restrictions regulating what may be printed. Printers and publishers must be alert to possible violations of the law. If there is any doubt, it would be wise to consult a law-

CHARACTERS BY PICAS

In those instances where the precise alphabet length is not given, use the next highest length figure. For example, an alphabet length of 109 would use 110.

ALPHABET LENGTH	1	10	12	14	16	18	20	22	24	26	28	30	32	34	36	38	40	42
73	4.35	44	52	61	70	78	87	96	104	113	122	131	139	148	157	165	174	183
75	4.25	43	51	60	68	77	85	94	102	111	119	128	136	145	153	162	170	179
76	4.20	42	50	59	67	76	84	92	101	109	118	126	134	143	151	160	168	176
77	4.15	42	50	58	66	75	83	91	100	108	116	125	133	141	149	158	166	174
79	4.05	41	49	57	65	73	81	89	97	105	113	122	130	138	146	154	162	170
80	4.0	40	48	56	64	72	80	88	96	104	112	120	128	136	144	152	160	168
81	3.95	40	47	55	63	71	79	87	95	103	111	119	126	134	142	150	158	166
82	3.9	39	47	55	62	70	78	86	94	101	109	117	125	133	140	148	156	164
83	3.85	39	46	54	62	69	77	85	92	100	108	116	123	131	139	146	154	162
84	3.8	38	46	53	61	68	76	84	91	99	106	114	122	129	137	144	152	160
86	3.75	38	45	53	60	68	75	83	90	98	105	113	120	128	135	143	150	158
87	3.7	37	44	52	59	67	74	81	89	96	104	112	118	126	133	141	148	155
88	3.65	37	44	51	58	66	73	80	88	95	102	110	117	124	131	139	146	153
90	3.6	36	43	50	58	65	72	79	86	94	101	108	115	122	130	137	144	151
91	3.55	36	43	50	57	64	71	78	85	92	99	107	114	121	128	135	142	149
93	3.5	35	42	49	56	63	70	77	84	91	98	105	112	119	126	133	140	147
94	3.45	35	41	48	55	62	69	76	83	90	97	104	110	117	124	131	138	145
96	3.4	34	41	48	54	61	68	75	82	88	95	102	109	116	122	129	136	143
98	3.35	34	40	47	54	60	67	74	80	87	94	101	107	114	121	127	134	141
100	3.3	33	40	46	53	59	66	73	79	86	92	99	106	112	119	125	132	139
102	3.25	33	39	46	52	59	65	72	78	85	91	98	104	111	117	124	130	137
104	3.2	32	38	45	51	58	64	70	77	83	90	96	102	109	115	122	128	134
106	3.15	32	38	44	50	57	63	69	76	82	88	95	101	107	113	120	126	132
108	3.1	31	37	43	50	56	62	68	74	81	87	93	99	105	112	118	124	130
110	3.05	31	37	43	49	55	61	67	73	79	85	92	98	104	110	116	122	128
112	3.0	30	36	42	48	54	60	66	72	78	84	90	96	102	108	114	120	126
114	2.95	30	35	41	47	53	59	65	71	77	83	89	94	100	106	112	118	124
116	2.9	29	35	41	46	52	58	64	70	75	81	87	93	99	104	110	116	122
118	2.85	29	34	40	46	51	57	63	68	74	80	86	91	97	103	108	114	120
120	2.8	28	34	39	45	50	56	62	67	73	78	84	90	95	101	106	112	118
122	2.75	28	33	39	44	50	55	61	66	72	77	83	88	94	99	105	110	116
124	2.7	27	32	38	43	49	54	59	65	70	76	81	86	92	97	103	108	113
127	2.65	27	32	37	42	48	53	58	64	69	74	80	85	90	95	101	106	111
129	2.6	26	31	36	42	47	52	57	62	68	73	78	83	88	94	99	104	109
132	2.55	26	31	36	41	46	51	56	61	66	71	77	82	87	92	97	102	107
135	2.5	25	30	35	40	45	50	55	60	65	70	75	80	85	90	95	100	105
138	2.45	25	29	34	39	44	49	54	59	64	69	74	78	83	88	93	98	103
142	2.4	24	29	34	38	43	48	53	58	62	67	72	77	82	86	91	96	101
ALPHABET LENGTH	1	10	12	14	16	18	20	22	24	26	28	30	32	34	36	38	40	42

CHARACTERS BY PICAS (Continued)

ALPHABET LENGTH	1	10	12	14	16	18	20	22	24	26	28	30	32	34	36	38	40	42
146	2.35	24	28	33	38	42	47	52	56	61	66	71	75	80	85	89	94	99
150	2.3	23	28	32	37	41	46	51	55	60	64	69	74	78	83	87	92	97
154	2.25	23	27	32	36	41	45	50	54	59	63	68	72	77	81	86	90	95
158	2.2	22	26	31	35	40	44	48	53	57	62	66	70	75	79	84	88	92
162	2.15	22	26	30	34	39	43	47	52	56	60	65	69	73	77	82	86	90
166	2.1	21	25	29	34	38	42	46	50	55	59	63	67	71	76	80	84	88
170	2.05	21	25	29	33	37	41	45	49	53	57	62	66	70	74	78	82	86
175	2.0	20	24	28	32	36	40	44	48	52	56	60	64	68	72	76	80	84
180	1.95	20	23	27	31	35	39	43	47	51	55	59	62	66	70	74	78	82
185	1.9	19	23	27	30	34	38	42	46	49	53	57	61	65	68	72	76	80
190	1.85	19	22	26	30	33	37	41	44	48	52	56	59	63	67	70	74	78
195	1.8	18	22	25	29	32	36	40	43	47	50	54	58	61	65	68	72	76
200	1.75	18	21	25	28	32	35	39	42	46	49	53	56	60	63	67	70	74
206	1.7	17	20	24	27	31	34	37	41	44	48	51	54	58	61	65	68	71
212	1.65	17	20	23	26	30	33	36	40	43	46	50	53	56	59	63	66	69
218	1.6	16	19	22	26	29	32	35	38	42	45	48	51	54	58	61	64	67
225	1.55	16	19	22	25	28	31	34	37	40	43	47	50	53	56	59	62	65
233	1.5	15	18	21	24	27	30	33	36	39	42	45	48	51	54	57	60	63
241	1.45	15	17	20	23	26	29	32	35	38	41	44	46	49	52	55	58	61
250	1.4	14	17	20	22	25	28	31	34	36	39	42	45	48	50	53	56	59
260	1.35	14	16	19	22	24	27	30	32	35	38	41	43	46	49	51	54	57
270	1.3	13	16	18	21	23	26	29	31	34	36	39	42	44	47	49	52	55
280	1.25	13	15	18	20	23	25	28	30	33	35	38	40	43	45	48	50	53
295	1.2	12	14	17	19	22	24	26	29	31	34	36	38	41	43	46	48	50
310	1.15	12	14	16	18	21	23	25	28	30	32	35	37	39	41	44	46	48
325	1.1	11	13	15	18	20	22	24	26	29	31	33	35	37	40	42	44	46
340	1.05	11	13	15	17	19	21	23	25	27	29	32	34	36	38	40	42	44
360	1.0	10	12	14	16	18	20	22	24	26	28	30	32	34	36	38	40	42
380	0.95	10	11	13	15	17	19	21	23	25	27	29	30	32	34	36	38	40
400	0.9	9	11	13	14	16	18	20	22	23	25	27	29	31	32	34	36	38
425	0.85	9	10	12	14	15	17	19	20	22	24	26	27	29	31	32	34	36
450	0.8	8	10	11	13	14	16	18	19	21	22	24	26	27	29	30	32	34
475	0.75	8	9	11	12	14	15	17	18	20	21	23	24	26	27	29	30	32
500	0.7	7	8	10	11	13	14	15	17	18	20	21	22	24	25	27	28	29
ALPHABET LENGTH	1	10	12	14	16	18	20	22	24	26	28	30	32	34	36	38	40	42

3-32. *A characters by picas table giving the number of characters per line.*

yer. The most common legal problems relate to counterfeiting, pornography, and copyrights.

COUNTERFEITING

Counterfeiting means to make an imitation or copy of a genuine article with the intent to deceive.

If a requested printing job seems to be questionable, contact the United States Secret Service, Treasury Department. This

UNIT SIZES FOR DISPLAY TYPE CONTAINING CAPITALS AND LOWERCASE LETTERS

1 unit 1/2 unit 1 1/2 units	all lowercase letters and numbers *except* f, l, i, t, and 1 set as a number m, w
1 1/2 units 1/2 unit 2 units	all capital letters *except* l M, W
1/2 unit 1 unit	all punctuation spaces

UNIT SIZES FOR ALL CAPITAL DISPLAY LINES

1 unit 1 1/2 units 1/2 unit	all letters and numbers *except* M, W 1, spaces, punctuation

3-33. *These tables are used in the unit count method of copyfitting display type.*

agency will give an opinion as to the legality of the job. Regulations concerning counterfeiting are part of the U.S. Code of Law.

Items most frequently counterfeited include money, securities, advertisements, and uncancelled stamps. Counterfeiting activities include making, selling, or possession of plates; printing, photographing, making, or passing paper designed specifically for the above items.

Federal Legislation

The Department of the Treasury sponsored legislation to clarify laws relating to the use of illustrations of paper money, postage and revenue stamps, checks, bonds, and other obligations of the United States and foreign governments. This legislation was passed by Congress on September 2, 1958 (Public Law 85-921). It was amended by Congress on June 20, 1968, to permit reproductions of postage stamps in color under certain conditions (Public Law 90-353).

The United States Secret Service is the federal agency charged with safeguarding the nation's currency.

Following are the conditions under which it is permissible to print illustrations and to make films of United States and foreign obligations and securities.

Paper Money, Checks, Bonds

Printed illustrations of paper money, checks, bonds, and other obligations and securities of the U.S. and foreign governments are permissible for numismatic, educational, historical and newsworthy purposes, and for numismatic or philatelic advertising but not for general advertising purposes. Numismatics is the study and collection of money and medals. Philatelic refers to the collection and study of postage stamps, postmarks, and related materials.

Illustrations must be in black and white and must be less than three-fourths or more than one and one-half times the size of the genuine article. No individual facsimiles of such obligations are permitted, and no illustrations of paper money, checks, or bonds may be in color.

To be permissible, an illustration must be accompanied by numismatic, educational, historical, or newsworthy information relating directly to the item that

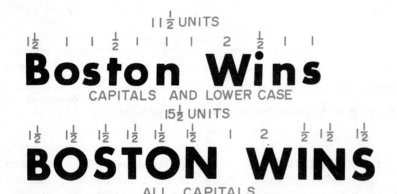

3-34. *Display type is counted in units.*

is illustrated. Illustrations used primarily for decorative or eye-catching purposes are not permissible.

Motion-picture films, microfilms, and slides of paper money, checks, bonds, and other obligations and securities of the U.S. and foreign governments are permitted in black and white or in color for projection upon a screen or for use in telecasting. They may not be used for advertising purposes, except philatelic or numismatic advertising.

Advertising

Printed illustrations or films of paper money, checks or bonds are not permitted in connection with advertising. However, printed illustrations of paper money, but not films, may be used in connection with numismatic advertising. Also, Treasury regulations permit the illustration of U.S. bonds in connection with a campaign for the sale of such bonds.

United States and Foreign Postage Stamps

Printed illustrations of cancelled and uncancelled U.S. postage stamps are permissible for articles, books, journals, newspapers, or albums for philatelic, educational, historical, and newsworthy purposes.

Black and white illustrations may be of any size. Colored illustrations of cancelled U.S. postage stamps may be of any size. However, illustrations in color of uncancelled U.S. postage stamps must be less than three-fourths or more than one and one-half times the size of the genuine stamp.

Printed illustrations of can-

celled foreign stamps in black and white or color are permissible in any size and for any purpose.

Black and white and color illustrations of uncancelled foreign postage stamps are permitted for philatelic, educational, historical and newsworthy purposes. They may be of any size, but color illustrations must be less than three-fourths or more than one and one-half times the size of the genuine stamp.

Motion-picture films and slides of U.S. and foreign postage stamps are permissible in black and white or in color for projection upon a screen or for use in telecasting. They are not permissible for advertising purposes except for philatelic advertising.

Philatelic Advertising

Black and white illustrations of cancelled and uncancelled U.S. and foreign postage stamps, as well as colored illustrations of cancelled postage stamps, are permissible in any size for philatelic advertising. Uncancelled colored illustrations of U.S. and foreign postage stamps are permitted for philatelic advertising, but must meet the three-fourths or one and one-half size restrictions.

Note: Cancelled U.S. and foreign postage stamps must bear an official cancellation mark; that is, the stamps must have been used for postage.

Revenue Stamps

Regulations for printed illustrations of U.S. and foreign revenue stamps are the same as for postage stamps, except that colored illustrations of U.S. revenue stamps are not permitted.

Destruction of Plates and Negatives

The plates and negatives, and glossy prints, of any U.S. or foreign obligations produced for any of the purposes just listed must be destroyed after their final use for the purpose for which they were made.

Coins

Photographs or printed illustrations, motion-picture film, or slides of U.S. and foreign coins may be used for any purpose including advertising.

With few exceptions, existing law generally prohibits the manufacture, sale, or use of any token, disk, or device in the likeness of any coins of the United States or of any foreign country which are issued as money.

PORNOGRAPHY

If asked to print any articles, drawings, or photographs which might be classified as offensive, legal advice should be secured. The attorney should contact the proper governmental agency prior to the printing.

The matter of what is obscene is a difficult thing to define. In the early 1960s the U.S. Supreme Court declared that to be obscene any printed matter must be totally without redeeming social value. This permitted a stream of pornographic publications. In 1973 the U.S. Supreme Court ruled that the standards for judging obscenity could be established by the citizens of each locality. This has enabled some areas to control pornography. Many cases have been taken to court. More will follow in the years ahead. The integrity and reputation of a printing company depend upon how the local citizens view its activities.

COPYRIGHTS

A copyright is the right granted by law to an author, composer, playwright, publisher, or distributor to exclusive publication, production, sale, or distribution of a literary, musical, dramatic, or artistic work. In the United States this right lasts the life of the author plus 50 years.

The printed copyright notice has three parts. The word "copyright" or an abbreviation "copr." or the symbol "©" is printed. This is followed by the name of the owner of the copyright and the year of the publication. Try to find the copyright in this book.

Applications for a copyright are filed with the Register of Copyrights, Library of Congress, Washington, D.C. Two copies of the work must be filed with the application plus a registration fee.

The copyright notice in books should be printed on the title page or the page immediately following. This is normally the reverse side of the title page. In periodicals it is placed on the title page, on the first page of the text, or under the title heading. Get some periodicals and find their copyright notice.

Contributions to periodicals can also be copyrighted. If this is done, the notice is placed on the contribution itself. If the contribution is a literary, dramatic, or musical work, the notice should appear on the first page of the contribution. Musical works require the notice be on the title page or the first page of music. Motion pictures have the notice on the title frame or near it.

Work of a United States citizen may be copyrighted in a way that secures protection both in the United States and in all of the other countries that are parties to the Universal Copyright Convention. It is necessary that all copies bear a particular form of copyright notice from the date of first publication. This notice consists of the symbol © accompanied by the name of the copyright owner and the year of publication. For example, © John Jones 1980.

THE SCHOOL SHOP

Because of the complexity of the laws and the need for legal advice, those working in school printing shops would be wise to avoid entirely any printing activity involving the items discussed in this section.

REVIEW QUESTIONS

1. Who usually prepares the artwork and the copy for reproduction?
2. What does the term *camera ready* mean?
3. What is the metric base unit of length?
4. How many millilitres are in a litre?
5. What is the metric base unit of mass?
6. How many picas (approximately) equal one inch?
7. How many points are in a pica?
8. For what is a plate type-high gauge used?
9. A 1320-word magazine article is to be set in 6-point type, leaded 2 points. Using the table in Fig. 3-29, find out how many square inches of space are needed for the copy.
10. What is alphabet length?
11. Whom should you contact if you think a printing job might be violating the laws against counterfeiting?
12. In the United States, how long does a copyright last?

Proofreading

After the words for a job are composed, it is necessary to check them for correctness. This is called *proofreading*. All composition must be checked for mistakes in spelling, punctuation, hyphenation, and spacing.

Copy set for printing is either set in metal type or some form of cold composition. Metal type is set by a slug casting machine or by hand in a composing stick. See Chapter 8, "Relief Composition—Machine" and Chapter 7, "Relief Composition—Hand." Cold composition involves the use of a photocomposition machine or the "strike-on" (like a typewriter) method. See Chapter 6, "Cold Composition."

METAL TYPE COMPOSITION

Metal type is very difficult to check. It is easy to confuse the letters n and u, b and d, or p and q, since everything is upside down. A simpler way to look at these characters is to "pull a proof;" that is, to make a print of the type. The *proof* is the reproduction of the type image. It presents the words in normal position. Since the proof is checked for errors, most shops call this step "reading proof" or "checking proof." The individual responsible for this job is called a *proofreader*.

GALLEY PROOFS

Newspapers, magazines, and books use a vast amount of type. Rather than taking proofs of individual stories or chapters when preparing for publication, the printers pull galley proofs. As the type comes from the machines, it is put in *galleys* approximately 20 inches long. A proof is pulled of each galley, which may contain one or more stories. These *galley proofs* are numbered for each individual job. They are sent to the proofreader for checking.

REVISED PROOFS

After proofs are marked, they are sent back to the composition area. Correction lines are set and inserted in the typeform on the galley. After the galley has been corrected, another proof is taken and marked "revised." This second, or revised, proof should be carefully checked against the first, or original, galley proof. Since entire lines are reset when making corrections, one must look for new errors that might occur in the corrected line. Sometimes the corrections are of such a nature they will not go into the space occupied by the original line. When this happens, additional lines will have to be set until they end at the same point as the first proof or until

the end of the paragraph is reached. All these reset lines must be checked closely for additional errors. The revised galley proofs are then returned to the composition area so that these corrections can be made. After all galleys have been corrected, the type is ready to be made up into pages.

PAGE PROOFS

After pages are made up, correctly spaced, with headings and page numbers, another proof is pulled and given to the proofreader. Now the proofreader must check headings, correct spacing, page numbers, illustrations, and any other items included in the page, such as footnotes and correct captions for artwork. A careful check should be made to be certain that copy continues from one page to another without lines missing or transposed. Printing plants will usually also have the author check page proofs before continuing with the job on the press.

OTHER PROOFS

Type that is to be used in job work such as library cards, absence slips, grade cards, and all kinds of forms is usually spaced out correctly before being sent to the proofreader. The proofreader's job is the same regardless of the kind of proof received—all errors must be found and corrected.

COLD TYPE COMPOSITION

If copy is set by a photographic method (photocomposition) or by "strike-on," it must be proofread. The final copy of "strike-on" composition is used as the camera copy to make a plate. Therefore it must be kept clean and protected from damage.

In order to protect the copy generated by either "strike-on" or photocomposition, proofs must be made. Corrections are marked on the proofs, thus preserving the original.

Proofs of "strike-on" and positive photocomposition material can be made by using a copy machine like a Xerox, Varifax, or Thermofax. These give a positive reproduction on paper.

Proofs of photocomposition negatives can be made by using vandyke paper or diazo paper. The negative and the paper are placed together and exposed to a light source. When the paper is developed, a positive image of the material on the negative is generated. The proofreader marks corrections on this positive image. The vandyke paper produces a brown image and the diazo a blue image. The vandyke prints are developed in water and the diazo by ammonia vapor.

Not only must proofreaders check the words on a job, but they must also check the entire job after it is asssembled. In offset printing the final product for making the plate is called a *flat*. Vandyke proofs of the entire flat are used to check the spacing, alignment, placement, and other aspects of the finished flat before it is used to make a plate.

PROOFING TAPE COMPOSITION

The two ways to check punched paper tape for errors are to use it to produce a positive copy or to use an editing terminal having a cathode ray tube (CRT) display screen. The first method is expensive because it involves the production of an image which will most likely have some parts discarded. It also takes production time from the expensive photocomposition machines.

With the use of an editing terminal, punched paper tape can be checked and corrected before the tape is used for the actual

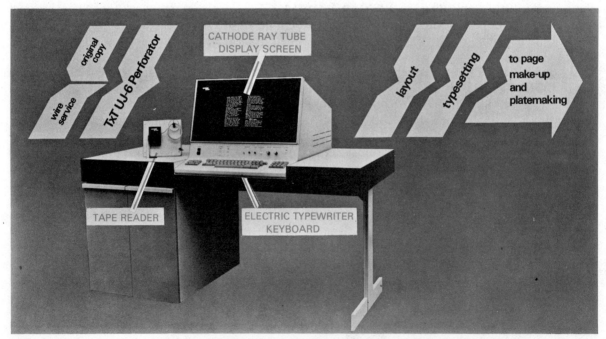

4-1. *This is an editing and proofing terminal. The text material is set on a Harris tape perforator. The tape is edited and proofread on this editing and proofing terminal.*

composition process. The system consists of a tape reader, a standard electric typewriter, and a cathode ray tube display screen. Fig. 4-1.

The punched paper tape is placed on the tape reader and is displayed on the CRT display screen. The system shown in Fig. 4-1 will display 50 lines at a time. The proofreader reads the display on the screen and must be constantly alert for errors. If an error is found, the correction is made immediately by the proofreader.

To correct an error, such as a misspelled word, the proofreader strikes a key on the typewriter keyboard which places a lighted rectangular spot on the incorrect letter. This light is called a *cursor*. Fig. 4-2. The proofreader then types the correct letter. The letter appears on the CRT display screen as it was typed. The editing terminal is connected to a repunch system. This system produces a new tape with the corrections.

In systems using computer storage, editing terminals are used to make corrections before composition takes place. Study the systems described in Chapter 6, "Cold Composition."

PROOFREADER AND COPYHOLDER

In small plants the proofreader could be anyone selected by the employer. Usually this person will have other duties besides proofreading. In larger plants proofreading is a full-time occupation.

Proofreading requires a special kind of reading. Over the years people form the habit of seeing reading material in words, blocks, or phrases. Some have been trained to scan or read rapidly. Thus, the eyes do not see each individual letter or punctuation mark. They tend to see what they think should be there.

Read the sentence below.

FINISHED FILES ARE THE RESULTS OF YEARS OF SCIENTIFIC STUDY COMBINED WITH THE EXPERIENCE OF YEARS.

Now count aloud the *F*s in that sentence. Count them ONLY ONCE; do not go back and count them again. How many did you see—three, four, five, six? There are actually six, but looking at words instead of letters will cause two or more to be missed.

Proofreaders must be careful not to fall into these old habits. They must look for each letter or combination of letters to make sure each is correct. The work of the proofreader, while unglamorous, is very important and carries a lot of responsibility. A letter left out can change a simple word into an obscene expression. The meaning of an entire sentence may be changed by an error left unchecked. Many hard feelings and even lawsuits have resulted from improperly corrected copy. Proper names are often pronounced alike but spelled differently. An error in a proper name can cause embarrassment. For instance, it was reported that "Mr. R. A. Bowyer" was arrested for drunken driving. The name when it appeared in the paper was spelled "Boyer." He was an entirely different person. One can imagine the outraged feelings of the innocent person.

In printing plants having a large number of difficult proofs to check, the proofreader has a helper called a *copyholder*. This person holds the original copy. As the proofreader reads aloud, the copyholder compares what the proofreader is reading to what is on the author's original copy. The proofreader even reads aloud commas, periods, quotation marks, question marks, and all other characteristics such as capitals, boldface, or italic. By following such a method, the author's original manuscript is accurately reproduced.

THE PROOFREADER NOTICES ON THE CRT DISPLAY SCREEN THAT THE WORD "FELL" IS MISSPELLED.

USING THE KEYBOARD THE PROOFREADER PUTS A CURSOR OVER THE WRONG LETTER.

THE CORRECT LETTER IS TYPED ON THE KEYBOARD.

THE CRT DISPLAY SCREEN SHOWS THE WORD IS CORRECTLY SPELLED.

4-2. The steps to correct a mistake when displayed on the CRT screen.

STANDARD PROOF MARKS

Punctuation and Spelling

⊙ Insert period

(set) ? Insert question mark

⋏ Insert comma

⋁ Insert apostrophe

;| Insert semicolon

:| Insert colon

⋁ ⋁ Insert quotation marks

|=| Insert hyphen

∂ or a Use superior figure or letter

∂ or a Use inferior figure or letter

⊥/M Insert em dash

⊥/N Insert en dash

••• Ellipsis

or stet Let it stand; OK as is. (Insert dots under word to be stetted.)

Typographical

lc Set in lowercase

cap Set in caps

sc Set in small caps

ital Set in italic

bf Set in boldface

rom Set in roman

⎯⎯ One underline signifies italic

⎯⎯ Two underlines, small capitals

⎯⎯ Three underlines, capitals

⁓⁓ Bold type

wf Wrong font; set in correct type

× Change broken letter

⃔ Reverse (type upside down)

ffi Use ligatures

Operational

¶ Start paragraph here

no¶ No paragraph; run in

run in No paragraphs or short lines

run over Carry over to next line

run back Carry back to preceding line

out-see copy Something left out; see copy

⌐ Start new line

☐ or ⊡ Indent one em quad

⊞ or ② Indent two em quads

⑧ Delete

⌒ Close up; delete space

⑧ Delete and close up

Insert space

eq# Make space between words or lines equal

hr# Insert hair space

ls Letterspace

⌐ Move right

⌐ Move left

⌐⌐ Center

⊓ Move up

⊔ Move down

= Straighten type; align horizontally

‖ Align vertically

tr Transpose

(sp) Spell out

∧ Insert correction indicated

(?) Query; is this right?

4-3. *Standard proof marks.*

COPY AND PROOF MARKS

Proof and copy marks are a kind of language all their own. Perhaps one should say they are a kind of shorthand rather than a language. Shown in Fig. 4-3 are the symbols and marks that are in standard use in the printing industry. By learning a standard set of marks, proofs can be sent from one part of the country to another and still be correctly understood. If workers move from one job to another, they will be working with familiar markings.

Copy marks are usually put in the lines of the original copy. They are marks made by the author to enable the operator or compositor to understand the author's wishes. Fig. 4-4. For example, if a word is to be set in italic, it would be underlined with a single straight line. Three lines would indicate capitals. A wavy line would tell the compositor to put the word in boldface type. Copy marks are instructions to the printer just as highway signs are instructions to the driver. They tell the printer what to do by use of a simple mark rather than a long, written statement.

Proof marks are symbols used to show an error in the copy after it has been set. A single symbol can tell what is wrong, whereas it might take several words or sentences to explain the error. Proof marks are made in the margin of the proof. Lines are drawn from the error to the symbol. The proofreader tries to avoid crossing one line with another or having too many lines drawn in the same general area. This can become confusing to those who must use the proof for setting and making corrections. Fig. 4-5.

The most commonly used means of printing have 4 stages of production. First an original image must be developed. An original image is the art work, illustrations, photographs and copy of the words to be reproduced. How this is done will vary with the reproduction process to be used. second, the original image must be converted into printing image carriers. A printing image carrier is the means used to make a copy of the Original image that can be inked and used to print the image.

Third, the printing image is iknhed. This forms an ink image on the face of the printing image carrier. This ink image is transferred to the material upon which it is to be reproduced. This produces the fourth step, the printed image, on some kind of material as paper, cloth or plastics.

4-4. *The original typed copy with the author's copy marks.*

The most commonly used means of printing have 4 stages of production. First an original image must be developed. An original image is the art work, illustrations, photographs and copy of the words to be reproduced. How this is done will vary with the reproduction process to be used. second, the original image must be converted into printing image carriers. A printing image carrier is the means used to make a copy of the Original image that can be inked and used to print the image.

Third, the printing image is iknhed. This forms an ink image on the face of the printing image carrier. This ink image is transferred to the material upon which it is to be reproduced. This produces the fourth step, the printed image, on some kind of material as paper, cloth, or plastics.

4-5. *The printed proof with proof marks.*

The most commonly used means of printing have four stages of production. First, an original image must be developed. An **original image** is the artwork, illustrations, photographs and copy of the words to be reproduced. How this is done will vary with the reproduction process to be used.

Second, the original image must be converted into printing image carriers. A printing image carrier is the means used to make a copy of the original image that can be inked and used to print the image.

Third, the printing image is inked. This forms an ink image on the face of the printing image carrier. This ink image is transferred to the material upon which it is to be reproduced. This produces the fourth step, the printed image, on some kind of material as paper, cloth or plastics.

4-6. The proof made after the errors shown in Fig. 4-5 were corrected.

An example of corrected copy is shown in Fig. 4-6.

WATCHING FOR ERRORS

While reading or checking proofs, the proofreader must be alert to many kinds of errors. These errors will usually fall into one of four categories: spelling, use of the wrong word, typographical, and hyphenation.

SPELLING ERRORS

A proofreader is not at liberty to change the author's original copy. However, it is important that all words used are correctly spelled. Even the best of authors occasionally spells a word incorrectly. Newspaper copy, with the pressure of time for deadlines, will often have errors in spelling.

The proofreader should have at hand a good standard dictionary and refer to it frequently when in doubt about spelling. Sometimes the author might make an incorrect statement, or the sentence is jumbled as to meaning. The proofreader should contact the author to find the correct meaning.

USE OF WRONG WORDS

Some words in the English language are pronounced the same, spelled differently, and have a different meaning. (This makes the job of the proofreader even more difficult.)

To illustrate: *to, too* and *two*

To err is human.

There are *too* many errors.

He found *two* errors.

The same is true of *there* and *their*. While pronounced the same, they are used differently.

There are too many errors.

Their errors are caused by carelessness.

These are simple illustrations, but the proofreader should be aware of all such words that can cause errors.

TYPOGRAPHICAL ERRORS

Typographical errors refer to mistakes made in setting type. Typical mistakes are a letter being omitted (runing instead of running), two or more letters being changed around, or transposed, (hte instead of the), or a wrong letter being used (enstead in place of instead). Most of the errors in a proof will be typographical in nature. One must keep a sharp eye and a clear head to find all of them.

HYPHENATION

Another thing the proofreader must check carefully is hyphenation. *Hyphenation* is the dividing of a word at a syllable by use of a hyphen (-).

Most of the composition in newspapers, books, and magazines is justified. That is, space is added between words so that the lines come out even on the right side of the column or page. However, if too much space is added to make the lines come out right, it can leave too much white space in the column. To avoid or reduce this, words at the end of a line may be hyphenated. The hyphen at the end of the line shows that the word is continued on the next line and helps the reader pronounce the word correctly.

The following words are divided according to syllables: a-gain, dif-fi-cul-ty, di-vi-sion, ac-ci-dent, be-cause, Wednes-day.

There would be no problem if the hyphen could be added wherever it was needed in the word. But hyphenation must follow correct English usage and occur only at syllables. The shorter the width of a column of type, the more difficult is the job of hyphenation. A newspaper column of standard width will need a hyphen every fourth or fifth line to keep from having too much space between words.

The hyphens must be placed to keep the pronunciation and meaning clear to the reader. However, this is sometimes difficult because of the way a word can be used. For example, consider the word *record*. When used as a noun, it is divided rec-ord; when used as a verb, it is divided re-cord.

A great help in determining word division is to pronounce the word correctly and use a good standard dictionary when in doubt.

TEN RULES FOR WORD DIVISION

Taken from *Linotype Keyboard Operation,* Mergenthaler Linotype Company, Brooklyn, New York.

1. Words should be divided according to syllables.

    con-ster-na-tion
    syl-lab-i-ca-tion

2. Divide after a vowel when possible, particularly when it is a single vowel coming before the last syllable.

mechani-cal, *not* mechan-ical
approxi-mate, *not* approx-imate

3. If the last syllable of a word contains only two letters, do not carry it to the next line.

vocifer-ously, *not* vociferous-ly

4. Carry over to the next line such word endings as *ible, able, tion, sion, ing.* When a letter is added before adding *ing,* carry it over also.

    run-ning, *not* runn-ing
    drum-ming, *not* drumm-ing
    stir-ring, *not* stirr-ing
    can-ning, *not* cann-ing

When the original word has the double letter, do not carry over.

    express-ing, *not* expres-sing
    pass-ing, *not* pas-sing

5. Divide at the hyphen when composing hyphenated or compound words.

    composing-room
    not compos-ing-room

6. One-syllable words cannot be divided, nor can plurals of such words, even though pronounced as if they were words of two syllables.

horse, horses; inch, inches; fox, foxes

7. The addition of *ed* to form the past tense of verbs does not add a syllable.

drown, drowned; slap, slapped; push, pushed

8. If the first syllable of a word contains but one letter, do not divide it on the first syllable; carry over the letter. Do not divide words such as:

E-gypt, a-mong, a-float, a-gain

9. Never have more than two divisions of words at the ends of successive lines.

10. Never divide four-letter words even though they have two syllables.

    in-to; ev-er; ov-er

Two words often found divided wrongly in newspaper columns are *children* and *Wednesday.* If the rules of word divisions are followed correctly, the words should be divided:

    chil-dren, *not* child-ren
Wednes-day, *not* Wed-nesday

In computer-assisted composition the proper hyphenation of words is stored in the memory. When a line is to be justified and a word must be hyphenated, the computer searches its memory and selects the proper place to put the hyphen.

STYLE BOOK

The proofreader is also required to follow any style adopted by a particular shop. There is a formal style used in publications of research manuscripts, textbooks, and other publications. There is also a journalistic style used in newspapers and pulp magazines which is much more casual in appearance. The formal style will use many more capital letters. It is very precise in its use of punctuation, capital letters, and type style, such as italic. The journalistic style will eliminate the use of many of these patterns and still keep the meaning clear.

These particular styles may be developed and used by the author, but not written down in a formal manner. On the other hand, almost all newspapers will publish a style book giving particular instructions on how to write certain words and phrases. For instance, the standard newspaper style is to spell out numbers up to ten and use figures for numbers over ten. Also most plants use figures when setting clock time. However, the a.m. or p.m. which follows can be set in different ways. Some capitalize the letters and use periods and a space between the letters. Others use lowercase letters with periods but no space between the letters.

Another style which varies among publications is whether to capitalize street names or leave them lowercase. Another example of variable style is use of the word *church.* It may be lowercase or capital. Example: First Methodist Church or First Methodist church.

A complete style book will tell how to handle each of these, and it becomes the responsibility of the proofreader to follow each correctly.

PRESS PROOF

A final check of the job is made after it is put on the press. This final check is for correct imposition, proper spacing and alignment of pages, trims, and to see that the finished product, when folded and trimmed, will be correct. This final press proof is not checked by the proofreader, but by the foreperson or supervisor.

REVIEW QUESTIONS

1. If an error appears in a line of type, that entire line must be reset. True or False?
2. One way to check punched paper tape for errors is to produce a positive copy from it. What is another, less expensive way?
3. Find the typographical error in the following sentence: Offset lithography is one the most widely used of the printing processes.
4. What do these proof marks mean: lc, bf, tr?
5. Which of these words is divided incorrectly: plan-ning, set-ting, cros-sing? How should the word be divided?

Graphic Design

Before the invention of movable type in the early fifteenth century, books and manuscripts were handwritten. The people who copied manuscripts—the scribes—each had their own style of forming letters. Individual style was often influenced by the area or country in which the scribe lived. Thus, certain writing styles became common in a particular country.

The typefaces—that is, the design of type—in use today evolved from letter forms of the scribes. With the invention of printing by movable type the handwritten letters were copied and cast in type. Since there were different styles of script writing, there soon was a variety of metal types. Over the next one hundred years, this variety in types began to fit into two major forms. These were the antique fonts of roman and italics, and Gothic. (Font refers to a complete assortment of type in one size and style.) The roman and italics were patterned after the round letters of the Italian Renaissance scribes. The Gothic style was patterned after the bold manuscript writing typical of the German and Netherlands manuscript writers.

The roman style letter remained popular in Italy and France for a long time. It remained the most commonly used style in the sixteenth century even though France became the leading center for typography. Roman type became standard for the development of nearly all typefaces since then, except for the text and cursive styles. The text developed from the Gothic. The cursive developed from the italic style.

Claude Garamond developed a series of roman fonts in the 1500s which influenced the development of type into the eighteenth century. Garamond was the first person to devote his full efforts to type design.

In the mid-sixteenth century the Civilite type was designed by Robert Granjon. This was the first of the display types. Display types are typefaces designed for use in headings and headlines. They stand out over the text that forms the body of a job.

Gothic was the major type used in Germany, Scandinavia, and the Slavonic countries through the mid-nineteenth century.

From the sixteenth to the nineteenth century, many variations of these typefaces were designed.

Early in the nineteenth century important design changes were made in the roman types, especially in the serifs. (Serifs are the fine strokes at the top and bottom of a letter.) *Modern faces* have very thin, horizontal serifs. Another change during this period was the development of letter forms with pronounced thick and thin members. A large number of decorative and ornamental types and bolder-face type were also developed. They were called *Egyptian faces*. The main strokes and serifs were of equal thickness. This group was also called slab serif or square serif faces. In another style, the serifs were eliminated, producing the *sans serif* group.

The late nineteenth century to the present has been a period of rapid change in type design. The designs began to reflect the changes in society. The development of the sans serif group reflected the mechanical age. A notable example is Futura, designed by Paul Revere. The classic faces which were widely used for several hundred years were no longer considered adequate to express the new era. Revolutionary new practices in fine and applied arts affected directly the development of typography. The growth of news media and advertising were strong influences for change. Typefaces were developed that were of bold and mechanical nature. They were designed specifically for the printing process rather than as a copy of handwritten manuscripts. Weight, size, width, and

69

THE TEXT LETTER
5-1. The text letter.

height of letter forms vary greatly within a given type family.

A large number of sans serif faces appeared. These were designed with condensed, extended, and italic versions. Swiss type designers were especially active in developing sans serif faces.

Many new editions of the classic roman faces have been introduced since 1900. Recent advances in the art of typography have been affected by technological developments in the science of type founding and type composition. Great strides have been made in nonmetallic composition. These systems employ photographic, electronic, or mechanical processes to produce nonrelief images. They have and will continue to influence the design of typefaces.

It is important for graphic designers to be familiar with typefaces. They must select the face or faces to use on each job. Type can reflect a mood. It can be graceful, powerful, loud, quiet, beautiful, ugly, old-fashioned, modern, simple, or decorative. The total image of a layout is influenced by the typeface selected.

The type available today has been developed from one of four basic letter forms: text, roman, italic, and script.

THE TEXT LETTER

This letter relates directly to the form used by scribes in writing early manuscripts, when each character was lettered by hand. Fig. 5-1. Text letters were also used in early churches, where they were cut into stone panels of the church. Sometimes this letter form is called Old English.

Text types are difficult to read. They are primarily used to set brief display lines that should be decorative. Formal announcements, such as wedding announcements, often use text letters. They are not usually used to set large masses of type.

THE ROMAN LETTER

The roman letter form was used in writing early manuscripts. It also was carved into the stone on early Roman buildings. It is very easy to read. Today it finds wide use in all types of printing jobs. Fig. 5-2.

VARIATIONS OF THE ROMAN FORM

The roman form is very popular. It has been made available by many manufacturers. Each one has changed the basic form to suit individual desires. Some of these changes are so small, it is difficult to tell them apart.

OLDSTYLE ANTIQUE ROMAN (BOOKMAN)

ABCDEFGHIJKLMN
abcdefghijklmnopqrstu

FORMAL OLDSTYLE ROMAN (GARAMOND)

ABCDEFGHIJKLMNOPQ RSTUVWXYZ 123456789 abcdefghijklmnopqrstuvwxy

INFORMAL OLDSTYLE ROMAN (CASLON)

ABCDEFGHIJKLMN OPQRSTUVWXYZ12 abcdefghijklmnopqrstuv

TRANSITIONAL ROMAN (BASKERVILLE)

ABCDEFGHIJKLMNO PQRSTUVWXYZ 1234 abcdefghijklmnopqrstuv

MODERN ROMAN (BODONI)

ABCDEFGHIJKLMNOPQ RSTUVWXYZ 123456789 abcdefghijklmnopqrstuvwx

5-3. The five basic classes of roman form letters.

THE ROMAN LETTER
5-2. The roman letter.

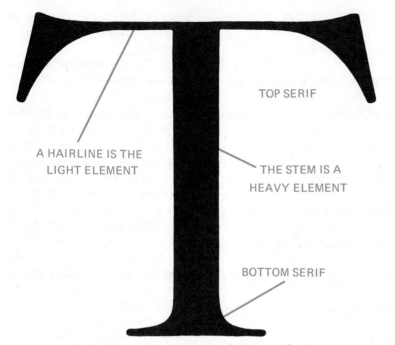

A HAIRLINE IS THE LIGHT ELEMENT

TOP SERIF

THE STEM IS A HEAVY ELEMENT

BOTTOM SERIF

5-4. *The major elements of a roman letter.*

THE SCRIPT LETTER

The script letter is a variation of the italic form. Fig. 5-6. Most lowercase script letters are connected as in longhand written material. Script is difficult to read when set in large masses. The primary uses of script letters are as display headings and formal announcements.

THE SANS SERIF LETTER

While some classify the sans serif letter, Fig. 5-7, as a variety of the roman, many feel it is in a

THE SCRIPT LETTER
5-6. *The script letter.*

There are five basic classes of roman form letters. Fig. 5-3. These are old style antique (Bookman), formal old style (Garamond), informal old style (Caslon), transitional (Baskerville), and modern (Bodoni). These vary in two ways. First, the thick (stem) and thin (hairline) strokes vary in proportion. Second, the shape of the serifs attached at the ends of the strokes varies. The locations of stem, hairlines, and serifs on a roman letter are shown in Fig. 5-4.

Many other new roman faces have been designed and are in use. Some of these are Caledonia, Century, Craw Clarendon, Dominate, Fairfield, Melior, Optima, Palatino, Times Roman, Torino, and Weiss.

THE ITALIC LETTER

As stated before, this letter form was used in early written manuscripts. Today it is a slanted variation of the roman letter form. Fig. 5-5. It is often used with roman type to call attention to certain words. Italic letters are also used as subheads and display heads. They tend to be more decorative than roman type.

THE ITALIC LETTER
5-5. *The italic letter.*

THE SANS—SERIF LETTER
5-7. *The sans-serif letter.*

class by itself. It has had wide use. Type designers have produced a number of variations. Some of these are Gill, Futura, Univers, Microgramma, News Gothic, Eurostile, Helvetica, Standard Sans Serif, Venus, and Grotesque. Fig. 5-8.

SELECTING AND USING TYPE

The selection of the type when designing a job requires the serious attention of the graphic designer. Following are some ideas the designer uses in selecting type.

1. Pick a typeface that matches the mood of the layout. A thin, light face gives the reader a different image than a thick, boldface type.

2. Headlines in color should be a little larger and have wider elements than those in black. *Headlines* are the major captions set above a newspaper or magazine article.

3. Generally the same type family is used for any one job. Variety is obtained by changes in type size and blackness. The use of condensed and expanded faces also gives variety. Italics are sometimes used for interest.

4. A skilled designer can mix a job by using one typeface for headlines and another for the body. Very rarely are three faces used on a job.

5. Seldom will headlines be made from two different faces.

6. Designers should consider how different faces go together, regardless of when they were designed. Just because two typefaces were designed in the eighteenth century does not mean they can work together on a job.

EUROSTILE NORMAL Eurostile

EUROSTILE

The Best and Fastest   1234

FUTURA

THE BROWN fox jumps over 456

GILL

THE QUICK fox jumps over 4

GROTESQUE

HELVETICA Helvetica

HELVETICA

MICROGRAMMA NORMAL

MICROGRAMMA

News Gothic ABCDEFG 12345

NEWS GOTHIC

SANS-SERIF MEDIUM abcdefg

SANS—SERIF

THE QUICK brown fox 6789

UNIVERS

The Best and Fast 1234

VENUS

5-8. *Some variations of the sans-serif letter form.*

Old style roman and modern roman do not go together well. Type mixing is a matter of taste.

7. Sans serifs are a neutral type. They go well with almost any other type. However, slab serifs are not usually mixed with sans serif.

8. Old English faces should be combined only with roman faces.

9. Typefaces selected should be readable.

10. Readability depends a great deal upon what the reader is used to seeing. Words made from capitals and lowercase letters are more readable than all capitals. Type running from left to right is more readable than in vertical rows or diagonals.

11. Readers expect the letters and words to be uniformly spaced. Extra space between the lines of the body will improve readability. One-point leading is common.

12. Type to form the body of a job is most effective if set in paragraphs.

13. Paragraphs should have the first line indented. If the indention is omitted, extra space between paragraphs is needed.

14. The size of the type affects the width of the body columns. The bigger the type, the wider the column needed. A general rule is to plan the width of the column to equal 39 lowercase characters. If wider copy is wanted, two or more columns can be used.

15. Long blocks of copy can be broken with subheads. These are usually a larger, bolder variety of the face used on the body.

16. Picture captions should be as near the picture as possible. They usually go below the picture, but they also can be on the side, top, or inside of the picture.

17. The designer has more freedom in working with display type. *Display* types are those larger than 14-point sizes. They are used for newspaper and magazine headings, posters, and other copy requiring a large attention-getting face. Display type can be crowded, slanted, or positioned in any way the designer feels is effective.

18. Plan the space needed for type on the copy. This is called copyfitting, as explained in Chapter 3, "Planning, Copyfitting, and Measurement."

19. Spacing between words and letters is vital to graphic design. The spacing used should be decided by a designer rather than a printer.

20. The spacing should be equal between lines in the body of the copy.

21. Spacing between a headline and copy should be unequal. The designer should strive to keep these in proper proportion. If a headline has several lines, the spacing between them should be equal.

If several blocks of copy have the same size headlines, the spacing for each should be the same.

22. Type set for the body of the copy is designed so that the spacing between letters is constant. Spacing between letters in display size type must also be constant. Actually, the spacing must be varied so that it *looks* equal. If it is really equal, it will not appear to be equal because letters have different widths.

23. To help sketch headlines on copy, rule guidelines on scrap paper. Sketch the letters on this scrap. Slide it beneath the copy paper. This will help determine if the letters are the right size. When the correct size is found, trace the letters on the copy. Do not hand-letter sizes below 14 points. Anything below 12 points is body type. This is shown with parallel ruled lines.

24. Usually three horizontal guidelines are needed. The top and bottom lines are the size of the capitals. The X-height is shown by the third line. Remember that space is needed for descending lowercase strokes.

25. Lightly rule some vertical lines over the guidelines. These help keep the letters from slanting. If slant letters are to be used, the vertical guidelines can be slanted as much as needed.

ART DESIGN

When a company has a need for an advertisement or some other type of printing job, it usually seeks the services of an advertising agency. The artists produce the original layout, the finished design, plus the lettering, photography, retouching, and paste-up. They produce *copy* ready for use by the printer.

Studios vary widely in size and services. They range from a one-person operation to large companies with many employees. In the one-person studio, the design is the work of this person. Some parts, such as the photography, may be sent out to be done by someone else. The designer produces the final materials ready for the printer.

A large company will employ specialists. A job will pass through the hands of many people.

DESIGNING A LAYOUT

A *layout* is a diagram or arrangement of the job to be printed. It can be for an entire page, part of a page, or advertisement. It serves as a guide to the printers. The layout also is used to give the person paying for the job a good idea of how the finished copy will look. The graphic designer revises and adjusts the layout until it is acceptable to both the designer and the customer.

Layouts include the following:

1. The exact size of the job.
2. The size and kind of border.
3. The placement of all illustrations.
4. The special effects for illustrations, such as duotones (two-tone color effect).
5. The amount of reduction or enlargement of illustrations.
6. The measure, size, and typeface of body and display type.
7. The kind and size of stock, including trim and fold allowances.
8. The areas to have color.
9. The type of color reproduction.
10. Properly keyed attached copy.
11. The type of film to be used, such as additive or reversal.
12. The date the copy is to be printed.
13. The proper color for each overflap.
14. The procedure for handling halftones and windows.
15. Any special effect areas, such as a reversed area.
16. The date the layout was made.

The layout is *planned* before any typesetting is done. As stated in the preceding list, it shows the typefaces to be used. The printer needs this information before starting the job.

Copy that is written for the layout must fit properly. Sometimes the layout is made with a certain amount of space allotted for the copy. The copy is then written to fit this space. Other times, the amount and contents of the copy are determined first and the layout must be made to accommodate the copy.

The page layouts for books are nearly always made after the copy is written. The design of the book and the illustrations are adapted to suit the text.

The layout of an advertisement is designed to present an idea. Developing the layout involves decisions about the kind and amount of illustrations, type style, contents of copy, and so forth. An approximate space is allowed for copy. Space must also be provided for any requirements of the advertiser, such as company trademark or slogan. A trial layout is made, and the copy is written to fit the space. As the layout is changed, the copy may have to be rewritten to fit the change in available space.

When the copy is written depends upon the judgment of the designer. As a general rule, if the designer feels the illustrations are most important, the layout is made before final copy is written. If the written message is of primary importance, then it is written first and the layout is made around it.

THUMBNAIL SKETCHES

Many designers like to start planning a layout by making several fast, small sketches. These *thumbnail* sketches are smaller than the proposed layout, but they are in the same proportion as the final job. Any type of tool—pencil, crayon, or ball point pen—can be used.

A thumbnail sketch gives the designer the chance to record rapidly several possible solutions. Details are not a concern at this point. Areas for halftones and outlines must be selected. A general practice is to show halftones as a gray, shaded area. Line drawings are shown by elliptical areas. Headlines are marked with zigzag lines. The copy is indicated by parallel lines.

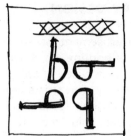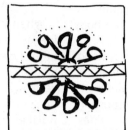

Commercial Art Department, Salina Vocational-Technical School, Salina, Kansas
5-9. *Three thumbnail sketches of a booklet cover.*

Some examples of thumbnail sketches are shown in Fig. 5-9.

ROUGH LAYOUTS

A rough layout is full sized. It is often as crude as a thumbnail sketch. Some designers prefer to skip the thumbnail sketch and start with the rough layout. It gives the printer a guide to use in the composing room. The heads are usually hand lettered. The lettering is rough, and no attempt is made to copy exactly the type size or face to use. This information is written on the margin of the drawing.

The area for the text is shown with double-ruled lines. Illustrations or halftones are sketched freehand. Fig. 5-10.

FINISHED LAYOUT

Some designers carry their rough layouts to a more finished condition. On these finished layouts the headings are hand-lettered in the type style wanted; so further identification is unnecessary.

The artwork and photographs are drawn in so that they look somewhat like the final copy. The area for copy is ruled with parallel lines. The spacing is carefully measured.

While the finished layout is more detailed than a rough layout, it is still quite rough when compared with a comprehensive layout. In practice many layouts end up somewhere between a rough and a finished layout. The important thing is to clearly present what is wanted.

Copies of the rough and finished layout are often sent to the customer. On many jobs, this provides enough information to secure approval.

COMPREHENSIVE LAYOUT

A comprehensive layout, Fig. 5-11, is made with great care. It shows a client exactly how the job will look. This is especially important when a client is paying thousands of dollars for a job and wants to approve it prior to printing.

Comprehensive layouts show the finished copy in every detail. The headings are hand-lettered in ink or tempera. Illustrations are printed or drawn in ink. Actual photographs are pasted in place. Sometimes the copy is set in type; a proof is taken and glued in place.

The comprehensive layout is fastened to a strong piece of illustration board for presentation

Commercial Art Department, Salina Vocational-Technical School, Salina, Kansas

5-11. *The comprehensive drawing of the rough layout, Fig. 5-10, selected for the cover.*

Commercial Art Department
Salina Vocational-Technical School
Salina, Kansas

5-10. *Rough layouts built upon the thumbnail sketches shown in Fig. 5-9.*

to the customer. Often it is framed and covered with a protective flap.

PASTE-UPS

It is necessary to make a paste-up if the job is to be printed by the offset method. A paste-up includes all the finished artwork and proofs of headlines and copy. It is sometimes called a *mechanical.* Making a paste-up is a very difficult job and requires a high level of skill.

The finished product is photographed for making into a plate. Anything on the paste-up is recorded by the camera and will therefore be printed. The paste-up technician is concerned only with what is photographed. The

client does not see the paste-up; it is used for production. Details for making paste-ups are found in Chapter 9, "Preparing Copy for the Camera."

MAKING A LAYOUT

1. Study all materials—the copy, artwork, photographs—and evaluate the importance of each.

2. Make a few thumbnail sketches. Try to find one sketch that is most effective in presenting the material.

3. If a job has several pages, arrange the layout in pairs.

CROP MARK

5-12A. *Photograph with crop marks.*

5-12B. *The cropped photo centers attention upon the chair.*

The two-page spread should be considered as a single design problem.

4. Use only one side of a sheet for layouts.

5. Draw the margins first. Then write on the page numbers. Draw in the columns if any are planned.

6. Next draw the headlines and illustrations. Usually they are more important than copy.

7. If copy is most important, lay out the space it requires first.

Then use remaining space for headings and illustrations.

8. Consider cropping or reducing the size of the illustrations. *Cropping* means removing some of the illustration, while permitting the most important part to remain large. The area to be removed is shown by marks on the margins of the photo. Fig. 5-12. *Reducing* means photographically making the entire illustration smaller to fit into a smaller space on the layout. Fig. 5-13.

Draw a box to show the space saved for each illustration. Label each space with a letter, as Photo A. Then label the photo with an A. It is even better if a copy of the illustration can be used in the layout. This makes it easier to see whether the layout is really effective.

9. Letter in the photo captions.

10. In the margin give the information about the typefaces wanted, spacing, and other directions. Be specific. Write clearly.

SOME LAYOUT POINTERS

1. Use a layout tracing pad. This will permit tracing parts of the layout when rearranging it on another sheet.

2. Use a variety of pencil weights.

3. Use a drawing board and T square.

4. Try to get one major design theme in the layout.

5. Mask unneeded parts of illustrations. Never butt photos together.

6. Do not print type across a photograph, drawing, or pattern. It is difficult to read and is distracting.

7. Use tint blocks rather than boxes. The blocks can be solid or screened.

8. Captions must be related directly to the illustrations.

9. Color adds a great deal to a layout.

10. If color cannot be used, consider screening the black to get a gray.

11. It is usually best to run type in black. Most colors make the text difficult to read. If color is used, go to a bold weight in the type.

12. Consider printing text in black on screened blocks of color. This attracts attention and is easier to read than printing the text in color.

13. If a job is to use color, use the color on the layout.

14. Get contrast into the type used. Consider dark and light, large and small, italic and capitals.

15. Do not combine two similar typefaces or two scripts. Con-

trast the type used, such as sans serif with old style.

16. If capitals are letter-spaced, use the same spacing in the entire layout. Do not letter-space lowercase letters.

17. Do not capitalize entire words within blocks of text. Use small caps instead.

18. Indent all paragraphs.

19. Be certain to specify every detail. Leave nothing to the imagination of the printer.

20. Do not use a line longer than 65 characters or shorter than 35.

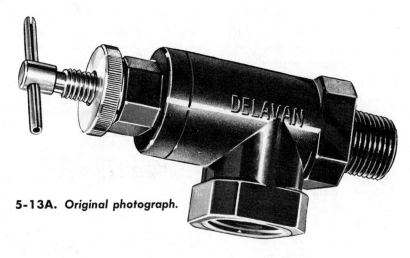

5-13A. *Original photograph.*

GRAPHIC DESIGN

When graphic designers undertake a project, they must focus their attention on the purpose it is to serve. The product's intended purpose will determine how it is to be designed and printed. The format and design, printing, and binding processes used are influenced by the purpose of the product.

In addition to considering purpose, the designer must present ideas clearly. The manner of arranging the parts of a printing job must add clarity and help attract the reader's attention.

Good graphic designers understand the basic rules of layout. As they gain experience, they can bend or violate some of the rules occasionally and still achieve a good layout. However, decisions to do this are based on a knowledge of the rules of layout.

DESIGN AND LAYOUT

A design is the original creation. The designer originates the material in the job and works on ways to assemble it. The person making the layout uses the ma-

terial made available by the designer. Often the size and shape of space the copy will occupy are decided. The layout artist does the best possible within the limits set. Both the designer and layout artist use the principles of design.

FACTORS INVOLVED IN DESIGN

1. *Lines* are an important part of the design. They can be made in many ways: smooth or rough, straight or curved, continuous or broken. Lines tend to influence the mood of the viewer. A horizontal line is calm. A vertical line imparts dignity. The diagonal line represents vitality. Curved lines indicate grace.

2. *Tone* refers to the modification of color to make it less brilliant. A solid black area can be changed into many variations of gray. Tones provide contrast to lines in a design.

3. *Color* is most effective in setting the mood of a printing job. Red, yellow, and orange are warm colors. They are associated with fire and sunshine. Violet, blue, and green are cool colors.

5-13B. *Photograph after reduction of 50 percent. It is half as long and wide as the original.*

They produce a cool sensation in the viewer.

4. *Texture* is a pattern that appears over part of a job. It can range from smooth to very rough. It can be hard or soft. It can be a printed image or the actual softness or roughness of the paper.

5. *Shape* is the result of several lines coming together, or a single line that bends. An area with a tone can assume a form or shape.

6. The *size* refers to the overall dimensions of the printed job, as well as the elements that make up the design. Usually the more important elements are the largest.

7. Parts of each design have *direction*. Lines and shapes tend to point. An important part of design is to control the direction of the elements in the job. Direction can greatly increase the effectiveness of a job. It can also reduce it to a message of confusion.

PRINCIPLES OF DESIGN

The following are general principles of design. They apply to each element of a printing job as well as to the entire composition.

The basic principles center around balance, proportion, sequence, unity, and emphasis.

Balance

A design is in balance when the different elements appear to be equalized. There are two kinds of balance: formal and informal.

Formal balance is symmetrical. Each item that appears on one side of the design also appears on the other. Fig. 5-14. Usually they are built around a center line. Equal parts of the design fall to the right and left of the center line. Formal balance is generally used where dignity is required.

In *informal balance* the design is not symmetrical. It does have the elements (items) distributed so that the weights (tone and mass) of the parts appear to balance each other. Fig. 5-15. Color, texture, size, and shape influence balance. Informal balance gives snap and pep to a layout.

A layout is balanced around its *optical center*. This is a line slightly above the actual center of a layout, since the actual center would give an illusion of being too low. Fig. 5-16. A designer

does not measure this. The location is estimated. It is moved until the designer feels the layout has balance.

If a layout has two masses, such as two pictures that are the same size, they are placed the same distance from the optical center. Fig. 5-17. This makes the layout appear to be in balance.

If a layout has pictures or blocks of type that are unequal in size, the larger is placed nearer the optical center. This is the

5-14. *This layout shows formal balance.*

Dynamic Graphics, Inc.

5-15. *This layout has informal balance.*

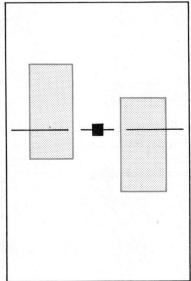

5-17. *Masses of equal size are placed the same distance from the optical center.*

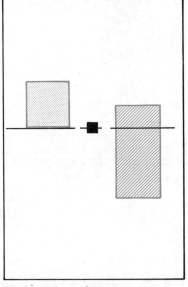

5-18. *When there are two unequal masses, the larger mass should be more nearly centered. In this drawing, the larger mass crosses the optical center line. The smaller mass is above the optical center line.*

same principle used on a seesaw. The larger unit must be placed nearer the center if it is to balance. Fig. 5-18.

Areas that are noticeable because they are bold, dark, or colorful are balanced by other areas of a similar nature. If a layout has a bold, dark heading at the top something must appear at

the bottom to balance it. Fig. 5-19.

Color also needs to be balanced. If color is at the top of a page, it should appear at the bottom. If it is on one side of a page, it should be on the other side.

Many layouts have several photos and lines of display type. These can be balanced on the

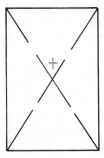

THE OPTICAL CENTER IS SLIGHTLY ABOVE THE ACTUAL CENTER.

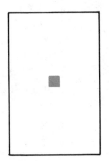

WHEN A MASS IS LO-CATED ON THE ACTUAL CENTER IT APPEARS TO BE LOW.

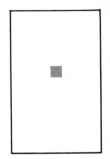

WHEN A MASS IS LO-CATED ON THE OPTI-CAL CENTER IT AP-PEARS TO BE STABLE.

5-16. *The location of the optical center is an important design consideration.*

5-19. *Bold, dark headings must be balanced with a bold feature at the bottom.*

C SHAPE

Dynamic Graphics, Inc.

5-20. Layouts can be made using the shapes of letters of the alphabet as the basic form.

T SHAPE

O SHAPE

L SHAPE

layout by arranging in the shape of letters of the alphabet. Fig. 5-20 shows the capitals L, T, O, and C used by the designer as a basic plan. As the layout is refined, the basic letter form used becomes less apparent. The shape of letter should not be apparent to the viewer of the final layout.

Proportion

Proportion is the relationship of sizes. For example, it is the relationship between the width of a layout to the depth. If the layout is 3″ deep and 6″ in length, it has a 1 to 2 proportion. Elements within a layout, such as the size of photos or area used for text, have a proportional relationship to each other.

Pleasing layouts have proportions that avoid division into obvious units such as halves, thirds, or fourths. The relationship is more subtle. The human hand is a good example. Notice that the distance between the knuckles of each finger is slightly different. The fingers are not divided into three equal parts. There is a slight, subtle difference in the proportion of the parts of the finger.

A layout of proper proportions must be pleasing to the eye. It must satisfy the artistic attitude of the viewer.

A square has a 1 to 1 proportion. It presents a rather dull appearance. It is not as effective as a rectangle. If a layout is square, a designer can break it up into rectangular elements. Fig. 5-21.

Finding Proportions

Proportions for a layout can be found by using the principle of dynamic symmetry. Dynamic

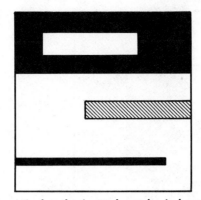

5-21. *A square area can be given vertical or horizontal emphasis by using rectangular elements.*

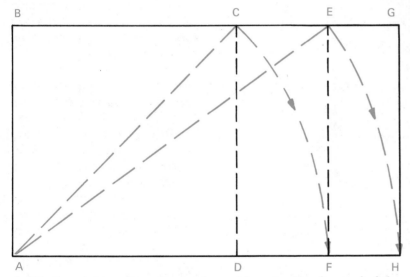

5-22. *Harmonious rectangles are formed by using the diagonal of the square as the length of the long side of the rectangle.*

HARMONIOUS RECTANGLES

Design Factors	Proportions Produced
Long Rectangle: 2.0	1:2
Printer's Rectangle: 1.7	2:3.5
Golden Rectangle: 1.6	3:5
Regular Rectangle: 1.5	4:6
Hypotenuse Rectangle: 1.4	5:7

5-23. *Rectangular design factors and proportions produced by the application of the factor to the short side of the layout.*

symmetry means dividing areas so that each part is in agreement with the others, as well as with the whole.

To use dynamic symmetry, one dimension must be known. This dimension is used to form a square. This square forms the basis for making rectangles that are in perfect harmony with the square.

The construction using dynamic symmetry is shown in Fig. 5-22. Edge AB is the known dimension. This distance is used to form the square ABCD. The diagonal AC is rotated to the bottom edge at F. A perpendicular from F forms a rectangle ABEF that is in harmony with the square area. Other harmonious rectangles can be formed. Use the diagonal of the rectangle just formed, AE, and swing point E to the bottom edge at H. A perpendicular here forms another harmonious rectangle. This process can be repeated over and over, giving many other rectangles.

Another means for developing rectangles of pleasing proportions is to multiply the short side by *design factors*. These factors will produce rectangles of various proportions. The proportion to use depends upon the judgment of the designer. The factors and proportions produced are shown in Fig. 5-23.

To determine the long side of a rectangle, *multiply* the *short* side by the design factor. For example, if a layout has a short side of 36 picas and a 3:5 proportion is wanted, multiply the 36 picas by the golden factor of 1.6. (See Fig. 5-23.) The long side is 58 picas.

If the long side is known and the short side is wanted, *divide* the *long* side by the design fac-

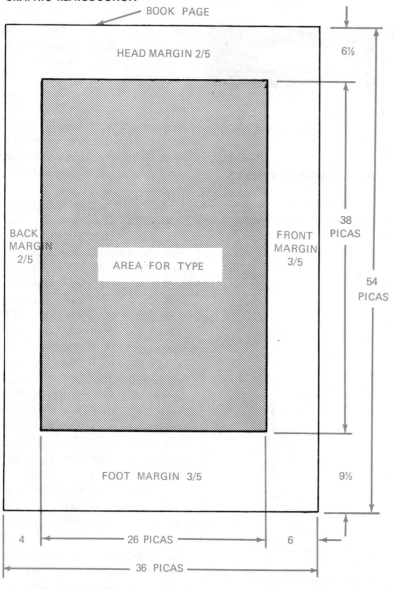

BOOK PAGE

HEAD MARGIN 2/5

6½

38 PICAS

BACK MARGIN 2/5

AREA FOR TYPE

FRONT MARGIN 3/5

54 PICAS

FOOT MARGIN 3/5

9½

4   26 PICAS   6

36 PICAS

5-24. *How to figure book page margins.*

Proportion involves the tone of the copy. As a general rule, about one-half of the copy should have a medium gray tone, one-fourth light gray, and one-fourth black. In any copy, one tone should dominate.

Figuring Type Area Proportions for Book Pages

There are two factors that must be decided when planning the area to be devoted to type on the pages of books. These are the proportions of the area of the page covered by type and the margins.

The type area proportions will vary somewhat. Very fine books have the type cover only one-half the area of the page. Most books devote more than this because of the cost. A good general rule is to set the type so that it measures 0.71 of the width and depth of the page. This gives slightly more than one-half the page to the type area. The type area is figured by multiplying the width and depth by 0.71. For example, assume a page is to be 36 × 54 picas. Each of these is multiplied by the factor 0.71.

$36 \times 0.71 = 25.56$, or 26 picas
$54 \times 0.71 = 38.34$, or 38 picas
The type will be set to a measure of 26 × 38 picas. Fig. 5-24.

tor. For example, if the long side is 58 picas and a 3:5 ratio is wanted, divide 58 by the design factor 1.6. This gives a short side of 36 picas. Sometimes both sides of a layout are known, and it is desired to find the design factor. To do this, divide the long side by the short side. For example, if the sides are 58 picas and 36 picas, division will show the design factor is 1.6. Looking in the table, Fig. 5-23, will show that

this is a golden rectangle having a proportion of 3:5.

Following is a summary of the methods to find the size of pleasing rectangles:

Unknown	Calculation Needed
Long side	= Short side multiplied by design factor
Short side	= Long side divided by the design factor
Design factor	= Long side divided by the short side

RUNNING HEAD

44 JOURNAL OF INDUSTRIAL TEACHER EDUCATION

5-25. A running head.

PILOT STUDIES

To pretest the inventory two separate pilot studies were conducted in succession for purposes of instrument refinement prior to developing the final form. Item phrases were written describing each element at the fourth level of the construction taxonomies. There were 33 elements of construction management practices. Construction production practices consisted of 46 elements at the fourth level. Construction personnel practices consisted of 59 elements of the fourth level. The total number of item phrases for the first draft consisted of 138. The sequential item phrase placement in the inventory was established by randomized using a randomization table.

Running heads are considered part of the type area. A *running head* is a caption above the copy on the page. Often the book title or chapter title is printed at the top of each page. Fig. 5-25.

Page numbers at the bottom of the page are not considered part of the type area. They are in the margin.

Figuring Book Page Margins

Page margins are figured by subtracting the actual type width and depth from the page width and depth. Then proportions of this difference are divided into the four margins. The proportions to use are head margin (top), 2/5; foot margin (bottom), 3/5; back margin, 2/5; and front margin, 3/5. Fig. 5-24.

The following figures are for the page margins shown in Fig. 5-24. The difference between the length of the page, 54 picas, and the type area, 38 picas, is 16 picas. The difference between the width, 36 picas, and the type area, 26 picas, is 10 picas.

$54 - 38 = 16$ picas for head and foot margins

Head = 2/5 of $16 = 6$ 2/5 picas, or 6 1/2 to the nearest pica

Foot = 3/5 of $16 = 9$ 3/5 picas, or 9 1/2 to the nearest pica

$36 - 26 = 10$ picas for back and front margins

Back = 2/5 of $10 = 4$ picas
Front = 3/5 of $10 = 6$ picas
These sizes are recorded on the layout. Fig. 5-24.

When the paper is cut and the job printed, it must be large enough to allow for binding. The amount to add to the back margin for this purpose varies with the type of binding. In any case, the back margin after binding should appear as calculated.

Sequence in Layout

Sequence refers to the plan the designer has for guiding the eyes of the reader over the layout. A skillful designer can direct the eyes of the reader much the same as a traffic control officer directs the flow of automobiles.

People generally start by looking at the top of a page. There is a natural tendency to look at the optical center of the page. Fig. 5-26. From the optical center, attention usually moves in a clockwise direction around the page. Generally, most of the top

half of a layout receives more attention from a reader than the bottom half. The reader tends to look to the top left area of a page first and directs attention there longer than any other area.

See Figs. 5-27 through 5-29 for some examples of how designers direct the attention of viewers. The eye is attracted to the dominant element on a page. The eye will then jump to the next most dominant element. Fig. 5-27. This tendency is so strong that the eye can be pulled to the bottom of a page if the copy there is strong enough. Dominance does not always refer to size. The subject matter in a smaller photograph can sometimes outpull a larger element. For example, a small picture of a girl in a bathing suit will outpull many larger pictures, such as a scene of a forest.

Color also attracts attention. The tendency is to go from color to uncolored areas. Fig. 5-28.

Designers use pointing devices (such as arrows, hands, or carefully placed lines of type) to direct attention. Fig. 5-29. Here the reader will usually start viewing at the largest element on the left, move across the page to the sec-

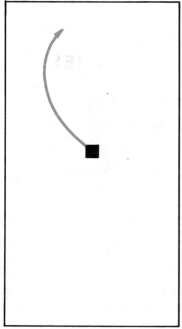

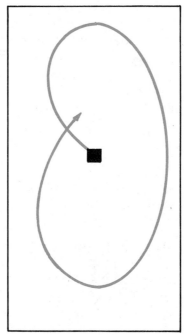

5-29. *Pointing devices are used to direct the eye.*

MOST PEOPLE START EXAMINING A LAYOUT AT THE OPTICAL CENTER.

THE READER TENDS TO EXPLORE A LAYOUT IN A CLOCKWISE DIRECTION.

5-26. *When examining a layout, there is a tendency to move the eye from the optical center in a clockwise direction around the page.*

ond dominant element, and up to the smallest at the top. The size of the elements, plus the direction devices, guide the reader.

A clever direction device is the use of eyes. Fig. 5-30. In this layout, it is natural to look in the same direction as the girl.

It is common to tell a story in pictures. Viewers start at the top left picture and move across the page to the right. They naturally move across the page to pick up

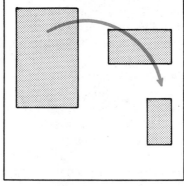

5-27. *The eye is attracted to the dominant element on the page.*

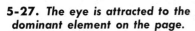

5-28. *There is a tendency to move the eye from color to uncolored areas.*

Dynamic Graphics, Inc.

5-30. *The reader's attention can be directed by the direction of eyes and hand.*

84

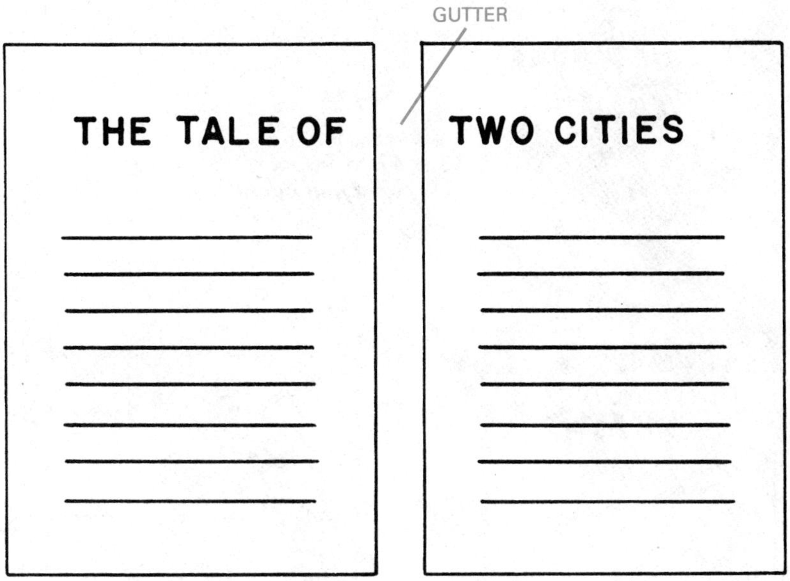

GUTTER

THE TALE OF | TWO CITIES

5-31. *A headline across the gutter tends to tie together an advertisement on two facing pages.*

the story on the second row at the left. The comic strip is built on this tendency, and the proper sequence must be followed to understand the story.

Often a designer has to prepare a layout for an advertisement that runs across two pages in a publication. The layout must tie the two pages together. One way to do this is by running a headline across both pages. Fig. 5-31. Another technique is to use common elements on both pages. Fig. 5-32. The elements on one page can point to or cross over the gutter between the pages. (The margin between the

Dynamic Graphics, Inc.
5-32. *The use of common elements on both pages helps hold together a two-page advertisement.*

GUTTER

5-33. *White space is a strong unifying agent.*

flowers by wire

5-34. *Layouts are built around an axis.*

Drugs

5-35. *Uneven groupings are common, as this three-point layout shows.*

HATS INC

5-36. *Color is used to provide emphasis.*

big jim beans

two facing pages is called the gutter.)

Unity

A layout has unity when the elements appear to be related and held together. To achieve unity, the graphic designer must select elements that go together and then arrange them so that they do not conflict with each other. If the elements in a layout have the same basic shape, size, texture, color, and mood, the layout will have unity.

Borders help unify a layout. An advertisement with a border will not merge with other ads on the page. Borders should be alike in thickness and tone. This helps the reader tie all the elements together.

White space is vital. It is a strong unifying agent. To be most effective, the white space should be on the outer edges of the layout. Fig. 5-33. The white space should take an irregular shape. A white band of equal thickness around a layout is not a strong unifying agent.

Layouts should be built around an axis. An axis is an imaginary line running through the layout either horizontally or vertically. Several axes can be used. Many of the elements of a layout should be built on the axis. While not all elements need to be related to the axis, it is essential that several do. Study the layout shown in Fig. 5-34.

One unifying technique is to build a three-point layout. Groupings of three are common and viewers expect them. They are comfortable with them. Uneven numbers are better than even numbers for groupings. Three-point layouts tend to form a triangle. Triangular elements reflect strength and add to the feeling of unity. Fig. 5-35.

Emphasis

Emphasis refers to the one item that is to be stressed in the layout. It can be the artwork, a headline, or the copy. If the artwork is to be emphasized, one part should be selected.

Once the element to be stressed is selected, the designer looks for effective ways to do this. The designer can increase its size, change the shape, or move other elements away from it. Color can be used. Fig. 5-36.

The designer must decide how much emphasis is needed and where to place the element to receive emphasis. The obvious location is near the optical center. However, skillful designers know they do not have to place it there, if the other elements are taken into consideration.

Emphasis can be generated from a sudden change in the direction of the element. A change in tone or texture produces emphasis.

COLOR

Understanding colors and their dimensions is important when planning a layout. Fig. 5-37. Color has three dimensions: hue, value, and chromaticity.

Hue refers to the quality of a color that enables the viewer to tell it from other colors. The names we give colors are hues. For example, red is a hue.

When one hue is placed against another, a contrast exists. The more dissimilar these hues are, the greater is the contrast. In other words, the farther

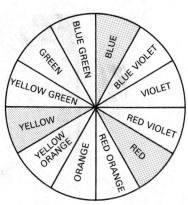

Dynamic Graphics, Inc.
5-37. A simple color wheel.

apart they are on the color wheel, the more dissimilar they appear.

Value is the degree of lightness or darkness. The prominence of parts of a layout can be changed by varying the value of the colors used.

Chromaticity is the measure of the intensity or strength of a color. Intense color is generally used sparingly on a layout.

When using color in a layout, color harmony must be carefully considered.

* *Monochromatic* color harmony is obtained by using shades and tints of one hue.
* *Analogous* color harmony is obtained by selecting adjacent colors on the color wheel. For example, yellow orange, orange, and red orange are analogous colors.
* *Complementary* color harmony is obtained by using two colors that are opposite each other on the color wheel. Red and green are complementary colors.
* *Triadic* color harmony is obtained by selecting three colors that divide the color wheel into three equal parts. Yellow, red, and blue are triadic colors.

BASIC TYPES OF LAYOUT

Following are nine basic formats for layout design. From these a limitless variety can be developed by the creative designer. A designer will try several different formats before deciding which one to use.

MONDRIAN FORMAT

The Mondrian format is based on the use of rectangular elements of pleasing proportions. (The name is derived from the painting style of the Dutch artist, Piet Mondrian.) The designer using this format is more interested in using the proportion of the rectangular elements as a design principle than in eye movement, emphasis, or any of the other principles. Fig. 5-38.

A Mondrian layout consists of a fitted set of vertical and horizontal rectangles. Sometimes a square element is inserted. These are all different sizes. The lines separating the rectangles can be of varying widths. All lines tend to be bold.

The rectangles generated can be filled with halftones, copy, or left blank in a solid color. The

87

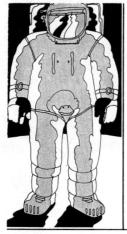

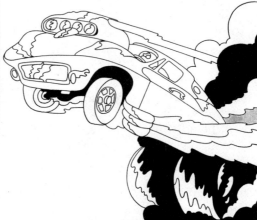

A life-style vs. "your thing"

Whom you work for is as important as what you do.

No man works in a vacuum. Associates. Policies. Environment. These and many more contribute to what is really your opportunity. Ultimately, they will determine rewards more significant than salary alone. Like recognition. Motivation. Satisfaction. Values and a way of life that reflects them.

At Stackpole, we produce electrical, electronic, electro-mechanical and ferro-magnetic componentry. Five million items daily. Since 1906.

Our young people tell us they chose Stackpole because work and training occur together, because the individual is important, and because life is unhurried and the sky still blue. Corny. Perhaps. But true.

For an exciting brochure on your opportunities at Stackpole, write: John Bezek, Stackpole Carbon Company, St. Marys, Pennsylvania 15857.

STACKPOLE

Stackpole, Developed by Ira Thomas Associates

5-38. *This advertisement uses the Mondrian format. Notice that each element is a rectangular shape.*

typefaces used should be related to the width of the ruled lines. If heavy ruled lines are used, a boldface type is needed.

As designers work, they will rule a series of horizontal and vertical lines over the layout sheet. They then begin to remove portions of some lines. Some areas can be enlarged. Thicker lines can be drawn. Adjustments are made to balance the layout and keep the rectangular elements in pleasing proportions. Headlines, pictures, and blocks of copy are inserted in the blocks. Again, this could change the balance, and adjustments must be made. The elements of this format are always informally balanced.

PICTURE WINDOW FORMAT

This format places emphasis on a picture that occupies most of the layout. Copy must be clever and tightly written, since

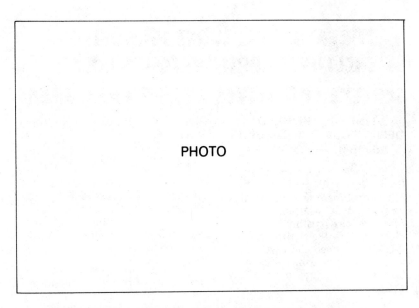

PHOTO

Experience is the best teacher.

No wonder KitchenAid makes such good dishwashers.
Look at all the experience we've had. We're the world's
oldest and largest commercial dishwasher manufacturer.
We got started making dishwashers for
restaurants over 80 years ago. That taught us
plenty about making dishwashers for the home.
Some of our original KitchenAid dishwashers are still in use after 20 years. With few
or no repairs.
If you'd like that kind of experience
with your dishwasher, see your KitchenAid
dealer. He's listed in the Yellow Pages. Or
write KitchenAid Dishwasher Division,
Dept. 1DRD-4, The Hobart
Manufacturing Company, Troy, Ohio
45373.

KitchenAid
Dishwashers and Disposers
Hot-water Dispensers

PHOTO

KitchenAid

5-39. A picture window format.

very little space in the format is allowed for it. Fig. 5-39. The picture is usually bled and cropped. (*Bleeding* means it runs off the edge of the page with no borders allowed.)

Sometimes a headline is printed over the picture. The picture is usually at the top of the page with the copy below. However, the picture can be placed at the bottom or centered, with copy above and below.

COPY-HEAVY FORMAT

The copy-heavy format usually uses no pictures or illustrations. It is often in formal balance. The headline is centered. Fig. 5-40.

This format is used when the message is long and detailed. Generally, the copy relates to an important message or one that needs dignity.

THREATS, PRESSURES IGNORED BY SHELTON AS PRICING FOR 4-COLOR SCREENED POSITIVES ENTERS GRAY AREA

LINE WILL BE HELD DESPITE OBVIOUS DANGERS AS FIRM LOOKS AHEAD

Hackensack, N.J. — Shelton Color Corporation of 16 Lafayette Street here announced this week that it will continue to offer its new customers a 50% discount on their first set of 4-color screened positives. For 4x5's, the first-set price will therefore continue to be a low $12.50.

Queried on certain rumored threats, a reliable source close to this, the oldest of the postcard manufacturers and producers of quality color separations, stated for the record that the firm continues to believe that natural color dominates our existence and is now more than ever in demand for promotions.

This belief will endure, according to the spokesman, despite the threats coming from outer space that gray is the dominant theme facing certain expeditionary forces.

Shelton will continue to attract new customers for its 4-color products with its half-price policy, combined with the firm's 5 day delivery and quality service.

Ignoring the pressures of re-entry, the firm also announced that it looks forward to seeing its new 8½x11 full-color flyers carry the news of its customers new products (at only 2¢ per copy) to markets on the moon and beyond.

To back its pledge, Shelton is offering free samples, prices, data and encouragement to all who write during this trying period. Merely signify whether you want separation or flyer information.

Shelton Color Corp.

5-40. *A copy-heavy layout.*

Often the copy is broken into easy-to-read segments. Copy for a long job should never be set solid. It is best if the copy is leaded to increase the space between the lines and make it easier to read.

Secondary headlines can be used to help the reader. The first few words of a paragraph could be set in bold type. The paragraphs can have extra spacing between them. If a paragraph is of special importance, the entire paragraph can be set in boldface.

It could be set to a narrower measure than the rest of the job.

A border is sometimes used. It must be in unity with the typeface.

FRAME FORMAT

The frame format uses some technique to border the copy to help the layout stand alone on the page. The frame format is often used on advertisements when several ads will be printed together on the same page.

A standard border can be used. Fig. 5-41. Another technique is to use a photograph with part of the center removed for the copy. Thus, the artwork is used as a frame. This format decreases the space available for the copy.

CIRCUS FORMAT

The circus format is filled with a wide variety of elements: oversize type, reverse blocks, tilted illustrations, sunburst designs, and other strong elements to attract attention. While this format

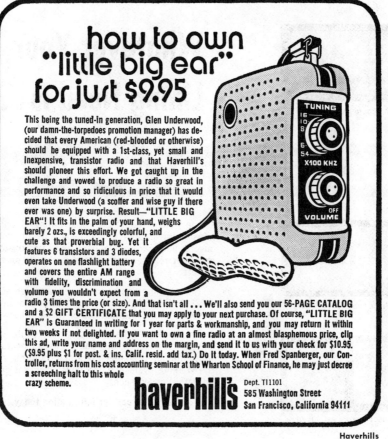

how to own "little big ear" for just $9.95

This being the tuned-in generation, Glen Underwood, (our damn-the-torpedoes promotion manager) has decided that every American (red-blooded or otherwise) should be equipped with a 1st-class, yet small and inexpensive, transistor radio and that Haverhill's should pioneer this effort. We got caught up in the challenge and vowed to produce a radio so great in performance and so ridiculous in price that it would even take Underwood (a scoffer and wise guy if there ever was one) by surprise. Result—"LITTLE BIG EAR"! It fits in the palm of your hand, weighs barely 2 ozs., is exceedingly colorful, and cute as that proverbial bug. Yet it features 6 transistors and 3 diodes, operates on one flashlight battery and covers the entire AM range with fidelity, discrimination and volume you wouldn't expect from a radio 3 times the price (or size). And that isn't all ... We'll also send you our 56-PAGE CATALOG and a $2 GIFT CERTIFICATE that you may apply to your next purchase. Of course, "LITTLE BIG EAR" is Guaranteed in writing for 1 year for parts & workmanship, and you may return it within two weeks if not delighted. If you want to own a fine radio at an almost blasphemous price, clip this ad, write your name and address on the margin, and send it to us with your check for $10.95. ($9.95 plus $1 for post. & ins. Calif. resid. add tax.) Do it today. When Fred Spanberger, our Controller, returns from his cost accounting seminar at the Wharton School of Finance, he may just decree a screeching halt to this whole crazy scheme.

haverhill's Dept. TI1101
585 Washington Street
San Francisco, California 94111

Haverhills

5-41. A frame format.

appears to be a miscellaneous array of attention-getting elements, it must follow the principles of good design. The elements are organized into units. These are combined to make a unified, balanced layout.

The big concern of the designer is variety. This is obtained by varying size, shape, and tone within the layout. Fig. 5-42.

This format is primarily used for advertisements that feature bargain prices or a big sale. Often prices become as important as any part of the layout.

COMIC STRIP FORMAT

The comic strip format features a series of drawings or photographs that tell a story. Following the style of the comic strips, a message is presented with photographs; the conversation is printed below each picture. Generally, the photos or drawings are all the same size. This prevents one from arresting the attention of the reader. All the photos must be examined to get the entire message. Fig. 5-43.

Sometimes a story is told by placing the pictures in a checker-

board fashion. This is effective when presenting pictures of products.

SILHOUETTE FORMAT

In a silhouette format, the elements of the layout are arranged to form an overall silhouette, or outline. A silhouette layout could be called a side-view layout. A silhouette that is irregular is more effective than a regular one. For example, consider the human head. If viewed from the front, a smooth, regular silhouette is made. When viewed from

5-42. A circus format.

The Graphic/Ricoh Plate-Producer: 6 reasons to like it and 1 way to get it.

1

You get the sharpest cleanest, most professional offset plates you ever saw. Anywhere. You can copy anything you need copies of. Screens, halftones, books, rigid material. Anything. And those large solid areas won't wash out. Ever.

2

Our new baby is really small. Just 31" long and 19" deep. It fits neatly in places you'd never think were big enough. But does the job of the big ultra-complicated ones.

3

CHICKEN SOUP

There are no messy liquid chemicals needed. You stay neat. The Plate-Producer stays neat. Your towels stay neat. (At least up to lunch.)

4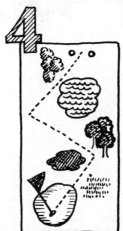

You easily get accurate electrostatic plates. In just 30 seconds. No problem at all to make additions, deletions or clean up. Lots of time to spend in improving your golf score.

5

ON

Just push. Our Plate-Producer does the rest. And there's nobody who can't learn to push a button and sit back.

6 No more quick burgers on the run. Or ordering in as you wait for the plates to come. Relax. You can sit like a person. Have a nice lunch. And drink a toast to our considerate, speedy Plate-Producer.

7 THIS IS THE WAY TO GET IT. JUST CUT THIS OUT AND PLACE ON THE DESK OF THE PERSON WHO DOES THE BUYING.

$1495.00

Plates cost 6¢ for short runs (about 200 copies) to 25¢ for long runs (5000 copies)

Any solution or ink you use with your own offset duplicator works just great with our plates.

graphic RICOH ELECTRONIC PLATE-PRODUCER

Call or write for a free demonstration:
GRAPHIC COMMUNICATIONS CORPORATION, 25 GRAPHIC PLACE, MOONACHIE, NEW JERSEY, 07074, (201) 343-5100

CIRCLE NO. 510 ON POST CARD

Graphic Communications Corp.

5-43. A comic strip format.

The anatomy of a photo typositor.

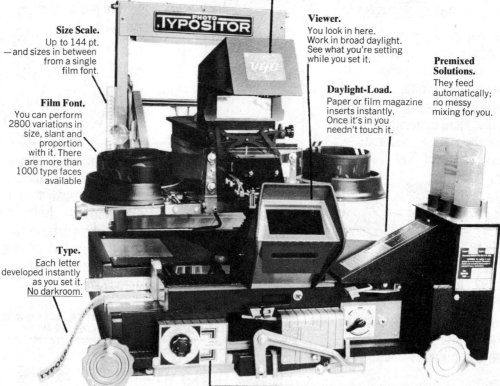

Special Lenses.
Expand, condense, italicize, back-slant as you compose. Match a layout, set a head to desired height or width.

Size Scale.
Up to 144 pt. —and sizes in between from a single film font.

Viewer.
You look in here. Work in broad daylight. See what you're setting while you set it.

Premixed Solutions.
They feed automatically; no messy mixing for you.

Film Font.
You can perform 2800 variations in size, slant and proportion with it. There are more than 1000 type faces available

Daylight-Load.
Paper or film magazine inserts instantly. Once it's in you needn't touch it.

Type.
Each letter developed instantly as you set it. No darkroom.

Anyone can learn to operate the Photo Typositor® in less than half a day. Purchase or lease is complete, without hidden extras, and includes free installation and thorough instruction.

Spacing Selector.
Set any desired letter or word spacing in points or picas. Accurate control for rules, bendays, shadows, step-and-repeat.

Photo Typositor Division, Visual Graphics Corporation
305 East 46th Street, New York, N.Y. 10017

☐ Send me your illustrated brochure.   ☐ Tell me about your leasing plan.

☐ I'd like a demonstration on my premises.

Company_____

Address_____

City/State/Zip_____

Your name & position_____

Visual Graphics Corp.
5-44. A silhouette format.

Worldwide sales, service, instruction. .   ®TM U.S. PATENT OFFICE VISUAL GRAPHICS CORP.

the side, the silhouette is irregular. The irregular silhouette is more descriptive and attracts more attention.

The silhouette arrangement is the result of all the elements of a layout. Fig. 5-44. The elements should not have too much white space between them or the unity of the layout will be destroyed. The best practice is to push the white space to the outside. This tends to form a frame.

TYPE SPECIMEN FORMAT

As stated before, the large number of typefaces available to designers is shown in type specimen books prepared by manufacturers. Designers appreciate the beauty of the curves, corners, serifs, and stroke variations of these typefaces. They can use this beauty in preparing layouts with large size letters, letting the beauty of the letters attract the reader. The designer often takes liberties in arranging words and spacing letters. However, the general principles of design must be observed.

Large, beautiful typefaces tend to overpower artwork. Many layouts emphasizing a typeface need no artwork. Fig. 5-45.

REBUS FORMAT

A rebus is a puzzle that uses pictures to suggest words. This technique can be used to produce an effective layout. Fig. 5-46. The designer can insert pictures in the copy to relay the message. The pictures can be all the same size, or they can vary. Generally, the copy in this layout is used for captions with each picture.

LAYOUT TOOLS AND TECHNIQUES

The basic tools needed for design layouts are not extensive or expensive. Some of the items that are needed include:

T square. Fig. 5-47. The T square is used to draw horizontal lines. It is placed on the edge of the drawing surface. The lines are drawn along the top edge of the T square, from left to right.

Triangles are used to draw vertical lines and some angles. Fig. 5-48. They are placed on the top edge of the T square. The triangle is held tightly to the T square with the free hand.

Vertical lines are drawn from bottom to top. Slanted lines are drawn as shown in Fig. 5-49.

Layout pads of tracing paper are needed for copying figures and letters. A bond paper layout pad is used for most design work, usually in sizes of 14″ × 17″ and 19″ × 24″.

Pencils. The designer selects a

When you need opacity, the answer is FINCH TITLE 95

Finch, Pruyn and Co., Inc.

5-45. A type specimen format.

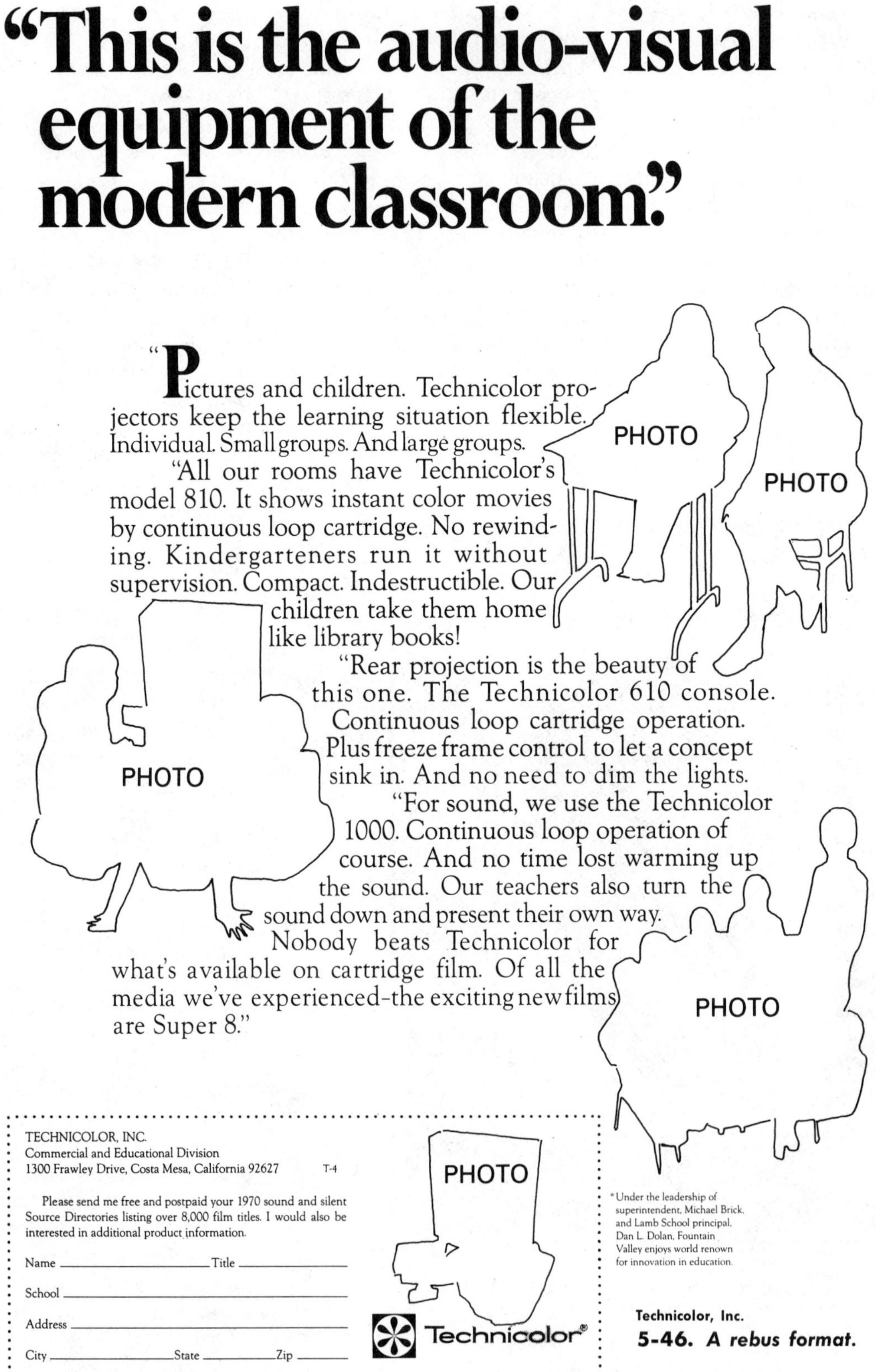

"This is the audio-visual equipment of the modern classroom."

"**P**ictures and children. Technicolor projectors keep the learning situation flexible. Individual. Small groups. And large groups.

"All our rooms have Technicolor's model 810. It shows instant color movies by continuous loop cartridge. No rewinding. Kindergarteners run it without supervision. Compact. Indestructible. Our children take them home like library books!

"Rear projection is the beauty of this one. The Technicolor 610 console. Continuous loop cartridge operation. Plus freeze frame control to let a concept sink in. And no need to dim the lights.

"For sound, we use the Technicolor 1000. Continuous loop operation of course. And no time lost warming up the sound. Our teachers also turn the sound down and present their own way.

Nobody beats Technicolor for what's available on cartridge film. Of all the media we've experienced-the exciting new films are Super 8."

TECHNICOLOR, INC.
Commercial and Educational Division
1300 Frawley Drive, Costa Mesa, California 92627   T-4

Please send me free and postpaid your 1970 sound and silent Source Directories listing over 8,000 film titles. I would also be interested in additional product information.

Name _____ Title _____

School _____

Address _____

City _____ State _____ Zip _____

*Under the leadership of superintendent, Michael Brick, and Lamb School principal, Dan L. Dolan, Fountain Valley enjoys world renown for innovation in education.

✦ Technicolor®

Technicolor, Inc.
5-46. A rebus format.

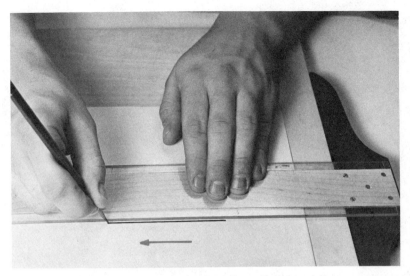

5-47. *A T square is used to draw horizontal lines.*

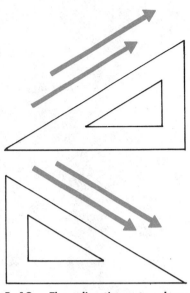

5-49. *The directions to draw slanted lines.*

pencil by size, depending on its use. For example, the B sizes are good for wide lines and shading, while the 2H is good for tracing. Large sets of color-leaded pencils are also available.

Two types of pencil points are used. One is a cone point and the other a chisel point. Fig. 5-50. The cone point will give thin lines. The chisel point gives wide lines and is also good for shad-

ing. The cone point is sharpened in a regular pencil sharpener. The chisel point is sharpened in a draftsman's pencil sharpener that cuts away only the wood.

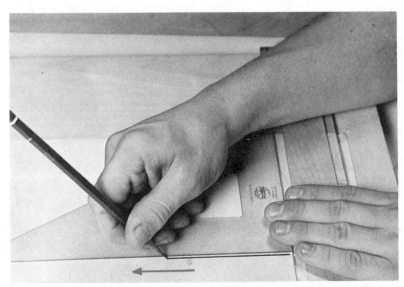

5-48. *Plastic triangles are used to draw vertical lines.*

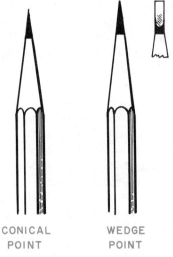

CONICAL POINT   WEDGE POINT

5-50. *Cone and chisel pencil points are used by the designer.*

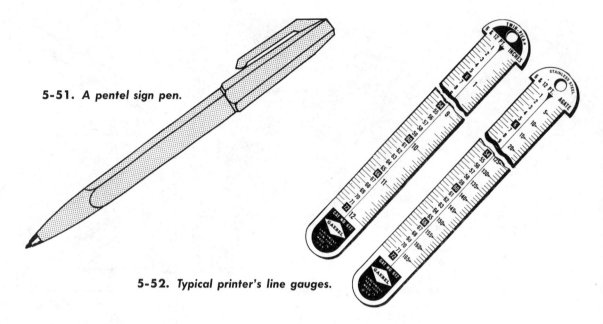

5-51. *A pentel sign pen.*

5-52. *Typical printer's line gauges.*

Then the lead is sanded to a chisel shape on a piece of sandpaper.

Erasers. There are many kinds of erasers available. The Pink Pearl is commonly used to erase pencil lines when corrections are needed. An art gum is used to clean up smears on the drawing. A kneaded eraser is used to make corrections in pastel, chalk, and charcoal areas.

Pentel. Fig. 5-51. This is a sign pen used a great deal for thumbnail sketches and preliminary roughs.

Line gauge. A line gauge is marked off in inches and picas. Some plastic rulers are also marked with both scales. Fig. 5-52. The line gauge is used for measuring distances.

Crayons can be used to show the colors on a layout. However, they only give an approximate color.

Pastel sticks are used to color large areas. They are much like

chalk. The points can be shaped to various widths with sandpaper.

Compass. Fig. 5-53. A compass has one leg with a sharp metal point. The other leg holds a pencil lead. It is used to draw circles and arcs. The pencil lead can be replaced with a device to ink circles and arcs.

Stick-on type and figures. A wide variety of typefaces, illustrations, and symbols are available on clear acetate sheets with an adhesive back. They speed the work of the designer.

Fixative is sprayed on the layout to prevent smears from handling.

Charcoal is used for fast rough sketches and shading.

Ink and pens. India ink is used a great deal because it is permanent. Sometimes colored inks are used. A variety of pen points are available for layout work. Fig. 5-54. A felt pen with a reservoir

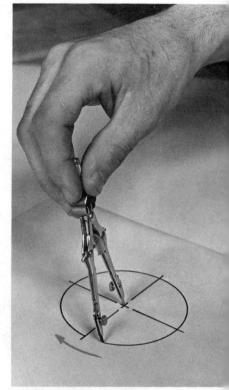

5-53. *A compass is slanted in the direction in which the point is being rotated.*

98

5-54. *A few of the types of pen points used for freehand layout.*

Speedball Pens

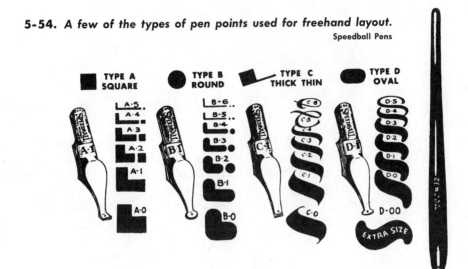

of ink that feeds a felt tip is very useful for light tones.

Tracing table (*light table*). This is a glass-topped table with a light below. Fig. 5-55. It is useful when tracing an illustration. The material to be traced is placed on the glass over the light while the paper for tracing is placed over the original illustration. The light makes it easy to see the lines. The same can be done by placing the drawing on a window and letting the outside light shine through.

The graphic designer also may use watercolors and tempera paints. The designer also needs general supplies, such as proper paintbrushes, scissors, drafting tape, and rubber cement.

Whatever materials designers choose, they must give them all proper care. Such basic practices as keeping pencils and pastel sticks properly sharpened, keeping pens and brushes cleaned, and keeping the layout free of smudges should be followed. As an aid to neatness, the designer

should use paper larger than the layout. The extra space allows room for notes and provides a place to hold the layout.

SHADING SHEETS

Shading sheets are made of transparent acetate. They have a shading pattern on the acetate. They are of special value for use on pen and ink illustrations. The pen and ink drawing is done in outline. The solid black areas are inked. Some brands of shading sheets have an adhesive back. They are applied to the area of

the drawing where shading is needed. With a sharp knife, they are cut to the shape desired. They are then rubbed lightly to make them stick in place. Fig. 5-56.

Shading sheets are available with black and white and color patterns on a clear background.

NuArc Co., Inc.

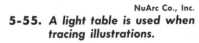

5-55. *A light table is used when tracing illustrations.*

How to use . . . Be sure artwork is absolutely clean and free of pencil marks, fingerprints and surface dirt. Remove enough of shading pattern from backing sheet to adequately cover area of original art that requires shading. Place over the portions of the copy to be shaded and flatten by rubbing shading sheet onto the artwork—adhesive side down—using mild pressure. Start at the bottom and rub from left to right, working upward as pattern adheres.

Then—using a burnisher—rub down shading screen onto copy until pattern is completely smooth and perfectly adhered. IMPORTANT—for best results and non-glare reproduction shading pattern must be completely flat against the artwork to which it is applied.

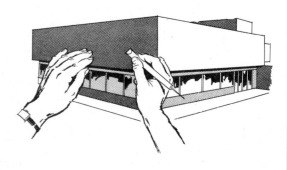

Where highlights are desired, they can be cut away or painted out with white opaque, using pen or brush. This assures smooth laying of the white and gives clean-cut edges. This also holds true if India ink is being used.

Remove excess or unwanted shading by cutting the shading pattern with cutting needle or stylus. Use needle at 60° angle. Heavy pressure is not necessary. Take care not to scratch original artwork. Peel off unwanted portions of shading sheet.

The Craftint Manufacturing Co.

5-56. *How to apply pressure-sensitive shading materials.*

How to Use One-tone Shading Sheets . . . Simply pencil your drawing on the one-tone sheet. Next use ink to make the permanent lines. Apply developer with pen or brush to the areas where you desire the tone. Blot the developer immediately. Do not let developer dry on the drawing.

5-57. How to use single-tone shading material.

Another method of preparing ink line drawings and shading them is shown in Figs. 5-57 and 5-58. The material used has a printed pattern that is photographically invisible. It is available on drawing paper or vellum. When the paper is dampened with special developer, the shad-ing printed in that area instantly turns black. After the areas have been developed, opaque white can be painted over them. Black waterproof ink can be painted either before or after developing the pattern. It is available in a single-tone and double-tone pattern. Figs. 5-59 and 5-60.

The film pattern to be used depends upon the amount the drawing is to be reduced. Remember that a fine pattern of shading, when reduced, becomes even finer. Fig. 5-60 shows how a 42-line screen pattern will look after several reductions.

How to Use Two-tone Shading Sheets . . . Here are the eight simple steps to achieve perfect results with two-tone shading sheets.

1. Select pattern of two-tone drawing board according to the way the drawing is to be reproduced. Example: Do not use extremely fine pattern when drawing is to be reduced 1/3 or 1/2. Use fine patterns for same-size copy only and use coarser patterns where reductions are required.

2. Make your drawing on two-tone drawing paper just as you would on any ordinary drawing paper. Use waterproof drawing ink and if erasing is necessary, use only art gum. Do not use hard or coarse erasers.

3. To bring out shadings, simply apply dark tone developer for dark shadings and light tone developer for light shadings. Apply freely with clean inexpensive brush or pen and blot immediately.

4. Important! Dark tones must be developed first throughout your drawings wherever such tones are desired. Do not begin to apply light tone developer until all your dark tone areas are completely developed.

5. Developers must be blotted immediately and not permitted to dry on your drawing of their own accord. Blotting is extremely important and absolutely necessary to insure satisfactory results.

6. Do not use the same brush to apply dark tone and light tone developers. Use an individual brush for each developer and wash each time after use.

7. It is not recommended that you apply dark tone developer over an area which has already been developed with light tone developer. Do not attempt this, unless you are positive that the light tone developer was immediately blotted after it was applied and are satisfied that the light area is absolutely dry before you proceed with the dark tone developer.

8. In developing large areas, blot as you go—small sections at a time. Do not wait until the entire area is developed before you start blotting.

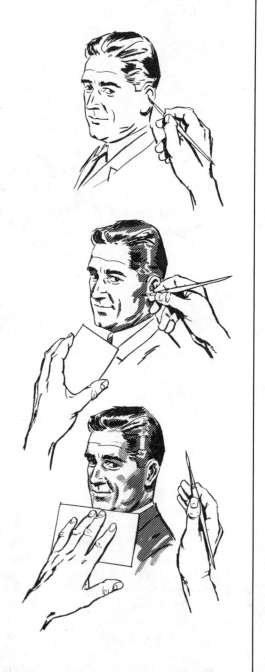

The Craftint Manufacturing Co.

5-58. *How to use double-tone shading material.*

The Craftint Manufacturing Co.
5-59. Selected examples of single-tone patterns.

Same Size

Reduced One-third

Reduced One-half

5-60. A 42-line screen double-tone paper at several stages of reduction.

REVIEW QUESTIONS

1. Some typefaces have fine strokes at the top and bottom of a letter. What are these strokes called?
2. A diagram or arrangement of the job to be printed is called a layout. True or False?
3. A rough layout is in the same proportion as a finished layout, but it is 50% smaller. True or False?
4. What is another name for a paste-up?
5. The paste-up is photographed for making into a plate. True or False?
6. Formal balance means that all items on a page are arranged vertically. True or False?
7. Why is a layout balanced around its optical center rather than its true center?
8. Assume a page is to be 45 × 60 picas. Using a factor of 0.71, figure the type area for the page.
9. All of the margins on a page (top, bottom, left, right) should be equal. True or False?
10. The margin between two facing pages is called the valley. True or False?
11. A picture that bleeds is one which runs off the edge of the page. True or False?
12. In a picture window format, a picture occupies most of the layout. Must this picture be centered on the page?
13. In the circus format, the main concern is variety. True or False?
14. A tracing table is a glass-topped table with a light below. True or False?
15. What is sprayed on the layout to prevent smears that may result from handling?

Chapter 6

Cold Composition

Cold composition produces images by means other than hot metal type, the primary image generation method used for many years. Cold composition is sometimes referred to as non-metallic composition. It is the means for producing camera-ready copy for offset printing.

The common methods of producing images for reproduction for offset printing include original art and illustrations, pre-printed materials, "strike-on" composition, continuous tone photography, and photocomposition. Any copy that can be photographed can be used for this purpose. (Also see Chapter 9, "Preparing Copy for the Camera.")

ORIGINAL ART AND ILLUSTRATIONS

Any kind of hand lettering or art can be used as copy for offset printing. Letter images can be generated by freehand or template lettering. Freehand lettering is usually done with special lettering and drawing pens. Fig. 6-1. Pen points of different sizes and shapes fit into a penholder.

Template lettering is performed by using a guide (the template) with the letters cut into it to control the movements of the pen (the inking device). Fig. 6-2 shows a lettering instrument having a template with recessed letters. The pen is held in a scriber. The pin on the scriber traces the shape of the letter in the template. The ink pen is thus guided through the same mo-

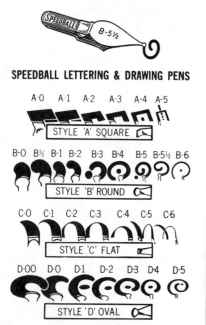

SPEEDBALL LETTERING & DRAWING PENS

A-0 A-1 A-2 A-3 A-4 A-5
STYLE 'A' SQUARE

B-0 B½ B-1 B-2 B-3 B-4 B-5 B-5½ B-6
STYLE 'B' ROUND

C-0 C-1 C-2 C-3 C-4 C-5 C-6
STYLE 'C' FLAT

D-00 D-0 D-1 D-2 D-3 D-4 D-5
STYLE 'D' OVAL

C. Howard Hunt Pen Co.

6-1. Speedball lettering pens are used to produce freehand lettering.

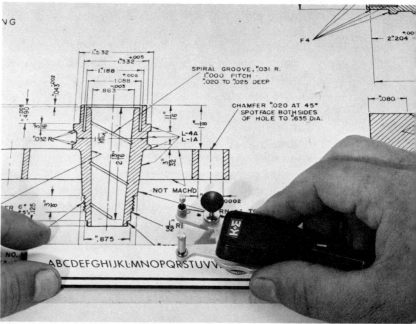

Keuffel and Esser Co.

6-2. A lettering instrument that uses a template to form the letters.

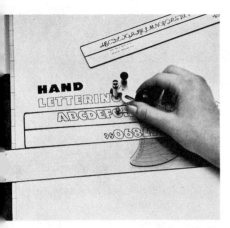

6-3. *The Letterguide template and scriber.*

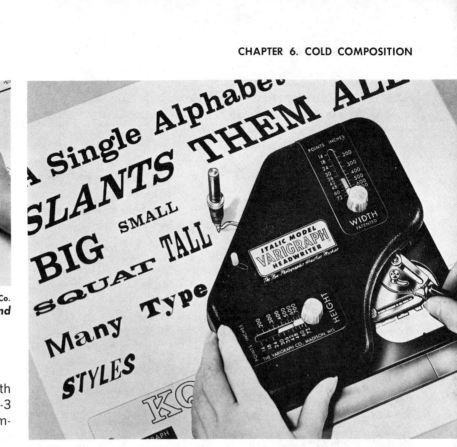

6-4. *The Varigraph italic model "Headwriter" lettering device.*

tions. Pens are available with different width points. Figs. 6-3 and 6-4 show other types of template lettering equipment.

Other templates have the symbols or letters cut through them. The point of a technical fountain pen is placed in and guided by the openings of the template.

Various types of technical illustrations, line drawings, and paintings are also used as copy for offset printing. Illustrations and lettering drawn with black India ink on white paper give the best results for reproduction purposes. All tools should be kept clean. Mistakes can be removed by erasing, scraping the ink away with a razor blade, or painting them out with white opaque or China white paint.

PREPRINTED MATERIALS
Clip Art

Clip art refers to material provided by companies that prepare illustrations of all sorts and print them on large sheets. Subscribers receive a continuous supply of new illustrations throughout the year. The various issues tend to reflect the seasons. For example, the fall issue will contain drawings relating to Thanksgiving, cold weather, and so forth. Many of the illustrations are available in several different sizes. The art is black on white paper, but some is prepared for color printing. To use clip art, the selected illustration is cut from the sheet and glued in place on the mechanical (paste-up). Fig. 6-5.

Preprinted Letters and Symbols

Letters are printed in sheets or pads for use in making headings

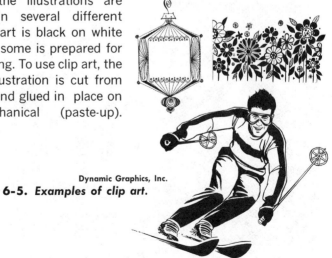

6-5. *Examples of clip art.*

and display lines. Each letter is mounted individually to form the words. One kind is made in pads, with one letter on each tab of the pad. Fig. 6-6. The letter that is visible is not the one which will appear on the copy. It is only to show what letter is on the *back* of the tab. The letters for the heading are assembled in a special composing stick. Fig. 6-7. After the heading is assembled, a

piece of transparent paste-up tape that is adhesive on both sides is applied over the letters in the stick. The line is lifted from the stick, turned over, and pressed into place on the copy. The letters on the rear of the tab are then facing up.

Transfer type is another kind of preprinted letter. To use it, first rule a faint guideline. For copy to be photographed, use a

Fototype, Inc.

6-7. Assemble letters and spaces in left hand, as right hand detaches characters from the perforated pads. Then snap each letter into the special composing stick.

nonreproducible blue pencil. (The blue will not show up on the photograph.) Align the letters by lining up either the top or bottom of the space bars on the sheets of lettering with the lines.

Place the sheet of letters over the mechanical. Locate the letter in the position wanted. Press down on the letter with a finger. Rub over the letter with a smooth, flat instrument. A spatula is a good tool to use. For small letters a pencil or a ballpoint pen will work. Start at the top of the letter and work down. Fig. 6-8. When the letter appears gray, it is free of the sheet and

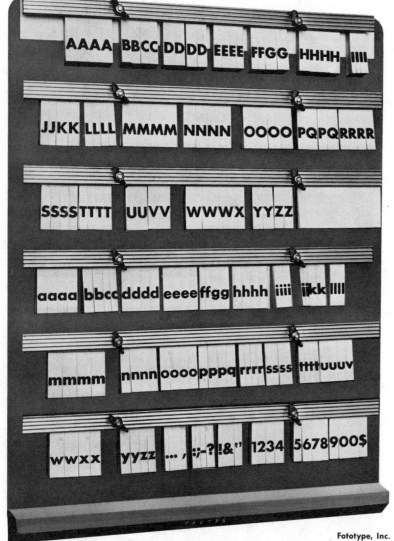

6-6. The Fototype letters are in pads.

Fototype, Inc.

Artype, Inc.

6-8. To transfer the letter, rub over it with a smooth, flat instrument.

Artype, Inc.

6-9. This letter has been transferred to the drawing paper.

Para-Tone, Inc.

6-10. Examples of preprinted adhesive borders.

has stuck to the artwork. Remove the sheet of letters. Fig. 6-9.

Borders are available in roll and sheet form. Fig. 6-10. Since they have adhesive backs, they are laid on the mechanical and pressed into place. Care should be exercised so that the border strips are not stretched when applied. Otherwise, they can cause the mechanical to curl.

It is easy to miter border corners. Let the pieces overlap at each corner. Then cut through both overlapping pieces, remove the unneeded tape, and press the miter to the mechanical. Fig. 6-11.

There are many symbols and illustrations available in the adhesive and transfer systems. Fig. 6-12. These are applied in the same manner as individual letters.

Material already printed can be used as part of the copy for a job. It can be cut from the original printed material and pasted up on the layout with the other reproducible images, such as a line drawing. The copy should be clean and from a job that has been well printed. It is preferred that it be black copy on a white background.

If the printed copy has halftones, they can be copied dot for dot (100 percent), but the results will not be of good quality. The dot structure tends to become coarse. Attempts to reduce the printed halftone may cause loss of the dot structure.

DIRECT-IMPRESSION TYPOGRAPHY

Direct-impression typography produces camera-ready copy when keys containing the characters strike paper. The most common example is copy produced by typing. The striking of keys directly produces copy. This process is also called "strike-on" composition.

Any typewriter can be used for direct impression, but electric typewriters are preferred. Some are especially designed to adjust the spacing between words to justify the lines on the right-hand margin.

DIRECT-IMPRESSION COMPOSITION PROCEDURES

Copy should be typed on good quality, smooth, dull white paper, such as a dull-coated book paper. If guidelines would be useful, they can be drawn with a non-reproducible, light blue pencil or printed in light blue ink. This color will not record when photographed.

The letters on the typewriter should be kept clean. They can be cleaned with a stiff fiber or plastic brush and then wiped with a clean cloth. The ribbon must produce a clear, dense image. The plastic, one-time ribbon is superior to all others.

The typist should keep a uni-

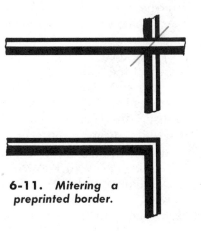

6-11. Mitering a preprinted border.

The Craftint Manufacturing Co.

6-12. Examples of preprinted symbols.

The process of image generation for offset printing is called cold composition. Cold composition is sometimes referred to as nonmetallic composition.

SINGLE SPACE

The process of image generation for offset printing is called cold composition. Cold composition is sometimes referred to as nonmetallic composition.

DOUBLE SPACE

The process of image

generation for offset printing

is called cold composition.

Cold composition is sometimes

referred to as nonmetallic

composition.

TRIPLE SPACE

6-13. The amount of space between lines changes the appearance of a job.

form pressure when typing on a manual typewriter. Electric typewriters give a uniform pressure to the stroke. Care must be exercised so that the keys do not pierce the paper. If this is a problem, a thin plastic sheet can be placed between the typewriter platen and the paper. Too light a stroke also causes difficulties. The image must be clear and dense for best reproduction.

If a different appearance is wanted, the typewritten copy can be photographically enlarged or reduced. The amount of space between lines also changes the appearance of the job. Fig. 6-13. Generally, typewritten copy uses headings produced on other cold composition systems, such as preprinted letters.

Since whatever is typed is printed, errors must be carefully corrected. The error can be painted over with a white, opaque correction fluid. When this dries, the correction is typed over the error. The correction can also be typed on a separate paper, cut out, and pasted over the error. Often the entire line is retyped and pasted in place. It is also possible to cut out the error and place a piece of tape over the back of the opening. The correction is cut to fit the opening, placed in it, and is held by the tape.

Direct-impression typography is also used to produce word images on paper offset plates. Pressure is critical on these plates. Too little or too much pressure will give defective characters. Corrections are made with an eraser, using light strokes and removing only the carbon, not the entire image.

TYPEWRITER JUSTIFICATION

As discussed in Chapter 4, justification refers to composing lines of text that are exactly the same length. This is difficult to do using a standard typewriter because the letters and spaces are usually equal width. It is possible to justify lines on a standard typewriter, but the space between some words will be much larger than others. To justify copy, rule a line on the paper to represent the right border. Type the copy and count the number of spaces left at the end needed to justify the line. This can be done by typing consecutive numbers in the spaces left. Fig. 6-14. When the copy is typed a second time, insert extra spaces between some of the words in each sentence. Insert these

Justification refers to12 composing lines of words that1 are exactly the same length.12 This is difficult to do using1 a standard typewriter because1 the letters and spaces are1234 usually equal width.

Justification refers to composing lines of words that are exactly the same length. This is difficult to do using a standard typewriter because the letters and spaces are usually equal width.

6-14. Justifying copy on a manual typewriter.

spaces between words that have tall letters at the end of one word or the beginning of the other. If a typed line extends beyond the right border, insert half spaces between some words to shorten the line. These are placed between words that have low letters on the end of one word and the beginning of the next word.

If the width of the copy is narrow, both the first and second typing can occur on the same paper. In this case, type the first line and then immediately retype it on the right side, justifying it. Then proceed with the second line.

The proportional-spacing typewriter produces a more uniform appearance in the finished copy. This machine gives the operator a choice of the amount of space to allow between words. Also, the individual letters are of different widths. For example, the letter "i" might take two units of space, while the "w" would take four units.

To get the right margin to line up using a manually operated, proportional-spacing typewriter, the copy is typed, and it is noted how many units each line is short or long. Then the job is retyped, and the operator adds or subtracts the necessary units between words. The details on this operation vary from one typewriter model to another.

The following material presents the major features of several different proportional-spacing machines. Before operating any typewriter, study the manufacturer's manual that accompanies the machine.

OLIVETTI "LEXIKON 94C"

The Olivetti "Lexikon 94C" features both proportional spacing and constant spacing. Fig. 6-15. The four spacing modes permit typing in proportion and three constant spaces, 9, 12, and 18 characters per inch.

The "Lexikon 94C" has an automatic correction device. The keyboard has a correction key, and the machine is fitted with a lift-off tape in addition to the typewriter ribbon. Typing errors are corrected by depressing the correction key. This backspaces the carriage and brings the lift-off tape into position. The character that was incorrectly typed

is now typed again. The lift-off tape removes it from the paper.

The unit uses interchangeable fabric or carbon ribbon cartridges. A unique built-in memory eliminates the following common typing errors before they occur:

$F_{lying} C_{aps}$
Sha**d**ing or gh**o**sting
Cro**w** ding or pil**i**ng
No space betweenwords

IBM "SELECTRIC COMPOSER"

The IBM "Selectric Composer" features proportional spacing. Fig. 6-16. This typewriter has a stationary carriage. The type characters are on a spherical element that moves across the carriage. Fig. 6-17. The element contains all the letters, numbers, and symbols for one typeface. A wide variety of typefaces are available. Elements come in

Olivetti Corp. of America

6-15. The Olivetti "Lexikon 94C."

RIBBON CARTRIDGE

TYPE ELEMENT

IBM Corp.

6-16. The IBM "Selectric Composer."

IBM Corp.

6-17. *The IBM "Selectric" spherical element containing the letters, numbers, and symbols.*

three escapement widths and in six- through twelve-point face sizes. (Escapement is the width of one character.)

To equip the typewriter with a different typeface, the operator removes the element and replaces it with one having the face desired. Fig. 6-18. When the element is being replaced, the machine must be in lowercase typing position. It is a good idea to turn the machine off when changing elements.

The machine uses a unique, solvent-film ribbon. The ribbon is contained in a cartridge and is easily removed and replaced. Fig. 6-16.

Justification of lines on the right margin is semiautomatic. The characters vary in width, depending upon their shapes. For example, the letter "I" requires less space than the "w". To justify copy, the operator first types a rough draft and stops before reaching the right-side margin. The number of spaces needed to

IBM Corp.

6-18. *On the IBM "Selectric," the lock lever on the element is lifted when the element is placed on or removed from the post.*

fill out the line is indicated by color and number on the *justification tube,* located directly above the keyboard. Fig. 6-19. The operator sets the justification control and retypes the material. The machine automatically justifies the line. Fig. 6-20.

IBM "EXECUTIVE"

The IBM "Executive" electric typewriter also features proportional spacing. Fig. 6-21. The characters are on typebars rather than a spherical element. This typewriter is available with changeable typebars so special symbols can be inserted in the typed copy. Fig. 6-22. It also may be equipped with a carbon or fabric ribbon. The carbon ribbon

is used only once. The fabric ribbon is used until it begins to produce poor quality copy. Fig. 6-23 shows the installation of the carbon ribbon, which is supplied on a large spool or in a cartridge.

The proportional spacing feature enables the typewriter to produce a printlike quality which is easier to read than normal typewritten material. Each character is allotted the correct

IBM Corp.

6-19. *The spaces needed to justify a line are indicated on the justification tube.*

You have just learned how to justify copy on

3 3 3 3 3 3 3 3 5

IBM Corp.

6-20. *The typewriter automatically adds the additional spaces between words as indicated by the setting on the justification control.*

You have just learned how to justify copy on

4 4 4 4 4 3 3 3 3

IBM Corp.

6-21. *The IBM "Executive" electric typewriter.*

TWO-UNIT
SPACING BAR

THREE-UNIT
SPACING BAR

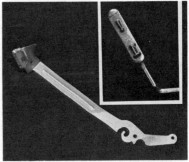

IBM Corp.

6-22. *The IBM "Executive" is available with changeable typebars.*

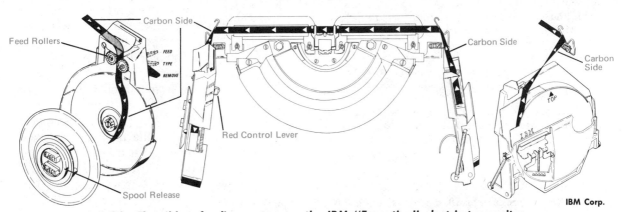

IBM Corp.

6-23. *The ribbon-feeding system on the IBM "Executive" electric typewriter.*

STANDARD SPACED TYPE

The weather during summer days
is usually warm and sunny. The
clear sky and white clouds bring
one close to nature

PROPORTIONAL SPACED TYPE

The weather during summer days
is usually warm and sunny. The
clear sky and white clouds bring
one close to nature

Standard: mmmmm   iiiii

Proportional: mmmmm iiiii

IBM Corp.

**6-24. Letters on proportional-
spacing typewriters produce copy
which is easier to read.**

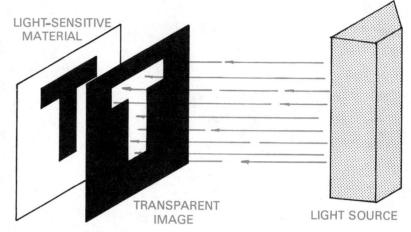

LIGHT-SENSITIVE
MATERIAL

TRANSPARENT
IMAGE

LIGHT SOURCE

**6-26. The projection of light through a transparent image onto a
light-sensitive material is the principle used for the phototypesetting
process.**

amount of space according to its
width. Fig. 6-24. The smallest
letter is allotted two units and
the largest five units.

Copy that must be justified
must be typed twice. The margins on line length are set, and
the copy is typed within this limit.
It is noted how many units the

line is short or over the margin.
When the line is retyped, these
units are added between words
with the space bars or subtracted
with the backspace key. Fig.
6-25.

THE PENCIL
LINE

JUSTIFICATION UNITS
ok
+3
+3
+6
-4
-1

The IBM "Executive" is a typewriter with proportional lettering. On ordinary typewriters,
all letters take precisely the same amount of
space. On the "Executive," every letter is
automatically given its natural amount of space
according to its width. All letters fit together
beautifully in a print-like manner.

The IBM "Executive" is a typewriter with proportional lettering. On ordinary typewriters,
all letters take precisely the same amount of
space. On the "Executive," every letter is
automatically given its natural amount of space
according to its width. All letters fit together
beautifully in a print-like manner.

20   40

IBM Corp.

**6-25. How to produce justified copy using the IBM "Executive" electric
typewriter.**

PHOTOTYPESETTING

The basic principle behind
phototypesetting is to send a
beam of light through a transparent image surrounded by an
opaque background. Fig. 6-26.
The light projects through the
image and strikes a light-sensitive film or paper. The image is
formed on this material.

DISPLAY PHOTOTYPESETTERS

There are many kinds of display phototypesetters. Some are
very simple and inexpensive,
while others are complex, high
speed, and more costly. Following are selected examples.

The Strip Printer photocomposition machine produces display
type from 6 through 96 points on
35-mm paper from film fonts.
Fig. 6-27. The font is moved
through the machine, exposing
one letter at a time. It can produce positive and reverse images
as well as fancy type, borders,
logotypes, and symbols. The exposure is automatically timed to

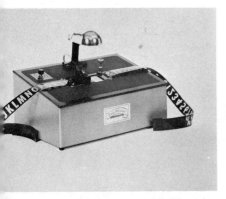

6-27. *The Strip Printer photo-composition machine for setting display type.*

assure uniform density. The machine can be operated in subdued light because a slow emulsion is used on both paper and film.

Another photocomposition machine, the Varityper "Headliner," Fig. 6-28, has a control panel. The exposure meter checks the voltage which controls the light intensity. Intensity can be adjusted for proper density of exposure. The unit will produce type sizes from 10 to 84 points. The characters are on a plastic disk. The disk is placed on a spindle in the center of the machine. The type is composed on 35-mm film or paper which is in daylight cartridges. Film and paper are available with plain or pressure-sensitive adhesive backs.

To compose on the Varityper "Headliner," the operator turns the type font disk to select the character and presses the print key to expose it. Position and spacing are regulated by the machine without visual lineup by the operator. There are control knobs to vary spacing between

words and letters in a word. When composition is complete, the cut-off lever is raised to cut off the strip and send it through the processing unit. This takes about 90 seconds. The developed material is ready immediately.

The Compugraphic "CG7200" is a keyboard-operated phototypesetting unit for display type. Fig. 6-29. The system has 150 typefaces available in sizes from 14 to 120 points. The line length is unlimited. The unit will accommodate four different type fonts at the same time. These are in the form of film strips. Operation is much like that of an electric typewriter. The output is in the form of exposed photo paper or film.

The unexposed film is held in a cassette and is fed into a second cassette as the copy is set. This cassette is designed to permit

the exposed film to be developed under daylight conditions.

TEXT COMPOSITION AND PHOTOTYPESETTERS

Text phototypesetting has gone through several stages of development. Early equipment used the operating principles applied to hot-metal linecasting machines but substituted negatives for matrices and photography for metal casting.

The second-stage phototypesetters were not adaptations of hot-metal typesetting machines but instead were designed specifically for setting type photographically. They have been largely replaced by newer systems, but a brief explanation is given here. The systems within the machine include input, character selection, image output, and spacing between lines. They

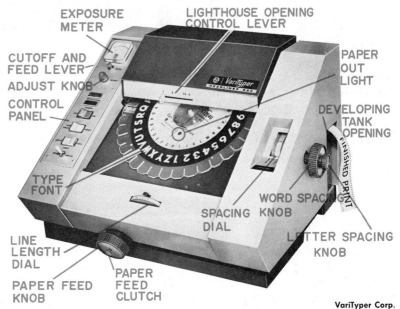

6-28. *The VariTyper "Headliner" display-type photocomposition machine.*

use codes from an input source, such as punched tape, to activate and control the machine functions to produce typeset copy. The input code sets the parameters for the operation. These include (1) characters to be set, (2) the type style and size, (3) spacing between words for line justification, and (4) spacing between lines.

The input sources for second-stage phototypesetting machines include: (1) keyboard entry directly into the machine, (2) a keyboard-controlled perforated paper tape, and (3) computer-controlled paper or magnetic tape. As the systems developed, the most frequently used source was punched paper tape.

The direct keyboard entry into the phototypesetting machine permitted one operator on one keyboard to control the machine. This required skilled operators who understood the function codes and who could divide the copy into justified lines. The process was slow because the justification decisions and coding strokes were made manually.

As the phototypesetters were improved, the use of separate keyboards to punch tape increased. A fast phototypesetting machine could handle all of the punched tape produced by several keyboards. Therefore, production was increased greatly over the direct keyboard entry system.

Second-stage phototypesetting machines use the following systems to select the characters to be composed: (1) a light source, (2) a master character set, and (3) control logic to synchronize the light source and the character set.

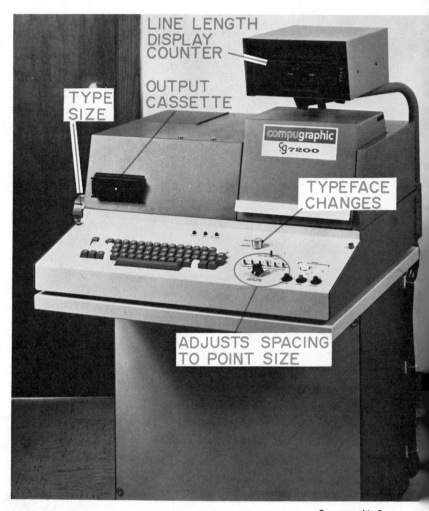

Compugraphic Corp.

6-29. The Compugraphic "CG7200" keyboard-operated, display type phototypesetting unit.

While details vary from one manufacturer to another, the basic process is similar. Fig. 6-30. The *light source* is of high intensity. It may operate continuously or stroboscopically (flash for one or two microseconds). The most commonly used light source is a xenon flash lamp.

Master character sets are negatives having clear characters on an opaque background. They are in the form of rotating disks, rotating drums with interchangea-

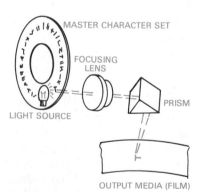

6-30. The basic process for second-generation phototypesetting machines.

DISC　　　　　DRUM　　　　　TURRET　　　　　GRID

6-31. *Types of photographic master character sets.*

ble film strips, rotating turrets, or stationary grids. Fig. 6-31. These sets can be replaced on the machine with fonts of a different size or type style. Some phototypesetting machines permit the use of several master character sets without the necessity of changing them.

The *logic control* receives the coded information from the input source (such as punched tape). The logic unit recognizes the character and the font code and moves it into postion in front of the light source. At the same time, the logic unit selects the proper light source if more than one is available and positions the apertures, mirrors, and lenses needed to isolate the desired character.

As the logic unit moves the desired character to the light source, a system of timing marks on the master character set synchronizes the motion between the light source and the character image on some phototypesetting machines. The timing mechanism positions the character in front of the light source for exposure. Machines using a stroboscopic light source time the flashes so that they occur at the exact moment the character image is in front of the light source. At this point, the *image output control* positions the pro-

jected character image on the output media (film or paper).

CURRENT PHOTOTYPESETTING SYSTEMS

The technology of text and graphics generation is changing rapidly. Many different approaches to input, assembly, image generation, and output are available. Those employed in the graphic arts industry must keep current on developments by reading professional journals

and attending conferences and seminars.

The following sections detail briefly some examples of systems using existing technology.

DIRECT INPUT SYSTEMS

The Compugraphic "CompuWriter" series of photocomposition machines use a keyboard much like a typewriter. Fig. 6-32. The typefaces are contained on film strips. The machines will set from 6- to 24-point typefaces. Some units will mix up to four type styles. It is possible to mix different style faces of the same size on one line. Each line can be a different type style and size.

The point size, line length, typeface, and leading are selected by touching the proper key or switches.

The "CompuWriter" has automatic hyphenless justification. It also permits manual justification

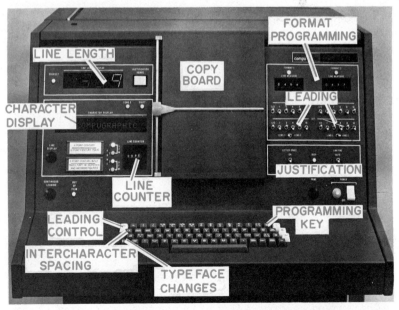

Compugraphic Corp.

6-32. *The keyboard for the "CompuWriter" direct-input photocomposition system.*

Compugraphic Corp.

6-33. The "Unisetter" uses a direct entry keyboard.

using hyphens if desired. The line length display permits the operator to hyphenate accurately and get the maximum number of characters in a line. As the characters are keyboarded, their unit width values are subtracted from the total line length. The unused part of the line is shown in the line length display.

The unit has an electronic character display. This allows the operator to see each word as it is composed. It helps reduce errors in composition and permits corrections to be made before the phototypesetting process is complete.

The leading is from 1/2 to 31 1/2 points in 1/2 point increments. Additional leading can be

inserted by hitting the leading key on the keyboard.

Formats can be programmed to speed up typesetting production. When the formats are programmed, the line measure, point size, and leading can be changed with a single key stroke. This makes it possible to produce camera-ready mixed-composition copy. It is especially useful for complex jobs such as display ads, catalogs, and directories.

It is possible to reduce the space between characters. A single key stroke reduces this space. This helps position a tight-fitting series of characters.

Another direct entry system uses an on-line keyboard console and a phototypesetter. Fig. 6-33. This is the Compugraphic "Unisetter" with DEK (direct entry keyboard).

The DEK provides instant control over all typographic activity. It includes fully automatic justification, quadding, and insertion of rules, leaders, and white spaces. It provides multiple justification functions and tabbing capabilities.

Displays on the keyboard show typographic activity, such as the vertical position in the copy block, the number of lines set, and the leading. They help with the end-of-the-line decisions by monitoring line length.

The phototypesetter will also accept six-level Teletype service (TTS) coded paper tape produced by off-line keyboards or wire service punches. It permits composition to be justified or unjustified.

The system has eight different typefaces in 12 sizes. These range from 6 to 72 points. The flexibility of the system permits

the production of camera-ready mixed typography for ads, brochures, and posters. Fig. 6-34. It will align indentions, columns, and tables.

When the "Unisetter" becomes part of a total system, with on-line interface to a visual display terminal and a "Uni-Scan," the output is three-, six-, and eight-inch photographic camera-ready composition.

TAPE-OPERATED SYSTEMS
Dymo Graphic Systems
"Pacesetter"

The Dymo Graphic Systems Mark 4 and 5 "Pacesetter" automated photocomposers, Fig. 6-35, use various kinds of input. They will accept six-, seven-, or eight-level paper tape. They can also be operated from recorded magnetic tape cassettes using a word processing interface. The "Pacesetter" will also accept manual data entries from an on-line justifying keyboard. This permits the user to alternately use paper tape and manual input. It is possible to interface the unit with a variety of electronic composition systems.

The "Pacesetter" has a wide variety of type fonts. The fonts are contained on glass matrix disks. Standard disks may contain four, eight, or sixteen typefaces, each with 112 characters. Also available are segmented disks. Fig. 6-36. They have eight segments, each containing a different typeface. Each typeface can be produced in 16 different sizes from 5 to 72 points.

Output may be on stabilization and resin paper or film. The unit will accept materials from 2 to 10 inches in width. The output is secured in disposable cassettes.

functions are controlled by the input device. The unit has normal controls for initial formatting of unjustified tape. These controls are also used when it is necessary to reformat already justified tape or to override incorrect tape codes.

The "Pacesetter" has a programmable computer. It stores character widths, locations, and typographic formats. This is especially valuable for repetitive formats and lines. The keyboard operator making the tape does not have to make the thousands of formatting key strokes needed on each job. The computer also automatically handles hyphenation, justification involving different typefaces and point sizes, the insertion of leaders and vertical rules, and the range of quadding and indentions.

The unit is programmed to hyphenate justified composition set from unjustified tape. This frees the keyboard operator from having to make the end-of-the-line decisions needed to produce a justified line. The production of punched tape is thus increased.

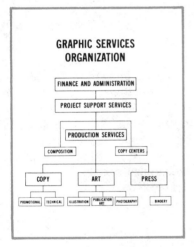

Dymo Graphics Systems, Inc.
6-35. *A tape-operated photo-typesetter.*

which can be handled in ordinary room light.

The units will produce copy at speeds of 35, 50, and 150 lines per minute. Special disks are used for the higher speeds.

The typesetting operation is completely automatic. The selection of typefaces, line length, leading, and other typographic

Compugraphic Corp.
6-34. *Camera-ready mixed copy can be set for a wide variety of jobs.*

Dymo Graphics Systems, Inc.
6-36. *A glass photomatrix segmented disc.*

The "Pacesetter" uses a photo-optical unit to project each character on film. As the typeface disk revolves, the flash unit fires a two-microsecond light burst at the exact time the wanted character is passing between it and the optical leverage mirror. The optical system uses a special high-power, variable xenon flash assembly. The image of the character is flashed onto the optical leverage mirror, which reflects it to the photo paper or film through the point-sizing lens. A complete line is produced by the lateral movement of the mirror. After a line is complete, the paper or film moves vertically to receive the next line.

Font shown actual size

Mergenthaler Linotype Co.

6-38. A typical photo composition font. This is an actual size reproduction.

Mergenthaler "V-I-P"

Another tape-operated system is the Mergenthaler "V-I-P" photocomposition unit. The standard input into the "V-I-P" is six-level coded perforated tape. It accepts tape produced on the simplest form of nonjustifying keyboard and delivers fully justified and hyphenated composition. It also can accept various forms of computer-generated tape, and it can be operated on-line with certain magnetic tape systems. It will also accept and set input from newspaper wire services.

The output is produced on conventional paper or film. The film cassette can be loaded and unloaded in daylight conditions.

There are many models of the "V-I-P." Fig. 6-37. Since the capacities vary, the following will give general specifications. A range of 6 to 72 points is possible; so text and display type can

TAPE INPUT   OUTPUT CASSETTE

Mergenthaler Linotype Co.

6-37. The Mergenthaler "V-I-P" phototypesetting machine.

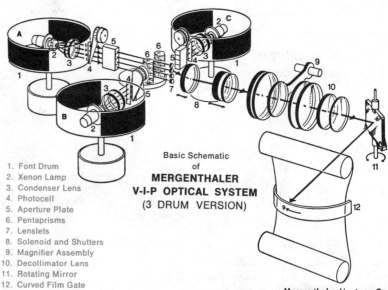

1. Font Drum
2. Xenon Lamp
3. Condenser Lens
4. Photocell
5. Aperture Plate
6. Pentaprisms
7. Lenslets
8. Solenoid and Shutters
9. Magnifier Assembly
10. Decollimator Lens
11. Rotating Mirror
12. Curved Film Gate

Basic Schematic
of
**MERGENTHALER
V-I-P OPTICAL SYSTEM
(3 DRUM VERSION)**

Mergenthaler Linotype Co.

6-39. The three-drum optical system available on the Mergenthaler "V-I-P" phototypesetting machine.

be set. This is available in 22 different sizes. The unit will maintain from 6 to 18 different fonts to give the operator a wide choice. A typical font is shown in Fig. 6-38. The fonts are placed on drums. Fig. 6-39. Each drum will hold from three to six fonts, depending upon the size of the font.

The optical system is an important feature of this unit. Figs. 6-39 and 6-40. This system, plus a special control program, provides proper character fit by producing automatic incremental letter space reduction for each increase in point size.

The "V-I-P" has a computer core capacity capable of mixing fonts and sizes in a line within certain font ranges. The leading (film advance) is set before the text material by commands on the tape or by setting the dial on the control panel. The unit can be commanded to increase or decrease letter spacing in increments of one-ninth of a point. Word spacing ranges may be selected from 3 to 15 units before letter spacing occurs.

Systems with CRT Editing Capabilities

Some phototypesetting machines use computers to generate the input and use a cathode ray tube (CRT) to produce the copy. A CRT is much like a television tube. Fig. 6-41.

The phototypesetting machine uses electronic selection and exposure of the character images on the face of the CRT. The phototypesetter uses four major subsystems: (1) data input, (2) character storage, (3) character generation, and (4) output pagination. Fig. 6-42.

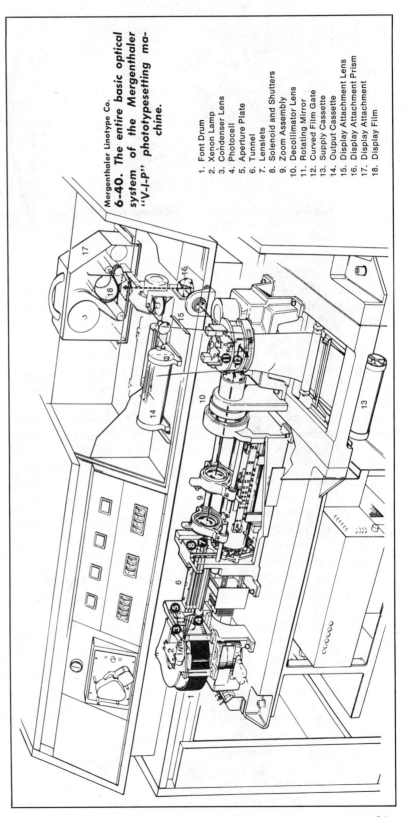

Mergenthaler Linotype Co.

6-40. The entire basic optical system of the Mergenthaler "V-I-P" phototypesetting machine.

1. Font Drum
2. Xenon Lamp
3. Condenser Lens
4. Photocell
5. Aperture Plate
6. Tunnel
7. Lenslets
8. Solenoid and Shutters
9. Zoom Assembly
10. Decollimator Lens
11. Rotating Mirror
12. Curved Film Gate
13. Supply Cassette
14. Output Cassette
15. Display Attachment Lens
16. Display Attachment Prism
17. Display Attachment
18. Display Film

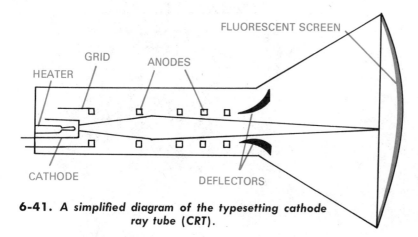

6-41. *A simplified diagram of the typesetting cathode ray tube (CRT).*

The *central processor* receives the information, sorts it, performs necessary calculations as indicated by the computer program, and outputs the results. The program and numerical data are read by the computer and transferred to storage locations in the memory. The control unit regulates the operation of the computer. It receives the program instructions one at a time and signals the memory unit to either store data or provide data already stored. It also activates the arithmetic unit to perform needed calculations.

When all the operations are completed by the central processor, the characters are generated on the face of the cathode ray tube and then exposed to the film or paper. (This is the output.) These phototypesetters are extremely fast. Speeds of 10,000 characters per second have been achieved in experimental models.

Data input is achieved with punched paper or magnetic tape. The tape contains the same character, function, and line spacing codes as discussed with second-stage phototypesetting machines.

Character storage is either photographic or digital. Those using photographic storage use master character sets which are positioned in the optical path. Digital storage describes the shape of the characters by digital coding, which is read and processed by a computer. Digital coding means each character is described by numbers which give the position of the various parts of the character. This requires extensive magnetic disk storage in the computer.

A computer has three main systems: (1) input, (2) a central processor, and (3) output. The central processor is made up of a memory unit, a control unit, and an arithmetic unit. In addition, it has other equipment which may be used in its operation. These are referred to as peripheral equipment. Peripheral equipment may be hardware or software. *Hardware* refers to pieces

of physical equipment, while *software* refers to the programs used to operate the computer.

Input can be punched cards or perforated or magnetic tape in off-line systems. An *off-line* system is one in which the input is developed by equipment not directly connected to the computer. Input in *on-line* systems is in the form of electronic pulses fed directly into the computer from a keyboard or scanning device. An *on-line* system is one which is directly connected to the computer.

Compugraphic EditWriter System

A self-contained composition

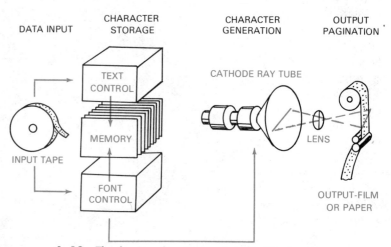

6-42. *The basic subsystems of a phototypesetter.*

Compugraphic Corp.

6-43. *The Compugraphic EditWriter self-contained composing system.*

puter. Lines of type are justified automatically.

The operator, using the keyboard, selects line length, typeface, size, and line spacing. Keyboard controls are used to store and retrieve from the memory. Material can be stored using operator-established file names. These names are automatically indexed and recorded on the floppy disk. The operator can recall the index to the screen for reference. This enables the operator to quickly find any job on the disk.

The unit also has tabulating capabilities. It can produce an unlimited number of columns across the full line length up to 45 picas. The system automatically computes column width and inserts white space equally between columns.

The photo output provides

station is the Compugraphic EditWriter System. Fig. 6-43. It has keyboard input, a visual display, a floppy disk storage, and a photo unit for output.

The keyboard gives the operator control over input, proofing, correcting, formatting, and final output from the photo unit. Fig. 6-44. The keyboard controls hyphenation, character fit, and an automatic depth calculator which allows formatting of complete pages. The operator can specify the copy depth in picas and points. The unit will scroll the copy to the specified depth and stop, ready for the operator to insert baseline rules, footnotes, and page numbers.

Hyphenation can be done manually by the operator or automatically by the internal com-

Compugraphic Corp.

6-44. *The keyboard and the video display give the operator complete control over the functions of the unit.*

eight typefaces in twelve sizes. It is possible to mix styles in a line. In this way tabular jobs, magazine ads, and display ads are camera ready when they leave the photo output unit.

Compugraphic Unified Composing System

Another system includes both composition and typesetting. This is the Compugraphic Unified Composing System. It is made up of an optical character recognition unit (OCR) called the "UniScan," an electronic composer called the "Unified Composer," and a phototypesetting unit such as the "UniSetter." Fig. 6-45. (OCR systems are discussed later in this chapter.)

The operator receives typed copy and processes it through to camera-ready material. The input device to the OCR is an IBM "Selectric II" with one-time carbon ribbons. The unit reads Printing and Publishing 3, which is a modified Courier-12 font. It accepts typed copy on standard bond paper or on control forms which are used for classified ad production. The typed lines can be one and one-half, double, or triple standard typewriter spaces. Typed copy with or without typesetting commands can be used for input. The system also accepts wire service printer copy. The "UniScan" is connected on-line to the "Unified Composer."

The "Unified Composer" has copy processing and file management capabilities. Its main components are a console keyboard, video display terminal, tape reader, a file management section, a computer, and an output control.

The keyboard permits the operator to control input, copy editing, formatting of copy, and data management. The final output is also controlled from the keyboard.

Using the keyboard the operator can edit the copy received from the OCR unit. The operator can correct, delete, insert, or move characters, words, lines, or full blocks of copy within the working memory of the computer, which is 128 lines. Using the keyboard the operator can also store and recall commands and blocks of copy.

The video display terminal will show 14 lines at one time out of a scrolling memory of 128 lines. Scrolling refers to passing composed lines across the video display for examination. The operator can examine the copy on the display and alter it using the keyboard.

The tape reader is an alternate input device. It permits the "Unified Composer" to accept six-level TTS-coded punched paper tape.

The file management section permits entered text or formats to be stored on floppy disks. The disks are divided into 128 alpha or numeric categories for automatic filing and recall to the terminal. The material entered is indexed. The index displays on the video display a list of all the files in the computer memory. This enables the operator to quickly find stored copy.

The computer makes possible the actions already described. In addition it can automatically sort daily files. For example, it could search a classified ad file and make insertions of new ads and drop ads that are no longer to be printed. After justified copy has been edited or revised, it will au-

PHOTOTYPESETTER   ELECTRONIC COMPOSER   OPTICAL CHARACTER RECOGNITION

Compugraphic Corp.

6-45. The Unified Composing System includes text composition and phototypesetting units.

Mergenthaler Linotype Co.

6-46. The "Linotron 404" digital typesetter.

150 characters each when digitized at 6 points. The "Linotron 404" will set typefaces in sizes from 4 to 96 points in 1/2 point steps. Point sizes and fonts can be freely mixed within a line or word.

The "Linotron 404" can attain speeds of up to 1500 newspaper lines per minute. It delivers full-page composition for tabloid newspapers with line lengths up to 70 picas. The high quality of work produced makes it suitable for book work, magazines, and financial composition.

Output is in the form of film or paper. The film or paper is stored in a cassette which holds 400 linear feet. The output is fed automatically into a cassette which holds 100 linear feet. The amount of material in each cassette is shown on the control panel.

The "Linotron 202" is shown in Fig. 6-47. It is a digital CRT typesetter that operates in much the same manner as the "Linotron 404." It is a smaller unit having a 48-pica line length, and it composes up to 450 newspaper lines per minute.

Mergenthaler "Linotron 606"

The Mergenthaler "Linotron 606" is another computerized photocomposition unit using a CRT system. The unit contains a high-speed magnetic disk, a minicomputer, interface and electronic controls, a cathode ray tube system, and a film magazine. Fig. 6-48.

Text for typesetting can be input using paper or magnetic tape or a direct connection to a computer. The input data are coded and justified before entry into the "Linotron 606."

tomatically re-hyphenate and re-justify the copy.

The output control enables the system to be programmed for on-line input to a phototypesetter. In addition the "Unified Composer" can output through a punch which produces six-level punched paper tape.

Mergenthaler "Linotron 404"

The "Linotron 404" is a digital CRT typesetter. It can be operated on-line to a front-end system or off-line with input from paper or magnetic tape. Fig. 6-46. The typeface fonts take the form of digitized information recorded on floppy disks.

The data from the floppy disks are loaded onto the "Linotron 404's" internal disk. A minicomputer calls the needed characters from this disk to a temporary buffer. The character generator draws data from the buffer and translates it into a series of vertical lines on a high-resolution CRT. Lines of type are thus built up on the screen and projected through an optical system onto film or paper that is controlled by a precision transport system. A transport system is the mechanism which moves the film or paper through the "Linotron 404."

Each font is digitized at a specific point size but may be set within a size range from 40% to 175% of the original size.

The internal magnetic disk can hold the typographic information for 700 individual fonts of up to

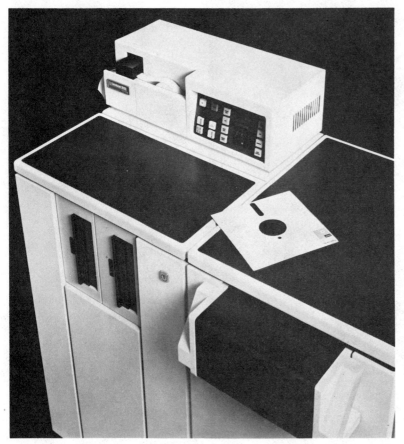

Mergenthaler Linotype Co.

6-47. The "Linotron 202" digital typesetter.

be in any measure up to 100 picas.

The photo material is stored on a cassette that holds up to 400 feet of film or paper. The machine threads itself after the cassette is inserted in place. After a run is completed, the exposed film or paper is advanced into the output cassette and automatically cut off. The output film could be run directly into a developing machine if so desired.

COMPUTER JUSTIFICATION

Line justification can be accomplished with a special-purpose computer. The initial information must be established—point size, type style, leading, and line measure. The operator then types the characters on the keyboard. They are recorded either as unjustified punched tape, displayed on a CRT, or fed directly into the computer. Fig. 6-49. As they enter the computer, the width of every character is subtracted from a counter on which the desired line measure was recorded. It also counts the number of spaces between words.

As the end of the line approaches, the subtractions made for line width are nearing the justified zone. The computer, having recorded the number of spaces between words, establishes minimum and maximum expansion values. If the space between words cannot be expanded properly, the line is too tight. If the line permits excessive expansion, it has been set too loose. Sometimes it is necessary to hyphenate words to get the line to justify.

There are two basic ways such lines are hyphenated using a

The characters are held in digital form on a magnetic disk. A single disk will hold 2000 fonts in sizes up to 12 points. It will set fonts up to 256 points and as small as 4 points. The larger fonts require more storage and thus reduce the number that can be stored. Expanded, condensed, and italic fonts are available. Standard fonts can be slanted by making electronic adjustments. Point sizes and fonts can be mixed within a line or a word.

The "Linotron 606" can output graphics under control of a graphic input scanner. This is used for logotypes and special characters and symbols. These can be up to 220 points in height. They are exposed in the same way as the regular characters, by means of vertical sweeps of the CRT microspot. The images can be input by the graphic scanner or from data stored on the magnetic disk in the digitized form.

The unit produces right-reading and wrong-reading outputs on film or paper. The photo material may be in any width from 8 to 17 inches. The text lines can

Mergenthaler Linotype Co.

6-48. The "Linotron 606" fully computerized photocomposition system.

computer. One is having a human operator make the hyphenation decision. The other is to have a programmed logic and a dictionary program stored in the computer memory. This requires a much larger computer than the first method.

If a line is set too tight for proper justification, there are three possible actions the operator can perform: (1) drop the last word to the next line, (2) hyphenate it and drop the last characters to the next line, or (3) force the line to justify.

The first choice is to hyphenate the line. One character at a time is dropped to the next line until a hyphenation point is reached. Space must be allowed for the insertion of the hyphen. The computer now will justify the line. The justified line is now ready to be recorded photographically. It is the same length as all other lines in the job, and the spacing meets acceptable composition standards. All of this takes place in approximately one-fourth of a second or less.

Words can be hyphenated by a computer without operator intervention. Many words hyphenate following logic rules of word division. The computer programmed to operate within these logic rules will locate possible points of hyphenation, choose one, and hyphenate the words accordingly. Since not all words break according to standard logic of word division, "exception" dictionary programs are used. Dictionary programs require the storing of a large number of words with proper hyphenation in the computer's memory. The word at the end of the set line which must be hyphenated is

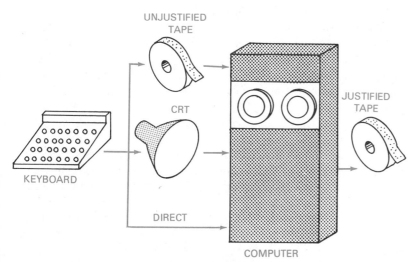

6-49. The computer is used to justify the text material and produce a justified tape, or it can operate on-line to a typesetter.

compared to the word in the memory. The computer indicates the correct break point, and the letters dropped go to the next line. In practice, this is a complex thing because of the large number of words in use. Decisions must be made as to which words to store.

OPTICAL CHARACTER RECOGNITION SYSTEMS

Optical character recognition is another way text material can be converted to a form usable by a typesetting machine. The optical character recognition system (OCR) "reads" the typed manuscript and produces a machine-readable tape. It converts information into electronic signals that will enable the recognition unit to recognize the typed character. This process eliminates the need for an operator to convert the text from the typed copy to tape using a keyboard.

In this system, the words to be printed are typed in manuscript form. The typed pages to be used on an OCR scanner must be in a form that is acceptable to the reader. They must have a typeface or code that the reader can recognize. The number of characters used must not exceed the character recognition abilities of the reader. The paper used for typing must be one that has been proven acceptable for this purpose. The length of the lines and their placement must be within the capabilities of the reader.

The sheet is placed on a *document transport* unit. It moves the sheet past the optical reader. The reader scans the typed images and converts them to electrical impulses which represent

each character. These are transmitted to a *character recognition logic unit.* This unit interprets the electrical signal as a particular character. The *systems control unit* formats the material, controls the sequence of operations, and provides the interface necessary to record the characters on some type of output device, such as magnetic tape, punched paper tape, or punched cards. The system's control unit may be a computer or a plug board.

There are a number of different character recognition systems, and they are designed for specific tasks. The two basic systems in use are reading the character by magnetic means and by optical means.

The most common use of *magnetic character recognition* is bank checks. The checks have identifying characters printed with a special magnetic ink. The characters have a special shape and magnetic qualities which make it possible to read them with a magnetic reader.

Optical character recognition systems recognize the character by its shape much the same as the human eye reads. OCR readers are classified as single font and multifont. Single-font readers read only one specific font style. Multifont readers read several styles.

Examples of two single-font type styles are the ANSI "OCR-

6-50A. *These are the characters in the American National Standards Institute "OCR-A" type font.*

6-50B. *The characters in the International Standards Organization "OCR-B" type font.*

A" font and the ISO "OCR-B" font. Fig. 6-50. The ANSI "OCR-A" font is the one recommended by the American National Standards Institute as suitable for typewriters and OCR. The "OCR-A" font is the most common font and is read by many OCR systems. The ISO "OCR-B" font was developed by the International Standards Organization. This is an international organization which sets standards in many areas in an attempt to coordinate business and industrial activities in the world.

These single-font type styles are generated by typewriters or line printers equipped with this face. The spacing between characters, between lines, and the reference to the side of the page must be exact. Since OCR readers respond to reflection, they are sensitive to the reflectivity of paper as well as the image. The degree of reflectivity between the paper and the image must be consistent.

Multifont readers can be programmed to read a number of different font styles even though they are intermixed. Multifont readers read several typefaces but only one at a time. The machine must be switched each time a face change is wanted. The readers have a large vocabulary. (The term *vocabulary* refers to the characters the machine will read.) Multifont readers will read upper and lower case characters, the number set, punctuation marks, and a number of special characters. They accept materials produced on standard office typewriters or line printers.

OCR scanning units have various ways to scan the typewritten page and convert the image into electrical signals. One system uses a cathode ray tube to generate a small beam of light. It is projected through a lens system onto the typed material. The material is exposed to the spot of light in a lightproof compartment. Here the reflected light is picked by photomultipliers and converted into electrical impulses.

Another type is a photocell scanning system. It uses a high intensity light source to light the typed sheet. The sheet moves, and the reflected image is focused by a lens system on a bank of photocells. Each character is sampled as it moves through the system. Each sample gives a vertical slice of the character. The electrical signals that are produced by the photocells are converted into a binary code. Each slice is stored until the entire character is scanned.

A vidicon television tube is used in another system. The characters are projected onto the tube. The image on the face of the tube is scanned by an electron beam which generates an electrical analog signal. The signals indicate black or white.

Another system uses a laser-beam optical system combined with a digital computer. After the scanning has occurred, the electrical representation of the character is transmitted to a recognition unit which identifies the character.

OCR recognition units receive the electrical signal from the scanner, which contains the representation of the text material. The recognition unit identifies each character. There are several types of recognition units available.

One system is *matrix matching*. The input is signaled from the scanner caused by reflections from the paper and lack of reflections from the character. The image shape is reduced to a dot pattern on a matrix. This process of converting the image to digital representation is called digitizing. The recognition unit stores these electrical signals received from the scanner in the first digital register, which is connected to a series of *resistor matrices*. Each matrix represents a single-reference character. Each resistor matrix is connected to a *second digital register*, which contains a voltage representation of the character. The voltage of the scanned character is compared with the second digital register and with the resistor matrix to identify the character. Recognition is based on the comparison of the voltage representations in the two registers.

A second recognition unit uses the principle of stroke analysis.

The recognition method is based upon the fact that characters can be distinguished by the number and position of their vertical and horizontal strokes. The information to recognize each character is stored in a computer. The formation of the character to be recognized is matched against the information in the computer and identified when a match is found.

The optical character recognition system is controlled by a *systems control unit*. This unit can perform editing functions, direct the formatting of composition, can direct the sequence with which operations are performed, and provide the means to transmit the character generation information to a means of output. Typically, the output will be magnetic or punched paper tape or punched cards. Generally, the computer serves as the main portion of the systems control unit. Some units utilize special software plus computer logic control.

CompuScan "170" OCR System

The CompuScan "170" OCR system is designed for conversion of typewritten text directly into on-line input to systems which use phototypesetting computers. One model is designed for off-line use and outputs magnetic tape or punched paper tape. Fig. 6-51. These are then used to drive phototypesetting machines. The system can also have direct input into a line printer which produces a readable image. It can also direct input into a tape cassette reader/recorder which provides a good way for post-editing the scanned text material.

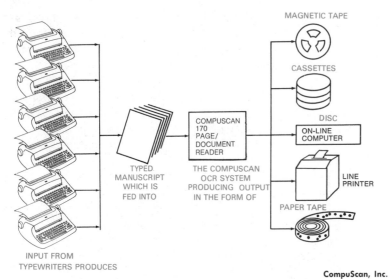

INPUT FROM
TYPEWRITERS PRODUCES

TYPED
MANUSCRIPT
WHICH IS
FED INTO

THE COMPUSCAN
OCR SYSTEM
PRODUCING OUTPUT
IN THE FORM OF

COMPUSCAN
170
PAGE/
DOCUMENT
READER

MAGNETIC TAPE

CASSETTES

DISC

ON-LINE
COMPUTER

LINE
PRINTER

PAPER TAPE

CompuScan, Inc.

6-51. *A system for converting typewritten text directly to output form for use in phototypesetters.*

In the system shown in Fig. 6-52, the original manuscripts are prepared on conventional office typewriters, using a standard type style together with special characters for use in editing and formatting. These are inserted in the stack feeder. They are then fed through the double-document detector to eliminate double feeds. Fig. 6-53. The optical display shows the typed characters, editing marks, and characters which will not read.

The scanning system uses a solid-state array of photocells. The scanning head is adjustable, allowing the operator to determine what portions of the page will be scanned. The system provides multifont capabilities, and with use of software packages it can also provide a hyphenation-justification capability. The system has the ability to read and recognize a multiplicity of fonts on the same machine. It

reads the text on the first pass so that no retyping is required.

The scanning program contains a set of code conversions. Code conversions can be refined, or a new set of conversion rules can be entered using code-conversion header sheets. Fig. 6-54. The conversion rules are typed on the header sheet. They are scanned using a header sheet routine. The routine decodes the equations typed on the sheets and stores the appropriate conversion rules in the memory of the computer. Once the conversion rules are entered, the scanner is ready for scanning the ordinary typed text.

A "Scan-Edit" unit permits errors discovered after typing to be corrected on the original manuscript page. The error is deleted by the proofreader by marking through it with a felt tip pen. Fig. 6-55. Corrections are written in with a nonrecording pen, and the

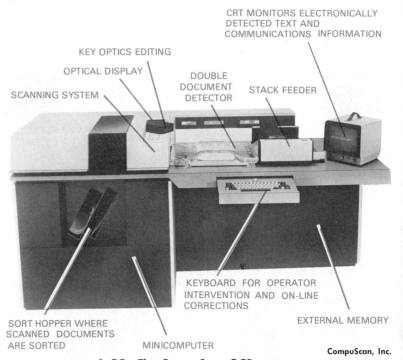

CRT MONITORS ELECTRONICALLY
DETECTED TEXT AND
COMMUNICATIONS INFORMATION

KEY OPTICS EDITING

OPTICAL DISPLAY

SCANNING SYSTEM

DOUBLE
DOCUMENT
DETECTOR

STACK FEEDER

KEYBOARD FOR OPERATOR
INTERVENTION AND ON-LINE
CORRECTIONS

EXTERNAL MEMORY

SORT HOPPER WHERE
SCANNED DOCUMENTS
ARE SORTED

MINICOMPUTER

CompuScan, Inc.

6-52. *The CompuScan OCR system.*

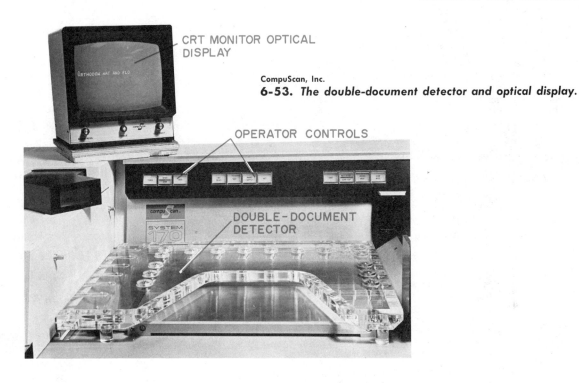

CRT MONITOR OPTICAL
DISPLAY

OPERATOR CONTROLS

DOUBLE-DOCUMENT
DETECTOR

CompuScan, Inc.
6-53. *The double-document detector and optical display.*

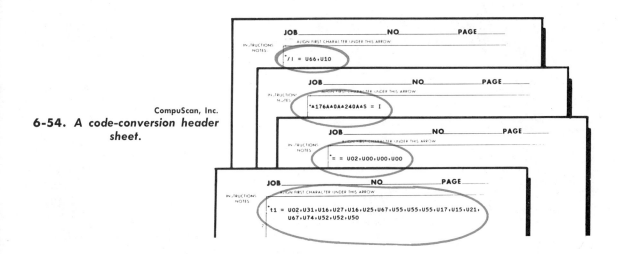

CompuScan, Inc.
6-54. *A code-conversion header sheet.*

manuscript is returned to the typist. The typist inserts a "Scan-Edit" symbol, types the correction, and puts a closing symbol. The "Scan-Edit" program holds the deleted characters in storage and searches for a "Scan-Edit" symbol. The unit recognizes the black crossout of an error as a delete command. Once a "Scan-Edit" command is found, the system accepts the typed correction and inserts it in the area where the error was crossed out.

A "Key Optics" display editing device permits the scanner operator to make last-minute corrections or minor editorial changes. These changes are noted on the original manuscript with a non-readable pen. Corrections are

129

TYPED COPY: Here is a one wprd correction

EDITED COPY: Here is a one ~~word~~ correction.
              ∆ word ∆

170 OUTPUT: Here is a one word correction.

> Here the proofreader discovered the error "wprd" and made the non-read penned correction. The sheet was then placed in a typewriter and the correction with Scan-Edit symbols typed between lines.

TYPED COPY: Here are multiple corrections on onx line.

EDITED COPY: Here are ~~multiple~~ corrections on ~~onx~~ line.
              ∆ two ∆ one ∆

170 OUTPUT: Here are two corrections on one line.

> Note that the corrections are typed in the same sequence as the crossed out words appear.

TYPED COPY: Paragraph insertion is a method of editing. ¶A
              You can insert up to 300 characters at one time.

PARAGRAPH   ++A
INSERTION: It is used when more than one line of text must
              be entered into the copy.
              ++A

170 OUTPUT:

> Paragraph insertion is a method of editing. It is used when more than one line of text must be entered into the copy. You can insert up to 300 characters at one time.

> The insertion page ++A is scanned first and stored. When the system encounters ¶A code in the original sheet, the insertion is retrieved from computer storage and inserted.

CompuScan, Inc.

6-55. The typist makes the corrections on the manuscript by inserting the proper symbols and typing the correction.

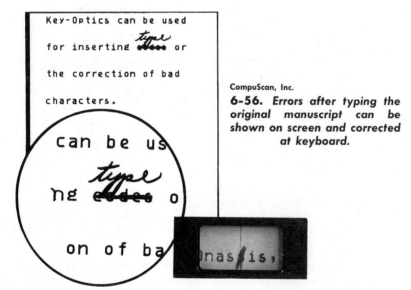

CompuScan, Inc.

6-56. Errors after typing the original manuscript can be shown on screen and corrected at keyboard.

crossed out with a black felt tip pen.

The scanner automatically stops when it reaches a crossed-out word. The console CRT displays the electronically detected text as the scanner reads it. The scanner's optical display screen shows the operator the actual typed text, including the surrounding correction marks. Fig. 6-56. The operator can now insert the correction through the scanner keyboard. Then the normal scanning operation continues.

ECRM OCR "Autoreader" System

The ECRM OCR "Autoreader" system converts typed and edited copy into machine-readable form for the typesetting computers. It produces edited, unjustified paper tape output or a direct-wire interface to the typesetting computer. Fig. 6-57. The flow of the image through the system is shown in Fig. 6-58. The typewritten copy is scanned. The signal generated is sent to the video buffer which, with the character recognition logic, establishes each character. Editing operations are made, and the application's software produces the typesetting commands. The stream of symbols now containing text and typesetting commands is shifted into an output device buffer which ultimately causes paper tape to be punched or some other output transmission be made.

The text material is typed normally on an electric typewriter with a carbon ribbon. The typewriter must have a typeface which is recognizable to the OCR

PUNCHED PAPER TAPE

STACK FEEDER

ECRM

ECRM, Inc.

6-57. *The ECRM OCR "Autoreader" system.*

SCANNER

↓

VIDEO BUFFER

↓

CHARACTER RECOGNITION LOGIC

↓

EDITING

↓

APPLICATIONS SOFTWARE

↓

OUTPUT DEVICE BUFFER

↓

ECRM, Inc.

6-58. *The basic flow diagram of the ECRM OCR system.*

system. Copy is usually double or triple spaced to allow room for normal editing on the original copy. Editing marks are made with a pen using nonreproducible ink. The OCR scanning device will not read it. Deletions are made with a black pen which is read by the scanner. A typist then types corrections between the lines on the edited copy with needed codes. The "Autoreader" will recognize the correction and perform the operation according to the code. Fig. 6-59.

The format selected is also typed on the copy. For example, a code indicating a subhead can cause the typesetting machine to set that line in boldface and center it.

The copy is then placed in the stack feeder of the "Autoreader." Fig. 6-60. The scanning system reads the typewritten text. The unjustified output is sent to a hyphenation and justification processor. This could be either a photocomposition machine with hyphenation and justification capabilities or a computer. This produces a justified tape for

AUTOREADER INPUT: Many ~~shiny~~ new faces ~~cropped up~~ in the group.
// /appeared/

AUTOREADER OUTPUT: Many new faces appeared in the group.

ECRM, Inc.

6-59. An example of edited copy. The word shiny was deleted and the symbol was placed below it to so signify. The words cropped up were deleted and appeared was typed on the copy. The symbols code the insertion.

use in a photocomposition machine.

The ECRM "Autoreader" uses a tiny beam of light from a laser to read the typewritten page. The light reflected from the paper strikes a photodetector which generates a corresponding electrical signal. This produces a modulated electrical signal corresponding to the black and white areas on the page.

This scanned signal is sampled to break up the black and white areas into a series of black and white dots. The dots represent digitized video or picture elements, with white corresponding to a binary 0 and black to a binary 1. The digitized video is stored in a magnetic core memory (video buffer). Fig. 6-61 shows a sample of a lowercase letter *a* stored in the video buffer. The video buffer's "height" is larger than the height of the largest possible character, and its "length" is equal to the width of the longest typed line the scanner will accept. The computer control console is shown in Fig. 6-62.

The scanning is accomplished by the laser beam, which sweeps from left to right. At the end of each sweep, the stepping motor in the paper-handling mechanism advances one step, and the laser sweeps again. The digitized video for each sweep is stored in the video buffer. It takes several sweeps to digitize the characters in a typewritten line since each sweep only records part of the height of each character.

When a character is detected, a "boxing" routine is started. This computer program sets the boundaries around the character; thus, the name *box*. After the character has been boxed, several measurements are made. For example, the height and width of the character are measured. The measurements are compared with a stored table of

ECRM, Inc.

6-60. The typed copy is placed in the stack feeder.

ECRM, Inc.

6-61. A character in a video buffer.

in the text to be reproduced are converted to the output code. This is transmitted to the output device buffer which causes the paper tape to be punched or sends the code to a wired interface into a computer.

Datatype OCR System

The Datatype OCR systems use IBM "Selectric" typewriters as the input copy preparation device. These typewriters are equipped with a special Datatype bar code typing element. This element produces readable characters as well as a special code beneath each character. Fig. 6-63. The code virtually eliminates OCR substitution errors.

The OCR reader can be combined with a minicomputer and a paper tape punch or a magnetic tape recorder to produce tape to operate phototypesetting machines. It can also be integrated with a video display terminal or a computer. Fig. 6-64.

PROOFREADING COPY IN PHOTOCOMPOSITION

When using a phototypesetter, the most economical time to have the copy proofread is before it is input into the phototypesetter. There are several main ways this is done. These are to use

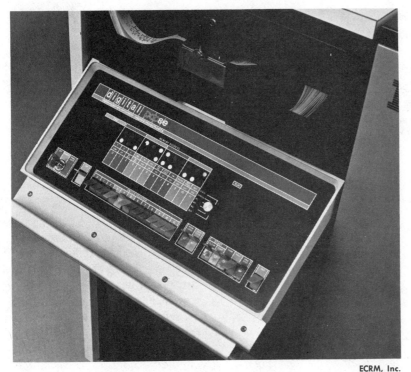

ECRM, Inc.

6-62. *The computer control console.*

character sizes to determine the character in storage which best fits the character in the box. By this method the reader recognizes the character. When all the characters in a typed line have been recognized, the resulting line buffer is transferred to the editing process.

The editing process includes character or word deletion as well as the performance of the editing directions typed on the original manuscript.

After the line is edited, it is operated on by the applications software computer program. This contains the character and typesetting commands. The format of the job and the characters

```
DF-3 PRINT ELEMENT

The DF-3 print element is a unique OCR font concept. This element

has a 'parity' bit incorporated in the bar code that appears below

the regular alpha-numeric characters. The presence of this 'extra'

bit virtually eliminates the possibility of code substitution during

the scanning process.
```

Datatype Corp.

6-63. *The Datatype character bar code.*

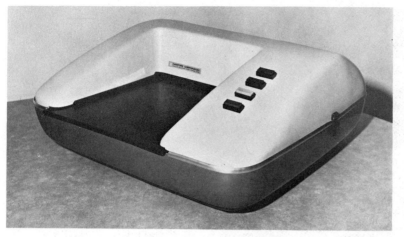

Datatype Corp.

6-64. *The Datatype OCR page reader.*

copy and is ready to input to the phototypesetting machine. Additional information on the matrix printer is given in Fig. 6-70.

The video display terminal method uses a VDT proofreader. The copy is set on a keyboard producing punched tape. The tape is fed into the VDT proofreader. There corrections in the tape are made before it is used by the phototypesetter to produce the camera-ready copy. Fig. 6-66.

A third method of proofreading punched paper tape is used when the tapes are prepared by an optical character recognition device. Fig. 6-67. The edited copy is typed, using the guidelines which suit the OCR system. This is proofread, and errors are marked according to the procedures for the OCR system. The marked, typed sheets are returned to the typist for corrections and necessary codes. The corrected, typed sheets then go to the OCR unit which produces

hard copy, a video display terminal (VDT), an optical character reader (OCR), or hard copy with a VDT.

When using the hard copy system, a copy of the text is put on punched tape. This transmits the copy to the computer, which

prints out the copy on an in-line matrix printer. Fig. 6-65. The hard copy is distributed to the proofreaders. They mark the corrections which go to the punched-tape operator, who keyboards them into the computer. The computer now has corrected

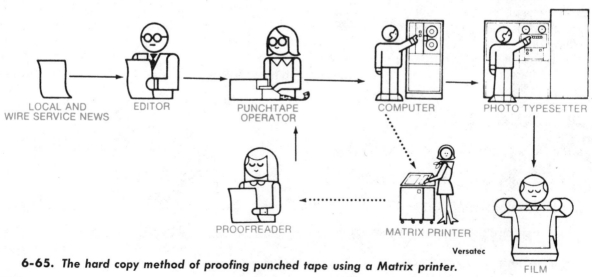

LOCAL AND WIRE SERVICE NEWS   EDITOR   PUNCHTAPE OPERATOR   COMPUTER   PHOTO TYPESETTER

PROOFREADER   MATRIX PRINTER

Versatec

6-65. *The hard copy method of proofing punched tape using a Matrix printer.*

FILM

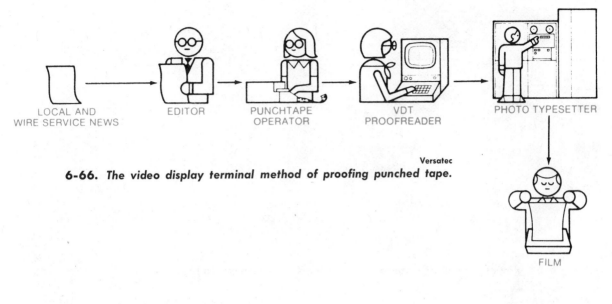

Versatec

6-66. *The video display terminal method of proofing punched tape.*

FILM

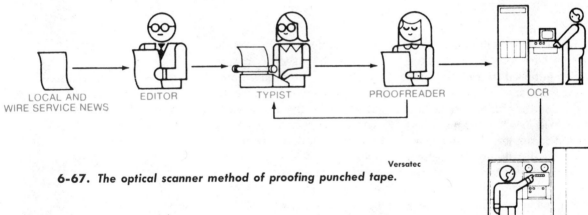

Versatec

6-67. *The optical scanner method of proofing punched tape.*

PHOTO TYPESETTER

FILM

punched tape to operate a phototypesetter or has a direct connection to a computer.

The last method of proofreading punched tape involves producing a hard copy on a matrix printer. This is proofread, and the tape and corrected copy are sent to a VDT unit. The operator keyboards the corrections in the tape, which then goes to the phototypesetter for the production of the reproducible copy. Fig. 6-68.

After the type has been set, it can be proofread and corrections marked on the phototypesetting paper with a nonreproducing blue pen. Customer proofs are usually made on an office copier.

VERSATEC "MATRIX PROOFER"

The Versatec "Matrix Proofer" is designed to produce hard copy of punched paper tape so that the copy can be proofread. The process is called matrix electrostatic writing technique (MEWT). It is true electrostatic writing.

There are no moving parts used to form the words. Fig. 6-69.

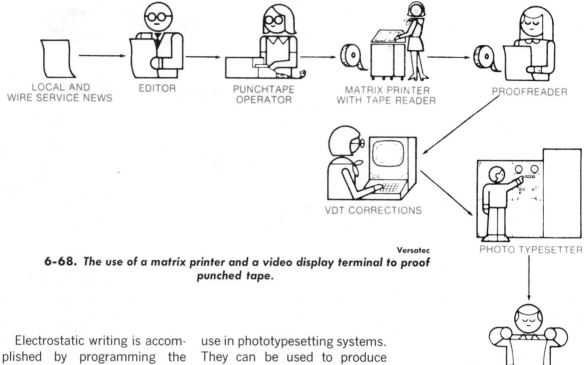

LOCAL AND WIRE SERVICE NEWS → EDITOR → PUNCHTAPE OPERATOR → MATRIX PRINTER WITH TAPE READER → PROOFREADER

VDT CORRECTIONS

PHOTO TYPESETTER

FILM

Versatec

6-68. *The use of a matrix printer and a video display terminal to proof punched tape.*

Electrostatic writing is accomplished by programming the voltage applied to a linear array of closely spaced writing nibs embedded in a stationary writing head. Fig. 6-70. As commanded by the computer, the nibs selectively create minute electrostatic dots on the paper as it passes over the writing head. Fig. 6-71. The paper is then exposed to a liquid toner to produce a permanent, visible image of the text. Sample printouts are shown in Fig. 6-72.

The proofer accepts 11″ wide paper in a roll or fan-folded. It produces copy at speeds up to 500 lines per minute. As the copy leaves the machine, it is ready for immediate use.

The proofer can be used in an off-line or on-line system.

VIDEO DISPLAY TERMINALS

Video display terminals are used for proofing, correcting, editing, merging, and marking up of text in tape form prior to its use in phototypesetting systems. They can be used to produce tape. However, they have limited character sets which reduce their usefulness for this purpose.

The terminal is a special type of television unit. It uses an electron gun to project a stream of electrons onto a phosphor coating on the inside surface of the face of the television tube. This causes the tube to glow. The image projected on the face of the tube will fade unless it is displayed repeatedly. To retain a steady visible image, the image must be held in a memory unit and recycled many times per second.

There are a number of ways characters are formed on the face of a video display terminal tube.

One system is to form the characters from a series of dots. Typically a rectangle five dots wide and seven dots high form the matrix. This makes it difficult to form lowercase letters, and

Versatec

6-69. *An off-line matrix proofer.*

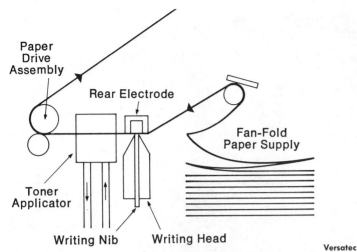

6-70. *The operating principles of a matrix proofing unit.*

Paper Drive Assembly

Rear Electrode

Fan-Fold Paper Supply

Toner Applicator

Writing Nib

Writing Head

Versatec

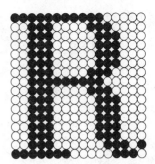

Versatec

6-71. *The dot matrix for the Roman text font in a matrix proofer.*

larger matrices are now being used.

A second system forms the characters on the tube using a series of line segments. This is called vector generation.

A third system develops characters with a series of horizontal or vertical strokes.

Video display units have three basic units: refresh logic, character generation, and editing electronics. As characters enter the video display tube, they are stored in the *refresh logic*. They are then projected on the face of the cathode ray tube sixty times a second. The refresh logic repeatedly reprojects the image so that it appears steady.

The *character generation* circuitry produces the shape and required characteristics of each projected character.

Most video display terminal *editing systems* use a cursor. A cursor is either an underline dash or a rectangle of light which appears on the screen. It points out the location of the character on the screen as the typeset-

ting progresses. The cursor is positioned by control keys that move it up, down, right, or left. The editing keys are used to correct errors. Generally, errors are corrected by placing the cursor over the incorrect letter and keyboarding the correct letter over it. This erases the incorrect letter and replaces it with the correct letter. The operator can delete a word, sentence, or paragraph with just a few key strokes. The typesetting function keys are used to establish commands, such as spacing or indention.

The following discussion relates to the Mergenthaler MVP Editing System.

There are several models available. The MVP-1 records and reads paper tape. It has a six-level paper tape punch. Floppy disk capabilities can be added. The MVP-2 is designed for keyboard to disk operation. It has no paper tape reader or punch.

Both units consist of a video display terminal and a controller. Fig. 6-73. The video display ter-

minal has a CRT screen and a keyboard. The operator has three text display choices. A single-column display has 23 lines with 80 characters per line. A two-column display has two 23-line columns with 40 characters per line separated by a gutter. A third display is a two-column display

Versatec Roman Text

In the fifteenth
his task of another pa
He had gotten as far a
the story of Gnaius Ju
Britain until 86 A.D.

Versatec Roman 128 Character Set

@ABCDEFGHIJKLMNOPQRSTU
abcdefghijklmnopqrstuv
!"#$%&'()*+,-./0123456'
ꞙⲨꞓꞒ⌘△꜔꜕ꞏ→↓↔←↕↦↧↨↩↪↫fl ffifl

Gothic Text

The clay was like leather wl
stick into the surface, and
Now the mid-day sun was beg;
and his fingertips whitened
harder to make the impressic

Versatec

6-72. *Sample printouts from a matrix proofing unit.*

Mergenthaler Linotype Co.

6-73. The MVP Editing System consists of a video display terminal and a controller.

duces a corrected tape. This is used on a phototypesetting machine to produce the film needed for printing. The system can have many different outputs. It can be on-line with a typesetter, a hard copy machine, or a computer that outputs to a typesetting machine.

FRONT-END SYSTEMS FOR NEWSPAPER COMPOSITION

Front-end systems provide editorial, classified advertisement, and display advertising depart-

with each half independent. Copy can be put into either side of the display through the keyboard, tape readers, or floppy disks. Either half can be scrolled forward or in reverse, and blocks of copy can be moved from one side to the other. This is helpful when merging copy from one job with another. For example, the original copy can be on one side and the new on the other. The operator can delete the obsolete material and insert the new. Fig. 6-74.

The keyboard has two sets of keys. One consists of a standard secretarial or TTS keypad plus special typesetting instruction keys. The other set includes controls for the cursor, editing, and reader-punch.

The tape reader-punch reads the original input tape, and it is this image which is displayed on the CRT. As corrections are made by the operator, the punch pro-

Mergenthaler Linotype Co.

6-74. Text material on a VDT opened to permit the insertion of new material.

TEXT OPENED FOR NEW INSERTION

ACTUAL SIZE

ments with the capability of providing corrected copy directly to the phototypesetter. This eliminates rekeyboarding, proofreading, and corrections which are commonly made in the composing room.

The Compugraphic Mini-Publishing System is made up of three basic units: a Mini-Disk Terminal, a Mini-Disk Reader, and a Mini-Disk Recorder.

When serving the *editorial function,* all copy flow is controlled in the newsroom from the origination of a story through copysetting. Fig. 6-75. All copy is recorded by reporters on reusable floppy disks. Fig. 6-76. This includes locally generated news and stories on the newswire. The editors insert the disks into their disk terminal, which displays the story on the video display screen. The editors can then edit the copy on the screen from the keyboard. Fig. 6-77. The keyboard has programmable keys which

6-76. Floppy disks can hold material that would require approximately one-half mile of punched paper tape.

are used to set column widths, indents, and other variables. The copy then goes to the Mini-Disk Reader, which translates the stored information into a language to operate a phototypesetter. Fig. 6-78.

When serving the *classified advertisement function,* a terminal is placed in the classified department. Through this terminal advertisements can be input, merged, corrected, updated, output, or killed with the controls on the keyboard. New ads can be entered with a single keystroke. They can be stored by classification during input.

A typeset command can instruct the system to search each classification for the ads scheduled to run on a particular date and combine them into a single file which will be output to the typesetter. The system will remove expired ads and put them in a billing file. This file is then

TYPESETTER

MDR

MINI-DISK READER

EDITOR'S TERMINAL

EDITOR'S TERMINAL

REPORTER'S TERMINAL

REPORTER'S TERMINAL

REPORTER'S TERMINAL

REPORTER'S TERMINAL

MINI-DISK TERMINALS

6-75. A typical editing system using video terminals having floppy disk storage capabilities.

Compugraphic Corp.

6-77. *The Compugraphic Mini-Disk video display terminal.*

disk from the recorder and insert it into their disk terminal and begin the editing process.

A *disk reader* is used to translate the information stored on the floppy disk into the language needed to operate a phototypesetter. Fig. 6-78.

COMPUTER ASSISTED MAKEUP

Computer assisted makeup systems enable operators to design and assemble camera-ready copy for advertisements. One such system is the "AdVantage," produced by the Compugraphic Corporation. This is a self-contained, code-free ad makeup system. The ad is assembled on a visual display screen. The steps of ad layout, markup, and makeup are performed by this system. Fig. 6-80.

The system is especially useful for newspapers because ads can be prepared faster than with

output to a forms printer to produce invoices for the ads.

The *display function* provides lines of copy on the video display of the disk terminal. The display shows the words, punctuation, a report on machine operations, the story name, segments of copy, commands, and programmable key definitions. Fig. 6-77. The display function permits copy to be edited, corrected, or changed as needed.

The copy is stored on a floppy disk. Each entry on the floppy disk has its own file name so that it can be located quickly. The disk directory of items stored appears as a visual listing on the screen. With the directory on the screen, the file wanted can be marked for output from the keyboard. Once marked, the disk is placed in a disk reader and only the marked files will appear in the final output.

A wire recorder is available that collects and stores wire

service reports. Fig. 6-79. It will supply an abstract of the story and file the entire story on the floppy disk under its own number. Editors can then remove the

Compugraphic Corp.

6-78. *The Compugraphic Mini-Disk Reader translates information stored on floppy disks into the language needed to operate phototypesetters.*

Compugraphic Corp.

6-79. *The Compugraphic Mini-Wire Recorder collects and stores wire service reports.*

After the ad is composed, the operator instructs the unit to output the ad for typesetting. The ad will be completely typeset in position except for the illustrations. The illustrations are pasted up with the copy, and the ad is finished.

The computer permits the operator to store ad copy and layout formats for recall. In this way entire blocks of copy or entire ads can be stored and reused as needed.

If an ad exceeds the 45-pica width and 11-inch depth of the system, the ad can be broken down and composed by parts. Each part is produced accurately, and all parts can be assembled into a finished ad with no additional work.

conventional means. This enables newspapers to set copy deadlines closer to the time of publication. It also reduces the need for paste-up supplies, typographic paper, and chemicals. The ads can be created by design-oriented, nontechnical personnel. Since only one person is involved with the ad during its creation, fewer errors are likely to occur.

The operator uses an electronic pen in conjunction with a makeup board. The operator controls all copy movements and the type size, type style, and positioning of the words in the ad. Artwork for the ad is positioned by tracing the outline with the pen. This puts it in the computer memory, enabling the operator to position it in the ad. All of these elements—art, text, and rules—are composed on the visual display screen.

Raw copy input from paper tape or floppy disks is automatically coded by the computer using plain English instructions given to it by the operator. Instructions include typesetting directions and layout instructions.

The operator can make any changes on the copy or layout with the electronic pen. If extensive copy changes are needed, a keyboard is available to do this.

Compugraphic Corp.

6-80. *The Compugraphic AdVantage computer assisted makeup unit.*

The "AdVantage" system has a protective storage function. Every two or three minutes the computer automatically writes the ad back onto the disk storage without interrupting the operator. If a power failure occurs, the ad will be in the computer memory and not be lost.

Another complete display composition system is the Compugraphic DCS (display composition system). Fig. 6-81. It is designed to produce complex composition. The DCS is a computer assisted area composition system suitable for text, classified and display ads, bar charts, forms, and periodical, catalog, and book pages. The three units making the system are the "Unified Composer" (an electronic composer), the "PreView" (a video display), and the "Video-Setter Universal" (a high-speed cathode ray tube phototypesetter).

VIDEO DISPLAY

ELECTRONIC COMPOSER

PHOTOTYPESETTER

Compugraphic Corp.

6-81. A total display composition system for text and ads.

After the copy is composed on the electronic composer, it is displayed on the video display. The type, rules, boxes, reverses, and the layout are shown exactly as they will appear in the final output. The copy can be proofed and corrected at this stage. When correct, it is sent in-line to the phototypesetter.

REVIEW QUESTIONS

1. Can printed matter be used as copy in preparing a layout?
2. In composition, what does justification mean?
3. A typewriter with *proportional spacing* lets the typist choose the amount of space to use between words. True or False?
4. In phototypesetting, light is beamed through a transparent image on an opaque background. True or False?
5. Today's phototypesetting machines can generate the type characters on a CRT screen. True or False?
6. What does OCR stand for?
7. An OCR system reads typed manuscript and converts it to a form usable by a typesetting machine. True or False?
8. What does VDT stand for?
9. Name one way VDT systems form characters.
10. All VDT systems output directly to a typesetting computer. True or False?

Chapter 7

Relief Composition—Hand

Composition refers to preparation of artwork and copy into a form that will be converted into printing. The accuracy and quality of the finished printed product depend heavily upon the skill of those working in composition. The person who does this work is called the compositor. Fig. 7-1.

Hand-set type is a *relief* composition process. In relief composition, the image is on a raised surface. During printing, this raised surface receives a layer of ink and is pressed against the printing surface. This process is repeated each time the image is reproduced. (See Chapter 1, "The Printing Industry.")

OVERVIEW OF THE HAND COMPOSITION PROCESS

When relief composition is done by hand, the compositor works from the layout of the pages to be set. The type size, typeface, and column width will be known by the compositor.

Copy is set by assembling individual pieces of type in a *composing stick*. Each word is put together one letter at a time. Words and lines are separated by inserting metal spacing materials.

After the stick is almost full, the type is transferred to a *galley*. This is called "dumping the stick." The galley is a metal tray used for storing type.

Next the type is placed on an imposing table and formed into pages. The type is then locked into a *chase*, a metal frame which holds the type in the press during the printing operation.

FOUNDRY TYPE

Hand composition uses *foundry type*; that is, metal cast in individual pieces. Each piece of type has one character on it. Fig. 7-2. The largest part of the type, the *body*, has a front and

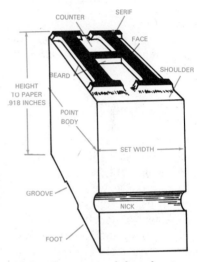

7-2. The parts of foundry type.

back side. The front side has a groove, called a *nick*. The nicks must all line up. If they do not, the type is upside down or from the wrong font. Figs. 7-3 and 7-4.

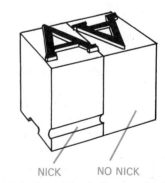

7-3. The nicks indicate whether all type is facing the same direction.

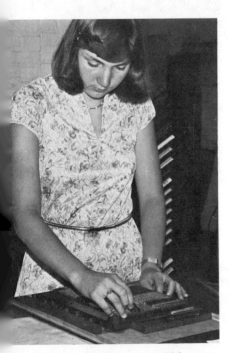

7-1. A compositor assembles type on an imposing table.

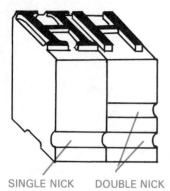

SINGLE NICK DOUBLE NICK

7-4. *When the nicks do not line up, it means the type has different style faces.*

(Font refers to an assortment of type of one size and style.) Since each design of type has different nicks, the nicks will not line up if two styles are mixed.

The *feet* are on the bottom of the type body and support it as it prints. The feet and names of other parts are shown in Fig. 7-2.

The size of foundry type is specified by three dimensions, *body size, set size,* and *height to paper.* Fig. 7-2. Body size varies according to the size of the type. Small type has a smaller body than larger type. The set size varies with the body size and the individual characters. The height-to-paper size is the same for all type sizes and faces. It is standardized in the United States as 0.918", which is called *type-high.* Since all type is the same height, the different sizes and faces can be mixed on a job.

FONTS OF FOUNDRY TYPE

Foundry type is sold in quantities by fonts. A *font* usually has capitals, lowercase letters, figures, and punctuation marks. Small capitals, ligatures, special

ABCDEFGHIJKLMNOPQRSTUVWXYYabcdefghijklmnopqrstuvwxyz $12345678
6 POINT

ABCDEFGHIJKLMNOPQRSTUabcdefghijklmnopqrstuvwxyz $901
8 POINT

AVWXYZABCDEFGHIJKabcdefghijklmnopqrstu $234
10 POINT

ALMNOPQRSTUVWavwxyzabcdefghijkl $567
12 POINT

ABCDEFGHIJKLMabcdefghijklmno $123
14 POINT

AXYZABCDEFGamnopqrstuvw $890
18 POINT

AHIJKLMNaxyzabcdef $123
24 POINT

AOPQRaghijklmn 45
30 POINT

ASTUVaopqr67
36 POINT

AWXastuv 9
48 POINT

AYawxy 0
60 POINT

AZazac1
72 POINT

7-5. *Typefaces are available in many sizes. Shown is a sans serif bold typeface.*

characters, and symbols may be bought in special fonts. All type in one font is the same size and typeface.

MAKING FOUNDRY TYPE

Foundry type is cast in a commercial foundry. Each letter is cast separately. Type manufacture involves six stages—design, photography, making pattern plates, engraving, fitting, and casting.

The typeface is drawn by a type designer. Most designers prefer to work with a capital-letter height of 2″. The artwork is enlarged or reduced by camera. The film positive is used to make the pattern plate. One pattern plate is used to engrave the complete range of point sizes for that character.

The engraving tool cuts the typeform in a blank brass plate, the *matrix*. After the matrix is engraved, it is placed under a highly accurate microscope equipped with a grinding attachment. The character's alignment is finalized by grinding the matrix. Its position in relation to the other characters of the alphabet is also set by grinding the matrix

until it has the exact overall dimension required. The matrix is then chromium-plated.

Now type can be cast using the matrix. After the type is cast, it is inspected, assembled into fonts, and is ready to ship to a customer.

TYPEFACES

Companies which design and manufacture foundry type identify different designs by name. Often two companies will have faces almost alike but give them different names. When ordering a typeface that is made by several companies, it is best to specify the typeface *and* the manufacturer.

Variations of typefaces from the original design include proportions, character width, and weight of the letters. A grouping of such variations for a typeface is called a *type family*.

Most typefaces are made in a wide range of sizes. Fig. 7-5. The usual sizes range from 6-point to 36-point. Some are made as large as 96-point. More information on typefaces can be found in Chapter 5, "Graphic Design."

SPACING MATERIAL

Words are separated from each other by inserting metal

☐America's☐industrial☐era,☐which☐began about 1800, is coming to a close. The beginning☐of☐the☐transition☐into☐the☐post-industrial age is already visible in the automated☐technology☐now☐producing☐many goods, in computer technology providing services, in more tenuous relationships between work and economic production, and in new meanings for work and for relationships within and between working organizations.☐☐☐☐

7-7. Metal spacing material is used between the words in sentences.

spacing materials called *quads* and *spaces*. The quads and spaces in hand-set type look much like a piece of type, except that they are not type-high. Fig. 7-6. The *em quad,* the basic unit, is square. The actual size will vary with its point size. If 8-point type is being set, 8-point spacing material must be used. The em quad for this size would be 8 points on each side. The *en quad* is half the em quad. Two-em and three-em quads (double or triple the basic size) are used to fill out the blank spaces at the ends of lines. They are also used to center lines or in places where a large blank area is wanted. Fig. 7-7. Extra-thin spaces, called *hair spaces,* are also made.

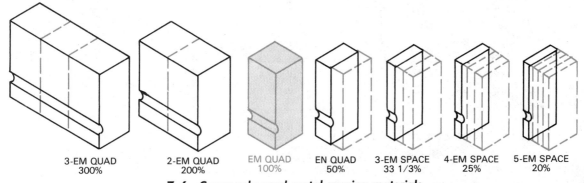

| 3-EM QUAD 300% | 2-EM QUAD 200% | EM QUAD 100% | EN QUAD 50% | 3-EM SPACE 33 1/3% | 4-EM SPACE 25% | 5-EM SPACE 20% |

7-6. Commonly used metal spacing materials.

145

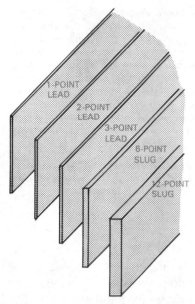

7-8. **Common lead and slug widths.**

7-9. *Leads and slugs are cut to length on a hand-powered slug cutter.*

7-10. *Leads and slugs can be cut with a power saw.*

LEADS AND SLUGS

Each line in hand composition may be separated from the next with spacing material called leads and slugs. These are long metal strips about 3/4" high. Common sizes are shown in Fig. 7-8. Leads are less than 6 points thick. Those 6 points and thicker are called slugs.

Leads and slugs are cut with a slug cutter. Fig. 7-9. The cutter has a scale marked in picas and half picas. A slug is cut by setting the stop at the length wanted, holding it firmly, and pushing down on the handle.

Power saws are a faster way to cut leads and slugs. Fig. 7-10. They produce a very smooth cut. Special care must be taken when using the saw.

TYPE STORAGE

Foundry type is stored in drawers with many compartments, called a *California job*
case. Fig. 7-11A. The compartments hold the different letters, spacing material, and other symbols on type. The location of each letter in the case is standardized. Compositors must memorize where each piece of type is stored. They can then choose letters from the case rapidly and without looking at a chart. Fig. 7-11B.

The best way to learn the lay of the California job case is to study the location of each part. Capital

7-11A. *Foundry type is stored in a California job case.*

ffi	fl	5-EM	4-EM	'	k		e		1	2	3	4	5	6	7	8		$			Æ	Œ	æ	œ
j		b	c	d					i		s		f	g	ff	9		A	B	C	D	E	F	G
?															fi	0								
!		l	m	n	h				o	y	p	w	,		EN QUADS	EM QUADS		H	I	K	L	M	N	O
z																								
x		v	u	t	3-EM SPACES				a	r			;	:	2- EM AND 3M QUADS		P	Q	R	S	T	V	W
q													.	-			X	Y	Z	J	U	&	ffl

7-11B. *Layout of the California job case.*

7-12. *Always slightly pull out the case below the one you are using.*

7-13. *Stand erect at the bank, and move both hands over the case as the type is set.*

letters are in alphabetical order on the right side. Numerals are in numerical order. Lowercase letters are located so that the most frequently used letters are near the center of the case.

Care must be taken when working with the job case so that it doesn't spill. Spilled type is called *pied* type. The sorting of pied type is a difficult task.

When removing a job case from the storage cabinet, pull out the case below it about 12″. This will catch the case, if it falls as it is being removed. Fig. 7-12.

The case is placed on a *bank* when in use. The bank is a slant-topped workbench. Fig. 7-13. It often has case storage below it. Leads and slugs are often stored above it.

HAND TYPESETTING

The actual setting of type into words and sentences is called *typesetting*.

Hand-set type is assembled in a composing stick usually made of steel or brass. Fig. 7-14. The most commonly used stick is the Rouse job stick. It has a series of

rectangular holes, one pica apart, in the body. The knee of the stick is held to the body with a clamp. The knee has little projections that fit into these holes. To secure the knee in place, insert the projections into the holes, and close the clamp.

Notice that the stick has a scale in picas stamped into it. Fig. 7-14. To set a line of type a particular length, place the face

of the knee on the measure wanted. Fig. 7-14 shows the knee on 21 picas. Be certain the knee projections are in the rectangular holes. Close the clamp. The stick is now set on the line length wanted, indicated in even picas. While most lines are set in even lengths, a half-pica lever can be

7-14. *A composing stick.*

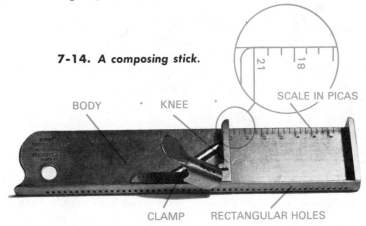

SCALE IN PICAS

BODY · KNEE

CLAMP   RECTANGULAR HOLES

147

used. Turning the lever sets the face of the knee projections halfway between the pica distances marked on the stick.

SETTING A LINE OF TYPE

The composing stick is held in the left hand. Fig. 7-15. A slug, cut to the length set, is placed in the stick. To set the first line of type on the slug, the right hand picks and places the first letter in the stick. It goes next to the knee. The nick is up. *Type is set from left to right.* This makes the type upside down and in reverse order from which it is read. Fig. 7-16. It takes practice to read the type in the stick, but after a while, it becomes easy.

The thumb of the left hand holds the type in place. Fig. 7-17. The stick is slightly slanted to help keep the type in place. The

7-16. *Hand-set metal type is set from left to right. The letters are upside down with the nicks showing.*

hand holding the stick follows the hand picking the type from the case.

The three-em space is placed between words. After a line of type is set, the spaces between words must be changed so that the line is the correct length. This is called *justification.* A justified line is exactly the same length as the opening in the composing stick.

When a line is properly justified, it is tight enough to stand alone. However, it must be loose enough so that the line can be easily removed from the stick. As changes in the spacing between words are made, spaces and characters must not be forced into place, or the spacing material could break.

PUTTING A LINE OF TYPE ON ITS FEET

It is important that the type be on its feet. If the type is leaning, the space at the end of the line will appear less than really exists. The face of the type will be above the type-high level, and it will be smashed when the job is printed. Fig. 7-18.

To get a line of type on its feet, start at the end next to the knee. Using your finger, push several

7-17. *The thumb holds the type in place as the line is set.*

characters straight. Then continue along the line until all are straight. If necessary, remove the end character to loosen the line a little. Do not try to push an entire line on its feet at one time. If you push too hard, the entire line will buckle and fall out of the stick.

SPACING BETWEEN WORDS

Under normal conditions type is set with three-em spaces between words. However, when the last word will not completely fit on the stick, the spacing between words must be reduced.

When hyphenation or space reduction between words fails to fit a word on a line, that word is

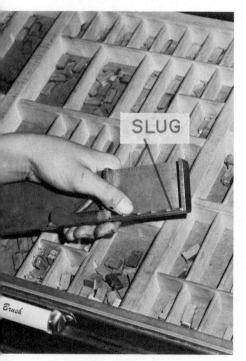

SLUG

7-15. *The composing stick is held in the left hand.*

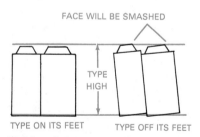

FACE WILL BE SMASHED

TYPE HIGH

TYPE ON ITS FEET   TYPE OFF ITS FEET

7-18. *If the type is leaning, it is off its feet.*

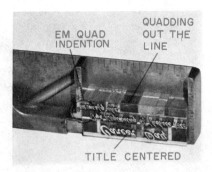

7-19. *Partial lines are completed with quads and spaces. Titles are centered by placing the same spacing materials on each side.*

7-20. *To dump the stick, hold the type between the thumb and forefinger.*

7-21. *Slide the type out of the stick, using the second fingers as guides to keep type from falling.*

set on the next line. Then spacing between the words must be increased to make up for the letters removed.

SETTING PARAGRAPHS

Paragraph indention uses the em quad. After the first line is set and justified, a two-point lead is placed over the type. The second line is then set and justified.

The two-point lead is the commonly used spacing between lines. The lead helps by giving a smooth, firm base upon which the line of type can be set. However, the copy can be set without it. A job set without leads between lines is said to be set *solid.* When type is set with leads, the leads are removed before printing.

Often a paragraph will end in the middle of a line. The remaining part of the line is filled with quads and spaces. Fig. 7-19. Use of the largest spacing material makes the line easier to handle.

The three-em space is used between the period ending one sentence and the first word of a new sentence. The white area above the period gives the appearance of more space.

DUMPING THE STICK

When the stick is one-half to three-fourths full, type is removed for storage on the galley. This is called dumping the stick.

To dump the stick:

1. Place the galley on a bank. Place the stick on the galley.

2. Put a slug on the open side of the type. Grip the entire unit of type between the thumb and forefinger. Fig. 7-20.

3. Begin to slide the type out of the stick onto the galley. Squeeze the type firmly so that the characters do not drop loose. Fig. 7-21.

4. As the type leaves the stick, place the second finger against the ends of the type to keep the end type characters from dropping loose. *Do not lift the type.*

5. Slide the type on the galley and place in a corner. Fig. 7-22.

6. Keep the galley on the sloped bank top so that gravity can help keep the type in place. Place some furniture around the typeform and hold it in place with spring-steel galley locks. Fig. 7-23. Information about furniture is found in Chapter 20, "Imposition and Lockup."

7-22. *Place the type in the corner of the galley.*

7-23. *Secure the form in the galley with a spring-steel galley lock.*

PROOFING RELIEF FORMS

A *proof* is a single printed impression of the typeform. It is carefully proofread, and errors are marked. (See Chapter 4, "Proofreading.") After the errors in the typeform are corrected, a second proof is taken and then proofread again. Common errors include misspelled words, characters that are upside down, type of a different design, type off its feet, and broken or worn typefaces. If some of the letters on the proof do not print clearly, the compositor must see if they are on their feet. If they are not, the proofing could smash the typeface. The typeface must be examined for wear and damage, and characters replaced that do not print clearly.

It is poor practice to place several sheets of paper on the typeform when pulling a proof. This will cause excessive pressure on the form and wear the typefaces.

A second kind of proof, called a *reproduction proof,* is a perfect printed copy. Details of each character must print perfectly.

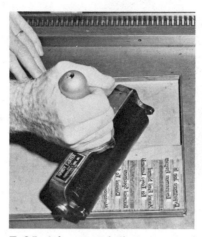

7-25 *Ink toward the corner of the form in the corner of the galley.*

7-26. *Place a sheet of paper over the inked form.*

The "repro" proof, as it is sometimes called, is used in offset printing. It is photographed, and the negative is used to make the offset plate.

An inexpensive proof press can be hand operated. Fig. 7-24. The typeform on a galley is placed on the bed of the press. The faces of the characters are inked with a *brayer*. The brayer has a composition roller. It is rolled through ink spread on an *ink plate*. Fig. 7-24. The brayer is then carefully rolled over the face of the typeform toward the corner supported by the sides of the galley. Fig. 7-25. A single sheet of paper is laid on top of the form. Fig. 7-26. The cylinder of the proof press is rolled by hand over the sheet of paper and the form. The paper is then lifted off the form by holding one corner and slowly pulling it clear. Fig. 7-27.

Some proof presses have grippers, which are metal clips that hold the paper to the cylinder. The grippers must be spaced so that they clear the typeform. If

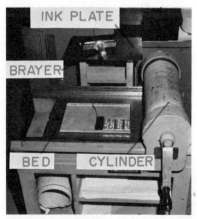

7-24. *A hand-operated proof press.*

a gripper hits the form, some of the type will be damaged.

The typeform is placed on the bed of the press. It is lined up with the *deadline*. This is a mark showing where to place the form. The side guide on the cylinder is set to print in the center of the sheet.

7-27. *After rolling the cylinder over the form, lift the proof off by its corner.*

7-28. *A power-operated proof press.*

7-29. *Using a proof planer.*

is one that requires the line be rejustified, it must be removed from the form and corrected in the composing stick. The line is then returned to the form on the galley.

If the correction does not change justification, it can be made on the galley. For example, a damaged character can be removed, and a new one the same size put in its place.

All corrections should be made in the order they appear on the proof.

CLEANING THE FORM AND PROOF PRESS

After a clear proof has been printed, the ink must be removed from the face of the type. Ink dried on the type will make it difficult to get clear prints the next time the type is used. Fig. 7-30.

Remove the ink with a rag dampened with type cleaner.

planer is moved around the form until all areas have been planed. Fig. 7-29.

MAKING CORRECTIONS

After a proof is taken, corrections are made. If the correction

Most proofs are made on a power-operated proof press. Fig. 7-28. The paper is held to the cylinder with grippers.

Some forms are too large for the proof press, but can be proofed on the imposing table. They are called *stone proofs.* (The imposing table, now made of steel, is frequently called the stone because the tops used to be made from stone.)

To make a stone proof, ink the type on the imposing table with a brayer. Lightly dampen the paper to be used for the proof with water. Carefully lay it over the form with the dampened side up.

The paper is pressed to the form with a *proof planer,* a wood block with a flat bottom. It is tapped lightly with a mallet. The

7-30A. *Dampen a cloth with type cleaner.*

7-30B. *Wipe across the face of the type toward the corner of the galley.*

7-31. *To distribute type, hold the line with the nicks up.*

Wipe across the face of the type toward the corner of the galley. Be certain to use a clean rag. Oil or dirt on the rag will damage the type. After the ink is removed, wipe the type with a clean, dry rag.

Do not pour type cleaner on the form. The ink will dissolve and run down between the pieces of type. When the ink is dry, the type will be stuck together.

The ink plate and the brayer's composition roller are cleaned with a rag dampened with type cleaner. Never use any type of abrasive cleaner on the ink plate. Wipe the surface of the roller carefully so that it is not broken.

All cleaners must be stored in closed containers to prevent evaporation. They are volatile and flammable. One type of container, Fig. 7-30A, has a spout that can be pushed in to let out the liquid. At all other times, a spring holds the spout closed.

DISTRIBUTING TYPE

After a job is printed and the type cleaned, the type must be distributed to the proper box in the type storage case. Type ready for distribution is called *dead matter*. Type not yet printed is called *live matter*. Type that has been printed and stored for future use is called *standing matter*.

Type to be distributed is placed on a galley. The storage case for the type is placed on the bank. It is essential to check the type in the form with the type in the case to make certain they are the same. It would be a serious error to distribute type in the wrong case. Before distribution begins, check to be sure the type has:

  * The same point *size.*

  * The same *face.*
  * *Nicks* that match.
  * *Feet* that match.
  * The same character *width.*

Special care must be taken when several different type sizes or faces are used on the same job.

Distribution requires practice. It is a rather slow process until the lay of the case is learned.

To distribute type:

1. Put slugs on each side of the first line. Pick up the line with the face toward you.

2. Hold the line. Fig. 7-31. Notice that the nick is up. The forefinger stays below the feet of the type to keep the line from sliding off.

3. Lift off *one word at a time* with the right hand. Read it and spell it out as you place each character in its box. Fig. 7-32.

4. Place all spacing materials on the galley. Compare their thickness with a space of known size. Distribute them in the same manner as individual type pieces.

5. Leads and slugs are placed in storage racks for reuse.

7-32. *Lift off one word at a time, and place each character in the proper compartment.*

REVIEW QUESTIONS

1. Copy that is set by hand is assembled one letter at a time in a galley. True or False?
2. What is a chase?
3. How many characters are on a piece of foundry type?
4. What does it mean if the nicks on the pieces of type don't all line up?
5. The height-to-paper size varies with the type size and face. True or False?
6. Spacing material must have the same point size as the type being set. True or False?
7. What are leads and slugs used for?
8. What does it mean when copy is said to be set solid?
9. Type that has been used, cleaned, and is ready for distribution is called dead matter. True or False?
10. What is type called if it has not yet been printed?

Relief Composition— Machine

Relief typesetting by machine is commonly referred to as hot-metal typesetting. While photo-composition is the most widely used composition system (see Chapter 6), hot-metal typesetting is still used.

Hot-metal typesetting involves a matrix, an adjustable mold, and hot metal. The *matrix* is made of brass or bronze. Recessed into it is the shape of the character. Fig. 8-1. The matrix is a reverse die. It is inserted in a mold, and hot metal is poured. The metal fills the cavity in the matrix, forming the shape of the character. Fig. 8-2. The mold also forms the body upon which the face is cast.

The hot-metal composition machines still in use are the Ludlow Typograph and the Linotype. These machines cast lines of type on a slug. A *slug* is a solid bar of metal with the typefaces on the top. Fig. 8-3.

THE LUDLOW TYPOGRAPH

The Ludlow Typograph machine, Fig. 8-4, casts a line of type on a single slug. The matrices are assembled by hand into a composing stick. Figs. 8-5 and 8-6. The stick is placed in the casting machine. The slug is cast on a 12-point body. Faces larger than 12 points overhang the body. Fig. 8-7. When the slug is

8-1. *A matrix is a reverse die of the letter to be cast.*

8-2. *A character formed by casting in a matrix.*

Mergenthaler Linotype Co.
8-3. *A slug cast on a Linotype machine.*

assembled in a chase for printing, blank slugs are placed below the overhang. This is called underpinning.

The main use for the Ludlow machine is to cast lines of display type. Fig. 8-8. Display type is used for headings and ranges in size from 14 points to 144 points. The Ludlow can cast type as small as 4 points. It is not used to cast large amounts of straight matter. This is generally done on a Linotype machine.

8-4. *A Ludlow casting machine and matrix storage cabinets.*

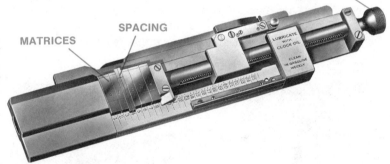

THUMBSCREW
ADJUSTMENT

SPACING

MATRICES

8-5. *The Ludlow composing stick with the letters to be cast in place. It is ready to be inserted in the casting machine.*

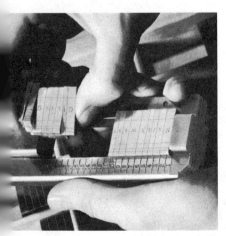

8-6A. *Assembling Ludlow matrices. The Ludlow operator gathers the matrices, forming a word from the case. These are inserted in the stick.*

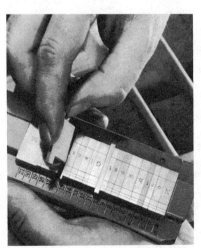

8-6B. *After the words are in the stick, word and letter spacing is done. The spaces are manually inserted between the matrices.*

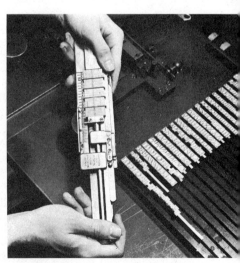

8-6C. *The thumbscrew on the end of the stick is tightened. This holds the matrices in the stick.*

155

8-7. *Ludlow slugs. Notice the overhang on the larger slug.*

THE LINOTYPE

Linotype machines are used to set large amounts of straight matter. A Linotype machine has four major sections: the keyboard, the magazine, the casting mechanism, and the distribution system. Fig. 8-9.

The Linotype operates as follows: The operator sits at the keyboard and punches the keys much the same as when operating a typewriter. Each time a key is punched, the matrix, also referred to as the mat, is released from the magazine. The magazine stores the mats that make up all the characters and letters of a single typeface. The mats drop through *delivery channels* to the *assembly elevator.* Here *spacebands* are dropped between the words. They are used to space the words equally and justify the line. The line of mats and bands is moved to the *casting mechanism.* Molten metal is injected into the mats, forming a slug. The slug contains all the words in the line cast in one piece. The slugs are trimmed to the proper thickness and made type-high. They are then dropped to the galley, where slug after slug is stored automatically.

After the slug is cast, the mats and spacebands are raised by the *first elevator.* They are transferred to the *distributing elevator,* which carries only the mats to the top of the magazine to the *distributor bar.* They are returned to the proper storage channels. The spacebands are not picked up by the distributing elevator, but are returned to their storage box.

After the type has been used to print a job, it is melted and cast into pigs. *Pigs* are bars of metal that are fed back into the metal pot on the machine. In this way the metal can be used over again.

One type of Linotype is called a mixer. It has four or more typefaces available. These are capable of setting different faces and sizes in one line.

Another linecasting machine is the Elektron. It is manually-operated, Fig. 8-10, and uses the

Ludlow Typograph Co.

8-8. *The Ludlow is used to cast lines of display type.*

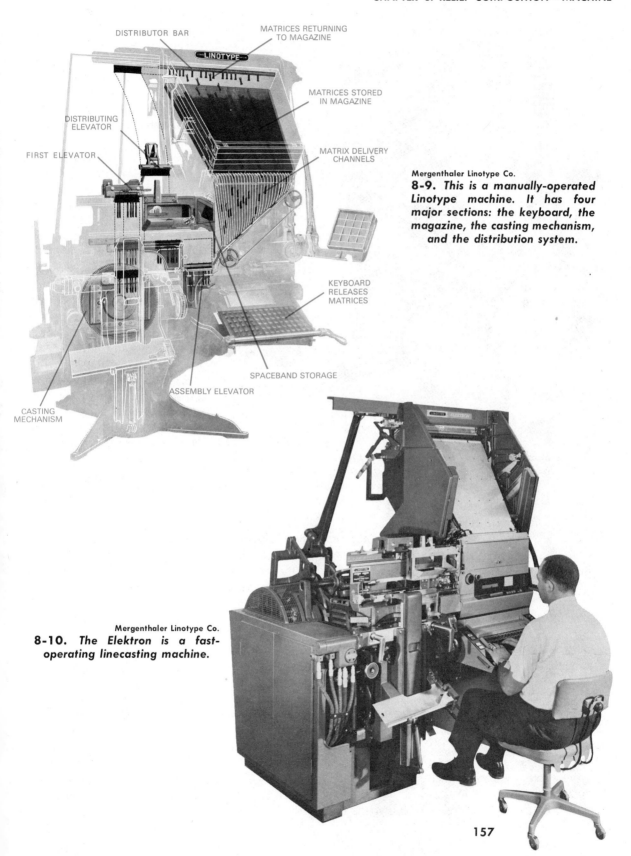

DISTRIBUTOR BAR

MATRICES RETURNING TO MAGAZINE

DISTRIBUTING ELEVATOR

MATRICES STORED IN MAGAZINE

FIRST ELEVATOR

MATRIX DELIVERY CHANNELS

Mergenthaler Linotype Co.
8-9. *This is a manually-operated Linotype machine. It has four major sections: the keyboard, the magazine, the casting mechanism, and the distribution system.*

KEYBOARD RELEASES MATRICES

SPACEBAND STORAGE

ASSEMBLY ELEVATOR

CASTING MECHANISM

Mergenthaler Linotype Co.
8-10. *The Elektron is a fast-operating linecasting machine.*

157

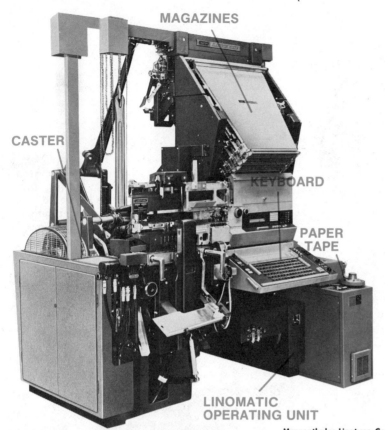

MAGAZINES

CASTER

KEYBOARD

PAPER TAPE

LINOMATIC OPERATING UNIT

Mergenthaler Linotype Co.

8-11. *An automatically controlled Elektron. All machine functions are controlled from codes punched in standard, six-level paper tape. The tape is read by the Linomatic operating unit.*

same general operating principles as the Linotype just described.

The most effective use of the Elektron is made when automatic controls are used. In the automatically controlled Elektron, Fig. 8-11, all machine functions are controlled from codes punched in standard, six-level paper tape. The tape is read by the Linomatic operating unit. This electromechanical decoder has four main parts: (1) the reader which reads the tape; (2) the relay panel which changes this information to electrical impulses; (3) the power supply to run the motors and energize the relays and solenoids of the system; (4) the decoder which changes the electrical pulses fed to it by the relay panels to the mechanical setting, initiating the release of the matrix. The major advantage is automatic collation at the machine. This function makes it possible to automatically collate (gather together) up to four different point sizes and eight different typefaces on the work being set.

THE MATRIX

The key to understanding the Linotype is the matrix. Fig. 8-12.

The matrices are made of brass and are 1 1/4" high, 3/4" across the lugs, and 9/10" across the body. All matrices have these same sizes. They vary in thickness, depending upon the width of the letters they are designed to mold.

The lugs on the matrix are used to release the mats. They are used in the assembly, justification, and casting processes. They carry the mat through the distribution and storage systems.

The top of the mat has a V-shape with teeth. These fit notches on the distributor bar. The mat moves along the bar until its teeth fit a set of notches. It then drops into the storage channel at this point. Fig. 8-13.

Each mat has a font slot in the bottom to identify the font.

Mats usually carry two letters. Common combinations are roman face and an italic face, or roman and boldface. The advantage of two-letter mats is that copy can be set in two faces from one magazine.

SPACEBANDS

Spacebands are dropped between words. When the line is nearly full, the operator delivers the line. The spacebands are pushed up by a block to fill the spaces between the words equally. The line is justified.

A spaceband consists of two parts. Fig. 8-14. They taper in opposite directions. When pushed together, they increase in thickness. The outer surfaces are always parallel.

Each part is wedge-shaped but different in size. The short part is called the *sleeve.* It is about the same length as the mats. The

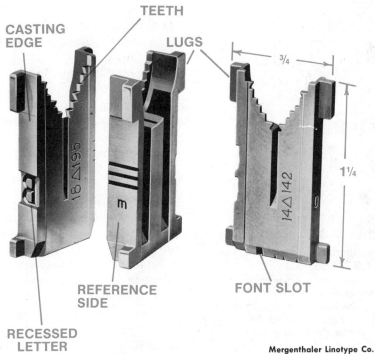

CASTING EDGE

TEETH

LUGS

3/4

1¼

REFERENCE SIDE

FONT SLOT

RECESSED LETTER

Mergenthaler Linotype Co.

8-12. Linotype matrices are accurately made and must be protected from damage.

8-13. The V notch on the matrix moves along the distributor bar until the teeth fit a set of notches. At this point, the matrix drops into the proper storage channel on the magazine.

Mergenthaler Linotype Co.

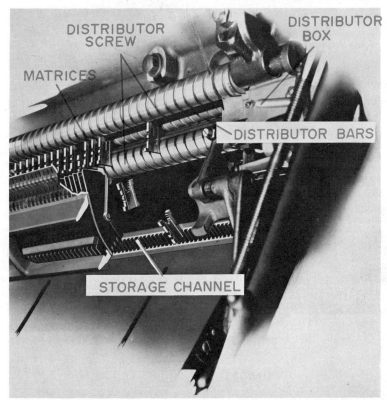

DISTRIBUTOR SCREW

DISTRIBUTOR BOX

MATRICES

DISTRIBUTOR BARS

STORAGE CHANNEL

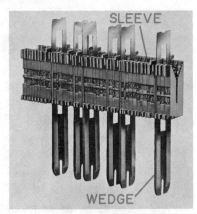

SLEEVE

WEDGE

Mergenthaler Linotype Co.

8-14. Spacebands in place in a line of matrices.

long part is called the *wedge*. It is about 3 1/2 times as long as the sleeve. As the line is justified, the sleeve does not move. The wedge is pushed upward against the sleeve. Fig. 8-15. The part pushing the wedges is called the *justification block*.

Spacebands are made in a number of widths. The extra-thin bands are used when small text type is being set, since it is usually rather close together. Wider bands are used when setting the larger display types.

8-15. A line is justified when the justification block pushes the wedges up tight against the matrices and the sleeve.

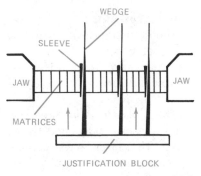

WEDGE

SLEEVE

JAW

JAW

MATRICES

JUSTIFICATION BLOCK

159

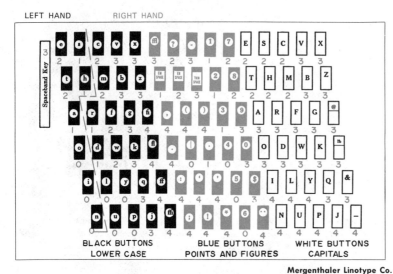

LEFT HAND   RIGHT HAND

BLACK BUTTONS
LOWER CASE

BLUE BUTTONS
POINTS AND FIGURES

WHITE BUTTONS
CAPITALS

Mergenthaler Linotype Co.

8-16. *This is the standard keyboard arrangement for two-letter matrices. It shows which fingers are used to strike the keys. The keys to the left of the dashed line are struck with the fingers of the left hand. All other keys are struck with fingers of the right hand.*

The Magazine

The matrices are stored in what is called the magazine. Each magazine contains one font. The magazine has flat channels into which mats flow. At the top, the mats are inserted into the various channels. Each channel holds the mats for one letter. At the bottom, a mechanism releases the mats when the operator punches a key on the keyboard. This is a continuous process. While mats are being returned at the top, others are released at the bottom.

The Keyboard

The standard keyboard of 90 keys has 6 horizontal rows with 15 keys each. Fig. 8-16. The spaceband key is at the upper left of the keys.

The keyboard is in three sections: black, blue, and white keys. The black keys contain lowercase letters. The blue keys

contain the figures, marks of punctuation, and other characters. Some of the blue keys con-

tain two characters. The white keys contain the capital letters. Notice that the position of the lowercase letters and the capital letters is the same.

Most magazines contain an extra channel. This provides a second supply of lowercase "e" matrices. This letter is used more than any of the others.

Casting the Slug

After the line is set and justified, it is moved to the casting unit. This is done by pressing a lever at the right of the keyboard. The line of matrices is automatically moved to the casting unit. The line is locked against the mold.

Next to the mold is the lead pot. It is either electric or gas fired. The liquid metal is forced into the mold by a plunger.

After the line is cast, it is trimmed to size and automati-

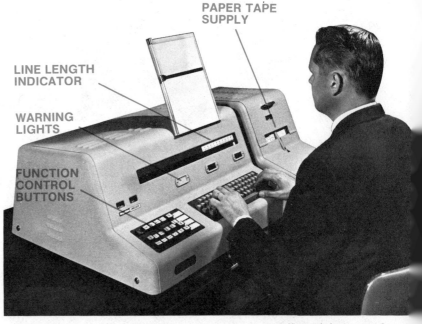

PAPER TAPE
SUPPLY

LINE LENGTH
INDICATOR

WARNING
LIGHTS

FUNCTION
CONTROL
BUTTONS

Mergenthaler Linotype Co.

8-17. *The Linoquick perforator produces perforated tape.*

cally ejected onto the galley. While this is happening, an elevator lifts the mats and spacebands off the mold. They are moved up and to the right, where the spacebands fall into the spaceband box. A second elevator (distributing elevator) lifts the mats to the top of the machine. Here they are placed on the distributor bar. As they move along this bar, they are dropped into their proper channels in the magazine.

TAPE-OPERATED LINECASTING MACHINES

Linecasting machines can be operated by a perforated tape. The tape allows the machine to assemble mats automatically. An operator is not needed to strike the keys on the keyboard.

The tape is prepared on a keyboard that punches holes in the tape. Fig. 8-17. The tape is then placed on tape-operating control equipment installed on a linecasting machine. Some linecasting machines are built especially for tape control. Fig. 8-11.

REVIEW QUESTIONS

1. What is a slug?
2. Name two hot-metal composition machines.
3. Each slug cast on a Linotype contains all the letters of one word. True or False?
4. Where are the slugs placed after being trimmed to proper thickness and height?
5. What happens to the Linotype slugs after they have been used for printing?
6. The Linotype is one type of linecasting machine. Name one other.
7. Linecasting machines can be operated by perforated tape. True or False?

Chapter 9

Preparing Copy for the Camera

Camera-ready copy is copy which is ready to be photographed. It contains image and nonimage areas. The base sheet (nonimage area) with mounted images can be copied photographically. Fig. 9-1. The assembly of image areas on a base sheet is called a *paste-up* or a *mechanical*. The image areas are made up of materials which absorb light; for example, black ink or black paper.

The finished camera-ready copy is photographed. The negative produced is used to make the offset printing plate. Chapter 14, "Offset Platemaking," discusses how various types of plates are made. A summary of how camera-ready copy is made into the plate is shown in Fig. 9-2.

MATERIALS USED IN COPY PREPARATION

Masking film is a clear or frosted polyester sheet which has a light-safe amber- or ruby-colored layer on one side. The polyester sheet is called the backing sheet. The color layer can be cut and peeled off the backing sheet. Masking film is used to make windows, drop-outs, color overlays, and large, solid image areas. (All are discussed later in the chapter.) Ordinary black paper can be used

for the same purpose, but the results will be of lesser quality.

Color base is a light-safe material with a pressure-sensitive, adhesive-back coating. It is used to make windows and image areas by sticking it directly to the base sheet.

Shading film is a preprinted sheet available in a wide variety of tones and patterns. It has a pressure-sensitive adhesive back and is adhered directly to artwork. See Chapter 5, "Graphic Design." It is also available in the form of tape, which is used to form borders.

Adhesives are used to hold image-producing copy to the paste-up base sheet. The com-

PASTE-UP BASE SHEET

PRESS SHEET

TRIM LINE

Assurance of High Quality Protects You
A distributor's reputation is built of two ingredients — dependable service and the quality of the tools and supplies he sells.

Power Tools

Local Sales Calls Help Avoid Emergencies
The regular and frequent local sales calls your distriutor makes can help prevent many of those production and maintenance emergencies from developing. Millions of dollars have been saved through the ability of distributors to anticipate many of their customers' needs. This has enabled them to have tools and other supplies on hand thus avoiding down-time and production stoppages.

Available Local Stock Cuts Delivery Time
Getting the correct tools and accessories where they're needed — when they're needed — is a specialty of your Distributor. The immediate availability of stocks at the local level cuts delivery time and enables you to carry smaller inventories. This releases capital and space for more profitable uses.

IMAGE AREAS

One Source For Many Products Simplifies Purchasing
Your Industrial Supply House stocks many products and supplies you use for plant maintenance as well as production. Using this one source can greatly simplify your purchasing system. Precious time will be conserved because this one source can supply ready information on a wide variety of the products and supplies your purchase.

FOLD LINE

9-1. A paste-up, or mechanical, has image areas, nonimage areas, and nonreproducible reference lines, such as fold and trim lines.

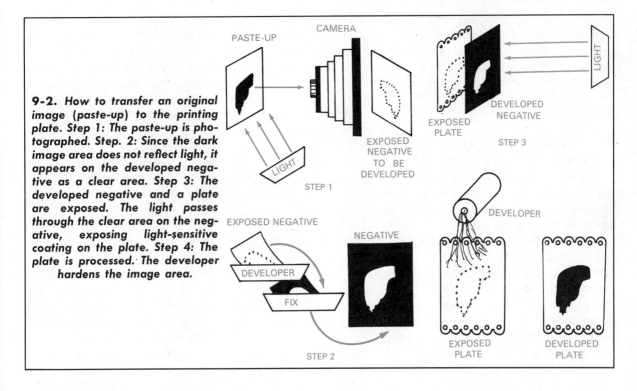

9-2. *How to transfer an original image (paste-up) to the printing plate. Step 1: The paste-up is photographed. Step. 2: Since the dark image area does not reflect light, it appears on the developed negative as a clear area. Step 3: The developed negative and a plate are exposed. The light passes through the clear area on the negative, exposing light-sensitive coating on the plate. Step 4: The plate is processed. The developer hardens the image area.*

mon types include a specially formulated wax, thinned rubber cement, and an aerosol spray adhesive. A waxer is a roll-coating device used to apply a thin layer of wax on the back of the image material. Fig. 9-3. A sheet with wax on both sides can be stuck to the back of the image material. It is then cut to the same size as the image material and stuck to the base sheet. Any excess image material can be trimmed away. Normally 1/4" of material is left around the image area.

A trimmer is used to trim paper materials. Fig. 9-4. It has a round, rotating cutter. Beneath the cutting edge is a line of light which shows through the paper and accurately locates the paper for cutting. Scissors and special knives may also be used for trimming.

Most paste-up work is performed on a *light table*. It has a frosted glass top with a strong light below.

Inks, opaques, and dyes are used to touch up image and non-image areas. Inks and dyes are used on the original images, and opaque is used on negatives.

Sheeting is used to prepare overlay sheets on photomechanicals. It is generally a clear or frosted acetate or mylar.

Base sheet material is used to form the base sheet for paste-ups. Any kind of white, hard, matte-surfaced cardboard or heavy paper can be used.

9-3. *A waxer applying wax to copy so that it will adhere to a base sheet. The cover is removed to show the waxing rollers.*

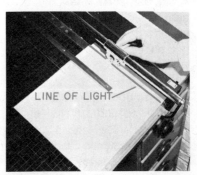

9-4. *A paper trimmer with a round cutter and a line of light to help align the paper.*

The hand tools used in paste-up work include those commonly used in drafting: T square, ruler, pens, protractor, triangles, dividers, and compasses. Other tools needed are a line gauge, scissors, knives, and rollers.

PREPARING ART FOR REPRODUCTION

There are many ways copy can be prepared for reproduction. Sometimes the artist makes the layout and produces part of the artwork. In this case the layout is marked indicating to the paste-up specialist, stripper, and platemaker what is wanted. Sometimes the artist prefers to prepare the paste-up. Regardless of who does the work, there are certain general considerations which are important:

1. The requirements of the customer must be clear and carefully recorded.

2. All data must be recorded—page, trim, and folding sizes; colors; and types of artwork to be used.

3. All line copy should be black images. The black must be intense and uniform to avoid tonal qualities.

4. Photographs must have the quality needed for the job. Avoid damaging them by accidental folding or bending. Keep free from finger marks. Do not use paper clips to hold them or write on the back. Any of these practices may damage the image-producing surface.

5. Keep all artwork clean. Carefully erase pencil marks. Paint out smudges which may photograph. Remove all excess adhesive. Cover all artwork with a tissue overlay to protect it while stored.

6. Store artwork flat.

7. Never paste up art or text material that is damaged. Repair or replace it before pasting it in place.

8. Spray a commercially made protective coating on proof copies of text material used in the paste-up. It will help keep the images from smearing. This is not necessary on text materials produced by photocomposition methods.

9. All marks and guidelines which are not to be reproduced should be made with a sharp, blue pencil.

10. Record the instructions to the stripper and platemaker outside the printing area of the paste-up.

11. Indicate the tint screen percentages and color on the overlay.

12. Samples of exact colors wanted should be included with the finished artwork.

13. Accuracy in placing the images is vital. Great care and attention must be given to the location and the squareness. Always line the images up with a T square. Never guess at alignment.

14. All pieces of art not pasted to a mechanical must have an identification mark on them which is keyed to the area for the art on the mechanical.

15. Be especially careful when locating register marks. The printing accuracy of the images depends entirely upon exact registration.

16. It is important to know how to impose the pages on the paste-up. See Chapter 20, "Imposition and Lockup."

17. The artist and paste-up specialist should have complete information about how the job is to be printed. They need to know such things as the composition and printing processes, cutting plan, and bindery operations. These influence how the artwork and paste-up will be made.

18. All the artwork and text material should be available before starting on the paste-up.

19. For efficient paste-up or art preparation the specialist should have a proper table with all the tools and materials needed within easy reach.

20. The people preparing the copy for reproduction should understand the total printing production process and what each member of the production staff can be expected to do. They should also know the processes the printing company can perform and the limits of their production equipment. There is no use preparing copy in such a manner that your company cannot produce it.

TYPES OF CAMERA-READY COPY

There are three major types of camera-ready copy: *line, continuous tone,* and *color.*

LINE COPY

Line copy is camera-ready copy made up of image lines and areas of a single density. There are no gradations of density. It is also called *high-contrast* copy because of the contrast between the density of the image area and the lack of density in the nonimage area.

Line copy to be printed entirely in one color is assembled in a paste-up on a single base sheet. Fig. 9-1. If line copy is to be used

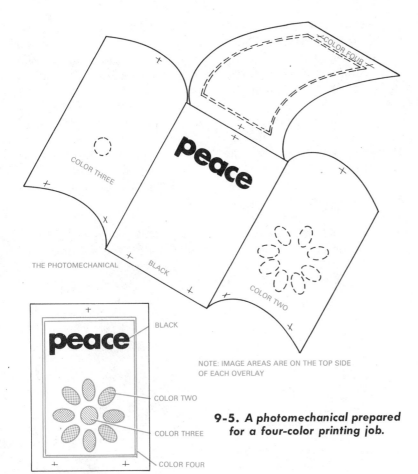

COLOR FOUR

peace

COLOR THREE

BLACK

COLOR TWO

THE PHOTOMECHANICAL

peace

BLACK

COLOR TWO

COLOR THREE

COLOR FOUR

THE PRINTED RESULT

NOTE: IMAGE AREAS ARE ON THE TOP SIDE
OF EACH OVERLAY

9-5. *A photomechanical prepared for a four-color printing job.*

Elastic Stop Nut Corp. of America

9-6A. *Airbrush shading. Other examples of continuous tone copy are shown in Figs. 9-6B and 9-6C.*

PREPARATION OF LINE COPY FOR PASTE-UP

Line copy images should be made from materials which reflect little light. They are assembled on a base sheet which does reflect light. One common way to prepare these images is to draw them with black ink on a white matte-finished paper. Red is another color which, because of low reflection of light, is satisfactory for line copy image preparation. In general, black or red images of any material will produce satisfactory copy.

paintings. Examples can be found in Chapter 18, "Color Separation."

for multiple-color work, a photomechanical is made up of a base sheet and a separate overlay sheet for each color. Each sheet contains the line copy for a different color. Fig. 9-5.

CONTINUOUS TONE COPY

Continuous tone copy contains gradations or variations in density within the image area. There are two types of continuous tone copy: one color and multiple color. Examples of one-color continuous tone copy are shown in Fig. 9-6. Examples of multiple-color continuous tone copy are color photographs and oil

Champion Home Builders Co.

9-6B. *Architectural rendering.*

9-6C. *Original photograph.*

graphically, which in turn reduces any small imperfections in the copy. Fig. 9-7.

Typical sources of line copy include transfer letters and other preprinted symbols with adhesive on the back, text matter that has been set, screened halftone positives, ink line drawings, and preprinted art. Fig. 9-8.

REVERSE PRINTS

Frequently an image in line copy is shown in reverse. The image is the color of the paper and the surrounding area the color of the ink. Fig. 9-9. To make

a reverse, the line copy is prepared in the normal way. Then a negative is made of this, and a film positive is made by contact printing. On the film positive the image to be in reverse appears black, and the surrounding area is clear. This is in reverse of the original negative. Fig. 9-9. The reverse negative is stripped into the flat and used to make the plate.

SURPRINTS

A surprint is a line image of the same color as a halftone image that is superimposed on

While line copy (artwork) can be prepared the actual size needed for printing, better results are obtained if it is drawn larger. Line copy is usually drawn 1 1/2 to 2 times larger than needed for printing. This permits the image to be reduced photo-

CAT

50% REDUCTION

CAT

ACTUAL SIZE

CAT

100% ENLARGEMENT

9-7. *Reductions lessen copy imperfections, while enlargements magnify them.*

ABCDabcdefg
Smart New
ABCabcdefghij
Style Heading

ADHESIVE AND TRANSFER LETTERS ARE AVAILBLE IN MANY SIZES AND STYLES

12½" 2 bevel rigid nickeled steel drawing scales. These steel scales are machine-divided for accuracy—sharp engraved black graduations. Registered against matte finish surface—scales are 1½" wide x 3/32nds thick with polished beveled edges for close work. Each scale is equipped with knurled finger-grip knob for easy handling. Hanging hole at one end. Recommended for all phases of professional drawing where exact measurement is required. Ideal for the graphic arts where sharp bladed instruments are used. A durable steel scale designed for years of continued service—recommended for every drafting room.

TEXT COMPOSED BY HOT TYPE, STRIKE-ON OR PHOTOCOMPOSITION

ADHESIVE SYMBOLS

SCREENED HALFTONE POSITIVE

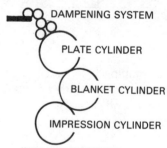

INK LINE DRAWINGS

PREPRINTED ART

9-8. *Typical line copy.*

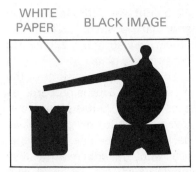

WHITE PAPER — BLACK IMAGE

THE ORIGINAL LINE COPY

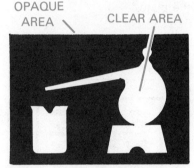

OPAQUE AREA — CLEAR AREA

THE NEGATIVE

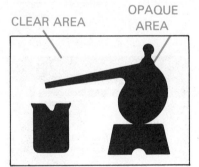

CLEAR AREA — OPAQUE AREA

THE CONTACT PRINTED FILM POSITIVE

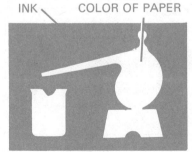

INK — COLOR OF PAPER

THE FINISHED PRINTED REVERSE

9-9. *How to produce a printed reverse.*

the halftone image. It is sometimes called an overprint.

To make a surprint, Fig. 9-10:

1. Reduce the continuous tone image to the actual size for reproduction.

2. Prepare an overlay containing the line copy to form the surprint. Register it over the continuous tone copy.

3. Photograph the continuous tone image through a halftone screen and the line copy without a screen. This produces two negatives.

4. Make film positives of each. This will produce a solid line image with a clear background.

5. Put the two film positives together in proper registration. Photograph together to produce a halftone negative with clear line copy. When this is used to make a plate, the line copy will reproduce solid, and the halftone's dots will reproduce the continuous tone image.

DROP-OUTS

A drop-out is that part of a halftone image that has been removed by masking.

To make a drop-out, Fig. 9-11:

1. Reduce the continuous tone image to the actual size for reproduction.

2. Prepare an overlay containing the line copy to form the drop-out. Register it over the continuous tone copy.

3. Photograph the continuous tone copy through a halftone screen and the line copy without a screen. This produces two negatives.

4. Make a film positive of the line copy, which produces a solid line image with a clear background.

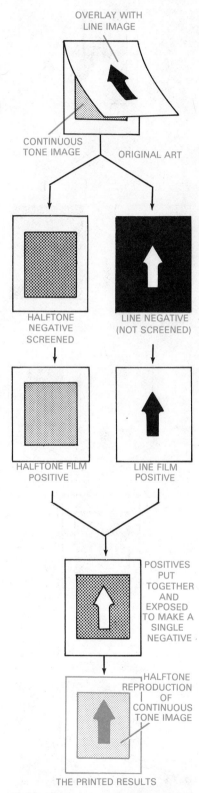

OVERLAY WITH LINE IMAGE

CONTINUOUS TONE IMAGE — ORIGINAL ART

HALFTONE NEGATIVE SCREENED

LINE NEGATIVE (NOT SCREENED)

HALFTONE FILM POSITIVE

LINE FILM POSITIVE

POSITIVES PUT TOGETHER AND EXPOSED TO MAKE A SINGLE NEGATIVE

HALFTONE REPRODUCTION OF CONTINUOUS TONE IMAGE

THE PRINTED RESULTS

9-10. *How to produce a surprint.*

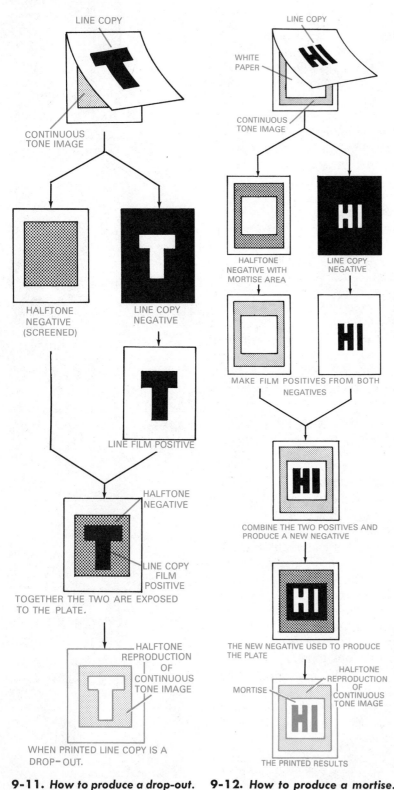

LINE COPY

CONTINUOUS TONE IMAGE

HALFTONE NEGATIVE (SCREENED)

LINE COPY NEGATIVE

LINE FILM POSITIVE

HALFTONE NEGATIVE

LINE COPY FILM POSITIVE

TOGETHER THE TWO ARE EXPOSED TO THE PLATE.

HALFTONE REPRODUCTION OF CONTINUOUS TONE IMAGE

WHEN PRINTED LINE COPY IS A DROP-OUT.

9-11. *How to produce a drop-out.*

LINE COPY

WHITE PAPER

CONTINUOUS TONE IMAGE

HALFTONE NEGATIVE WITH MORTISE AREA

LINE COPY NEGATIVE

MAKE FILM POSITIVES FROM BOTH NEGATIVES

COMBINE THE TWO POSITIVES AND PRODUCE A NEW NEGATIVE

THE NEW NEGATIVE USED TO PRODUCE THE PLATE

MORTISE

HALFTONE REPRODUCTION OF CONTINUOUS TONE IMAGE

THE PRINTED RESULTS

9-12. *How to produce a mortise.*

5. Put the halftone negative and film positive together in proper registration. Expose to the printing plate.

This example assumes the drop-out line copy is prepared as black artwork. If it is prepared in reverse, a white image on a black background, the line copy negative would produce a positive image which can be used with the halftone negative to make the plate.

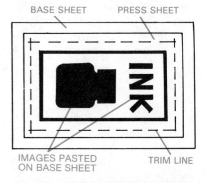

BASE SHEET   PRESS SHEET

IMAGES PASTED ON BASE SHEET

TRIM LINE

THE PASTE-UP

THE NEGATIVE

THE PRINTED RESULTS

9-13. *How to produce a one-color job.*

MORTISES

A mortise is an area of a continuous tone copy which has been left blank. This is done so that other copy can be printed in the blank area.

To make a mortise, Fig. 9-12:

1. Reduce the continuous tone image to the actual size for reproduction.

2. Prepare an overlay with the line copy to be printed in the mortise area. Register it over the continuous tone copy.

3. Cut a piece of white paper or masking film the shape and size desired for the mortise. Place it on the continuous tone copy.

4. Photograph the continuous tone copy through a halftone screen and the line copy without a screen.

5. Make film positives of both negatives.

6. Place the two film positives together in proper registration and make a negative.

7. Expose the plate with this negative.

MAKING A PASTE-UP OF LINE COPY FOR ONE-COLOR REPRODUCTION

A paste-up for single-color line copy reproduction is made on a single base sheet. The finished paste-up is photographed to produce a negative which is used to make a plate. Fig. 9-13.

To make a one-color paste-up:

1. Tape the white base sheet at each corner on the light table. Square it with the edge with a T square. The size of the base sheet is determined by the job.

2. Lay out the reference lines

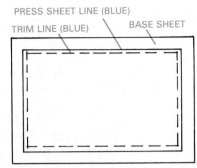

1 TAPE BASE SHEET TO THE LIGHT TABLE. LAY OUT THE REFERENCE LINES IN LIGHT BLUE PENCIL.

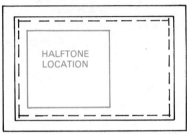

2 LOCATE POSITION OF HALFTONES AND TINT SCREENS WITH THIS RED LINE.

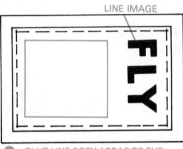

3 GLUE LINE COPY AREAS TO THE BASE SHEET.

4 TAPE THE PROTECTIVE OVERLAY SHEET OVER THE PASTE-UP.

9-14. How to make a one-color paste-up.

using a light blue pencil. Fig. 9-14. The reference lines needed are the fold, press sheet, trim, and image area lines. If the pages are to be perforated, a reference line is needed to show where the perforation will be.

Fold lines, drawn as long dashes, show where the job has to fold. The *press sheet lines* are drawn as solid lines and give the size of the press sheet upon which the job will be printed. The *trim lines* show where the press sheet will be cut after printing. They are drawn as short, dashed lines. The *image reference lines* are placed in the image area to help locate the images when they are pasted on the base sheet. Fig. 9-14.

3. Locate the position of halftones, tint screen areas, and reverses with a thin red or black line. The stripper uses these lines as a guide when stripping in the negatives for these items. Fig. 9-14.

4. Place rules and borders on the base sheet. They are usually made from self-adhering rolls of tape or inked. Fig. 9-15.

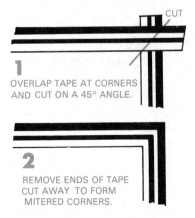

1 OVERLAP TAPE AT CORNERS AND CUT ON A 45° ANGLE.

2 REMOVE ENDS OF TAPE CUT AWAY TO FORM MITERED CORNERS.

9-15. How to miter borders made from self-adhering border tape.

5. Place all line copy images in their proper location on the base sheet. Use the T square to keep them straight. They are held in place by coating their backs with an adhesive. As mentioned earlier, the most common used adhesives are specially formulated wax, thinned rubber cement, or an aerosol spray adhesive.

6. Burnish or roll down all image-producing materials so that they are flat on the base sheet. Cover the surface with a sheet of paper when burnishing to prevent damage to the images.

7. Check the completed paste-up for correctness and accuracy. Touch up any defects or damage to the image areas, using an appropriate material like black India ink.

8. Tape a protective tissue overlay to the finished paste-up. Fig. 9-14. If the paste-up will be handled a great deal, a second, heavier cover sheet will help protect it.

9. Write any instructions to the camera operator, such as sizing the negative. These are written on the base sheet with blue pencil.

PREPARATION OF CONTINUOUS TONE COPY FOR REPRODUCTION

Continuous tone copy is made ready for reproduction by converting it to a *halftone*. A halftone is made by photographing the image through a halftone screen. Read Chapter 11, "Halftone Photography," for technical details. The screen reduces the continuous tones to a dot formation on a negative.

9-16A. *Halftone using a 65-line screen.*

The heavy tones of the image print as large dots, while the light tones print as smaller dots. This variation in dot size produces tonal values. Fig. 9-16. The negative is used to produce the dot formation on the printing plate.

HALFTONE SCREENS

Halftone screens are classified by the number of dots that appear per linear inch. A screen in the range of 55, 65, or 85 lines produces a coarse halftone. Screens numbering 100, 110, and 120 are used for super-calendered papers and 133- and 155-line screens are used for printing high quality work on coated papers. Study Chapter 11, "Halftone Photography," for complete details.

CROPPING COPY

The artist designing the job will indicate by crop marks what part of the continuous tone image to use on the printed job. Fig. 9-17. The proportions of the cropped area should be in the same width and height ratio as the area in which it will be printed.

ENLARGEMENTS AND REDUCTIONS

Any continuous tone image can be enlarged or reduced proportionally to fit the area allowed for it. This process is called sizing or scaling. If the image has been screened, it is not possible to use it for additional enlargements or reductions. This action distorts the tonal gradation of the halftone dot pattern. It is

9-16B. *Halftone using a 150-line screen.*

9-16C. *An enlargement of part of the above continuous tone image.*

9-17. *Crop marks are used to indicate which part of a photograph the designer wants to use.*

9-18. *How to figure the percentage of enlargement or reduction.*

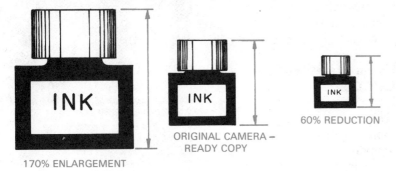

170% ENLARGEMENT

ORIGINAL CAMERA –
READY COPY

60% REDUCTION

ENLARGEMENT CALCULATIONS

$$\frac{\text{LENGTH OF ENLARGED SIDE}}{\text{LENGTH OF SAME SIDE ON ORIGINAL}} = \frac{17}{10} = 170\% \text{ OF ORIGINAL SIZE}$$

REDUCTIONS CALCULATIONS

$$\frac{\text{LENGTH OF REDUCED SIDE}}{\text{LENGTH OF SAME SIDE IN ORIGINAL}} = \frac{6}{10} = 60\% \text{ OF ORIGINAL SIZE}$$

necessary to use the original image for enlargements and reductions.

SIZING

Sizing determines the percentage of enlargement or reduction required to fit the image to the space available. Sizing is expressed as a numerical percentage and written on a non-image area of the original copy. Fig. 9-18. Artwork sized for 100 percent will be reproduced the same size as the original. Seventy-five percent means a reduction to 75 percent of the original size. One hundred fifty percent means an enlargement that will be 50 percent bigger than the original.

The percentage is based on the relationship between the length of the sides of the original copy to the length of those same sides on the reproduction. The first step in sizing is to know the length of the sides on the original image and the length of one or both sides wanted on the reproduction. If crop marks are indicated, the material must be sized according to the area within the crop marks, not by the entire original area.

The percentage of enlargement or reduction can be found by reading it directly from a proportional scale or by mathematical calculations. To calculate the percentage, divide the desired reproduction size by the size of the original copy. These calculations are shown in Fig. 9-18. The length of the sides can be stated in inches, millimetres, or picas.

Such calculations can be figured rapidly by using a proportional scale. Figs. 9-19 and 9-20. The inner circle is for the original

9-19. A proportional scale shows a percentage of reduction. The size of reproduction wanted is 3 1/4", to be reduced from a 5" original. The percentage of reduction is 65 percent.

size of the copy. The outer circle is for the size of the reproduction. To find the percentage, line up the original size of one side

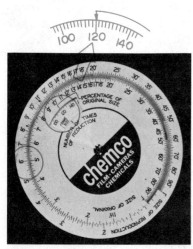

9-20. A proportional scale shows the percentage of enlargement. The size of the enlargement wanted is 6", to be enlarged from a 5" original. The percentage of enlargement is 120 percent.

with the desired reproduction size of the same side. The percentage can be read in the window. It is designed for copy measured in inches.

It is often necessary to enlarge or reduce original copy to fit a predetermined area on a job. This can be found by calculation or the use of a proportional scale. The width and depth of rectangular areas enlarge or reduce in direct proportion to each other. If the original copy was 3" wide and 6" deep, and the 3" width had to reduce to 2", how deep is the reduced copy? The following statement of proportion is used.

$$\frac{\text{Original width}}{\text{Desired width}} = \frac{\text{Original depth}}{\text{Desired depth}}$$
$$\frac{3''}{2''} = \frac{6''}{\text{depth}}$$
$$3 \times \text{Depth} = 12$$
$$\text{Depth} = 4''$$

The proportional scale, Fig. 9-19, can also be used to find these sizes. Set the original width on the inner circle opposite the desired width on the outer circle. Without moving the scale, find the original depth on the inner circle. Directly opposite it on the outer circle is the desired depth.

USING HALFTONES AS LINE COPY

Occasionally the original continuous tone image is no longer available when it is necessary to reproduce it again. It is possible to photograph the printed halftone as *line copy*. In this case, it is photographed dot for dot—that is, 100 percent—without a screen, and the negative produced is a halftone negative.

It is possible to paste up halftone prints with the line copy on

Dynamic Graphics, Inc.
9-21. The background of this line drawing was covered with a screen tint.

the base sheet. The quality of this work, while usually acceptable, is not as satisfactory as that made by screening the original image.

9-22. This photograph was reproduced using a screen tint to provide a background color.

U.S. ELECTRIC CO.
FIELD, OHIO

TINT

PARTS LIST

PART NAME	QUANTITY

9-23. *A screen tint was used to give emphasis to the title of this form.*

SCREEN TINTS

A screen tint is mechanical shading of a single tone applied to the artwork. It produces an area with a uniform pattern of small dots. It is used to provide emphasis to part of a layout or to provide a background. The tint background may be printed in a color. Figs. 9-21 through 9-23.

Screen tints are based on the percentage values of gray. Fig. 9-24. White is 0 percent and black is 100 percent. In Fig. 9-24 the tint values are shown across the top. The line screen size is shown on the left.

Screens that are coarser, as 65 or 85 lines, are generally used in letterpress newspaper printing. Commercial offset work uses 110- through 133-line screens. Better quality work printed on smooth, coated paper would use a 150-line screen.

Screen tints can be applied to the original art or can be stripped in the flat and produced by the platemaker.

To produce screen tints during paste-up, shading film with an adhesive back is used. It is cut to size, placed over the art, and

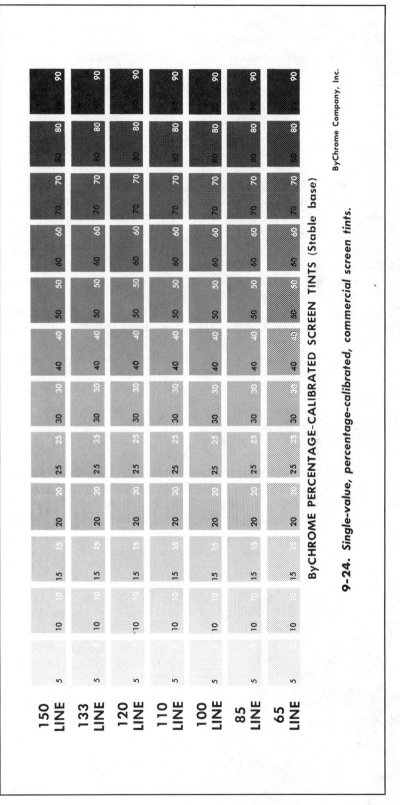

ByChrome Company, Inc.

ByCHROME PERCENTAGE-CALIBRATED SCREEN TINTS (Stable base)

9-24. *Single-value, percentage-calibrated, commercial screen tints.*

pressed in place. The film is cut away from the areas which should not be screened. Fig. 9-21. When putting the shading film on the artwork, be certain the surface is free from dirt or pencil marks. Any imperfections will photograph. If the art is to be reduced, use a percentage film which will permit the reduction without filling in between the dots. Companies selling these materials have charts which show the screens at various reductions. Do not attempt to produce a special effect by applying one film on top of another. A moiré pattern will occur.

If the screen tint is to be produced by the platemaker, the artist will note on the art the percent and line screen desired. The platemaker places a commercial screen tint sheet between the negative of the art and the offset plate during the exposure. Fig. 9-24.

Another procedure is to expose the plate to a flat containing the screened areas, and then make a second exposure of the art negative. The work shown in Fig. 9-23 was done in this manner. The

screened band was stripped on a flat and exposed. Then, the negative of the rest of the copy was exposed to the plate.

Screen tints can also be used to subdue halftones. Fig. 9-25. This is helpful when overprinting on a halftone. Overprinting means printing on top of a previous print.

Another technique for preparing copy for screen tints is to use masking film. Masking film has a thin, clear, polyester base covered with a light-resisting layer that is adhesive-backed. To use masking film, Fig. 9-26:

1. Apply registration marks to the art.

2. Cut a piece of masking film, and tape it, dull side up, over the art as overlay.

3. Using a sharp knife, cut through the color layer, outlining the area to be tinted. Do not cut through the polyester base sheet.

4. With the tip of the knife blade or a piece of tape, lift up a corner and peel away the unwanted color layer from its base. The color will remain over the areas to be tinted.

5. Make a negative of the overlay. To do this, place a sheet of white paper under it to block out the artwork. Do not cover the registration marks. This will produce a negative with the tint areas clear. It can be used to produce a plate to print in 100 percent color or any tint desired.

6. If several colors are being printed, make a separate overlay for each.

SILHOUETTE DROP-OUTS

A silhouette drop-out is a technique used to remove the background of artwork. The following steps explain how to do this.

1. Cover the artwork with a masking film overlay. Tape the overlay on one edge, forming a "hinge" so that the artwork can be folded back.

2. Using a sharp knife, cut through the colored layer of the masking film, following the outline of the area to be silhouetted.

3. Remove the emulsion from the background.

4. Slip a piece of white paper between the overlay and the artwork, and make the first camera exposure.

5. Being careful to not move the artwork, remove the white paper, fold away the overlay, and make a second camera exposure. This produces a negative upon which the background has been removed and image remains.

OUTLINING HALFTONE NEGATIVES

Outlining can be used to remove the background of halftone negatives. The following steps, shown in Fig. 9-27, explain one way to do this. (NOTE: In the

9-25B. *Photograph screened with 150-line, 20% screen so that the overprinting would be more prominent.*

9-25A. *Original photograph.*

how to lay-in color or tints

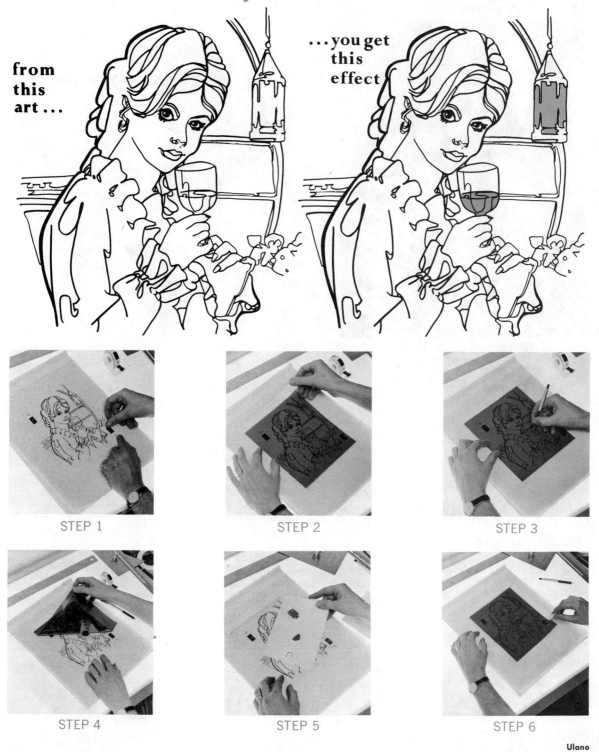

from this art ...

...you get this effect

STEP 1

STEP 2

STEP 3

STEP 4

STEP 5

STEP 6

Ulano

9-26. *How to use masking film to prepare a part of an illustration for a screen tint.*

how to outline halftone negatives accurately

from this photo...

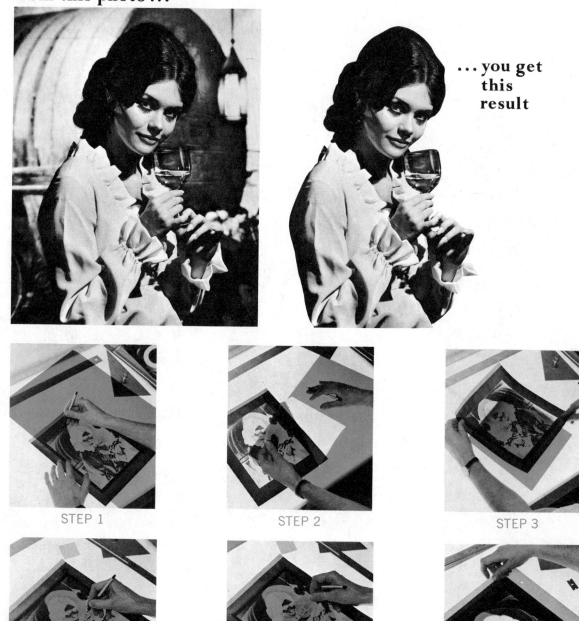

...you get this result

STEP 1

STEP 2

STEP 3

STEP 4

STEP 5

STEP 6

Ulano

9-27. How to use masking film to produce an outline halftone.

illustrations, the masking film is printed in blue. In real life it is red or amber.)

1. Place the negative of the artwork, emulsion side down, on a light table. Lay a sheet of masking film, dull side up, on top of the negative. Using a sharp knife, cut the color layer of the masking film at least one inch wider than the area to be outlined.

2. With tip of blade, lift up a corner and carefully remove the color layer from its base. Smooth it out, adhesive side up.

3. Holding the negative emulsion side up over the color layer, carefully place the negative on the light table in such a way that all the artwork is "inside" the color layer. Smooth out to insure good adhesion of the color material to the negative.

4. With the color layer facing you, outline the exact area to be included in the final picture. Be careful not to cut through the negative.

5. With tip of blade, lift up a corner of the color layer you have just cut and peel away.

6. Insert negative in position in plate exposing flat.

PREPARING CAMERA-READY COPY FOR A JOB HAVING BOTH LINE COPY AND CONTINUOUS TONE COPY

There are three commonly used ways to prepare camera-ready copy when both line copy and continuous tone copy are in one job. These are the one-exposure method using windows, the two-exposure method, and the screened print method.

ONE-EXPOSURE METHOD USING WINDOWS

The line copy paste-up is prepared as explained earlier in this chapter. Then the halftone negative is stripped to the line work negative in a clear area prepared for it. This area is called a *window*. To prepare a halftone window, follow these steps, Fig. 9-28:

1. Position the line art under a sheet of masking film. The masking film should be dull side up. With a sharp knife, carefully outline an area slightly larger than the halftone as it will finally print. Peel the color layer and apply it to the line art paste-up.

2. Accurately outline the exact area that is to be the halftone window.

3. Burnish the center area of the color film with your fingertip to assure good adhesion to the art. Peel off the excess film from the just-cut window.

4. Expose and develop the line negative. Opaque any imperfections. It may be necessary to bleach or etch away pepper spots in the window that were caused by dust or incorrect development.

5. Position the halftone negative in the window of the line negative. Place trim marks on the halftone negative. *Do not* trim the halftone negative on top of the line negative. Cutting through the halftone would scratch the emulsion of the film underneath.

6. Tape the trimmed negative in position on the line negative. Both should be emulsion side up.

Instead of using masking film, you could cut a piece of black paper the exact size of the window and glue it on the paste-up. However, the paper tends to produce fuzzy edges because of its thickness and is not used on quality jobs.

TWO-EXPOSURE METHOD

The line copy paste-up is prepared, and the continuous tone image is converted to a halftone negative. Fig. 9-29. The halftone negative is exposed to the plate alone, and the line copy negative is exposed to the plate as a second, separate exposure.

SCREENED PRINT METHOD

The line copy paste-up is prepared, and the continuous tone image is converted into a halftone screened print. This is a positive reproduction of the continuous tone image that has been converted to halftone dots. This screened positive image is pasted onto the line copy paste-up. Fig. 9-30. Together they are photographed, and a single negative is produced. This negative is exposed to the plate.

MAKING PHOTOMECHANICALS

A photomechanical is made when a job has more than one color. The base sheet contains the images to be printed black. Each additional color requires an overlay sheet that is attached to the base sheet.

The artist indicates the colors and the percent of screen tint on the layout sheet. Fig. 9-31 (Page 180). The paste-up staff studies the artist's layout to determine the requirements for the photomechanical. The mechanical is constructed to produce the job exactly as it was shown on the layout.

how to prepare halftone windows on art.

from this art ...

... you get this effect

STEP 1

STEP 2

STEP 3

STEP 4

STEP 5

STEP 6

Ulano

9-28. *The one-exposure method of preparing camera-ready copy when the job has both line copy and continuous tone copy.*

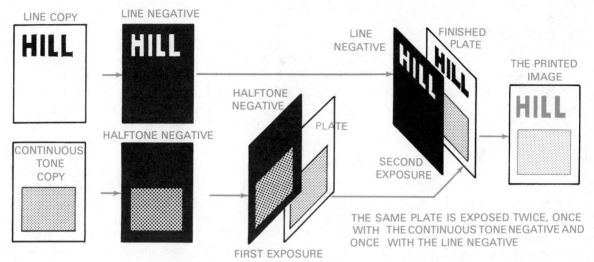

9-29. *The two-exposure method of preparing camera-ready copy when the job has both line copy and continuous tone copy.*

The art and text material for the base sheet are pasted in place. This is the same as preparing a one-color paste-up. Fig. 9-32. Sometimes this is done by the artist. Registration marks are attached. Notice on the artist's layout the title, "Flowers," is to be reproduced in black using an 80 percent screen. The paste-up staff can produce these letters from 80 percent screened shading film, or the letters can be solid black and the camera operator can photograph them through an 80 percent screen. This latter process is the one chosen for this example.

Since this is a two-color job, one overlay sheet must be made for the second color. The overlay sheet is made from a transparent material. Usually this is a clear mylar or acetate sheet. If the overlay will contain large solid image areas, it can be of masking film.

Tape one edge of the overlay sheet to the base sheet to form a hinge. Fig. 9-33. Smooth it over the base sheet, and secure each corner with a small piece of tape.

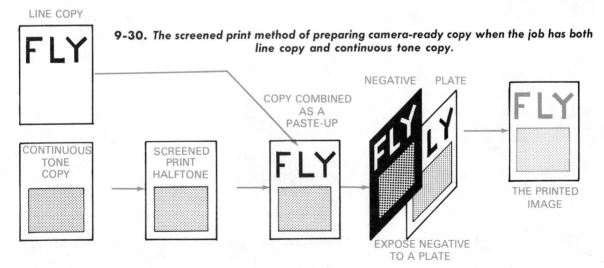

9-30. *The screened print method of preparing camera-ready copy when the job has both line copy and continuous tone copy.*

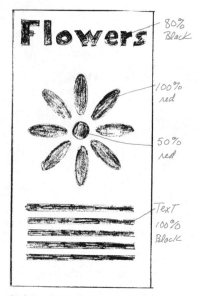

9-31. *The artist indicates the colors and the percent of screen tint on the layout.*

tape or wax. One advantage to film paste-up is that light can pass through all areas of the film except the image areas. This often eliminates the need for further camera work and provides for considerable latitude in platemaking, as explained later in the text.

PUBLICATION PASTE-UP

Publication paste-up is normally made on preprinted page base sheets or on thin paper or clear plastic page base sheets placed over a backlighted master grid. Fig. 9-34. Publication paste-up refers to newspaper paste-up. Advertisements which are less than full-page size are normally constructed on separate ad base sheets. These separate sheets are often precut to full-page depth for each column width. When an ad is to be less than full-page depth, the ad base sheet is cut to the appropriate depth size before it is constructed. Fig. 9-35. Paste-ups for ads are normally constructed as a separate operation. After construction, the ad base sheet is waxed and attached to the page

Attach registration marks directly over those on the base. The overlay sheet is now ready to receive the image areas that are to be printed in color. They can be pasted on or drawn directly on the overlay sheet.

If the job had a third color, a third overlay sheet would be attached from a different edge. Remember that each separate color requires a separate overlay sheet.

Each overlay sheet on the photomechanical is photographed separately. The individual negatives are used to make a plate for each color to be printed.

FILM PASTE-UP

Pasting up with film is similar to pasting up with paper. The main difference is that all construction materials are film. They are assembled with cellophane

BASE SHEET PASTE-UP   OVERLAY PASTE-UP

9-32. *The pasted-up base sheet and the overlay for a second color for the layout shown in Fig. 9-31.*

9-33. *The steps to complete the photomechanical.*

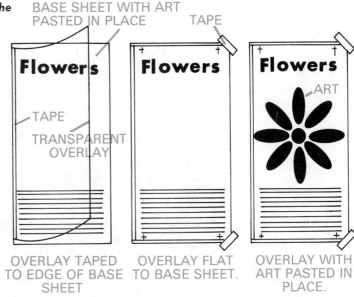

BASE SHEET WITH ART PASTED IN PLACE

TAPE

Flowers

TAPE

TRANSPARENT OVERLAY

OVERLAY TAPED TO EDGE OF BASE SHEET

Flowers

OVERLAY FLAT TO BASE SHEET.

Flowers

ART

OVERLAY WITH ART PASTED IN PLACE.

base sheet. This permits ads to be rearranged on a page or "picked up" from issue to issue.

To paste up a typical, single-color newspaper page using a preprinted base sheet and separate ad sheets:

1. Attach the page base sheet squarely to the paste-up table.

2. Using a light blue pencil, mark the areas of the page base sheet to be used for ads. Use an X or similar symbol to identify the areas as specified by the page dummy. Fig. 9-34.

3. Locate the running heads and folios. Fig. 9-36. Running heads are the words at the top of a newspaper giving the date and the name of the paper. A folio is a page number. Odd-numbered folios are normally on the right in publication work. Running heads are sometimes printed in black ink directly on the page base sheet.

4. Place the ads into their designated locations.

5. Using the page dummy layout as a guide, locate the heads, illustrations, underlines, features, and straight matter (text) in their approximate position on the base sheet. Fig. 9-37. Screened prints are used to reproduce artwork. This is a common practice in many modern newspaper plants.

6. Align all copy for final position, using the preprinted reference lines on the base sheet as alignment guides. Illustrations and straight matter are often cut

down, shortened, or moved to get all elements to fit into their desired position.

7. Burnish all image elements so that they adhere tightly to the page base sheet. Corrections are made prior to burnishing.

8. Make multiple-color overlays if the job is in two or more colors.

9. Cover the base sheet with a protective tissue and add any instructions necessary for those who will process the job following paste-up. A completed page paste-up is shown in Fig. 9-38.

REVISING A PASTE-UP

When the wax used on paste-ups is slightly warmed, the paste-up can be revised or corrected with comparative ease. The warming action converts the wax to its original state so that all image-producing materials may be removed or shifted as neces-

sary. A metal plate placed over a hot plate can be used to warm the wax on the paste-up. The

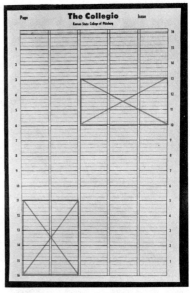

9-34. *A preprinted page base sheet for publication paste-up.*

9-35. An advertisement pasted up on a separate ad base sheet. This base sheet is then pasted on the full-page base sheet. Notice that some of the copy was left loose on the end to show how the copy is produced and pasted in place.

9-36. Folios and running head are glued in place.

9-37. Locate and glue the copy to the base sheet.

paste-up is simply placed on the warm plate and covered with a sheet of cardboard.

If the burnishing pressure used to make the original paste-up was not too firm, the image-producing materials may be removed or shifted without the need for heating. Simply pick up the corner of the material and peel it away from the base sheet.

CORRECTING A PASTE-UP

Corrections or alterations can be made by cutting the correction directly into the incorrect portion of the image material or by pasting the correction directly

9-38. *A complete page paste-up for a newspaper.*

over the incorrrect portion. The cut-in method is preferred since it has less chance of producing a shadow. Fig. 9-39. The steps to cut-in corrections are:

1. Outline the incorrect area with a blue, nonreproducible pencil.

2. Wax the correction, and adhere it exactly over the incorrect area.

3. Cut through both the correction and the incorrect materials. Do not cut through the base sheet.

4. Remove both images from the base sheet. Separate the correction.

5. Fit the correction in the opening left on the base sheet and press into place.

9-39. *How to cut-in a correction on a paste-up.*

The Graphic Arts field offers career
opportunities fr young people wh are willing
to master the technology of the field.

INCORRECT AREA MARKED

The Graphic Arts field offers career
opportunities for young people who are willing
to master the technology of the field.

CORRECTION PLACED OVER THE
INCORRECT LINE. CUT THROUGH
BOTH ON THE COLORED LINE.

The Graphic Arts field offers career

to master the technology of the field.

REMOVE BOTH LINES

The Graphic Arts field offers career
opportunities for young people who are willing
to master the technology of the field.

PUT CORRECTION IN PLACE

REVIEW QUESTIONS

1. Camera-ready copy contains only those elements which will form an image on film. True or False?
2. What is another name for a mechanical?
3. Name the three major types of camera-ready copy.
4. Name the term that matches this definition: camera-ready copy made up of image lines and areas of a single density.
5. Name the term that matches this definition: copy that contains gradations or variations in density within the image area.
6. Why is it a good idea to photographically reduce line copy?
7. What is another name for an overprint?
8. Why are mortises sometimes used in continuous tone copy?
9. Continuous tone copy is converted to a halftone for reproduction. How is a halftone made?
10. An illustration is 8″ wide and 10″ deep. If it is reduced to a width of 6″, how deep will the illustration be?
11. A 2″ × 3″ halftone is to be photographed as line copy. At what percentage should it be photographed?
12. When a job is to be printed in more than one color, a separate overlay is needed for each color. True or False?
13. If a job is to be printed in more than one color, a separate plate must be made for each color. True or False?
14. What is a folio?
15. Once a paste-up is made, it cannot be corrected. True or False?

Chapter 10

Line Photography

WHAT IS GRAPHIC ARTS PHOTOGRAPHY?

Graphic arts photography is the photomechanical method of converting camera copy to produce images suitable for reproduction by printing processes. This method produces a photographic rendering that meets the needs of ink, paper, and press in order to produce a print. It is an intermediate step between copy and press plate that is basic to modern printing today.

LINE PHOTOGRAPHY

Offset and relief presses print by attaching ink to paper. These presses are not capable of printing light and dark areas by varying the amount of black ink. They cannot print the tones from black, through gray, to white. The black ink prints black where applied. Line photography, like black ink on a press, has no intermediate tones. The image of line copy is produced by contrast with the background. These images may be drawn, typed, printed, or formed by any solid, dense material.

The film used for line photography has an emulsion (coating) made of light-sensitive silver salts. The emulsion is on a base sheet of paper or acetate. The emulsion side of the film is dull; the coating can be scratched off.

The base side is glossy. Film emulsion is discussed in more detail later in this chapter. Film is supplied 0.003″ to 0.008″ in thickness. Line film is a high-contrast film. It produces a negative that is clear in the image areas and dense black in the nonimage areas. The film does not produce good intermediate tones or continuous tones such as the film used in making snapshots.

Graphic arts films are produced to be sensitive to different colors of light. These are: regular or colorblind film, orthochromatic, and panchromatic films. *Regular film* is sensitive only to ultraviolet, violet, and blue light. *Orthochromatic films* are sensitive to yellow light but not to orange, green, and red light. The *panchromatic films* are sensitive to all kinds of visible light.

The emulsions of high-contrast films are made with a fine grained silver. Such films reproduce very thin lines accurately. This ability is called the film's resolving power. All these films have an *antihalation backing.* Halation refers to an undesirable reflection or spreading of light from the negative, causing a halo effect. Antihalation coating on the back of film stops light from reflecting back through the film base.

GRAPHIC ARTS (PROCESS) CAMERAS

Most of the cameras for graphic arts photography are designed for darkroom operation. Fig. 10-1. The rear of the cam-

10-1. A 24″ process camera. These cameras are used in photomechanical departments of printing companies. They are used to photograph copy prepared to be printed in such things as newspapers, brochures, and pamphlets.

Brown Manufacturing Co.

era—the part holding the film—opens inside the darkroom. The rest of the camera is outside the darkroom, and is opened in room light.

The parts of the camera shown in Fig. 10-2 are identified by numbers. The same numbers are used here to explain the function of the various parts.

1. The rear case separates the camera back, in the darkroom, from the camera front.

2. A hinged, light-tight door.

3. The vacuum film holder is perforated for air suction to hold the film flat.

4. The vacuum hose supplies suction to the film holder.

5. This pump and motor are similar to a vacuum cleaner.

6. The base or foot of the camera frame.

7. The track allows the carriage of the front case and the copy carriage to move or travel on the track.

8. This carriage travels on the camera track.

9. Adjustable lamp arms hold the camera lights in proper position.

10. The front base of the camera frame.

11. A latch to hold the copyboard upright.

12. A latch to hold the copyboard horizontal.

13. The arms that support the copyboard.

14. A framed base to hold the copy in exposure position.

15. The glass cover of the copyboard.

16. The frame that supports the lens board and travels on the camera track.

17. A lamp designed to direct light into the lens for flash exposure.

18. The front case holds the lens.

19. The bellows is an adjustable light-tight tunnel between the shutter and the camera back.

20. The bellows hanger supports the bellows underneath when extended.

21. The bellows support holds the bellows hanger.

22. The ground glass is used in place of the vacuum door to view the image.

23. These controls position the copyboard and front case on the camera track.

The size of a camera is determined by the largest size of film that can be used. The cameras designed for larger sized film often are supported by an overhead bed. This provides walking space between the lens board and copyboard. Figs. 10-3 and 10-4.

Vertical cameras are designed to save space. The copyboard is placed near the floor and the

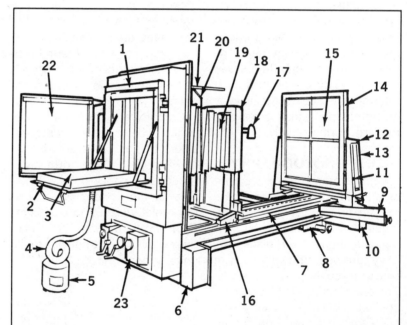

1. rear case	13. copyboard carriage uprights
2. vacuum film holder door	14. copyboard
3. vacuum film holder	15. copyboard cover
4. vacuum hose	16. front case carriage
5. vacuum pump and motor unit	17. flash lamp
6. rear pedestal	18. front case
7. camera track	19. bellows
8. lamp carrier carriage	20. bellows hanger
9. lamp carrier arms	21. bellows support
10. front pedestal	22. ground glass
11. copyboard vertical lock	23. copyboard and front case
12. copyboard horizontal lock	controls

Robertson Photo-Mechanix, Inc.

10-2. *Parts of the process camera.*

OVERHEAD BED

COPYBOARD CARRIAGE

VACUUM FILM HOLDER

Brown Manufacturing Co.

10-3. An overhead camera, 41" model, supported by an overhead bed.

camera is directly above. These are usually small cameras and are placed within the darkroom. Fig. 10-5.

Cameras made for high-speed production use roll film instead of sheet film. They have mechanical and automatic operations which save time and work. Some carry several sizes of roll film which is positioned, exposed, cut from the roll, and carried to a film processor without being handled by the camera operator. These cameras are used when a large amount of copy

Brown Manufacturing Co.

10-4. Another overhead camera.

Robertson Photo-Mechanix, Inc.

10-5. A vertical camera.

must be handled in a short time, such as in newspapers and large, commercial plants.

Some cameras, known as gallery cameras, are made to operate either completely inside or outside the darkroom. When this type is operated outside the darkroom, the film must be carried to and from the camera in lightproof boxes.

PARTS OF THE CAMERA

The copyboard is a baseboard on which the copy is placed. Fig. 10-6A. The board is marked in convenient sizes to position the copy accurately. Some copyboards are fitted with a vacuum to hold the copy flat. The copyboard cover is a glass frame hinged to one side of the board. It clamps over the copyboard. The glass holds the copy against the copyboard. Light is reflected from the copy on the copyboard through the camera lens. A copy image that reflects light is called *reflection copy.*

The copyboard may have a removable center area. This center area is removed when transmission copy (transparent image), such as a film transparency, is used. Figs. 10-6B and 10-6C. The lighting is positioned behind the copyboard so that light is transmitted through the copy to the lens.

The copy carriage travels on the bed so that the distance from the lens can be adjusted. This is used when working on enlargements and reductions.

The camera *bed* is the rigid structure used to support the copyboard front case and back case. It provides a level, parallel track for movement of copyboard

Brown Manufacturing Co.

10-6A. *Standard pressure-back copyboard being moved to vertical shooting position.*

and the lensboard. It may be cushioned by springs to prevent camera vibration. Fig. 10-7.

The front case is a movable frame to hold the lens, shutter, and front of the bellows. Fig. 10-7. It is moved on the bed toward or away from the rear of the camera for reductions and enlargements.

Since the bellows is a flexible, light-tight hood enclosing the area between the front case and camera back, light is prevented from reaching the camera back except for the light that passes through the lens. Fig. 10-8.

The camera back assembly includes a framed ground glass, Fig. 10-9, marked for positioning and focusing the image. Part of the rear case is a hinged door which is used to hold the film in position. The inside facing of the

Brown Manufacturing Co.
10-6B. *An overhead camera's 60" × 84" copyboard, pressure-backed with transparency insert underneath.*

Brown Manufacturing Co.
10-6C. *Overhead camera's transparency holder.*

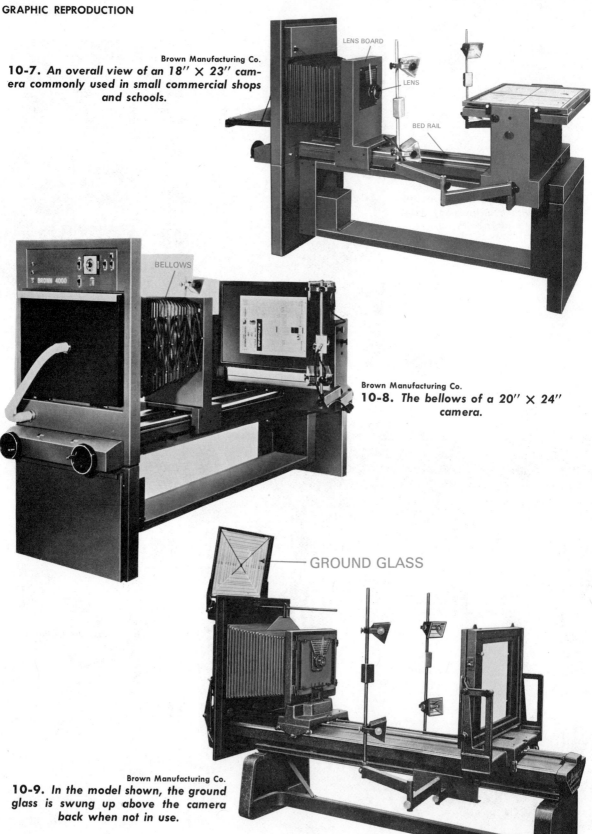

Brown Manufacturing Co.

10-7. *An overall view of an 18″ × 23″ camera commonly used in small commercial shops and schools.*

LENS BOARD

LENS

BED RAIL

BELLOWS

BROWN 4000

Brown Manufacturing Co.

10-8. *The bellows of a 20″ × 24″ camera.*

GROUND GLASS

Brown Manufacturing Co.

10-9. *In the model shown, the ground glass is swung up above the camera back when not in use.*

FILM DOOR

Robertson Photo-Mechanix, Inc.
10-10. *Camera film door.*

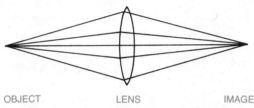

OBJECT   LENS   IMAGE

Robertson Photo-Mechanix, Inc.
10-11A. *The lens gathers light reflected from a point on the object to converge it to a point on the film, creating an image.*

door may be fitted with a vacuum, register pins, or a tacky material for holding the film. The door may be hinged left or right, at the bottom, or both for easy operation. Fig. 10-10.

The center of the camera is the *lens.* Fig. 10-7. It is made of several curved and polished glass circles mounted in a tube called a lens barrel. The lens gathers reflected or transmitted light from the copy and projects it onto the camera back, where the film is placed. The curved surface of the lens causes light to converge or focus on the film. Fig. 10-11A.

Spherical aberration is the loss of focus, when the outer edges of the lens transmit light. Fig. 10-11B. Distortion and curvature, Figs. 10-11C and 10-11D, are caused by the difference in lens curvature and thickness. Fig. 10-11E shows the separation of light into colors, *chromatic aberration,* caused by the prism effect of the curvature of the lens near its edges.

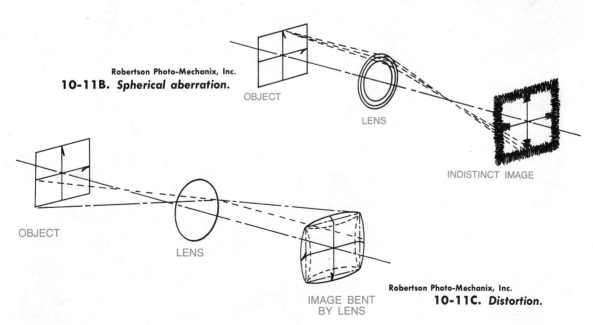

Robertson Photo-Mechanix, Inc.
10-11B. *Spherical aberration.*

OBJECT

LENS

INDISTINCT IMAGE

OBJECT

LENS

IMAGE BENT
BY LENS

Robertson Photo-Mechanix, Inc.
10-11C. *Distortion.*

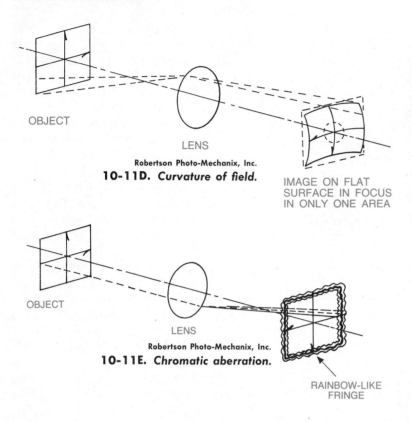

OBJECT

LENS

Robertson Photo-Mechanix, Inc.

10-11D. *Curvature of field.*

IMAGE ON FLAT
SURFACE IN FOCUS
IN ONLY ONE AREA

OBJECT

LENS

Robertson Photo-Mechanix, Inc.

10-11E. *Chromatic aberration.*

RAINBOW-LIKE
FRINGE

The copyboard and camera back must be parallel so that light passing through the lens does not form a distorted image. Modern lenses are coated to reduce *flare*. Flare is stray light reflected through the lens to the film, reducing contrast of the negative. The lenses are ground to avoid spherical aberration (fuzzy image from outer lens perimeter). They are tinted to reduce chromatic aberration. The lenses are also made "flat" in that they have little *depth of field*. Since they are used for flat copy, they do not have to record a third dimension, as do snapshot cameras. Depth of field is the distance in front of and behind the image that is in focus. The lenses have relatively long focal length and are considered "slow," as opposed to short focal

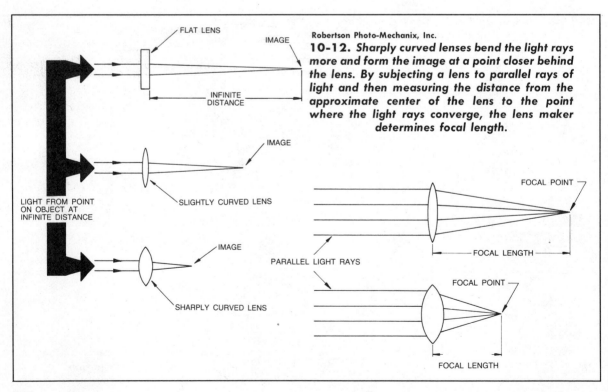

FLAT LENS

IMAGE

Robertson Photo-Mechanix, Inc.

10-12. *Sharply curved lenses bend the light rays more and form the image at a point closer behind the lens. By subjecting a lens to parallel rays of light and then measuring the distance from the approximate center of the lens to the point where the light rays converge, the lens maker determines focal length.*

INFINITE
DISTANCE

IMAGE

LIGHT FROM POINT
ON OBJECT AT
INFINITE DISTANCE

SLIGHTLY CURVED LENS

IMAGE

SHARPLY CURVED LENS

FOCAL POINT

PARALLEL LIGHT RAYS

FOCAL LENGTH

FOCAL POINT

FOCAL LENGTH

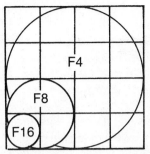

10-13. *The lens opening at f/16 is 1/16 the area of the opening at f/4. Consequently the exposure time at f/16 must be 16 times as long. At f/8 the area is 1/4 as large as at f/4; so the exposure must be four times as long.*

length, high-speed lenses of snapshot cameras. Fig. 10-12. The focal length of a lens is the distance from the lens' optical center (nodal point) to the film when the image is in focus. The optical center is the point where the light rays cross.

The lens barrel usually contains the *iris diaphragm.* This is a device for restricting light gradually from the outer edges of the lens toward the center. The closure of the iris is measured in focal ratios called f-stops. The f-stop indicates the size of the aperture through which light passes. The larger the f-stop number, the smaller the opening of the iris. Each larger f-stop number allows one-half of the previous amount of light to go through the lens. Each larger f-stop number also doubles the exposure time. For example: a 10-second exposure at f/11 would require a 20-second exposure at f/16, or a 40-second exposure at f/22.

The *speed* of a lens is determined by the largest opening of the iris, which admits the maximum amount of light. Most graphic arts cameras have f-stops from f/11 to f/45. The lenses are ground so that the sharpest focus and most effective working f-stop is two f-stops from the lens' largest aperture (opening). The largest aperture corresponds to the smallest f-stop number.

Light from the copyboard is "gathered" by the lens and restricted by the aperture of the iris. When the opening of the iris is small, say f/22, it causes the light to bend or diffract around the edges of the iris. The image is slightly distorted on its outer edges. This fuzziness may be transferred to the film in the camera. Each higher f-stop number (smaller aperture) doubles the exposure time and increases the diffraction of light. Fig. 10-13. Long exposures at small apertures should be avoided.

The longer the *focal length* of the lens, the larger will be the image. At two focal lengths from the lens, the focused image is the same size as the copy. The focal length of a lens is one-fourth the distance between copy and same-size focused image. Fig. 10-14.

Enlargement and reduction of the focused image are determined by movement of the front case and copy carriage. These movements must be in focal length ratios to each other if the image is to remain in focus. In the diagram shown in Fig. 10-14, the ratio of focal length distances between the image, lens, and copy determines reduction or enlargement of the image. When the lens moves closer toward the film, the image is reduced. Movement away from the film enlarges the image. Fig. 10-15.

The focal length of the lens governs the fixed positions of focus and enlargement and reduction (coverage). Fig. 10-16. These positions are scaled on the camera. The scales are fixed to the bed rails. Indicators are put on the lens and copyboards. Flexible tapes or wheels with markings may be used. Some camera scales are viewed and controlled in the darkroom. The operator can set the lens and copyboard by remote control.

CAMERA LIGHTING

Process cameras require a great amount of light to expose film in the camera back. Carbon

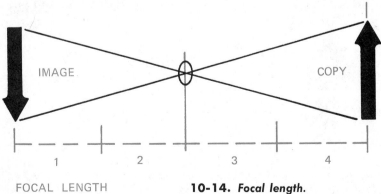

IMAGE   COPY

1   2   3   4

FOCAL LENGTH OF LENS

10-14. *Focal length.*

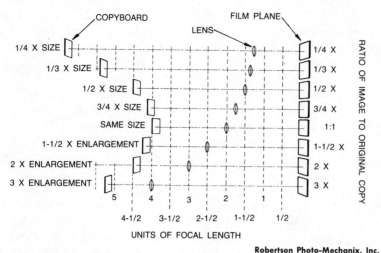

10-15. *Copyboard, lens, and film distance for reduction and enlargement.*

Robertson Photo-Mechanix, Inc.

arcs, tungsten lamps, pulsed xenon, quartz-iodine, and mercury lamps are in use today. The illumination from each of these light sources varies in amount of light (*intensity*) and kind of light (*extent of visible spectrum*). To understand the effects of lighting and film sensitivity, it is necessary to describe that part of the visible radiant energy we call light.

Energy radiates from emitting bodies, such as the sun or a light bulb. Radiation is measured by the length of the carrier wave on which it travels. The full spectrum (series of waves arranged by length) ranges from short gamma waves to long radio waves. The visible spectrum consists of a narrow band of waves. The waves in the visible spectrum are made up of pure colors. Each color corresponds to a particular spectral wavelength.

The wavelengths in angstrom units for the six common colors in light are:

Red	6500 Å
Orange	6000 Å
Yellow	5800 Å
Green	5200 Å
Blue	4700 Å
Violet	4100 Å

The waves are from about 400 to 700 nanometres in length. The *nanometre* is one billionth of a

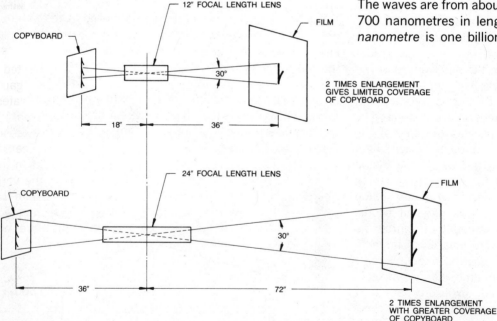

10-16. *The angular field of good definition for both the 12" and 24" lenses is 30°, but the coverage is much greater for the 24" lens. However, distances between copyboard, lens, and image are less for the 12" lens when making the same enlargements or reductions.*

Robertson Photo-Mechanix, Inc.

metre. One nanometre is equal to 10 angstrom units (Å).

In suitable proportions, the sum of all the colors (wavelengths) is seen as white light.

SPECTRAL DISTRIBUTION OF LIGHT

Incandescent light sources (tungsten and carbon arc) have a continuous output of waves. Emission is throughout the visible spectrum. The intensity of wavelengths along the spectrum depends on the temperature at which these lamps burn. Fig. 10-17.

Gas discharge lamps, such as mercury vapor and xenon arcs, produce separated spectral wavelengths. Such light is called a discontinuous, or line, spectrum. The nature of the gas, rather than the temperature, determines the spectral distribution. Fig. 10-18.

COLOR TEMPERATURE

Incandescent lights can be measured for color quality. Their appearance is compared to a black body heated to incandescence. The temperature of the black body (called an ideal radiator), when it appears the same as the lamp, is then listed as the lamp color temperature by degrees in the kelvin scale. This temperature scale begins with absolute zero (equal to −273 degrees Celsius or −459.4 degrees Fahrenheit). Some color temperatures for various light sources are:

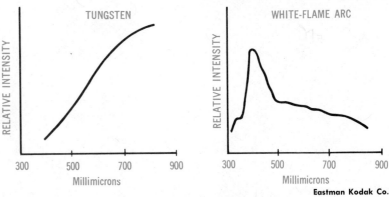

10-17. *Continuous light source.*

Eastman Kodak Co.

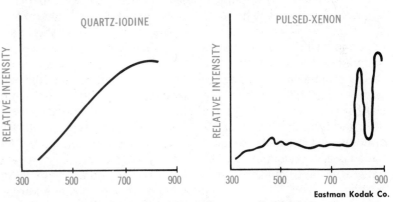

10-18. *Carbon arc and xenon distribution.*

Eastman Kodak Co.

CARBON ARC LIGHTS

The spectral distribution of light for the carbon arc is shown in Fig. 10-19A. The light intensity is high, allowing short exposures. The light covers the entire spectrum. These lights are adequate for color photography.

Carbon arc operates by electrically heating the tips of two carbon rods in contact until the tips melt and form a gas. The tips are then slightly separated to make the current jump a gap between the points. This creates greater heat until the points vaporize and produce an intense light.

High-intensity carbon arcs have metallic salts in their cone. The salts raise the vaporization temperature. Despite the level of and range of illumination of carbon arcs, they are not widely used today.

Sunlight (at noon)	5 400 K	Intensified carbon arc	5 500–6 400 K
Daylight	6 100 K	100-watt tungsten lamp	2 796 K
Pulsed xenon	6 000 K	Quartz-iodine	3 400 K
Blue-sky light	12 000–24 000 K	Photoflood—No. 1	3 400 K
Fluorescent (daylight)	6 500 K	White light (standard	
Flame carbon arc	5 000 K	black body)	6 000 K

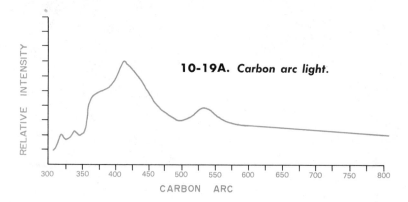

10-19A. *Carbon arc light.*

CARBON ARC

TUNGSTEN LIGHTS

A tungsten filament is used in regular light bulbs. The same metal is used as a filament in three kinds of lighting for the graphic arts. These three are the photoflood lamp, the power converted lamp, and the quartz-iodine lamp.

The *photoflood lamp* obtains a high intensity of light by using a filament too small for the voltage. The over-voltaged filament heats hotter, has shorter life, and emits more light than an ordinary bulb. In the same manner, a *power converter* can be used to select the temperature and output of the bulb by selection of the voltages used. As these bulbs age, they tend to darken and the intensity of light becomes less.

The *quartz-iodine lamp* uses a tungsten filament inside a quartz glass envelope. Fig. 10-19C. (An envelope is the glass shell over the filament.) This lamp has several advantages over regular tungsten lamps. Iodine crystals inside the bulb are vaporized and energized by heat and the electric current. The iodine forms tungsten iodide when it comes in contact with tungsten being vaporized from the filament. The tungsten iodide then decomposes at thinnest and hottest

The ash and smoke from carbon arcs are troublesome. Arcs create problems where cleanliness and dustless conditions are mandatory. The arc gap must be closely maintained. The level of voltage must not vary for constant illumination. The period from the time the arc is struck until the peak intensity of illumination is about one minute. This time lag delays high-speed production.

Arc light has large amounts of ultraviolet and blue-violet light. Most films are very sensitive to light of this color. Your eyes are also particularly sensitive to arc light. Do not stare at arc lamps; your eyes may become damaged.

Arc lights should be disconnected before changing or trimming the arcs. Clean and keep reflectors free of ash. Avoid drafts on the lamps. Do not handle or work with the lamps while they are electrically connected.

PULSED XENON LIGHTS

Pulsed xenon light is a gas-discharge type. It is similar to the electronic flash tube used in photography. The pulsed xenon lamp is designed to light, or pulse, with each half cycle of alternating current applied. The light pulses 120 times per second with 60-cycle alternating current. The illumination appears continuous to the eye.

Carbon arcs and pulsed xenon lights are about equal in film exposure time. The xenon lamp has a spectral distribution across the visible light range. Fig. 10-19B. It has less energy in the violet range than carbon arc light. It has more energy than carbon arc light in the red areas of the spectrum.

Pulsed xenon lamps have several advantages. They are clean and are not affected by voltage variation. No warm-up time is required. The level of light is constant. The primary disadvantage of pulsed xenon camera lighting is the high initial cost of installation.

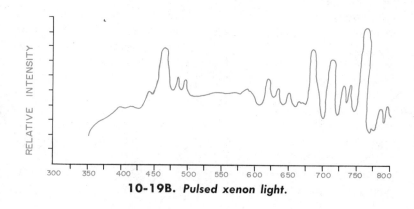

10-19B. *Pulsed xenon light.*

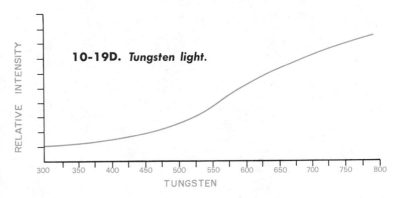

10-19D. *Tungsten light.*

TUNGSTEN

RELATIVE INTENSITY

Brown Manufacturing Co.

10-19C. *Copyboard lights, quartz and iodine lighting in adjustable reflectors.*

part of the filament. This replaces the tungsten filament and gives the lamp longer life. Because the tungsten is replaced, these bulbs do not darken or lose intensity of light during their lifetime. Because the quartz will withstand more heat, the envelope can be very small and used with higher voltages. Using several quartz-iodine lamps, a great amount of light can be generated from a small area.

Tungsten filament lighting systems are relatively inexpensive. They are clean and easy to operate. They require little maintenance other than bulb replacement. Tungsten, which makes an incandescent source of light, has a continuous spectral distribution. Much of the energy is dispersed along the red area of the spectrum. Fig. 10-19D. Sufficient energy is dispersed in the green and blue areas to be useful for color separation. These systems are often used for black and white photographic illumination.

PLACEMENT OF LIGHTING

The placement of lighting is important for proper film illumination. The copyboard should be properly illuminated to achieve correct film exposure. The diagram in Fig. 10-20 shows the intensity of a beam of light and the distance it travels to the film in the camera back. The shortest distance is between the center of the copyboard through the center of the lens and to the center of the camera back. The inverse square law of light (illustrated in Chapter 12, Fig. 12-51) states the intensity of the light is inversely proportional to the square of the distance. The distance from a corner of the copyboard to the opposite corner of the camera back is further than the center to center distance. It can be seen that the level of illumination at the copyboard should increase from the center to the outer edges in proportion to the square of the distance

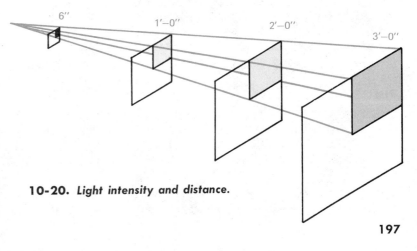

10-20. *Light intensity and distance.*

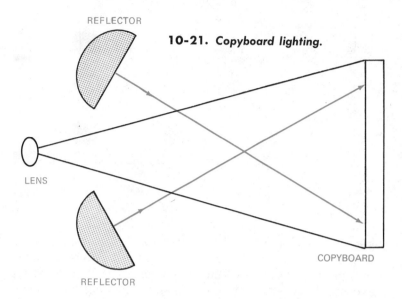

10-21. *Copyboard lighting.*

REFLECTOR

LENS

COPYBOARD

REFLECTOR

from the copyboard to the center of the camera lens. While present illumination sources are not capable of such discrimination, certain steps can be taken to assure adequate illumination.

By illuminating the copyboard, light is reflected from the copy to the film. Normally, lighting is placed so that the light rays strike the copyboard at a 30- to 45-degree angle. The lights are

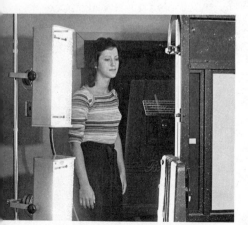

10-22. *Looking for light reflection on glass copyboard cover.*

set about three feet away from the copyboard. The centers of the reflectors are aimed to point at an imaginary line about one-fifth the distance in from the edge of the copyboard. Fig. 10-21.

CAMERA FOCUS

To focus the camera, the copyboard must be parallel to the camera back. The copyboard glass should be clean. The lights must be adjusted so that the copyboard is evenly illuminated. This can be checked by placing one eye as close to the lens as possible and looking at the copyboard. If the direct reflection of a light can be seen in the copy glass, the light should be moved. Fig. 10-22. Another way of checking for even illumination is to turn on the lights, open the shutter, and look into the bellows of the camera from the dark-room. Any stray light will show up as a flare of light on the bellows. Move the lights until the flare is gone.

Focusing is begun with the iris diaphragm wide open. The image

is then focused on the ground glass. The rough side of the glass faces the lens. The ground glass should be in the exact location as the emulsion surface of the film will be when it is placed in the camera. If not, ground glass focus and film focus will not be the same. Fig. 10-23.

Since a lens focuses best at its center, the copy image should also be examined about one-fourth the distance across the glass from each of the four sides. At these four points, place a small piece of transparent tape on the rough side of the glass and make a pencil mark on the tape. Using a 8- to 10-power magnifier, focus on the pencil mark. When the pencil mark is in focus, move the copy image so

10-23. *Viewing through ground glass camera back.*

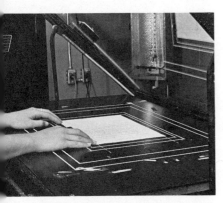

10-24. *Placing copy on board.*

that it appears in focus at this location. Critical focus can then be checked by parallax viewing of the pencil mark and the copy image. Parallax is the apparent movement of the mark and image when looked at from different directions. The magnifier enlarges the apparent movement. Looking through the magnifier, move your head slightly

10-25. *Locking cover on copyboard.*

from side to side. If the pencil mark and copy image are not the same focus, they will appear to move in relation to each other. If the pencil mark appears to move, the lens should be moved away from the ground glass. If the copy image appears to move, the lens must be moved closer to the ground glass. If both the copy image and the pencil mark move together, they are in focus at this location. If the copy image is not in parallax focus at the other penciled locations, a focus must be chosen midway between the extremes of differing location focuses. Most modern cameras have accurate scales or tapes which focus the copy image sharply on the film. These tape readings should be checked periodically. Make certain the camera elements have not been forced or misaligned, causing improper readings and focusing.

MAKING A LINE SHOT

These procedures are used when making a same-size reproduction of line copy:

PREPARATION

1. Clean both sides of the copyboard glass. Use graphic arts glass cleaners.

2. Center the copy face up on the copyboard. Fig. 10-24. Make certain the copy is free of dirt and finger marks. Close the copyboard cover and fasten it shut. Fig. 10-25.

3. Put the copy and lens holders in position for a 100 percent reproduction. Use the scales on the camera.

4. Arrange lights. Fig. 10-26. Illuminate copyboard evenly. Place your eye near the lens and

10-26. *Setting lights.*

check for reflection of lights. Fig. 10-22.

5. Set aperture two numbers from largest opening (this will probably be f/22) and for reproduction size. Fig. 10-27.

6. Under safelight, cut a strip of film for a test exposure strip. Handle film by the edges.

7. Close shutter. Place film strip on camera back. Dull, or emulsion, side must face the lens. Fig. 10-28.

8. Cover all but 1″ of the film strip with black paper. This is

10-27. *Setting f-stop. The marker will be lined up with the 100 mark at f/22.*

10-28. *Place film in position.*

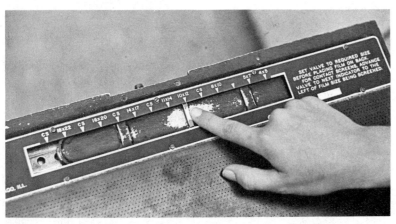

10-29. *Select film size for vacuum control.*

10-30. *Lay film on vacuum back.*

the correct exposure can be selected by examining the strip. The selected exposure can be used for all line shots at this camera setting and f-stop. Set correct exposure on timer.

EXPOSURE OF LINE COPY

1. Adjust vacuum size to film. Fig. 10-29.
2. Place sheet of film in camera back, in reference to copy location. Fig. 10-30. Turn on vacuum.
3. Roll film to be sure it is flat. Fig. 10-31.
4. Close camera back, and make the exposure. Fig. 10-32.
5. Open camera back and remove film.

DETERMINING BEST F-STOP NUMBER

Lenses, due to grinding, are "sharpest" at one f-stop number. This f-stop should always be used. To determine the sharpest f-stop, a series of test exposures can be made.

1. Set camera for same-size reproduction.
2. Position copy in copy holder. (Use 6-point text or similar type size.)
3. Place film in vacuum back. Use a large sheet. Position film for exposure in upper right corner. Mask the rest of the film.
4. Expose with largest f-stop number.
5. Reposition film to expose in a clockwise direction around the sheet of film.
6. Reduce f-stop number for each exposure. Do not change exposure time.
7. Develop film by standard method and select sharpest image. Always use the f-stop that made this image.

called a *mask*. Secure mask with tape.

MAKING A TEST STRIP

1. Close camera back. Set the timer for five seconds and expose the film.
2. Move mask to uncover another inch of film. Repeat exposure for five seconds. Continue moving mask and making exposures, each five seconds long.
3. Remove film strip from camera back and develop. (Chapter 12 discusses film developing.)
4. After film development,

200

ENLARGEMENT AND REDUCTION

A process camera can change the size of the image in relation to the copy size. As discussed in Chapter 9, reproduction size is usually expressed as a percentage, with a 100 percent reproduction being the same size as the original. A 200 percent reproduction is twice the copy size. A 25 percent reproduction is one-fourth the copy size. Fig. 10-33.

Changes in image size require setting the lens and copyboard differently. When the image is the same size as the copy, the lens is centered. Fig. 10-34. The lens is two focal lengths from the copy, and two focal lengths from the image. When a *reduction* in image size is required, the lens is moved *closer to the image* than to the copy. When an *enlargement* is wanted, the lens is moved *closer to the copy* than to the image. Fig. 10-15.

Modern cameras have scales for the lens board and copy-

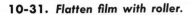

10-31. Flatten film with roller.

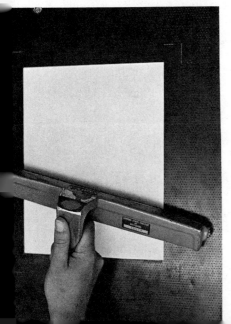

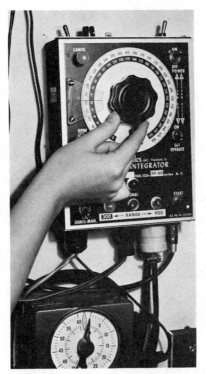

10-32. Setting exposure time.

board. These scales are usually marked in hundredths for accurate reproduction sizes. When the copyboard or lens is moved, the light intensity for the film changes. The time necessary for proper exposure is changed unless a change in the amount of light allowed through the lens is made. As stated before, each

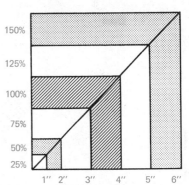

10-33. Percentage and size of reproduction.

larger diaphragm opening (smaller f-stop number) doubles the light and halves the exposure time. Fig. 10-13.

The camera usually has an f-stop scale indicator for reproduction size. This indicator is set in relation to the exposure time and f-stop used at 100 percent reproduction. A constant exposure time can be maintained for different reproduction sizes by changing the f-stop. Fig. 10-35A. This applies to cameras that have lights which move with the copyboard.

If the camera f-stop is not to be changed for enlargement or reduction, then the exposure time must be changed. The chart, Fig. 10-35B, shows the ex-

10-34. Setting for a 100 percent reproduction.

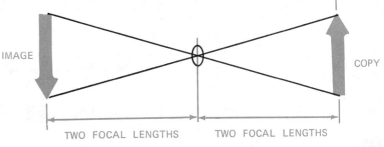

IMAGE

COPY

TWO FOCAL LENGTHS   TWO FOCAL LENGTHS

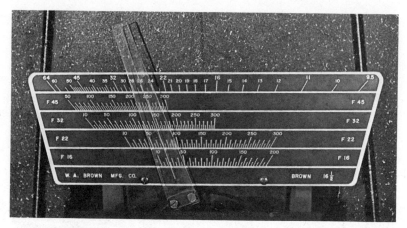

10-35A. *The f-stop indicator.*

EXPOSURE FACTORS

Reproduction Size	25%	50%	75%	100%	125%	150%	200%
Exposure Factor	0.4	0.55	0.7	1.0	1.3	1.6	2.3

10-35B. *Exposure factors for various reproduction sizes.*

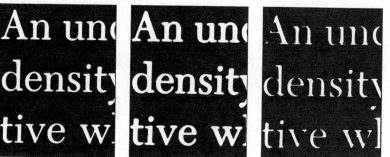

Eastman Kodak Co.

10-35C. *Positives and negatives of correct exposure, overexposure, and underexposure.*

CORRECT EXPOSURE

This segment was exposed correctly. The negative areas are either clearly transparent or densely opaque. Edges are sharp, and detail proportions are true to the original.

UNDEREXPOSURE

This segment was underexposed. Although transparent areas are clear, the dark areas have low density. A positive made from a negative of this type shows thickening of all detail.

OVEREXPOSURE

This segment was overexposed. Although dense areas are opaque, density appears in some areas which should be clear. A positive made from a negative of this type shows loss of fine detail.

posure factors for common enlargements and reductions. When the correct exposure is known for a 1 to 1, or 100 percent, reproduction, an exposure factor can be selected for a different size reproduction. Fig. 10-35C shows the results obtained with correct exposure, underexposure, and overexposure for line negatives and positives.

SENSITIVITY GUIDE

A sensitivity guide can be used with line copy. This guide reproduces with the image and aids in establishing correct or basic exposure. These guides, such as the Stouffer guide, are made in steps of density. Black type on

white paper is exposed at 100 percent in a series of tests. With controlled temperature the film is developed by time according to instructions from the manufacturer. It is important that the film and developer are fresh. Exposure is selected that will develop a black step 4 (called a solid 4). Step 5 will not be completely black. This will give the correct basic exposure for 100 percent. Fig. 10-36.

When enlargement or reduction is necessary, the guide provides additional help. Fine copy, like rules and pencil drawings, is finer still when reduced. To keep from reducing these fine lines so they tend to be lost, the exposure time can be shortened somewhat. The film can be developed by inspection to a solid step 2 on the Stouffer guide.

The relationship between exposure and scale steps is shown in Fig. 10-37. Copy that is light or heavy requires different exposure at different reproduction size to develop to the same density. Normal copy reproduced at 100 percent is a step 4 on the scale. Normal copy reproduced at 25 percent should be exposed to develop at step 3 on the guide. The basic exposure time is altered by using the time factor shown in Fig. 10-37 beside step 3, which is 71 percent. Multiply 71 percent times the basic exposure, say 22 seconds: $0.71 \times 22 = 15.6$ seconds, or 16 seconds exposure.

This development time roughly will be the same as normal copy at 100 percent developed to a step 7 by film manufacturer's time. Fig. 10-38.

If the light to copyboard distance must be changed, the ex-

10-36. *A solid 4 on the step scale.*

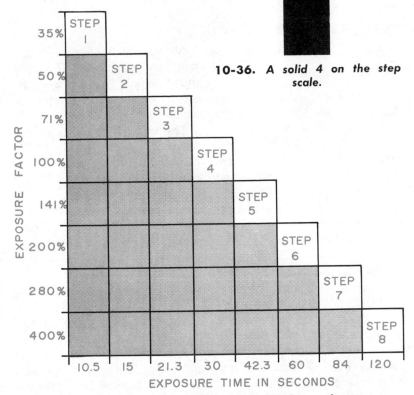

10-37. *Chart of exposure factors as related to scale steps.*

posure time will be changed. To determine the new exposure time, the following method is helpful:

1. Measure the original distance of lights to center of copyboard. (Example: 24″ exposure, 40 seconds)

2. Measure the new distance of lights to copyboard center. (Example: 30″)

3. Square original distance and new distance. Proportion old distance to new distance and original exposure time to new unknown exposure time. For example:

$$\frac{\text{Original Time}}{\text{Original Distance}^2} = \frac{\text{New Exposure Time}}{\text{New Distance}^2}$$

$$\frac{40 \text{ sec.}}{24″^2} = \frac{x}{30″^2}$$

$$\frac{40}{576} = \frac{x}{900}$$

$$576x = 36{,}000 \text{ seconds}$$

$$x = 62.5 \text{ seconds}$$

FILM EMULSION FOR LINE PHOTOGRAPHY

The emulsion for line photographic films includes silver halide salts. These salts, in crystal form, are encased in gelatin. The gelatin forms a colloid with the sliver halide salts in suspension to form an emulsion. The emulsion is coated to the film base, which has flexible support.

Three forms of silver halides are generally used. Silver chloride is a halide sensitive to blue light. Silver bromide is sensitive to blue and green light. Silver iodide is sensitive to blue, green, and red light. Film made with these halides also has dyes

added to increase the film's sensitivity to certain colors of light.

Blue-sensitive film records only the near ultraviolet and blue light. It is insensitive to red and green light. All silver halides are sensitive to blue light. Blue-sensitive films are normally used in making contacts of negatives and copying black and white photographs. (Contacts are explained in Chapter 12.)

Silver bromide halide salts provide blue, yellow, and green sensitivity. These orthochromatic (red-blind) films are "faster" (require less light) than the blue-sensitive films because of the increased color sensitivity. They may be safely handled in a darkroom with a red light of the proper intensity. Ortho films are universally used for black and white copy, and they can also record copy that is yellow or green in color.

Silver iodide is used for panchromatic films. These films are sensitive to all colors, including ultraviolet. They must be handled in complete darkness. They have about the same sensitivity as our eyes to light. Panchromatic film is widely used to reproduce colored copy and for color separation work.

Films are exposed by allowing

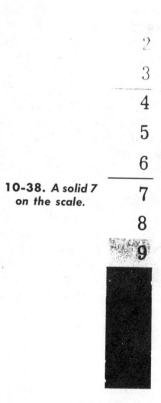

10-38. *A solid 7 on the scale.*

light to strike the film for a certain length of time. The light must contain the wavelengths (color, or angstrom units) for which the film is sensitive.

The amount of exposure is determined by the intensity of the light and the time. This equation is: exposure equals intensity multiplied by time, or $E = I \times T$. Either the time or the intensity can be varied to give approximately the same exposure.

Example:
$$E(50) = I(10) \times T(5)$$
or
$$E(50) = I(5) \times T(10)$$

This is only approximately right because photographic films are exposed somewhat faster with high intensity light than with low intensity light. This is known as the reciprocity law failure. For the camera operator it means that lower light intensity requires more than the time calculated to achieve the proper density.

FILM CONTRAST

The amount of density in relation to exposure determines the contrast of the film. A series of exposures can be plotted on graph paper. The base line is measured in log exposure (each division twice the amount of the previous division). The height is measured in units of density. This forms a *characteristic curve* of three distinct parts. The lower or toe part shows less increase in density than in log exposure. The upper or shoulder also indicates less density change than log exposure. The central, straight-line portion of the curve shows a consistent ratio between log exposure and density. The angle or steepness of the straight portion is called *gamma*. The correct exposure of graphic arts line and halftone films is in this area and can be determined by the interaction of gamma with the log exposure and density desired. Underexposure is found in the toe portion; overexposure is in the shoulder portion. High-contrast films have a steep gamma which is common for line and halftone works. Medium- or low-contrast films are used in continuous tone photography.

For direct application of contrast to camera work, a contrast index is used. This is the average slope of the portion of the characteristic curve that measures the limits of densities required for making negatives. The minimum density may include part of the toe portion. This is particularly true of continuous tone film. The maximum and minimum densities required are achieved from development times determined by the contrast index number.

FILM SPEED

Film speed refers to the amount of light required to affect the emulsion of the film. It is the rate of response of a particular emulsion to a predetermined amount of light and method of development. Films are rated by an index (ASA) which determines the length of exposure. The ASA ratings vary with different light sources that contain different amounts of light wavelengths.

Film speed has no direct relation to film contrast or color sensitivity. The emulsion response is built into film according to film usage.

REVIEW QUESTIONS

1. Name the parts of the graphic arts camera described in the following:
   a. The copy is placed on this part.
   b. This part can be moved along the bed so that the copy-to-lens distance can be adjusted.
   c. A flexible, light-tight hood enclosing the area between the front case and the camera back.
   d. This part is marked to aid in positioning and focusing the image.
   e. Gathers the light coming from the copy and projects it onto the film.
2. The lenses of graphic arts cameras have little depth of field. True or False?
3. The larger the f-stop number, the smaller the opening through which light passes. True or False?
4. Lighting should be placed so that the light rays strike the copyboard at a 30- to 45-degree angle. True or False?
5. Will moving the lens closer to the copy enlarge or reduce the image size?
6. If the f-stop is not to be changed for enlargement or reduction, what must be changed instead?

Chapter 11

Halftone Photography

Before attempting to understand halftone photography, it is helpful to be knowledgeable in the area of line photography. Line photography is explained in detail in Chapter 10.

Halftone photography converts an image with continuous tones, such as a black and white glossy photograph, into a form by which the image can be printed and still resemble the continuous tones. A continuous tone image may have a wide range of tones. Fig. 11-1. These tones tend to flow into each other without clearly defined boundaries. *Tones* are values of gray from light to dark, or stated in another way, from white to black. Tone does not refer to changes from one color to another.

Du Pont Co.

11-2. A coarse screen has been used to make the dots visible to the eye in this halftone.

The press cannot vary the amount of ink printed to show tone difference in the print. But the image can be divided into dots of various sizes. The print will appear to have light and dark areas corresponding to the size of the dots. The mixture of light reflecting from images and paper gives the illusion of tone. An area of larger dots close together with less white paper showing would appear dark. Very small dots widely separated with a good deal of paper showing in between would appear light. Fig. 11-2.

THE HALFTONE PROCESS

The halftone process converts the continuous tone image into a pattern of very small dots. The size and shape of the dots vary, depending upon the results

Du Pont Co.

11-1. A normal halftone print that appears to have continuous tones.

11-3. A portion of a halftone print greatly enlarged. Highlight areas have small dots. Shadow areas are large, connected dots.

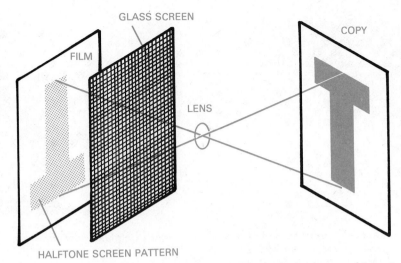

GLASS SCREEN

FILM

COPY

LENS

HALFTONE SCREEN PATTERN

11-4. *Reflected light from the copy goes through the lens and is patterned by the screen on the film.*

pends upon the distance from which the printed material will be seen under normal conditions. Halftones to be used in reading material use very small dots. They are planned for viewing from the normal reading distance of 15″. If a poster or larger display material is printed using halftones, the dots will be considerably larger.

THE HALFTONE NEGATIVE

A halftone negative is made by placing a halftone screen in the camera between the image and the film. Fig. 11-4. When an exposure is made by the camera, the light from the copy is broken by the screen into a pattern of dots on the film. The developed film will have a dot for each hole in the screen. This is the negative. Fig. 11-5. The size of the dot depends upon the size of the holes in the screen and the amount of light projected through these holes. The darker areas on the copy reflect little light. These dots on the exposed film are very small. Lighter copy areas reflect more light. These areas produce a larger dot on the exposed film.

wanted and the density of the tones to be printed. Fig. 11-3. These dots are reproduced upon the printing plates and, when printed, appear as solid areas. The surface around the dots is the color of the paper. To the naked eye the individual dots are not seen, and the printed image

resembles the original continuous tone image. The dots can be seen by examining a printed halftone image with a magnifying glass. Examine the image shown in Fig. 11-1 with a magnifying glass, and notice the dot patterns and sizes.

The size of the dots used de-

THE HALFTONE PRINT

When the film negative is used to make a printing plate, the clear areas become the areas to be printed. The pattern of dots on the plate exposure will be reversed from those on the film negative, producing the positive image plate. When printing, the plate image receives the ink and prints black dots. The resulting print will have light tones from the small printed dots and dark tones from the large printed dots. Study the black dot pat-

LIGHT MODULATED BY A PHOTO

DOT SIZES FORMED ON A NEGATIVE

SHADOW

HIGHLIGHT

MIDTONE

Du Pont Co.

11-5. *Halftone size dot in relation to print tone.*

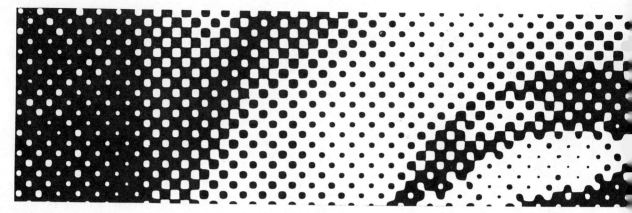

Du Pont Co.

11-6. *Small negative shadow dots print the dark areas of the halftone. Large negative highlight dots print the light areas of the halftone.*

terns on the enlarged image shown in Fig. 11-6.

HALFTONE SCREEN PROCESSES

There are three common halftone processes: (1) glass cross-line screen, (2) contact screen, and (3) use of prescreened halftones. These three are photographic processes.

GLASS CROSS-LINE SCREEN PROCESS

The glass cross-line screen process photographs a continuous tone image through a cross-line screen in a camera. A *cross-line screen* is made of two glass sheets ruled with a number of grooved lines per inch. The ruled grooves are filled with a black material which blocks the passage of light. The width of the ruled lines and the spaces between the lines are the same. The two sheets are joined together with their lines at right angles. The lines are on the inside surfaces. Fig. 11-7.

Screens are identified by the number of ruled lines per inch. This is called the *rule number.*

The larger the number, the finer the screen is. The most commonly used screens are 85, 120, and 133 lines per inch. Offset newspapers generally use a 110-line screen. Very fine screens with 150 to 200 lines per inch are available. These show great detail and give excellent tone to the printed image.

The cross-line screen is placed at carefully determined distances from the film. It serves much like a lens and focuses the reflected light on the film. The distances used must be carefully determined to produce a clear image. Cameras using glass screens usually have a scale and table for determining the correct screen distance from the film. The glass screen is expensive and requires care in use. When not in use, a compensating glass is used to avoid resetting the camera.

A *compensating* glass allows the same amount of light

11-7. *A cross-line glass screen. Enlarged circles show the engraved lines on edges of the two glass sheets sandwiched together.*

through as would a glass screen. It is used as a "stand-in" for the screen unless an actual exposure is being made. This minimizes breakage of the expensive glass screen. Glass screens are made in rectangular or circular mounts. The circular mounts permit angling the screen for color work.

CONTACT SCREEN PROCESS

Contact screens, sometimes called *vignetted* screens, are of two types, the magenta screen

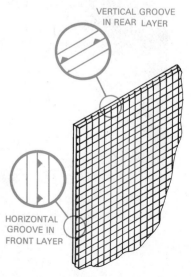

VERTICAL GROOVE IN REAR LAYER

HORIZONTAL GROOVE IN FRONT LAYER

ENLARGED AREA OF A CONTACT SCREEN

Du Pont Co.

11-8. A contact screen consists of a pattern of vignetted, dotlike apertures. The vignetted dots vary in density from very light in the center to dark near the edges.

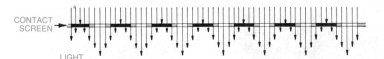

CONTACT SCREEN

LIGHT

Du Pont Co.

11-9. More light passes through the center of each contact screen dot than through its more dense edge.

DOT FORMATION ON THE ADJACENT LITHO FILM

HALFTONE SCREEN

SMALL BLACK DOTS START HERE

DOTS INCREASE IN SIZE AS STRONGER LIGHT PENETRATES GRADIENT

SMALL CLEAR DOTS HELD OPEN HERE

Du Pont Co.

11-10. Film exposure through contact screen.

and the gray screen. A vignette is a tone that gradually fades away.

The magenta screen uses color filters to control contrast. The gray screen takes the place of the magenta screen in direct-color separation photography. See Chapter 18 for details.

The Contact Screen

The contact screen is a single thickness of film. It is placed in direct contact, emulsion to emulsion, with the film upon which the halftone exposure is to be made. This eliminates the need to adjust the distance between the film and the screen as is done in the cross-line glass screen process.

A contact screen has a pattern of vignetted dots. Fig. 11-8. A vignetted dot has its maximum density at its edges and least at the center. Fig. 11-9. Weak light will penetrate only the center portion of the dot. Stronger light will pass through larger portions of the dot. Thus, the amount of light coming from the copy determines the size of the dots reproduced on the negative. Figs. 11-10 and 11-11.

Contact screens are identified by the number of dots per linear inch. The lines of dots serve the same function as the lines on cross-line screens.

Different screens are used when making halftone negatives and positives. A *positive screen* is used to make halftone positives from continuous tone negatives. A *negative screen* makes halftone negatives from black and white images such as continuous tone prints (not continuous tone negatives). Some screens have a dot pattern desirable in making halftone negatives. A different screen pattern is used in making halftone positives.

Contact Screen Care

The contact screen is a film base with a dye image emulsion. It scratches easily and can be damaged by chemicals and careless handling.

Handle screens only by their edges. Keep them flat in a protective cover when not in use. If dusty, wipe lightly with a dry, soft chamois. If water spotted, use an approved film cleaner. The best care is continual precaution and protection. Large size screens

Halftone dot formation begins when a small amount of light penetrates the lightest areas of the screen, producing small black dots on the adjacent litho film after processing.

As the intensity of the exposing light increases, more light penetrates the screen and forms larger and larger dots until they join and form the familiar 50% dot shown here.

Dot growth continues with increasing exposure until the large black dots merge, leaving only small clear areas such as these.

Du Pont Co.

11-11. *Halftone dot formation by exposure.*

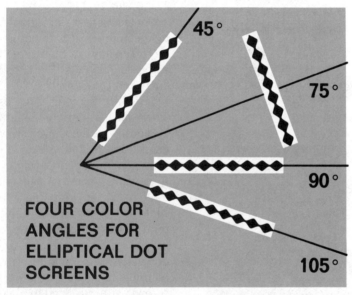

FOUR COLOR ANGLES FOR ELLIPTICAL DOT SCREENS

Du Pont Co.

11-12. *Enlarged area of a contact screen.*

ORIGINAL GRAY SCALE

← EXCESS DENSITY → ← SCREEN RANGE →

HALFTONE REPRODUCTION

are expensive and should not be used with small sized films. Avoid placing a screen on dusty surfaces or areas that have been taped. Clean the vacuum back of the camera carefully. Watch for exposed pins in the camera back. Do not handle screens with damp or wet hands. Always replace the screen in its cover or box immediately after use.

Screen Angle

The screen pattern is not as noticeable when the dot pattern is printed at a 45-degree angle. Most black and white or single-color halftones are printed with this screen angle. The screen angle is measured from the screen base through the diagonal corners of the dot pattern. Most screens have a reference edge (base line) for positioning the screen to assume correct screen angle. When halftones are printed over each other as in process color, a different angle for each printing must be used. A moiré (undulating) pattern will result if similar screen angles are used for each color. For four-color process work the screen angles are: yellow, 90 degrees; magenta, 75 degrees; cyan, 105 degrees; and black, 45 degrees. Duotone (two-color) screen an-

Du Pont Co.

11-13. *Screen range is the copy density range that a halftone screen will reproduce (with halftone dots) with a single, white-light exposure.*

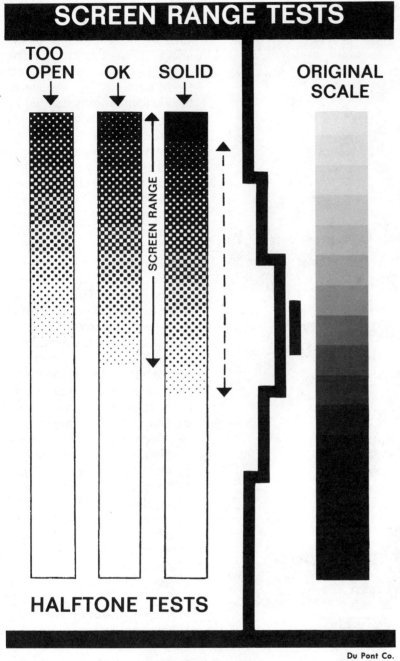

SCREEN RANGE TESTS

TOO OPEN   OK   SOLID   ORIGINAL SCALE

SCREEN RANGE

HALFTONE TESTS

Du Pont Co.

11-14. Screen range.

lows one screen to be used for the four angles. Other methods use angle marks on the camera back or punch holes that align the screen to pins in the camera. Sets of screens (preangled) are available which are made with the different angles correct from the base line of the screen. Each screen is marked with an identifying screen angle from the base line.

Screen Range

The *range* of a screen is the copy density range it can reproduce. Normally, this is from a pinpoint dot to a 95-percent dot. Fig. 11-13. The *speed* of a screen refers to the exposure time necessary to produce a halftone dot of a certain density, usually a 50-percent dot. Each screen must be tested before use to determine speed and range. Fig. 11-14.

The Magenta Screen

The magenta screen is most widely used. The positive screen uses magenta color to give control over contrast when making positives. Filters are used to change the density of the screen. A yellow filter extends the screen range. A magenta filter shortens the screen range. These are color-compensating filters which allow the camera operator to obtain positives of high or low contrast. The magenta *negative* contact screen is used without filter. Control of contrast is determined by exposure and development.

The Gray Screen

The gray screen is also called the neutral density screen. It may be a positive or negative

gles are usually 105 degrees and 45 degrees. An exception is the gray contact screen with elliptical dots. The magenta screen angle must be 90 degrees or at right angles to the 75-degree angle. Fig. 11-12.

For color work, the screen can be turned on a template for the correct screen angles. This al-

POSITIVE SCREEN

NEGATIVE SCREEN

Du Pont Co.

11-15. Reproduction differences of a positive and negative screen.

Screen Dot Patterns

Halftone dot patterns are related to the tonal values of the image to be reproduced. The differences in tones require different halftone dots. As stated before, light tones are shown by small ink dots, darker tones are shown with larger dots. The actual shape of the dots changes with their area. Fig. 11-6. Notice that the dots are not all the same size and shape. The different sizes and shapes represent different tonal values. The dots are indicated in percentages. For example, in the 50-percent pattern, the dot occupies about 50 percent of the area. Fig. 11-17. The shape of the dot is determined by the way the screen is made. Square dots are the most common. They are formed by square-ruled screens and produce good reproductions, except in the midrange. A drastic density change takes place when the 50-percent square dots line up. When the four corners of square dots join together at this range, the printed effect is noticeable. When this is objectionable, a screen is used that is ruled at less than right angles. This screen has a diamond pattern (elliptical dot) instead of the square dot. Fig. 11-18.

The Elliptical Dot Screen

The *elliptical dot* screen is used to offset the sudden change in dot structure in the middle tones. The screen is made so that two corners join at about 35 percent and the other two corners at about 60 percent. The diamond-shaped dots appear to form a chain, linking first across the broad portion of the diamond. This provides a larger

screen. A *positive screen* makes halftone positives from continuous tone negatives. A *negative screen* makes halftone negatives from black and white copy. Figs. 11-15 and 11-16. This screen is used for direct photographic color separation. It is always used when photographing an original in color on panchromatic film. It can be used for black and white work.

Du Pont Co.
11-16. *A negative screen is used to make halftone negatives. The screen gradient gives the effect of a built-in bump.*

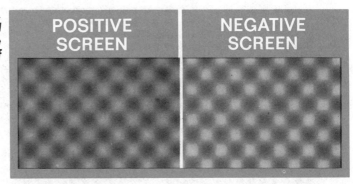

POSITIVE SCREEN | NEGATIVE SCREEN

POSITIVE SCREEN HALFTONE

NEGATIVE SCREEN HALFTONE

range of density change. Fig. 11-18. This pattern is used in the same manner as the square dot pattern. It is particularly suited to vignette copy and subtle tonal subjects, such as portraits.

There are other types of screens available. Some of these produce bull's-eye patterns, wavy lines, spirals, and mezzotints. Fig. 11-19.

SENSITOMETRY

Sensitometry is the science of measuring the reaction of materials to light. Specifically, it deals with the chemical action of light on light-sensitive materials. Light-sensitive activity includes color, contrast, reaction speed, and extent of change and density.

DENSITOMETRY

Densitometry is a branch of sensitometry. It includes the measurement of optical density.

Optical density refers to the light-blocking ability of a material. It can be measured as loss of light going through a material (transmission density) and by the amount of light reflected from a material (reflection density). There are three general ways to measure density.

The easiest way to measure density is to compare visually the tone of the material in a photograph with a measured tone scale. A gray scale, such as the

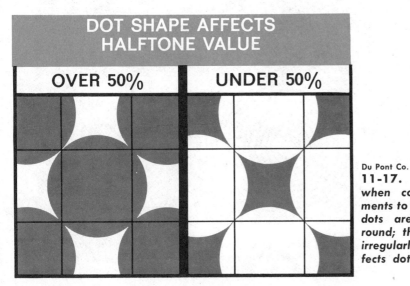

DOT SHAPE AFFECTS HALFTONE VALUE

OVER 50% | UNDER 50%

Du Pont Co.
11-17. *Caution must be used when converting dot measurements to dot percentage. Halftone dots are usually not perfectly round; they may be elliptical or irregularly shaped. Dot shape affects dot area and effective dot percentage.*

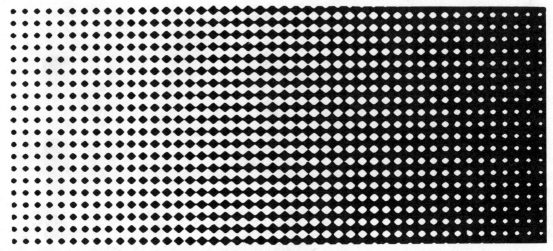

Du Pont Co.

11-18. *Elliptical dot screens (also called chain dot or diamond dot) form diamond-shaped dots in the midtones. Smoother tone transition can be made with elliptical dots.*

Kodak calibration gray scale, can be used to approximate the tone of a photograph. Fig. 11-20.

A second way to measure density is with a visual tone projector. This device projects a tone from the photograph on a gray scale. The density is read by adjusting the scale to match the photographic tone. Since both these methods require sound visual judgment, they are not accurate.

A third way to measure density is with an electric densitometer with reflection and transmission heads. These devices compare tones photoelectrically. They accurately and quickly measure amounts of light. Fig. 11-21. They are used by most printing plants today.

DENSITY AND OPACITY

Density and opacity are different measurements of light-blocking effect of tone in copy, negatives, or prints. *Opacity* measures the difference in the amount of light that strikes an object and the amount of light that goes through the object. Opacity is the result of *incident* light (light arriving at an object) divided by the *transmitted* light (light going through an object). The opacity number increases as the transmitted light decreases.

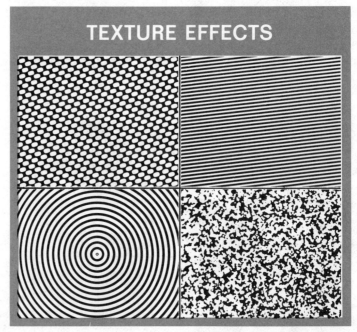

Du Pont Co.

11-19. *Special effect screens are numerous. Among the patterns available are straight line, wavy line, spiral, brick, and mezzotint designs. Special effect screens add texture for artistic renditions.*

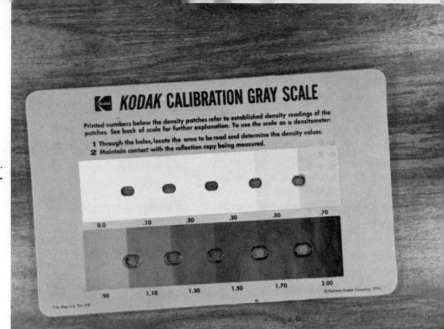

Eastman Kodak Co.

11-20. *A gray scale used to compare photo densities.*

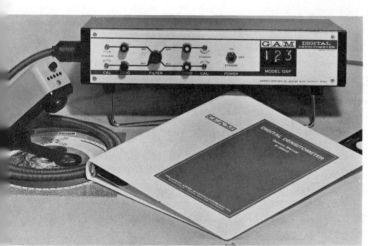

11-21A. *An electric densitometer that measures density by reflection of light.*

11-21B. *An electric densitometer that measures density by transmission of light.*

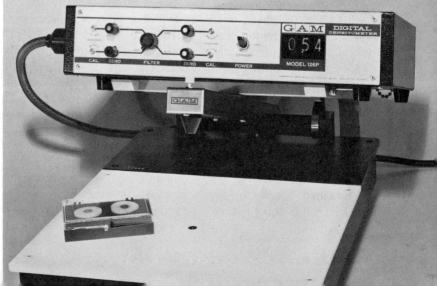

When measuring paper, opacity is usually expressed as a percentage of the incident light. Density uses a logarithmic scale to measure opacity. Density is the logarithm of opacity. The log scale for density is used to reduce the long range of opacity numbers that must be used. Log scale numbers can be added or subtracted. Opacity numbers must be multiplied or divided. The log is simply the number of times the base number is multiplied by itself.

This can be shown in the following example. Suppose a sheet of paper (A) transmits about 31.6 percent of the 100 percent incident light. Its opacity number would be 3.16.

$$\text{Opacity of 1 sheet of paper (A)} = \frac{\text{Incident light}}{\text{Transmitted light}}$$

$$\text{Opacity of (A)} = \frac{100\%}{31.6\%}$$

$$\text{Opacity of (A)} = 3.16$$

A second sheet (B) would transmit only about 31 percent of the 31.6 percent transmitted by the first sheet. The two sheets would have an opacity of 9.9, or about 10.

$$3.16 \times 3.16 = 9.99$$
$$AB = 10 \text{ opacity}$$

Each additional sheet would multiply its opacity by the opacities of the previous sheets. The first sheet (A) has an opacity of 3.16. The first and second sheets combined opacity is 3.16 × 3.16, or 9.99. Three sheets would be 3.16 × 3.16 × 3.16, or about 31 opacity.

Density is a logarithm measure that uses 10 as the base number. The combined opacity of four sheets of paper is equal to about 100. The log of 100 is 2, using a base of 10.

$$10^2 = 100$$

Density is the log of opacity. The density of four sheets is 2.0.

In like manner, the opacity of five sheets (3.16 × 3.16 × 3.16 × 3.16 × 3.16, or 3.16^5) equals approximately 316. The log of base 10 for 316 is 2.5 ($10^{2.5} = 316$). The density is 2.5 for 5 sheets.

As you can see by these examples, the total of several opacities is geometric rather than arithmetic. The opacities must be multiplied, not simply added, to find their total. Another way to find the total is by using logarithms. Add the logs of the opacities; the antilog of the sum will be the total opacity. The antilog is the number corresponding to a given logarithm. For example, the antilog of the logarithm 2 is 100 (log 100 = 2).

Suppose the opacity of one sheet of paper is 3.16. The log of 3.16 is 0.5. To find the opacity of five sheets, add their log numbers. The sum is 2.5. This is the logarithm of the total opacity. The antilog of 2.5 is 316. Thus, 316 is the combined opacity of the five sheets. Fig. 11-22.

If a sheet of exposed film has an opacity of 3, it will transmit one-third of the incident light. Suppose the incident light is 27 candlepower.

$$\text{Opacity} = \frac{\text{Incident light}}{\text{Transmitted light}}$$

$$3 = \frac{27}{\text{Transmitted light}}, \text{ or } \frac{27}{9}$$
$$\text{Transmitted light} = 9$$

$$\text{Transmission} = \frac{\text{Transmitted light}}{\text{Incident light}}$$

$$\text{Transmission} = \frac{9}{27} = \frac{1}{3}$$

Opacity is always greater than one (1), since the stronger incident light is divided by the weaker transmitted light. Transmission is always less than one (a fraction) since it is the relationship of the transmitted light to the more powerful incident light.

Imagine two sheets of film, one placed above the other. Each has an opacity of 3. Each will transmit one-third of the light that falls on it. The light that goes through the upper film is one-third the original 27 candlepower, or 9 candlepower. The 9 candlepower incident light going through the second film is again reduced to one-third of incidental light, or 3 candlepower.

The effect of the two film opacities on the original 27 candlepower is to reduce it to 3 candlepower. This is a nine-fold reduction in power.

If the opacity numbers of the films are simply added (3 each), the total is only six. This is incorrect. The opacities cannot be added; their effects are *multiplied*. Therefore, the logs of opacity numbers (density) must be used in order to add and subtract opacities. Since the use of and conversion of opacity numbers into logarithms is tedious,

COMBINED OPACITY OF SHEETS (MULTIPLIED)

COMBINED DENSITY OF SHEETS (ADDED)

3.16 OPACITY OF ONE SHEET

.5 DENSITY OF ONE SHEET

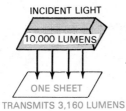

INCIDENT LIGHT
10,000 LUMENS

ONE SHEET

TRANSMITS 3,160 LUMENS

3.16 OPACITY ONE SHEET
X 3.16 OPACITY ONE SHEET
10.00 OPACITY TWO SHEETS

.5 DENSITY ONE SHEET
+ .5 DENSITY ONE SHEET
1.0 DENSITY TWO SHEETS

INCIDENT LIGHT
10,000 LUMENS

TWO SHEETS

TRANSMITS 1,000 LUMENS

10.00 OPACITY TWO SHEETS
X 3.16 OPACITY ONE SHEET
31.16 OPACITY THREE SHEETS

1.0 DENSITY TWO SHEETS
+ .5 DENSITY ONE SHEET
1.5 DENSITY THREE SHEETS

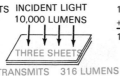

INCIDENT LIGHT
10,000 LUMENS

THREE SHEETS

TRANSMITS 316 LUMENS

31.16 OPACITY THREE SHEETS
X 3.16 OPACITY ONE SHEET
100 OPACITY FOUR SHEETS

1.5 DENSITY THREE SHEETS
+ .5 DENSITY ONE SHEET
2.0 DENSITY FOUR SHEETS

INCIDENT LIGHT
10,000 LUMENS

FOUR SHEETS

TRANSMITS 100 LUMENS

100 OPACITY FOUR SHEETS
X 3.16 OPACITY ONE SHEET
316 OPACITY FIVE SHEETS

2.0 DENSITY FOUR SHEETS
+ .5 DENSITY ONE SHEET
2.5 DENSITY FIVE SHEETS

INCIDENT LIGHT
10,000 LUMENS

FIVE SHEETS

TRANSMITS 31.6 LUMENS

316 OPACITY FIVE SHEETS
X 3.16 OPACITY ONE SHEET
1,000 OPACITY SIX SHEETS

2.5 DENSITY FIVE SHEETS
+ .5 DENSITY ONE SHEET
3.0 DENSITY SIX SHEETS

INCIDENT LIGHT
10,000 LUMENS

SIX SHEETS

TRANSMITS 10.0 LUMENS

1,000 OPACITY SIX SHEETS
X 3.16 OPACITY ONE SHEET
3,162 OPACITY SEVEN SHEETS

3.0 DENSITY SIX SHEETS
+ .5 DENSITY ONE SHEET
3.5 DENSITY SEVEN SHEETS

INCIDENT LIGHT
10,000 LUMENS

SEVEN SHEETS

TRANSMITS 3.16 LUMENS

3,162 OPACITY SEVEN SHEETS
X 3.16 OPACITY ONE SHEET
10,000 OPACITY EIGHT SHEETS

3.5 DENSITY SEVEN SHEETS
+ .5 DENSITY ONE SHEET
4.0 DENSITY EIGHT SHEETS

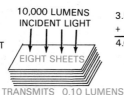

10,000 LUMENS
INCIDENT LIGHT

EIGHT SHEETS

TRANSMITS 0.10 LUMENS

11-22. *Transmitted light, opacity, and density readings compared.*

density numbers are used outright in halftone photography.

COPY DENSITY

The lightest tone in copy is called a *highlight*. The darkest tone is called *shadow*. The amount of tonal difference between the two extremes is the *density range* of the copy. The highlight area and shadow area can be measured by a densitometer or compared with a gray scale. A gray scale, Fig. 11-20, shows successive density steps, usually from 0.05 density to 2.10 density. The tone range of the copy is the difference between the copy highlight-density value and copy shadow-density value. For example, if the shadow density is at the 1.55 density scale step and the highlight density is at the 0.13 density scale step, the density range for this copy is 1.42 (1.55–0.13). Finer and more accurate density readings require measurement by the reflection densitometer. Good photographs often have a tonal range from near 0.01 to 1.5 or 1.7 density. Often this range is greater than can be reproduced by halftone printing. Fig. 11-23.

Several factors limit the tonal range of reproductions. The materials (paper and ink) affect tone range. No printed highlight can be lighter than the paper. No shadow will be darker than the density of the ink's film, usually about 1.4 density.

The printability of the plate, the press run, and paper used affect the density range that can be printed. Precision presses with excellent plates, high quality inks and blankets, operated by a skilled technician and running on cast-coated stocks can consistently reproduce halftone dots from a 5 percent to 95 percent range. If printed halftone dots tend to plug or print solid, a series of printings should be run with different percentages of shadow dots. This will determine the percentage of shadow dot that will remain open on coated and uncoated stocks.

HALFTONE EXPOSURES

Producing a good halftone usually requires more than one kind of exposure. Three different kinds of exposure may be used: *main, flash,* and a *screenless* or no-screen, "bump" exposure.

THE MAIN EXPOSURE

The main (detail) exposure is timed to reproduce the highlight printed dot. It is timed so that the lightest copy (original) areas reflect sufficient light to expose almost completely the negative highlight area. This area will make the smallest dot on the print.

The main exposure time will not reflect enough light from the shadow area of the original to expose the film. This will be a clear area in the negative and will print solid.

THE FLASH EXPOSURE

The range of dots can be extended into the print shadows by additional flash exposure. This exposure is made directly (not reflected from copy) through the screen. It mainly affects the unexposed film areas. These are the shadow areas. This exposure is timed to expose the smallest dot on film that will, as a shadow dot, stay open during printing. The flash exposure has the effect of extending the dot pattern further into the film area that corresponds to the darker areas of the halftone print. The flash extends the tonal range of the halftone negative (sometimes called extending the screen range). The flash exposure time is calculated

COPY RANGE

$$\frac{1.60}{\begin{array}{r} -0.10 \\ \hline 1.50 \end{array}}$$

SCREEN RANGE

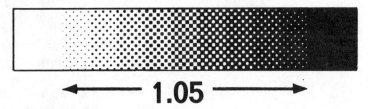

$$\longleftarrow 1.05 \longrightarrow$$

$$\frac{\begin{array}{l} 1.50 \quad \text{COPY RANGE} \\ -1.05 \quad \text{SCREEN RANGE} \end{array}}{0.45 \quad \text{ADJUSTMENT REQUIRED}}$$

Du Pont Co.

11-23. *Density readings and screen range determine photo-mechanical adjustment for reproduction.*

as a percentage of the main exposure. This exposure can extend up to 0.70 units of density in range of the negative. Larger flash times cause a continual dot pattern in all the density and resulting loss in detail and tone.

THE SCREENLESS EXPOSURE

A third exposure may be necessary to achieve accurate reproduction. This exposure is used to increase the highlight contrast. The screen is removed without disturbing the film position on the camera back. The film is exposed to reflected light from the copy as a percentage of the main exposure. This is called a highlighting, screenless, or "bump" exposure. Fig. 11-24. At times, the main exposure must be reduced to compensate for the highlight exposure. This exposure affects the highlight negative dots, increasing their size and density. It affects the midtones less and the shadow negative areas hardly at all. This is because the copy reflects great amounts of light from the copy highlights, less from the midtones and hardly any from the shadows. This exposure is a small percentage of the main exposure. It compresses the tonal or screen range. Longer highlight exposures cause the film to become completely exposed in the highlight areas. This blocking of the negative highlight area causes loss of dot pattern in the highlight print area. This effect is used in making a posterization (line effect), highlight drop-outs (to remove light backgrounds), and in some duotone work.

The small percentage of the

main exposure used for the highlight exposure often causes problems of very short highlight exposure times which are inaccurate. One solution is to "step down" the camera lens (use a smaller diaphragm opening). Each smaller opening requires

POSITIVE SCREEN AND 5% BUMP

POSITIVE SCREEN AND 5% BUMP WITH ADJUSTED EXPOSURE

Du Pont Co.

11-24. *Comparison of "bump" exposures with and without adjustment of the main exposure.*

NEUTRAL DENSITY FILTERS FOR BUMP EXPOSURES

2%—1.70 N.D.
2½%—1.60 N.D.
3%—1.50 N.D.
4%—1.40 N.D.
5%—1.30 N.D.

USE SAME *f*-STOP AND MAIN EXPOSURE TIME

Du Pont Co.

11-25. *Filters used for the screenless exposure.*

double the exposure time of the previous f-stop. The light to the lens can also be filtered to reduce its intensity and prolong exposure. A gray filter called a *neutral density* filter is used. The neutral filter is a color combined of white and black. It does not selectively alter the light from colored copy. The filter absorbs some of the light which passes through it. The filters are measured and marked with neutral density numbers. The scale in Fig. 11-25 shows the neutral density filter required for the percentage highlight exposure desired.

HALFTONE DOT FORMATION

RANGE

The range of copy tones is the extent of contrast available to the camera lens. The contrast range of the halftone negative is controlled by the flash and highlight exposures. The main exposure is determined by highlight density of copy. Its length in time is dependent on the volume of light received through the lens. The volume of light is affected by filters, magnifications, and lens operatives (stop). The flash (no copy, screen) exposure extends the halftone contrast into the shadow area. The highlight (copy, no screen) exposure increases halftone contrast in the highlight area. The range of overall contrast is determined by size of dot that is printable as highlight and shadow. This is a print density range of 1.4 or less.

SCREENED "BUMP"

Some screens, such as the Kodak magenta contact screen (negative), are manufactured with additional highlight contrast built into the screen. The extent of contrast varies by screen rulings and is highest in 120- and

133-line screens. It is equivalent to about 7 percent "bump" (screenless) of the main exposure. Most negatives made with this screen do not require a highlight ("bump") exposure. If required, however, 2 percent to 15 percent of the main exposure can be added as a no-screen, copy exposure ("bump").

DENSITY THROUGH FILTERS

The filtered density method of changing the density range of a halftone *positive* makes use of color-compensating filters with a magenta *positive* screen. Yellow filters reduce the halftone positive contrast. Magenta filters increase the contrast of the halftone positive. The filters, in effect, change the density of the magenta screen. Yellow light increases the screen density, while magenta light reduces the effective density of the magenta screen. Filter control of density is advantageous for halftone positives. The use of color filters avoids the effect of flash and "bump" exposures on screen positives. Because the yellow filter reduces the contrast of the halftone positive, the negative used as copy can have higher contrast than normal. Magenta filters that increase the contrast of the halftone positive can use negatives of lower contrast.

SUMMARY OF HALFTONE EXPOSURE

Following is a summary of the techniques used to expose a halftone negative:

1. A single exposure may be used for copy that has a density range similar to that of the

screen, which also reproduces well on paper. This is the main or detail exposure. Some negative screens, such as the magenta negative, have highlight contrast built in.

2. To extend the screen density range and place dots in the shadow area, an additional flash exposure is made through the screen. The magenta *positive* screen uses CCY (color-compensating yellow) filters to extend the screen range.

3. To compress the screen range and increase the highlight contrast, a screenless or "bump" exposure is made. Additional screenless exposures will produce drop-out effects. Use a CCM (color-compensating magenta) filter with a magenta positive screen to compress the screen density range.

4. All exposures are related to the main exposure. Filters alter the amount (neutral density) and color (color compensating) of light available to the film.

5. Exposures are related to copy light, camera settings, development, press requirements, and film sensitivity.

HOW TO COMPUTE A HALFTONE EXPOSURE

The exposures necessary to reproduce the halftone print desired depend on several factors.

The kind of copy being photographed is important. The copy's tonal range, color surface reflectance, and size are important. The camera, lights, kind of screen and ruling, film, flare, aperture and exposure affect the halftone reproduction. The plate, press, and paper affect the print. Finally, the desired pictorial effect changes the exposure.

The correct halftone exposures are those that result in producing a press print which is the exact pictorial effect desired. Generally, an exposure system can be used that will produce acceptable press prints from normal copy. The Kodak halftone negative computer is a simple method of determining exposure to produce a satisfactory halftone negative. Fig. 11-26.

This computer is designed to give correct exposures for halftone negatives from photographs, artwork, or other reflection copy. It is made to be used with gray and magenta negative contact screens. It also can be used with "Kodalith Autoscreen" ortho film (estar base). An additional dial is used for the magenta positive screen.

COMPUTER CALIBRATION

The computer must be calibrated before use to a specific camera and exposure condition. In sequence, this consists of:

1. Making a test negative with exposures for main and basic flash.

2. Identifying highlight and shadow dot areas on the test negative.

3. Selecting the time for the correct flash exposure.

4. Transferring to the computer the correct shadow dot

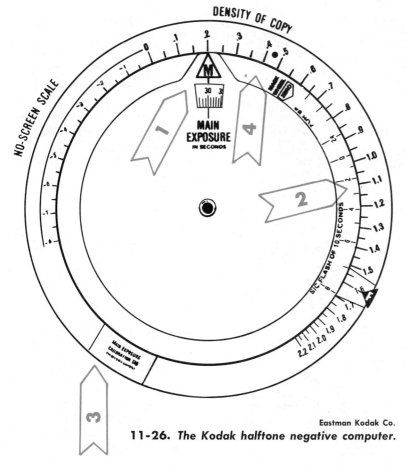

Eastman Kodak Co.
11-26. *The Kodak halftone negative computer.*

measurement in alignment with the flash section.

5. Setting the main exposure indicator on the density scale and calibrating main exposure to this setting.

The computer can be used without recalibration as long as lighting, screen film, and camera combination remains the same.

COMPUTER READINGS

The main exposure is read from the highlight density of the copy. The flash exposure is read from the shadow density of the copy. The interrelationship of main and flash exposure is built into the computer. The density scale is compressed in the shadow range to compensate for average camera flare. The scale is expanded in the highlight range for the reciprocity effect common to many litho film emulsions.

COMPUTER SCALES

The computer has three dials and two scales.

The main exposure dial, marked 1 on Fig. 11-26, is read in the window when the pointer is set at the proper copy highlight density.

A quadrant scale dial, 2, is read for the proper flash exposure.

The calibration tab, 3, is set to conform to the test negative exposure time.

The density of copy scale (upper right) reads from 0 density to 2.2 density. The copy highlight and shadow density are recorded on this scale.

The "F" indicator (lower right) shows exact flash exposure time.

The no-screen scale (upper left) on the dial base is used for

screenless or "bump" exposures, if required.

Before the computer can be used, it must be calibrated from a test negative.

HOW TO MAKE A TEST NEGATIVE

To make a test negative:

1. Set up the camera and lights for optimum conditions at 100 percent reproduction.

2. Center a reflection scale on the copyboard. Fig. 11-27.

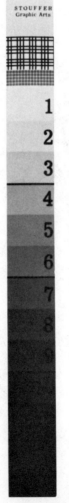

Stouffer Graphic Arts
11-27. A gray scale.

3. Set lens at best f-stop, usually two full stops from wide open. An approximate exposure could be 30 seconds with two pulsed xenon (1500-watt) lamps at 48". Recheck settings and test shutter and lights.

4. Center a sheet of film, such as "Kodalith" ortho film, Type 3, in camera back and cover with larger size magenta negative contact screen. Using black paper, cover a 1" wide edge strip of the film and screen. Close camera and make the exposure as described in Step 3. Open camera. Cover exposed area of film with black paper. Move paper that covered 1" strip of film to expose one-fourth of the 1" strip. Flash expose this area at 10 seconds. Using two pieces of paper, continue to expose one-fourth of the strip at a time, making additonal exposures of 15, 20, and 25 seconds each. Process the film according to manufacturer's directions.

5. Examine the negative. It will resemble Fig. 11-28. Locate the proper highlight dot in the 0.0 to 0.30 density range. If no suitable dot is in this range, another test negative must be made, reducing or increasing exposure as indicated.

6. Locate the proper shadow dot, Fig. 11-28, and note the density.

7. Locate the same shadow dot in the flash strip and record time of this exposure. If none of the exposures renders correct flash dot, change intensity or distance of flash lamp accordingly, and reshoot flash portion on another film. Both the highlight and shadow negative dot should compare to the dot size of other negatives that made high-

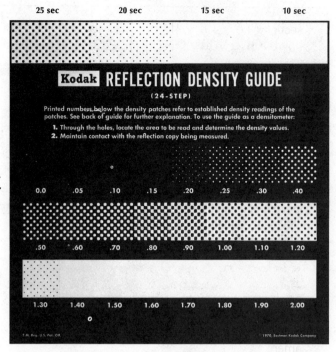

Eastman Kodak Co.

11-28. A 24-step reflection density guide.

quality press prints. A good test negative will have qualities like those shown in Fig. 11-28.

For correct use of the Kodak halftone negative computer, refer to the manufacturer's instructional brochure.

MAJOR STEPS IN HALFTONE EXPOSURE

Figs. 11-29 through 11-31 (Pages 226–229) illustrate the steps and correct procedures of halftone exposure and development. Carelessness or neglect in following an established procedure will lead to poor halftone production.

SUMMARY FOR SHOOTING SAME-SIZE HALFTONES

1. Examine the continuous tone photograph. The photo should have shadow, intermediate, and highlight tones. Avoid photos that are cracked, dirty, indented, or out of focus.

2. Select and measure highlight and shadow areas.

3. Compute main and flash exposures with Kodak negative halftone computer and set the camera. Set camera scale to 100 percent. Set f-stop and remove lens cap.

4. Clean copyboard glass. Center copy and gray scale on the copyboard. Fasten glass and lock in position.

5. Set up materials in the darkroom, making sure all equipment and supplies are working and available. Wipe screen with photo chamois. Turn on safelights and turn off room lights.

6. Turn on vacuum. Center film on camera back, ortho emulsion facing you. Cover film with larger sized screen, emulsion side toward film. Check that screen is held by suction all around film. Carefully roll out any wrinkles.

7. Close camera, set timer, and make exposure.

8. Open camera parallel to flash lamp and reset timer for flash exposure.

9. Make flash exposure, turn off vacuum, and remove screen and film.

10. Process the film. Developer temperature and time of development determine negative density and quality.

ENLARGEMENT AND REDUCTION TIME

Most modern cameras have a diaphragm dial which is calibrated to a percentage size chart. Fig. 11-32 (Page 230). This permits changing the f-stop in relation to the distance between the lens and copyboard. When the f-stop is changed in relation

MAJOR HALFTONE PRODUCTION STEPS

1

CENTER COPY
ON COPYBOARD

2

ADJUST LAMPS

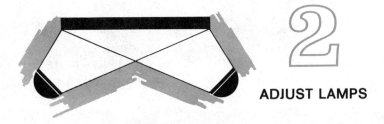

3

SET LENS

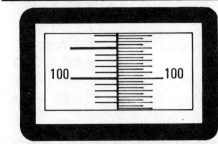

100   100

4

SET COPY SIZE

DO
- Position copy squarely.
- Remove dirt and fingerprints from copy.
- Clean copyboard glass.
- Include a gray scale.

DON'T
- Don't overlap copy and cause shadows.
- Don't use copy that is too thick.
- Don't use white copyboard.

DO
- Use angle for even illumination of film plane.
- Use angle indicators.
- Keep reflectors clean.

DON'T
- Don't change lamp angle unnecessarily.
- Don't fingerprint lamp tubes.

DO
- Use a lens diaphragm control system or a lens formula to determine f-stop.
- Use a lens shade.

DON'T
- Don't fingerprint lens.
- Don't leave lens cap on the lens.
- Don't allow reflections from camera parts to strike copyboard.

DO
- Check camera focus.
- Center image on ground glass.
- Lock carriages.

DON'T
- Don't use wrong lens scale.
- Don't try to move locked carriages.

Du Pont Co.

11-29. Major halftone production steps.

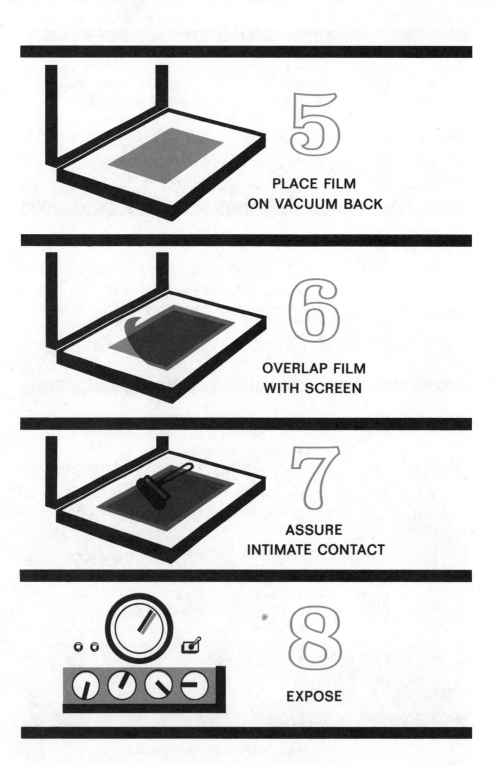

5 PLACE FILM ON VACUUM BACK

6 OVERLAP FILM WITH SCREEN

7 ASSURE INTIMATE CONTACT

8 EXPOSE

DO
- Position film squarely.
- Make sure camera back has a dull black finish.
- Keep camera clean.

DON'T
- Don't use vacuum strong enough to pull film into grooves or holes of camera back.
- Don't rub film surface with your hand.
- Don't kink film.

DO
- Use large enough screen to provide ample overlap.
- Keep screen lined up with bottom of camera back.
- Avoid dust and dirt.

DON'T
- Don't splash screen with processing chemicals.
- Don't kink or scratch screens.

DO
- Use a clean rubber roller or photo chamois and cover sheet to achieve intimate contact between film and screen.

DON'T
- Don't use stiff bristle brushes or rough cloths on screen.
- Don't scratch screens by sliding.

DO
- Use a light integrator or a computer-type exposing unit.
- Place sensor near copy.

DON'T
- Don't change lamp angle and cause inaccuracy in sensor unit.
- Don't guess at exposures; use a system.

Du Pont Co.

11-30. *Halftone production steps.*

9 FLASH

10 PROCESS BY MACHINE

OR TRAY

11 INSPECT

DO
- Determine time by flash computer.
- Use flash times long enough to be reproducible.
- Have even exposure light coverage.
- Use yellow light with magenta screens.

DON'T
- Don't overflash.
- Don't remove screen before flashing.
- Don't use very short flash times.

DO
- Use control strips.
- Replenish methodically.
- Check machine operating conditions.
- Mix and dilute chemicals accurately.

DON'T
- Don't use exhausted replenisher.
- Don't vary development times to compensate for exposure errors or incorrect developer activity.

DO
- Change developer systematically.
- Maintain constant temperature.
- Agitate reproducibly.
- Continue agitating in short stop and fix.

DON'T
- Don't use plastic tray for developer because of poor temperature control.
- Don't use chipped or rough surfaced trays.

DO
- Check mid-tones as well as scale ends.
- Check for missing dots due to dirt.
- Check final size.

DON'T
- Don't scratch film on a rough-surfaced viewer.
- Don't use an excessively bright viewing light.

Du Pont Co.

11-31. *Halftone production steps.*

Brown Manufacturing Co.
11-32. *Lens diaphragm control using a percentage-calibrated chart. Note the use of a combination lens shade and filter holder.*

focused on the ground glass and measured for the correct size.

Changing reproduction size affects the exposure. Some camera lenses reproduce better when the aperture is increased for an enlargement and reduced for a reduction. As discussed earlier in Chapter 10, some cameras have an aperture scale at the lens. A related percentage of reproduction scale allows the same exposure time by changing the aperture (f-stop).

A Kodak graphic arts exposure computer can be used to calculate new exposure time for enlargement or reduction. When the exposure time for same size (100 percent) has been calculated, it is used to determine exposure times of other sizes. Fig. 11-34. The steps are:

1. Determine the enlargement or reduction size of the copy by percentage. Use a proportion calculator, ruler, or follow job instructions.

2. Line up the f-stop used for 100 percent reproductions on the inner computer dial against the 100 percent figure.

3. Place the zero density number on the outer dial opposite the exposure time calculated for 100 percent size.

4. Rotate both dials to place the f-stop used opposite the desired enlargement or reduction.

5. Read the new exposure time opposite the zero (0) on the density dial.

to the reproduction size, the exposure time remains the same regardless of reproduction size. In effect, the f-stop is determined by the intensity of light reaching the lens. The procedure is:

1. Scale the area of copy to be reproduced.

2. Using a guide to compute percentage, determine the percentage reproduction size. Fig. 11-33.

3. Set the camera scales to the proper percentage reproduction size.

4. Set the diaphragm dial to the percentage size, using the same scale (f-stop) used to make a 100-percent size exposure.

5. Follow same procedure as in making 100-percent exposure.

Sometimes it is necessary to change the exposure time when reducing or enlarging. This may be due to copy and camera back masking, or copy and camera requirements.

DETERMINING REPRODUCTION SIZE

The reproduction size of the copy is usually predetermined for the camera operator. It is figured as a percentage of the original size. This topic is discussed in Chapters 9 and 10.

The extent of reproduction possible is determined by the camera capabilities and screen sizes available. The reproduction size is set on the lensboard and copyboard scales. If the camera has no scales, the image can be

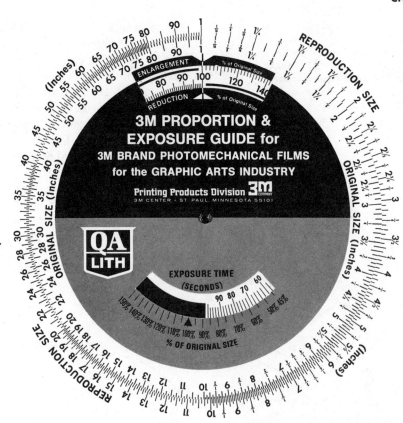

11-33. *A guide for determining percentage of reproduction.*

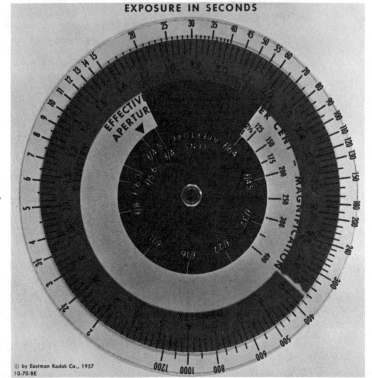

Eastman Kodak Co.

11-34. *Kodak graphic arts exposure computer.*

EXPOSURE IN SECONDS

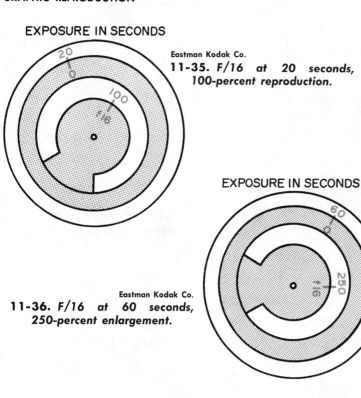

Eastman Kodak Co.
11-35. F/16 at 20 seconds, 100-percent reproduction.

EXPOSURE IN SECONDS

Eastman Kodak Co.
11-36. F/16 at 60 seconds, 250-percent enlargement.

EXPOSURE IN SECONDS

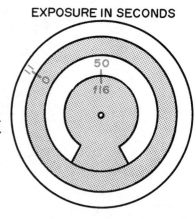

Eastman Kodak Co.
11-37. F/16 at 11 seconds, 50-percent reduction.

For example: For same-size (100-percent) reproduction, the exposure at f/16 is calculated to be 20 seconds. The dials in Fig. 11-35 show f/16 opposite 100 percent and zero density opposite 20 seconds. For an enlargement of 250 percent, Fig. 11-36 shows both dials rotated so that f/16 is opposite 250 percent. The exposure time indicated opposite zero density is 60 seconds. Using the same f/stop, a 50-percent reduction in original size would produce an exposure time of 11 seconds. Fig. 11-37.

REVIEW QUESTIONS

1. Halftone dots are all the same size. True or False?
2. A glass cross-line screen is made from two sheets of glass. What is a contact screen made of?
3. What are the two types of contact screens?
4. Density can be measured by visual comparison with a gray scale or by using a visual tone projector. Name a third way to measure density.
5. What is the lightest tone in copy called?
6. What is the darkest tone called?
7. Three different kinds of exposure may be required for a halftone. Name these.

Chapter 12

Developing Film

THE DARKROOM

Developing film requires a lightproof area called a darkroom. A good darkroom is carefully planned and organized. It must be located to serve both the camera and the stripping area. Fig. 12-1. It is often arranged so that the same processing area can be used with two or more cameras. Fig. 12-2. The equipment selected for the darkroom is determined by the needs of the printing plant.

PHYSICAL CONDITIONS

A well-equipped darkroom should contain:

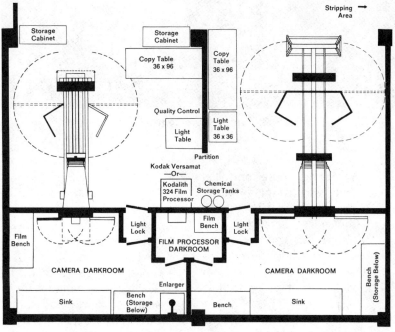

Eastman Kodak Co.

12-2. *Floor plan for process camera rooms.*

12-1. *Floor plan for production facilities in a lithographic plant.*

Eastman Kodak Co.

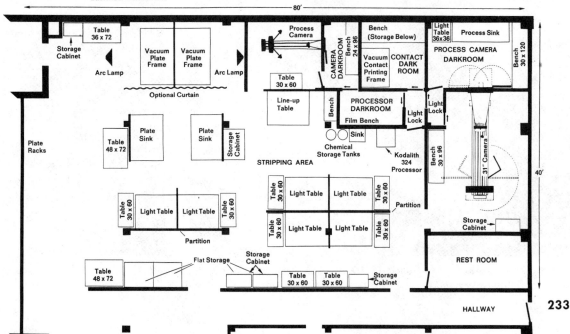

12-3. *Temperature-controlled sink.*

12-6. *Storage in film boxes in the darkroom.*

* A temperature-controlled sink with running water. Figs. 12-3 and 12-4.
* Convenient safelights. Fig. 12-5. A safelight has a filter which restricts the emitted light so that it does not cause film exposed to it to be activated.
* Lightproof film storage. Figs. 12-6 through 12-8.
* Timer. Fig. 12-9.
* Inspection area. Figs. 12-10 and 12-11.
* Vacuum frame. Fig. 12-12.
* Point-source light. Fig. 12-13.
* Storage area should be available for solutions, trays, screens, film, and other necessary items. A refrigerator can be used for film storage. Film should be allowed to return to room temperature before use.

Equipment in the darkroom is generally located to provide a flow of work from the camera to the stripping area. Aisles follow the work flow and provide safe movement of workers in the dark. The air should be changed every ten minutes and exhaust hoods used where toxic chemicals are a hazard. A good tem-

12-4. *Nitrogen-burst, controlled-temperature sinks.*

12-5. *Safelight positioned near timed flash lamp in the darkroom.*

12-7. *General bulk film storage in light-tight drawers.*

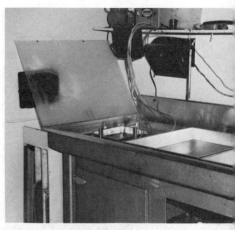

12-10. *A sheet of rigid plastic with a safelight behind it is used for inspection of film during development.*

12-8. *Special types of films and papers are stored in light-tight drawers located near specialized equipment.*

perature is in the range of 70 to 75° F. (21 to 24 °C). The relative humidity should be kept between 45 and 50 percent. These conditions will help prevent worker fatigue and will aid in processing photosensitive materials. It is critical that the air be clean as well as conditioned. Dust is the greatest enemy of quality work.

Besides filters on air conditioners and dustproof ventilators, the air inside the room must be clean. Often an inside fan and filter combination is used to trap dust inside the room. The darkroom may have "positive pressure," or a higher air pressure than connecting rooms. This stops dust from entering when a

12-9. *Timers and variable voltage transformer for point-source lights.*

12-11. *Checking film for extent of development.*

12-12. A contact vacuum frame with point-source light controls located for convenient use.

door is opened. Contamination by dust must be avoided. Arc lights, traffic, and dirty materials are common sources of dust.

The darkroom floor is designed to be waterproof and easily cleaned. A resilient covering of

12-13. An enclosed point-source light with powered rotating filter wheel. The unit shown is attached to the ceiling.

sheet tile in neutral color will give comfort, safety, and cleanliness.

The darkroom ceiling is usually white to reflect safelights. Walls are painted white or tan except where light reflection is not desired.

Openings to darkrooms are made so as to allow entrance without light coming in from other areas. The entrance may be a light lock or a light trap. The light lock, Fig. 12-1, may be a revolving door or double doors. The revolving door has an outer shell with openings for each room. An inside drum with a single entrance rotates inside the circular shell. Double doors require a warning device to prevent both doors from being opened at the same time. When a single door is used, it is locked from the inside.

A light trap, Fig. 12-14, does not require a door. However, due to reflected light, it is not as effective. A light trap does permit air circulation and free entrance to a room. Curtains can be used where a light lock or light trap cannot be installed.

Water supplied to the darkroom sinks and for use in processing needs to be reasonably free of impurities and contain less than 150 parts per million of calcium carbonate. Solids such as clay or silt must be removed by filtration.

Water usage in the darkroom may be excessive unless carefully conserved. Control of water usage produces better film products with minimal expense.

A completely grounded electrical system is necessary for safety. Switches can be marked with luminescent material. Safety covers or latches can be

12-14. Light trap. The inside should be painted black to trap stray light.

used as covers to block white light switches. Another method is to install all white light switches high (six feet off the floor) and all safelight switches at normal height. Some darkrooms have a master switch to shut off all lighting. Safelights have special filters for different purposes. The chart in Fig. 12-15 compares filter numbers and colors from one manufacturer for use with different photosensitive materials.

FILM DEVELOPMENT

There are three common methods of film development. One method uses trays in a temperature-controlled sink. Fig. 12-3. Another uses controlled agitation in a temperature-controlled sink. The third method is fully automatic, using a film processor. Fig. 12-16.

A *temperature-controlled* sink uses circulating water maintained at a constant temperature. Three trays and a water wash bath are used. The first tray holds the developer. The second tray holds a stop bath; and the third, a fixative.

Film developers vary according to the brand of film used. Follow the manufacturer's recommendations. Several common developers are available as two concentrated solutions. The two solutions are mixed together with water before use. The tray bottom should be larger than the film size to be developed. Do not fill the tray over half full of developer.

The developer acts on the grains of silver in the film emulsion which have been exposed to light. (See Chapter 10 for a discussion of film emulsions.) Developer action reduces the light-affected silver halides to black metallic silver. Developers have an accelerator to soften the gelatin. This permits the developer agent to reach the silver salts within the emulsion. A preservative controls the speed of development and retards emulsion softening. A restraining agent is included to stop the developer

12-15. *Safelights have special filters for different purposes. This chart shows which filters are used for various photographic materials.*

USE OF SAFELIGHT FILTERS

Kodak Safelight Filter No.	Color	For Use With
OA	Greenish yellow	Kodak black and white contact and duplicating materials and projection films.
OC	Light amber	Kodak black and white contact and enlarging papers. Kodak high resolution plate, and opalure print film.
1	Red	Blue-sensitive films and plates, Kodagraph projection positive, Kodagraph projection papers (standard and extra thin), and most linagraph papers.
1A	Light red	Kodalith and Kodagraph ortho-sensitive materials.
2	Dark red	Orthochromatic-sensitive materials, green-sensitive X-ray films, Ektaline papers, and Linagraph 1832 and 1884 papers.
3	Dark green	Panchromatic films and plates.
6B	Brown	X-ray film (except dental), blue-sensitive film for photoradiography, Kodak Electrocardiograph 553 Paper.
7	Green	Infrared materials (except Kodak high-speed infrared film).
8	Dark yellow	Eastman color print film, types 5385 and 7385.
10	Dark amber	Kodak Ektacolor slide film, Kodak Ektacolor print film, Kodak Ektacolor paper, Kodak Ektacolor professional paper, Kodak Resisto rapid pan paper, Kodak Panalure paper.
Type ML-2	Light orange	Dental X-ray films.

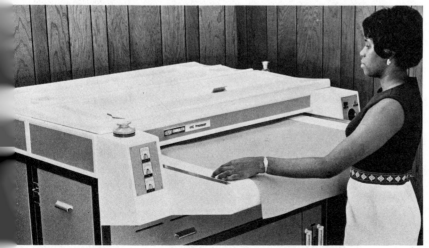

agent from acting on the unexposed silver.

The development can be stopped by placing the film in a *short stop bath*. The short stop solution is put into the second tray. It is made of one ounce of 28-percent acetic acid to 16 ounces of water. Developers have an alkaline agent that reduces the silver salts or halides.

Du Pont Co.
12-16. *Automatic film processor.*

12-17. *Film being air-dried on a darkroom "clothesline."*

The acid nature of the stop bath kills the action of the developer.

The third tray contains a fixative, commonly called hypo or fixer. This bath stops development, hardens the emulsion, and removes the undeveloped silver salts. Sometimes the short stop bath is not used. Then fixative is used to stop development. Afterwards, the film is placed in a water bath to rinse away the fixative. The completed processed film is a negative.

FIXATIVE ACTION

The gelatin emulsion is softened and swelled by water and by the accelerator in the developer. The softened gelatin is easily scratched. This is one reason a fixative is needed.

Water in the fixative carries the fixative chemicals into the emulsion. The hypo (actually sodium thiosulfate) dissolves the undeveloped crystals. A preservative, sodium sulfite, slows the formation of sulfur. Acetic acid makes the solution acidic. A gelatin hardener makes the film scratch-resistant.

The fixative dissolves the unexposed crystals and "clears" the film. That is, the grayish-tan crystals in unexposed areas become clear. For good results, film should be left in the fixative twice as long as it takes to clear the film.

THE RINSE

Washing the film after fixing removes the dissolved crystals, or soluble silver salts, and the other chemicals. The rinse bath temperature should be between 68 and 75° F. (20 and 24 °C). Washing time needs to be about a half hour when complete water change occurs every five minutes. To remove water drops after washing, the film can be dipped in a wetting agent solution.

Apeco Div., Brown Manufacturing Co.
12-18. *Film dryer.*

12-19. *Print dryer.*

Fig. 12-18. A print dryer is shown in Fig. 12-19.

HOW TO DEVELOP FILM

1. Prepare solutions of developer, stop, and fixative according to manufacturer's recommendations. Place these in trays in a temperature-controlled sink. Fig. 12-20. Set the temperature control according to film and developer specifications. This is usually 68° F. (20 °C). If a controlled sink is not available, place developer tray in a larger tray. Regulate temperature by adding warm or cold water to the large tray. Use a photographic thermometer in the developer tray. Fig. 12-21.

2. Use only safelight recommended for film. Do not allow any other light in the development room during film processing.

3. Set timer for manufactur-

FILM DRYING

Film may be room-dried, Fig. 12-17, or dried in an enclosure using heated air. Drying shrinks the emulsion to its original thickness. Dust, water drops, and chemicals present on the film during drying will leave a residue that creates problems in usage of the film. A film dryer is shown in

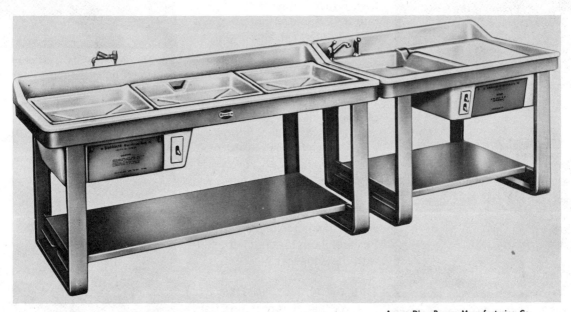

Apeco Div., Brown Manufacturing Co.

12-20. *Temperature-controlled sinks for developing, fixing, and washing films and prints.*

er's recommended development time.

4. Put film into developer, and start the timer. Tilt the tray, and slide in film with the emulsion side up in the high side of the tray. Figs. 12-22 and 12-23. At the same time, rock the tray toward the film. The wave of developer will roll over the film, covering it evenly and quickly. Avoid uneven wetting of film and air bubbles. Rock the tray lightly, alternately side to side and front to back. Make this action as regular as possible. Wait until the developer ripple returns before rocking in another direction.

5. When development time is complete, remove film. Lift film by a corner. Gently drag each side over the edge of the tray to remove excess developer as film is removed. Be careful not to scratch the soft emulsion. Figs. 12-24 and 12-25. Another way to remove excess developer from film is to let the film drip for about five seconds before putting it in the next tray. With this method, you do not risk scratching the film.

6. Slip film into short stop tray. Rinse hands in water. Agitate tray. Remove film after several seconds. Let film drip.

7. Slip film into fixative tray. Agitate tray until film clears. Do not use room light until film clears. Remember, film should remain in fixative twice as long as it takes to clear the film.

8. Rinse the film in the recirculating water tray. Follow recommended time for film. Fig. 12-26.

9. Squeegee film on both sides and hang to dry. Fig. 12-27. Be careful not to scratch the film with the squeegee.

TIPS ON HANDLING FILM

Never take film or hands from short stop or hypo back to the

12-21. A stainless steel photographic thermometer.

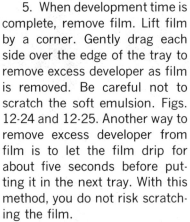

12-22. Placing film in tray.

12-23. Sliding film in tray under developer.

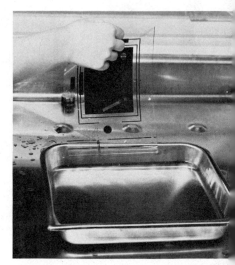

12-24. Lift film against side of tray to slide off developer.

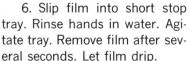

12-25. Reverse film and drag off developer against stops at side of tray.

12-26. Rinsing film.

240

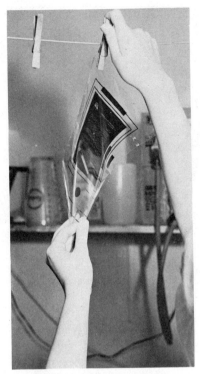

12-27. Hang film to dry.

developer. This action will contaminate the developer and destroy its activity. Always rinse your hands in water after hypo immersion. Short stop and fixative will discolor and eat holes in clothing. Handle film by edges and corners with *dry* hands before and after processing. White light will fog film not completely fixed. Hypo stains will show if film is not completely washed.

DEVELOPMENT BY EXAMINATION

Development by time and temperature is the best method. In some instances, however, development by examination is necessary. Lighting on the camera may vary. The sink may not be temperature-controlled. The developer may be weak or exhausted. Film may be old or development time unknown. If these variables cannot be controlled, standard development cannot be accomplished.

The film must then be visually inspected during development. This method requires an inspection window. The translucent window is lighted by safelight. A magnifying glass is used for close examination. A rinse tray of water is also used.

The negative in the developing tray is inspected when it appears to have almost reached the proper density. The negative is lifted from the developing tray. It is rinsed in the water tray. This stops development. The negative is placed on the inspection window. Fig. 12-28. If further development is necessary, the negative is returned to the developing tray. When proper development is reached, the negative is stopped and fixed.

Inspection development can be aided by the use of a *step scale*. Regular, increasing steps of density are measured on the scale. Fig. 12-29. The scale is photographed with the copy. As development progresses, the less dense steps on the scale become black on the negative. A number on each step of the density scale indicates development.

Proper exposure and development of negatives are critical. Good negatives have the following characteristics.

1. Sharp edges of letters and lines.

2. Letters not fattened (underexposure).

3. Letters not thinned or broken (overexposure).

4. Good reproduction of fine detail. (Loss results from underexposure.)

5. Clear image. (Clouded image is the result of overexposure.)

12-28. Inspecting the negative.

Stouffer Graphic Arts

12-29. Ten-step scale.

STOUFFER
Graphic Arts

1
2
3
4
5
6
7
8
9

12-30. *Excess pinholes in the negative caused the flaws in this print.*

6. Dense black areas (will not transmit light).

7. Few pinholes.

Development problems often appear to be exposure problems. Dust on the film or copyboard causes excessive pinholes in the negative. Fig. 12-30 shows an example of good reproduction of dust. It shows sharp exposure, good development, and poor housekeeping. Cold, weak, or poorly mixed developer causes negatives to appear underexposed. Underdevelopment yields negatives with insufficient density and an underexposed appearance. Overdevelopment causes fine lines to fill and the negative to become cloudy.

FILM DEVELOPMENT VARIATIONS

Careful camera settings and exposure make for quality film reproductions. The film, however, must be processed with equal care. Variations in development time, developer temperature, agitation, or chemicals used cause differences in the film image. Processing of film needs to be standardized to produce uniform film products.

TIME AND DEVELOPMENT

Most film and developer combinations have a time recommended by the manufacturer. The lapsed time is measured by

Du Pont Co.
12-31. *These prints are from halftone negatives that had identical exposures but different developer temperatures.*

a timer which alerts by sound on completion of the development period. For convenience, the timer can be set for slightly more than the development time. This will allow you time to reach the developer tray. Immerse the film as the second hand reaches the starting time for development. Variation in development time rapidly affects the screen range and quality of the dot. When de-

68°

82°

A NORMAL HALFTONE PROCESSED AT 68°.

SHORTENED DEVELOPMENT TIME TO COMPENSATE FOR HIGHER TEMPERATURE.

veloping by inspection, rinse the film in water before visual inspection. This will wash away the developer and stop development during the inspection phase.

Developer Temperature

Time and temperature of development are related. Automatic processors use higher temperatures to reduce development time. Most tray developers have longer development times. The temperature used is determined by the time necessary in handling the film, the capability of the temperature control equipment, and nature of the film emulsion.

A precision tray thermometer must be used to check the sink temperature control. The developer solution may not be the same as the sink temperature. Fresh developer placed in a tray may require a cooling period to equal the maintained sink temperature. It is the variation of temperature during development or between development of identical exposures that causes changes in the film image. Fig. 12-31 illustrates different temperature and development times used to make similar prints from halftone negatives of identical exposure. The four prints in Fig. 12-32 show a range of change in print quality by varying the temperature. All four negatives shown had the same exposure and development time. Variation in temperature caused the range from underdevelopment through overdevelopment of the negatives.

Variation in Agitation

Movement of the developer across the emulsion is necessary to carry away exhausted chemicals and provide a continuous rate of development. Changes in halftone contrast are the result of variation in agitation. Rapid agitation has the effect of shortening the halftone scale. Highlights tend to close up, with a

Du Pont Co.

12-32. *Results of different developer temperatures, using same exposure and development time.*

| **NORMAL AGITATION** | **BRISK AGITATION** | **STILL DEVELOPMENT** |

Du Pont Co.

12-33. *These prints are from halftone negatives that had identical exposure and development time but different agitation.*

resulting loss of highlight print dot. A reduction in exposure time is required to compensate for rapid agitation.

Still development, in which the developer is agitated only for the first 15 or 20 seconds of development, lengthens the halftone scale. This method produces a negative with highlights that are too open. Print dots will be over-size in the highlight areas. An increase in exposure time is required to compensate for still development. Fig. 12-33 shows the effect of still development and rapid agitation as compared to normal agitation. Each of the prints shown was made from a halftone negative with identical exposure and development time. Each was developed in the same temperature.

EXHAUSTION OF CHEMICALS

Developer exhaustion is the chemicals' loss of ability to change silver halides at the proper rate. While exposure and development time can be extended for weakened solutions, poorer quality negatives are often a result. Each sheet of film developed uses up some of the original developer activity. Fig. 12-34 shows the effect on the first, seventh, and fifteenth sheets of film developed in the same limited solution of developer. Highest standards of quality require that a fresh developer solution be used for each sheet of film.

Developers, particularly diluted solutions, age rapidly while in storage. Used developer should never be poured back into fresh developer for storage. Aged developer causes variations and problems in processing film. Developers should be kept in sealed containers or tanks with floating lids. Fig. 12-35. This practice reduces the effects of oxidation, which ages developers.

Contamination of developers by metals or chemicals reduces or destroys their usefulness. The developer is alkaline in nature. Acids from the stop bath and the fixative are contaminators. Remember, never place film or hands from the stop bath or the fixative tray to the developer tray without first rinsing in water. Developers must be systematically replaced in trays or replenished in automatic processors. This will prevent exhaustion and maintain consistent development.

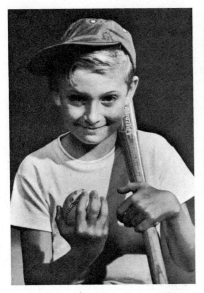  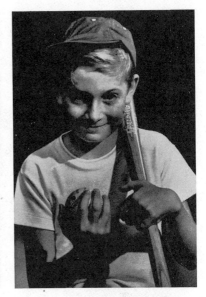

1ˢᵗ SHEET   7ᵗʰ SHEET   15ᵗʰ SHEET

Du Pont Co.

12-34. Examples of developer exhaustion through use. These prints are from halftone negatives that had identical exposure and development times and were tray-processed in the same limited quantity of developer.

Bromide, developer, and adjacency effects, Fig. 12-36, are usually caused by directional sheet movement during development. The bromide effect is the result of exhausted chemicals flowing from the dense image to the less dense area. The exhausted materials prevent sufficient development of areas behind the direction of film movement.

The developer effect is the reverse of the bromide effect, as fresher chemicals flow across and cause increased development. The adjacency effect is the loss of development around a dense image. This is caused by exhausted chemicals during still development. The bromide and developer effects are usually the product of tank or automatic processors. These effects can be minimized through use of fresh developer, proper temperature, development time, and regular agitation.

MIXING PHOTOGRAPHIC SOLUTIONS

The proper preparation of chemicals is critical to good film production. The manufacturer's instructions must be followed carefully. The containers and stirring rods must be clean and made of glass, plastic, or stain-

12-35. A and B developer solutions with hoses and clamps for controlled measurement.

less steel. Each material should be completely dissolved before adding the next chemical. Accurate measuring graduates should be used. Storage bottles must be completely filled and capped to keep out air. Proper temperature and cleanliness of water are important for dissolving and retaining purity of solutions. Materials, particularly powders, should not be mixed in the darkroom. Chemical dust causes spots and stains on photographic materials.

CONTAMINATION

If possible, each solution should have its own mixing containers. This is the best way to avoid contaminating other solutions. If mixing in a common container, wash thoroughly between use of chemicals. Mix chemicals in the sequence they are used in processing film. A little developer in hypo (fixative) is not harmful, but hypo in developer fogs film.

MIXING DEVELOPER

Lith-type (graphic arts) developers differ from continuous-tone developers in several ways. They generally deteriorate more rapidly, have only one developing agent (hydro-quinone) and have a long initial developing rate. The rapid deterioration is due to the small amount of preservative used. Because of this, the two parts should not be mixed together until necessary for use.

Mixing should follow the manufacturer's instructions. *Tempered* water (heated) from 90–100° F. (32–38 °C) is used. Do not attempt to mix part of a package. Agitate well while pouring powder slowly. Avoid splashing air into the solution as this weakens the developer. Never mix in developer trays or tanks. Store stock solutions (A & B) in small bottles that can be used up completely for each tray supply.

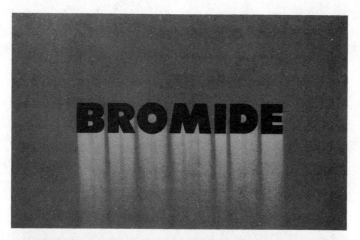

Du Pont Co.

12-36. Bromide, developer, and adjacency effects.

When A & B stock solutions are mixed for tray use, the tray size determines the amount required:

For an 8″ × 10″ tray
475 millilitres (16 oz.)

For an 11″ × 14″ tray
950 millilitres (32 oz.)

For a 16″ × 20″ tray
1900 millilitres (64 oz.)

For a 20″ × 24″ tray
2850 millilitres (96 oz.)

Some graphic arts developers are supplied in liquid form. These should be mixed according to the manufacturer's directions.

DARKROOM MATERIALS

Darkrooms require a wide variety of chemicals, films, papers, and proofing materials, depending upon the kind of work done. A list of such materials would be extensive and beyond the scope of this book. All photographic materials require careful study of the directions and usage according to package instructions. Complete specifications concerning the material are available in manufacturers' and suppliers' catalogues.

While many of the chemicals are available in simple dry or liquid mixes, others are prepared as needed. Several of these solutions are included in the following section.

STOP BATH

The acid bath to stop development is made of the following: acetic acid 28%, 125 millilitres; water, 1 litre. Add the acetic acid to the water. Do *not* use glacial acetic acid.

KODAK FARMER'S REDUCER R-4A

STOCK SOLUTION A		
	Liquid Measure	
	Customary	Metric
Kodak Potassium Ferricyanide (Anhydrous)	1¼ ounces	37.5 grams
Water to make.	16 ounces	500 millilitres
STOCK SOLUTION B		
Kodak Sodium Thiosulfate (Hypo) (Pentahydrated)	16 ounces	480.0 grams
Water to make.	64 ounces	2.0 litres

For use take: Stock solution A, 1 oz. (30 ml), stock solution B, 4 oz. (120 ml), and water to make 32 oz. (1 litre). Add A to B, then add the water, and pour the mixed solution at once over the negative to be reduced, which preferably should be contained in a white tray. Watch closely. When the negative has been reduced sufficiently, wash thoroughly before drying. (Reduction is discussed in a later section.)

For less rapid reducing action, use one-half of the previously mentioned quantity of stock solution A with the same quantities of stock solution B and water.

Solutions A and B should not be combined until they are to be used. They will not keep long in combination.

ETCH-BLEACH FORMULAS

SOLUTION A		
	Customary	Metric
Water, at 122° F. (50 °C).	24 ounces	750 millilitres
Cupric Chloride	145 grains	10 grams
Kodak Citric Acid (Anhydrous)	145 grains	10 grams
Water to make.	32 ounces	1 litre
SOLUTION B		
Hydrogen Peroxide 3%		

For use, mix equal parts of A and B. One quart of mixed solution is sufficient for about 16 sheets of 8″ × 10″ film.

CHANGING THE IMAGE

The processed photographic image in litho films can be changed three ways. It can acquire added density, called *intensification*. The image can be subtracted in size and density, called reduction or *etching*. Finally, the image can be changed from negative to positive, or to the opposite in density. This process is called *reversal*.

INTENSIFICATION

This process is common for continuous tone but not for litho films. It uses two steps. Step one bleaches the film. Step two uses an intensifier to change the bleached image to an opaque, metallic image.

REDUCTION

Two types of reduction, or etching, are used. They are *flat* and *dot* etching. Flat etching is used to reduce the image overall.

Dot etching is used on small areas to change load densities. It is often done for color separations, to change color, or add highlights. See Chapter 18, "Color Separation."

Flat etching is used primarily for line negatives. Some negatives have excessive density in the image (clear) areas. This is called *fogging* and may be caused by exposure or contamination of the developer. An etch called Farmer's Reducer is used to "clear" line negatives. It acts on the silver, producing a soluble salt, which is rinsed away. The activity of the solution on the film stops after a few minutes. Farmer's Reducer is not used on halftones as it tends to leave a stain around the dots.

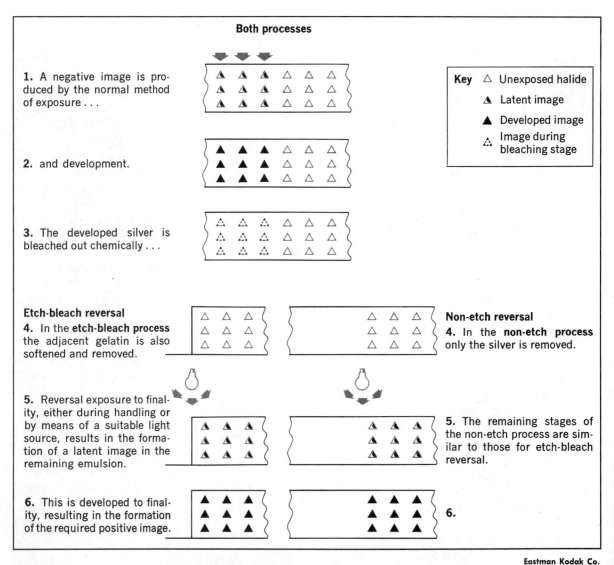

12-37. *Outline of the bleach reversal and etch-bleach reversal processes, shown by means of diagrammatic representations of a section through the emulsion.*

The reducer is mixed from A & B stock solutions and used immediately. The negative must be completely covered with solution. When the negative is cleared, remove and wash carefully. For critical work and slower action, decrease the amount of A solution in relation to the B solution.

IMAGE REVERSAL

When high density, fine definition, and a tough image are required, a reversal process can be used. Positives for screen process work can be made in this manner. An added advantage is the absence of pinholes in the positive.

The reversal of the image begins with the bleaching and etching of the developed film. This softens the gelatin around the developed silver and bleaches the developed silver. Rinsing removes the gelatin and bleached silver. The film is re-exposed to light to form a latent image on the remaining (previously unexposed) silver. The film is developed again with density becoming reversed. If the image was originally negative, it becomes positive. Fig. 12-37.

SAVING SILVER

Conservation of silver is important. It is a natural resource and a valuable metal. The films used in graphic arts are coated with silver particles. The fixative, or hypo, collects silver particles removed from the film. Neither used film nor hypo should be thrown away. Used film can be sold by the pound to recovery companies. They burn the film and smelt the ashes.

Silver can be recovered from the fixing bath. Three methods can be used. These are metallic replacement, electrolytic plating, and precipitation.

REPLACEMENT

A simple method of removing silver from fixative is to replace it with another metal. Usually, fine steel wool is used as replacement.

Steel wool is put in a container as a filler material. The spent hypo trickles over the filler. Acid in the hypo etches the steel, causing silver to be "squeezed" out (precipitated) as a sludge. When the steel wool is dissolved, it can be replaced.

While this method is simple, the amount of silver recovered depends on the silver content available, pH of the hypo (a measure of acidity), and speed of flow. The pH should be between 4.5 and 6.5 for best results. Silver test strips of paper are available to determine silver content of hypo by color of the strip.

ELECTROLYTIC PLATING

The exhausted fixer usually has between 1/2 to 1 troy ounce of silver per gallon. The electrolytic method of recovery uses a charged anode and a cathode. The anode and cathode are submerged in the fixer to attract the silver. The silver in the fixer solution has a positive charge (+ ions). The positively charged carbon anode (+) repels the silver ions. Fig. 12-38. The stainless steel cathode (−) attracts. A layer (plating) of silver builds on the cathode. Fig. 12-39. The stainless steel cathode resists corrosion and allows the silver to be peeled off easily. Most electrolytic methods use agitation to provide continual silver-bearing

12-38. A portable electrolysis unit that can be placed in the hypo tank.

solution contact with the cathode. Excessive voltage or low silver content will cause a "rotten egg" smell. This is characteristic when excessive sulfides of silver are created. For litho films, an ounce of silver usually can be recovered from processing 150 sheets of 5″ × 7″ film or 75 sheets of 8″ × 10″ film.

SILVER PRECIPITATION

Silver can also be recovered by precipitation with caustic chemi-

12-39. The portable electrolysis unit showing the stainless steel cathode.

Apeco Div., Brown Manufacturing Co.
12-40. Hand-fed film dryer.

tion.") Paper in the processor is transported by rollers through an activator chemical tray and a stabilizer tray. It is used in the darkroom to provide quick, continuous tone prints from continuous tone negatives.

A diffusion-transfer processor is used to make screened prints, reflex proofs, and to copy line work. The processor has a single tray of activator chemical. The exposed negative paper is faced with receiver paper, and the two sheets are fed through the processor together. Eastman Kodak markets a line of photomechanical transfer (PMT) materials for various diffusion process uses.

PMT Screened Prints

Photomechanical transfer screened prints are produced by exposing PMT negative paper in a process camera with a gray screen. The camera operations are similar to shooting film halftones.

1. The exposed PMT negative paper is faced emulsion to emulsion with PMT receiver paper in proper safelight.

cals. Due to the danger to films and health, this method is not used in the darkroom.

The silver sludge or plated silver is collected by reclaiming companies and refined to 99.9 percent pure silver. With the electrolytic method, the used fixer, unless it is sulfided, can be reused.

The tray rocker, Fig. 12-41, provides control of the agitation of chemicals. These and other devices generally save time and manual labor.

SIMPLE PROCESSORS

A stabilization processor may be used in the darkroom to make continuous tone prints. It is more commonly used to process phototypesetting paper. (See Chapter 6, "Cold Type Composi-

MECHANICAL PROCESSING

Mechanical devices for processing prints and films vary from air-powered tray rockers to automatic "dry to dry" processors that develop, fix, and dry photographic materials.

MECHANICAL ASSISTS

Mechanical devices, such as a hand-fed film dryer, Fig. 12-40, aid in certain processing phases.

12-41. Air-driven tray rocker.

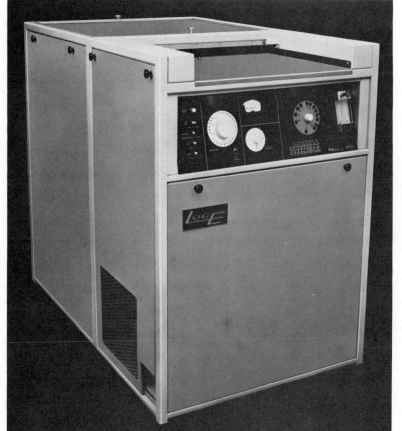

12-42. *An automatic processor with dial-in replenishment.*

2. The PMT negative and receiver papers are fed together through the diffusion processor.

3. After 30 seconds the papers are pulled apart.

The result is a screened print. Advantages of this method are that it is a fast process, and when used as camera copy, it permits line shots of line and tone paste-ups. In the same manner, line copy can be reproduced in different sizes. Poor copy can be reproduced as PMT copy for better camera work.

PMT Reflex Proofs

PMT reflex paper is used to reproduce reflection copy or film negatives and positives in a printing frame. The procedure is as follows:

1. Place copy face up in frame.

2. Cover copy with reflex paper (emulsion down).

3. Draw down vacuum and expose about 30 seconds.

4. Place reflex paper emulsion to emulsion with receiver paper and feed into diffusion processor.

5. After 30 seconds pull receiver proof from reflex paper.

Advantages of this method are time saved in processing proofs and low sensitivity of reflex paper to subdued light.

A transparent receiver material can be used with PMT nega-tive and PMT reflex paper. It is exposed and processed like opaque receiver material. The transparencies can be positive or negative, according to the copy. Transparencies are used for projection and as positive and negative film. As film, they are used directly to expose plates, for screen process work, and diazo reproduction of mutliple proofs.

MECHANIZED PROCESSORS

As stated before, there are mechanical processors that develop and fix photographic materials continuously. Fig. 12-42. Many provide "dry to dry" operation.

The exposed film enters the developer and is transported through a rinse, a fixative, a wash, and finally a dryer. Fig. 12-43.

Processors are used for lithographic films, photographic films, and radiographic films that record radio wave movement. In the graphic arts, two different types of films and papers are processed. These are the litho, or high-contrast materials, and the continuous tone, or low-contrast photo materials.

Litho chemicals, called "the chemistry," process camera negatives, duplicates, reversals,

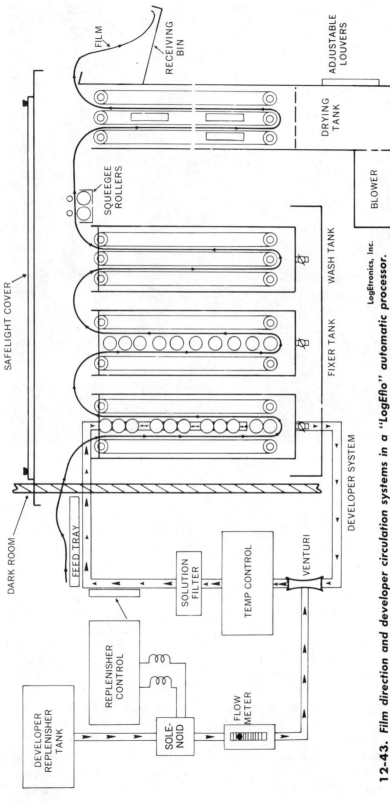

12-43. Film direction and developer circulation systems in a "LogEflo" automatic processor. LogEtronics, Inc.

and stripping films. Continuous tone chemistry is used mainly for color separation work, such as masks, color-separation negatives, positives, and copy negatives. In addition, special chemistry is used for processing phototypesetting and scanner materials. Processors are usually filled with one type of chemistry and used for litho or continuous tone operations. Two general types of processors are in use. One type uses rollers to transport the film. Fig. 12-44. The other style uses rollers and belts to transport the film. Fig. 12-45.

ADVANTAGES IN AUTOMATIC PROCESSING

Processors have several advantages over manual processing. These can be grouped in the areas of time, cost, space and quality.

Time Reduction

Generally, processors can complete a sheet of film in four to six minutes. Additionally, processors will continuously process film by the hour. The processing rate is normally faster than the manual rate. Also, the operator is freed from tray tending and can utilize this time for other work. Rapid processing and continuous volume save time.

Cost

In tray work, the depleted developer is discarded, and a new batch is mixed after developing several films. A mechanical processor automatically replenishes the developer as required. Figs. 12-46 and 12-47.

The enclosed system retards exhaustion of developer, since

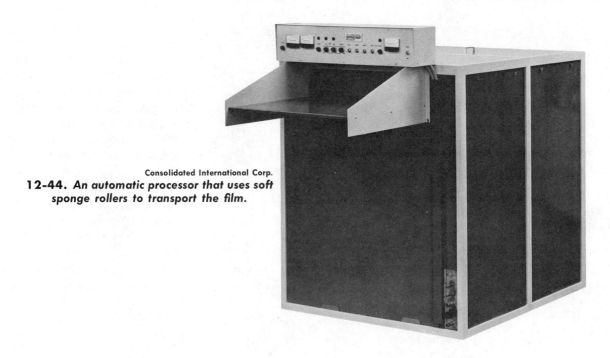

Consolidated International Corp.

12-44. *An automatic processor that uses soft sponge rollers to transport the film.*

Du Pont Co.

12-45. *The automatic-contact, litho film processor that handles films up to 24" wide and provides 90-second access for contact and camera line work. It has a rewash/redry slot.*

Du Pont Co.

12-46. Total automation for litho film processing. The processor is coupled to a blender. A scanner reads the actual processed silver image and signals the blender, which mixes fresh replenisher from concentrates and pumps it to developer tanks.

With the control of variables, film density can be consistent. Exhausted developer makes soft, mushy dots; sharp, hard dots come from fresh developer. Hard dots make good plates. Film products with consistent density lead to consistent quality in plates.

MACHINE OPERATION

Cleanliness and control are the key words for good machine operation. Dirty rollers, belts, sludge, and contamination render a machine useless. When replacing all the chemistry, the following steps are used:

1. Dump developer and fixer chemicals. Flush tanks and processor with warm water. Fill tanks with warm water and run machine for 10 minutes. Repeat this cycle three times.

2. Dump replenishment and proceed as in Step 1.

3. Use a sulfanic acid cleaner and follow label directions.

4. Remember to flush all lines and entire system of cleaner.

5. Drain all lines and tanks. Install filters and clean outside of machine.

6. Mix lith or continuous-tone developer according to directions.

7. Mix fixative according to directions.

8. Transfer chemistry to the processor.

9. Mix and add replenisher solution.

10. Fill wash section and run until temperature is 75° F. (24 °C) or recommended temperature.

When the machine is first started in the morning or after a weekend, it must be run until the

air contact is less than in tray development. Filtering systems are provided in mechanical processors to recirculate clean developer and provide more active chemistry.

Most processors use less water than in tray processing, since the film is rinsed for a shorter period of time. Tempered water usage for controlling chemistry temperature is reduced during stand-by periods. A reduction in chemistry and water costs are the result of the enclosed design and automatic systems of a mechanical processor.

Quality and Consistency

The quality and consistency of machine-processed negatives are

the result of control of variables in processing. In machine processing, the time, temperature, agitation, chemical strength, and drying are controlled. Negatives of consistent quality can be produced. This quality is evident as the negative is used in related work.

Pinholes in negatives are caused mainly by dust. Machine-processed negatives have fewer pinholes, due to developer flow. Less opaquing is required.

Heat control in drying produces better control in maintaining film size and reduces streaking. Film registration is aided by consistent size. Duplicates can be processed to the same size consistently.

temperature is normal before using.

Control

A number of conditions must be met before a machine can be controlled. The machine must be operating according to the manufacturer's directions. Temperature, water flow, and transport speed must conform to specifications. Machine control is basically the control of developer activity.

Developer activity slows down as films are processed. To prevent this, developer replenisher is added. The amount added is related to the square inches of film developed. Replenishment balances developing agents for uniform activity over a period of time.

Replenishment Rate

Replenishment is triggered by the entering film and continues for the length of the film. The amount of replenishment must be determined by average film width and film area that is exposed. Normally, area exposure is rated at 25 percent for positives, 50 percent for halftones, and 75 percent for line negatives. The operator determines the area of the film and type of exposure to set the replenishment rate. It is easily seen that for the same amount of film, line negatives require three times the amount of replenishment as do film positives. To avoid overcontrol, mixed film sizes and exposure types should be averaged to determine proper replenishment. Replenishment may be controlled by switches or rate dials and regulated by flow valves.

Density Control

Running control of the processor is accomplished through the use of process-control strips. These strips are pre-exposed by the manufacturer under exact conditions. The strips are processed at regular intervals. The density is compared visually or read with a densitometer. An aim point is used, usually the fourth step on the gray scale of the strip.

Overdevelopment is indicated when the processed strip reads in excess of one step in density more than the reference strip. To regain control, run exposed scrap film through the processor without replenishment.

Underdevelopment is indicated when the processed control is more than one step below compared density with the reference strip. Adding replenisher without processing film increases the development rate and film density. Various films differ in their development characteristics. Lith-type films can generally have a greater variation in density than continuous tone film for acceptable production work.

CONTACTING

Contacting is the darkroom process that reproduces same-size images. It is so named because the original image and reproduction are placed in contact with each other. The process is widely used to reproduce negatives or film positives for stripping and other photomechanical operations.

The film or paper exposed is processed in a similar manner as other photo materials. The equipment used is much the same as for other darkroom processes. Contact materials may be tray developed or automatically processed.

LogEtronics Inc.

12-47. Dial-in feature for semiautomatic replenishment.

12-48. *Placing materials in a printing frame.*

ment. The light is more direct on the work. It is used when duplicating in exact size.

The broad-source light is scattered by diffuser glass and is used when the duplicate requires a spread image. Point-source light exposure is most commonly used. Image spreading is controlled with a point-source light by spacers between the original and the reproduction image. While point-source lights tend to record dust particles, they have several advantages. Since the light is contained in an area (the frame), it does not affect other operations in the darkroom. With proper regulation, point-source lights can be used for all contact work. This includes proofing, screening, and film contacting as well as duplicating. In addition, the lack of diffusion or scattering of light allows dot-for-dot duplication. White carbon arc, quartz-iodine, and photoflood lamps are used for point-source light. Fig. 12-13.

EQUIPMENT

The equipment for contacting includes a printing frame, a light source, and processing equipment.

PRINTING FRAME

The printing frame is either a pressure frame or vacuum frame. Fig. 12-48. The pressure frame may be portable and is used primarily for line work. The closed vacuum frame, Fig. 12-12, has a vacuum back with a glass cover. An open vacuum frame has no cover and is similar to the vacuum back on a camera. Used correctly, a vacuum frame provides close contact of surfaces and greater accuracy of reproduction. Fig. 12-49.

LIGHT SOURCE

Light sources for exposing photosensitive material are either point source or broad source. Fig. 12-50. Point source, called specular, is light from a point, such as an arc or fine fila-

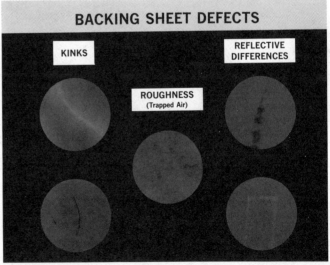

BACKING SHEET DEFECTS

KINKS

REFLECTIVE DIFFERENCES

ROUGHNESS (Trapped Air)

Du Pont Co.

12-49. *Poor contact in the vacuum frame leads to kinks, roughness, and reflective differences in the backing sheet.*

12-50. *Examples of broad-source and point-source light.*

Du Pont Co.

such as negative to positive or positive to negative. The other type of material reproduces like the original, that is, positive to positive or negative to negative. This type makes duplicate images of the original material.

Film or photographic paper which produces an opposite image is often called contact reversal. The reverse image is similar to the action of regular negative-image-producing film used in a camera.

CONTACT PAPER REVERSALS

A paper print can be contacted from either a positive or negative film image. The paper prints may be used for proofing, corrections, records, duplicate material, or as a product for the customer. The type of photo paper used depends on the quality requirements of the print.

Velox, azo, and ortho type papers which have a high contrast index are used. The photo paper is placed in the contact frame with the emulsion side toward the light source. The negative or positive image film is placed over the photo paper, with the emulsion facing away from the light source. The two emulsions are thus in contact. The lateral orientation of the film image was reversed by turning the film emulsion away from the light. When the print is produced, the image will then have the same orientation as the film. Fig. 12-52.

For example, an ortho paper may be exposed to a point-source light 5′ away for 7 seconds using the lowest number on the voltage regulator. The paper would be developed in a "Kodalith" devel-

INTENSITY AND EXPOSURE

Exposure is determined by the amount (intensity) of light at the frame and the time it is on. The inverse square law of light, Fig. 12-51, shows that the distance between the light and the film affects intensity. To achieve proper exposure, the light source should be about four feet from the film and regulated by a variable voltage transformer. This gives longer and more accurate exposures which are easier to control.

MATERIALS

Two general types of reproducing materials are used. One type reproduces opposite values,

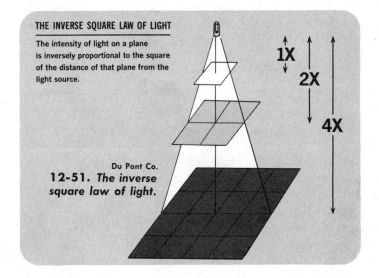

THE INVERSE SQUARE LAW OF LIGHT

The intensity of light on a plane is inversely proportional to the square of the distance of that plane from the light source.

1X
2X
4X

Du Pont Co.
12-51. *The inverse square law of light.*

EXPOSURE LIGHT

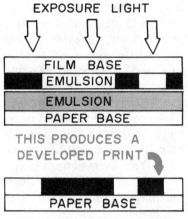

12-52. *Reverse paper print.*

oper for 1 minute. It would be stopped, fixed, and washed. The print would be hung to dry or put into a print dryer.

To speed the development cycle, a stabilization paper may be used. For example, "T" grade Kodak "Ektamatic" paper is exposed 15 seconds using the lowest number controlling the point-source light. The paper is processed in an "Ektamatic" processor, using A10 activator and S40 stabilizer solution. The processing time is usually less than 10 seconds for an 8" ×

12-53. *Negative placed emulsion side up.*

10" size print. If the print is to be saved for later use, it should be fixed and washed.

CONTACT FILM REVERSALS

A film positive may be contacted from a film negative for reversals or for use with plates that require positives. A special, thin-base contacting film is used. It is 0.003" to 0.004" thick with a clear base. This thin, clear-base film retards the spreading effect of thicker films with antihalation backing. This is particularly evident when light must go through the base of either the film original or contact film. This spreading effect of light is utilized in making spreads and chokes, as explained in a later section.

The ortho-type contact film is placed on the contact frame emulsion side up (toward the light). The film negative is placed over the contact film, also emulsion side up. Figs. 12-53 and 12-54. The two emulsions face the same way. They do not face away from or toward each other. Fig. 12-55. For example, the ortho contact film is exposed to a point-source light for 15 seconds using the lowest number on the transformer. The film is developed in "Kodalith" for 2:45 minutes, stopped, fixed, washed, and dried.

CONTACT DUPLICATES

Duplicates are the products of "like" image reproduction, since a negative produces a negative, or a duplicate and a positive produce a positive duplicate. Films for duplicate contacting have a black latent image. Light exposure removes or "clears" the black. Unexposed areas remain

12-54. *Cover of contact printer fastened over negative.*

black when developed, making a duplicate of the original.

The black unexposed areas offer the advantage of minimal pinholes in the developed film duplicate.

Duplicates have a great variety of uses. Among these are:

1. Producing duplicate line or halftone negatives and positives.

2. Making spreads or chokes (as described in a later section).

EXPOSURE LIGHT

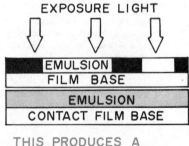

12-55. *Reversal film print.*

3. Producing laterally reversed duplicates.

4. Producing higher density duplicates.

5. Producing window masks.

6. Producing a single duplicate of combined negatives or positives.

7. Duplicating press proofs or line drawings.

8. Producing a combination positive and negative duplicate.

Duplicating Films

Three general types of duplicating films are used. The regular film, such as Kodak duplicating film or Du Pont "Cronar Contact Reversal W" film, requires high intensity light exposure. High speed duplicating films require less intensity and can be exposed by a point-source light. Exposure time is less. Neutral density filters can be used to increase exposure time. Fig. 12-56.

There are some paper films and plates that are called "autopositive." When autopositive materials are developed without any white light exposure, they become dense black. Exposure to yellow light "clears" or reduces density. Autopositive materials can repeatedly be exposed to yellow (clearing) and white (adding density) light prior to development. They are useful for making laterally reversed duplicates, halftone tints, combined negative and positive film, outlines, and reverses made in room light.

Daylight Film

A recent development in film for contact work is "daylight" film. It is a high-contrast, stabilized film that can be safely handled under yellow fluorescent light for short periods of time. The maximum safe handling time is about 12 minutes in 50 footcandles of yellow light. The film is manufactured both as contact and duplicating film.

Exposure and development are the same as with other contact films. Follow the manufacturer's instructions for exposure times and for tray and mechanized processing methods. Some daylight contact films can be reduced (negatives) and dot etched (positives or negatives) using a ceric sulfate dot etching solution.

While this film cannot be safely handled in actual daylight, the yellow light source used provides better vision while doing contact work.

Making Duplicates

If the duplicate is to read left to right as in the original, the emulsions of the original and the duplicate face the same way. Fig. 12-57. When the duplicate needs to be laterally reversed, the emulsions of the original and the duplicate face each other. Fig. 12-58. Make sure the image of the duplicate is oriented correctly for later work.

To make a duplicate negative or positive, place duplicating film in the contact printer. See Figs. 12-57 and 12-58. Exhaust closed contact frame until Newton's rings disappear. (Newton's rings are colored rings caused by light interference.) Expose with

ADJUSTING CONTACT EXPOSURE WITH NEUTRAL DENSITY FILTERS

Neutral Density Filter	Add Filter to increase exposure time by this amount*	Remove Filter to decrease exposure time by this amount**
0.1	1.25 times	1.25 times
0.2	1.6	1.6
0.3	2.0	2.0
0.4	2.5	2.5
0.5	3.2	3.2
0.6	4.0	4.0
0.7	5.0	5.0
0.8	6.3	6.3
0.9	8.0	8.0
1.0	10.0	10.0
1.1	12.5	12.5
1.2	16.0	16.0
1.3	20.0	20.0

* To increase effective exposure given the film by the number of times indicated, *remove filter* listed and use the same time setting.
** To decrease effective exposure by the number of times indicated, *add filter* listed and use the same time setting.

Du Pont Co.

12-56. Use of neutral density filters changes exposure times.

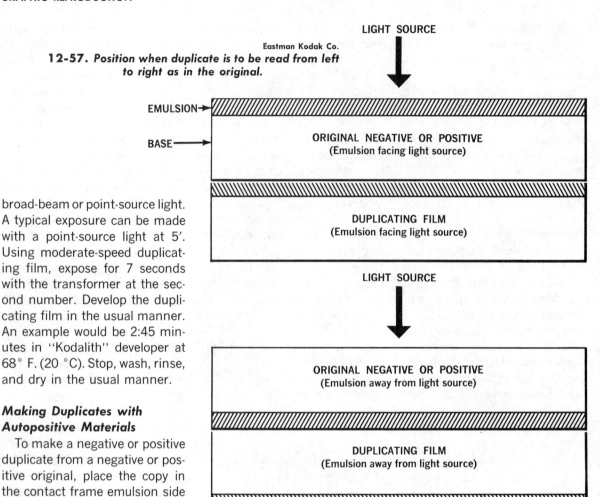

12-57. Position when duplicate is to be read from left to right as in the original.

broad-beam or point-source light. A typical exposure can be made with a point-source light at 5′. Using moderate-speed duplicating film, expose for 7 seconds with the transformer at the second number. Develop the duplicating film in the usual manner. An example would be 2:45 minutes in "Kodalith" developer at 68° F. (20 °C). Stop, wash, rinse, and dry in the usual manner.

Making Duplicates with Autopositive Materials

To make a negative or positive duplicate from a negative or positive original, place the copy in the contact frame emulsion side up. Place a sheet of autopositive

film, emulsion side down, over the copy. Cover with a piece of transparent yellow sheeting, such as "Kodagraph" yellow sheeting. Close the vacuum frame and draw out the air. Expose for about 2 minutes with a high intensity carbon-arc or a quartz-iodine light for 30 seconds. Develop for $1\frac{1}{2}$ minutes in "Kodalith" developer at 68° F. (20 °C). Use continuous agitation. Stop, fix, and rinse in the usual manner. Before drying, carefully wipe the surface with a photo sponge or chamois. To laterally reverse the duplicate

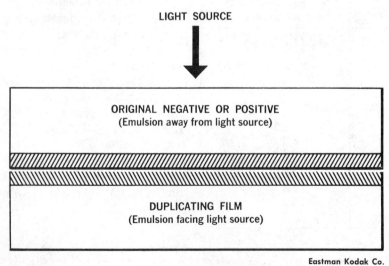

12-58. Position when duplicate is to be laterally reversed.

image, place the negative over the yellow sheeting with the emulsion side down.

Making Halftone Tints with Autopositive Film

To make halftone tints that are free from pinholes, use autopositive film. Place the copy in a contact frame emulsion side up. Place autopositive film over the copy, emulsion side down. Cover with a gray or magenta contact screen emulsion side down. Cover the screen with yellow sheeting. The length of exposure will determine the percentage dot size of the duplicate tint. The longer the exposure, the smaller the dot will be.

Autopositive Reflex Duplicates

This procedure can be used to make duplicates of black and white line copy without using a camera. Reflex copying means that light from the white areas of the copy is reflected back through the autopositive film.

The copy is placed in the contact exposure frame with the image facing the light source. It is covered with autopositive film, with the emulsion facing the image. The exposure is made through yellow sheeting. The difference in the amount of yellow light that is reflected back from the white areas of the copy "clears" the autopositive material and makes a positive duplicate. Due to differences in paper color and reflection properties, a series of trial exposures should be made. Processing is similar to other autopositive procedures.

Making Combination Negative and Positive Images on the Same Negative

By using masks, the autopositive negative can be part negative and part positive imaged. Use an opaque film mask for the duplicate image which is to be positive. Expose the rest of the negative with yellow light. Remove the mask, and cover the areas just exposed. Uncover the area to be printed as a positive. Expose the positive area in yellow light. Replace the original, and expose the same area to white light. Process in the usual manner.

Since this procedure requires several masking operations, the autopositive film must be fastened to a base or register frame. Each mask is taped to the base or punched in register with the film. Remember that white light adds density, and yellow light "clears" autopositive material.

EXPOSURE CONTROL IN CONTACT WORK

An easy method to control exposure in contact work is to use the Kodak contact control guide. Fig. 12-59. This guide is stripped to the edge of the original flat and is exposed to the duplicating film. Area A of the guide is used to evaluate line width and line intersection. Area B indicates image-change size and is used when making spreads and chokes. Area C shows the degree of image change. Area D has opposed highlight scales. Area E is a clear area and can be used for mounting a continuous-tone gray scale.

To use the guide accurately, make trial exposures. When the exposure duplicates line width and tone of the guide, use this exposure time as a standard. A densitometer may be used to measure step densities on the duplicate scale. A duplicate which reads plus or minus 0.3 of an original 1.0 density is acceptable. If you don't have a densitometer, a visual comparison can be made of the step densities.

To continually maintain constant exposure in order to have repeatable densities for duplicates, the following practices must be maintained:

1. Use a voltage regulator.
2. Do not vary the lamp-to-film distance.
3. Use the longest practical lamp-to-film distance.
4. Do not use very short exposures.
5. Use neutral density filters to adjust exposure.
6. Keep lights, reflectors, and contact glass clean.

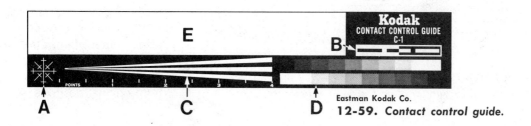

12-59. Contact control guide.

SPREADS AND CHOKES

Spreading is a method of enlarging line copy. It is used to create a heavier, larger line. *Choking* is a method of reducing line copy to make a lighter, smaller line. Spreads and chokes are used with type to make the letters fatter or slimmer. A spread and choke are combined to make outline letters. A spread is used for line work when it is to be imposed over a background. A spread line overlaps the background and makes it easier to register on the press. Fig. 12-60 illustrates the equipment and procedure to make spreads and chokes in the darkroom.

A contact printing frame of any type can be used. This may be a pressure or vacuum frame. The illumination is furnished by a point-source light that is equipped with variable voltage and a time clock. A diffuser sheet is used over the frame to scatter the light. Opalized plastic or standard diffusion sheets are used. A spacer, made of unexposed (clear) film that has been fixed and washed, is placed between copy and the film to be exposed. The Kodak Company recommends a contact control guide, which designates in type points the spread and choke when placed with the copy. Contact film or high speed duplicating film is placed below the spacer, next to the frame back. Always place the emulsion side of films *away* from the light. This aids in keeping the image sharp.

Part A in Fig. 12-61 illustrates the use of an original negative to make a spread negative on duplicating film. Part B in Fig. 12-61 shows the use of an original positive to make a choke positive on duplicating film.

If a reversed image is required for spread or choke, contact film is used. Part C in Fig. 12-61 demonstrates a spread positive made from an original negative using contact film. Part D in Fig. 12-61 shows a choked negative made from an original positive using contact film. Spreads are always made from an original negative, while chokes are made from original positives.

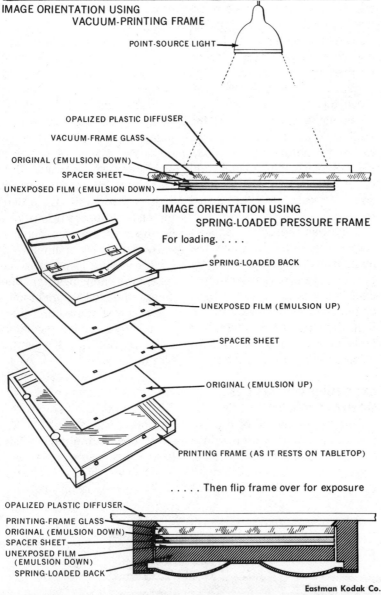

IMAGE ORIENTATION USING VACUUM-PRINTING FRAME

POINT-SOURCE LIGHT

OPALIZED PLASTIC DIFFUSER
VACUUM-FRAME GLASS
ORIGINAL (EMULSION DOWN)
SPACER SHEET
UNEXPOSED FILM (EMULSION DOWN)

IMAGE ORIENTATION USING SPRING-LOADED PRESSURE FRAME

For loading. . . . .

SPRING-LOADED BACK

UNEXPOSED FILM (EMULSION UP)

SPACER SHEET

ORIGINAL (EMULSION UP)

PRINTING FRAME (AS IT RESTS ON TABLETOP)

. . . . . Then flip frame over for exposure

OPALIZED PLASTIC DIFFUSER
PRINTING-FRAME GLASS
ORIGINAL (EMULSION DOWN)
SPACER SHEET
UNEXPOSED FILM (EMULSION DOWN)
SPRING-LOADED BACK

Eastman Kodak Co.

12-60. *The image orientation for making spreads and chokes using either a vacuum printing frame or a pressure frame.*

Procedure to Make a Spread

1. Make a negative of the line copy.

2. Set up the frame as shown in Fig. 12-60.

(a) Place duplicating film emulsion down against frame back.

(b) Put on spacer. Use 0.004" thickness for medium spread, 0.008" for large spread.

(c) Place the negative over the spacer, emulsion against the spacer.

(d) Expose according to the table given in Fig. 12-62.

3. If a spread positive is needed, use contact film in place of the duplicating film.

Procedure to Make a Choke

1. Make a contact positive from the original negative of the line copy.

2. Set up the frame as shown in Fig. 12-60.

(a) Place duplicating film emulsion side down against the printing frame back.

(b) Put on spacer. Use 0.004" thickness for medium choke, 0.008" thickness for large choke.

(c) Place the positive on top of the spacer, emulsion side toward the spacer.

(d) Expose according to the table shown in Fig. 12-62.

3. If a choke positive is needed, use contact film instead of duplicating film.

To place line work over a window (clear, unexposed area) in a background, make a spread on duplicating film of the line work to be superimposed. If the line work cannot be spread, then the background can be choked.

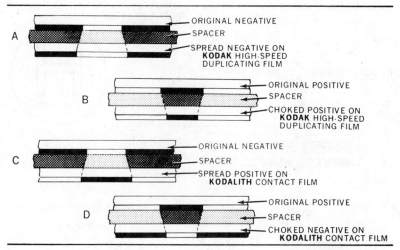

Eastman Kodak Co.

12-61. Spreads and chokes with positives and negatives.

Make a positive of the background and choke it, using duplicating film.

OUTLINING

Outlining is the procedure of exposing only the outer edges of the image. The outlined image is larger than the original when a spread is used. It is smaller than the original when a choke is used. Fig. 12-63 shows the procedure for a spread outline. Fig. 12-64 shows the procedure for a choke outline.

1. Contact a positive from the original negative.

2. For a spread outline, use the original negative or spread negative with duplicating film.

EXPOSURE TABLE

Film	Voltage Setting	Lamp Distance	Filter	Exposure
KODALITH Contact Film 2571 (ESTAR Base)	20 volts	5 feet	KODAK WRATTEN Neutral Density Filter No. 96 (0.60 density)	20 seconds
KODAK High Speed Duplicating Film 2575 (ESTAR Base)	20 volts	5 feet	None	40 seconds

Eastman Kodak Co.

12-62. An approximate exposure table for making spreads and chokes. Note that a No. 96 neutral density filter is used with contact film to reduce illumination.

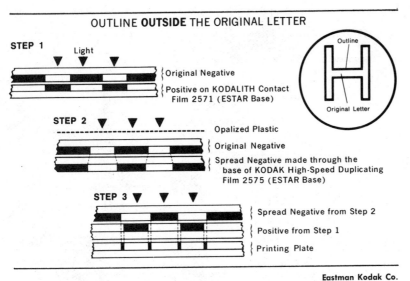

OUTLINE OUTSIDE THE ORIGINAL LETTER

STEP 1

Light

{ Original Negative

{ Positive on KODALITH Contact
Film 2571 (ESTAR Base)

Outline

Original Letter

STEP 2

- - - - - - - - - - - - - - - Opalized Plastic

{ Original Negative

{ Spread Negative made through the
base of KODAK High-Speed Duplicating
Film 2575 (ESTAR Base)

STEP 3

{ Spread Negative from Step 2

{ Positive from Step 1

{ Printing Plate

Eastman Kodak Co.

12-63. *Making a spread outline. Step 3 shows the position of the negative and positive when exposing a plate.*

When exposing the plate, register the spread negative over the positive, emulsion to emulsion, to produce an outline exposure.

3. For a choke outline, make a choked positive by exposing the

positive from the first procedure to duplicating film. Register the original negative over the choked positive, emulsion to emulsion, to expose a choke outline on the plate.

OUTLINE INSIDE THE ORIGINAL LETTER

STEP 1

Light

{ Original Negative

{ Positive on KODALITH Contact
Film 2571 (ESTAR Base)

Outline

Original Letter

STEP 2

- - - - - - - - - - - - - - - - - Opalized Plastic

{ Positive from Step 1

{ Choked Positive made through
the base of KODAK High-Speed
Duplicating Film 2575 (ESTAR Base)

STEP 3

{ Original Negative

{ Choked Positive from Step 2

{ PRINTING PLATE

Eastman Kodak Co.

12-64. *Diagram for making a choke outline. Step 3 shows the position of the negative and positive for exposure of a plate.*

The amount of spacer material used, the exposure time, and amount of diffusion determine extent of spread or choke. A record of these factors should be kept in order to repeat previous results. A reference guide to make chokes and spreads is shown in Fig. 12-65.

SCREENED PAPER PRINTS

Screened paper prints are useful in pasting up mechanicals for the camera. Prints can be made with an enlarger and vacuum register board using a continuous tone negative. Another method utilizes the camera with reflection copy, using PMT paper developed in a diffusion processor.

With a continuous tone negative available, an enlarger is used with Kodak "Ektamatic" photomechanical paper, grade T. The negative is placed in an enlarger film holder. A No. 213 enlarger bulb is required for exposure.

The image is focused on white paper placed on the vacuum board. The enlarger is turned off and T grade "Ektamatic" paper is put in place of the white paper. The paper is covered with a gray contact screen, placed emulsion to emulsion. A series of test exposures can be made by covering the screen with a card in the following sequence of time. After 5 seconds, cover one-fourth of the screen. After an additional 3 seconds, cover another one-fourth of the screen. After 4 more seconds, cover another one-fourth. Expose the last one-fourth for 6 seconds. The series of exposures are now 5, 8, 12, and 18 seconds.

Without moving the screen, a test series of flash exposures is made at right angles to the main exposure. These should be 4, 6, 9, and 13 seconds. These are made by placing the register board 5' from the flash lamp.

The proper exposure will give highlight and shadow dots larger than usual, since these will diminish in line reproduction of the mechanical. After selecting the proper main and flash exposure time, make a print using these values. Experience will indicate necessary exposure adjustments.

The print is developed in "Dektol" according to label recommendations or in an "Ektamatic" processor.

MAKING SAME SIZE HALFTONES FROM CONTINUOUS TONE FILM

It is practical to make halftones in a vacuum print frame when the same size is desired. As stated before, halftones can be made from continuous tone film negatives or positives. The procedure is similar to camera exposure.

1. Clean both sides of the glass in the frame. Use a glass cleaner and a lintless cloth.

2. Check lamp distance and voltage for desired exposure.

3. With the safelight on, place film (such as Kodalith Orth, Type 3) emulsion side to light.

4. Place contact screen over film with emulsion side toward film. Have the screen's base line parallel to the film. (Be certain screen is clean. Use photo chamois to clean, and handle only by the edges.)

5. Lay continuous tone film negative or positive over the screen, emulsion side toward screen. (Be certain film is per-

fectly clean.) Put glass cover in place and exhaust air.

6. Expose with tri-level, point-source lamp or a modified safe lamp.

7. Make the main exposure as determined by test negative and exposure computer.

8. Make the flash exposure using the correct voltage (usually 20 volts).

A screenless exposure cannot be made since the negative would be moved. If a screenless exposure is required, an open vacuum frame is used.

SAFETY

The camera and darkroom area can be hazardous because of:

1. Light—excess at camera and insufficient light in darkroom.

2. Glass—in bottles, covers, and lights.

3. Heat from film dryers, lamps, water.

SPREADS AND CHOKES

Original	Result Desired	Procedure
Film Negative	Choked Negative	1. Make a normal contact positive on KODALITH Contact Film. 2. Make a choke on KODALITH Contact Film.
Film Negative	Choked Positive	1. Make a normal contact positive on KODALITH Contact Film. 2. Make a choke on KODAK High Speed Duplicating Film.
Film Negative	Spread Negative	Make a spread on KODAK High Speed Duplicating Film.
Film Negative	Spread Positive	Make a spread on KODALITH Contact Film.
Film Positive	Choked Negative	Make a choke on KODALITH Contact Film.
Film Positive	Choked Positive	Make a choke on KODAK High Speed Duplicating Film.
Film Positive	Spread Negative	1. Make a normal contact negative on KODALITH Contact Film. 2. Make a spread on KODAK High Speed Duplicating Film.
Film Positive	Spread Positive	1. Make a normal contact negative on KODALITH Contact Film. 2. Make a spread on KODALITH Contact Film.

Eastman Kodak Co.

12-65. A reference guide for spreads and chokes from negatives and positives.

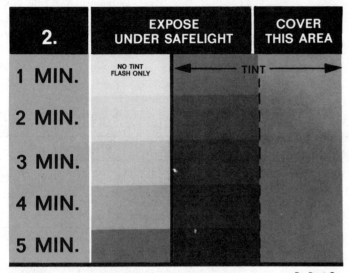

12-66. A safelight test.

Du Pont Co.

Avoid spilling and splashing while measuring and mixing.

11. Determine hazardous chemicals (acids, bases, poisons) and store safely. Store active chemicals near floor level.

SAFELIGHT TESTS

Safelights, even with proper filters, will fog film over a period of time. To determine the safe working time of film in safelight, the following test is used:

1. Make a standard camera exposure on film using a uniform tint screen. Block off one-third of the area on the side of the film so that it is not camera-exposed.

2. Place the film in a working location under the safelight. Block off one-half of the tint-exposed side.

3. Cover four-fifths of the remaining film at right angle to its side and expose to the safelight for one minute.

4. Uncover one-fifth more of the film for each minute of continued exposure.

5. Develop film under standard conditions.

As shown in Fig. 12-66, this test will reveal the dot formation from safelight exposure. It will determine the permissible time film can be safely worked under the safelight.

COLOR PROOFING

Proofs for multiple-color works are often required for use in dot etching, stripping, preplating, and customer inspection. Color proofs are also used for comparison in the plateroom, pressroom, and as a check for screen angles and registration.

"Color Key" and "Transfer Key" are colored proofing materials manufactured by the 3M

4. Chemicals — poisoning or sensitivity from contact by inhalation, absorption, and swallowing.

5. Electrical shock, from numerous locations.

Some general rules to follow are:

1. Make certain all electrical appliances and all circuits are properly grounded. Do not use any ungrounded appliance in the darkroom.

2. Make certain camera lights are disconnected before adjustment or maintenance. Watch out for hot arcs and lights.

3. Avoid staring at camera lights.

4. Wear rubber apron in darkroom.

5. Wear rubber gloves when mixing or handling chemicals. Avoid breathing fumes and dry chemicals.

6. Always add acid slowly *to* water.

7. Carry one bottle at a time.

8. Do not move in darkroom until eyes adjust. Walk with arms extended. *Do not rush.*

9. Do not lean or put weight on glass surfaces. Avoid warping glass covers.

10. Mix chemicals where spills can be rinsed away. Keep area clean to avoid contamination.

12-67. *Laminating of "Cromalin" proofing film.*

Du Pont Co.

emulsion and removing it (subtractive process) from the material. This can be accomplished by hand or by a special processor.

A thinner, single-unit color proof can be made using "Transfer Key." The sheets are separated from their bases and laminated together. This method provides a single-sheet proof.

"CROMALIN" PROOFING SYSTEM

Cromalin film, made by the Du Pont Company, is laminated to a base surface. Fig. 12-67. It is exposed through a positive in a vacuum frame with ultraviolet light. A toner of dry powder of the color required is applied. Fig. 12-68. The system provides for lamination of the subsequent films and toners for additional colors.

Company. "Color Key" material is a colored emulsion made of presensitized ink pigment coatings on a transparent base. Each colored material is made to match the expected color of the ink on the printed job. For example, four-color process negatives or positives would be contacted to magenta, cyan, yellow, and black "Color Key" sheets. After processing, the four color keys are placed in register to show the completed process coloration. Exposure is made in a plate-exposing unit. Ultraviolet light hardens the exposed areas of the material. For example, 30 seconds exposure with pulsed xenon may sufficiently harden the image areas. "Color Key" materials are processed by dissolving the unhardened part of the

Du Pont Co.

12-68. *Toning "Cromalin" proofing film.*

REVIEW QUESTIONS

1. Darkroom walls are usually painted black. True or False?
2. In the tray method of development, what do the three trays used contain?
3. Why must film be washed after developing?
4. When developing film by inspection, why should you rinse the film in water before examining it?
5. Automatic processing is generally more expensive than manual processing. True or False?
6. Contact printing produces images the same size as the original. True or False?
7. To make a negative from a negative, use duplicating film. True or False?
8. *Spreading* is a method of creating a larger, heavier line in line copy photos. True or False?
9. Even safelights will fog film over a period of time. True or False?

Chapter 13

Laying Out and Stripping the Flat

A *flat* is an assembly of image-bearing *film* (as a film negative or positive) and *film-supporting material*. Fig. 13-1. The flat is used to produce printing image areas onto lithographic printing plates by the contact exposure method. Fig. 13-2.

Before studying this chapter, it would be helpful to study Chapter 20, "Imposition and Lockup." The basic principles of imposition apply to both letterpress and

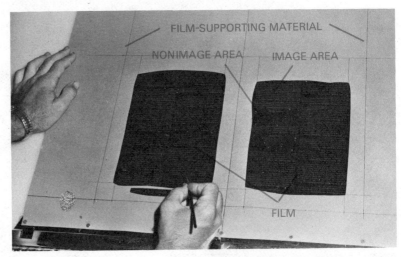

13-1. A flat. The film is taped to the film-supporting material. Each piece of film is comprised of an image area and a nonimage area.

offset printing. In offset printing the principles of imposition are applied to the production of the flat, which is used to produce the offset plate.

STRIPPING

Stripping is the process of positioning and attaching the

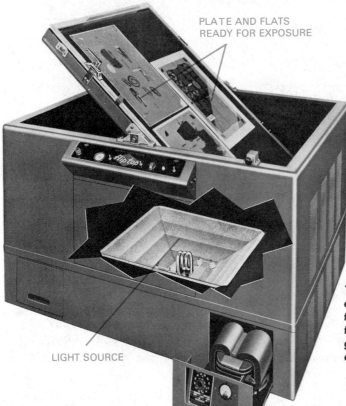

13-2A. The flat is placed in direct contact over the plate. Light shines through the clear image area of the film and exposes the photographic emulsion on the plate by action of the light source in the platemaker.

image-bearing film to the film-supporting material. The person who performs the stripping operation is called a *stripper*.

The two basic categories of stripping are *single-flat* and *multiple-flat*.

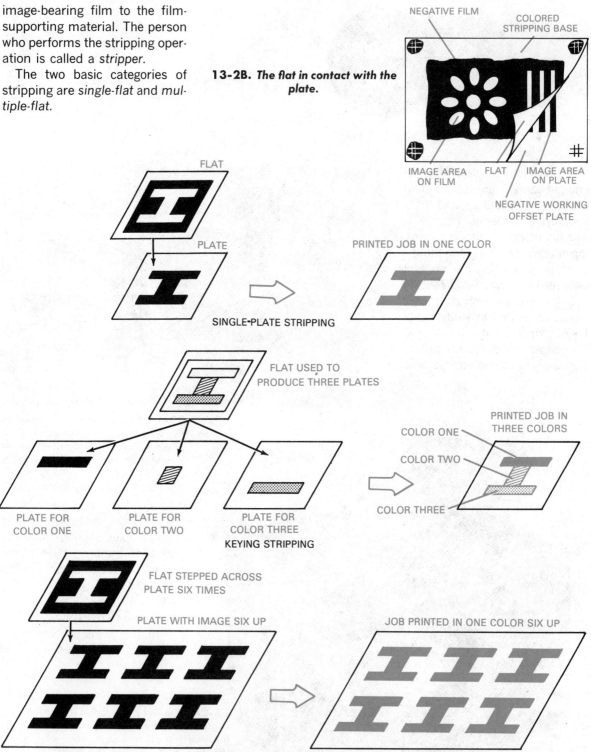

13-2B. *The flat in contact with the plate.*

NEGATIVE FILM

COLORED STRIPPING BASE

IMAGE AREA ON FILM   FLAT   IMAGE AREA ON PLATE

NEGATIVE WORKING OFFSET PLATE

FLAT

PLATE

PRINTED JOB IN ONE COLOR

SINGLE-PLATE STRIPPING

FLAT USED TO PRODUCE THREE PLATES

PRINTED JOB IN THREE COLORS

COLOR ONE

COLOR TWO

COLOR THREE

PLATE FOR COLOR ONE   PLATE FOR COLOR TWO   PLATE FOR COLOR THREE

KEYING STRIPPING

FLAT STEPPED ACROSS PLATE SIX TIMES

PLATE WITH IMAGE SIX UP

JOB PRINTED IN ONE COLOR SIX UP

STEP-AND-REPEAT STRIPPING

13-3. *The three categories of single-flat stripping are single-plate, keying, and step-and-repeat. Here are examples.*

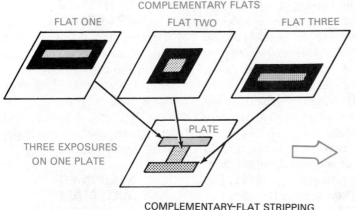

COMPLEMENTARY FLATS

FLAT ONE   FLAT TWO   FLAT THREE

THREE EXPOSURES ON ONE PLATE

PLATE

COMPLEMENTARY-FLAT STRIPPING

13.4. Complementary-flat and multiple-flat stripping.

PRINTED JOB IN ONE COLOR

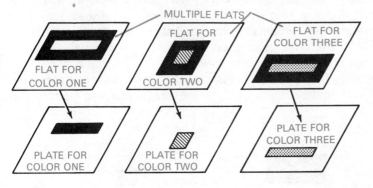

MULTIPLE FLATS

FLAT FOR COLOR ONE   FLAT FOR COLOR TWO   FLAT FOR COLOR THREE

PLATE FOR COLOR ONE   PLATE FOR COLOR TWO   PLATE FOR COLOR THREE

MULTIPLE-FLAT STRIPPING

PRINTED JOB IN THREE COLORS

COLOR ONE
COLOR TWO
COLOR THREE

SINGLE-FLAT STRIPPING

Single-flat stripping includes all stripping functions that require just one flat to produce a printed job, regardless of how many printing plates are necessary to print the job.

There are three types of single-flat stripping; *single-plate*, *keying*, and *step-and-repeat*. *Single-plate* stripping means that one flat is used to make one plate. *Keying* means that one flat is used to make several plates, but each plate is different. *Step-and-repeat* stripping means that one flat is used to make one printing plate, but the one plate has a multiple-up imposition. A multiple-up imposition is one in which the same image is re-peated several times on the same plate. Fig. 13-3.

MULTIPLE-FLAT STRIPPING

Multiple-flat stripping includes all stripping functions where more than one flat is used to make the necessary plates. This category of stripping is used primarily in multi-color work and in single-color work where separate flats are required to make the single-color plate.

There are two basic types of flats used in multiple-flat stripping, *complementary* and *multiple*. Complementary flats are separate flats used to expose the *same* press plate. This is necessary when film cannot be han-dled in a single flat. Examples include halftones with close-fitting captions or films that require such long exposure times that they cannot be combined on the same flat as those which require normal exposure times. Multiple flats are separate flats used to expose *separate* plates. They are used mostly in color work where a separate plate is required for each color. Fig. 13-4.

STRIPPING OPERATIONS

There are two basic operations involved in the stripping process. These are *laying out the flat* and *preparing the flat*.

LAYING OUT THE FLAT

In laying out the flat, the stripper consults the designer's layout, the bindery dummy, and the basic imposition plan. The information contained in these three items is used by the stripper for drawing reference lines onto the stripping base. The lines are used as positioning guides for placing the film onto the flat. The designer's layout is used as a guide for determining the location of image elements *within each page* on the flat. The bindery dummy and imposition plan are used for determining the location of the *entire page* on the flat.

PREPARING THE FLAT

In preparing the flat, the stripper performs all the operations needed to prepare the film for attachment to the film-supporting material. The completed film is then attached, using reference lines as placement guides. How these steps are actually accomplished depends to a great extent on the method of stripping, explained later in the chapter.

BASIC KNOWLEDGE REQUIRED BY THE STRIPPER

In addition to the basic techniques, strippers must master: mathematics fundamentals, drafting techniques, and the appropriate use of stripping marks and symbols.

They must have a working knowledge of geometry, as well as fundamental knowledge of basic mathematics. As the United States converts to the metric system, the stripper must be able to work with metric units.

Strippers must develop a working knowledge of basic drafting techniques, such as making measurements, drawing

lines, and using drafting tools. These drafting skills are necessary for use in laying out the reference lines onto the stripping base. A review of the book, *Drafting Technology and Practice,* by William P. Spence, will help you understand these fundamentals.

Strippers must know how to interpret and use standard stripping marks and symbols. Fig. 13-5. They are used as processing guides for identifying the various stripping elements and for placing film products onto the flat. These symbols print on the press sheets and are used in processing through the pressroom and bindery.

STRIPPING DEPARTMENT

The stripping department is normally located between or adjacent to the camera and plate-making departments. The stripper uses the film produced in the camera department to make the flats that are used in the plate-making department.

STRIPPING MATERIALS

As stated before, stripping materials are divided into film and film-supporting materials.

FILM

Film positives are opaque in the image area and clear in the

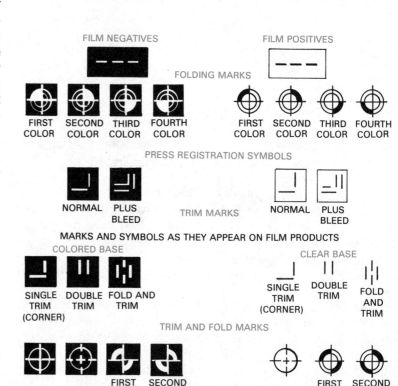

13-5. Standard stripping marks and symbols. The images are in negative form for film negatives and colored stripping base, and in positive form for film positives and clear stripping base.

272

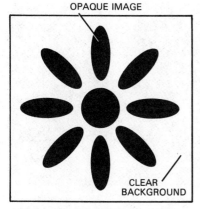

OPAQUE IMAGE

CLEAR BACKGROUND

A FILM POSITIVE

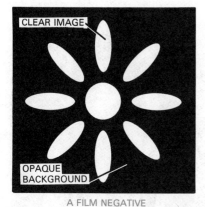

CLEAR IMAGE

OPAQUE BACKGROUND

A FILM NEGATIVE

13-6. Films are either positive or negative.

nonimage area. *Film negatives* are clear in the image area and opaque in the nonimage area. Fig. 13-6.

Film can be produced photographically, by the use of hand-cut masking films, by scribing emulsion off developed film, by drawing image areas onto clear acetate, or by the use of specialty products such as stripping film. Masking films, scribing techniques, and drawing procedures are discussed later in the text.

Stripping film has a photographically sensitive emulsion membrane that can be removed from its temporary film base after the film has been exposed and processed. Once removed, the membrane is adhered directly to film-supporting material or to clear acetate to form film positives or film negatives.

Specialty products possess light-sensitive emulsions. Portions of the photographically processed emulsion are peeled away to produce special effects. Fig. 13-7.

Film products may be right- or wrong-reading. To determine the "read," arrange the film so that the emulsion (dull) side is facing you and attempt to read the image area. Fig. 13-8. If the image area reads conventionally from left to right, the film is right-reading (R-R). If not, it is wrong-reading (W-R).

FILM-SUPPORTING MATERIAL

Film-supporting material, commonly called *stripping base,* is used to support and fasten film in the correct position for plate-making.

Stripping base can be colored or clear, depending on whether the flat requires film positives or film negatives. *Positives* are used with *clear* stripping base, and *negatives* are used with *colored* stripping base.

The colored stripping base material is usually a translucent orange, yellow, red, or goldenrod color. It is colored so that it will not transmit actinic rays to the blue-light-sensitive emulsion coated on lithographic plates.

Direct Reproduction Corp.

13-7A. Making a "Striprite" specialty film. The end results can be positive or negative, depending on which areas are peeled. The first step is to make a photographic film positive from line artwork.

Direct Reproduction Corp.

13-7B. Expose the "Striprite" material to the film positive in a vacuum frame.

Direct Reproduction Corp.

13-7C. *Develop the exposed "Striprite" material to clear the unexposed areas.*

Direct Reproduction Corp.

13-7D. *Peel away all areas desired to produce a film positive or a film negative.*

(Actinic rays are light rays of the violet and ultraviolet spectrum that produce chemical changes.) Colored film-supporting material is commonly called *goldenrod* or *stripping vinyl.*

Goldenrod stripping material is used in conjunction with film negatives so that only the clear image area on the flat allows light to be transmitted through to the offset plate. Fig. 13-2 shows how the goldenrod is cut away from the image area on the film to allow only light in the image area to strike the plate.

Unlike the colored material, clear stripping base allows actinic rays to go through the non-image area of the flat. Therefore, clear stripping material is used in conjunction with film positives. Only the nonimage area on the flat allows light to strike the offset plate. Clear stripping base is generally made from dimensionally stable acetate or glass.

Direct Reproduction Corp.
13-7E. *The finished product.*

STRIPPING TOOLS, SUPPLIES, AND EQUIPMENT

To perform stripping work correctly, the proper tools, supplies,

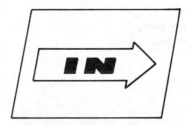

RIGHT-READING FILM POSITIVE

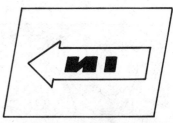

WRONG-READING FILM POSITIVE

RIGHT-READING FILM NEGATIVE

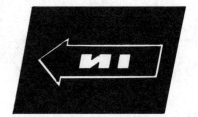

WRONG-READING FILM NEGATIVE

13-8. *To determine the "read" of a film, examine it with the emulsion side facing you.*

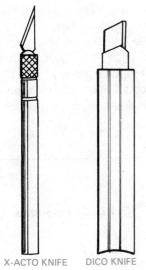

X-ACTO KNIFE   DICO KNIFE

13-9. *Stripping knives.*

and equipment should be used. The following are essential items:

STRIPPING TOOLS

Stripping knives are special knives used for cutting film products and stripping base. Fig. 13-9.

Scissors should be of industrial size and sturdiness.

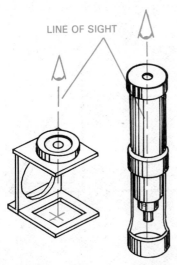

LINE OF SIGHT

13-10. *Collimating devices.*

Collimators are devices that direct the visual line of sight in a straight path to limit parallax error. Fig. 13-10. Parallax error is the *apparent* change in position of an object. It is an illusion caused by a change in the direction or position from which the object is viewed. Collimators are generally used to insure that flats or film products placed in registration over each other are in exact alignment.

Artist's brushes are used for applying opaque to film. An assortment of sizes should be provided.

Magnifying glass devices, usually with $10\times$ or $12\times$ power, are used for close examination of film.

Screen-angle indicators are devices used for determining the screen angle of tint and halftone screens. Screen angles are explained later in the text.

Halftone and tint-screen dot indicators are devices for determining the percentage and linage of halftone and/or tint screens. Screen percentage and linage are explained later in the text.

Needles and scribes are used for scraping the emulsion off film. They are manufactured in a variety of styles and sizes. Fig. 13-11. The different tips on each style are designed to remove specific amounts of emulsion.

Standard drafting tools, including irregular curves, triangles, compasses, calipers, rulers, adjustable-angle protractors, tape dispensers, straightedges, and so forth, are used to lay out flats. Fig. 13-12. Fine ball-point pens and medium-hard lead pencils are the most commonly used marking devices.

STRIPPING SUPPLIES

There are seven different types of *stripping base.* Three are colored, and four are clear. The three types of colored stripping base are paper, vinyl, and emulsion. *Paper* is translucent and can be purchased in a variety of sizes in either rolls or sheets. Some sheets are printed with reference lines. Fig. 13-13. Paper stripping base is inexpensive, but it is not dimensionally stable. Therefore it is rarely used for jobs that require multiple flats.

Vinyl stripping base is made from dimensionally stable vinyl. It can be purchased in various precut sizes with or without preprinted reference lines. It is more expensive than paper base, but it lasts longer. Vinyl stripping base

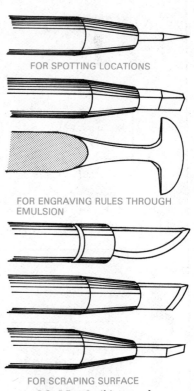

FOR SPOTTING LOCATIONS

FOR ENGRAVING RULES THROUGH EMULSION

FOR SCRAPING SURFACE

13-11. *Scribing tools.*

is ideally suited for multiple-flat work.

Emulsion is a clear stripping base material that has a uniform light-safe membrane over the clear base. The membrane is not light sensitive, but it can be scraped or peeled away to reveal clear, light-transmitting areas. This material is available in orange, amber, or red translucent colors. It is more expensive than vinyl stripping base and is used mainly for high quality or specialty work. This material is also called masking film.

The four types of clear stripping base are : acetate, mylar, frosted, and glass.

Acetate is an inexpensive, clear plastic material produced in

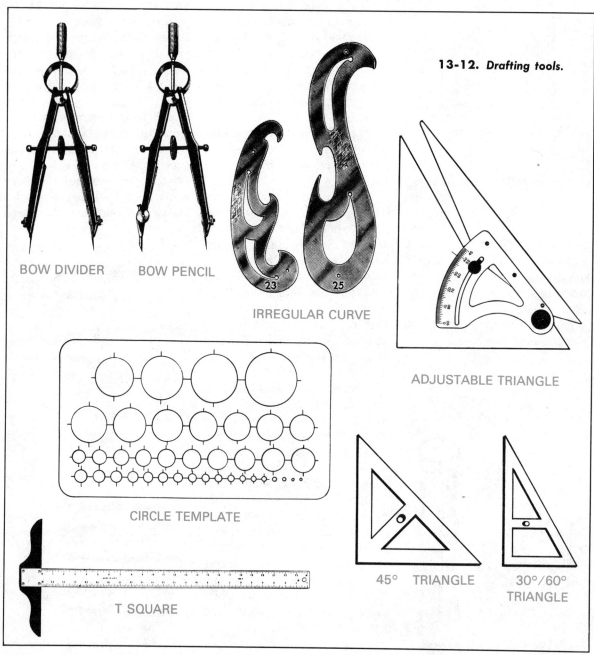

13-12. *Drafting tools.*

BOW DIVIDER

BOW PENCIL

IRREGULAR CURVE

ADJUSTABLE TRIANGLE

CIRCLE TEMPLATE

T SQUARE

45° TRIANGLE

30°/60° TRIANGLE

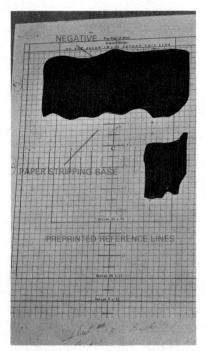

13-13. *A paper stripping base.*

rolls or sheets. It is not dimensionally stable.

Mylar is a clear plasticlike material that is dimensionally stable. It is considerably more expensive than acetate and comes in thicknesses varying from 0.0005″ to 0.020″.

Frosted acetate or mylar is diffused on one side to permit easy ink ruling. The matte (dull) side of this material will either reflect or transmit light.

Stripping rubber cement is simply conventional rubber cement that is thinned. It is commonly used to butt halftone film, adhere film positives to clear stripping base, or help hold processed stripping film emulsion that has lost its stickiness.

Opaque is a water-soluble red or black material that is used to prevent light from transmitting through film products. Black

opaque is composed of a graphite base and produced in paste form that must be kept moist at all times. Once it becomes dry in the container, it is no longer usable. Red opaque is produced as a solid and requires dilution with water for proper application. It does not need to be kept moist and can be thinned without losing opacity. In stripping work, the red opaque is recommended because it provides contrast against the black emulsion on the film.

Opaques should be light-safe after a single application and should lie flat and smooth on the base side of the film after application. Methods of opaque application are discussed later in the text.

There are four types of stripping tape:

Clear tape is the conventional pressure-sensitive transparent type. It is available in either cellophane or polyester base. The polyester type lasts longer, is more transparent, and is less affected by changes in humidity than the cellophane type.

Translucent tape is red, orange, or brown. It, too, is pressure-sensitive. The translucent color of the tape permits visual inspection but prohibits actinic ray transmission. The better varieties are produced with the coloring properties in the base material and not in the adhesive.

Paper tape has an adhesive on one side. The adhesive side is moistened and rubbed against the film to be adhered to the flat. The adhesive leaves the paper base and sticks to the film.

Drafting tape is used to hold the stripping base material to the surface of a stripping table.

Inks are designed to "bite" into acetate, mylar, and glass. These inks are used for drawing image areas or reference lines onto clear base materials.

Tint screens are screened films that possess a uniform dot pattern and dot size. They are available in a variety of sizes, angles, percentages, and linages. These screens, called *master tint screens,* can be used with a flat to expose dot patterns onto offset plates, or to make consumable tint-screen duplicates. These duplicates are then cut up and attached directly to the flat.

Register pins, Fig. 13-14, can be either pointed or flat. They are used to achieve very close registration in stripping as well as other lithographic applications.

STRIPPING EQUIPMENT

Line-up tables are equipped with a frosted glass surface and some form of ruling and measuring device which is attached in a horizontal and/or vertical position. Fig. 13-15. The measuring device is used to lay out reference lines onto the base. It is also used to check the layout of

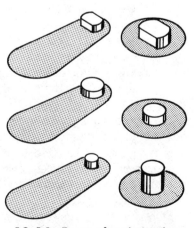

13-14. *Types of register pins.*

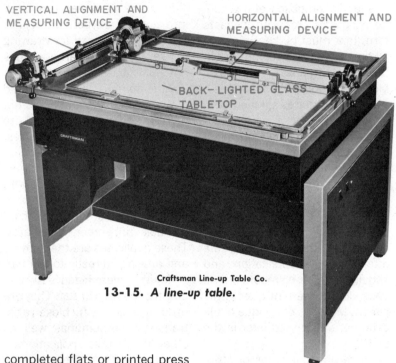

VERTICAL ALIGNMENT AND MEASURING DEVICE

HORIZONTAL ALIGNMENT AND MEASURING DEVICE

BACK-LIGHTED GLASS TABLETOP

Craftsman Line-up Table Co.

13-15. A line-up table.

completed flats or printed press sheets. The checking action is called *lining up*. If the line-up table is back lighted, it can also serve as a stripping table.

Stripping tables are back-lighted tables that are exactly like line-up tables, except they are not equipped with measuring or ruling devices. Stripping tables are normally equipped with sturdy metal T squares and triangles. The stripping table surface is the place where most stripping operations take place.

Storage cabinets containing many shallow drawers are used for storing photomechanicals, film, screen tints, and finished flats.

Devices to punch holes in the edges of flats or offset plates are shown in Fig. 13-16. One type produces only round holes, and the other produces round and slotted holes. Fig. 13-17.

Step-and-repeat devices are used to enable a single film to be exposed several times across an offset plate.

HOW TO DO STRIPPING WORK

The development of the overall printing plan is the responsibility of the impositor, regardless of what method of printing is selected. When lithography is selected, however, the actual placement of the image area onto the press sheet is the responsibility of the stripper, who prepares the platemaking flat and lines up the press sheet.

There are five basic steps in stripping work.

PREPARATION

The stripper prepares the work area and assembles in one convenient location all materials necessary to complete the job. The film must be checked for completeness, scratches, dirt, and opacity. Finally, the stripper checks the film for the correct read and placement of the emulsion. The emulsion side of the film should be prepared so that it reads correctly and is directly against the emulsion of the offset plate during exposure.

PLAN THE FLAT

The more image placement that is accomplished on the photomechanical, the more ef-

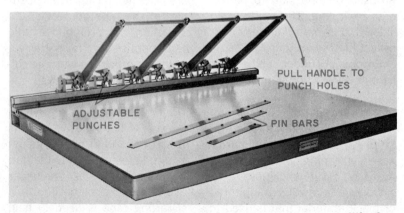

PULL HANDLE TO PUNCH HOLES

ADJUSTABLE PUNCHES

PIN BARS

Hulen Corp.

13-16. A hole-punching device. The hole locations are adjustable to conform to the location of the pins on the pin bars.

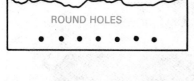

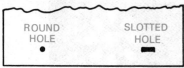

13-17. *The two basic types of hole arrangements produced by hole-punching devices.*

ficient the entire stripping operation will be. Complete photomechanicals which preassemble, space, and position all image elements are more practical than those which rely on stripping operations to combine the image elements. For example, halftones produced as screened prints on the paste-up are preferred over halftones using windows on the paste-up. The latter method is more cumbersome because it requires that separate halftone film be produced and placed beneath the window on the line film during stripping. This same basic planning philosophy holds true for the imposition requirements as well as the reproduction of special effects like surprints, drop-outs, and reverses, explained later in this chapter.

The stripper first consults the job ticket to determine the production details. Once the production details are identified, they are compared with the bindery dummy and the imposition plan. With this information the stripper then knows how to plan for the stripping details. It is necessary to plan for the size and number of flats and where each major image area should be placed on each flat. Then, using the designer's layout as a guide,

the stripper plans for the placement of the various elements within each major image area. The head or top part of the job is customarily laid out to run to the gripper edge of the press sheet.

Accuracy in planning as well as all other stripping operations is extremely important. Once a lithographic printing plate is made, the image areas on the plate cannot be moved relative to each other. This means no adjustments in the individual location of image areas are possible. However, the entire image area can be moved relative to the press sheet by shifting the plate, changing the side guide, adjusting the head stops, or rolling the blanket cylinder on the press.

A planning checklist can be used to insure all stripping factors are considered. The stripper must determine:

1. The category of stripping (single or multiple flat).

2. The type of film (positive or negative).

3. The type of stripping base (colored or clear, dimensionally stable, and so forth).

4. The number of flats required (single or multiple flat).

5. The press sheet size (imposition plan).

6. The press plate size.

7. The press requirements: bend over, gripper, maximum and minimum printing area, and plate positioning marks.

8. The bindery requirements, covered in the imposition checklist.

9. The stretch allowance, if needed. Stretch allowance is discussed later in the chapter.

10. The flat requirements.

    A. Correct screen angles, linage, and percentage.

    B. Method of stripping: emulsion up or down, conventional or step-and-repeat, special effects.

11. The margin requirements (imposition plan), such as fold (lip and shingling), bleed, gripper, trim, and binding.

SELECT THE STRIPPING METHOD

The selection of the stripping method is related to whether the film will be attached to the stripping base in an *emulsion up* or *emulsion down* position. If the emulsion is *up*, the film is attached to the top of the base. Fig. 13-18. If it is stripped emulsion *down*, the film is attached to the underside of the stripping base. Fig. 13-19.

Regardless of which method is selected, the film must be wrong-reading and arranged so that emulsions are in direct contact with the emulsion on the plate during exposure. Consequently, when flats are stripped with the film on top (emulsion up), pagination is laid out in a stone-lay fashion. Fig. 13-18. When the flat is stripped with the film beneath the stripping base (emulsion down), the pagination is laid out in a sheet-lay fashion. Fig. 13-19.

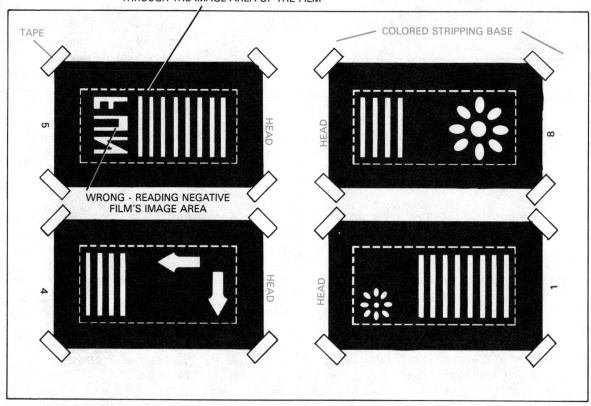

THIS PORTION OF THE BASE HAS BEEN CUT AWAY TO PERMIT LIGHT TO TRANSMIT THROUGH THE IMAGE AREA OF THE FILM

TAPE

COLORED STRIPPING BASE

HEAD

HEAD

HEAD

HEAD

WRONG - READING NEGATIVE FILM'S IMAGE AREA

13-18. *An "emulsion up" flat stripped for an outer form of an eight-page, sheetwise signature. Note that it is imposed in a stone-lay fashion.*

There are advantages and disadvantages to both methods, and considerable controversy exists regarding which method is best. A brief summary of the characteristics for each is shown in Fig. 13-20.

Another point to consider in selecting the stripping method is whether positive- or negative-working offset plates are to be produced. Positive-working plates are those that are made from film that has positive images. Negative-working plates are those that are made from film that has negative images. Positive-working plates are made with clear stripping base, and negative-working plates are

made with colored stripping base.

Still another factor to consider is whether the flat will be prepared in a conventional fashion or in a step-and-repeat manner, discussed later.

The last major factor to consider is whether pack assemblies or complementary flats are to be used to produce special effect image areas. A pack assembly is a combination of film designed to achieve special effects. Fig. 13-21 shows how a pack assembly requires only one specially prepared flat to produce special effect image areas. Special effects can also be produced by making complementary flats.

Fig. 13-4. Ideally, the best method for producing special effects is to produce them directly on the photomechanical.

RADEN C PRINTING CONTROL SYSTEM

Every printing job requires special preparation to make certain the printed images appear in the proper places on the paper. If finishing operations are called for (folding, trimming), they require accurate alignment with the printed image.

The Raden C system is designed to provide control of alignment during production. This includes art production, camera work, layout and strip-

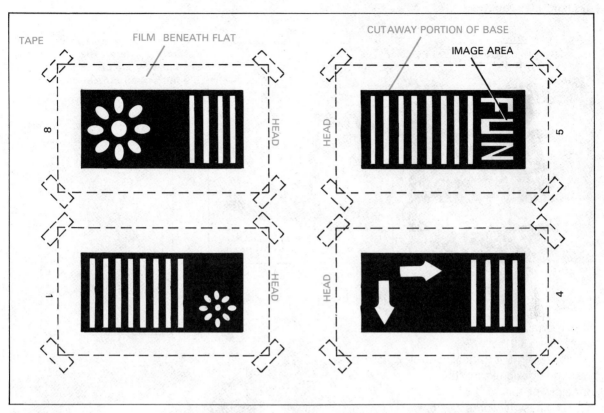

13-19. *An "emulsion down" flat stripped for an outer form of an eight-page, sheetwise signature. Note that it is imposed in a sheet-lay fashion.*

ping, platemaking, stepping and repeating, plate mounting, press registration, folding, and trimming. The system is based upon creating and maintaining perpendicular alignment.

On a printing press, each cylinder can represent a series of imaginary parallel lines. They run parallel to the axis of rotation of the cylinder. Fig. 13-22A. When the press cylinder rotates, a vertical set of imaginary parallel lines is created. They cross the horizontal lines at 90°. Fig. 13-22B. If the surface of the cylinder were flattened out, a grid

13-20. *Advantages and disadvantages of stripping methods.*

ATTACHMENT OF FILM TO BASE

	Advantages	Disadvantages
EMULSION UP	1. Film easily moved. 2. Film easily taped. 3. This method is recommended when film positives are used.	1. Awkward layout to contend with. 2. Reference lines are obscured by film. 3. Emulsion subject to damage. 4. Film must be prepared for alignment.
EMULSION DOWN	1. Base side of film is up for opaquing. 2. Working with a sheet-lay style. 3. Film needs no alignment preparation. 4. Reference lines are not obscured by film. 5. This method is recommended when film negatives are used.	1. Film difficult to move. 2. Film hard to tape. 3. Emulsion can be scratched.

TINT SCREEN TAPED TO NEGATIVE

LINE NEGATIVE

OFFSET PLATE

SCREENED IMAGE

SOLID IMAGE

13-21A. *A one-exposure pack assembly. Here the image is screened by the use of a consumable tint screen attached to the line film.*

SCREENED IMAGE

of perpendicular lines would appear. Fig. 13-22C.

The Raden C printing control system is designed to utilize the principle of this grid of perpendicular lines. It works by registering from a center point created by the intersection of a horizontal and vertical grid line.

A Raden C alignment frame is shown in Fig. 13-22D. The frame has a series of holes along the outer edges. These holes are used to position a straightedge and hold it in parallel locations every 1/16 inch. The alignment frame is used in layout and stripping to assure accurate perpendicular formatting.

LAY OUT AND PREPARE THE FLAT

There are many different systems for laying out and preparing a flat. The following

SCREENED IMAGE NEGATIVE FLAP

TAPE STRIPS

PLATE

STRIPPING BASE

TAPE HINGE

LINE FILM NEGATIVE FLAP

LINE IMAGE

THE FINISHED SURPRINT FROM THIS PLATE

13-21B. *A two-exposure pack assembly. Each film has a separate flap. A surprint is produced by combining a screened film with a line film. A surprint is a solid image area printed over a screened image.*

13-22A. A press cylinder surface can be thought of as a series of parallel lines.

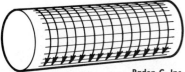

13-22B. When a press cylinder rotates, the surface represents a series of vertical parallel lines which are perpendicular to the horizontal lines.

13-22C. *The grid on the surface of a press cylinder represented as a flat surface (as on a layout table).*

prepare the flat for this job follow.

Step One: *Select, punch, and attach the stripping base to the stripping table.*

The base should be slightly larger than the size of the plate and conform to the type of film (clear for positives and colored for negatives).

The gripper end of the base is punched. Be sure that the base is inserted completely and squarely into the punching device before punching.

The punched base is then attached to the flat-topped metal pins that are taped to the stripping table. The gripper edge of the flat should be closest to the stripper. The pins are initially aligned and secured to the stripping table using tape and a T square. This alignment insures that all reference lines drawn with the T square or triangle are square with the gripper edge of the base sheet. The pin registration system provides for consistent registration between the flat and the plate.

Step Two: *Draw the basic reference lines onto the stripping base.*

Reference lines allow the stripper to visualize directly on the base where the film images must be placed to insure that the press sheet prints, cuts, folds, or trims correctly. The lines are used to place the film onto the base and to allow for the press

explanation is one standard way this is done.

Assume a flat for a job has a print-one-side (P1S) imposition. The size of the press sheet for this job is 8 1/2″ × 11″, and it is to be trimmed on all sides and folded in half after printing. Assume also that the job requires only one color and that it is to be printed on an offset press, using a negative-working plate. The finished size of the job is 8″ × 10 1/2″ before folding.

The eight steps to lay out and

13-22D. *The Raden C alignment frame.*

Raden C, Inc.

and bindery requirements. Fig. 13-23A.

Plate bend-over line indicates what portion of the base must be set aside to permit the plate to be mounted onto the press. No printing is possible in the plate bend-over area.

Press sheet lines indicate the size of the sheet to be printed. The press sheet line which is closest to the gripper end of the plate is called the *paper line*. The paper line is the same as the bend-over line.

The *gripper line* marks the area that must be set aside for the press grippers to grab and feed the paper through the press. No printing is possible in the gripper area.

The *center line* indicates the vertical center of the press sheet on the base. It is used to align vertically the film image areas onto the base.

Trim lines indicate where the press sheet will be trimmed. They are usually drawn in with short dashes.

Fold lines indicate where the press sheet will be folded. They are drawn in with long dashes.

Image placement lines indicate where the image area must be located on the base to print in the correct place on the press sheet. They are used as guides for placing the film onto the base. The extent to which these lines are placed on the base depends a great deal on the type of film and whether it is attached to the top or bottom of the stripping base. The placement lines generally indicate the base line of the image area.

Although none are required for the sample problem, the lip, shingling, and binding margin

requirements are considered at the time the image placement lines are drawn on the base. The locations of the image areas must be adjusted to compensate for these requirements.

Press plate placement lines on the base help the press operator to position the plate on the press. These lines are normally placed so their images transfer to the plate in a nonprinting area. Their primary purpose is to prevent the unnecessary movement of press guides or plate cylinders when several press plates are required to print the same press sheet.

Three press plate placement lines are required. The first is

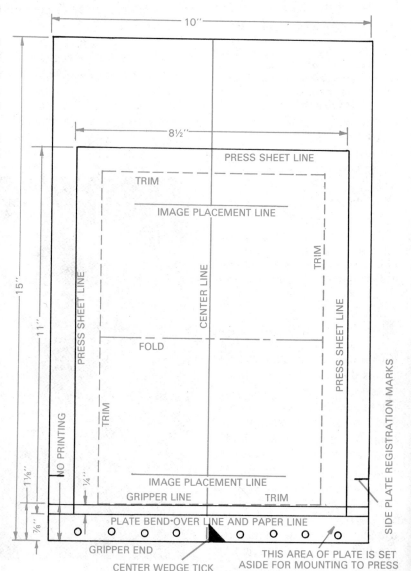

13-23A. *The basic reference lines.*

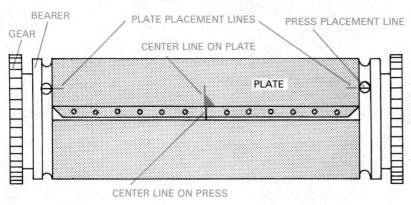

BEARER

GEAR

PLATE PLACEMENT LINES

CENTER LINE ON PLATE

PRESS PLACEMENT LINE

PLATE

CENTER LINE ON PRESS

13-23B. *The center and side placement lines on the plate are aligned with the center and side placement lines scribed onto the press plate cylinder.*

called the *center wedge tick*. It is produced by cutting a small, wedge-shaped section out of the stripping base at the center line of the gripper edge. This mark, when transferred to the plate, identifies the center of the plate gripper edge for the press operator. The second and third placement lines are the *side plate registration marks*. These are produced by cutting very fine slits on each side of the colored stripping base. Fig. 13-23A. These lines, when transferred to the plate, are aligned with corresponding lines permanently placed on the press cylinder. Fig. 13-23B. When all three lines on the plate are matched to the three corresponding lines on the press, it minimizes the shifting of guides used for registration.

If the center wedge tick and the side plate registration marks are modified so that they print in the trim on the press sheet, they can be used to check the placement of the image on the press sheet. The press operator merely insures that the center wedge and the side placement lines are printing the prescribed distance from the guide edges. Guide

edges are explained in Chapter 20, "Imposition and Lockup."

Side plate marks are used on plates for medium and large presses only because the blanket cylinders and head stops are rarely changed on these presses. Center wedge ticks are placed on every plate regardless of size because they assist the press operator in identifying the gripper edge of the plate.

To draw the basic reference lines on the flat:

1. Determine the individual values for each horizontal and vertical reference line. This is done by consulting the imposition plan, the designer's layout, and the stripper's planning checklist. These values for the sample problem have been computed and are shown in Fig. 13-24.

2. Using an accurate ruler and a ball-point pen, point off onto the base the accumulative *horizontal* line values determined

REFERENCE LINE VALUES

Reference Line	Value	Source
Bend-over/Paper	7/8''	From press manufacturer.
Press Sheet	8 1/2 × 11''	Given in imposition plan.
Center Line	5''	Compute to one half of plate width.
Gripper	1/4''	From press manufacturer.
Trim	1/4'' all sides	Computed by comparing final size with press sheet size.
Fold	5 1/2''	Given in imposition plan.
Image Placement		Based on designer's layout.
Press Plate Placement	5''	Center wedge only.

13-24. *Values for horizontal and vertical reference lines.*

in Step One. To avoid parallax error, use the procedure shown in Fig. 13-25.

The ruler is placed so that the zero index is even with the edge of the flat. Then each reference line's point mark is made with regard to each preceding value. The ruler is not moved during marking since that increases the possibility of error. Examine Fig. 13-24 closely to see why the accumulative ruler readings for each horizontal reference line for the sample problem are:

Bend-over/Paper, 7/8".
Press sheet, 7/8" and 11 7/8" (7/8 + 11).
Gripper, 1 1/8" (7/8 + 1/4).

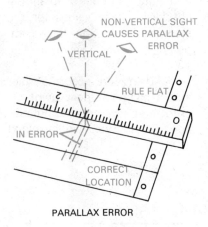

NON-VERTICAL SIGHT CAUSES PARALLAX ERROR
VERTICAL
RULE FLAT
IN ERROR
CORRECT LOCATION

PARALLAX ERROR

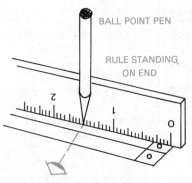

BALL POINT PEN
RULE STANDING ON END
NO PARALLAX ERROR

13-25. *How to avoid errors in dimensioning caused by parallax.*

Trim, 1 1/8" and 11 5/8" (1 1/8 + 10 1/2).

Fold, 6 3/8" (7/8 + 5 1/2).

Image Placement (These values are determined by examining the designer's layout to see where the image looks best.)

Fig. 13-26 shows why the base sheet must be kept flat when the measurements are made.

3. Using the T square and a fine-point ball-point pen, draw horizontal lines through the point marks. When drawing these lines, the T square must be pushed snug against the left edge of the stripping table to avoid the wobble effect shown in Fig. 13-27. The square should be held firmly with the left hand. T squares equipped with strong magnets on the T bar help hold the T square against the metal edge of the stripping table.

4. Mark off the vertical reference line values. First, find and mark the center of the base sheet. Fig. 13-28. Then mark the press sheet lines. Fig. 13-29. The mark on the ruler which is one-half of the press sheet width is placed on the center line mark. The mark on the ruler to the zero and the width of the press sheet can be used to establish the left and right press sheet marks. Fig. 13-30. The trim line marks are made at 1/4" less than the press sheet marks.

5. Using the T square and the triangle, draw the vertical reference lines through the center line, trim line, and press sheet's point marks. Fig. 13-31.

Step Three: *Align and attach the stripping mark and symbol devices to the flat.*

When these devices are not already on the film, they must be

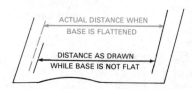

ACTUAL DISTANCE WHEN BASE IS FLATTENED
DISTANCE AS DRAWN WHILE BASE IS NOT FLAT

13-26. *This illustration indicates why the base sheet must be kept flat during measurement.*

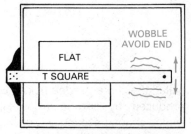

STRIPPING TABLE
WOBBLE AVOID END
FLAT
T SQUARE

13-27. *Wobble effect caused by the T square not being held firmly against the left edge of the stripping table.*

stripped into the base in an area that is trimmed away so that their images will transfer to the press sheet. These images are used by the press operator and bindery worker as guides for insuring that the press sheet is printed, cut, folded, assembled, bound, and trimmed correctly.

The devices are aligned and attached emulsion side down beneath the reference lines on the stripping base. After each device is correctly aligned beneath the appropriate reference line, a small diamond or box is cut out of the stripping base over a non-image area on the device. Fig. 13-32. Apply only enough pressure to cut through the base. Colored tape is then placed over the opening and securely pressed down into the diamond or box to attach temporarily the device to the flat.

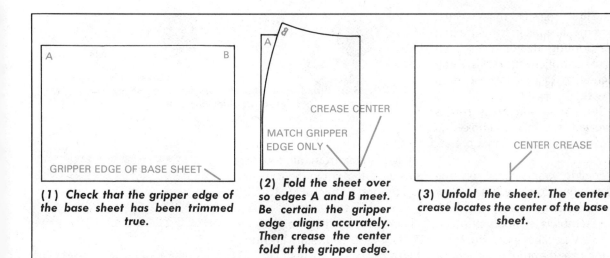

(1) *Check that the gripper edge of the base sheet has been trimmed true.*

(2) *Fold the sheet over so edges A and B meet. Be certain the gripper edge aligns accurately. Then crease the center fold at the gripper edge.*

(3) *Unfold the sheet. The center crease locates the center of the base sheet.*

13-28. *How to find the center of the base sheet.*

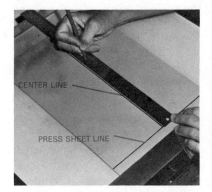

13-29. *Marking off the press sheet lines.*

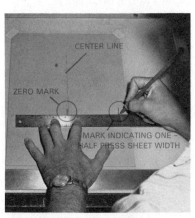

13-30. *Mark off the right and left press sheet marks.*

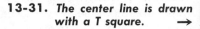

13-31. *The center line is drawn with a T square.* →

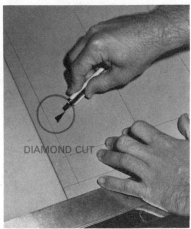

13-32. *A diamond-shaped area is cut out of the base over a non-image area on the device.*

The common stripping mark and symbol devices include press registration marks, folding marks, and assembling symbols.

Press registration marks are used to register press sheets that are printed by more than one printing plate. In practice, the correct alignment of the printed image on the first run is verified by lining up the sheet. Then the registration devices are used to register each remaining press run. The object is to align all subsequent register marks with

287

the first register mark. Great care must be taken to insure that the printing images align when all registration marks are attached to their respective base sheets.

Since only one press run is involved for this example, no press registration marks are required.

Folding marks print on the press sheet to show the bindery worker where the sheet will fold.

Assembling symbols print on the very backbone of signatures to indicate the order of assembly. None are required for the indicated example.

Step Four: *Attach the quality control devices.*

These devices are used to help the platemaker and press operator produce quality plates and press sheets. There are two types of quality control devices. One is used for plates, and the other is used for press sheets. Both types are attached to the base during stripping.

The device for plates is called a *platemaking sensitivity guide*. It is actually a transparent 21-step gray scale that is used for controlling the exposure and development of the offset plate. The scale is stripped into the base so that the image projected through the guide will expose onto the plate in a nonprinting area. This is further explained in Chapter 14, "Offset Platemaking."

There are four commonly used press quality control devices for checking and maintaining high quality press runs. They are the *star target*, the *slur gauge*, the *dot gain scale*, and the *color test strip*. These devices were developed by the Graphic Arts Technical Foundation (GATF). The

Graphic Arts Technical Foundation

13-33A. GATF Star Target. Shown from left to right are normal, simulated, double, and slur.

image areas from all four are designed to print in the trim area of the press sheet. Fig. 13-33.

The GATF *star target* is used to check print quality. It quickly detects ink spread, slur, and doubling on press sheets. Fig. 13-33A. The design of the target is such that it magnifies an ink spread about 23 times, thus making it easily visible to the press operator. The target can be used in platemaking to check the contact of film and plate and can also be used in the camera gallery to check resolution.

The GATF *dot gain scale* provides a means of control of the dot size when reproducing halftones and process color work. Fig. 13-33B. The dot area has a tendency to spread each time it is transferred to another surface. There are several transfer steps in most jobs. Typically, the job could flow from the original copy to a negative, a positive, a duplicate positive, a plate, and an offset blanket which finally transfers the dot to paper. The spread of the dot must be carefully controlled if the original image is to be faithfully reproduced. Dot gain causes lines to broaden and tones to become darker.

The dot gain scale visually indicates the dot area changes by observing displacement of an "invisible number" to a higher or lower value. Fig. 13-33B. The ap-

Graphic Arts Technical Foundation

13-33B. The printed images of the GATF Dot Gain Scale showing the different effects of ordinary dot gain and slur. The top scale is sharp, the second scale shows dot gain without slur, and the bottom scale shows dot gain caused by slur.

parent movement of the "invisible number" reliably measures the degree of dot size change, which is inevitable in contact printing in the camera gallery, platemaking, and on the press.

The GATF *slur gauge* is attached to the dot gain scale. Fig. 13-33B. Slur appears when slurring or dot doubling occurs as the job is being printed. Slurring refers to a blurring of the image. As a job is being printed, the press operator checks the printed image of this device as a quality control check.

The GATF *compact color test strip* is used whenever color work is printed. Press operators and quality control personnel use a color bar for visual and densitometric (optical density) control of color and printing factors during the press run. Hues and densities of printed inks, hues of secondary colors, trapping, uniformity of inking across the sheet, dot gain or loss, slur, and dot doubling are checked on the printed sheet with the control strip.

Step Five: *Attach the film to the stripping base.*

1. Turn on the stripping table light. Trim the excess nonimage area off the film. Do not trim closer than 1/4″ to any image area unless absolutely necessary. Only that portion of the film that overlaps other film needs to be trimmed when film is stripped emulsion down.

2. Align the film beneath the image placement reference lines on the flat. Be sure they are squared and correctly aligned in accordance with the designer's layout.

3. After each film has been aligned, cut a small diamond or box out of the flat over a nonimage area on the film. Hold the film in place while cutting by applying pressure onto the base from the top.

4. Using colored tape, temporarily secure the film to the base. Several diamonds or boxes may be required for larger sized film.

Film that is stripped emulsion down requires very little attention from the stripper. The primary reason for this is that the reference lines are not masked from view by the nonimage portion of the film. Reference lines are hidden from view when film is stripped emulsion up.

When the flat is stripped emulsion up, the preparation of the film is quite extensive. Note in Fig. 13-34 that considerable attention is given to drawing ad-

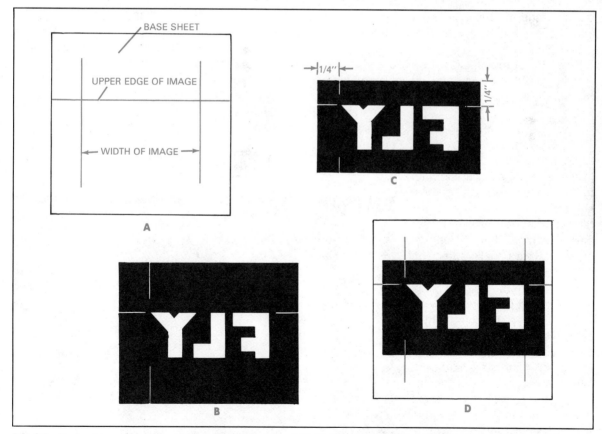

13-34. *Preparing a film to be stripped emulsion up: (A) Make additional image placement reference lines on the base. (B) Scribe image boundary reference lines in the emulsion side of the film. (C) Trim each film to 1/4″ of the image area. (D) Trim is required on each film so the reference line on the base sheet is not obscured by the film itself.*

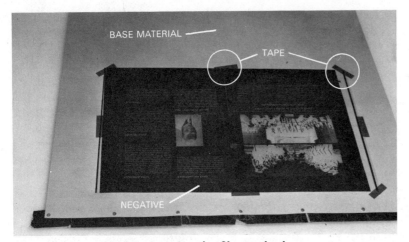

13-35. *Securing the film to the base.*

While this step is not required for the example, it is essential that stripping personnel know what a registration matrix is and how it is used. The matrix is actually a positive-image registration device used for stripping jobs requiring more than one flat. It is made by several different exposure methods in contact with the first flat to be stripped. All subsequent flats are then stripped to this matrix using its positive image as a guide. The major advantage of this device is that it eliminates the difficult task of trying to register one negative film to another negative film. Registration devices are discussed in greater detail later in the chapter.

Step Eight: *Proof the flat.*

Silver prints, vandykes, brown prints, and/or color keys are used to proof the flat. The proofing operation allows the stripper and the customer to check the flat for completeness and correct placement of all elements before

ditional reference lines onto the flat, scribing reference lines on the film, and trimming the non-image area away from the film.

Step Six: *Open the flat.*

When the stripping base is removed from the image areas on the film, it is called opening the flat.

Several steps are involved.

1. Turn the flat over.

2. Using pressure-sensitive transparent tape, secure all film to the base. Use only enough short pieces of tape to hold the film to the base. One or two pieces no more than 2″ long on each side are usually sufficient. Fig. 13-35.

3. Restore the flat to its original stripping position.

4. Using a stripping knife, cut the base material away from all image areas that are to transfer to the plate. Use sufficient cutting pressure to cut cleanly through the colored base without cutting the film. Cut to within 3/8″ of all image areas to prevent a shadow from forming during exposure. Fig. 13-36. Be sure that no narrow strips of base

capable of tearing or twisting are left between adjacent image-area openings. These strips must be removed and replaced with colored tape to prevent them from covering the image area during platemaking.

5. Check the flat for fingerprints and overall cleanliness.

Step Seven: *Make the registration matrix.*

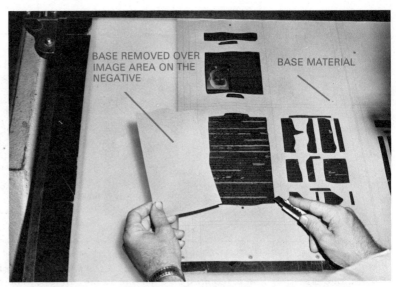

13-36. *A flat after it has been opened over the image area.*

13-37. *The original photograph with crop marks.*

13-38. *The trimmed negative.*

expensive plates are made. It also provides a sheet that can be used to make a bindery dummy.

LINE UP THE PRESS SHEET

It is the stripper's responsibility to place the image on the flat so that it will print in the correct place on the press sheet. The press sheet is a copy of the job printed on a press.

The stripper aligns and secures the press sheet printing side up to a line-up table, with the gripper edge closest to the stripper. Horizontal and vertical lines are ruled onto the press sheet through the printed fold and trim reference marks to insure the image areas are located correctly. The imposition and stripping checklists are consulted to insure that all image area locations are correct. The stripper checks the press sheet for position of the printing image only. The quality of the image is

the responsibility of the press operator.

When the center wedge and side placement lines are allowed to print on the press sheet, they are used as quick indicators for checking the location of the image area on the press sheet. For example, if the center wedge mark does not print the planned distance from the side-guide edge of the sheet, then the sheet must be shifted horizontally until the correct image distance is achieved.

SPECIAL STRIPPING TECHNIQUES

A stripper must know how to handle a variety of special production requirements. Following are a few examples.

ADDING HALFTONES TO WINDOWS

Fig. 13-37 shows how the crop marks placed on photographs

tell the strippers how much of the halftone film is to print through the window. To attach the halftone, the stripper first trims the halftone film to not less than 1/4" on all sides of the image area. Fig. 13-38. Then the stripper aligns and tapes the trimmed halftone over the window on the emulsion side of the line film so that both emulsions are facing in the same direction. Transparent tape is used. The tape is placed on only two opposite sides of the window. Fig. 13-39. Tape should never be

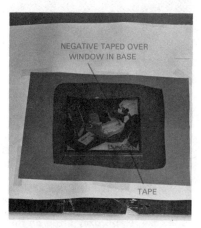

13-39. *The negative taped over the window in the base.*

placed anywhere within the image area because it casts shadows and cuts down on the amount of exposure light.

Many printers produce their halftones by adding screened prints to photomechanicals instead of adding halftones to windows. The screened print approach greatly simplifies stripping techniques. Screened prints are generally not used by publication printers using a condensing lens because this type of lens distorts a screened-print halftone image. The condensing lens is used to shrink the width of a page without shrinking the depth in order to produce more revenue-producing columns of advertising within a fixed page width.

BUTTING HALFTONES TO WINDOWS

Butting halftones refers to the action required to place one halftone film directly against another so that each shares a common edge. To make this common edge as inconspicuous as possible, the joining edges should whenever possible be matched for screen angle, image density, and dot size.

No white or black lines along the common edge should show on the finished job. White lines are caused by halftones that slightly overlap each other and block out the exposure light. Black lines are caused by halftones that do not quite touch each other, allowing exposure light to get through the crack between the halftones.

To insure a correct fit, the halftones are temporarily fitted over the window in an emulsion up configuration so that the image areas are correctly aligned to each other and to the window. Fig. 13-40A. Then the halftones are temporarily taped together, and a fine reference scratch is made in the trim portion of the emulsion on two opposing sides of the halftones. These marks show where the butt should occur. After that, the halftones are removed from the window and securely taped emulsion down to a cutting surface. Then, using a sharp knife and a straight edge aligned with both reference scratches, both halftones are cut simultaneously. The common edge produced by cutting both halftones at the same time insures they will align exactly when resecured to the flat. Each halftone is then taped over the window in the flat. Fig. 13-40B.

Sometimes, because of limited space, tape cannot be used to attach the halftones to the line film. In this case a minimum amount of diluted rubber cement or the adhesive from paper tape is used within the image area to secure the film together. Neither diluted cement nor the adhesive from paper tape casts shadows or reduces the amount of exposure light that transmits through a flat.

MAKING SURPRINTS

Single flats using pack assemblies (Fig. 13-21) or multiple flats (Fig. 13-4) can be used to produce surprint effects. Each flat is used to make separate exposures onto the plate. The *surprint* effect is produced when the image from a given film is exposed over the image already formed by another film. This is possible because the area on the plate not struck by light in the first exposure is exposed by the second exposure.

MAKING DROP-OUTS OR REVERSES

Any device that stops actinic rays from striking a plate will

THE OVERLAPPING NEGATIVES

13-40A. *The overlapping halftones are temporarily fitted on the window, and the image areas are lined up ready to be cut.*

THE BUTTED NEGATIVES AFTER CUTTING

13-40B. *The butted halftones are taped over the windows in the flat after they are cut.*

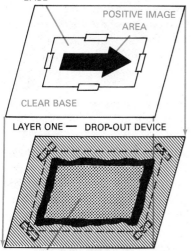

PHOTOGRAPHIC FILM POSITIVE
OR HAND–CUT EMULSION STRIPPING
BASE

POSITIVE IMAGE
AREA

CLEAR BASE

LAYER ONE — DROP-OUT DEVICE

SCREENED IMAGE ON NEGATIVE

LAYER TWO — FLAT

THESE TWO LAYERS TOGETHER ARE
EXPOSED TO THE PLATE

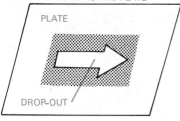

PLATE

DROP-OUT

PLATE PRODUCED BY A SINGLE
EXPOSURE OF THE PACK ASSEMBLY

13-41. *How to make a drop-out pack assembly.*

halftone, or tint blocks are required. The emulsion material is cut to the size of the plate and attached to the pins on the stripping table in the same manner as conventional stripping base. The emulsion is peeled away to make the sharp-edged window for a film or to produce an actual solid image area. Only the ruby or dark red emulsion stripping base material is suitable for platemaking since the amber or light-colored material is not absolutely light-safe.

produce a drop-out or reverse. Photographic film positives or hand-cut emulsion stripping base is excellent for this purpose. These materials are placed in a pack assembly so that their positive images stop exposure light from reaching the plate. Normally, the film positive is placed over the conventional film in the pack assembly so that only one exposure is required. Fig. 13-41.

USING EMULSION STRIPPING BASE

Emulsion stripping base (hand-cut masking film) is used when windows for large solid,

SCRIBING THE FILM

One of the most effective ways to produce the film necessary for printing lines or rules is to scribe the emulsion off film negatives. Fig. 13-42. The scribing devices used for this are made in many different styles and thicknesses. The stripper must select the appropriate device that will produce the desired thickness of rule with only one stroke.

The first step is to tape the film squarely onto a line-up or stripping table so that the emulsion side is up. Next, with only one continuous stroke and using a straightedge as a tool guide, scribe the lines as shown in Fig.

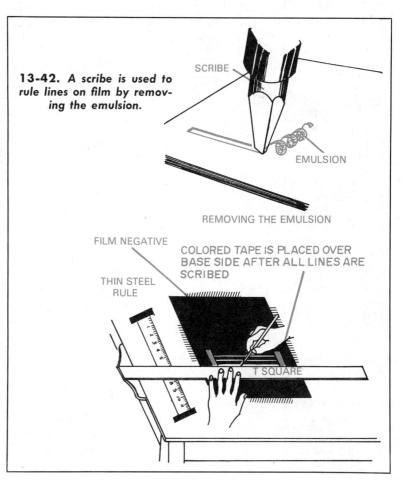

13-42. *A scribe is used to rule lines on film by removing the emulsion.*

SCRIBE

EMULSION

REMOVING THE EMULSION

FILM NEGATIVE

THIN STEEL
RULE

COLORED TAPE IS PLACED OVER
BASE SIDE AFTER ALL LINES ARE
SCRIBED

T SQUARE

13-42. Begin the stroke before the left edge of the rule, and extend the stroke beyond the right edge. Hand-cut masking film or lithographer's tape is then placed over the base side of the film to sharpen the edges.

COMPENSATING FOR PRESS SHEET EXPANSION

Strippers must compensate for the paper expansion that often occurs with press sheets which run through the press several times. This expansion is generally the result of the press sheet absorbing excessive moisture the first time it runs through the press. It is always greater in one direction; the paper fibers which produce grain in paper expand in diameter to a greater extent than they expand in length.

When too much stretch occurs after the first press run, the subsequent flats must be adjusted for the lengthening of the image area on the press sheet. These flats are adjusted by measuring the overall stretch difference between the originally stripped flat and the already printed press sheet. After this value is determined, the stripper applies the difference between each element on the new flat. Fig. 13-43. Never adjust a flat by registering it directly over the image on the first plate because offset printing presses always print image areas that are longer than the plate, even on the first impression.

Ideally, the best solution for press sheet expansion rests with the press operator rather than the stripper. In particular, the press operator should initially overpack the blanket cylinder and underpack the plate cylinder for the first impression on a multiple-impression job. Then as the job progresses and expansion begins, the press operator can remove some of the packing from the blanket cylinder and add it to the plate cylinder. This increases the length of the image on the blanket cylinder, which automatically compensates for the lengthening of the image on the stretched press sheet.

PROVIDING FOR SUFFICIENT TRAPPING

In stripping, *trapping* refers to the activities which insure that image areas printed on a press

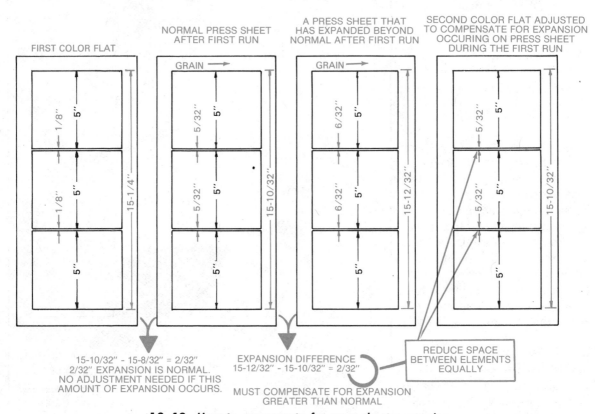

13-43. *How to compensate for press sheet expansion.*

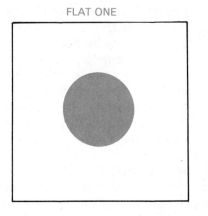

FLAT ONE

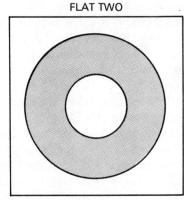

FLAT TWO

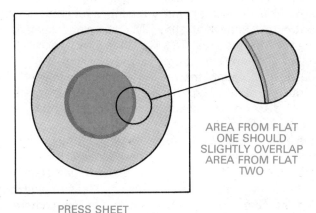

AREA FROM FLAT
ONE SHOULD
SLIGHTLY OVERLAP
AREA FROM FLAT
TWO

PRESS SHEET

13-44. *Trapping insures that printed image areas register by allowing them to overlap slightly.*

sheet register with already printed image areas. To accomplish this, strippers should examine the film to insure that all joining image areas overlap approximately one point into the surrounding printing area. Fig. 13-44. This overlap compensates for slight variance in press registration and prevents paper from showing between the printing areas. Strippers often request that the person operating the camera spread and choke the film to insure that sufficient trapping overlap is provided for each printing area. *Spread* and *choke* refer to enlarging or re-

ducing image areas on the film. (See Chapter 12.)

STRIPPING FILM POSITIVES

When film positives are used, exposure light reaches the offset plate in the nonprinting area. The printing area on the film must be completely opaque, and the nonprinting area must be clear. Because of this, the chance for registration error is decreased because the stripper can easily see through the non-image area to line up the image area with the image placement lines.

Positive film is normally stripped emulsion up. The procedures are as follows:

1. Rule the basic reference lines onto a colored base sheet, and pin it to the stripping table.

2. Punch and place the clear stripping base over the ruled base sheet. When the clear stripping base itself is ruled with light blue translucent reference lines, no separate colored base sheet is required.

3. Trim the film so that it does not overlap after it is attached to the base. Cut the film edges at a 45-degree angle toward the image to minimize the shadow.

4. Attach the quality control devices and film to the stripping base. These are attached emulsion up in a stone-lay fashion. Use short pieces of clear tape. A collimating device is used to guard against parallax errors between the film and the reference lines on the base sheet.

5. Proof and check the flat. Follow the procedures for proofing and checking the flat outlined previously.

IMPROVING THE FILM

Often a stripper has to give special corrective attention to the film in order to prepare it for stripping. Typical improvements made are as follows:

Repairing Scratches

Scratches on film are harmful because they cast shadows on plates. Scratches are repaired by filling, or retouching. When the scratch is on the base side, glycerine, oils, jellies, or commercial scratch fillers are used. The scratch must be thoroughly cleaned of dirt or opaque before filling. When the scratch is on the emulsion side, it is repaired by using opaque to replace the emulsion. In a halftone area, opaque is applied to the base side with a No. 0 sable brush or a Rapidograph pen. A 12× power magnifying glass is recommended when a fine dot structure is repaired. In a solid area, opaque is also applied with a brush, but the use of a magnifying glass is usually not required.

Clearing the Film

Large clear areas of film are often speckled with fine dots of unwanted emulsion. These dots are usually caused by dust. Sometimes the clear areas are veiled by a faint, chemically pro-

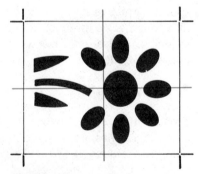

13-45. *Convert the image into a rectangle. Then find the center of the rectangle. The intersection of these lines determines the center of the image area.*

duced tint. For either of these problems, Farmer's reducer is used to clear the film. Farmer's reducer is a mild etch or reducing solution. It is available commercially.

To correct a veiled film, pour the reducing solution into a flat pan, and momentarily soak the defective film in the solution. Then remove and flush the film with fast-running, clean water. Repeat this operation until the clear areas are no longer veiled.

To remove fine dots, first apply a water-soluble lacquer or varnish onto the emulsion surrounding the affected area. This will protect the emulsion from the reducer. Next, apply the reducer onto the dots or specks until they dissolve or release from the base. Then thoroughly rinse the film with water to remove the reducer and the varnish or lacquer.

Cleaning the Film

Dirty film produces undesired effects on the plate. A film expected to print a five percent halftone or tint screen dot will also print dust specks that same size. Also, opaques will not adhere to a dirty, greasy, or oily surface on a film. Use commercial film cleaner or carbon tetrachloride. Never rub film to remove dust as this generates static electricity and causes more dust to adhere to the surface. Electrically charged brushes should be used to remove dust from film if cleaning solutions are not used.

Opaquing the Film

As stated before, opaque prevents light from transmitting through film. It is used for mak-

ing corrections and spotting out defects, such as pinholes. Opaque can be applied with any number of devices. However, a No. 4 or No. 6 sable-haired fine-pointed brush is recommended for fine work, and the flat sign-painter's brush is suggested for covering large areas.

STEP-AND-REPEAT WORK

There are many styles of step-and-repeat devices. All involve vertical or horizontal stepping movements of a film containing a unitized image area. The stepping action is accomplished directly across a plate or a sheet of film.

Although many different step-and-repeat systems are manufactured, only the basic principles of one will be briefly explained in this section. This is the "Raden C" system.

In the Raden step-and-repeat system the stripping principles are based on compressing all image areas into rectangles or squares. The computations and settings are then based on movements originating from the center of these rectangles or squares. Fig. 13-45.

The system utilizes the following major components:

The *master template* is a dimensionally stable plastic jig containing precision-punched holes around its perimeter in absolute parallel and vertical alignment. Fig. 13-46. These holes permit the film to be moved from one position to another in registered parallelism through the use of a step sheet. The gripper edge of the master template is at the bottom. The zero reference lines are centered on the long edges of the master template.

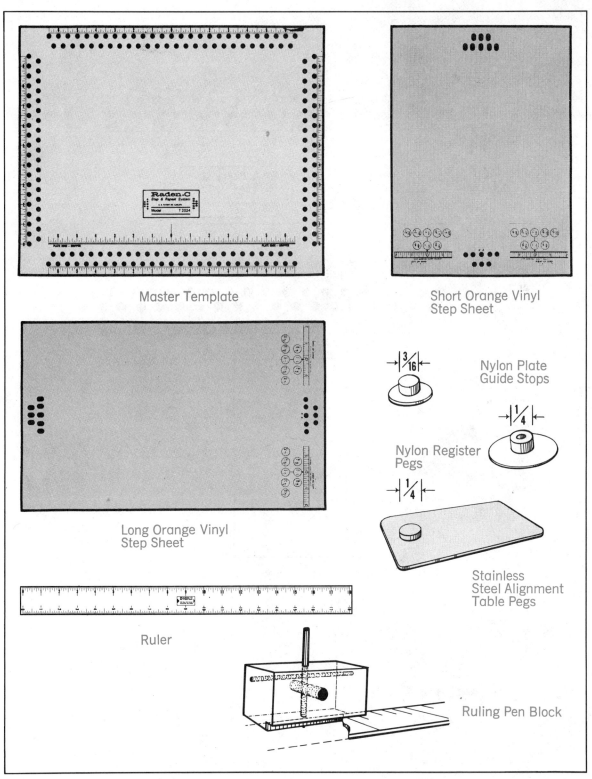

Master Template

Short Orange Vinyl Step Sheet

Long Orange Vinyl Step Sheet

Nylon Plate Guide Stops

Nylon Register Pegs

Stainless Steel Alignment Table Pegs

Ruler

Ruling Pen Block

Raden C, Inc.

13-46. *Materials for the "Raden C" step-and-repeat system.*

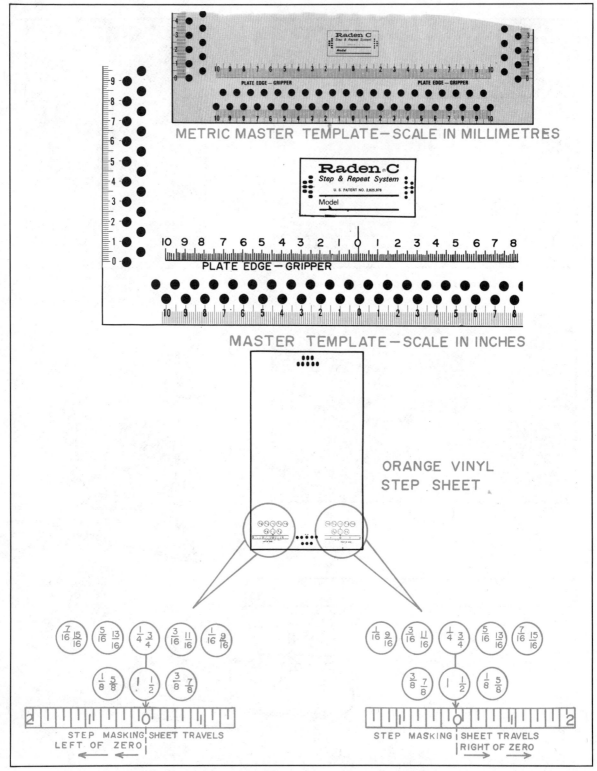

METRIC MASTER TEMPLATE—SCALE IN MILLIMETRES

MASTER TEMPLATE—SCALE IN INCHES

ORANGE VINYL
STEP SHEET

STEP MASKING SHEET TRAVELS
LEFT OF ZERO

STEP MASKING SHEET TRAVELS
RIGHT OF ZERO

Raden C, Inc.

13-47. Close-up view of the master template and the step sheet.

An enlarged view of the master template is shown in Fig. 13-47. Templates are available with scales in inches and millimetres.

Step sheets are precut, punched sheets of orange-colored stripping base materials. Fig. 13-46. They are used to hold the film while it is stepped across the plate. The punched holes at the ends of each step sheet coincide with those in the master template. Movement of the step sheet with the film is determined by matching a set of holes in the step sheet with a set of holes in the master template.

There are two types of step sheets, long and short. Short sheets are used for horizontal stepping movements. Long sheets are used for vertical stepping movements.

Register pegs are inserted in the holes in the step sheets and master template to register the sheets to the template. Fig. 13-46.

Companion devices are special supplemental templates and masking sheets designed to increase the versatility of the basic system.

Following is only a simplified explanation of how the system works. The many technical details and possibilities must be obtained from the manufacturer.

1. Place the master template face up in the vacuum frame. Insert the plate guide stops in the holes provided on the master template. Fig. 13-48A.

2. Position the plate on the master template so that it touches the guide stops. Tape the plate to the master template. Fig. 13-48B.

3. Position a step sheet on a light table. Steel alignment pegs

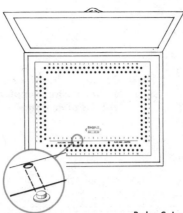

Raden C, Inc.

13-48A. The Raden step-and-repeat system. Step 1. Place the master template on the plate guide stops on the vacuum frame.

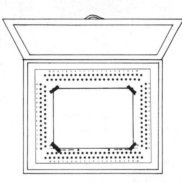

Raden C, Inc.

13-48B. Step 2. Tape the offset plate to the master template.

are inserted in the center holes at each end. Butt a straightedge against them. Rule a center line on the step sheet with the ruling pen block. Fig. 13-48C.

4. Remember that the round holes on the step sheet correspond to the gripper edge of the plate. All measurements must be made from this end of the step sheet. The space measurements include template allowance, plate clamp allowance, and paper gripper allowance. Fig. 13-48D.

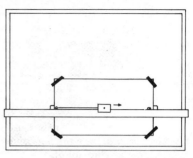

Raden C, Inc.

13-48C. Step 3. Rule a center line on a step sheet.

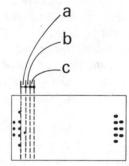

Raden C, Inc.

13-48D. Step 4. Space requirements are measured on the step sheet: (a) The template allowance is the distance from the top edge of the inner row of holes to the edge of the plate line on the template. (b) The plate clamp allowance is the space required for plate clamps when plate is put on the press. (c) The paper gripper allowance is the unprinted area required for gripping the printed sheet.

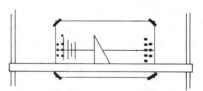

Raden C, Inc.

13-48E. Step 5. Scribe the space requirements on the step sheet.

5. Scribe these distances on the step sheet. Fig. 13-48E.

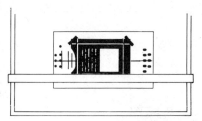

Raden C, Inc.

13-48F. *Step 6. Tape the negative to the step sheet.*

Raden C, Inc.

13-48G. *Step 7. Transfer the step sheet to the master template on the vacuum frame.*

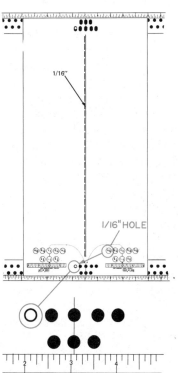

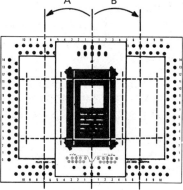

Raden C, Inc.

13-48H. *Step 8. Expose the negative and the plate. Move the step sheet left and right, as shown by lines A and B, for additional exposures.*

6. Tape the negative to the step sheet with the emulsion side up. Center it over the scribed line. Turn the step sheet over, and cut away that portion of the sheet which blocks the part of the negative to be exposed to the plate. Fig. 13-48F.

7. Transfer the step sheet with the negative to the master template in the vacuum frame. Fig. 13-48G. The exact placement of the step sheet will depend upon the number of exposures. In this illustration it is placed in the center, and an exposure is made. Register pins are placed in holes in the master template at each place the center of the step sheet is to be located.

8. The step sheet is then moved left, and another exposure is made. A third exposure is made after the sheet is moved right. Fig. 13-48H. The distance from the center line of the first exposure to the center line of the other exposures is equal to one-half the width of the printed image plus one-half the width of the margin between them.

The location and movement of the step sheet across the master template are controlled by the numbered holes on the template and the set of eight round holes in the step sheet. An enlarge-

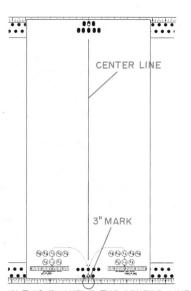

CENTER LINE

3" MARK

IN THIS EXAMPLE THE CENTER LINE IS ON THE 3" MARK. THE 1"–1/2" HOLE ON THE STEP SHEET IS USED.

1/16"

1/16" HOLE

TO MOVE TO 3–1/16" TO THE RIGHT USE THE HOLE MARKED 1/16". IT IS THE LEFT HOLE ON THE TOP SERIES.

Raden C, Inc.

13-49. *How to use the template scale on the "Raden C" system step sheet.*

ment of this is shown in Fig. 13-47.

The basic function of the holes in the template and step sheet is to hold them together firmly. The holes also provide an accurate registration of the step sheet with the negative to the plate. Minimal movements of the sheet on the template are permitted by the holes. Various step sheets are available which provide differing amounts of movement. The one shown in Fig. 13-47 is designed for movements in increments of 1/16″.

The step sheet shown in Fig. 13-49 has the center line on the 3″ mark on the template scale. When on even inches or half inches, the only hole to line up is the one marked 1″—1/2″. This is the lower center hole. The two holes will line up and accept a nylon register peg.

If it is desired to move the center line of the step sheet 1/16″ to the right, find the hole on the series labeled right of zero with the 1/16″ indicated. Fig. 13-49. The location of this hole shows that the nylon register pin must be placed in the upper left hole. This is the only hole which will line up and accept the pin. The center line is now on 3 1/16″. This principle is repeated for any distance—right or left—on all step sheets.

Step-and-repeat is also accomplished by machinery which automatically steps and exposes the unitized film across the plate or film. A step-and-repeat machine is shown in Chapter 14, "Offset Platemaking."

CUTTING IN CORRECTIONS

Often a stripper must cut corrections into the film. To do this,

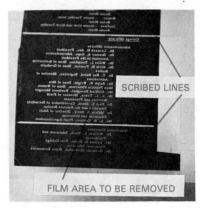

13-50A. *Scribe lines around area to be removed.*

13-50B. *Slide the film correction beneath the area to be removed.*

he or she cuts out the incorrect section and replaces it with a corrected section. Great care is taken so that the corrected film section does not overlap the original film.

A recommended method for stripping in corrections follows:

1. Securely tape the film to be corrected onto a lighted stripping table, emulsion down. The film should be accurately aligned with the T square before taping. Place a sturdy, transparent cutting sheet beneath the film to protect the glass on the stripping table from becoming scratched by the stripping knife.

2. Scribe lines in the emulsion surrounding the incorrect image area. Fig. 13-50A. These lines are used to help align the corrected film segment. They are not needed if line-for-line corrections are made.

3. Slide the film correction beneath the area to be removed.

Align it so that the spacing and borders are correct. Fig. 13-50B.

4. Temporarily tape the correction in place under the section to be removed with transparent tape. Fig. 13-50C.

13-50C. *Temporarily tape the film correction in place.*

13-50D. *Cut through both layers of film.*

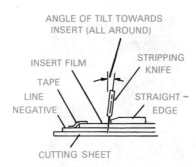

ANGLE OF TILT TOWARDS
INSERT (ALL AROUND)

INSERT FILM

STRIPPING
KNIFE

TAPE

LINE
NEGATIVE

STRAIGHT —
EDGE

CUTTING SHEET

STRIPPING KNIFE TILTED TO CUT
OPENING LARGER THAN INSERT FILM

5. Using a stripping knife, cut through both pieces of film. Fig. 13-50D.

6. Remove the incorrect section.

7. Tape the correction in place, using thin strips of colored tape. Tape all nonimage places that will transmit light, but do not tape over any image areas. Fig. 13-50E.

PUBLICATIONS STRIPPING

The stripping functions required for newspaper or magazine publication are relatively standardized because the stripping details generally remain the

COLORED
TAPE

FILM CORRECTION

13-50E. *Remove the areas to be replaced, and tape in the film correction.*

same each time. As a result, publication stripping is reduced to assembly-line techniques. This means the image placement requirements are simplified to a point where registration devices are used in conjunction with a special pin-register system. This system reduces most stripping computations to one-time requirements and eliminates most layout requirements completely. Its application begins with the photomechanical; continues through the camera, stripping, and platemaking departments; and ends with the pressroom.

The system is based on first determining where the image area should appear on the plate. Then the registration devices are mounted with complete-page photomechanicals and placed in the camera. This permits the image on the photomechanicals to be exposed onto the film in such a fashion that the film ends automatically align with the ends of the plates. As a result, the full-sized film is used in place of the stripping bases.

The trick to publication stripping is to expose the film so that it can be pin-registered to the plate during exposure. The registration devices are used to ac-

complish this. They are ruled so that specially printed photomechanical base sheets can be aligned in their relative printing position directly on the devices. The devices are made the same size as the plate. This makes it convenient to draw the image boundaries onto the devices. The boundaries are used for aligning the base sheets onto the devices.

The registration devices containing the complete-page photomechanicals are then pin-registered to a pin bar on the copyboard of the camera. The film is also pin-registered to a pin bar on the film plane in relation to the registration device. The positions of both pin bars are adjusted until the films register to the plate while both are attached to the pin bar on the plate exposure unit.

The procedures for stripping two companion pages for a tabloid newspaper to be printed on a web press are:

1. Align and attach the two companion page photomechanicals onto their respective left and right registration devices. Fig. 13-51.

2. Pin one of the registration devices to the pin bar taped to the copyboard on the camera. Fig. 13-52.

3. Pin special prepunched film to the pin bar in the vacuum back of the camera. This one sheet of film will cover half the plate. Then expose, develop, and opaque the film. Repeat Steps two and three for the second registration device holding the other companion page.

4. Attach both of the films to the pins, emulsion down, on the stripping table. Fig. 13-53. Note that the films are aligned side by

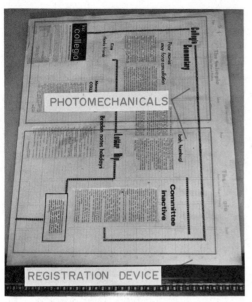

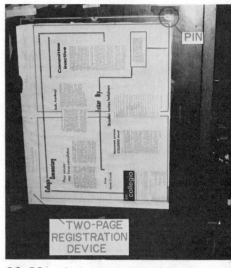

13-51. Companion pages attached to the registration devices.

13-52. A registration device pinned to the camera copyboard.

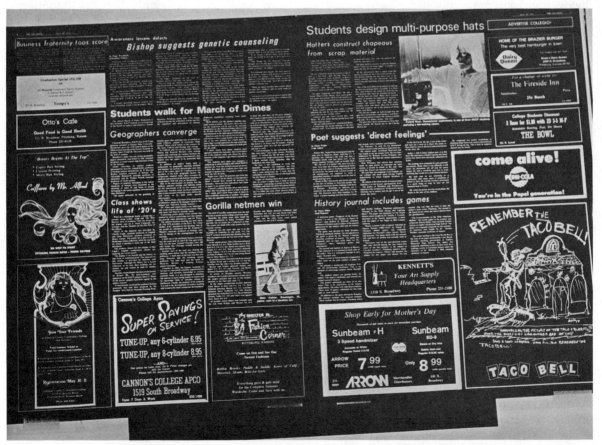

13-53. Film arranged in platemaking position on the stripping table.

side. If only one color is involved, the taping together of the film and minor opaquing are all that is required to prepare the film for platemaking. Observe that no stripping base is required for one-color work since colored tape makes the joining edges between the two pieces of film light-safe.

If more than one color is required, the flats for the color printing plates can be made by covering the film with pin-registered stripping bases that are the same size as the plate. Portions of the base are cut away from all areas that are to print in color. Flaps that open and close on one base sheet can be used instead of several base sheets. This permits the one set of film to produce the different printing plates. This method of color stripping is called *keying* and is generally used in publication stripping only.

BOOKLET STRIPPING PROCEDURES

Except for the layout requirements, the procedures for booklet stripping are the same as those shown in the beginning of this chapter. An example of booklet stripping is shown in Fig. 13-54. Observe how the flat for the 16-page, separate-covered booklet is laid out. Film utilizing four-page segments is used because the original photomechanicals were produced using four-page formats.

However, when the films are not laid out, the stripper is required to proportion the printed image area to the paper page during the stripping operation to produce suitable margins. Normally, the image area is positioned on facing pages so that

the three vertical margins are equal, and the top margins are less than the bottom margins. Fig. 13-55. Also, if not already determined, the image area is planned to be approximately one-half the area of the booklet page. To find the width of the image area, multiply the width of the page by the factor 0.71. To find the depth, multiply the length of the page by the same factor. Folios (page numbers) are not included in the image area since they are considered white space.

For example, assume a booklet page of 6″ × 9″ (36 × 54 picas) is to be produced, and the stripper must determine the image area. It is determined as follows:

$$36 \times 0.71 = 25\ 1/2\ \text{picas}$$
$$54 \times 0.71 = 38\ \text{picas}$$

The result is a printing image area 25 1/2 × 38 picas. This means that each facing page of the booklet will have an image

area 25 1/2 × 38 picas. These image areas must then be positioned on the booklet pages to produce margins in pleasing proportion. These margins may be determined by making a diagram of the two facing pages and superimposing cutouts of the image areas onto the diagram until pleasing proportions are produced. In practice, it is customary to make three even, vertical margins and then appropriate the space for top and bottom margins on a basis of two-fifths for the top and three-fifths for the bottom. Since the depth of the book page measures 54 picas and the type page 38 picas, the 16 remaining picas are divided so that two-fifths, or 6 1/2 picas, represents the top margin and three-fifths, or 9 1/2 picas, the bottom margin. The three vertical margins are seven picas apiece. Fig. 13-55.

$$\frac{(36 \times 2) - (25\ 1/2 \times 2)}{3} = 7$$

13-54. *The interior flat for a 16-page, separate-covered booklet.*

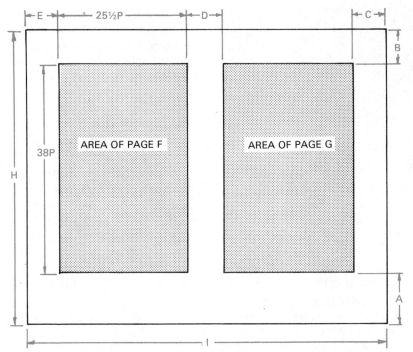

13-55. How to proportion facing pages: (1) E = D = C = 7 picas. (2) A = 9 1/2 picas; B = 6 1/2 picas. (3) Area F + Area G = (H × I)². **(4) I = 72 picas. (5) H = 54 picas.**

COLOR STRIPPING PROCEDURES

There are two categories of color stripping—flat and process—but the stripping techniques for both are essentially the same. As a result, only three major color-stripping factors must be considered. These are color registration, halftone and tint screen applications, and determination of the film and stripping base requirements.

Color Registration

Some form of positive-image registration matrix is used for registering film negatives. These matrices can be produced in two different ways.

The first way is by producing a light-image photographic film positive from the first flat that is stripped. This film positive is produced by contact-exposing a sheet for the film in pin-registration with the flat. On flats that are made for large plates, the individual film positives are often made separately and then registered to sheets of clear stripping base cut to plate size to produce the matrix.

The second way to produce a registration matrix is by the use of commercial, blue-line products. These are dimensionally stable film products that are coated with a special photographic emulsion which, after contact exposure to the stripped flat, produces a light blue, positive image. Sometimes 3M "Cyan Color Key" is used for this purpose. After processing, the color key is stripped in registration

with the first flat to a dimensionally stable sheet of clear base the size of the plate.

To use a commercial, blue-line type registration matrix:

1. Attach the appropriate colored base sheet to the pins on the stripping table. Then rule all basic reference lines onto the base sheet.

2. Attach the film for the color containing the fullest or most prominent printing image to this base sheet.

3. Attach the stripping symbol devices to the base sheet and open the flat.

4. Make the blue-line registration matrix.

(a) Expose the light-sensitive matrix in pin registration with the flat produced by Steps one, two, and three. The exposure should be made in a plate-exposure unit, following directions supplied with the matrix material. Because of the pin registration during exposure, the bottom edge of the blue-line matrix will correspond to the bottom (gripper) edge of the flat.

(b) Develop the matrix in accordance with the instructions that accompany the product.

(c) The processing of the blue-line material will produce a matrix that possesses a light blue, positive image on a clear base. This image will be in exact registration with the first flat to be stripped.

5. Place the matrix onto the pins on a lighted stripping table, emulsion up, and cover it with a new stripping base sheet.

6. Attach all the film for the

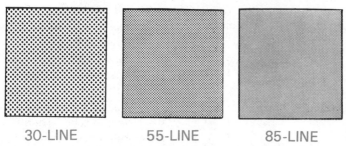

30-LINE 55-LINE 85-LINE

13-56. *Screen linage refers to the number of dots a halftone screen will produce within one running inch.*

next color to be stripped onto the new base sheet. Use the positive image on the matrix as a guide for registering the negative film onto the base.

7. Repeat Steps five and six for each flat to be stripped.

Halftone and Tint Screen Applications

Once correct registration has been assured, the stripper must consider the halftone and tint screens. The three major screen factors to consider are linage, percentage, and angle.

Screen linage refers to how many dots a halftone or tint screen will produce within one running inch. The number of dots produced by a screen actually controls the detail or resolution of the color reproduction. The more dots, the greater the

detail and color intensity are. This is true for both halftone and tint screens. Fig. 13-56.

Screen percentage refers to the amount of light that transmits through a halftone or tint screen. This controls the size of the dot and the saturation of the color produced by the screen. The larger the dot, the darker the color saturation is. In tint screens the percentage of dot size is constant for each screen. Therefore, dot percentages are controllable by the stripper only by changing screens. The percentage of dot produced by halftone screens is determined by the contrast of the continuous-tone copy and is not controllable by the stripper. Fig. 13-57.

Screen angle refers to the angle that is formed between a horizontal base line and any one

of the straight rows of dots on the screen. Fig. 13-58. Screen angles control the pattern that is formed when screened images are printed over other screened images. Each screen-angle image must be rotated from other screen-angle images by thirty degrees. This prevents a *moiré* from forming. Fig. 13-59 shows how screens overprinted at incorrect angles produce the undesirable moiré pattern, which is a watered or wavy effect. Normally, the screen image for the strongest color is stripped so that it prints at a 45-degree angle from the base line. This is the least noticeable angle.

In *flat color* stripping requiring screen overprinting, correct screen angles are produced for each flat by rotating the tint screen on the flat when each is

13-58. *Screen angle is the angle between the horizontal base line and a straight row of dots.*

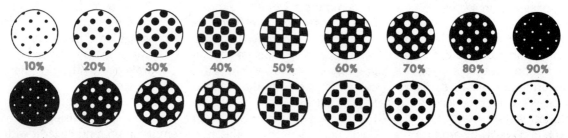

10% 20% 30% 40% 50% 60% 70% 80% 90%

13-57. *A greatly enlarged example of halftone dots. This gives an approximate comparison of dot sizes for various screen percentages. The dots in the top row are positive, and those in the bottom row are negative.*

A NORMAL SCREENED PRINT

A PRINT CONTAINING A MOIRÉ

13-59. A moiré pattern.

ous-tone color image. If all colors were screened at the same angle, the resulting overprinting would produce a black and white reproduction instead of color. Halftones for duotones must be rotated 30 degrees also. Detailed information is available in Chapter 18, "Color Separation."

Film and Stripping Base Requirements

Several factors are involved with regard to determining the number of film and stripping bases. As previously indicated, a single film can be used to produce several different color flats by changing the bases or making flaps, that is, keying. Keying works only when no colors overlap (trap) on the finished, printed job. When colors overlap or trap, both separate stripping bases and separate pieces of film are required. The procedures for producing these separate film units are explained in the Chapter 9, "Preparing Copy for the Camera." The procedures for stripping the separate film units are the same as those explained

stripped. A triangle or a protractor is used to determine the angles. If only one screen is used to produce a tint block, it is usually placed at a 45-degree angle.

In *process color* stripping, the halftone screen angles, Fig. 13-60 are already produced on the film at the camera. Each halftone film is then registered by eye when it is stripped. Note that the film that will print the yellow ink (yellow printer) is rotated only 15 degrees on four-color work. This is because yellow is a weak color and will not produce a noticeable moiré pattern.

The purpose of selecting different halftone screen angles is to place the dots for each of the three strong process colors (cyan, magenta, and black) at angles which will produce the least moiré pattern. The differ-

ence in angles permits each set of the four colored dots to produce a rosette pattern, which results in additive and subtractive halftone color combinations that duplicate the original, continu-

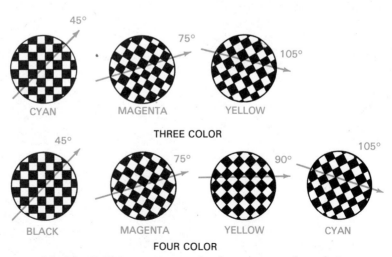

13-60. Halftone screen angles for process color printing.

for using a registration matrix. Sometimes when time is limited, negative film units are stripped in register with other negative film units without benefit of a registration matrix. In this case, the first flat to be stripped is placed on the stripping table, and it is used as the registration matrix. This method is not recommended when quality work is required.

REVIEW QUESTIONS

1. Single-flat stripping includes all stripping work that requires just one flat. True or False?
2. What are complementary flats?
3. What are multiple flats?
4. Clear stripping base is used with positives, and colored stripping base is used with negatives. True or False?
5. If the film is to be attached to the stripping base with its emulsion side *down*, to which side of the base will it be attached?
6. Name the reference lines described in the following:
   a. Indicate the size of the sheet to be printed.
   b. Indicates the area to be set aside for the press grippers.
   c. Marks the portion of the base that must be set aside to permit press mounting of the plate.
   d. Indicate where the press sheet will be trimmed.
   e. Indicate where the image area must be located.
7. What is meant by the term *opening the flat?*
8. Positive film is usually stripped emulsion up. True or False?

Offset Platemaking

Platemaking facilities should be located in temperature-controlled rooms which are close to the camera, stripping, and press departments. They should be well ventilated and lighted with yellow lights. Yellow lights are recommended because they emit light in the red and green range only. They will not expose the coatings which are used on most offset plates.

The plate room should also have a white light system. This will allow the platemaker to see yellow-colored material not visible under yellow light only.

A typical platemaking room layout is shown in Fig. 14-1.

MATERIALS AND CHEMICALS

Large, soft rubber squeegees, fine-grain cellulose sponges, developing pads, cheesecloth polishing strips, disposable cotton wipes, rolls or stacks of absorbent paper, and the plates themselves are the major items needed for the processing of conventional offset plates.

All plate material should be stored flat in a cool, dry place. Presensitized plates should be kept wrapped in their light-safe packaging material, dated and arranged so that the plates are lying emulsion side down.

Process gum, fixing solution, gum arabic, asphaltum, devel-

oper, tusche, scratch remover, deletion fluid, stop-out solution, film cleaner, and glass cleaner are the major chemicals used.

Process gum is designed to desensitize the nonimage portion of a plate coating. It also protects a completely processed plate from the air. *Fixing solution* also desensitizes the nonimage portion of the plate coating, but it generally does not protect the processed plate from the air.

Gum arabic is a covering solution used to retard oxidation of the nonimage areas on a plate. The solution should have a reading of 14 degrees Baumé if used

to gum a plate on a workbench. (Baumé refers to hydrometer scales used to indicate specific gravity.) When gumming a plate on a press, use a 7° or 8° Baumé solution. This is made by adding one part water to two parts of a 14° Baumé solution. When the solution smells sour, it is too old and should be discarded.

The Baumé reading is made by placing a Baumé hydrometer in an empty jar. Pour the solution slowly in the jar until the float rises from the bottom and is floating. Read the marking on the hydrometer at the top of the

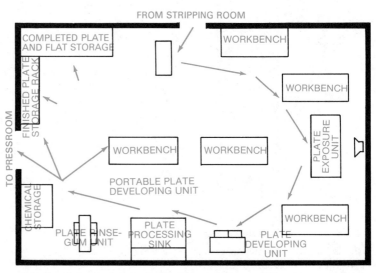

14-1. *A typical shop layout for a platemaking department.*

liquid's level. Fig. 14-2. This reading is the specific gravity of the liquid.

Asphaltum is a mineral substance produced from petroleum and gum arabic. It is used to protect the image area of stored plates.

Developer is made of developing ink or developing lacquer. Both apply a specially formulated, ink-receptive material to the surface of the image area on the plate. Sometimes traces of copper are added to developing solutions to strengthen the image's protective coating.

Tusche is used for adding or correcting image areas on a plate. When tusche is applied to a plate and treated with a plate

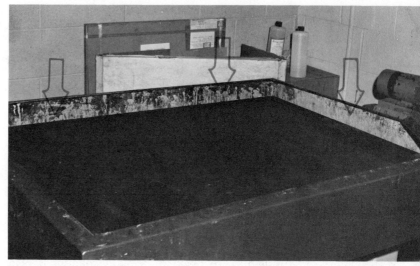

14-3. *Fumes are pulled down around the outside rim of the downdraft developing sink.*

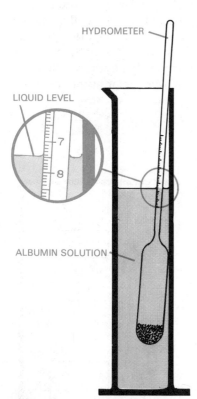

14-2. *A Baumé hydrometer is used to measure the Baumé reading of a solution.*

etch, it becomes ink receptive, then becomes an image area.

Scratch remover, deletion fluid, and *stop-out solution* are thickened solvents used to remove unwanted image and non-image areas on the plate. The solvents actually soften the light-hardened coating so that it can be removed from the interlay or plate base.

The following general rules apply to the handling of all plate-making chemicals and materials.

* Discard chemicals and materials when they become outdated or worn.
* Mix or shake liquid chemicals thoroughly before using.
* Use chemicals and materials only as directed.
* Keep chemical containers closed when they are not in use.
* Keep chemicals from freezing or overheating.
* Keep chemicals from direct sunlight.

* Keep materials and supplies clean and free from moisture.

SAFETY IN THE PLATE ROOM

The misuse of equipment and toxic platemaking materials can result in permanent crippling. These materials contain very dangerous chemicals that must be used only in well-ventilated areas.

Some safety precautions are:
* Avoid looking directly into the energized light source on exposing units.
* Wash hands thoroughly after handling platemaking chemicals.
* Avoid breathing fumes given off by platemaking chemicals. The best protection is to use a downdraft sink. Fig. 14-3. It pulls fumes down, away from your face.
* Use extra caution when handling the sharp-edged plates.

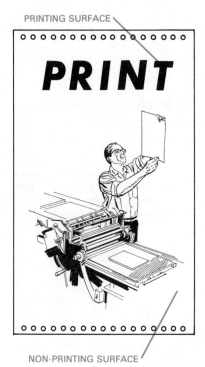

14-4. *A typical offset printing plate. The image to be reproduced has been developed on the surface.*

plastic, or metal on which a printing and a nonprinting surface can be produced. Fig. 14-4.

The printing surface is called the image area. The nonprinting surface is called the nonimage area. The nonprinting area of an offset plate accepts and holds a thin film of water. This serves to repel the greasy, water-resistant lithographic ink. The image area rejects water and accepts the ink. Fig. 14-5.

Offset plates vary in thickness from 0.005″ to values in excess of 0.025″. The thickness, which is often called caliper, is governed primarily by the type of plate. The size of an offset plate is determined by the size of the offset press. Some offset plates are even manufactured in rolls and are cut off in various lengths as needed.

PLATE ENDS

Although there are many different kinds of offset plates, there are only four styles of plate ends. Fig. 14-6. The plate end is used to attach the plate to the

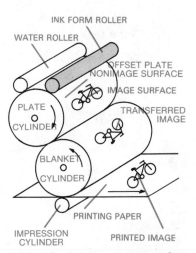

14-5. *The printing image surface accepts ink from the ink form roller. The nonimage background rejects ink.*

press. Before selecting a plate, it is necessary to know which style of plate end the press was designed to use.

PLATE SURFACES

The surface finish of offset plates varies from smooth to coarse. The smooth surface is called *grainless*, *anodized*, or

* Avoid handling electrical platemaking equipment with wet hands.
* Hang completed plates so their bottom edges are readily visible and safely out of the way.
* Avoid spilling water or other liquids on the floor.
* Keep the cover closed on discarded developing pads and other waste materials.
* Always pour platemaking chemicals slowly.
* Never lean on glass-topped surfaces such as vacuum frames and light tables.
* Keep all drinking containers out of the platemaking area.

OFFSET PLATES

An offset (lithographic) printing plate is a thin sheet of paper,

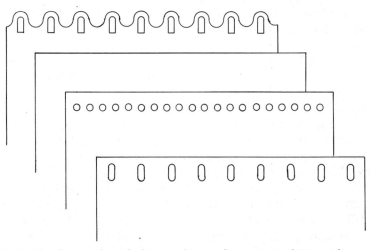

14-6. *The four styles of plate ends are, from top to bottom: loop or serrated, straight, round hole, and oval hole.*

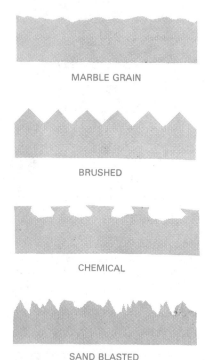

MARBLE GRAIN

BRUSHED

CHEMICAL

SAND BLASTED

14-7. Cross-section views of marble, brushed, chemical, and sandblasted graining.

smooth. The coarse surface is called grained. The grained plate surface holds more moisture than the smooth. Graining also improves the platemaking characteristics, helps control the ink-water balance when the plate is on the press, increases the ink gloss, and provides for greater image area retention on the plate.

A plate can be grained mechanically or chemically. Fig. 14-7. Mechanical graining is done with graining machines, using an abrasive with steel, glass, or wood marbles. The marbles are made to oscillate rapidly on the plate. This movement causes the marbles to roll over the abrasive powder, which roughens or grains the surface. Mechanical graining is also done

by revolving steel or nylon brushes against pumice or an aluminum oxide abrasive. Brushed grains are shallower and less expensive than marbled grains. A third mechanical graining process is to blast an abrasive against the plate, much like sandblasting a building.

Chemical graining is an etching or anodizing process. Sandblasted and chemical grains are generally coarser than brushed grains. They are most often used with wipe-on plates. Wipe-on plates are discussed later in this chapter.

Paper and plastic plates are made so that their surface retains a film of moisture. They are classified as grainless plates.

Plates are grained in three grades and five textures. The grades are thrift, news, and commercial. The thrift is the least expensive, news is next in cost, and the commercial is the most expensive. The texture values are extra fine (#7), fine (#8 1/2), medium (#10), coarse (#12), and very coarse (#14–17). The extra fine grain is generally best suited for color process work and rarely makes an indention into the plate surface more than 0.0005″.

PARTS OF AN OFFSET PLATE

The major parts of an offset plate are the base, covering, and coating. Fig. 14-8.

The base used for most metal plates is aluminum. Aluminum is used because it is easily wetted and grained, prefers moisture over grease, resists cracking, and is flexible. Other materials, such as plastic, paper, or combinations of plastic, paper, or

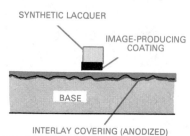

SYNTHETIC LACQUER

IMAGE-PRODUCING COATING

BASE

INTERLAY COVERING (ANODIZED)

14-8. A cross-section view through an offset plate showing the base, interlay covering, image-producing coating, and the synthetic lacquer protective covering.

metal, are also used as the base for offset plates. Long-run plates are made from combinations of aluminum, copper, zinc, stainless steel, and chromium.

A covering is a special material on a plate that helps hold the image area on the base metal. This covering is called an interlay. Two types of coverings are shown in Fig. 14-9.

A coating is the image-producing layer on the surface of a plate. It can be image producing

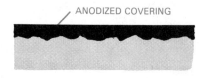

ANODIZED COVERING

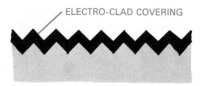

ELECTRO-CLAD COVERING

14-9. Two special coverings that are coated onto grained plates. The anodized covering is smooth and water receptive. The electro-clad covering enables the plate to hold the image area longer, thus increasing the number of impressions.

or water receptive, depending upon the type of plate.

IMAGE-PRODUCING COATINGS

If a coating is image producing, it means that a portion of the light-sensitive coating can be converted into an ink-receptive image area after it has been exposed to an actinic light source and processed. As explained in Chapter 13, actinic rays are in the ultraviolet region and cause chemical change in photosensitive materials.

There are four major categories and six different types of image-producing coatings. The categories are the *negative-working*, *positive-working*, *additive-working*, and *subtractive-working* coatings. The six types are the *diazo, halide, bichromate, photopolymer, electrostatic*, and *differential adhesion* coatings.

CATEGORIES OF COATINGS

Negative-working coatings are those that produce an image area in all places on the plate that are struck by light during exposure. Any place not struck by light on a negative-working coating produces a nonimage area. On the coating struck by light, a latent image is produced. This imaged coating is hardened during the developing process. The unhardened coating not struck by light is washed away or desensitized during development to produce the nonimage area. The term *negative-working* is derived from the fact that film negatives are commonly used to make this type of plate.

Positive-working coatings are those that produce an image area in all places not struck by

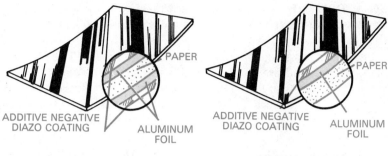

TWO-SIDED "L" PLATE   ONE-SIDED "E" PLATE

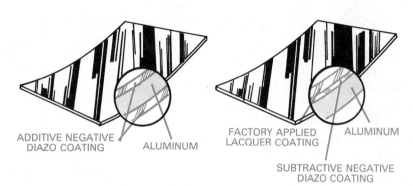

TWO-SIDED "R" PLATE   SUBTRACTIVE "K" PLATE

14-10. *Four typical diazo-coated plates.*

light during exposure. The area of a positive-working coating struck by light during exposure becomes the nonimage area. The term *positive-working* is derived from the fact that film positives are commonly used to make positive-working plates. As stated before, a film positive is the reverse of a film negative. The image is black and the background is transparent.

Negative- and positive-working coatings must be either in the additive or subtractive categories

A plate is in the *additive-working category if a special ink-holding coating is added during the plate developing process.* This coating is either a synthetic lacquer or a copperized resin sub-

stance. It is placed onto the image-producing coating of the plate in the light-hardened image area. Fig. 14-8. A disadvantage is that the additive process produces a variation in the thickness of the protective coating.

Subtractive-working coatings have the synthetic lacquer applied at the factory. Fig. 14-10. This produces a layer of lacquer uniform in thickness. When processing a subtractive plate, the nonimage area and its lacquer coating are removed during development. The lacquer on the image area remains as applied at the factory.

All image-producing coatings must be either positive- or negative-working and have additive or subtractive coatings.

SENSITIVITY OF IMAGE-PRODUCING COATINGS

Image-producing coatings are high contrast and are manufactured in two levels of light sensitivity. One is sensitive to blue light and is referred to as *contact speed*. A plate with this type of coating uses a stripped flat placed *in contact* with the plate during exposure. The light source used is very high in ultraviolet (UV) properties since contact-speed coatings are especially sensitive to radiant energy. The other level is sensitive to blue and green light and is referred to as *projection speed*. Projection speed coatings are generally exposed by a photo-direct plate-making camera, explained later.

TYPES OF IMAGE-PRODUCING COATINGS

There are six different types of image-producing coatings. A brief discussion of each follows.

Diazo coatings are either negative-working or positive-working. In negative-working coatings, image areas are formed because diazo molecules in the coating have a tendency to give up nitrogen when struck by actinic rays in the blue range. When any part of the coating is struck by light, nitrogen is released from that part and it becomes inactive. The coating not struck by light remains active. When the surface of an exposed, diazo-coated plate is swabbed with desensitizing process-gum solution, the still-active non-image area becomes soluble, permitting it to be washed away during plate processing. However, the inactive image area will not react with the desensitizing solution and will not wash away. As a result, the light-struck, inactive image area will remain on the surface of the plate.

The opposite nitrogen release reaction occurs with positive-working diazo coatings. The end result is still the same. The image area remains on the plate just as with negative-working diazo coatings.

Once an exposed diazo coating is desensitized, it is developed with a synthetic lacquer and resin solution that is mixed with a wetting agent composed of water and gum arabic. This developer solution puts a layer of lacquer over the image area to prevent it from wearing away during the printing process. The water in the developer solution helps to wash away the non-image area, while the gum arabic protects the entire plate.

Diazo-coated plates are generally grainless, have limited shelf life, are contact speed, and require minimum amounts of printing ink and fountain water on the press. Fig. 14-10 shows four typical diazo-coated plates.

Silver halide coatings are composed of silver salts, such as iodides, bromides, and chlorides. The salts suspended in this coating are ultimately converted into metallic silver image areas during development. When used to make photo-direct offset plates, this type of coating can be projection speed or contact speed. If the coating is projection speed, it is generally developed by the stabilization process. Contact-speed silver halide coatings are used on offset plates made by the "diffusion silver" or the "gelatin silver" transfer process.

These methods of platemaking are explained later in this chapter.

Photopolymer coatings. A polymer is a chemical compound made up of repeating structural units called monomers. The monomers in the coating link together in chains when struck by light. In platemaking, the term *polymer* means a material which will form a tough printing image that does not necessarily need to be reinforced by a lacquer. Photopolymer coatings are unlike other light-sensitive plate-making coatings which form image areas that are tender and require protection or reinforcing with resin or lacquer during developing. Instead, photopolymer coatings produce sturdy, long-lasting image areas that do not require a protective coating of lacquer.

Some versions of the photopolymer offset plate require no special developing chemicals at all. One type is simply put on the press after exposure and wiped with distilled water. Other types of photopolymer plates need only be exposed to conventional fountain solution found on the press dampening rollers to complete development. The wetting action of the dampening rollers plus the standard chemicals found in the press fountain solution are all that are required to develop these plates.

Electrostatic coatings. Electrostatic coating is really not a coating, but just one of the many non-light-sensitive substances capable of producing image areas on an offset plate. It is used in conjunction with the *water-receptive* coating to produce direct-image plates, ex-

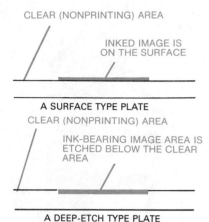

CLEAR (NONPRINTING) AREA

INKED IMAGE IS ON THE SURFACE

A SURFACE TYPE PLATE

CLEAR (NONPRINTING) AREA

INK-BEARING IMAGE AREA IS ETCHED BELOW THE CLEAR AREA

A DEEP-ETCH TYPE PLATE

14-11. Surface and deep-etch offset plates.

plained later in this chapter. Basically, electrostatic materials are manufactured in the form of carbonized powders or liquids. They can be applied to the surface of a direct-image offset plate electrostatically. Electrostatic materials are mentioned here because a light-sensitive coating is used in the platemaking process. This light-sensitive coating is not on the plate but on a drum or plate on the platemaking machine. The image-forming, plate-coating material itself is carbonized and not light sensitive.

Water-receptive coatings. The water-receptive coating is not sensitive to light; therefore, it is not image producing. It is merely a coating which has a surface tension designed to be especially receptive to water. Being receptive to water means it is not receptive to ink. Offset plates manufactured with this type of coating are often called *duplicating masters.* These plates or masters are ungrained and usually made of paper or paper laminated on plastic.

The image area on water-receptive coated plates is produced by covering the water-receptive coating so that it no longer is water receptive. This "covering up" can be achieved by many different ways, such as writing, drawing, typing, proofing, and electrostatic adhesion of an image on the plate.

TYPES OF OFFSET PLATE IMAGES

There are two major types of offset plate images, *surface* and *deep etch.* Fig. 14-11.

SURFACE PLATES

The printing image on surface plates is raised slightly above the plate's surface. Fig. 14-11. The amount the image is raised is so small that it cannot be distinguished by feel. This lack of "feel" is why the term *surface plate* is used.

There are several different types of surface plates and deep-etch plates. Fig. 14-12. Each type is used for a particular printing application.

Mechanical direct-image plates (masters). This kind of plate is most often covered with a non-light-sensitive, water-receptive type of coating. It is manufactured in short- and long-run styles. The short-run style is capable of producing up to 1,000 quality impressions. The base materials for short-run plates are usually made of paper, paper laminated with aluminum foil, or paper impregnated with plastic. The long-run style uses acetate or aluminum as the base material. It will print up to 25,000 impressions.

Printing images are placed on direct-image plates by typewriters using one-time carbon ribbons, recording pens or pencils containing generous amounts of carbon, crayons, carbon papers, rubber stamps, typeforms, printing inks, copying machines, diffusion transfer devices, or any other material that will cover the water-receptive coating and attract ink.

Presensitized plates. This type of offset plate generally has a

TYPES OF OFFSET PLATES

Surface Plates	Deep-Etch Plates

A. Mechanical Direct Image
B. Presensitized
C. Albumin
D. Wipe-On
E. Photo-Direct
F. Transfer
   1. Silver Gelatin
   2. Silver Diffusion
   3. Thermographic
G. Electrostatic Direct Image
H. Scanned
I. Waterless
	A. Single Metal
	B. Multimetal
	   1. Raised Image
	     a. Positive-Working
	     b. Negative-Working
	   2. Recessed Image
	     a. Positive-Working
	     b. Negative-Working

14-12. Types of surface and deep-etch offset plates.

presensitized diazo or photopolymer coating placed on one or both sides of the plate in the commercial printing industry. This plate is ready for exposure immediately upon removal from the container. It is available in many varieties from different manufacturers. The presensitized plates are capable of producing more than 100,000 quality impressions. All the plates shown in Fig. 14-10 are presensitized.

Wipe-on plates. A modern shop-coated type, wipe-on plates utilize diazo coatings that are commonly applied by sponge or roll-coating devices. Fig. 14-13. The base metal for this type of plate is usually grained aluminum. Since the wipe-on coating deteriorates after mixing, it is mixed immediately before use.

The coating itself is a relatively active chemical solution that will react with exposed and untreated aluminum. As a result, the grained aluminum base plate is usually treated with a special interlay solution that prevents the diazo coating from reacting with the unprotected aluminum plate.

While on the press, wipe-on plates generally require more moisture than other types of surface plates to keep the nonimage area free from ink during printing. A wipe-on plate is capable of producing 100,000 quality impressions.

Photo-direct plates. Photo-direct plates are commonly coated with a silver salts emulsion that is projection speed. This coating permits photo-direct plates to be made directly from photomechanicals on special platemaking cameras. This

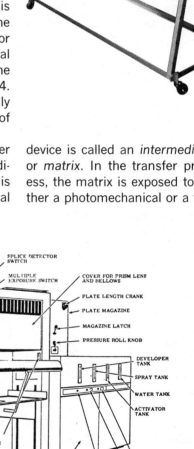

Western Litho Plate and Supply Co.
14-13. *A roll-coating device used to apply wipe-on diazo coatings in the shop.*

means no stripped flats are required since the plates are exposed by light reflected from the photomechanicals. Since the plate material is stored inside the light-safe platemaking camera, no separate darkroom facilities are required to process this type of plate.

In addition to the simplicity and speed, a major advantage to the photo-direct type of plate is that the printing image on the plate can be easily enlarged or reduced from that on the original photomechanical during the platemaking process. Fig. 14-14. Photo-direct plates are generally not used for runs in excess of 50,000 impressions.

Transfer plates. In the transfer platemaking system, an additional image-producing device is used. Fig. 14-15. This additional device is called an *intermediate* or *matrix*. In the transfer process, the matrix is exposed to either a photomechanical or a flat

CAMERA POWER SWITCH
SPLICE DETECTOR SWITCH
LENS POSITION INDICATOR
MULTIPLE EXPOSURE SWITCH
COVER FOR PRISM LENS AND BELLOWS
LENS POSITION SWITCH
PLATE LENGTH INDICATOR DIAL
PLATE LENGTH CRANK
PLATE MAGAZINE
LOAD COPY BOARD INDICATOR LIGHT
MAGAZINE LATCH
READY TO EXPOSE INDICATOR LIGHT
PRESSURE ROLL KNOB
EXPOSURE TIME INDICATOR DIAL
DEVELOPER TANK
PRE-FOCUSED TUBE LIGHTS
SPRAY TANK
COPY BOARD POSITION SWITCH
COPY
WATER TANK
PLATE COUNTER INDICATOR
ACTIVATOR TANK
REFLECTOR
COPY BOARD POSITION INDICATOR
COPY BOARD
DRIVE SWITCH
FOOT SWITCH
PROCESSOR DOORS
DEVELOPER READY LIGHT
HEATERS SWITCH

ITEK Corp.
14-14. *A photo-direct unit capable of making plates larger or smaller than the photomechanical.*

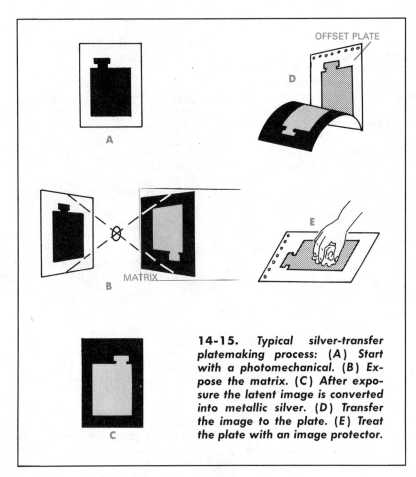

OFFSET PLATE

D

A

E

MATRIX

B

C

14-15. *Typical silver-transfer platemaking process: (A) Start with a photomechanical. (B) Expose the matrix. (C) After exposure the latent image is converted into metallic silver. (D) Transfer the image to the plate. (E) Treat the plate with an image protector.*

sion produced when the printing plate and the matrix are placed against each other and immersed in a developing bath. After immersion, the matrix is removed from the plate. Then the plate is treated with an image-intensifying solution that also clears the nonimage area at the same time it is intensifying the image area.

The silver diffusion printing plate is actually developed by the stabilization process. The plate is placed against the matrix, and both are run through a processor containing an activator solution and a stabilizing bath. While the matrix and plate are in the processor, the activator solution develops and transfers the image from the matrix to the plate. Then the matrix and the plate are transferred to the stabilizing bath. This solution stops the development of the image area and fixes the image to the plate. Little skill is needed by a platemaker since the sandwiched matrix and plate are automatically fed into the processor by motor-driven rollers. The whole operation is done in less than 60 seconds. The major steps involved in a typical transfer platemaking system are shown in Fig. 14-15.

The *thermographic* process relies on infrared energy and direct-image plates. A specially coated matrix is exposed to become image bearing. This exposed matrix is then placed in contact with a direct-image plate, and both are sent through a special machine containing an infrared energy source. While in the machine, the image area on the matrix is chemically changed and fused to the printing plate by the radiant energy emitted from

to produce both an image and a nonimage area on the matrix. Exposure of the matrix can be accomplished either by projection or by contact, depending on the type of matrix. After exposure, the matrix is then placed in contact with a printing plate, and the image area is transferred to the plate.

Transfer plates are short run and commonly used for reproducing ordinary line work or coarse-screen halftone work. There are three types of transfer plates: silver gelatin, silver diffusion, and thermographic.

In the *silver gelatin* process, a silver-laden matrix is exposed

and developed so that all the gelatin except the image area is hardened. This developed matrix is then placed against a printing plate, and both are sent through a processor. By action of light roller pressure in the processor and by chemical adhesion, the soft, sticky image-area gelatin is transferred to the printing plate and then hardened.

The *silver diffusion* process is very similar to the gelatin process. The major difference is centered on how the image is transferred from the matrix to the printing plate. In the silver diffusion process, a chemical transfer occurs as a result of an adhe-

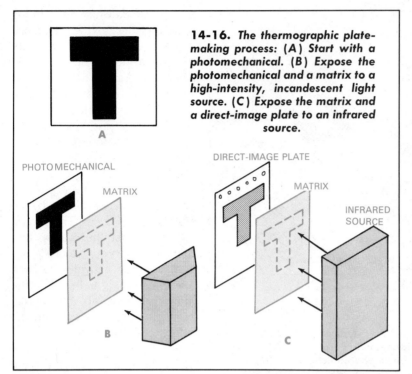

14-16. *The thermographic plate-making process: (A) Start with a photomechanical. (B) Expose the photomechanical and a matrix to a high-intensity, incandescent light source. (C) Expose the matrix and a direct-image plate to an infrared source.*

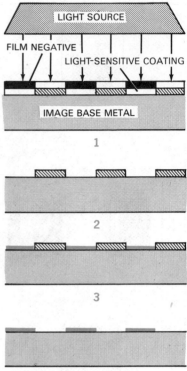

14-17A. *A bimetal plate. (1) Coat the plate and expose it through the negative. (2) Develop the positive image on the plate. (3) Electroplate the nonimage metal on the clear areas. (4) Remove the acid resist from the image areas.*

the infrared energy source. Fig. 14-16.

Electrostatic direct-image plates are produced by combining a direct-image master with an electrostatic copying machine. The theory of this system is explained in detail later in this chapter. Press runs in excess of 2,000 impressions are rare with this type of plate.

Scanned plates are offset plates which have a coating that is sensitive to an engraving beam of light. The printing image is formed on the surface of the plate by this engraving beam. The beam heats the coating of the plate until it becomes ink receptive.

Reflected light from the photomechanical is picked up by the tracing beam and fed into a photomultiplier. The amount of light reflected varies according to the material making up the photomechanical. The photomultiplier increases the signal to the proper level and feeds it to the engraving beam. Scanned plates are short-run plates.

DEEP-ETCH PLATES

There are two basic types of deep-etch plates: single metal (Fig. 14-11) and multimetal (Fig. 14-17). Both types can be made with a raised or a recessed image area.

The raised image area on a surface plate will not last as long as the raised image area on a deep-etch plate. Fig. 14-18. The raised printing area on the surface plate is simply a chemically bonded lacquer. This lacquer can easily flake off the light-hardened coating. The raised printing area on a deep-etch plate is securely electroplated to the surface. Fig. 14-17. However, if the printing image area is recessed below the nonimage area, Fig. 14-11, the plate can transfer more ink to the paper because more ink is held in the recessed image area. When more ink is transferred, fine line and halftone images reproduce more brilliantly. Recessed image areas also permit exceptionally long runs to be produced from each

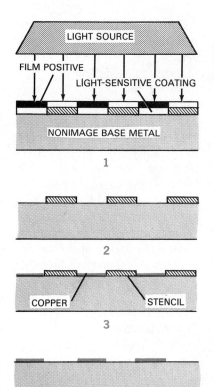

14-17B. *A bimetal plate. (1) Coat the plate and expose it through the negative. (2) Develop the negative stencil. (3) Electroplate the image metal on the clear areas in the stencil. (4) Remove the stencil from the nonimage areas.*

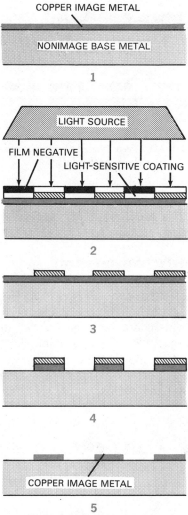

14-17C. *A bimetal plate. (1) Electroplate an image metal on a nonimage plate. (2) Coat the plate and expose through a negative. (3) Develop a positive image. (4) Etch through the image metal in the nonimage areas. (5) Remove the resist from the image areas.*

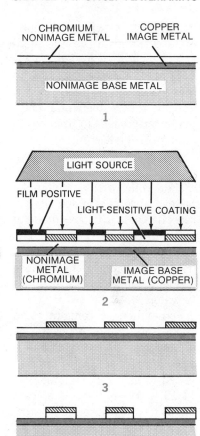

14-17D. *A trimetal plate. (1) Electroplate a nonimage metal on an image metal. (2) Coat the plate and expose through a positive. (3) Develop the negative stencil. (4) Etch through the nonimage metal in the image areas. (5) Remove the stencil from the nonimage areas.*

plate. Many recessed image deep-etch plates last for several million impressions before image breakdown occurs.

Subtractive-type coatings are generally used to produce deep-etch plates. These coatings can be either positive- or negative-working, depending on the type of plate that is to be made. Although there are many different ways to make deep-etch plates, the most popular of the single metal varieties have the image areas etched below the non-

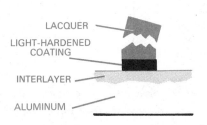

14-18. *A section through a raised image offset plate. The lacquer layer can easily break away from the light-hardened coating.*

image surface, while the multi-metal varieties have the non-image etched away. Fig. 14-17.

Aluminum is normally used to make the single metal plates. Copper, zinc, steel, and chromium are used to make the multimetal plates.

Unpolished chromium is generally used as the outer layer metal with most multimetal plates, while the image or ink-receptive area is usually made of soft, ungrained copper. Fig. 14-19. Unpolished chromium is used as the outer metal because it is very hard and very receptive to water.

Sometimes chromium and copper are laminated over zinc or steel to provide for additional strength. These plates are referred to as *trimetal* plates. Fig. 14-19. When the deep-etch plates have a raised image area,

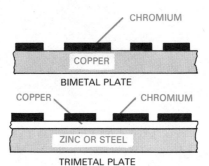

14-19. *Two types of multimetal deep-etch plates.*

they are known as *copperized* deep-etch plates.

SELECTING THE PLATE

A synopsis of the major types of offset plates is shown in Fig. 14-12. A summary of the many plate characteristics is shown in Fig. 14-20. By examining Figs. 14-12 and 14-20, it can be readily understood that many combinations of plate ends, surfaces,

coatings, and sensitivities are possible. Because of this great variety of combinations, the process of selecting the right plate for the job involves three major considerations. These are *cost, length of run,* and *processing characteristics.* Cost involves the expense required to produce the plate, and length of run refers to how many impressions the plate can produce. Processing characteristics involve two considerations: how difficult the plate is to make, and how well the plate will reproduce fine lines or screened images.

PLATE HANDLING TECHNIQUES

There are five primary plate handling techniques. These are:

1. Always lift large plates by opposite corners to keep them from kinking or scratching.

OFFSET PLATE CHARACTERISTICS

Plate Ends	Surfaces	Sensitivity	Coatings

A. Looped
B. Straight
C. Pin Bar
D. Slotted
	A. Grainless
	B. Grained
	  1. Grades
	    a. Thrift
	    b. News
	    c. Commercial
	  2. Textures
	    a. Extra Fine
	    b. Fine
	    c. Medium
	    d. Coarse
	    e. Very Coarse
	  3. Mechanical
	  4. Chemical
		A. Contact
		B. Projection
			A. Water Receptive
			B. Image Producing
			  1. Additive (Negative- or
			    Positive-Working)
			    a. Diazo
			    b. Halide
			    c. Bichromate
			    d. Photopolymer
			    e. Electrostatic*
			    f. Differential Adhesion
			  2. Subtractive (Negative- or
			    Positive-Working)
			    a. Diazo
			    b. Halide
			    c. Bichromate
			    d. Photopolymer
			    e. Electrostatic*
			    f. Differential Adhesion

*This uses a light-sensitive (image-producing) coating in the process, but the coating itself is not image producing.

14-20. *A summary of offset plate characteristics.*

CONTACT SYSTEM

Negative-Working Plates	Positive-Working Plates

Presensitized subtractive—diazo
Presensitized subtractive—
  waterless
Presensitized subtractive—polymer
Wipe-on additive—diazo
	Presensitized subtractive—diazo
	Presensitized subtractive—
	  polymer
	Wipe-on subtractive—deep etch

14-21. *Contact system of offset platemaking.*

2. Lift small plates by the short edge, using only the thumb and index finger.

3. Keep fingers off the plate coating both before and after processing.

4. Hang developed plates. Do not stack or slide them against each other.

5. Keep the protective slip-sheet over plates for protection before and after processing.

Remove small dents in offset plates by tapping them with a leather mallet. Another method is to smooth them out from the backside with a roller. Still another method is by tapping them out using an ordinary teaspoon. If the tapping method is used, the plate should be covered on both sides with cardboard to prevent scratching or nicking.

OFFSET PLATEMAKING BY THE CONTACT SYSTEM

One of the major systems of making offset plates is the contact system. Fig. 14-21. With this system, plates are made using a stripped flat placed in contact with the plate during exposure. Four major factors to consider regarding contact platemaking are the condition of the flat, the contact between the flat and the plate, exposing techniques, and developing operations.

(Other major systems—projection, transfer, and direct-image—are discussed later in the chapter.)

EXAMINING THE FLAT

The film to be used for plate-making should be produced by the contacting method. This is recommended because the half-tone dots, lines, and solids produced by the projection method have edges which shade off into the surrounding area. Sharp, clear-cut edges are needed. Only a contact film will produce a sharp and long-lasting image on an offset plate. Fig. 14-22.

TROUBLESHOOTING POOR CONTACT

Newton's rings are small, rainbowlike circles that appear be-

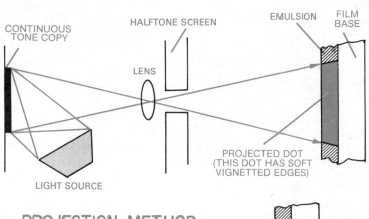

PROJECTION METHOD

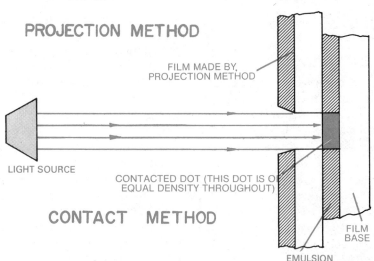

CONTACT METHOD

14-22. *The projection and contact methods of producing film.*

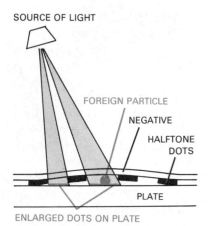

14-23A. *Foreign particles under the plate can cause undercutting.*

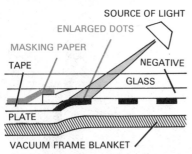

14-23B. *Careless stripping can result in double thickness or extra layers of tape or paper. This buildup between the plate and the vacuum glass can cause undercutting.*

NuArc Co., Inc.

14-24. *This platemaker is used to expose the plate. The unit contains a vacuum frame, timer, and a mercury vapor light source.*

tween the film on the stripped flat and the vacuum frame glass. They are caused by light reflecting back through the glass from the surface of the tightly contacted flat. The absence of Newton's rings indicates poor contact, while their presence indicates proper contact has been achieved. Poor contact could be caused by air trapped between the plate and the stripped flat. To correct this condition, "bleed" air into the sys-

tem or open the glass on the vacuum frame for a moment.

Sometimes a faulty gauge on a vacuum indicator will result in poor contact because the reading on the indicator does not correspond to the actual vacuum inside the frame. Check the gaskets on the edge of the vacuum frame for splits, cracks, or ridges. If that is not the trouble, check to see if the vacuum gauge hose is collapsed or plugged.

If the rubber diaphragm on the bed of the vacuum frame is worn, replace it. Undercutting can be caused by poor contact,

resulting from poor stripping techniques or foreign material trapped between the plate and the stripped film. Fig. 14-23.

EXPOSING THE PLATE

Exposing techniques are relatively standardized for all varieties of contact-made plates. A typical plate exposing device is shown in Fig. 14-24. To expose the plate:

1. Punch pin register holes into the plate. Guide from the same corner used to punch the pin register holes into the flat. Some prefer to punch the plate

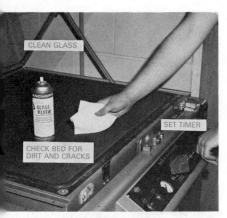

14-25. *Before making an exposure, make certain the glass and bed are clean.*

AGFA-Gevaert

14-26. *A two-sided plate exposure unit. The top flips, allowing the operator to position a plate for exposure on the top side while the plate on the lower side is being exposed.*

and flat together before the flat is stripped.

2. Set up the exposing machine (platemaker). Fig. 14-25.

    A. Set the timer for the correct exposure.

    B. Check the light to insure they are working properly.

    C. Clean the glass.

    D. Prepare the bed of the vacuum frame by checking the rubber blanket for unwanted cuts or tears. Be certain the vacuum holes are not covered by the blanket. A special two-sided exposure unit is shown in Fig. 14-26.

3. Mount flat-topped registration pins to the rubber bed of the vacuum frame. Flat-topped pins are recommended because they are less likely to damage the glass on the platemaking machine. Fig. 14-27.

4. Attach the plate to the registration pins so that the emulsion side of the plate will be toward the light source during exposure. Fig. 14-28.

5. Attach the stripped flat to the pins so that the flat covers

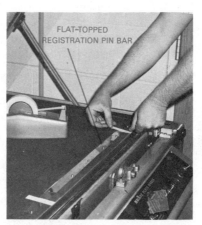

14-27. *The registration pin bar is taped to the bed.*

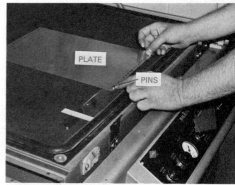

14-28. *Attach the plate to the registration pin bar so that the emulsion side will face the light source during the exposure.*

323

14-29. *Lay the stripped flat over the plate, and attach it to the registration pin bar.*

the plate in correct registration. Keep the emulsion side of the negatives facing the plate. Fig. 14-29.

6. Make sure that the sensitivity guide is stripped into the flat so that it will expose on the plate in a nonprinting area.

7. Close the glass lid, apply the vacuum, and check for proper contact. The vacuum setting should show approximately 20 pounds of vacuum on the

14-30. *After closing the glass lid, pull a vacuum and examine for Newton's rings.*

gauge. Newton's rings should appear over the flat if proper contact is achieved. Fig. 14-30.

8. Face the emulsion side of the plate toward the light source and make the exposure.

9. Remove the flat and the plate.

If plate punching systems are not available, a plate can be held in place on the bed of the plate-making machine by taping the corners to the bed. The flat can then be taped in position over the plate.

DETERMINING THE EXPOSURE TIME

The correct exposure time should be determined before a plate is made. This is done by making trial exposures using a platemaking *sensitivity guide.* Fig. 14-31. This guide is simply a transmitting type gray scale that is similar to the projection (reflective) type sensitivity guide used in camera and darkroom work. It is used to determine how much light strikes the photographic emulsion on a plate during exposure. During the exposure process, light passes through the sensitivity guide on the flat and strikes the plate. Then when the plate is developed, that portion of the light-sensitive coating on the plate which has not received sufficient exposure will wash away. Areas which are struck with sufficient light will produce an image in direct proportion to the light that gets through the guide.

If the image produced by the scale on presensitized, negative-working plates develops to a solid step 6, the exposure time is satisfactory. If the scale develops to a higher numbered step, the

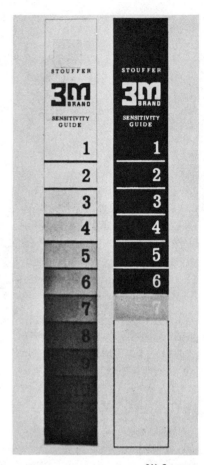

3M Company

14-31. *A gray scale sensitivity guide. The left side shows how the device looks when it is stripped in the flat. The right side shows the image the scale makes on the plate after the plate is exposed and developed. This scale is developed to the sixth step.*

exposure time is too long. The term *step* refers to the numbered parts of the scale. If it develops to the 6, it is said to be a step 6. Exposures that are too long will cause screened areas to spread and fill. When numbered steps are too low, this indicates that insufficient light has hit the plate. Emulsion not completely exposed will wash away when the plate is developed. The correct

EXPOSURE FACTORS

Steps	1	2	3
Exposure Factors	1.4	2	2.8

14-32. *Exposure factors. The text explains how to use this chart.*

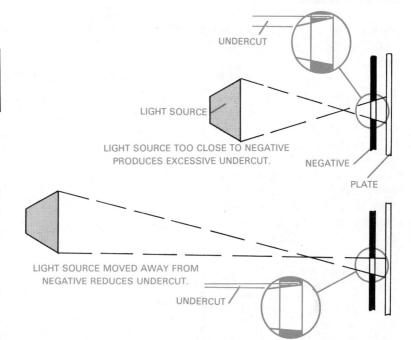

UNDERCUT

LIGHT SOURCE

LIGHT SOURCE TOO CLOSE TO NEGATIVE PRODUCES EXCESSIVE UNDERCUT.

NEGATIVE

PLATE

LIGHT SOURCE MOVED AWAY FROM NEGATIVE REDUCES UNDERCUT.

UNDERCUT

14-34. *The correct distance from the light source to the plate must be found. A light source that is too close produces undercut. Undercut can be reduced by moving the light source away from the negative and plate.*

step number to achieve depends on each product and on shop conditions.

ADJUSTING EXPOSURE TIME

If an *additive plate* is exposed, developed, and the image produced on the density scale indicates a need for a change in the exposure time, the typical additive exposure factors, Fig. 14-32, are used. To *increase* the step number on the plate, *multiply* the original exposure time by the exposure factor. To *decrease* the step number, *divide* the original exposure time by the exposure factor. For example, if a solid step 6 were desired and an exposure time of 60 seconds were used to produce a solid step 5, the exposure time must be increased to produce one more step. The 60 seconds is multi-

plied by the exposure factor 1.4. The new exposure time is 84 seconds.

If a subtractive plate is used, exposure times are changed using typical subtractive exposure factors. Fig. 14-33. For this type of plate, a step 7 exposure is normally satisfactory. Therefore if the developed plate produces a

solid step 6 at 30 seconds exposure time, the time must be multiplied by the factor 1 1/2 to get to a step 7. The corrected exposure time will be 45 seconds to achieve a step 7.

DETERMINING THE CORRECT LIGHT DISTANCE

When establishing the proper exposure time, the correct distance of light source to plate also must be considered. Undercut can be caused by an exposing light source that is too close to the plate. Fig. 14-34. If the light source is too far away from the plate, exposure time will be excessively long. To be correct, the distance from the light source to the glass surface of the contact frame must be equal to the diagonal measurement of the biggest plate that is to be made in that frame. This will permit all expos-

SUBTRACTIVE EXPOSURE FACTORS

Solid Step Exposure	3	4	5	6	7	8	9	10	11
Adjustment Needed	increase				OK	decrease			
New Exposure* Factors	4X	3X	2X	1 1/2X	same	3/4X	1/2X	3/8X	1/4X

*Note: X = 1st trial exposure

Eastman Kodak Co.

14-33. *Exposure control scale used with the Kodak subtractive LN plate. Notice that the sensitivity guide should develop to a solid step 7 for best results with this plate.*

ing light rays to be parallel to each other when they strike the plate. Fig. 14-34.

Often an acceptable exposure time is determined for an *incorrect* light source to plate distance. When this happens, a nomograph, Fig. 14-35, can be used to compute the new exposure time after adjustments have been made to correct the distance. If a nomograph is not available, the following formula can be used.

New exposure time = Old exposure time $\times \dfrac{(\text{New distance})^2}{(\text{Old distance})^2}$

To use this formula, both distances must be in either inches or in feet.

For example, if an exposure were made at 90 seconds at a distance of 4 feet, and the lights were moved to a distance of 5 feet, what would be the new exposure time?

$$\text{New time} = 90 \times \frac{5^2}{4^2}$$
$$= 90 \times \frac{25}{16}$$
$$= 90 \times 1.56$$
$$\text{New time} = 140 \text{ seconds}$$

DEVELOPING NEGATIVE WORKING CONTACT PLATES

The main steps for producing a plate using the contact system are summarized in Fig. 14-36.

Developing procedures vary with each type of contact plate. Following is a general discussion of these procedures.

(Remember, negative-working plates produce an image area in all places on the plate that are struck by light during the expo-

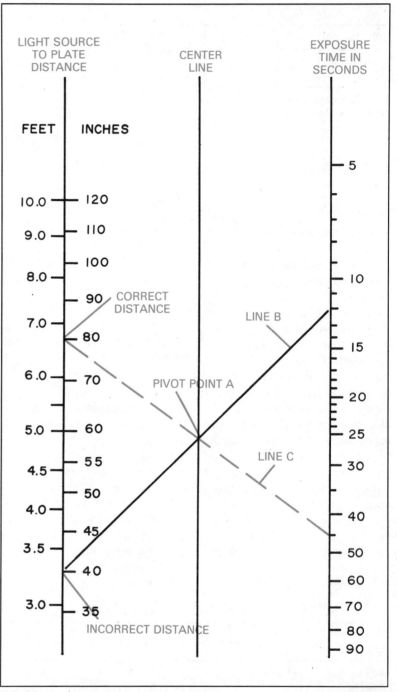

14-35. A nomograph is used to compute exposure time after light to plate distances are corrected. For example, assume a correct exposure was determined at 12 seconds for an incorrect light source to plate distance of 40". Locate these on the nomograph and connect them with a line (line B). Where this crosses the center line is pivot point A. The correct distance was determined to be 80". Locate this on the nomograph. Draw a line (line C) from the 80" mark through pivot point A to locate the new exposure time (45 seconds).

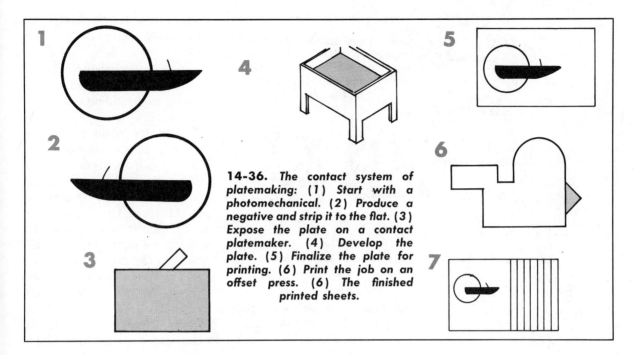

14-36. *The contact system of platemaking: (1) Start with a photomechanical. (2) Produce a negative and strip it to the flat. (3) Expose the plate on a contact platemaker. (4) Develop the plate. (5) Finalize the plate for printing. (6) Print the job on an offset press. (6) The finished printed sheets.*

sure. Subtractive coatings are factory applied. Additive coatings are applied by the platemaker.)

Presensitized Subtractive Diazo Plates

The 3M Company has a presensitized, negative-working, subtractive plate. To process the plate, first expose it to produce a solid step 6 after development. Then develop as shown in Figs. 14-37 and 14-38. Pour predeveloper on a developing pad.

14-37. *Developing the 3M "T" negative-working, subtractive, presensitized plates.*
3M Company

A
Develop under yellow lighting. Place the exposed plate on smooth, firm surface.

Pour pre-developer on pad and plate.

Spread the pre-developer with a pad. Pause briefly until the image becomes visible—about 30 seconds.

D
Begin development. Use firm pressure and tight circular motion, always holding pad flat against the plate.

E
Squeegee plate and sink area. Remove all visible pre-developer from the plate surface.

F
Add subtractive developer. Complete development using light pressure on a second pad.

G
Squeegee plate. Complete drying of the plate using disposable wipe.

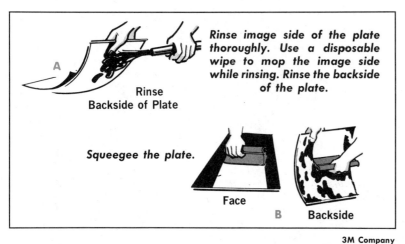

Rinse image side of the plate thoroughly. Use a disposable wipe to mop the image side while rinsing. Rinse the backside of the plate.

Rinse Backside of Plate

Squeegee the plate.

Face

Backside

B

3M Company

14-38. Cleaning the 3M "T" plate after it is developed.

Spread it over the plate. Let it stand until the image appears. Rub the plate with the pad in tight circular motions for about 20 seconds. Squeegee the predeveloper from the plate. Soak a pad with subtractive developer and rub the plate. Squeegee the plate again. Rinse the plate with fresh water. Wipe the image side with a water-soaked cotton wipe. Dry the plate on both sides with a soft cloth. Then pour the gum on the plate and spread it with a cotton wipe. Buff both sides dry with a cloth.

Presensitized Subtractive Waterless Plates

These plates, produced by the 3M Company, are known as dry plates. To develop these plates:

Expose the plate to yield an open step 5 after development. Then pour the developer on the plate. Rub the plate with a developing pad in a circular motion to remove the image area coating. Only the image area needs to be developed. When the image is developed, rinse the plate with clear, running water. Do not

leave the developer on the plate more than four minutes. Should some small image area still be plugged, brush a small amount of image cleaner on that area. Rewash the plate, and dry with a soft cloth. Do not gum the plate.

Presensitized Subtractive Polymer Plates

There are many different kinds of photopolymer plates. The processing procedure for each varies. Following is a generalized explanation.

Expose the plate to yield a faint step 9 after development. Then spread developer over the plate with a developing pad. About two ounces of developer per square foot of plate is required. Allow the developer to soak on the plate until a "halo" effect is produced. A "halo" occurs when the nonimage area discolors and breaks away from the image area. Now rub the plate with the developing pad in a circular motion for 30 seconds. Squeegee the plate. Once again add developer, and with a fresh pad continue the development until the image coating is com-

Du Pont Co.

14-39. A photopolymer plate is developed, gummed, and dried in one continuous process in the processing unit shown. The unit processes the Du Pont "Lydel" photopolymer plate.

pletely removed. Rinse with clean, running water. While the plate is still wet, apply the gum with a cloth. Wipe off the excess gum and buff both sides of the plate dry.

This process can be done in an automatic processor. Fig. 14-39. It develops, gums, and dries the plate in one pass through the machine.

Presensitized Additive Diazo Plates

Following are generalized procedures for developing the 3M plates. Fig. 14-40.

Expose the plates to yield a solid step 6 after development. Clamp the plate over a pad of absorbent paper or on the table of a downdraft developing sink. Desensitize the entire plate using a developing pad and the process gum recommended by the manufacturer. Wipe off the excess gum. Before the gum dries, pour developer recommended by the manufacturer on the plate. Spread the developer with a pad. Rub until a strong, dark, uniform image appears. Sponge off the excess developer. Wash the plate with running water and buff or squeegee it dry. If halftone or screened areas are plugged, wipe with a cotton wipe soaked with a plate ink solvent. Then desensitize and redevelop the plate again. Apply a thin coat of process gum and buff it dry.

Wipe-on Additive Diazo Plates

With this type of plate the light-sensitive coating must be applied to the plate. Then the exposure and development of the image can occur.

The coating is a special carrier liquid and a light-sensitive diazo

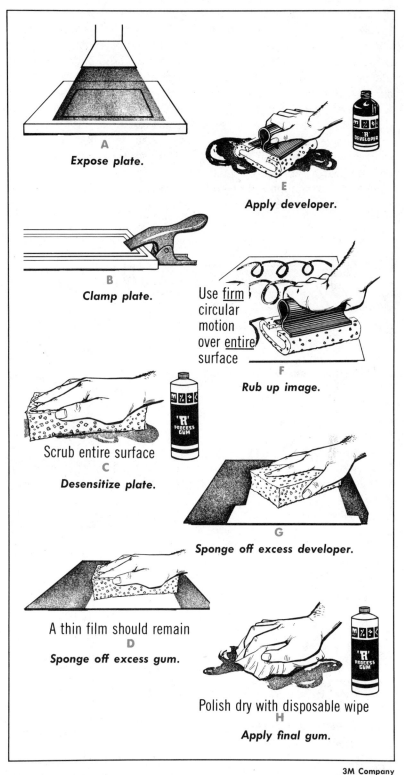

A — **Expose plate.**

E — **Apply developer.**

B — **Clamp plate.**

Use firm circular motion over entire surface

F — **Rub up image.**

Scrub entire surface
C
Desensitize plate.

G — **Sponge off excess developer.**

A thin film should remain
D
Sponge off excess gum.

Polish dry with disposable wipe
H
Apply final gum.

3M Company

14-40. Processing the 3M Company "R" and "L" negative-working, presensitized plates.

powder. They are mixed under yellow safelights. This should be done 24 hours before use. The best way to apply the coating to the plate is with a coating machine. It has rollers which run in the liquid coating mixture. The plate is run between the rollers for an even coating. Some plates require two coatings. This coating can also be applied by hand using rags or sponges. It is important to get an even coating.

After the plate has been coated, let it dry for 30 seconds. It is then ready for exposure.

Exposure time is based on experience. A step 6 is often satisfactory. Wet a sponge with water and squeeze until it is damp. Put the sponge in the developer and let it soak up a liberal amount. Rub the surface of the plate in a circular motion with the sponge. Sprinkle a little water over the plate and rerub its surface using

the developer-soaked sponge. While the plate is still damp, gum the surface. Polish the plate dry with a soft cloth.

DEVELOPING POSITIVE-WORKING CONTACT PLATES

The positive-working coating is intended for use with plates that will have film positives placed over them during exposure. The printing image on positive-working plates is produced by the

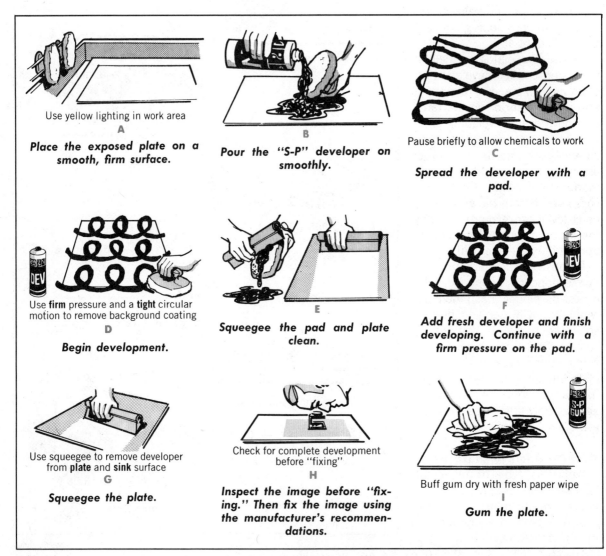

Use yellow lighting in work area

A

Place the exposed plate on a smooth, firm surface.

B

Pour the "S-P" developer on smoothly.

Pause briefly to allow chemicals to work

C

Spread the developer with a pad.

Use **firm** pressure and a **tight** circular motion to remove background coating

D

Begin development.

E

Squeegee the pad and plate clean.

F

Add fresh developer and finish developing. Continue with a firm pressure on the pad.

Use squeegee to remove developer from **plate** and **sink** surface

G

Squeegee the plate.

Check for complete development before "fixing"

H

Inspect the image before "fixing." Then fix the image using the manufacturer's recommendations.

Buff gum dry with fresh paper wipe

I

Gum the plate.

3M Company

14-41. Processing the 3M Company "S-P" plate.

coating that is *not struck by light*. As a result, the nonimage area on flats stripped for positive-working plates must be transparent. Instead of being desensitized, most positive-working plates are "staged." This means any undesired image area which is visible after exposure is removed through the use of a staging solution.

Generally, the coating on positive-working plates is subtractive. This means that during processing, the light-struck, nonimage area is washed away, leaving only the factory-coated image area that was protected by the opaque image areas on the flat.

Presensitized Subtractive Polymer Plates

Following are general procedures for developing these plates.

Expose the plate to produce a step 4 after development. With these plates it is better to overexpose a little rather than underexpose them.

To develop the plate, use the same procedure as described for negative-working polymer plates. While the plate is still moist with the developer, coat it with a positive-working photopolymer conditioner. Then stage the plate. Use a staging solution on all places in the nonimage area that still have a coating. Rinse the plate with water and squeegee dry. Gum the plate.

Presensitized Subtractive Diazo Plates

Following is the general procedure for developing positive-working, subtractive plates produced by the 3M Company. Fig. 14-41.

First, expose the plate to yield an open step 3 after development. Develop the plate under yellow light. Soak the plate with 3M "S-P" developer. Spread the developer with a pad. Rub in circular motions to remove the coating from the nonimage area. Squeegee the plate and pad clean. Add fresh developer and rub the plate some more. Squeegee again. Spread 3M "S-P" fixing solution over the plate, using a fresh pad. It should soak two to three minutes. Squeegee the fixer solution off the plate. Stage the plate using staging solution. Gum the plate.

Wipe-on Subtractive Deep-Etch Plates

This type of plate is often produced by the platemaker. The metal base is pre-etched for 60 seconds and washed with water. It is then placed in a whirling device. The coating solution is poured onto the center of the plate. The spinning distributes it over the plate. Heat is used to dry the plate.

The finished plate is exposed the same as any positive-working plate. After exposure a stop-out solution is applied. It removes any undesired nonimage areas left.

The plate is developed using a special deep-etch positive developing solution. Rubber gloves are needed to work with this solution. Apply developer and squeegee it off several times. Now etch the plate. The etch removes parts of the image area the developer missed. Next remove the coating from the image area. Redevelop the plate to neutralize the etch. Squeegee and wipe the plate with anhydrous alcohol. Dry

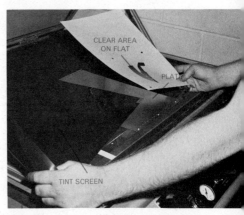

14-42. A tint screen is inserted between the plate and the window in the flat.

the plate with a blower. Then apply a coat of lacquer.

Scrub the plate with water and a brush to remove the light-hardened coating from the nonimage area. Gum the plate.

Using Tint Screens

If a tint screen is required to produce a Ben Day area on a contact-type plate, the screen is inserted between the screenless window in the flat and the surface of the plate during exposure. Fig. 14-42. A Ben Day is a method of adding a tone to a printed image by imposing a transparent sheet of dots or other patterns on the image during the photographic reproduction process. Additional information on screen tints is given in Chapter 9, "Preparing Copy for the Camera."

Color Work

In the contact system, as with the other systems, multiple color work must be accomplished by making a separate plate for each color required. Film must be made to produce the plates for each color. It is possible for the

TO PRINT IN BLACK

TO PRINT IN COLOR

THE DEVELOPED
FILM NEGATIVE

DEVELOPED FILM STRIPPED
TO A PLATEMAKING FLAT

FLAP 1 OPEN

FLAP 2 CLOSED

FILM STRIPPED SO THE
PLATE FOR THE BLACK
INK CAN BE EXPOSED

FLAP 1 CLOSED

FLAP 2 OPEN

FLAT STRIPPED SO THE
PLATE FOR THE COLORED
INK CAN BE EXPOSED

PRINTING PLATE

BLACK INK OFFSET PLATE
PRODUCED USING FLAP 1.

COLOR INK OFFSET PLATE
PRODUCED USING FLAP 2.

14-43. Two different plates can be made from one negative by stripping the negative so that the flat has flaps. With Flap 1 open, an exposure for the plate to print black can be made. With Flap 1 closed and Flap 2 open, a plate can be made to print a color.

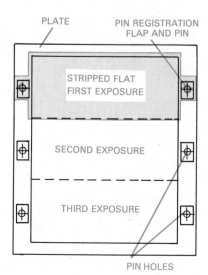

PLATE

PIN REGISTRATION
FLAP AND PIN

STRIPPED FLAT
FIRST EXPOSURE

SECOND EXPOSURE

THIRD EXPOSURE

PIN HOLES

14-44. A flat in position for the first of three step-and-repeat exposures. This procedure produces multiple images on one plate.

platemaking procedures are to repeatedly expose the unitized negative image to portions of the plate while protecting all other portions of the plate with a light-

EXPOSURE HEAD

14-45. A photocomposition machine that will produce step-and-repeat plates. This picture shows the exposure head.

same film to be used to make all the plates required. To do this, the flat is prepared so that there are flaps, or masks, covering each image area on the single film. These flaps are then opened and closed in direct relationship to the areas that are to print in color. Fig. 14-43 shows how different plates can be made from the same flat by opening and closing the flaps. Review Chapter 13, "Laying Out and Stripping the Flat," to understand the relationship of tints, color, flats, and plates.

Step-and-Repeat Work

As discussed in' Chapter 13, step-and-repeat refers to the process in which one unitized image is exposed several times across a single plate. The platemaker should know how the stripper sets up the step-and-repeat job. The basic contact

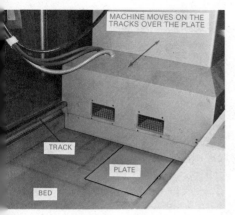

VIEW OF MACHINE REAR

14-46. *The rear of the photo-composition machine.*

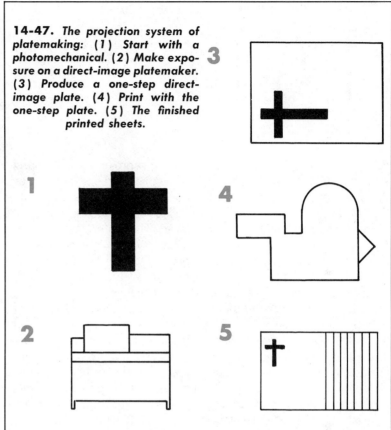

14-47. *The projection system of platemaking: (1) Start with a photomechanical. (2) Make exposure on a direct-image platemaker. (3) Produce a one-step direct-image plate. (4) Print with the one-step plate. (5) The finished printed sheets.*

safe mask. Fig. 14-44. Special photocomposition machines can be used to produce contact plates using the step-and-repeat process. Figs. 14-45 and 14-46.

THE PROJECTION SYSTEM OF PLATEMAKING

The photo-direct projection system produces a plate by projecting light from the photomechanical onto the photosensitive paper plate. The light is projected through a lens in the platemaking machine. The exposed plate is processed by the machine to produce a finished plate. Fig. 14-47. The plate coating is high contrast. It is capable of printing both line and halftone work.

The plate chemistry used for projection emulsions is comprised of three separate layers. Fig. 14-48. After exposure the plate is automatically fed through two solutions for processing. The first solution is an activator which develops the plate. The second solution is a

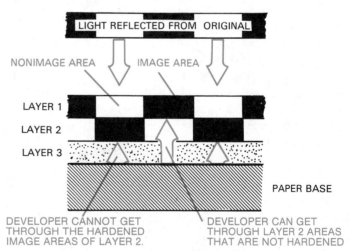

IMAGE ON PHOTOMECHANICAL

LIGHT REFLECTED FROM ORIGINAL

NONIMAGE AREA   IMAGE AREA

LAYER 1
LAYER 2
LAYER 3

PAPER BASE

DEVELOPER CANNOT GET THROUGH THE HARDENED IMAGE AREAS OF LAYER 2.

DEVELOPER CAN GET THROUGH LAYER 2 AREAS THAT ARE NOT HARDENED

14-48. *A photo-direct projection plate has three layers: the top pre-fogged printing layer, the middle image-hardened layer, and the bottom developer layer.*

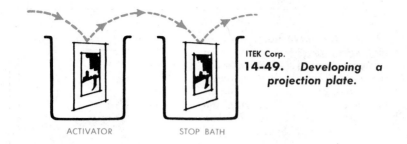

ITEK Corp.

14-49. *Developing a projection plate.*

ACTIVATOR   STOP BATH

combination stop bath, fixer, and stabilizer solution that finalizes the plate for printing or storage. Fig. 14-49.

To understand how the projection plate actually works, an examination of the three layers is required. Fig. 14-48.

Layer one (top). This outermost layer is designed to be especially receptive to water. However, this layer will reject water and attract ink on any part of its surface that is exposed to a special photographic developer. In other words, any part of this layer struck by special developer will form a printing image area on the plate.

Layer two (middle). The middle layer is composed of silver halides suspended in gelatin. This layer is very similar to the high-contrast emulsion found in standard graphic arts film.

Layer three (bottom). This layer is comprised primarily of the previously mentioned special developer solution. This developer is suspended in a gelatin substance and is used to develop the top layer.

A Photo-direct Projection System

During the exposure sequence, light is reflected from the background of the photomechanical and projected through a lens onto the plate material. Fig. 14-

50. This projected light passes through all three layers and produces a latent image in the silver halides suspended in the middle layer. The outer layer is unaffected by this light because it is prefogged at the factory. The bottom layer is unaffected by the light because it is not image-producing. Therefore after the exposure process, a latent image is formed in the middle layer only, and this image is a direct copy of the nonimage background on the photomechanical.

After exposure, the roll-fed plate is cut off and immersed in the activator fluid. Fig. 14-49. Here the latent image in the middle layer is developed and hardened. This hardened area, which corresponds to the non-image area of the photomechanical, forms a barrier to the passage of developer from the lower layer. Specifically, it is this hardened barrier that prevents the developer suspended in the bottom layer from passing through the middle layer to develop the top layer. The unhardened portion of the middle layer, which corresponds to the image area on the photomechanical, does permit passage of the released developer from the bottom layer to the top layer. Fig. 14-48. In other words, when developer from the bottom layer migrates out of its suspended state and passes through the middle layer, it mixes with the top layer and changes it from a water-receptive substance to an ink-receptive substance. Thus, an offset printing plate is produced.

The procedures for making projection plates containing halftones in combination with line work are complicated and beyond the scope of this text. Following is a brief explanation of how they are made with a camera platemaker. Fig. 14-51.

The platemaker contains the plate materials and processing chemicals needed. The photomechanical is positioned on the copyboard. Fig. 14-52. The machine is set to produce the enlarged or reduced image needed. The operator has to position the lights, set the camera controls, and make the exposure. Fig. 14-53. The machine performs all the operations needed to produce the plate.

THE TRANSFER SYSTEM

The basic steps for producing a job by the transfer system are shown in Fig. 14-54. As described earlier in the chapter, the

PLATE MATERIAL

LENS AND MIRROR

LATENT IMAGE

ORIGINAL COPY

ITEK Corp.

14-50. *A photo-direct, optical projection system.*

ITEK Corp.

14-51. *The photo-direct ITEK Platemaster unit produces offset plates in a single step from photomechanicals. The processing is automatic, and no film or other intermediate materials are required.*

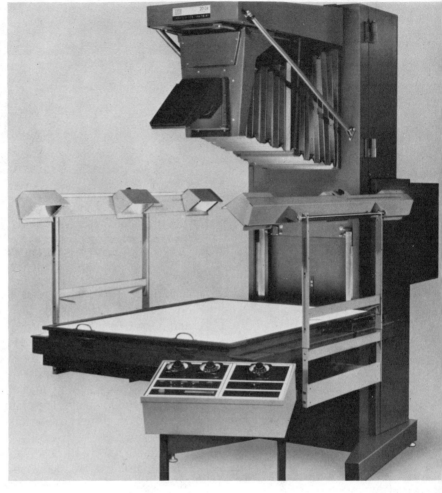

ITEK Corp.

14-52. *Positioning the photomechanical onto the copyboard.*

1 SET PLATE LENGTH CONTROL

MAGAZINE

COPY LENGTH CONTROL

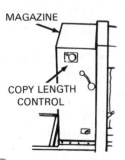

2 SET COPY LENGTH CONTROL

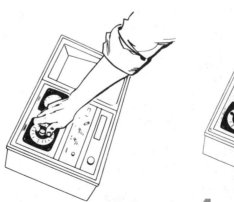

3 SET EXPOSURE TIMER

4 PRESS EXPOSURE BUTTON

ITEK Corp.

14-53. *The controls of the ITEK platemaker.*

light-sensitive coating is held on the matrix for temporary support during the developing process. The photomechanical is exposed to the coating on the matrix, and the image is developed.

The developed image is then transferred to the offset plate.

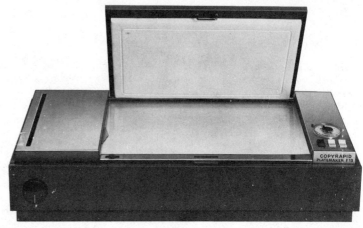

14-55. *This machine exposes and develops transfer plates. The flat is placed in register with the matrix and put on the glass frame. The lid is closed, and the exposure is made. The exposed matrix and the plate are then fed into the processor end of the machine. The matrix-plate sandwich exits through the slot on the left of the machine.*

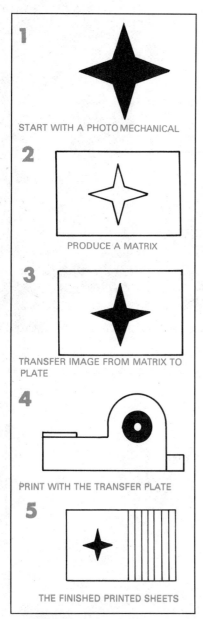

1 START WITH A PHOTOMECHANICAL

2 PRODUCE A MATRIX

3 TRANSFER IMAGE FROM MATRIX TO PLATE

4 PRINT WITH THE TRANSFER PLATE

5 THE FINISHED PRINTED SHEETS

14-54. *The transfer system of platemaking.*

The image is placed in register on the plate. Together the plate and image pass through a developer solution in an automatic feeding machine called a processor. Fig. 14-55. The temporary support is peeled away, leaving the image on the plate. The plate is treated to protect the transferred image.

While the matrix and plate are passing through the developer, the exposed silver salts are converted into hardened black silver, and the unexposed silver salts are released from their suspended state in the gelatin. Then, as a result of an electrochemical reaction, the unexposed silver salts are liberated and forced to adhere to the surface of the offset plate. Fig. 14-56. The transfer system produces a right-reading, silverized image area on the surface of the plate.

THE DIRECT-IMAGE SYSTEM

In the direct-image system the material to be printed is pro-duced directly on the surface of a direct-image plate by a mechanical or electrostatic process. The steps for printing with this system are shown in Fig. 14-57. As stated before, the items used to produce the image on the plate must leave an ink-receptive coating which is then printed by the offset process.

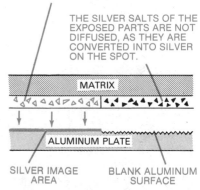

THE SILVER SALTS OF THE UNEXPOSED PARTS ARE TRANSFERRED TO THE PLATE BY DIFFUSION.

THE SILVER SALTS OF THE EXPOSED PARTS ARE NOT DIFFUSED, AS THEY ARE CONVERTED INTO SILVER ON THE SPOT.

MATRIX

ALUMINUM PLATE

SILVER IMAGE AREA

BLANK ALUMINUM SURFACE

14-56. *This system transfers the silver salts of the unexposed parts of the matrix by diffusion. The exposed areas of the matrix convert to silver and remain with the matrix.*

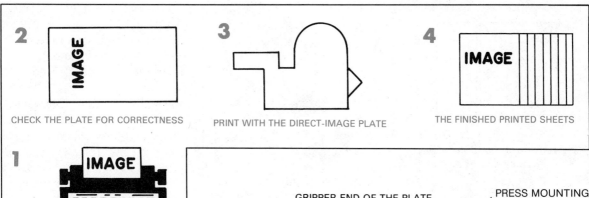

2 CHECK THE PLATE FOR CORRECTNESS

3 PRINT WITH THE DIRECT-IMAGE PLATE

4 THE FINISHED PRINTED SHEETS

1 PLACE THE IMAGE DIRECTLY ONTO THE PLATE

14-57. *The direct-image plate-making system.*

A direct-image plate, Fig. 14-58, has reference lines to guide the worker in placing the ink-receptive image area onto the surface of the plate. As a minimum, the *plate mounting, gripper margin,* and *image placement* reference lines should be considered at the time the image area is placed onto the plate. The *plate mounting* reference line indicates to the worker how much of the plate has to be set aside for mounting the plate to the press. The *gripper margin* reference line lets the worker know how much of the plate cannot be used because of the press gripper margin restriction. Finally, the *image placement* reference lines allow the worker to place the image onto the plate longitudinally and laterally. The image placement reference lines actually indicate the size and relationship of the press sheet to the plate. Fig. 14-58 shows how the various press sheet sizes are referenced onto the plate.

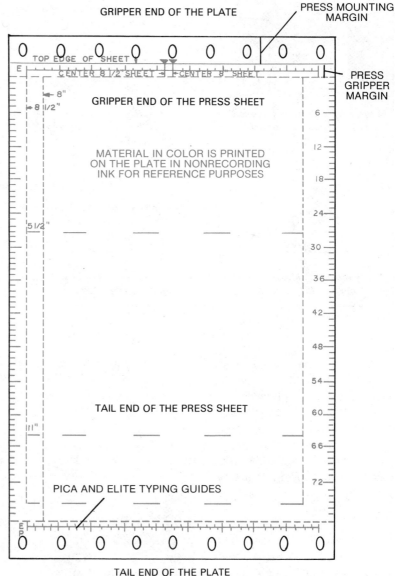

14-58. *A typical direct-image plate. The scales for locating material are printed on the plate in nonrecording ink.*

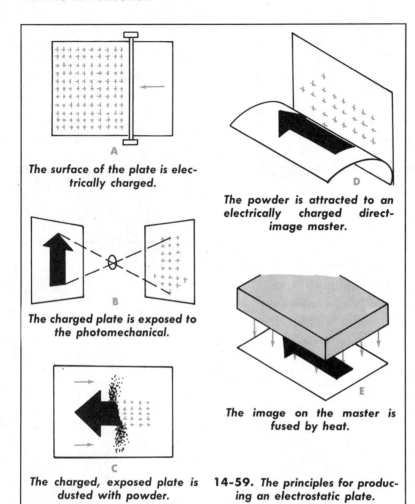

A

The surface of the plate is electrically charged.

B

The charged plate is exposed to the photomechanical.

C

The charged, exposed plate is dusted with powder.

D

The powder is attracted to an electrically charged direct-image master.

E

The image on the master is fused by heat.

14-59. *The principles for producing an electrostatic plate.*

is put face down on the copy glass. Fig. 14-60. Cover the photomechanical and make the exposure. The plate will automatically be processed and delivered to the receiving bin.

An electrostatic platemaking machine is shown in Fig. 14-61. A total reproduction system using the electrostatic principle is shown in Fig. 14-62. This unit accepts the photomechanical, automatically makes the plate, and prints the desired number of copies.

TROUBLESHOOTING

There are three factors that will affect the performance of an offset plate. These are the *manufacturing quality*, the *method of platemaking*, and the *treatment the plate receives on the press*.

If an unsatisfactory plate is produced, it is sometimes difficult to pinpoint exactly which of the three factors are at fault.

Some conventional contact platemaking problems and solutions are as follows:

Problem: A portion of the

Almost any mechanical device can be used to add the recording material onto the plate. For example, rubber stamps, proof presses, carbon paper, pens, pencils, crayons, pantographs, and/or typewriters can be used. Electrostatic copying machines can add the electrostatic powders and liquids.

The procedures for making an electrostatic direct-image plate using a Xerox copying machine are shown in Fig. 14-59.

The masters are loaded in the machine. The photomechanical

RECEIVING BIN

ORIGINAL TO BE COPIED

COPY GLASS

14-60. *Register the photomechanical onto the copy glass.*

image area is not on the plate after development.

Cause: Missing image area is not on the original paste-up; image area is not opened during development or is accidentally masked on the flat during plate-making.

Correction: Scratch the area into the plate with a sharp-pointed tool held at an angle, and fill the scratched area with press ink. If the area is pitted solid, rub the pitted area with a plate tusche, neutralize the area with water, and then rub in press ink. Another solution is to re-make the plate.

Problem: An unwanted image area is on the plate after development.

Cause: Poor opaquing on the stripped film, or the stripped mask is accidentally left open.

Correction: Rub the undesired image area with a soft rubber eraser or scratch stone. If the area is extensive, remove it with a drop-out solution.

Problem: An image area is on the plate, but the plate will neither accept ink from the form rollers nor transfer ink to the paper.

Cause: (1) Too much final gum is added to the plate; chemicals are contaminated or outdated. (2) Incorrect pressure (rollers, plate, blanket, etc.).

Correction: (1) Rub the plate with a 5-percent phosphoric acid or strong fountain solution to remove the excess gum film; re-place all contaminated or out-dated chemicals. (2) Reset pressures.

Problem: Image area on the plate is broken.

Cause: Stripped film is stained or yellowed; the stripped film is

Addressograph Multigraph Corp.

14-61. The electrostatic plate-maker will make plates up to 15″ x 18″. Enlargements to 150 percent or reductions to 45 percent are possible.

incorrectly opaqued; tape is covering the image area on the stripped film; exposure time is insufficient; fingerprints are on film; the glass is dirty on the vacuum frame; the stripped film is improperly developed; the developing sponge is dirty.

Correction: Take the appropriate action to eliminate the cause—clear the film, opaque the stripped flat correctly, and so forth.

Problem: Image is too light

after development or the image takes too long to appear on the plate during development.

Cause: There is an improper balance between the desensitizing gum and the developer; the developing pads are worn; the plate was uneven or not flat during development.

Correction: Balance the amount of process gum and developer; develop the plate on a flat surface.

Problem: The image area is spread or thickened.

Cause: There is poor contact between the flat and the plate; excessive exposure light is striking the plate at an oblique angle; the flat is opened too close to an image area which causes a shadow; lights are too close to vacuum frame.

Correction: Use a masking sheet that is less than 0.004″; strip the flat properly; use sufficient vacuum; replace worn or uneven blankets on the bed of the vacuum frame; lengthen the light source to plate distance. If all else fails, place pieces of 0.2″ clear, pliable plastic over any

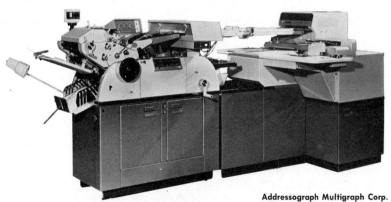

Addressograph Multigraph Corp.

14-62. A total copy reproduction system. It automatically makes plates directly from the photomechanical, mounts the plates onto the press, and prints the desired number of copies.

stripped film area where "halos" appear. This plastic will help absorb the uneven thickness of the stripped film. Additional exposure time might be required.

Problem: Screened areas are plugged after development.

Cause: Dried developer is left in the developing sponge or pad; chunks of developer are falling onto the plate from the rim or caps on the containers; the developing pads are worn; dirt is on the plate surface.

Correction: Dissolve the developed image area with a plate ink solvent and desensitize the dissolved area with process gum. Then redevelop the affected area with fresh materials and chemicals.

Problem: Scratch marks are visible in the image and nonimage areas.

Cause: Plates are being handled improperly.

Correction: Avoid sliding plates across each other; use scratch remover.

Problem: An ink-receptive area appears in the nonimage area on the plate.

Cause: Plate is not completely densensitized in the nonimage area, or there are press or ink-related problems.

Correction: The press and the ink should be checked first since most scumming problems are not caused by a faulty plate. To determine if the plate is at fault, gently rub the area with a wet hone. (A hone is an abrasive stone used for this purpose.) If the plate continues to scum, the plate is *not* at fault.

REVIEW QUESTIONS

1. Besides white, what color of lights should be used in the platemaking room?
2. The image area of an offset plate is the printing surface. True or False?
3. A grained surface on an offset plate improves platemaking characteristics. True or False?
4. On a negative-working plate, any area struck by light during exposure becomes a nonimage area. True or False?
5. When is the ink-holding coating applied to an additive-working plate?
6. The printing image on surface plates is exactly even with the surface of the plate. True or False?
7. On a deep-etch plate, the printing image can be either raised or recessed. True or False?
8. What are Newton's rings? What do they indicate?
9. One system for making offset plates is the contact system. Name another one.

Chapter 15

Offset Press Systems

THE OFFSET PROCESS

Offset printing, a lithographic process, has three major characteristics: (1) the image carrier is a single unit (plate); (2) it uses the principle that ink and water do not mix (lithography); (3) it prints by having the plate trans-fer the inked image to a rubber blanket, which then offsets it to the paper. Fig. 15-1. Review the general discussion of the offset process found in Chapter 1, "The Printing Industry."

This chapter shows the systems that make up an offset press and provides an understanding of the general procedures used in setting up these systems prior to operating the press. Operation of specific presses commonly found in commercial printing and publication work is discussed in the next chapter.

There are three kinds of presses that print by the offset process: duplicators, sheet-fed offset, and web offset presses.

Offset duplicators are designed for simplicity of operation. They originated as office machines for single-color printings. Fig. 15-2. A chain delivery is

15-1. A three-cylinder offset press system.

WATER ROLLER   INK ROLLER

PLATE CYLINDER

BLANKET CYLINDER

PAPER

IMPRESSION CYLINDER

15-2. A "Multilith" duplicator.
Addressograph Multigraph Corp.

INKING SYSTEM

DAMPENING SYSTEM

TRANSFER SYSTEM

PRINTING UNIT

FEEDER

DELIVERY

341

CHAIN DELIVERY

Addressograph Multigraph Corp.
15-3. A duplicator with chain delivery.

added for longer runs. Fig. 15-3. For color printing, two-color machines are made. Fig. 15-4 shows a press which places images from two plate cylinders on a common blanket, printing two colors with one impression. For in-plant and quick-print operations, several manufacturers have automated models. Fig. 15-5.

The sheet-fed offset press is a generalized machine designed for a wide variety of work. Fig. 15-6. As larger sheet sizes and more colors are run, these presses become longer and more complicated. Figs. 15-7 through 15-10.

Web presses print from a roll of paper. A color is printed by

SECOND-COLOR UNIT

Addressograph Multigraph Corp.
15-4. A duplicator with second-color unit.

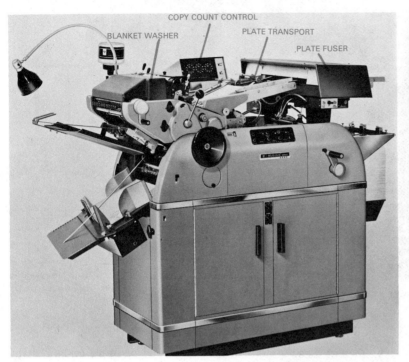

BLANKET WASHER — COPY COUNT CONTROL — PLATE TRANSPORT — PLATE FUSER

Addressograph Multilith Corp.

15-5. A "Multilith" automated offset duplicator.

15-6. Attaching the plate on a single-color press.

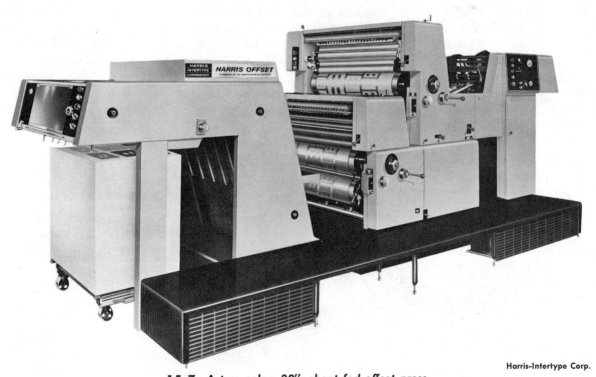

Harris-Intertype Corp.

15-7. A two-color, 38", sheet-fed offset press.

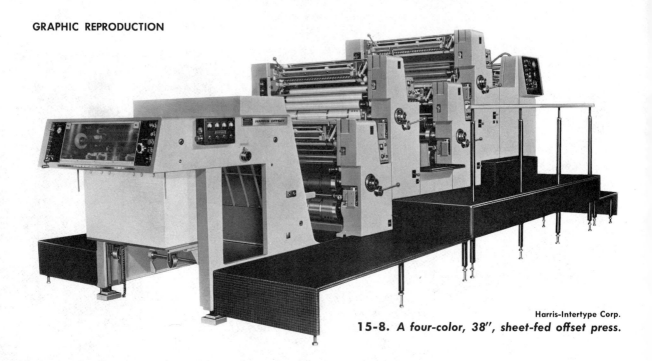

Harris-Intertype Corp.

15-8. A four-color, 38", sheet-fed offset press.

each unit. Publication web presses often are designed to print both sides of the paper in each printing unit. Fig. 15-11.

OFFSET PRESS SYSTEMS

The offset press is made up of a series of systems, each functioning as part of the total printing process. These systems are named by their function: feeder, transfer and registration, inking, dampening, printing, and delivery. Each of these systems must be set up, or "made ready," before printing can begin.

The function of these systems can be understood by following the flow of sheets of paper as they go through the press. The *feeder* system separates a sheet from the pile. The *transfer and registration* system guides the paper into the proper location. The *inking* system and *dampening* system supply ink and water to the *printing* system, which transfers the plate image to the sheet. The *delivery* system removes and stacks the printed sheets.

THE FEEDER SYSTEM

The function of the feeder is to separate one sheet from the pile and move it to the transfer and

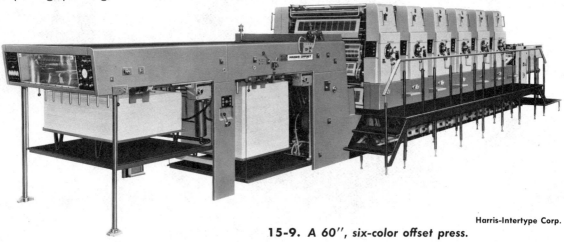

Harris-Intertype Corp.

15-9. A 60", six-color offset press.

Harris-Intertype Corp.

15-10. *A 78", six-color, sheet-fed offset press.*

registration system. There are two general types of feeders: the single sheet feeder, Fig. 15-12, and the stream feeder, Fig. 15-13. Either type may use a contin- uous feed table, designed so that it may be loaded while the press continues to run. Fig. 15-14. The stream feeder moves several sheets on the transfer table to

15-12. *A single-sheet feeder.*

15-11. *A four-unit publication press. Each unit has two blanket cylinders for printing both sides of the paper.*

15-13. *A stream feeder.*

345

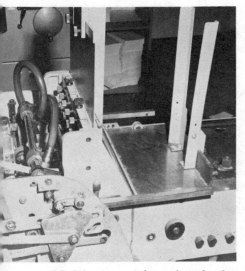

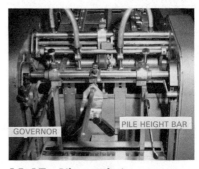

15-14. *A special envelope feeder mounted on a "Multilith" duplicator. Envelopes are fed from the bottom of the pile as more envelopes are added to the top of the pile for continuous feeding.*

15-16. *Guide bars on the feeder.*

15-17. *Pile-regulation governor.*

slow the individual sheet's travel speed. The sheet feeder moves one sheet at a time from the feeder to the impression cylinder at press speed.

THE SHEET FEEDER

The sheet feeder is a self-regulating elevator and sheet separation system. The *elevator*

is a moveable platform which holds the pile of paper. Fig. 15-15. *Guide bars* keep the pile in position. Fig. 15-16. The amount of elevation, or pile height, is determined by a governor which controls the lifting mechanism. Fig. 15-17. Usually the elevator mechanism will continue to lift until the top of the pile lifts the governor, which disengages the lift mechanism. As sheets are fed off the pile, the governor lowers and the lift mechanism is engaged. Correct pile height is critical to uninterrupted feeding.

The top sheets are kept in alignment by *corner guides* and *guide plates*. Fig. 15-18. These prevent the sheets from being out of position as they are separated and fed.

Separation of the sheets from the pile and the feeding of a single sheet are controlled by mechanical devices, suction, and air blast. These include combers, spring fingers, and suckers. *Combers* are rotating wheels which cause the sheet to buckle near the corner for mechanical separation. Air blast may be directed to blow apart the top sheets. Fig. 15-19. *Holddowns* control the top sheet and aid in

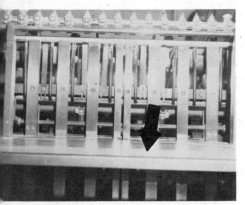

15-15. *The paper feed platform.*

15-18. *Duplicator guide plates.*

15-19 *Feeder devices on an offset press.*

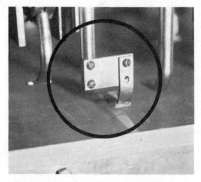

15-20. *Sheet-tail holddown on one type of offset press.*

15-22. *Feed suckers on a KOR Heidelberg.*

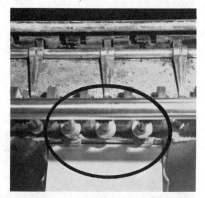

15-21. *Feed suckers on the A.B. Dick duplicator.*

ward motion, the tail of the next sheet is exposed to be lifted and forwarded. Each lead edge of the sheet is blown up underneath the previous sheet and moved between rollers onto the transfer table. Sheet speed is reduced for registration, since several are fed and in transit between the feeder and the guides. Like the sheet feeder, the stream feeder is aided by fingers, air and suction, holddowns, and similar devices to keep the sheet in proper position. The lifting device and pile height governor are similar to those on the pile feeder.

CONTINUOUS LOADING

The continuous loading method provides continuous press operation. It may be used with either the sheet or stream feeding method. Stopping the press to reload the feeder wastes production time and hampers uniform print quality. Some presses are equipped with auxiliary devices which permit loading while the press is running. These use extra platforms which can be fastened to the lift system under the platform in use. When

The sheet feeder which *forwards* (moves the sheet ahead) from the lead edge cannot feed another sheet until the tail edge has passed by the forwarding suckers. Each sheet must move as fast as the press is running. As press speeds increase, it becomes difficult to stop or accurately register the sheet at the guides.

THE STREAM FEEDER

The stream feeder forwards sheets from the tail (opposite the gripper) edge. Fig. 15-23. As soon as the sheet begins its for-

preventing multiple sheet feeding. Fig. 15-20. *Spring fingers,* or separators, are used to hold and separate the underneath sheet from following the top sheet being fed. Fig. 15-19. *Suckers* are used to lift, hold, and move the sheet. Duplicators use forwarding suckers to lift and move the sheet by the lead (gripper) edge after separation. Figs. 15-21 and 15-22. Some presses use separating suckers to lift the back corners of the top sheet. Air blown under the sheet from *blast nozzles* aids in separation, makes an air cushion, and helps the sheet make contact with the forwarding suckers. Fig. 15-19.

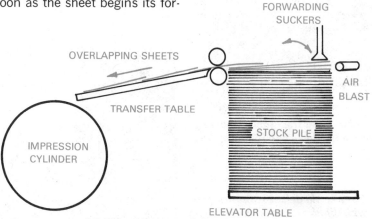

15-23. *Diagram of a stream feeder.*

15-24. *The feed-table bars are removable from the pins on the elevator chains for continuous loading.*

15-25. *An electric caliper and pull-in wheel on one type of feeder.*

15-26. *Transfer table showing rotary brushes, bands, balls, and wheels.*

15-27. *Heidelberg transfer table with brushes and slowdown fingers.*

empty, the upper platform must be removed before running is resumed. Fig. 15-24. Continuous feeding can be accomplished by supporting the remainder of the stock with rods between the platform and the stock. The rods are attached to the lifting mechanism and support and raise the stock pile while the platform is lowered to reload. The new stock pile is raised to the rods and they are removed, allowing continuous feeding.

TRANSFER AND REGISTRATION SYSTEM

The transfer and registration system carries the sheet from the feed pile to the impression cylinder grippers in exact position for printing. The sheet is forwarded from the feed pile to pull-in wheels at the rear of the transfer table. Fig. 15-25. Moving tapes on the table carry the sheet to the front guides. The sheet is aided in maintaining proper position on the table by holddown bands, rollers, balls, or brushes. Fig. 15-26. Slowdown fingers may also be used. Fig. 15-27. The sheet is stopped by the head stops and pushed or pulled sideways into position with the side

15-27. *Heidelberg transfer table with brushes and slowdown fingers.*

guide. Fig. 15-28. Various detectors may be installed to spot double-fed, torn, or cocked sheets. These detectors may be located on or above the feed table or on the forwarding roller. Fig. 15-29. Some detectors cause the multiple sheets to jam up, while others deflect the offending sheets off the feed table.

15-28. *An adjustable side guide.*

15-29. *Duplicator double-sheet eliminator.*

15-30. *Electric sheet detector.*

Electrical models may signal the press to stop feeding and trip the press off-impression. Fig. 15-30.

The feeder, transfer, and registration systems are timed to the press cylinders in order that each sheet will be in position as the impression cylinder grippers rotate past the guides on the feed table. Some duplicators do not have front guides and insert the paper into the grippers by timing. Smaller and slower presses use the impression grip-

pers to take the sheet from the guides. Other presses use cams and rollers or swing grippers to pick up the sheet from the guides and transfer it to the impression cylinder grippers. Sheet registration (exact placement of the sheet on the impression cylinder) is determined by timing the position of the sheet on the feed table in order to secure it under the impression cylinder grippers without change.

Most cylinder grippers are of the tumble type which close parallel to the sheet on the feed table or beside the swing grippers. With swing grippers, posi-

tive control is maintained by having the impression cylinder grippers grasp the sheet while it is still held by the swing grippers. Both sets of grippers "dwell" on the sheet for a short interval of time, assuring a positive transfer. A similar method is often used to pass the sheet from the impression cylinder to a transfer cylinder for delivery of the printed sheet.

Some sheet-fed presses are roll fed to the feed table, where the web is cut into sheets. This design is economical and fast but tends to standardize the length of the sheet as determined by the cutoff.

THE INDIRECT PRINTING SYSTEM

The plate cylinder, the blanket cylinder, and the impression cylinder make up the indirect printing system. Fig. 15-31. These cylinders are geared together. The inked image is transferred from the plate cylinder to the blanket cylinder and then to the paper on the impression cylinder. Different press designs

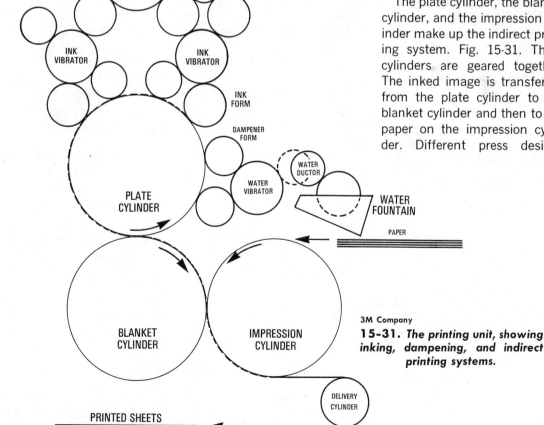

3M Company

15-31. The printing unit, showing inking, dampening, and indirect printing systems.

allow for rotational movement of one or more of the cylinders so that the location of the image on the sheet can be adjusted. Most presses also move the impression cylinder away from or towards the blanket cylinder for different thicknesses of paper.

The plate and blanket cylinders may have bearers, which establish the distance between them. Plate clamps and blanket clamps are used to hold the plate and blanket on the cylinder. Packing may be placed under the plate, blanket, or (on some presses) the impression cylinder to obtain proper contact and image transfer. Each revolution of the plate is right-reading and transfers an image which is wrong-reading to the blanket cylinder, which then transfers (offsets) a right-reading image to the sheet on the impression cylinder.

A system of levers and cams are used to "trip" or move the blanket cylinder to prevent the transfer of the ink image to the paper. Some presses trip only the blanket cylinder to disengage it from both the plate and impression cylinders. On small presses the blanket and impression cylinders are engaged manually, while tripping is usually automatic and is determined by sheet detectors on the feed table. The trip system prevents image transfer to the impression cylinder when sheets are not fed. While the press is tripped, inking and dampening of the plate can occur without image transfer to the blanket cylinder.

THE DAMPENING SYSTEM

The dampening system is designed to provide moisture to the plate. It also provides chemical protection to the background (nonimage area) of the plate to preserve its water-receptive properties. Both conventional and alcohol dampening systems are widely used. Remember, the nonimage area of a plate must remain water receptive so that it will reject ink during the inking stage.

The conventional dampening system consists of a water fountain pan, a ductor roller, a vibrator roller, and form rollers. Fig. 15-32. The fountain provides water storage and a pan roller to pick up water. The pan may be supplied automatically to maintain a constant water level. The pan roller transfers fountain solution to the water ductor as it rocks between the pan roller and vibrator roller. The vibrator roller oscillates laterally as it rotates, transferring fountain solution to the form rollers. Dampening rollers may be covered with cloth, paper, or sleeves to aid the transfer of solution. The amount of water transferred can be controlled several ways. It is controllable by: the speed of the pan roller, the dwell time of the ductor against the pan roller, water stops on the pan roller, and the number of form rollers.

Normally, the plate cylinder turns counterclockwise from the operator's side, and the plate is dampened before it is inked to protect the nonimage areas. Usually the pan and vibrator rollers are driven and drive the ductor and form rollers.

The alcohol dampening system is composed of a pan (fountain), a chrome pan roller, a metering roller, and an ink form roller. This system is designed to place a thinner film mixture of alcohol and water on the plate, reducing excess moisture problems.

THE INKING SYSTEM

The inking system is designed to transfer ink from storage (the ink fountain) through a series of rollers to form a thin, even film on the image area of the plate. Fig. 15-33. It is made up of rollers that are named by their location and function. Fig. 15-34. The fountain roller carries ink from the fountain through the fountain blade. The blade is a flexible plate used to control the amount of ink on the fountain roller. A ductor roller transfers ink from the fountain roller to a vibrator roller. The ink is then

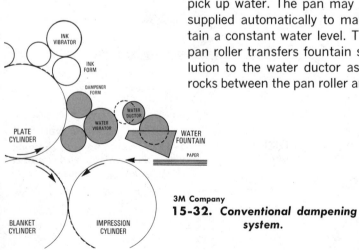

3M Company
15-32. Conventional dampening system.

divided between distribution rollers and is transferred through other idler rollers and vibrators to the form rollers. The numerous rollers of different sizes work the ink to a fine film, providing a steady supply to the plate. Usually the vibrator rollers (drums) are metal, and the distributor and form rollers are rubber. To remove ink from the press, a wash-up blade is used to scrape ink and solvent off a vibrator, which causes ink to be removed from all the rollers.

An automatic or manual lever raises and lowers the form rollers to the plate. Ink feed is usually controlled by the fountain screws against the blade, rotation of the fountain roller, and dwell time of the ductor roller.

THE DELIVERY SYSTEM

The delivery system is used to remove the sheet from the im-

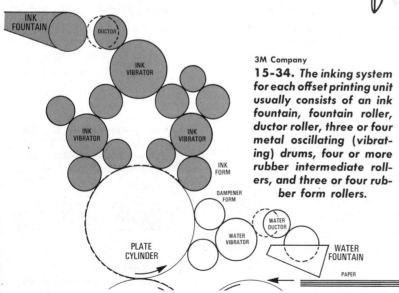

3M Company

15-34. *The inking system for each offset printing unit usually consists of an ink fountain, fountain roller, ductor roller, three or four metal oscillating (vibrating) drums, four or more rubber intermediate rollers, and three or four rubber form rollers.*

pression cylinder to a storage location for the printed sheets. On duplicators with chute deliveries, only small amounts can be stored. On offset presses with elevated deliveries, a substantial number of sheets can be jogged and stored over a period of time. Fig. 15-35. The delivery system is made up of the delivery cylinder, delivery transport, joggers, and elevator.

The delivery cylinder is a reel, made up of spider wheels. It is used to support the sheet and drive the chains of the transport

15-35. *Delivery truck removed from the delivery elevator with stacked, printed sheets.*

system. Fig. 15-36. The transport system has delivery gripper bars between the chains, timed to transfer the sheet from the impression cylinder to the delivery grippers on the delivery gripper bars. Fig. 15-37. The method of transfer is similar to the action of the swing-over impression cylin-

SPIDER WHEEL

15-36. *A delivery cylinder.*

der gripper in feeding the sheet to the impression cylinder. The delivery grippers and impression cylinder grippers both overlay the sheet when the two sets of grippers are parallel to each other. The impression grippers then tumble open as the delivery bar transports the sheet.

The delivery or front end of the press has a delivery elevator on which the sheets are stacked and jogged. A lowering system allows the delivery table to descend as the printed sheets are piled. Joggers aid in stacking the sheets evenly. The delivery gripper bars are attached to chains that revolve between the impression cylinder and the front end of the press. Sheets transferred to the delivery bars at the impression cylinder are carried to the delivery table, the grippers open, and the sheet is dropped. The chains then carry the gripper bars back around to transfer another sheet from the impression cylinder. Unless the press has a double delivery or continuous delivery system, it must be stopped periodically to remove the filled delivery truck. On small presses, delivery trucks are platforms on wheels that can transport the printed pile. Larger presses may use skids that are moved with forklift trucks.

Overall, the press is a semiautomatic machine that has regulating devices to control paper handling through the press while determining the flow of ink and water to the printing unit. Larger presses have more devices to handle the paper. They have more controls to regulate the press and sophisticated equipment to detect irregularities in the handling of paper.

GENERAL MAKEREADY INFORMATION

Makeready means the preparation required in order to produce acceptable prints. It involves maintenance, setting up the press, and adjustments in registration, ink, water, and image before production begins. It covers the activities of the press operator between starting the job and running the job.

Offset presses that run successive jobs having the same size and kind of paper and similar image coverage have little change in makeready from job to job. Longer runs reduce the percentage of makeready time in relation to running time. Where there are constant changes in size and kind of paper, images, and colors of ink, additional time must be spent on makeready.

One of the differences between duplicators and offset presses is the relative flexibility of the press. It can accept a wide range of different types of printing jobs. The size, weight, and kind of paper often determine whether a job must be printed on a duplicator or a press. The paper differences are combined with differences in image size and coverage, ink requirements,

15-37. *Grippers on the delivery bar (indicated in black rectangle).*

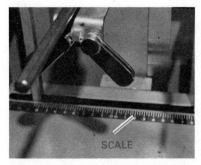

15-38. *A centering scale for positioning paper in the feeder of a duplicator.*

and registration accuracy. The combination of these differences usually determines press capabilities or requirements. The duplicators tend to be standardized in paper handling capabilities, ink coverage, and registration. Offset presses are more generalized, having a wider latitude in range of papers and inks while registration and image transfer are more precise. Modern, larger size duplicators now are similar to the smallest offset presses and have about the same capabilities. Office duplicators and medium size presses designed for job work demonstrate the greatest differences in ability to handle a wide variety of work.

JOB INFORMATION

Proper makeready requires a knowledge of the press and the job to be printed. The press must be adjusted to handle the stock, transfer the image, and produce reliably.

Details concerning the job are usually available to the press operator as instructions on a job tracer, or job ticket. Information is given about the work to be done. An example might be a two-color, work and turn, eight-

page brochure. Materials are specified, such as: 5,400 press sheets, size 23" × 35", 70-pound white enamel; first down yellow ink, PMS number 102, with halftone black ink, PMS number 412. Information concerning image position, sheet lay, and press changes are also stated. With proper information and directions, the press settings can be tailored to the job. The quality and economy of production depend to a large extent on setting up and adjusting the press.

PAPER TRAVEL

Before the press is moved, it is inspected. Loose blankets are tightened, and clamps are checked for clearance. Rollers, fountains, and wash-up blades are examined for position and security. A visual check is made for tools, rags, or loose objects on the press. Accumulations of paper dust, ink, or spray are removed. The press is stripped of any auxiliary items which will not be used, such as perforators, brushes, special feeder attachments, and so forth. The press is never started until the press operator is certain no damage will occur to the equipment and no injuries will happen to persons near the press.

When the makeready is simple, it involves only a plate change and the above steps are not necessary. A partial makeready involves plate, blanket, and ink changes but does not involve adjustments for the proper flow. A complete makeready requires paper, plate, ink, and image changes.

The press can be adjusted to feed, register, and deliver sheets

before it is plated, inked, or run. Some press operators prefer to proceed with the cleaner work first to avoid smudging sheets and getting press controls dirty.

FEEDER SETUP

Most jobs are designed so that the paper is centered across the press cylinder. The paper in the feeder can be positioned so that it will register centered on the press. The sheet is folded in half, and the fold mark is placed to one side of the center mark on the feeder, usually about 1/4" from the guide that will push or pull it into registration. Some presses have a *scale* marked on the feeder which indicates location of the paper side-guide edge according to paper width. Fig. 15-38. The *feeder guide bars* are adjusted to the paper width. The *sheet-separating mechanism* is also adjusted for paper width. In single-sheet feeders this may require changing positions of the feeding suckers as well as the kind of suckers or amount of suction required. Fig. 15-39. Generally, metal or soft rubber suckers are used for heavyweight and porous paper. The single-sheet feeder often uses air jets at the sheet gripper edge to separate paper. These are set to blow

15-39. *Feeder setup for narrow stock on an A. B. Dick duplicator.*

a few sheets apart at the top of the paper pile after the pile height is determined. The feeder platform is then lowered, and the stock is prepared for loading.

STOCK LOADING

The press operator inspects the stock as it is loaded. Curly stock is bent against the curl. Each lift is winded, placed in position, and smoothed out. (Winding is a hand operation used to separate the edges of sheets in a stack of paper.) Special attention is given to nicked edges. The stock is always loaded according to the gripper and guide edges marked on the stock. Care must be taken not to damage stock edges, particularly the guide and gripper edges.

As the stock is loaded, the pile is kept as level as possible. Wedges may be placed in the pile to aid in leveling. Cords may be fastened to these wedges and to the press to prevent the wedges from following the paper through the press. If large piles cannot be leveled, smaller piles are fed. The sheets must be in a uniform pile for constant feeding. Uneven, rough-edged, curly stock causes

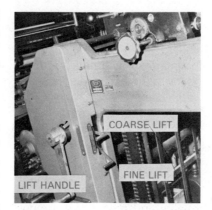

15-41. *Pile height adjustment controls.*

misfeeding and continued press stops. The lost time and uneven print quality are more costly than the sheets saved. Wasted sheets (previously printed, unused paper) are placed on the top of the pile. These sheets are used to set up the press and make ready the printing.

PILE HEIGHT AND SHEET SEPARATION

After the feeder is loaded, the pile is elevated to slightly below feeding position. The pile height for feeding is determined by the pile height governor. The press or feeder is turned on, and the governor is adjusted to maintain correct pile height. Air blast is adapted for proper separation. Separation fingers are checked for height and position. Separation suckers are positioned to make contact with air-separated sheets. Forwarding suckers are adjusted to grasp the separated sheet. Tail guides are located to hold sheets in position. Fig. 15-40.

Most of these adjustments are determined by pile height. Proper height is critical to con-

tinuous feeding. While no two press operators adjust or run presses exactly alike, many prefer the pile height to be at the bottom of a full stroke of the pickup or separating suckers. This provides maximum air separation and adjustment while running. Gauges or marks on the feeder may be used to determine pile height. A pile that is too high is prone to misfeeding and doubles (two or more sheets fed as one). A pile that is too low can easily be raised during the run to correct misfeeding. See Fig. 15-41 for coarse and fine elevator adjustment.

PULL-IN WHEEL AND DETECTORS

The pull-in wheels, which move paper from the pile to the feed table, are set with proper tension to pull in the stock evenly. Unequal pressure will cause the paper to twist. Heavy pressure may cause jams, tearing, or buckling at the paper gripper edge. Often the multisheet detector is located near the pull-in wheels. Fig. 15-42. On single-sheet feeders, the detector is a two-sheet detector, eliminator, or

15-40. *Sheet tail guides on a duplicator.*

15-42. *Multisheet detector and pull-in wheel.*

15-43. *Belt and ball sheet transport on a duplicator.*

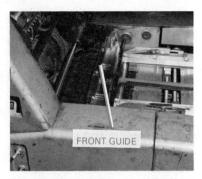

15-46. *Front guide on a duplicator.*

table to the guides. It may be moved by belts and rollers or by grippers. Fig. 15-43. Belt or tape transport uses friction between the driven belt under the sheet and rollers above the sheet. Flat and rotary brushes, holddown rollers, balls, and flexible or rigid bands are devices to aid in controlling and moving the sheet across the feed table. Some are adjustable to supply pressure or weight to aid in sheet control. Figs. 15-44 and 15-45.

To register the sheet to the guides in time with the printing unit requires that the sheet be fed and transported in sequence with the printing cycle. Loss of sheet control on the ramp will result in mistiming. Excessive pressures should be avoided. Roller-marked sheets or cocking and dragging of the sheet can result. When feed table grippers are used to transport single sheets, they open just before the

choke. With stream feeding, the detector is adjusted to the number of sheets overlapping on the feed table.

To set the two-sheet detector, the press operator passes a narrow folded strip of the stock under the detector. It is adjusted to pass one thickness and detect a double thickness of paper. Stock that has nicked edges can cause detection when passing a single sheet. Ink, spray, or lint build-up on the face of the detector can cause false detection.

A stream-fed detector is usually set to clear the number of overlapping sheets under the detector. The number overlapping depends on the depth of the sheet being fed. Some stream detectors are adjusted to trip the press when either too many or too few sheets are fed.

The sheet detector should be checked occasionally for accuracy and reset whenever a different stock is fed. Excessive paper between the cylinders can cause major press damage.

THE FEED TABLE

The sheet is transferred from the pull-in wheels or feeder suckers across the feed (transfer)

15-44. *Tape wheel with adjustable tension and movement.*

15-45. *Rotary brush is adjustable for pressure and register.*

sheet lead edge touches the front guides. Most problems on the feed table begin at the pile or pull-in wheels. Different papers require different adjustments of control devices on the feed table.

REGISTRATION

The gripper edge of the sheet is stopped by the front guides (head stops) before the side guide pushes or pulls the sheet into register. The term *register* means to locate the printed image in its proper position in relation to the gripper edge and side-guided edges of the sheet. Each sheet must be in register, or guided to the same image location, so that the image prints in the same place on every sheet. Successive printings register when their images are in the proper location in relation to the previous printing. While many factors influence register, positive and accurate feeding to guides is always required.

Most small presses have guides located at the front of the feed table, near the impression cylinder. Figs. 15-46 and 15-47. These front or "drop" guides (head stops) and the side guide provide registration at three

15-47. Overhead roller used for timing and registration on a duplicator.

places on the sheet. The front guides determine the parallel position between the image and the gripper edge of the sheet as well as the margin between the image and gripper edge. Adjusting the guides toward the front of the press (the delivery end) increases gripper image margin and gripper bite (area of the sheet covered by a gripper). Moving the guides toward the back of the press (away from the cylinders) reduces margin and gripper bite. The front guide must be out of the way when swing-arm gripper or cylinder grippers take the sheet from the feed table. The guides must be back in place to stop the next sheet coming down the ramp.

After the front guides stop the sheet, the side guide pushes or pulls the sheet sideways into position. During this movement, the gripper sheet edge must be dragged across the front guides and maintain contact. The pull side guides which grasp the side of the sheet must be off the sheet when it is picked up by the grippers. Some presses have a slowdown mechanism which retards sheet speed on the ramp

just before the sheet contacts the guides. Single-sheet feeders running at high speed may cause the sheet to strike the guides hard, bouncing heavy stocks and buckling thin stocks.

Front guides are positioned close to the impression cylinder so that the grippers grasp the sheet closer to the feed table. Guides locate the sheet so that the tumbling grippers of the impression cylinder grasp the sheet parallel to the cylinder surface. Some presses use swing-arm grippers to take the sheet from the guides. The swing arm arcs forward in a parallel position to the open impression cylinder grippers. After the impression cylinder grippers close, the swing grippers open and continue up and away from the cylinder.

Front guide adjustment for gripper bite is limited. Many presses have normal gripper bite of 1/4" to 3/8". Too little gripper bite causes misregister, sheet slippage, and misses when the sheet transfers to the delivery grippers. Excessive gripper bite causes nicked and bunched sheets as well as jammed sheets during delivery transfer. Good register requires a flat sheet at the guides with *normal* gripper bite. This occurs when the front guides are centered in their adjustment. Antibuckle devices are used to hold the sheet flat on the ramp during registration. They prevent the sheet from bending while being guided into position. Many side guides have a cover plate over the sheet to prevent buckling. This is usually adjusted to two thicknesses of stock. Pull and push guides are set by a paper scale on the feed table. The paper edge, if positioned

correctly in the feeder, will be located about 1/4" inside the side-register stop. Some presses have a fine adjustment for the side plate. This control may be located on the side of the press, so fine side adjustment may be made while the press is running.

INCHING PAPER THROUGH THE PRESS

Feeding adjustments are made by running a sheet of paper through the press but stopping it at critical points to check adjustments. This is called "inching" paper through the press. To do this, get the feeder running and run a sheet down the feed table to the guides. At this point the press is stopped. The position of the paper is examined relative to the front guides, with clearance for the side guide. The bands or rollers are checked and are "inched" so that the action of the side guide can be seen. At slow speed the paper is transferred to the impression cylinder and through the printing cycle. From the front of the press the transfer of the sheet to the delivery bar grippers is examined. If necessary, the press is stopped at this point, and the sprockets on the skeletal cylinder are set. Fig. 15-36.

Do not work on or make adjustment on any press that is running or is ready to run. Make certain control buttons are locked on "safe." Do not allow anyone else to jog or run a press on which you are working. Always stand clear before giving instructions to the press crew. When making adjustments that require the removal of safety guards, replace these before operating the press.

15-48. Rotary suction wheels to control stock in the delivery section.

After examining the delivery transfer, the press is inched toward the position where the sheet is released on the delivery truck. The press is stopped just short of this point, and the delivery joggers or pile guides are set. Delivery air blast and suction wheels or nozzles may be used to slow down and control the sheet in the delivery. These are usually adjusted at this time. Fig. 15-48.

After the delivery is set, a few sheets are fed through the press at slow speed. As these sheets go through the press, the press operator visually checks the sheet movement through the press. Readjustment is made with the press stopped. The use of "try sheets"—previously run spoilage for making ready the press—saves clean sheets to be used on the job. When the press operator is certain the sheets will feed, register, and deliver, he or she begins makeready on the printing unit.

PRINTING UNIT MAKEREADY

Where successive similar printings occur, as in book work, the blanket is not disturbed. With a new job, both the blanket and blanket packing may be changed. Alternating blankets is a way to extend blanket life. The old blanket is unreeled and removed from the cylinder, along with the blanket packing. The blanket is scrubbed with solvent and water to remove any ink or glaze, gum, or paper residue. It is hung to dry and "rest" for the next job. No press prints well with a poor blanket.

PACKING THE BLANKET CYLINDER

The blanket cylinder on the lithographic press enables the precise transfer of the inked image from the plate to the offset blanket. The offset blanket provides minimum abuse of the plate image and also permits printing on a wide variety of textured stocks. Fig. 15-49.

Correct packing under the blanket is very important. If the blanket cylinder is overpacked, the halftone dots will spread. If it is underpacked, the ink will not correctly transfer from plate to blanket.

The blanket cylinder must be examined for rust, ink, and gum. It should be cleaned with solvents, making certain all foreign materials are removed from the undercut surface

Use blanket or roller wash to scrub down the blanket. Com-

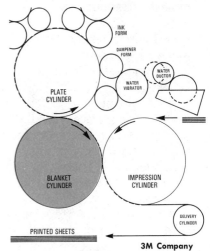

3M Company

15-49. The blanket cylinder direction.

plete the cleaning by thoroughly washing the blanket with water to remove ink and gum residue. If the blanket is new, this procedure will remove any chemicals or oils used in processing the blanket. If it is old, ink will be removed from the surface. (Try pumice powder mixed with solvent if the blanket is extremely glazed or dirty.)

The blanket surface should have a velvety feel when in good condition. This identifies quality printing characteristics and reduces paper handling problems.

The thickness of the alternate blanket is measured with a micrometer. Fig. 15-50A. All four corners of the blanket should be measured to find its average thickness. Slide the micrometer sideways on the blanket to as-

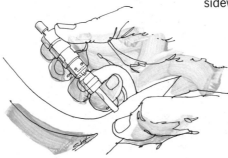

3M Company

15-50A. Avoid excessive pressure in measuring the blanket.

sure accurate caliper reading at minimum pressure.

Examine for damage and swelling. The surface must be free of indentations, cuts, or blisters. The surface should feel and look clean. Blanket bars must be clean and tight.

Packing paper is uniform and comes in different calipers. Thicknesses of 0.002″, 0.003″, 0.004″, and 0.005″ are common. The edge of the sheet is dyed, and colors identify different thicknesses. The blanket cylinder body has a smaller circumference than its bearers. The difference in radius between bearer and cylinder is called *undercut*. In packing a press with an undercut of 0.075″, for example, the blanket and packing combined thickness would need to measure 0.076″. This would be 0.001″ over bearer height, which is common. If the blanket measured 0.065″, then 0.011″ thickness of packing would be required. This could be a sheet each of 0.005″, 0.004″, and 0.002″ thickness. Fig. 15-50B.

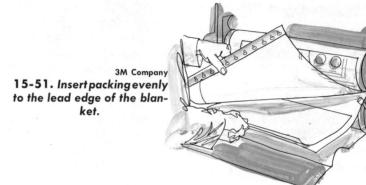

3M Company
15-51. *Insert packing evenly to the lead edge of the blanket.*

After the right amount of packing has been selected, insert the blanket into the lead edge cylinder clamp and tighten securely.

Then lift the blanket and insert packing, Fig. 15-51. Be sure to insert the packing sheets deep enough so that the blanket adequately holds the packing. (If packing slips, the blanket will wrinkle and produce a poor impression, besides causing excessive plate wear.)

The blanket, with its bar and packing, is fastened at the lead edge of the blanket cylinder. The press is rolled forward, and the blanket and packing are wrapped around the cylinder. Care is taken so that the packing is smooth and flat. The tail of the blanket is fastened in place and reeled tight. Both a loose blanket and one reeled too tight will cause problems. Loose blankets cause slurs, while excessive tightening will cause a blanket to break down. Blankets stretch under tension; new blankets may need to be retightened during the run. Fig. 15-52.

When installing a new blanket, don't take all the stretch out with the first tightening. Draw it up snug, then run 40 or 50 impressions and take up a notch or two on the ratchet. Repeat this procedure several times until the blanket is properly tightened.

It should be remembered that the blanket cylinder is between the plate cylinder and impression cylinder. Any defect in its surface or any packing error affects transfer of the image from the plate to the paper.

PACKING THE PLATE CYLINDER

The plate cylinder provides uniform support for the plate during dampening and inking, enabling it to transfer the inked image onto the offset blanket smoothly and evenly. Fig. 15-53.

The plate cylinder is also undercut. Clean the undercut in the same fashion as the blanket cylinder. Some presses require the

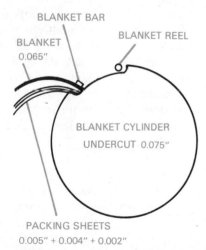

BLANKET BAR

BLANKET
0.065″

BLANKET REEL

BLANKET CYLINDER
UNDERCUT 0.075″

PACKING SHEETS
0.005″ + 0.004″ + 0.002″

15-50B. *Packing the blanket cylinder.*

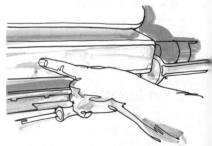

3M Company
15-52. *Press on the blanket in the cylinder gap to determine uniform blanket tension.*

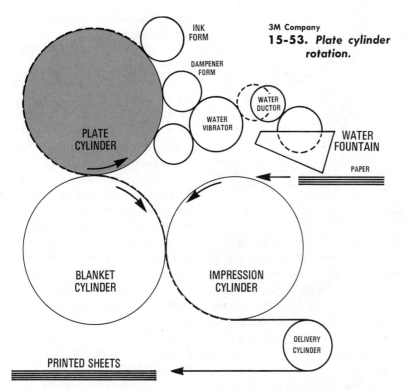

INK FORM

DAMPENER FORM

WATER DUCTOR

WATER VIBRATOR

WATER FOUNTAIN

PLATE CYLINDER

PAPER

BLANKET CYLINDER

IMPRESSION CYLINDER

DELIVERY CYLINDER

PRINTED SHEETS

3M Company
15-53. *Plate cylinder rotation.*

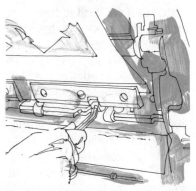

3M Company
15-55. *Clamps should be set for the thinnest plate used.*

3M Company
15-56. *Insert plate cylinder packing when lead edge is at the bottom.*

plate to be bent at the lead and tail edge in order to mount it on the plate cylinder. Like the blanket, the plate is measured with a micrometer for thickness. Fig. 15-54. (Avoid scratching the plate with the micrometer.)

Packing is added to the plate to pack 0.001″ over the plate cylinder bearers. For example, if the plate is 0.012″ and the undercut 0.017″, add 0.006″ packing. It is wise to cut the packing slightly narrower than the plate to prevent water from swelling the packing along the plate edges. Adjust the plate edge so that it is parallel to the edge of the cylinder. The plate is seated and fastened in the lead edge plate clamps. Fig. 15-55. The packing is inserted under the plate. Fig. 15-56. The press is then rolled forward on impression. The plate is held to its cyl-

inder by the blanket cylinder pressure. The tail of the plate is fastened in the tail clamps, and the impression is tripped off. The plate clamps are drawn down to hold the plate securely in position. Fig. 15-57. If a plate is mounted crooked, it will transfer a crooked image.

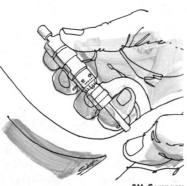

3M Company
15-54. *The plate and packing are measured together with a micrometer.*

3M Company
15-57. *Plate tension is adjusted uniformly across the plate.*

NOTE: If you find it difficult to mount the plate in the rear clamps, apply dampener-to-plate pressure and jog the cylinder until the trailing edge of the plate is in a convenient working position. The dampeners prevent the plate from moving or shifting during the completion of the mounting process.

After the plate has been tightened up on the cylinder, put press on "Impression." Make sure the ink and water form rollers are *off*, and then run for five to ten revolutions. Stop press and check for any looseness.

BEARER PRESSURE

Printing quality and plate life from presses that have plate and blanket cylinder bearers are dependent on correct bearer-to-bearer pressure. Fig. 15-58.

Properly adjusted bearers keep the blanket and plate cylinders in uniform parallel contact. The pressure holding the bearers in contact is greater than the pressure required to transfer the inked images from the plate to the printing stock. This maintains a smooth transmission of power.

Bearers that are in proper contact will be relatively shiny with few or no signs of rust. If they are shiny only in the gaps, the bearers are probably coming into contact at those points, but are thrown apart when the plate and blanket meet.

NOTE: If a press is new or if the cylinder ends are routinely cleaned with oil wipes, a more extensive check will have to be made to determine if the bearer pressure is correct.

If the bearers are not properly adjusted, the cylinder gears,

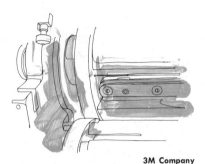

3M Company
15-58. *Bearers should be inspected for contact and pressure.*

even when the backlash setting is correct, will not mesh properly. This will cause the plate cylinder shaft to be forced against the top of its bearings and the blanket cylinder shaft to be forced against the bottom of its bearings when printing pressure is applied.

If these bearings are worn, the resilience of the blanket will make it very difficult to maintain a uniform printing pressure. The plate cylinder will float or bounce each time it enters or leaves the gap. This causes slippage between the plate and blanket that will produce undue wear and eventually premature breakdown of the image.

All the pains that have gone into the exposure and development of the plate and into press roller settings cannot assure quality and long plate life if correct bearer pressure is lacking.

Many of the problems in image transfer and poor printing can be traced to the pressure, or lack of it, between plate and blanket. It is critical that the correct pressure be applied and maintained between the blanket and plate cylinder. A careless job of makeready in this area results in poor printing.

ADJUSTING CYLINDER PRESSURE

The impression cylinder, Fig. 15-59, is examined and cleaned to remove any foreign substances. The stock to be run is measured by micrometer, and the impression cylinder is set to this clearance. Fig. 15-60. All safety bars and grills are replaced before proceeding with the makeready.

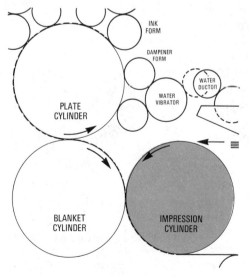

3M Company
15-59. *Impression cylinder rotation.*

15-60. *Stock thickness gauge for setting impression cylinder pressure.*

PRESS PACKING PRESSURE CHECK

Minimum plate-to-blanket pressure improves printing quality and extends plate life. Excessive pressure will cause blanket skid on the plate, creating copy register and quality problems.

The following procedure will establish the actual running condition of press packing and the trueness of the cylinders. It will identify optimum printing pressures.

1. Select a plate with large solid and halftone screen areas (not line copy). Use a dark ink.

2. Pack the plate and blanket cylinders to the press manufacturer's specifications.

3. Wash off the gum, roll up the plate, and pull several impressions (until the copy is no longer washed out).

4. Stop the press. Remove 0.004″ of packing from under the plate.

5. Relock plate, wash old image off blanket, and run about 10 more sheets.

6. Inspect copy. If the image is broken, the plate and blanket packing were correct. Replace the packing that was removed and run the press.

If the print is still good after the 0.004″ has been removed from the plate packing, it's an indication that the blanket or plate cylinder is overpacked. Continue to pull packing from the plate until the print becomes broken.

Replace 0.001″ to 0.002″ under the plate to obtain a good print. Measure the thickness of excess packing. Fig. 15-61. The primary advantage to this method of determining correct printing pressures lies in the fact that only one printing point (A) is affected by removal of packing from the plate cylinder during your check, whereas two printing points (A and B) would be involved if packing were removed from the blanket cylinder.

Now, replace all the packing that was taken from under the plate, and remove the excess amount from the over-packed blankets. Then reset the blan-

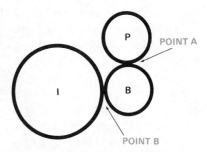

3M Company

15-61. *A two-point check for packing removed from the blanket cylinder.*

ket-to-impression cylinder pressure.

PACKING WEB-FED PRESSES

Although correct packing is vital to the proper operation of any litho press, it is especially critical with web-fed presses. The concern here goes beyond just obtaining the most desirable printing pressures. Fig. 15-62.

Absolute uniformity of packing among the various units on

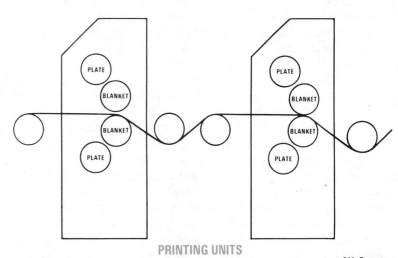

PRINTING UNITS

3M Company

15-62. *Common impression between blankets on two-unit web press.*

large, multicolor machines must be established. Packing affects the cylinder diameters, which in turn affects their relative speeds and the rate at which they feed paper to the next unit. Any variance in diameters, speeds, and the resultant uneven paper feed can produce web breaks if one unit feeds faster than those that precede it, or web lag if the unit is slower than those that precede it. Shorter plate life, poor printing quality, and press downtime problems result.

WATER AND INK MAKEREADY

The dampening unit, consisting of a fountain and rollers, is checked for cleanliness. If needed, a fountain solution is mixed according to specifications. The fountain is filled with solution. The ink fountain is locked in place, and a visual examination is made of the ink rollers. The correct ink is selected. All dried ink in the can must be removed before filling the ink fountain. If fast drying inks are to be used, substitute a small amount of slow drying ink for makeready.

If the fountain blade is unevenly adjusted, it should be corrected at this point. Open the blade (backing off the ink keys) whenever it scrapes the fountain roller. This can be determined by turning the fountain roller manually and watching the thickness of the ink film. Sometimes it helps to have the ductor contacting the fountain roller. If the ink film on the fountain roller is thick, close the blade. Start adjusting from the center of the blade so that it will not buckle.

Alternating from the center towards either side, close one key at a time. The thickness can be checked by sliding your finger across the top of the fountain roller. If it drags across a location, the film is too thin. If it pushes through a location, leaving a pronounced "gulley" in the film, it is too thick. Try to set the ink film thickness so that the ink feed control, when running, will be in the center of its range of control. When the blade is satisfactorily adjusted, the ink and water can be "run up" together. Most presses have ink and water controls that will feed with the ink and water rollers off the plate.

Start the press and run up the water and ink. Do not apply ink to rollers while the press is running. Do not touch moving rollers. On many presses, the ink will "sing" or "whistle" when a sufficient amount is on the rollers. With the press stopped, the dampened rollers should feel wet but not soggy or dripping. Avoid excessive water and ink films.

PRINT REGISTRATION

The plate is washed with a wet sponge to remove the protective gum coating. The press is started, and the water form rollers are dropped on the plate. A shiny plate indicates sufficient water. The ink form rollers are then dropped on the plate. The operator inspects the plate closely to see if the correct water-ink balance is present. The image should cover with ink while all nonimage areas stay open. Three "try sheets" are fed, printed, and delivered. The position is checked for squareness

and location. All position adjustments are made with the press stopped.

Coarse adjustments to move the image toward or away from the gripper edge of the sheet are made by rotating the plate cylinder. Bolts in slots fasten the plate cylinder to its bearers. The bolts are loosened, and the cylinder rotated in accordance with a scale provided. If the cylinder is rotated in the direction of sheet run, less margin from the image to the gripper edge of the sheet will result. After rotation adjustment, the bolts are retightened. The blanket is washed to remove the old image, since the new image position will differ.

Fine gripper-register adjustment is made by adjusting the guides. Any slight adjustment for squareness should be made before final margin adjustment. Movement toward the impression cylinder increases margin. After squaring the image, both adjusting screws on the gripper guides are turned the same amount to correct the margin. If proper margin cannot be gained without extreme adjustment, the plate cylinder should be rotated.

The complete side guide may be moved for coarse side adjustment. In severe cases, this may require moving the pile guides and paper in the feeder to maintain clearance between the side guide and sheet travel.

Fine adjustment is made by moving the side-guide plate. Some presses have fine guide adjustment controls on the operator's side of the press. These can be adjusted slightly while the press is running. Some side-guide plates can be tilted to parallel sheets fed at an angle to the impression cylinder.

Pull side guides grasp the sheet and pull it to the side-guide plate. The tension on a pull guide is adjusted so that sufficient friction is maintained to pull the sheet to the plate. Excessive tension will nick the side of the sheet or cause it to buckle or bounce. Pull fingers on the side guide which extend through the plate are set so that they are free of the paper before it is picked up by the impression grippers. Tension is determined by watching the finger action and examining the side of the sheet. The antibuckle plate height is usually adjusted to two thicknesses of the stocks being run.

Between side and drop guide movements the press operator feeds, runs, and delivers several sheets. During this time, adjust and examine the press sheet handling controls and guides from the feeder through the delivery cycle. Examine the transfer of ink and water and the printed image to maintain an ink-water balance on the press. Make certain the image is in proper location and the press is registering (guiding successive sheets accurately).

PRINT QUALITY

The final part of the makeready deals with the quality of reproduction, or print quality. If the press operator has been careful in setting up the press and has controlled the ink and water, most of the work is done. The printed image is examined.

The ink fountain screws are opened for very heavy areas and closed slightly for very light areas. The sheet can be tacked up under the ink fountain to use as a guide for setting the ink during the run. A number of "try sheets" are fed and printed to achieve a good water-ink balance. The image should be dense, sharp, and clean. It should not appear gray, washed out, blurred, or spread out. Halftone dots should print clean (no ink between dots, or dot spread). When the press operator is satisfied as to color and quality, fresh stock is fed and printed. A final OK is obtained to run the job. The job ticket is rechecked for information about the run. The counter is set. The job is ready to run.

REVIEW QUESTIONS

1. Name three kinds of presses that print by the offset process.
2. Name the press systems described in the following:
   a. Separates a sheet from the pile.
   b. Removes and stacks printed sheets.
   c. Transfers plate image to press sheet.
3. Name the two general types of feeders.
4. Name the cylinders that make up the indirect printing system of an offset press.
5. Preparation is required before a job can be run on the press. What is this preparation called?
6. Blankets should be fastened as tightly as possible to the cylinder. True or False?
7. Why is correct, uniform packing especially important on web-fed presses?

INTRODUCTION

Chapter 15, "Offset Press Systems," described the basic systems of offset presses and general makeready procedures for these presses. This chapter concerns the *operation* and *adjustment* of a specific press. The press is a Harris Model L-125-B. This press was selected because it contains operating systems which are like those on other small offset presses. Careful study of this chapter will enable you not only to operate this press, but also to understand the operation and adjustment of many similar presses.

In order to understand press operation, the press operator must become familiar with the *major sections* of the press and *press specifications*. Before operating the press, the location and function of the press *operating controls* must be known. In addition, the press operator must understand the proper *operation* and *adjustment* of each controlling or operative part of each major section of the press.

MAJOR PRESS SECTIONS

The Harris Model L-125 offset press, Fig. 16-1, is a single-color offset lithographic press designed to print one color at a time on sheets up to a maximum size of 19" × 25". The press includes a stream feeder, tape table, sheet register mechanism, ink distribution system, water distribution system, main press section, and delivery section.

The *pile feeder elevator* is where the stock to be printed is loaded. A sheet separator lifts one sheet at a time and moves it to the tape table.

The *tape table* moves the unprinted sheet to the register system. The table has a series of endless moving tapes, friction drive wheels, and flat brushes.

The *sheet register* aligns the sheets and insures that each sheet is fed into the press at the proper time. It also positions the sheet so that the printed image is located on it in the place desired. The components of the sheet register are side guide, choke, corrugating bar, sheet detector, front guides, and sheet holddowns.

The *inking system*, including the ink fountain, feeds ink to the plate through a series of rollers.

The *water distribution system* includes the dampener and a series of rollers. A roller picks up the fountain solution, which contains alcohol. After carrying it past a metering roller, it deposits the correct amount of moisture on the first ink form roller.

The *main press elements* include the blanket cylinder, plate cylinder, and impression cylinder. The printing plate is fastened to the plate cylinder. The plate is inked and offsets the ink image onto the blanket cylinder. The sheet to be printed is on the impression cylinder. It rolls the sheet against the blanket cylinder, thus transferring the ink image to the paper.

The *delivery unit* receives the printed sheets and piles them on a delivery pile board. The unit consists of a delivery gripper assembly and the delivery pile board assembly.

The parts of the Harris Model L-125-B press are described and illustrated in the following section. They are divided in the following way:

* Operating controls, Figs. 16-2 through 16-5.
* Pile feeder operations and adjustment, Figs. 16-6 through 16-16 (Shown on Pages 367–369).
* Tape table operation and adjustment, Figs. 16-17 through 16-21 (Shown on Pages 370, 371).
* Operation and adjustment of the registering mecha-

Harris-Seybold Co., Div. Harris-Intertype Corp.

16-1. *An offset press.*

nism, Figs. 16-22 through 16-34 (Pages 371–374).

* Main press operation and adjustments, Figs. 16-35 through 16-43 (Shown on Pages 375–377).

* Delivery operation and adjustment, Figs. 16-44 through 16-48 (Shown on Pages 378, 379).

* Inker operation and adjustment, Figs. 16-49 through 16-53 (Shown on Pages 379, 380).

* Ink fountain operation and adjustment, Figs. 16-54 through 16-60 (Shown on Pages 381, 382).

OPERATING CONTROLS

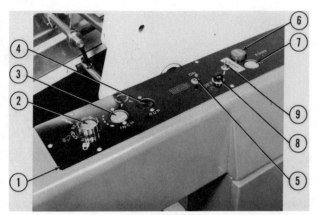

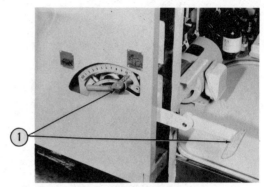

Harris-Seybold Co., Div. Harris-Intertype Corp.

16-3. *The press speed regulator controls the speed of the press.*
   1. Press speed regulator.

Harris-Seybold Co., Div. Harris-Intertype Corp.
16-2. *The main control panel has electric push buttons which control the major operating units of the press.*
   1. Main control panel. 2. Press stop and "safe" control. 3. Press inching control. 4. Press running control. 5. Sheet counter switch. 6. Air and vacuum pump start. 7. Air and vacuum pump stop. 8. Counter "off" indicator light. 9. Off-set spray switch.

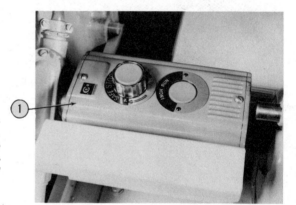

Harris-Seybold Co., Div. Harris-Intertype Corp.
   16-4. *Printing area push-button control station. The inching button permits the operator to run the press in short stops. The control station also permits stopping the press or putting it on "safe" without moving to the main control panel.*
   1. The "inching" push button.

Harris-Seybold Co., Div. Harris-Intertype Corp.
16-5. *The press speed regulator controls the speed of the press when on printing pressure.*
   1. Stop locking lever. 2. Speed regulator pedal. 3. Rod.

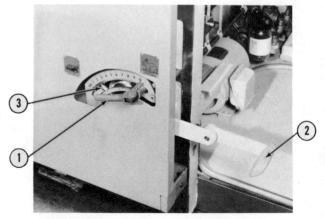

PILE FEEDER OPERATION
AND ADJUSTMENT

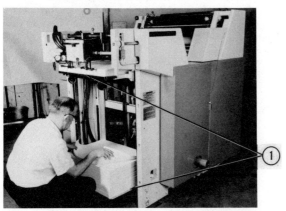

Harris-Seybold Co., Div. Harris-Intertype Corp.

16-6. *Loading stock in the feeder. Stock must be loaded evenly in the feeder. Carelessly loaded material causes trip-offs. (A trip-off means the press automatically shuts off because of some malfunction.) A crooked sheet will not feed, thus shutting off the press.*
1. Feeder tables.

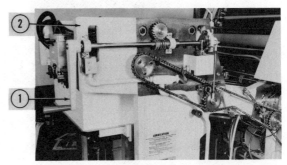

Harris-Seybold Co., Div. Harris-Intertype Corp.

16-7. *Pile feeder elevator control raises and lowers the feed pile.*
1. Elevator hand lever. 2. Pile feeder frame.

Harris-Seybold Co., Div. Harris-Intertype Corp.

16-8. *Front piling guides maintain the pile of stock on the pile board.*
1. Front piling guides. 2. Crossbar. 3. Pile of stock. 4. Pile board.

Harris-Seybold Co., Div. Harris-Intertype Corp.

16-9. *Pile feeder front guide rails. The front edge of the sheet must contact the front guide rails. The side-guide edge of the pile must be kept straight. The scale aids in positioning the guide rails and sheet. Set the gear-side pile guide 1/4" off the sheet dimension on the scale toward the side guide being used.*
1. Front edge of sheets. 2. Front pile-guide rails. 3. Scale. 4. Thumbscrews.

367

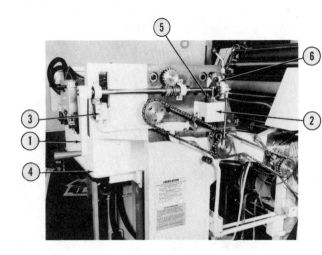

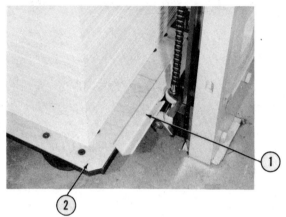

Harris-Seybold Co., Div. Harris-Intertype Corp.

16-10. *Adjusting the pile to separator height. The elevating handle turns the automatic pile feeder's elevating mechanism "on" and "off." When "on" the pile will elevate automatically as signals are received from the pile-raising solenoid.*

1. Pile feeder's elevating handle. 2. Automatic pile-elevating solenoid. 3. Switch. 4. Pile. 5. Pile solenoid. 6. Pile-height indicator.

Harris-Seybold Co., Div. Harris-Intertype Corp.

16-11. *Preparing additional pile. A second pile can be made ready on another pile board.*
1. Pile-board support. 2. Pile board.

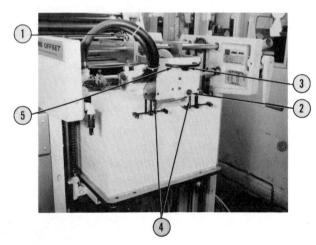

Harris-Seybold Co., Div. Harris-Intertype Corp.

16-12. *The separator control locks the separator in position to handle various sheet lengths.*
1. Lock clamp. 2. Pile height adjusting knob. 3. Air pressure control. 4. Separating air tubes. 5. Grip handle.

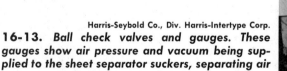

Harris-Seybold Co., Div. Harris-Intertype Corp.

16-13. *Ball check valves and gauges. These gauges show air pressure and vacuum being supplied to the sheet separator suckers, separating air tubes, and blast foot.*

1. Ball check valves. 2. Air pressure and vacuum gauges.

Harris-Seybold Co., Div. Harris-Intertype Corp.

16-14. *Pretimed rotary air valve controls and times the air and vacuum to suckers, separating air tubes, and blast foot.*

1. Pretimed rotary air valve. 2. Feed side of the separator frame.

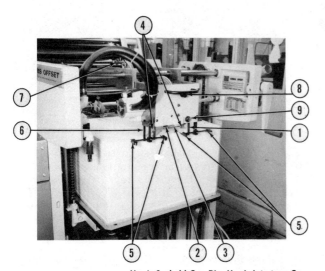

Harris-Seybold Co., Div. Harris-Intertype Corp.

16-15. *Separator components. Air is forced into the rear of the pile through perforated separator tubes until the top 1/4" of the pile is separated. The vacuum pickup suckers then lift the top sheet from the pile. The presser foot descends to the top of the second sheet on the pile. At this moment, a blast of air from the base of the presser foot separates the top sheet from the second and forms a cushion effect. This helps the sheet move forward to the pull-in wheels. Strippers hold top sheets in place so they will not be blown out of position.*

To set up the separator: Place pile backers against the rear of the pile. Adjust ball check valves (Fig. 16-13) so that air and vacuum are working properly. Position strippers on each side of the presser foot. Turn on the air separation control to separate top sheets. The unit is now ready to operate.

1. Perforated separator tubes. 2. Vacuum forwarding suckers. 3. Presser foot. 4. Vacuum pickup suckers. 5. Strippers. 6. Pile backers. 7. Separator lock handle. 8. Air-separating control. 9. Pile-raising control.

Harris-Seybold Co., Div. Harris-Intertype Corp.

16-16. *Flap shaft. The flaps act as a ramp for the sheet as it is moved forward after separation from the pile. The flap shaft is operated by a cam. When the flaps are in a vertical position, they should be perpendicular with the flap shaft.*

1. Flap shaft. 2. Pull-in wheels. 3. Flaps. 4. Flap adjustment screws.

TAPE TABLE OPERATION AND ADJUSTMENT

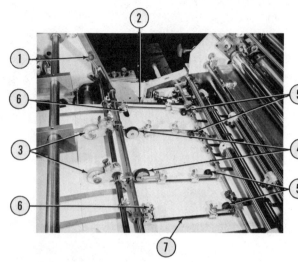

Harris-Seybold Co., Div. Harris-Intertype Corp.

16-17. *Tape table controls. The pull-in wheels have a shaft lever that raises or lowers the wheels from the tape table. The friction-driven wheels and brushes control the movement of the sheets on the table.*

1. Pull-in wheels shaft lever. 2. Pull-in wheels shaft. 3. Pull-in wheels. 4. Friction drive wheels. 5. Friction drive wheels. 6. Brushes. 7. Trim rack.

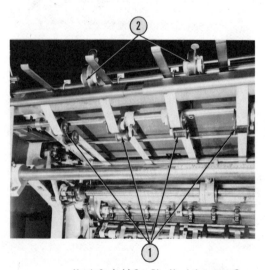

Harris-Seybold Co., Div. Harris-Intertype Corp.

16-18. *Tape table tapes. The pulleys are adjusted to put tension on the tapes and insure uniform speed as tapes travel.*

1. Adjustment pulleys for tape tension. 2. Pull-in wheels.

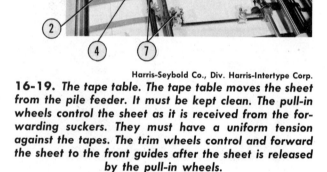

Harris-Seybold Co., Div. Harris-Intertype Corp.

16-19. *The tape table. The tape table moves the sheet from the pile feeder. It must be kept clean. The pull-in wheels control the sheet as it is received from the forwarding suckers. They must have a uniform tension against the tapes. The trim wheels control and forward the sheet to the front guides after the sheet is released by the pull-in wheels.*

To set up the tape table: Move the outer two tapes suitable for the width of paper. Place a piece of paper to be printed against the front guides. Mount two rubber-tired, friction-driven wheels over the same tape with the pull-in wheels. Position them to clear the rear edge of the sheet. Adjust the tension on the wheels. Now put two wood, friction-driven wheels over the two outer tapes. They are normally placed near the front edge of the sheet. Locate brushes so they rest against the rear edge of the sheet when it is in contact with the front guides.

1. Pull-in wheels. 2. Tension adjusting screws. 3. Handle to raise and lower pull-in wheels. 4. Set-screws for positioning pull-in wheels. 5. Trim wheels. 6. Trim wheels. 7. Brushes. 8. Front guides. 9. Rack-positioning set collars.

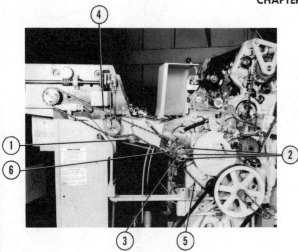

Harris-Seybold Co., Div. Harris-Intertype Corp.

16-20. *Timing the sheet to the front guides.* To print in register, the lead edge of the sheet must reach both front guides and remain in contact with them until the sheet is side-guided and picked up by the impression cylinder grippers.

To check timing, run a sheet from the pile to the front guides. The gripper edge of the sheet should have 1/4" to travel to contact the front guides when they have completed their downward motion to the register plate.

Timing is adjusted by moving the drive sprocket.

1. Drive chain's idler sprocket. 2. Cap screws. 3. Feeder drive sprocket. 4. Drive chain. 5. Drive chain. 6. Drive sprocket.

Harris-Seybold Co., Div. Harris-Intertype Corp.

16-21. *Feeder latch handle.* The handle has three positions. Position 1 starts the pile feeder, camshaft, and the sheet separator mechanism. The sheet can run through the press without printing pressure being applied. In position 2 the printing pressure is applied between the plate, impression, and blanket cylinders. Position 3 is the trip position. This stops the feeding of sheets and shuts off the printing pressure. The on-the-fly side-guide control is used to make adjustments in side guiding while the press is running.

1. Feeder latch handle. 2. On-the-fly side-guide control. 3. Speed indicator.

OPERATION AND ADJUSTMENT OF THE REGISTERING MECHANISM

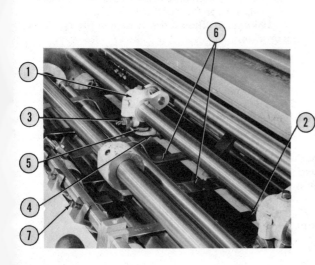

Harris-Seybold Co., Div. Harris-Intertype Corp.

16-22. *Adjusting the front guides.* The front guides can be positioned over the two inside guide tongues for minimum size sheets. They are positioned over the two outer tongues for normal and maximum size sheets. Guides should be in their "up" position. The front guide adjusting screw is used to set the guides so the sheet will be parallel with the front edge of the impression cylinder gripper's contact blocks after the impression cylinder grippers have closed on the sheet.

The flat-spring guide on the bottom of the front guides must be adjusted. It should clear the register plate to permit the sheet to be free yet not buckle. Adjust the sheet holddowns. Place three sheets of paper under the holddowns and tighten them. This gives the proper spacing for the sheets to flow under them.

1. Front guides. 2. Outer tongues. 3. Front guide adjusting screw. 4. Adjustable, flat-spring sheet guide. 5. Knurled adjusting nut. 6. Sheet holddowns. 7. Holddown lock screw.

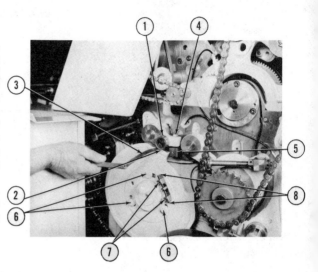

Harris-Seybold Co., Div. Harris-Intertype Corp.

16-23. *Timing the front guide cam.* The impression cylinder grippers must be in adjustment before the front guide cam can be timed. To set the front guide cam, put a 0.004″ thick sheet of paper at the front guides. Then manually turn the press until the grippers start to close. Turn the press slowly until the grippers touch the sheet but have not completely closed. Loosen the cam adjusting screws and the Allen setscrews. Turn the adjusting screws until the cam is just contacting the front guide cam roller. Lock the cam.

1. Cam roller. 2. Front guide cam. 3. Feeler gauge. 4. Front-guide stop screw. 5. Stop block. 6. Cap screws holding the cam. 7. Allen setscrews. 8. Cam adjusting screws.

Harris-Seybold Co., Div. Harris-Intertype Corp.

16-24. *Side guides.* The side guides move along the guide bar. They are locked to it when in their desired position.

1. Side-guide bar. 2. Side guides. 3. Side-guide lock. 4. Locknut. 5. Adjusting screw.

Harris-Seybold Co., Div. Harris-Intertype Corp.

16-25. *Side-guiding linkage.* The linkage that determines the direction of the side-guide movement is located between the edge of the tape table and the inside of the feed-side press frame. This linkage is set for the feed-side linkage.

1. Linkage. 2. The feed-side hole in the operating bracket.

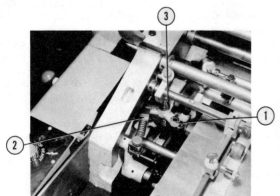

Harris-Seybold Co., Div. Harris-Intertype Corp.

16-26. *Side guiding to the gear side.* The feed and gear side guides operate from the same side-guide bar. The direction of movement of the side guides must be reversed so that the feed side guide can push the sheet toward the gear side of the press, and the gear side guide will push toward the feed side of the press. The side-guide operating lever controls this movement.

1. Side-guide operating lever. 2. Operating arm. 3. Spring clip.

Harris-Seybold Co., Div. Harris-Intertype Corp.
16-27. *Side guiding to the feed side. This linkage is for side-guiding from the gear to the feed side.*

Harris-Seybold Co., Div. Harris-Intertype Corp.
16-28. *Timing the side-guide cam: Run a sheet down to the front guides. Turn the press manually until the impression cylinder grippers close on the sheet and start to move it forward. Stop the press. Loosen the side-guide cam and turn it in the direction of rotation. When the cam comes off the high point and the side guide starts to move away from the sheet, stop the press. Tighten the cam.*

1. Side-guide cam. 2. Cam roller. 3. High point of cam. 4. Operating lever spring.

Harris-Seybold Co., Div. Harris-Intertype Corp.
16-29. *The sheet holddowns control and flatten the sheet while it is in contact with front stops. The corrugating bar flattens the sheet as it is being placed against the side guide.*

1. Push-type side guides. 2. Sheet holddown adjusting screw locknut. 3. Sheet holddown adjusting screw. 4. Corrugating bar. 5. Push guide bar.

Harris-Seybold Co., Div. Harris-Intertype Corp.
16-30. *The corrugating bar is cam operated. The bottom of the bar in the down position will have a slight pressure on the sheet when it is being side-guided. The bar height is changed by turning the adjustment screw.*

1. Corrugating bar. 2. Lock screw. 3. Adjustment screw. 4. Corrugating bar cam.

Harris-Seybold Co., Div. Harris-Intertype Corp.

16-31. Sheet controls. *The two-sheet choke permits only one sheet at a time to pass into the sheet registering mechanism. The holddowns flatten the sheet while it is in contact with the front stops. The front guides stop each sheet and pre-register the front edge before it is taken by the impression cylinder grippers. The sheet detector releases the printing pressure if the feeder misses a sheet.*

1. Two-sheet choke. 2. Short, center sheet guides (holddowns). 3. Long holddowns. 4. Sheet holddown bar. 5. Front guides. 6. Front-guides shaft. 7. Sheet detector. 8. Choke-position sheet holddown.

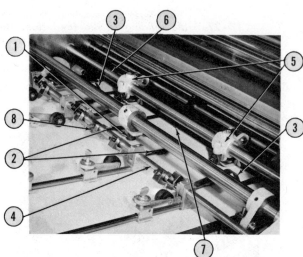

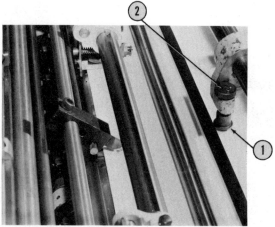

Harris-Seybold Co., Div. Harris-Intertype Corp.

16-32. *To adjust the choke: Loosen the knurled portion. Place a sheet of stock under the choke. Adjust the clearance so that only one sheet will pass. Tighten the knurled portion.*

1. Choke. 2. Knurled portion of the choke.

Harris-Seybold Co., Div. Harris-Intertype Corp.

16-33. *To time the choke: Set the feeder in the first notch. Run a sheet down to the front guides. Turn the press by hand until the tail of the sheet clears the choke. The choke should be down to caliper the second sheet. Loosen the choke cam. Rotate it in the normal direction until the choke is all the way down. Center the cam on the cam roller and tighten the cam.*

1. Choke cam. 2. Cam roller.

$1/32''$

Harris-Seybold Co., Div. Harris-Intertype Corp.

16-34. *The sheet detector. If the separator fails to forward a sheet, if the sheets are stopped by the choke, or if they are slow coming to the impression cylinder, the press will automatically stop. The sheet detector senses the missing sheet and stops the press.*

1. Trip latch. 2. Collar

MAIN PRESS OPERATION AND ADJUSTMENTS

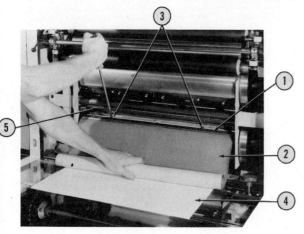

Harris-Seybold Co., Div. Harris-Intertype Corp.

16-35. Blanket installation. *For good printing a squeeze of 0.002" to 0.003" between the plate and blanket is necessary. Overpack the blanket by this amount.*

To install the blanket: Place the blanket bar on the front edge of the blanket. Slide the bar in its slot in the cylinder. Tighten the setscrews. Place the packing behind the blanket. Hold the loose end of the blanket and install the main drive shaft. Rotate the cylinder by hand, using the drive shaft until the reel rod appears. Insert the blanket bar in the reel rod. Tighten the blanket by turning the reel rod.

1. Blanket bar. 2. Blanket. 3. Setscrews. 4. Packing. 5. Reel rod.

Harris-Seybold Co., Div. Harris-Intertype Corp.

16-36. The main drive shaft. *The drive shaft is turned manually to rotate the blanket cylinder.*
1. Handle. 2. Main drive shaft.

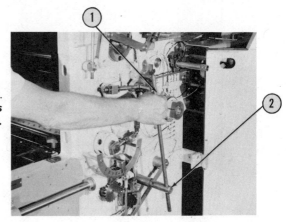

Harris-Seybold Co., Div. Harris-Intertype Corp.

16-37. Blanket cylinder reel and ratchet. *The ratchet secures the blanket and adjusts its tension on the cylinder.*
1. Blanket reel rod. 2. Reel-rod ratchet. 3. Wrench on the square shoulder of the reel rod.

Results of an improperly installed blanket or a poor blanket:
1. A loose blanket will cause a blurred print.
2. Poor contact between the blanket and plate will cause ink to build up on the plate.
3. Blankets that are swollen in places cause excessive pressure on the stock, giving a poor printing.
4. A poor blanket, such as one that is uneven, will be impossible to pack correctly.
5. A glazed blanket will not accept ink properly. It can be reconditioned sometimes by cleaning with a blanket conditioner.

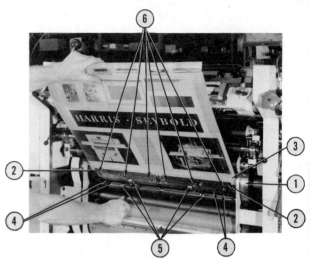

Harris-Seybold Co., Div. Harris-Intertype Corp.

16-38. *Installing the plate. The plate cylinder runs on bearers. The thickness of the plate plus packing should bring the plate up to the bearer height. For example, if the bearers are 0.015" above the cylinder and the plate to be used is 0.008", the packing will be 0.007".*

To install a plate, loosen the clamps, eccentrics, and screws. Adjust the clamps parallel with the edge of the cylinder. Insert and lock the front edge of the plate in the clamps. Place the packing behind the plate. The end of the packing must extend over the front edge of the cylinder. Manually roll the cylinder forward. Press the plate and packing against the cylinder. When the clamps for the rear edge of the plate appear, stop the rotation. Place the plate in the clamps. Close the clamps on the plate. Using the knurled screws, tighten the plate around the cylinder. The entire plate must be tight to the cylinder.

1. Bearers. 2. Front clamps. 3. Front edge of plate. 4. Knurled screws. 5. Eccentrics. 6. Adjusting screws.

Harris-Seybold Co., Div. Harris-Intertype Corp.

16-39. *Installing the plate in the rear plate clamps. These clamps hold the rear edge of the plate, and the knurled screws tighten the plate to the cylinder.*

1. Rear plate clamps. 2. Tension screws. 3. Knurled screws to tighten plate. 4. Rear clamp eccentrics.

Harris-Seybold Co., Div. Harris-Intertype Corp.

16-40. *Around-the-cylinder lay adjustment. The plate cylinder can be rotated 4" to adjust where the image will print on the sheet. Loosen the cap screws, place a pin wrench in the threaded hole in the cylinder, and rotate the cylinder as needed.*

1. Plate cylinder. 2. Cap screws. 3. Backlash gear. 4. Screw heads. 5. Plate cylinder's backlash gear.

Harris-Seybold Co., Div. Harris-Intertype Corp.

16-41. *Stock thickness adjustment. The bearers on the impression cylinder are 0.015″ below the cylinder body. This allowance provides the clearance necessary to change the packing between the plate and blanket cylinders. Normally a 0.002″ to 0.004″ squeeze is required between the blanket and impression cylinders.*

To arrive at the correct pressure, loosen the cap screw, and move the blanket cylinder away from the impression cylinder until a light or broken image is being printed. Then gradually move the capstan in order to move the blanket cylinder toward the impression cylinder. Inspect the printed images. When they are printed properly, tighten the cap screws.

1. Cap screw. 2. Pressure capstan. 3. Blanket cylinder.

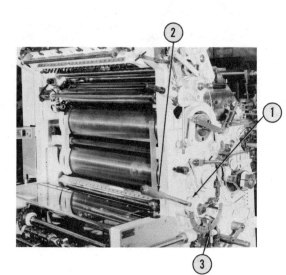

Harris-Seybold Co., Div. Harris-Intertype Corp.

16-42. *Impression control. This control varies the printing pressure between the blanket and impression cylinders. This permits some adjustments for difference in thickness of stocks being run. The thickness-setting indicator shows the setting normally used to print the stock being run.*

1. Impression control. 2. Handle. 3. Thickness-setting indicator.

Harris-Seybold Co., Div. Harris-Intertype Corp.

16-43. *The impression cylinder grippers. These grippers must have exactly the same tension because they hold the sheet while the ink image is being printed.*

1. Screws holding gripper to shaft. 2. Gripper shaft. 3. Gripper shaft's stop pin. 4. Stop lever. 5. Tumbler cam.

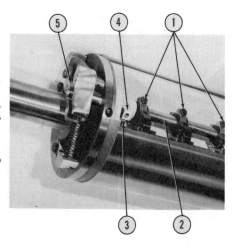

DELIVERY OPERATION AND ADJUSTMENT

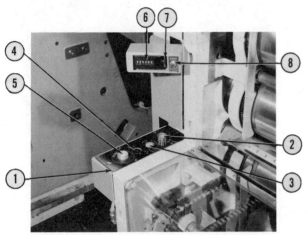

16-44. *Delivery push-button control station for major press operations. The sheet counter tells how many sheets have passed through the press. The "trip" button permits the operator to trip the press off printing pressure from the delivery end of the press.*

1. Delivery push-button control station. 2. Stop press control. 3. Inching press control. 4. Running press control. 5. Reverse-inching press control. 6. Sheet counter. 7. Reset for the sheet counter. 8. "Trip" button.

16-45. *Jogger controls. The side jogger is adjusted by sliding it along the operating shaft. The rear jogger is adjusted by turning the control knob.*

1. Rear jogger control. 2. Rear jogger's adjustment thumbscrew 3. Side jogger plate. 4. Side jogger's adjustment thumbscrew. 5. Operating shaft.

16-46. *Positioning the joggers. Joggers assist in producing a neat, straight pile on the delivery pile board. To adjust, first place a sheet of the stock to be printed on the delivery pile board. Move the gear-side jogger until it touches the edge of the sheet. Lock it in position. Inch the press forward until the feed-side jogger reaches the center of the pile board. Stop the press. Move the jogger until it contacts the edge of the stock. Lock it in this position. Repeat this procedure to locate the rear jogger.*

1. Feed-side jogger. 2. Thumbscrew. 3. Thumbscrew. 4. Rear jogger's adjusting knob. 5. Rear jogger. 6. Sheet-releasing cam. 7. Delivery gate. 8. Sheet-releasing cam's adjusting knob. 9. Delivery chains. 10. Gripper bars. 11. Adjustable spring rods.

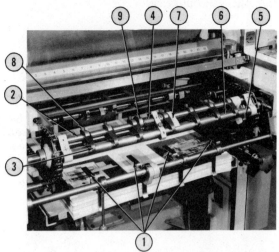

16-47. *Delivery mechanical controls. The delivery grippers release the sheet after it is printed, and it floats against the delivery gate. The cam control knob times the release of sheets from the delivery grippers. The pile-lowering crank manually raises or lowers the delivery pile. A down-feed switch automatically controls lowering the delivery pile when the press is operating on printing pressure.*

1. Delivery gripper's opening cam control knob. 2. Pile-lowering crank. 3. Delivery pile's support rails. 4. Down-feed switch.

16-48. *The delivery stripper fingers and grippers. The delivery stripper fingers guide and retain the sheets as they are released by the delivery grippers. They are located between the grippers and above the sheet. Each finger must have 1/16" clearance from the gripper bars. The delivery grippers receive the printed sheet from the impression cylinder.*

1. Delivery stripper fingers. 2. Gripper bars. 3. Spring grippers. 4. Master torsion spring. 5. Cam rolls. 6. Gripper contact shaft. 7. Master gripper. 8. Cap screws. 9. Master torsion spring's adjusting collar.

INKER OPERATION AND ADJUSTMENT

16-49. *Inker controls. The form rollers can be lowered manually by the inker throw-off handle. When the press is printing, they are lowered to the plate automatically and raised when the printing pressure is removed.*

1. Inker throw-off. 2. Bearings. 3. Adjusting screws.

16-50. *Ink ductor and form-rollers control. The ink ductor roller control will start to feed ink when the printing pressure is applied and stop when the pressure is released.*

1. Ink ductor-roller control. 2. Form-rollers control.

Harris-Seybold Co., Div. Harris-Intertype Corp.

16-51. *Installing the form rollers. Once the form rollers are properly installed, they may be removed and replaced without losing their setting. The rollers are held with the eccentric clamp assembly.*
   1. Eccentric clamp. 2. Bearing pin. 3. Screw. 4. Allen setscrews.

Harris-Seybold Co., Div. Harris-Intertype Corp.

16-52. *Adjusting form rollers. To set the form roller to the vibrator, loosen the eccentric clamp. Place the form roller in the mid-position. Use strips of tissue paper 8" long and 3/4" and 1 1/2" wide. Place one narrow strip between two wide strips about 2" from the ends of the roller. Place them between the roller and the steel drum. Pull on the strips. Adjust until each has an identical light pull.*
   To set the form roller to the plate, set four strips of tissue between the roller and the plate, beginning 2" from each end. Manually lower the roller against the plate. Adjust the roller so the tissue strips have an identical light pull. The strips in the center should have the same pull as those on the ends.
   1. Roller. 2. Plate. 3. Steel drum. 4. Roller bearings. 5. Spring-loaded brackets. 6. Mounting pins. 7. Adjusting nut.

Harris-Seybold Co., Div. Harris-Intertype Corp.

16-53. *The inker feed control and washup. The washup machine permits the cleaning of the inker rollers without removing them from the press. To clean the rollers, start the press and apply solvent on the upper vibrator roller. The solvent is carried through the inking system and loosens the ink. Then place the blade against the vibrator roller. Let the press run, and apply more solvent on the upper vibrator roller. When the rollers are clean, remove the washup unit and clean it.*
   The feed control knob is used to increase or decrease the flow of ink.
   1. Washup machine. 2. Support pins. 3. Levers. 4. Ink-feed control mechanism. 5. Fountain roller's indexing handle.

INK FOUNTAIN OPERATION AND ADJUSTMENT

Harris-Seybold Co., Div. Harris-Intertype Corp.

16-54. *Ink fountain controls. The ink fountain keys control the flow of ink. The fountain blade distributes the ink on the fountain roller.*

1. Ink fountain keys. 2. Ink fountain. 3. Knurled nuts to release fountain. 4. Fountain blade. 5. Fountain blade screws.

Harris-Seybold Co., Div. Harris-Intertype Corp.

16-55. *Ink fountain controls. The fountain roller has a manual lever, enabling the operator to charge the inker quickly. The ink-feed control adjusts the amount of ink coming from the ink fountain roller to the ductor roller.*

1. Manual, ink-charging lever. 2. Fountain roller shaft. 3. Fountain roller. 4. Ink feed control.

Harris-Seybold Co., Div. Harris-Intertype Corp.

16-56. *Ink fountain blade adjustment. The ink fountain blade is adjusted to the roll by using the fountain adjusting keys. The keys are turned gradually, starting at the center and working toward the ends of the blade.*

1. Fountain adjusting keys. 2. Cap screws. 3. Adjusting screws at end of blade.

16-57. Cleaning the ink fountain. The ink fountain opens away from the fountain roller. This makes it easy to clean.

1. Ink fountain. 2. Fountain roller. 3. Knobs. 4. Bar.

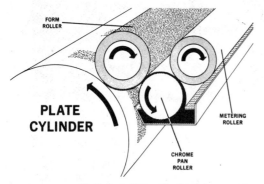

16-58. The dampener. The dampener controls the amount of moisture transferred to the plate cylinder. The chrome pan roller runs in the fountain solution. The metering roller squeegees the excess solution off the chrome pan roller. The solution remaining on the chrome pan roller is transferred to the ink form roller. This provides the correct mixture of moisture and ink to the printing plate.

16-59. The dampener system.

1. Water pan. 2. Dampener speed control. 3. Frame. 4. Chrome pan roller. 5. "On" and "off" control handle. 6. Form roller. 7. Metering roller's setting controls. 8. Metering roller. 9. Screw. 10. Metering roll hanger.

16-60. Dampener controls. The throw-off lever moves the form roller on or off the plate. The pan roller's speed selector controls the rotation speed of that roller. The skew adjustment controls skew of the metering roller. This regulates the amount of moisture from the feed side to the gear side. The metering roller has a pressure adjustment. It is used to obtain the proper film of moisture to be transferred to the first ink form roller.

1. Throw-off lever. 2. Pan roll's speed selector. 3. Metering roll's pressure adjustment. 4. Skew adjustment.

SETTING UP THE DAMPENER TO RUN A JOB

1. *Make certain the fountain solution tank is full.*
2. *Turn on the press fountain circulation system.*
3. *Set the metering roller to the pan roller.*
4. *Run the press on idle, and set the pan roller's speed control at a medium speed.*
5. *Ink the inker.*
6. *Observe the water film squeegeed by the metering roller. Adjust until it is even across the roller.*
7. *Wash and dampen the plate evenly on the plate cylinder.*
8. *Engage the dampening unit. Print a few sheets. Reduce the pan roll speed until the open areas being printed start to pick up. Make adjustments to get uniform inking across the printed image.*
9. *Increase the pan roller speed and run a few more sheets. When the pickup disappears, the job is ready to print.*

MAKEREADY AND OPERATING THE PRESS

Pre-Makeready

Anything that can be done by the press operator to prepare for makeready before it actually starts is referred to as "pre-makeready." The makeready of any job should be as systematic and routine as possible and should not be interrupted by anything that should have been done during the pre-makeready.

Pre-makeready for a new job, for the most part, involves those duties and responsibilities of the press operator that can be performed before the press is actually shut down at the completion of the previous job. This does not mean that a press operator should neglect the job that is running in order to prepare for the next one. In fact, pre-makeready for a certain job should start long before that job is in the pressroom. For instance, check whether the correct size, weight, and type of stock is on hand for the job. Is it piled correctly and ready to be put into the pile feeder? Is the correct color ink

for the job in the shop or does it have to be ordered? If the ink is in the shop, has the color been checked against the sample? Has the ink been brought to the press? Have the plates been brought to the press? Will the paper be properly conditioned by being in the pressroom at least overnight?

Some questions a press operator should consider are:

1. Are plate and blanket packing sheets handy to the press, and are they cut to the correct size?
2. Is a full set of tools available?
3. Are waste sheets of the correct size for the job available?
4. Has a new blanket been punched and mounted on the blanket bars in case the one on the press needs replacing?
5. Does fresh fountain solution have to be made up?
6. Is sufficient press wash-up solvent and blanket wash available?
7. Has the paper been tested for pick, curl, printability, absorbency, drying, and so forth?
8. Has the first load of paper

for the next job been made up with several waste sheets on top?

Pre-makeready should also extend into the area of press maintenance.

1. Have ink rolls become hard, glazed, or cracked?
2. Are cylinders rusted or caked with dried ink?
3. Do ink form rolls need resetting?
4. Have the filters on the air-vacuum pumps been cleaned recently?
5. Are the correct weight oils being used to lubricate the press and the pumps?
6. Has the press been greased according to a maintenance schedule?
7. Do the feedboard tapes need replacing? If so, have they been ordered?
8. Does the blade in the wash-up unit need replacing?

A press operator should keep the press and the area around the press clean. The inspection table, platforms, and shelves should be orderly. Buckets, sponges, and tools should have a proper storage place very near the press.

Remember, the time to think about the next job is while the press is running the job ahead of it.

MAKEREADY

Makeready can be divided into three general classifications. There is the simple makeready which only involves a plate change, a partial makeready which involves a color change in addition to a plate change, and the full makeready which involves setting up the press from feeder to delivery.

For a simple makeready:

1. Color of ink and ink fountain settings remain unchanged.
2. Dampener settings remain unchanged.
3. Size and type of paper remain unchanged; stock is in the feeder.
4. Install new plates.
5. Position plates and/or pile to register and run the job.
6. Clean blanket.

For a partial makeready:

1. Change ink and ink fountain settings.
2. There is a possibility of a second inker washup if the new color is lighter than the previous color.
3. Install new plates.
4. Wash the blanket. It may or may not have to be changed.
5. Sheet size and type of stock remain unchanged.
6. Feeder must be loaded.

For a full makeready:

1. Blanket may or may not have to be changed but must be well cleaned.
2. Install new plates.
3. Change size and weight of stock.
4. Separator must be repositioned.

5. Pile-height mechanism may have to be reset.
6. Sheet-separating air may have to be readjusted.
7. Tape-table trimmings must be repositioned.
8. Choke must be reset.
9. Side-guide mechanism must be reset.
10. Pressure between blanket cylinder and impression cylinder will have to be changed.
11. Delivery joggers will have to be reset.
12. Delivery gripper's opening cam may have to be repositioned.
13. If required, add driers and varnishes to ink.
14. Put ink in fountains, and make preliminary adjustments to the fountain keys.
15. Make preliminary adjustment to fountain roll sweep.
16. Remove gum from plate.
17. Drop ink rolls on plate for two or three revolutions.
18. Dampener is lowered to the plate.
19. Print about 50 sheets of waste and four or five good sheets.
20. Check position of image on sheet, and make necessary moves of plate, plate cylinder, and side guides to get correct position.
21. Get OK from supervisor as to correct image position.
22. Run more waste and minimum amount of good sheets while making necessary changes in ink fountain and water fountain settings to get correct color.
23. Get OK from supervisor as to correct color.
24. Run the job.
25. Be thinking about your next makeready while the job is running on the press.

OPERATING THE PRESS

1. Set the speed control on the speed at which the press is to operate.
2. Wash the gum from the plate and dampen it.
3. Start the press and run at slow speed. The pile feeder should raise the pile until the pile-height governor stops the rising action. Adjust as required.
4. Start the dampener circulating system.
5. Move the dampener throw-on lever to the "on" position, and adjust control for the desired moisture.
6. Turn on the air and vacuum pumps. Jog a sheet onto the tape table, then turn off the air and vacuum pump. Make final adjustments of the pull-in wheels, the trimming wheels, the side guide, and the choke, if required.
7. Engage the feeder latch in the first notch; turn on the air and vacuum pump and start feeding sheets.
8. When the lead edge of the first sheet is opposite the side guide, move the feeder latch handle to the second notch and release it quickly.
9. Check the pile-delivery jogger settings to make certain the sheets are being properly jogged on the delivery board.
10. To stop the press, first depress the "off" vacuum and pressure pump button. When the last sheet that was fed into the pull-in wheels goes through the sheet detectors, the press will automatically throw off printing pressure. Second, press the "stop" button and turn its ring to the "safe" position.
11. Manually put the dampener in "off" or "idle" position

and gum the plate in order to preserve it.

12. After the job has been completed, clean up the press, and perform the makeready for the next job.

Sheet Sequence

Press operators will improve their ability to make ready and run the press by studying and understanding the sheet sequence of the press. The following is a complete operational sequence of the press.

1. Position stock in the feeder approximately 1/4″ off center toward side guide to be used. Set the piling guides.

2. Push elevating handle "in" and raise pile manually to within 3/8″ of the top of the flap. Pull handle "out" to the automatic elevating position.

3. Position the separator so that the back gauges are in contact with the rear edge of the pile. Lock separator in this position.

4. Turn on press motor.

5. Adjust pile-height governor to bring pile up to operating height. Lead edge will be approximately 1/4″ below top of flaps.

6. Turn on air and vacuum pump.

7. Adjust ball check valves for pressure and vacuum to approximately 4 psi of pressure and 8″ to 10″ of vacuum.

8. Turn separator air control to obtain separation of approximately 1/4″ of the top of the pile of sheets.

9. Adjust clock-spring strippers to the rear edge of the pile.

10. Engage the operating handle in the first notch.

11. Pickup suckers will lower to the top of pile, and the pres-

sure foot will be in the raised position.

12. Vacuum will come on the pickup suckers, and as they start to lift the top sheet, the presser foot will return to the top of the second sheet on the pile.

13. As the top sheet is lifted by the pickup suckers to the height of the forwarding suckers, vacuum will come on at the forwarding suckers and momentarily all four suckers will control the sheet.

14. Vacuum to the pickup suckers will cut off; the flap shaft will rotate to tilt flaps forward to act as a ramp for the sheet; and the forwarding suckers will move the sheet to the pull-in wheels. Simultaneously, the forwarding air will come at the base of the presser foot to form a cushion of air to help forward the sheet.

15. When the sheet is approximately 1/8″ to 1/4″ under the pull-in wheels, the vacuum to the forwarding suckers is released.

16. The sheet is forwarded down the tape table by the pull-in and tape table's trim wheels.

17. Sheet passes under the choke; choke lowers to caliper the sheet thickness.

18. As the gripper edge of the sheet reaches the side-guide bar, engage the feeder latch in the second position to put press on pressure.

19. The sheet continues to move forward. The corrugating (sheet-flattening) bar is up.

20. The front guides lower to the register plate to intercept the sheet. The detector comes down to detect the presence of the sheet.

21. The sheet settles momentarily against the front guides. The corrugating bar lowers to

stiffen the sheet, and the side guide moves into contact with the sheet and pushes it approximately 3/16″ sideways.

22. The side guide stops, the impression cylinder grippers close on the sheet, the front guides and corrugating bar lift. Simultaneously, as the impression cylinder grippers start to move the sheet, the side guide moves away from the sheet.

23. The sheet is printed, then transferred to the delivery grippers.

24. At this point, both sets of grippers hold the sheet for approximately 1/4″ of cylinder travel.

25. The impression cylinder grippers release, and the sheet is carried to the delivery where it is released by the delivery grippers and deposited on the pile.

26. The pile is kept uniform by the rear and side joggers. As sheets are deposited on the top of the pile, the pile board lowers.

HOUSEKEEPING

Regardless of how well a piece of equipment is engineered, designed, and manufactured, there will be times when servicing will be required because of normal wear, maladjustments, or readjustment. Most of the causes of trouble could be greatly reduced or eliminated through proper housekeeping and maintenance.

There is time to perform many housekeeping functions during regular operational periods. Some of these duties are:

1. Keeping cylinder bearers and cylinders *clean*.

2. Washing ends of inker rollers to prevent cuffs from forming.

3. Cleaning the underside of

ink fountain blade each time the fountain is opened; also clean end shoes.

4. Keeping tape table, tapes, and register plate free of paper, spray powder, ink, or other dirt that may impede sheet travel or cause loss of sheet drive.

5. Inspecting and cleaning side guides regularly to remove lint, paper, ink, and so forth.

6. Cleaning grippers and gripper pad area regularly.

7. Cleaning air and vacuum pump filters and jars, as required.

8. Wiping up immediately all spills of ink, solvents, liquid chemicals, gum, fountain solution, oils, grease, and spray powder.

9. Sweeping and mopping platforms, steps, walkways, and immediate press area.

10. Maintaining neat, orderly work tables and a set of tools in good working order.

MAINTENANCE

Preventive maintenance consists of day-to-day observation and regularly scheduled machine inspections.

A press operator must constantly observe the equipment while it is operating. This can often prevent a routine problem from becoming serious. Unusual mechanical actions or strange noises are often the forerunner of troubles.

Abnormal wear is generally an indication of a condition which must be corrected. If such things are noted by the press operator and reported to supervision, unscheduled downtime will be greatly reduced.

A careful inspection must be carried out at regular intervals to make a good preventive maintenance program work. Since press usage and conditions in various plants differ greatly, the scheduled maintenance periods should be adjusted to fit the circumstances.

TROUBLESHOOTING

Troubleshooting, to be very effective, must be done in a logical step-by-step process.

Trouble should be diagnosed by a sound thought process, not by jumping to conclusions and making adjustments that may only further complicate proper diagnosis and remedy for the trouble.

Following is a list of problems, possible causes, and remedies (Pages 387–391). They are not all-inclusive; but, if properly applied, the principle can serve to guide the press operator in diagnosing the trouble and the action required to remedy it.

LUBRICATION AND PREVENTIVE MAINTENANCE

The productive life of the machine and any of its components will be shortened by lack of lubrication, use of inferior lubricants, or by carelessness in use of lubricants. Correct lubrication will reduce wear on all moving parts. To obtain the best results from lubricating the machine, follow the manufacturer's recommendations in the press operating manual.

SAFETY

Accident control in the print shop should be given high priority from top management on down. Accident prevention is important because it involves people as well as machines.

Unsafe acts refers to the actions of people. *Unsafe conditions* refers to the condition of tools, machinery, or other inanimate objects.

The following is a listing of unsafe acts and unsafe conditions that can result in accidents.

UNSAFE ACTS

1. Failure to lock the stop buttons when working on equipment, or failure to turn off equipment when not in use.

2. Failure to warn others of your intended action. You should warn others when you are doing something that may put them in danger.

3. Failure to wear protective devices, such as safety shoes and eye goggles when grinding or cleaning machinery.

4. Wearing dangerous accessories and unsafe clothing. Remove rings, wristwatches, and unsafe clothing, such as loosely rolled sleeves, loose shirttail, or a dangling belt. Wear a hairnet on long hair.

5. Operating someone else's equipment without permission or using tools or equipment for which you have not been properly trained.

6. Operating at excessive speeds or taking unsafe shortcuts.

7. Using tools, machinery, or materials that have become defective.

8. Overloading pallets or tables until they become topheavy. Placing tools, equipment, or materials in a position where they may accidentally roll or fall.

PROBLEM	POSSIBLE CAUSE	REMEDY
Double sheet feeding.	Sheets stuck together in pile.	Wind stock thoroughly to release edges that may be sealed together or to separate sheets that may be sticking together due to offsetting.
	Pile too high.	Reset pile height so that front edge of pile is 1/4'' below top of flaps.
	Insufficient separating air.	Adjust separating air pressure to separate top 1/4'' of pile.
	Excess vacuum.	Reduce vacuum to the suckers.
	Stripper fingers not positioned properly.	Position inside stripper fingers behind the pickup suckers and extending approximately 1/8'' on the pile.
	Static electricity in sheets.	Stock is probably too dry. Allow paper to condition itself to the pressroom overnight.
		If problem occurs commonly, thought should be given to purchase of a static eliminator for press.
Erratic sheet feeding.	Insufficient vacuum.	Increase vacuum to the pickup suckers.
	Pile too low.	Reset pile height so that front edge of the pile is 1/4'' below top of flaps.
	Insufficient separating air.	Position separating air tube and adjust separating air pressure to separate top 1/4'' of pile.
	Top of pile not level.	Use wedges to keep pile level.
	Low air pressure and/or vacuum from pump.	See air-vacuum pump trouble-shooting in manufacturer's manual.
	Sheets stuck together.	Wind stock thoroughly.
Crooked sheet feeding.	Sheets stuck together in pile.	Wind stock thoroughly.
	Pull-in wheels not set properly.	Be sure wheels are on tapes. Set tension on pull-in wheels so that both wheels have an identical drag when rotated manually. Make certain that both wheels rotate freely when lifted.
	Pull-in wheels positioned near edge of stock.	If at all possible, run pull-in wheels on the two center feeder tapes.

PROBLEM	POSSIBLE CAUSE	REMEDY
	Tape table trimming wheels do not turn freely.	Remove wheels from shafts. Clean thoroughly. Polish shafts and reassemble.
	Loose feeder tapes.	Tighten tapes by means of the tape tensioning wheels under the tape table.
	Worn or frayed feeder tapes.	Replace tapes.
	Pull-in wheels are worn or have flat spots.	Replace wheels.
Misregister around the cylinder (front end misregister).	Sheets bouncing away from front guides.	Position rubber-tired trimming wheels just off the tail edge of the paper when it is at rest against front guides. Position brush trimmings half on the paper and half on the tapes. Add tension gradually to wooden trimming wheels.
	Sheets not getting to the front guides.	Retime sheets to front guides. Reset register plate holddowns. Check for freeness of trimming wheels. Check for frayed or worn tapes. Replace if necessary. Reset sheet thickness clock-spring holddown in front guides. Should have a slight drag on three thicknesses of stock being run. Reset drop bar. Drop bar should lightly contact paper while it is being side guided. Drop bar should not corrugate sheet. Reset tension on pull-in wheels. Check squareness of sheet to the impression cylinder. Front guides may have to be paralleled.
	Sheet buckling at side guide.	Reset register plate holddowns. Position rubber-tired trimming wheels just off the tail of the sheet with the sheet at rest against the front guides. Position a short, register-plate holddown next to the side guide.

PROBLEM	POSSIBLE CAUSE	REMEDY
Sheets torn at lead edge.	Sheet coasting away from side guide.	Reset drop bar to just contact the sheet when the bar is in its "down" position. Apply also for sheet coasting. Add some pressure to the wooden trimming wheels.
	Delivery grippers not set correctly.	Reset according to instructions in the manufacturer's manual.
	Impression cylinder grippers not set correctly.	Reset according to instructions in the manual.
	Delivery gripper transfer cam not positioned correctly.	Reset cam so that delivery grippers and impression cylinder grippers have hold of the sheet for 1/4" travel.
	Sheets hitting delivery stripper fingers.	Reset delivery stripper fingers.
	Sheets hitting delivery gate stop.	Reset delivery gripper opening cam to release sheet earlier.
Scumming or tinting.	Improperly set rollers. Form rollers set too light to vibrator rollers.	Set rollers according to instructions in manual.
	Percentage of alcohol too low in fountain.	Add isopropyl alcohol to the fountain solution to keep the specific gravity above 15% (25% alcohol).
	Dirty dampener system rollers.	Clean metering roll with isobutyl alcohol or pumice and water. Clean pan roll occasionally with concentrated fountain acid and a kitchen cleanser. Gum the roll thoroughly.
	Ink too "greasy".	Add a heavy varnish or contact the ink manufacturer.
	Incorrect pH (acidity of fountain solution) for ink being used.	The pH of the fountain solution should be 4.6 for aluminum plates and 3.8 for zinc plates.
Ink emulsifying.	Incorrect percentage of alcohol in fountain solution.	Use hydrometer to check if low isopropyl alcohol should be added to the fountain solution to keep the specific gravity above 15%.
	Incorrect pressure setting between metering and pan roll.	Reset pressure according to instructions in manual.
	Too much water.	Keep plate moisture to a minimum.
Too much water on plate.	Dampener speed control setting has changed.	Reset.

PROBLEM	POSSIBLE CAUSE	REMEDY
Not enough water on plate.	Incorrect pressure between form roller and pan roller.	Reset according to instructions in the manufacturer's manual.
	Dampener speed control setting has changed.	Reset.
	Dirty pan roll and/or metering roll.	Clean same as dampener system rollers.
	Drive belts are worn or saturated with oil.	Clean or replace.
Steel vibrator rollers refuse to take ink.	Fountain acid and gum accumulation on ink rollers have desensitized them.	Rollers must be counteretched. Contact your lithographic supply dealer for commercial copperizing solutions. Reduce the amount of gum and/or acid used in mixing the fountain solution. Maintain proper pH of fountain solution.
Large solids do not ink up evenly.	Ink rollers not set correctly.	Reset rollers according to instructions in manufacturer's manual.
	Ink fountain keys (thumbscrews) not adjusted properly.	Care must be taken in adjusting the fountain key in the area of a solid to make certain that the ink film on the fountain roll is as even as possible.
Ghosting.	Emulsified ink.	Reduce amount of fountain solution used to run job, wash up, change ink.
	Glazed ink rollers.	Glaze formed on rubber ink rollers by poor washups, dried inks, and/or varnishes must be removed by scrubbing with solvent and pumice powder, or having roller manufacturer regrind rolls.
Ink does not dry properly.	Excess amount of fountain solution used in running job.	Keep plate moisture to a minimum.
	Fountain solution is too strong.	Maintain proper pH fountain solution.
	Wrong type drier used in mixing ink.	Contact ink manufacturer.
	Relative humidity in pressroom is too high.	Relative humidity in pressroom should be between 45 and 50%.
Ink "stripping" off rollers.	Excessive fountain solution used and/or pH too low (too acid).	Keep moisture to a minimum and use pH meter to check acidity.

PROBLEM	POSSIBLE CAUSE	REMEDY
Sheets curl in delivery.	Too much fountain solution used to run job.	Reduce amount of fountain solution used.
Blurred or mushy print on first few sheets.	Pressure mechanism not going over toggle.	Reset toggle mechanism and check bearer pressure settings.
Blurred or mushy print on all sheets.	Plate and/or blanket may be under- or overpacked.	Recheck plate and blanket packings.
	Loose blanket.	Tighten.
	Blanket too long and rear blanket bar hitting center support bearing on reel rod.	Make certain blanket size is correct.
Plate image wearing prematurely.	Rollers not set correctly.	Reset rollers.
	Plate and/or blanket packing excessive.	Repack plate and/or blanket.
	Lack of bearer pressure.	Reset bearer pressure.
	Fountain solution too acid.	Check pH of fountain solution.
	Plate not firmly in contact with cylinder.	Retighten plate clamps' tensioning screws.
Image on sheet lighter on one side.	Rollers not set properly.	Reset all rollers.
	Ink fountain not properly set.	Reset ink fountain.
	Blanket cylinder not parallel to plate and/or impression cylinder.	Reset cylinder parallelism and reset bearer pressure.
Length of image around the cylinder does not match previously run color.	Paper has stretched or second plate was not stripped properly. Or, second plate was not packed properly.	If second image is longer than first image, remove some packing from the blanket and install under the plate. Recheck length of second image to the first. If second image is shorter than the first, reverse procedure.

9. Smoking where flammable materials are stored, using unsafe solvents to clean machinery, or allowing working areas that are required to be clean and dry to become contaminated with oil, water, or grease.

10. Bypassing safety devices. Do not deactivate any safety devices. Always inspect signals, fuses, switches, valves, and other safety devices and keep them in good repair.

11. Avoid improper conduct, such as teasing, abusing, or startling fellow workers, playing practical jokes, boxing, wrestling, throwing material, quarreling, shouting, or making any unnecessary noises.

12. Avoid oiling, cleaning, and adjusting equipment while it is in motion. Do not work on electrically charged equipment without cutting the power. Avoid unnecessary handling of materials when they are in the act of being processed by moving machinery.

Unsafe Conditions

1. Lack of guards. This applies to catwalks and platforms where no guards are provided. It

also covers machines where moving parts or other dangerous conditions are not guarded. Presses should not be operated with guards removed.

2. Inadequate guards. Often a hazard that is only partially guarded is more dangerous than one that has no guard at all. A person seeing this guard may have a false sense of security and fail to take precautions that would ordinarily be taken if there were no guards.

3. Hazardous arrangement of machines and auxiliary equipment. This includes improper machine layout, cluttered floors and work areas, and blocked aisles and fire exits. Other dangerous production facilities include unsafely stored tools and materials, overloaded platforms or tables, and inadequate dis-

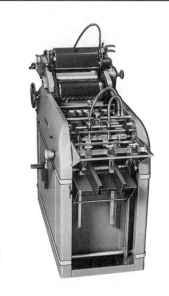

Minimum Sheet Size	3″ x 5″
Maximum Sheet Size	9½″ x 13″
Paper Weights	13 lb. to 110 lb.
Maximum Printing Area	9½″ x 13″
Gripper Margin	5/16″
Plate Size	10″ x 15⅜″
Plate Thickness	.006″
Blanket Size	10″ x 15″
Blanket Thickness	.065″
Speed Range	5,000 to 10,000 IPH
Feeder Capacity	20″
Delivery Capacity	2″
Drive Motor	½ HP
Pump Motor	⅓ HP
Length	60″
Width	27½″
Height	48″
Weight	640 lbs.
Inking Unit	10 Rollers
Dampening Unit	4 Rollers

3M Company

16-62. Addressograph-Multigraph Model 1250 (Multilith).

3M Company

16-61. ATF Chief Model 15.

Minimum Sheet Size	3″ x 5″
Maximum Sheet Size	11″ x 15″
Paper Weights	11 lb. Manifold to 2 ply card
Maximum Printing Area	9¾″ x 13¼″
Gripper Margin	3/16″ to 5/16″
Plate Size	10″ x 15″
Plate Thickness	006″
Blanket Size	10″ x 15 3/16″
Blanket Thickness	065″
Speed Range	4500 to 9000 IPH
Feeder Capacity	21¾″
Delivery Capacity	2⅞″
Drive Motor	⅓ HP
Pump Motor	⅓ HP
Length	61″
Width	28″
Height	50″
Weight	740 lbs.
Inking Unit	10 Rollers
Dampening Unit	4 Rollers

posal facilities for waste products.

4. Improper illumination. This includes excessive light, inadequate light, wrong colored lights, direct or reflected glare, and lighting systems that produce shadows or excessive contrast.

DUPLICATORS

This section covers the operation and maintenance of four brands of offset duplicators. Figs. 16-61 through 16-64. While each press differs somewhat, general information can be given concerning principles of operation. For specific information, refer to operating manuals for the particular press.

The duplicator is a small offset press. It is particularly adapted to short-run and standard-size jobs. It is widely used in offices, in-plant facilities, and small commercial plants. Like larger offset presses, the duplicator functions on the principle that oil and water do not mix. The image area of the plate is sensitive to ink, and nonimage areas repel ink and pick up water.

To produce good, sharp copies with clean backgrounds, the balance of ink and water must be carefully controlled. The correct ink roller and blanket pressures must be maintained.

As the cylinders revolve, the dampening rollers supply moisture to the plate, and the inking rollers supply ink to the plate. And with each revolution, the rubber-covered blanket receives the inked image from the plate.

Since the impression cylinder

3M Company
16-64. A. B. Dick Model 360.

Minimum Sheet Size	3″ x 5″
Maximum Sheet Size	11¾″ x 17″
Paper Weights	12 lb. bond to 110 lb. index stock
Maximum Printing Area	10½″ x 16½″
Gripper Margin	¼″
Plate Size	10¾″ x 18⅝″
Plate Thickness	.006″
Blanket Size	10¾″ x 18″
Blanket Thickness	.065″
Speed Range	4,500 to 9,000 IPH
Feeder Capacity	20″
Delivery Capacity	2″
Drive Motor	⅓ HP
Pump Motor	⅓ HP
Length	45″
Width	28″
Height	52″
Weight	611 lbs.
Inking & Water	12 Rollers

3M Company
16-63. Davidson Dualith 500.

Minimum Sheet Size	3″ x 5″
Maximum Sheet Size	11″ x 15″
Paper Weights	8 lb. Manifold to 6 ply card
Maximum Printing Area	9¾″ x 13″ or 14″
Gripper Margin	⅜″
Plate Size	10″ x 16″
Plate Thickness	.004″ to .006″
Blanket Size	10″ x 16″
Blanket Thickness	.064″
Speed Range	5,000 to 10,000 IPH
Feeder Capacity	24″
Delivery Capacity	3¾″
Drive Motor	¾ HP
Pump Motor	⅓ HP
Length	64″
Width	34″
Height	57″
Weight	710 lbs.
Inking Unit	9 Rollers
Dampening Unit	4 Rollers

rotates against the blanket cylinder, paper fed between them receives the image inked on the blanket.

All modern duplicators have five basic systems: inking, dampening, cylinder, plate, and paper. Fig. 16-65.

INKING SYSTEM

The principal parts of the inking system are identified by number in Fig. 16-66 (Page 396).

The ink fountain uses a series of thumbscrews (called keys) which push against a thin blade to control the amount of ink to the fountain roller. Each thumbscrew allows more or less ink to be carried to a specific area on the plate.

The fountain roller has a ratchet lever on one end to con-

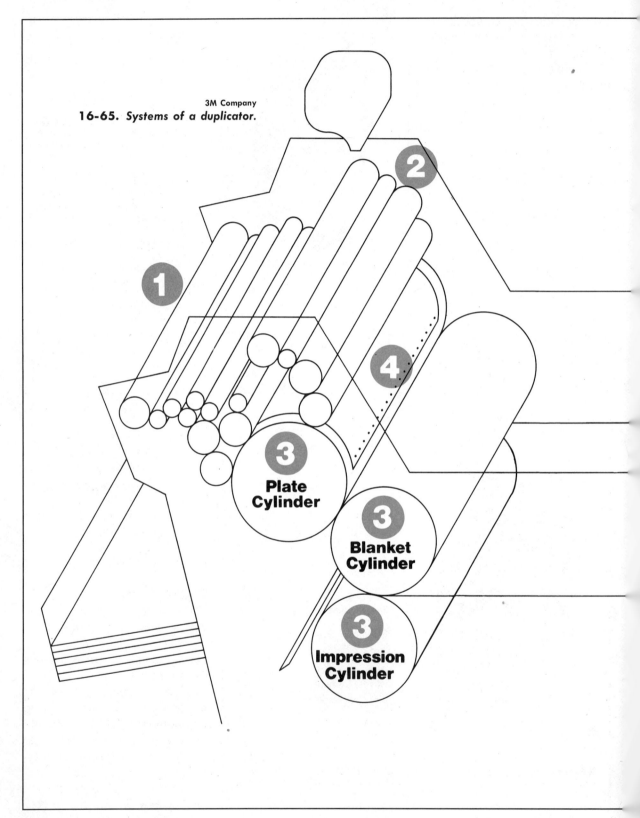

3M Company
16-65. *Systems of a duplicator.*

1 Inking
2 Dampening
3 Cylinder

4 Plate
5 Paper

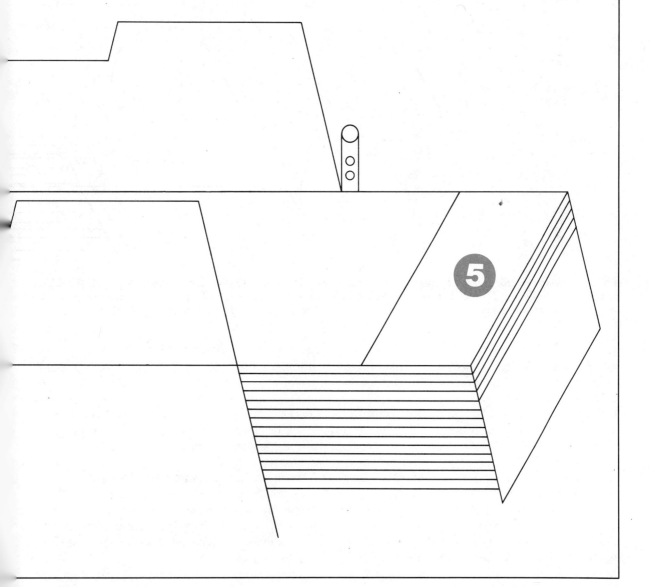

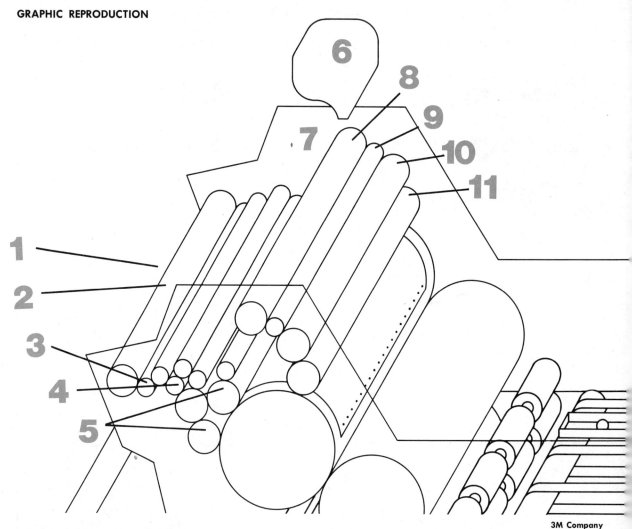

16-66. *Inking and dampening systems: (1) Ink fountain. (2) Fountain roller. (3) Ductor roller. (4) Distributor and vibrator rollers. (5) Ink form rollers. (6) Dampener solution bottle. (7) Dampener fountain pan. (8) Fountain roller. (9) Ductor rollers. (10) Vibrator roller. (11) Dampener form roller.*

trol its speed. When the roller turns faster, it picks up more ink.

The ductor roller rocks back and forth between the fountain roller and the first distributor roller and acts as an additional ink flow control.

A series of distributor, intermediate, and vibrator rollers breaks down the heavy ink into a thin, workable film. The number of these rollers will vary, depending on the duplicator manufacturer.

Ink form rollers transfer a thin film of ink to the plate.

Ink Form Roller Checks

To assure proper ink laydown and prevent plate wear, check the ink form roller pressure on the plate cylinder. Determine the correct setting by an *ink band check*. To do this, ink up the press. Gently drop the ink form rollers to the plate cylinders; then lift them. Turn the handwheel to bring the plate around

for inspection. If there are uniform parallel bands of ink exactly 1/8″ wide, the rollers are correctly set. Irregular bands indicate either uneven settings or worn rollers. Fig. 16-67.

DAMPENING SYSTEM

The dampening system is shown in Fig. 16-66.

The fountain solution is supplied by the dampener solution bottle.

The dampener fountain pan

IDEAL SETTING
Uniform parallel band exactly ⅛″ wide.

ROLLER WORN AT ENDS
Caused by form roller being set too tightly to oscillator roller. Correct by resetting rollers, replacing them if no longer possible to obtain desired setting.

LOW AREA IN CENTER
Indicates improper grinding or improper manufacture. Replace.

ROLLER SWOLLEN AT ENDS
Results from continuously setting roller too tightly. Replace.

SETTING UNEVEN
Too heavy on one end; too light on the other end. Reset rollers.

3M Company
16-67. Ink form roller checks.

holds the fountain solution and delivers it to the fountain roller.

The fountain roller transfers the fountain solution from the pan to the ductor roller.

The ductor roller meters water to the vibrator roller.

The vibrator roller assures an even flow of water to the dampener form roller.

The dampener form roller transfers moisture to the plate.

Dampener Form Roller Checks

Dampening roller pressure to the plate cylinder should be checked. Insert two paper strips one at each edge of the dampening roller between the dampening roller and the plate cylinder. Apply pressure to slowly remove each strip. If the pressure is correct, a uniform, firm pull on both

strips is felt. Fig. 16-68. If it is unequal, too heavy, or too light, follow the procedure in the section on common duplicator adjustments.

CYLINDER SYSTEM

All offset duplicators have three main cylinders: the plate, blanket, and impression cylin-

der. The exception is the Davidson, which has a two-cylinder design combining plate and impression on one oversize cylinder. Fig. 16-69.

Plate-to-Blanket Cylinder Pressure Check

This check is usually performed after the ink form roller

3M Company
16-68. Dampener form roller checks.

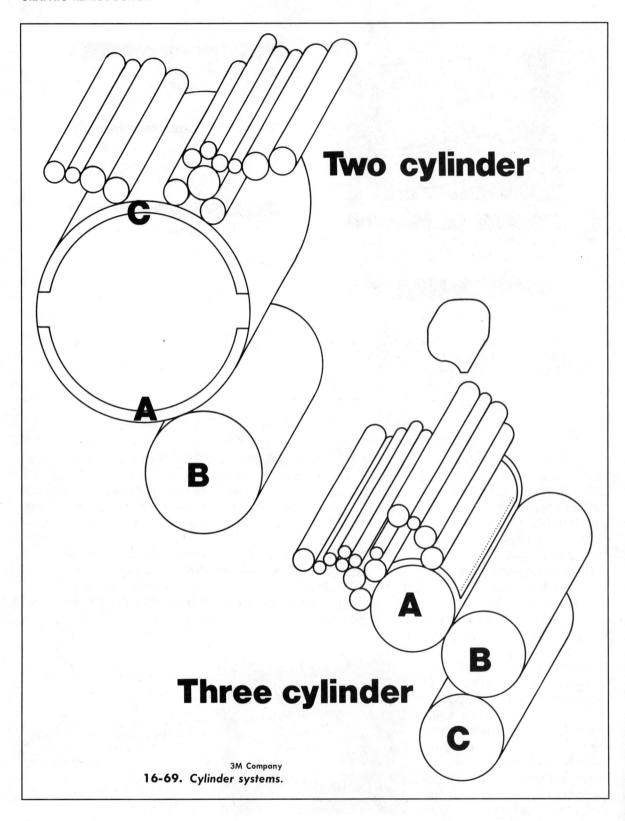

Two cylinder

Three cylinder

3M Company
16-69. Cylinder systems.

checks. The dampener form rollers must be in the "off" position. The ink form rollers must be in the "on" position.

Start the duplicator and ink up the entire plate, including the nonimage area.

Now, stop the duplicator and gently lower the plate cylinder to the blanket cylinder and immediately raise it to inspect the ink band. (The blanket cylinder will have to be rotated into view by turning the handwheel.)

There should be a parallel ink band 1/4" wide across the blanket. If it is irregular, see the section on duplicator adjustments.

Blanket-to-Impression Pressure Check

Set the impression cylinder pressure at the lowest setting. Clean the plate and blanket cylinder. Start the duplicator and feed a sheet through. Adjust the pressure up to obtain the sharpest copy.

PAPER SYSTEM

Paper passes through the duplicator as indicated by the numbers identified in Fig. 16-70. Paper is stacked on the feed platform (1) which raises automatically (2) to the correct height for feeding. The air blowers (3) separate the top sheets for feeding. The suction hose (4) lifts the lead edge of the paper, inserting it into the pull-out rollers (5). The paper is moved on to the feed table where a double sheet eliminator (6) prevents more than one sheet from going through at the same time. Tapes (7) and straps (8) carry paper to stop fingers (9) that time the sheet for the gripper. Feed rollers (10) move the

sheet to gripper fingers on the impression cylinder. The plate cylinder (11) transfers the image to the blanket cylinder and to the paper (12). Ejector wheels (13) carry paper from the impression cylinder across the stripper fingers (14) and the ejector roll (15) to the jogger (16).

HOW TO RUN THE DUPLICATOR

Although operating adjustments and parts differ from one duplicator to the next, all of them have the same basic operating principles. To become completely familiar with all the controls and adjustments on a machine, read its instruction book. To run a duplicator:

1. Put ink in the fountain.
2. Replace the dampener rollers (if removed the night before).
3. Fill the water fountain bottle and replace.
4. Mount a test plate for pressure checks. (Next, if running a Davidson duplicator, check dampener form roller to vibrator pressure).
5. Check the dampener form roller-to-plate pressure.
6. Turn on the machine.
7. Ink up the rollers (but not plate).
8. Turn the machine off. (Next, if running a Davidson duplicator, check ink form roller to vibrator pressure).
9. Check the ink form roller-to-plate pressure.
10. Turn on the machine and ink up the plate completely.
11. Check the plate-to-blanket pressure.
12. Remove the test plate and wash down the blanket.

13. Load the paper and mount the plate for a production run.

The duplicator operator should check the copy frequently while a job is running.

Experienced operators use the ink and water ratchet levers to get proper ink and water balance. The ratchet lever controls the speed of the fountain rollers, which is the best way to regulate ink-water balance.

The ink and water fountain hand knobs should be used only to add larger amounts of ink and water to the system quickly. Too much reliance on hand knobs is one reason many operators must constantly add or cut back ink and water.

Keep in mind that the amount of ink delivered to the image governs the amount of water needed to keep the plate clean in the nonprinting area.

A common mistake is to add ink in an attempt to achieve a darker color than the ink film can give. The remedy here is to use a darker shade of ink.

Another mistake is having excessive pressure between the plate and the ink and dampener rollers. Light pressure is one of the first requirements for good ink-water balance.

PRINTING PROBLEMS

There are many things to consider when a job does not print properly. Some common problems, with solutions, are shown in Figs. 16-71 through 16-86.

Fig. 16-71 (Page 402)—a good print: crisp, dark lines and solids; a clean background; clean halftones, screens, and reverses; good registration. Each sheet is dried completely.

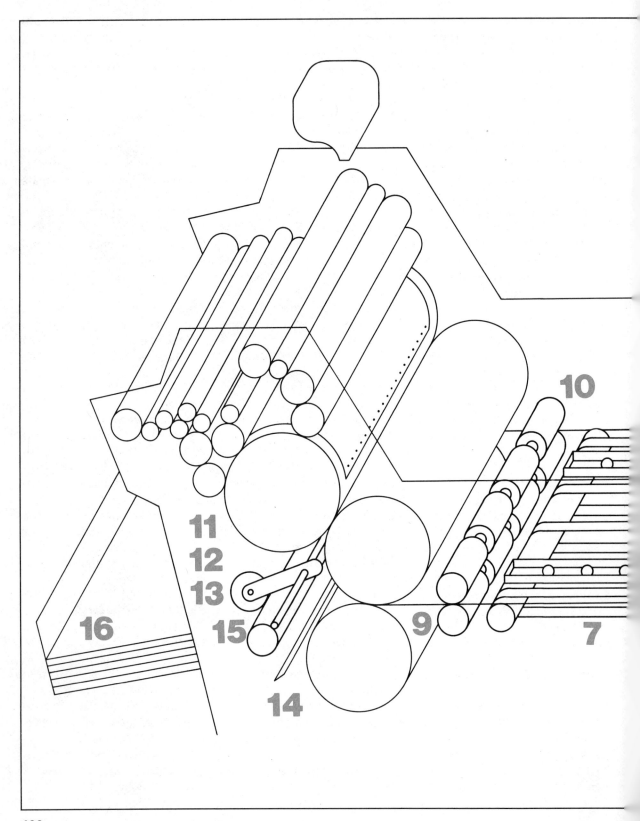

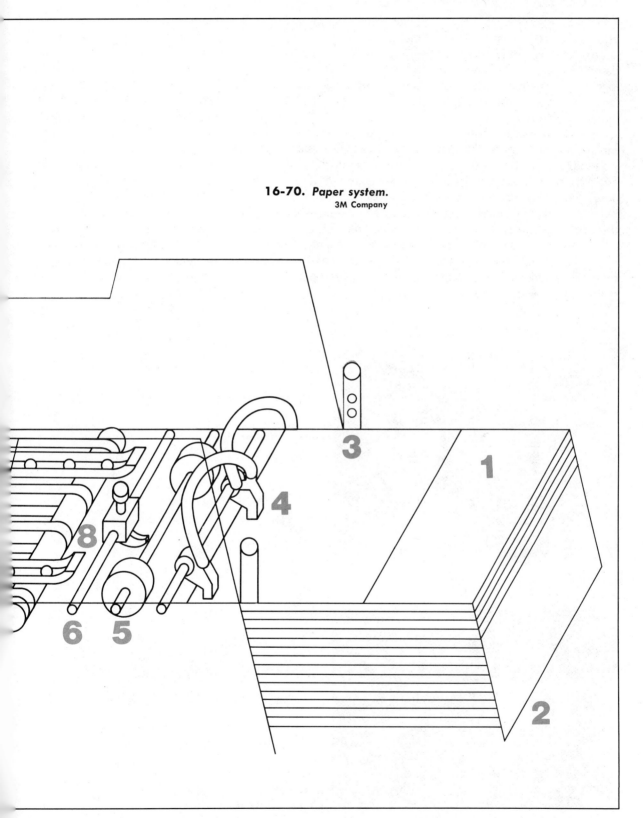

16-70. *Paper system.*
3M Company

Fig. 16-72—a gray print: not enough ink, too much moisture, wrong color of ink, incorrect dampener form roller pressure, incorrect plate-to-blanket pressure, incorrect impression-to-blanket pressure.

Fig. 16-73—a dark print: too much ink, too much impression-to-blanket pressure, not enough plate-to-blanket pressure, too many revolutions on blanket without paper going through (build up on blanket).

Fig. 16-74—a double image: loose blanket, too much ink and fountain solution, not enough plate-to-blanket pressure, loose plate, incorrect impression-to-blanket pressure.

Fig. 16-75—scumming: too much ink, not enough moisture, dirty dampener roll covers, dampener covers tied too tightly on ends.

Fig. 16-76—a gray and dirty print: glazed ink rollers, glazed blanket, too much ink form roller pressure, too much dampener form roller pressure.

Fig. 16-77—an uneven print: incorrect ink distribution, glazed rollers, incorrect dampener form roller parallel pressure, incorrect plate-to-blanket parallel pressure, incorrect impression-to-blanket parallel pressure, dirty impression cylinder.

Fig. 16-78—printing weak: incorrect plate-to-blanket pressure, incorrect impression-to-blanket pressure, low spots in blanket, tacky ink, tacky blanket, dirty impression cylinder, "blind" image on plate caused by dried gum or too strong fountain solution.

Fig. 16-79—image breakdown: too much dampener form roller pressure, too much ink form roller pressure, too much plate-to-blanket pressure, fountain solution too strong, end play in form rollers.

Fig. 16-80—misregister: loose blanket, side guides not set properly, paper not cut straight, cam band not set.

3M Company
16-71. A good print.

16-72. Gray, washed-out print.
3M Company

3M Company
16-73. Copy too dark.

402

3M Company

16-74. *Double image (blurred copy).*

3M Company

16-77. *Uneven printing.*

3M Company

16-75. *Background dirty—scumming.*

3M Company

16-78. *Weak spots (spotty copy).*

3M Company

16-76. *Gray, washed-out plus dirty background.*

3M Company

16-79. *Image breaks down while plate is running.*

3M Company

16-80. *Improper register.*

3M Company

16-83. *Streaking.*

3M Company

16-81. *Paper curling in receiver.*

3M Company

16-84. *No image at all.*

3M Company

16-82. *Paper missing grippers.*

3M Company

16-85. *Paper nicking on edge.*

16-86. *Paper wrinkling.*
3M Company

Fig. 16-81—paper curl: too much moisture, curl in paper.

Fig. 16-82—paper missing the grippers: stop fingers incorrectly set, feed rollers out of adjustment.

Fig. 16-83—streaking: incorrect ink form roller pressure, incorrect dampener form roller pressure, incorrect plate-to-blanket pressure, incorrect impression-to-blanket pressure, improper ink, loose blanket.

Fig. 16-84—no image: not enough ink roller form pressure, not enough plate-to-blanket pressure, not enough impression-to-blanket pressure, too much moisture, glazed blanket, glazed ink rollers.

Fig. 16-85—nicked paper: paper stop fingers too high, feed rollers not set properly, paper hitting back stop in receiver too hard.

Fig. 16-86—wrinkled paper: too much moisture, paper damp, too much pressure between blanket and impression cylinder, register board not set properly.

COMMON DUPLICATOR ADJUSTMENTS

Dampener Rollers to Plate Cylinder

It is important to have equal pressure at all points between the dampening roller and the plate cylinder. After mounting a plate on the cylinder, place two 1″ wide strips of paper (or two 0.005″ 3M dampening gauges) between the roller and plate. With the roller in the "on" position, slowly pull on the strips. You should feel a uniform, firm pull on both strips. An unequal pull on the paper strips means the roller is not parallel with the plate cylinder. If the pull is too heavy, or if the strips pull too easily, overall pressure between the roller and plate cylinder must be adjusted.

To adjust the ATF Chief 15, Fig. 16-87:

1. Loosen locking nut (a).

2. Turn the dampener form roller adjusting screw (b) clockwise if the test strip is too tight or counterclockwise if too loose.

3. Tighten the locking nut (a) and repeat the paper test to be sure that the proper amount of adjustment has been made.

To adjust the Addressograph-Multilith 1250, Fig. 16-88:

1. Loosen setscrew (a) in the form roller knob.

2. With a screwdriver turn eccentric shaft (b) counterclockwise until a fairly strong pull can be felt as the strips are withdrawn.

3. Tighten setscrew (a) to lock the adjustment.

3M Company

16-87. *Adjusting dampener rollers to plate cylinder on the ATF Chief 15.*

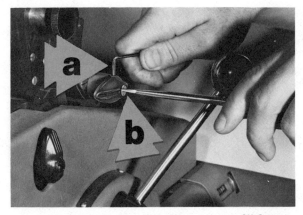

3M Company

16-88. *Adjusting dampener rollers to plate cylinder on the Addressograph-Multilith 1250.*

3M Company

16-91. *Adjusting ink form rollers to plate cylinder on the ATF Chief 15.*

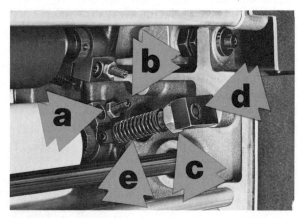

3M Company

16-89. *Adjusting dampener rollers to plate cylinder on the Davidson Dualith 500.*

3M Company

16-92. *Adjusting ink form rollers to plate cylinder on the Addressograph-Multilith 1250.*

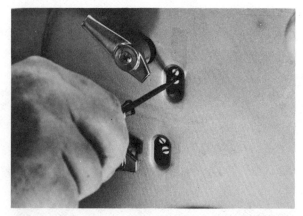

3M Company

16-90. *Adjusting dampener rollers to plate cylinder on the A. B. Dick 360.*

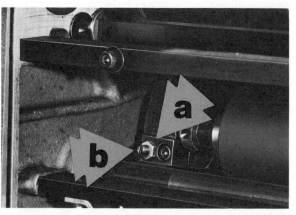

3M Company

16-93. *Adjusting ink form rollers to plate cylinder on the Davidson Dualith 500.*

To adjust the Davidson Dualith 500, Fig. 16-89:

1. Loosen locknuts (a) and turn screws (b) counterclockwise until the bottoms of the screws (b) do not touch the round metal banking stud directly under the dampening form roll brackets.

2. Loosen locknuts (c) and turn the adjusting screws (d) until the springs (e) exert an even pressure slightly more than is normally needed for running.

3. Tighten locknuts (c).

To adjust the A. B. Dick 360, Fig. 16-90:

1. The dampening roller does not contact the master cylinder, but there should be a 1/64" gap between the aquamatic oscillator and the aquamatic ductor roller. After turning the handwheel until the ductor operating levers have travelled as far as they can toward the oscillator roller, adjust the eccentric screws so there is a 1/64" gap across the entire length. This adjustment must be rechecked and adjusted whenever ink form roller pressure adjustments are made.

Ink Form Rollers to Plate Cylinder

It is important to have machines properly adjusted. When performing the ink form roller check, uniform parallel bands of ink should be seen. Irregular bands indicate either uneven settings or worn rollers.

To adjust the ink form rollers to the plate cylinders on the ATF Chief 15, Fig. 16-91:

1. Loosen ink form roller lock

screw (a) on the side requiring adjustment.

2. Then turn the ink form roller adjusting screw (b) clockwise to decrease the width of the stripe or counterclockwise to increase the width of the stripe.

3. Tighten lock screw.

To adjust the ink form rollers to the plate cylinders on the Addressograph-Multilith 1250, Fig. 16-92:

1. Loosen setscrew (a) in the form roller knob.

2. With a screwdriver, turn eccentric shaft (b) counterclockwise to increase width of bead or clockwise to decrease width of bead.

3. Tighten setscrew (a) to lock the adjustment.

To adjust the ink form rollers to the plate cylinders on the Davidson Dualith 500, Fig. 16-93:

1. Loosen locknuts (a) in the form roll brackets.

2. Turn the adjusting screw (b) clockwise to decrease pressure and counterclockwise to increase the pressure.

3. Tighten the locknuts (a) and recheck the pressure until both form roll marks are exactly 1/8" wide.

To adjust the ink form rollers

to the plate cylinders on the A. B. Dick 360, Fig. 16-94:

1. Loosen lock screws (a) both sides and adjust screws (b) as necessary.

2. Turn screw (b) on operator side of machine in clockwise direction.

3. Turn screw (b) on the non-operator side of the machine in a counterclockwise direction to increase width of bead line.

4. Tighten lock screws.

Plate Cylinder to Blanket Cylinder

After the ink band checks and adjustments are completed, the duplicator is turned on and the rest of the plate is inked up. To make a plate-to-blanket check, the entire plate must be covered, not just the image area. This is done by not dropping the dampener rollers. Turn the duplicator off, and then gently lower the plate cylinder to the blanket and raise it immediately. Rotate the blanket cylinder by the handwheel and inspect the ink band. Again, it should be a uniform parallel band.

To adjust the plate-to-blanket cylinder on the ATF Chief 15, Fig. 16-95:

3M Company

16-94. Adjusting ink form rollers to plate cylinder on the A. B. Dick 360.

1. Loosen the locking screw (a).

2. Turn the plate-to-blanket impression adjusting screw (b) clockwise to increase the width of the stripe or counterclockwise to decrease.

3. Retighten locking screw (a).

To adjust the plate-to-blanket cylinder on the Addressograph-Multilith 1250, Fig. 16-96:

1. Loosen lock bolt (a).

2. Move single lever control (b) to left to increase pressure; move lever to right to decrease pressure.

3. Tighten lock bolt (a).

To adjust the plate-to-blanket cylinder on the Davidson Dualith 500, Fig. 16-97:

1. Loosen the two allen screws (a) in the blanket latch.

2. Loosen the locknut (b) and turn the hex-headed screw (c) clockwise to increase pressure and counterclockwise to decrease pressure.

3. Tighten the locknut (b) and the two allen screws (a), and recheck for correct pressure.

The plate-to-blanket cylinder adjustment on the A. B. Dick 360, Fig. 16-98, should be made

by the company's service representative.

Blanket Cylinder to Impression Cylinder

Improper pressure adjustments may result in poor quality copy. If a heavier than normal stock is run, it will be necessary to readjust the blanket cylinder-to-impression cylinder adjustments. Improper blanket cylinder-to-impression cylinder pressure adjustments may result in smashed blankets and poor quality copy.

To adjust the blanket cylinder to the impression cylinder on the ATF Chief 15, Fig. 16-99:

1. Loosen locking screw (a).

2. Turn the impression adjusting screw (b) toward you until the print obtained is very light.

3. Turn the adjusting screw (b) back, away from you, until the desired impression on the paper is obtained.

4. Retighten the locking screw (a).

To adjust the blanket cylinder to the impression cylinder on the Addressograph-Multilith 1250, Fig. 16-100:

1. Loosen clamp screw (a).

2. Turn micrometer adjusting screw (b) clockwise to decrease pressure and counterclockwise to increase pressure.

3. Tighten clamp screw.

To adjust the blanket cylinder to the impression cylinder on the Davidson Dualith 500, Fig. 16-101:

1. Underpack the impression segment with packing sheets under the metal drawsheet. Refer to owner's manual for specifics.

To adjust the blanket cylinder to the impression cylinder on the A. B. Dick 360, Fig. 16-102:

1. Insert allen wrench into the control dial opening.

2. Turn the dial to the lower numbers to increase pressure and to the higher numbers to decrease pressure.

WEB OFFSET PRESSES

The web-fed offset presses are designed primarily for commercial and job work, for publication work, or for business forms work. The commercial webs have drying systems made for coated paper and fast-drying ink. Publication (newspaper and similar)

3M Company

16-95. Adjusting plate cylinder to blanket cylinder on the ATF Chief 15.

3M Company

16-96. Adjusting plate cylinder to blanket cylinder on the Addressograph-Multilith 1250.

3M Company

16-97. *Adjusting plate cylinder to blanket cylinder on the Davidson Dualith 500.*

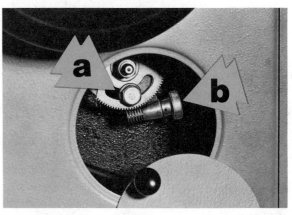

3M Company

16-100. *Adjusting blanket cylinder to impression cylinder on the Addressograph-Multilith 1250.*

3M Company

16-98. *Adjusting plate cylinder to blanket cylinder on the A. B. Dick 360.*

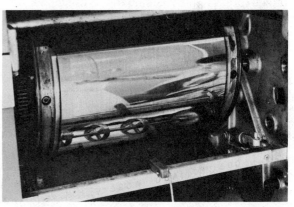

3M Company

16-101. *Adjusting blanket cylinder to impression cylinder on the Davidson Dualith 500.*

3M Company

16-99. *Adjusting blanket cylinder to impression cylinder on the ATF Chief 15.*

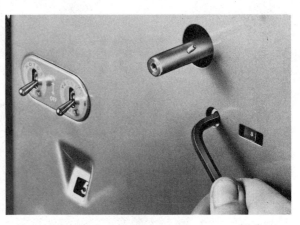

3M Company

16-102. *Adjusting blanket cylinder to impression cylinder on the A. B. Dick 360.*

presses rely on the absorption of the ink for drying. Form presses are specialized webs and may have letterpress units as well as offset units.

It is beyond the scope of this text to explain the operation of the various web offset presses, even all the presses of similar operation in any category. Small publication presses, however, are numerous. One of the popular small web presses, the Harris V-15A, is discussed in this chapter. Fig. 16-103.

The Harris V-15A is a web-fed, blanket-to-blanket, lithographic offset press which simultaneously and continuously prints

both sides of the web (perfecting press). Its folder gathers, folds, cuts, and counts the printed products and delivers them on a conveyor belt. A V-15A press with the 24-page, JF-7 folder can combine from one to six printing units, depending upon required printing capacity. These units are normally installed in line. Each unit prints either a standard four-page newspaper or an eight-page tabloid at speeds up to 15,000 impressions per hour. Fig. 16-104.

When multicolor printing is desired, two or more printing units operate to print successive impressions on a web. Adjust-

ments are provided to assure proper register between the press units.

Printed webs from all printing units move horizontally to a jaw folder. This unit gathers, center-folds, and cuts the webs. It then half-folds (quarter-folds with quarter-folder engaged) to deliver finished copies. A conveyor transports these copies from the folder.

PRINTING UNIT

Printing is done when the web is fed between the blanket cylinders, which simultaneously print both sides of the web. The ink and water fountains and their associated rollers are housed in the printing unit. One printing unit is capable of printing four pages of standard, one-color print. Each additional printing unit will expand the capability of the press either to print an additional color or to add four pages of one-color printing capacity as desired. Each printing unit is supplied with its own control panel. Provision is made on the work side of the unit for adjusting each plate cylinder for *side lay* (side guide). This insures correct back-to-back alignment of the printed material. Two adjustable compensator rollers are located on the folder side of the unit where the web exits from the printing unit. The compensator provides for circumferential color image adjustment and for correct cutting of the web at the folder. Detailed descriptions of

Harris-Intertype Corp.
16-103. *Harris V-15A web press.*

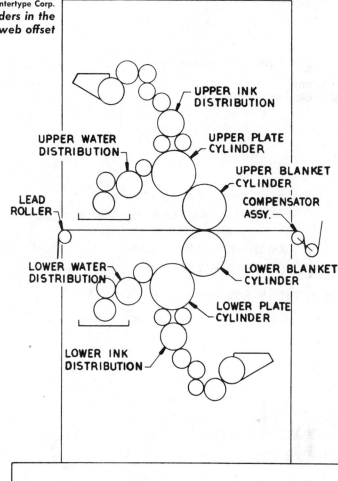

Harris-Intertype Corp.

16-104. *Location of rollers and cylinders in the Harris blanket-to-blanket, perfecting, web offset press.*

the rollers in the printing unit, the ink and water distributors, and the compensator are given in the paragraphs that follow.

Each printing unit contains upper and lower plate and blanket cylinders. Fig. 16-104. The plate cylinders allow for quick plate changes. One-, two-, or four-page (tabloid) plates are locked into position by means of a quick set and release plate lockup. The rubber-faced blanket cylinders transfer plate images from the printing plates to the web. One blanket cylinder acts as an impression cylinder to the other.

INK SYSTEM

Each printing unit has an upper and lower ink fountain. Fig. 16-105. These ink fountains are adjustable through a series of 25 fountain keys which allow the press operator to control ink flow across the plate. Each ink fountain roller is driven by a separate gear motor to provide close control of inking. The inking system consists of one ink fountain roller which rides in the ink fountain, one transfer roller which conveys ink from the fountain roller to the rest of the system, three distributor rollers, one vibrator roller, and two form rollers.

WATER SYSTEM

Each printing unit also has an upper and lower water system. Fig. 16-105. This system applies the proper amount of dampener solution to the nonimage areas of the plate suface. The dampener solution repels ink, thus enabling the nonimage areas to run clear. The water fountain roller, which is driven by a motor, collects dampener solution on its surface as it rotates. As it turns, the fountain roller carries the solution to the cloth-covered transfer roller, which is driven by the vibrator roller. The solution then is transferred from the vibrator to the water form roller, which in turn applies it to the plate. The water system is designed so that there is continuous circulation of the filtered solution.

FOLDER

As stated before, the folder is capable of producing either a standard, tabloid, or quarter-folded product. The folder and quarter-folder are engaged and disengaged by separate clutches on the lower folder assembly. One clutch is for the folder as-

411

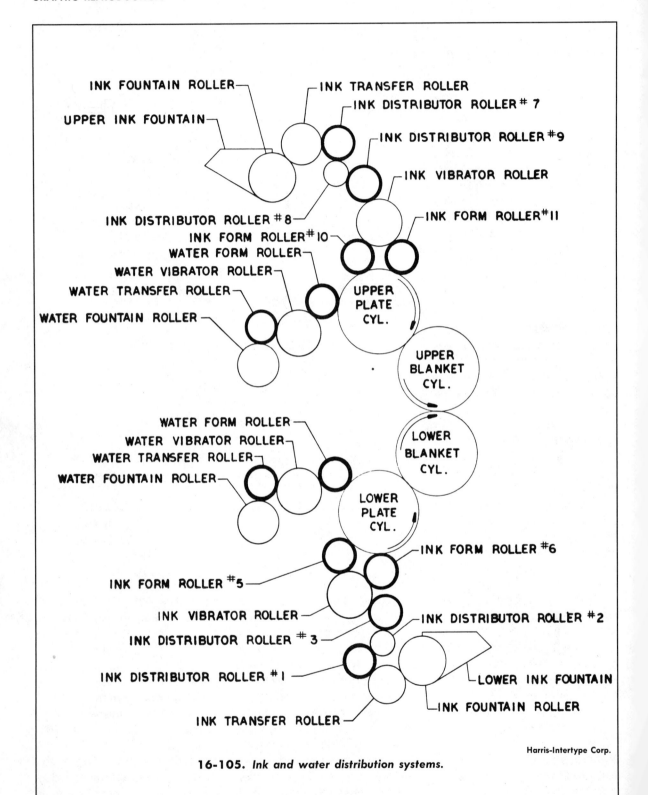

16-105. *Ink and water distribution systems.*

Harris-Intertype Corp.

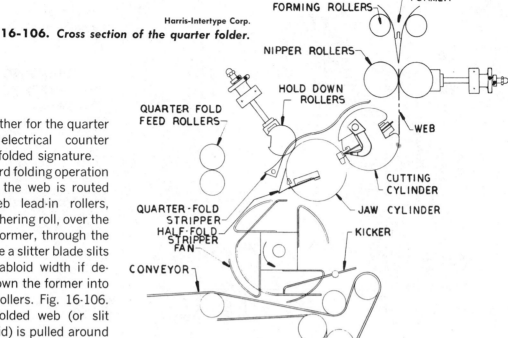

Harris-Intertype Corp.

16-106. *Cross section of the quarter folder.*

FORMER

FORMING ROLLERS

NIPPER ROLLERS

HOLD DOWN ROLLERS

QUARTER FOLD FEED ROLLERS

WEB

CUTTING CYLINDER

JAW CYLINDER

QUARTER-FOLD STRIPPER
HALF-FOLD STRIPPER
FAN

KICKER

CONVEYOR

sembly, the other for the quarter folder. An electrical counter counts each folded signature.

The standard folding operation begins when the web is routed over the web lead-in rollers, under the gathering roll, over the roller top of former, through the trolleys (where a slitter blade slits the web to tabloid width if desired), and down the former into the nipping rollers. Fig. 16-106. The former-folded web (or slit web for tabloid) is pulled around the cutting cylinder by six pins spaced across the width of the cutting cylinder. These pins are projected from the cylinder by a cam mechanism to pierce the web and keep the sheets correctly positioned until they pass through the cutting mechanism. The tucker blade on the cutting cylinder tucks the web into the jaw blades of the jaw cylinder, and the cutting knife cuts the former-folded web at the proper point. The jaw cylinder takes the cut and folded signature from the cutting cylinder and carries it around and through the hold-down roller and either into the fan, which lays it down on the conveyor assembly, or to the quarter-folder table.

MAKEREADY PROCEDURE
PREPARATION FOR THE MAKEREADY

Check the webs through the press and the folder to see that the impositions are correct and that color is on the pages where it is required. Check the new press plates to verify the page imposition. Determine where each plate is to be mounted on the machine, and mark it for identification.

If the last job that was run is very similar to the new job coming up, it is possible that many of the settings on the press can be left as they are. A checklist of the things to be done should be filled out so that each member of the press crew is aware of the items to be checked for this makeready. From this it is possible to make assignments. The list will also be useful in checking to see that every step or assignment in the makeready process has received the required attention.

Before the press can be operated, the paper roll must be installed on the roll stand, the press must be *webbed,* and the tension and side lay of the web must be properly adjusted. Fig. 16-107.

WEB SIDE-LAY ADJUSTMENT

Side lay of the web, Fig. 16-108, should be adjusted whenever a new paper roll is installed.

a. With the press running at a slow speed, the head press operator should observe the web as it passes over the former or visually inspect finished folded products.

b. The operator signals the person at the roll stands as to which web to adjust and in which direction.

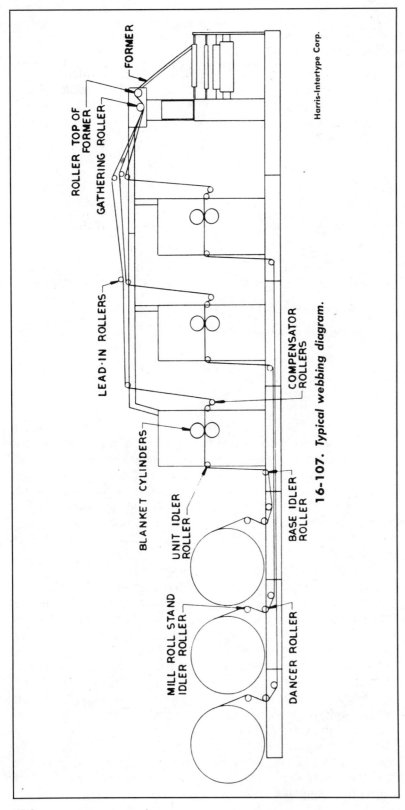

16-107. Typical webbing diagram.

FORMER

ROLLER TOP OF FORMER

GATHERING ROLLER

LEAD-IN ROLLERS

COMPENSATOR ROLLERS

BLANKET CYLINDERS

UNIT IDLER ROLLER

BASE IDLER ROLLER

MILL ROLL STAND IDLER ROLLER

DANCER ROLLER

Harris-Intertype Corp.

c. The head press operator should then make a second observation and verify the new setting.

PRINTING UNIT PREPARATION

Preparation of the printing unit consists of preparing the ink and water fountains, the ink and water rollers, and installing the plates and blankets.

INK FOUNTAIN

Fill the ink fountain with the quantity of ink needed for the run. Be sure the ink is spread evenly across the width of the ink fountain. (If the fountain has ink in it from a previous run, be sure to stir its contents before starting up.) After the fountain has been filled and the fountain keys preset, the rollers are inked up as follows:

1. Run press at a slow speed with folder disengaged. The blanket cylinder throw-offs should be in the "off" position. The ink and water form throw-offs should also be in the "off" position.

2. Turn each ink fountain motor switch to the "on" position and set the speed-control knob at a low setting.

3. Turn the ink switch located on the master control panel to the "on" position.

4. Allow motors to run until the rollers have picked up a thin film of ink.

The quantity of ink carried by the ink fountain roller is determined by the clearance between the fountain roller and the ink fountain blade. Fig. 16-109. This clearance is regulated by a series of thumbscrews on each ink fountain. The clearance between

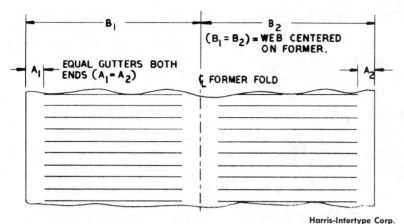

16-108. *Side-lay adjustment for printing a full web.*

Harris-Intertype Corp.

the ink fountain roller and the ink fountain blade is factory set at 0.002″ nominal. However, each run will require adjustment of this clearance because of differences in plate image areas. If one side of a plate contains a larger image area than the other, it will require more ink. This requirement of more ink can be met by increasing the space between the fountain blade and roller by adjusting the thumbscrews.

The fountain blade setting is adjusted by the following procedure when the press is running:

1. Visually examine a printed copy. Take note of areas where too much or too little ink appears.

2. Once these areas have been recognized, determine which unit they are being printed on and their position on the plate cylinder.

3. Then go to the appropriate ink fountain (upper or lower), and make the necessary thumbscrew adjustments. Turning the thumbscrews to the right (clockwise) decreases the amount of ink, and turning them to the left (counterclockwise) increases the ink flow to the ink transfer roller.

DAMPENING SUPPLY PREPARATION

Preparation of the dampening system includes preparing the dampener fountain solution and moistening the dampener rollers. The operator must obtain the correct ink-water balance to provide the desired image. The proper amount of moisture is the least amount possible to keep the nonimage areas clean. Running too much moisture will cause undue emulsification of the ink, which results in a frayed, washed-out copy.

Following are steps to prepare the dampening system:

a. Fill the tank located on the gear side of the unit with dampening solution. Prepare the solution following the directions given by the manufacturer of the chemicals which are added to the water. (Each tank provides water to two printing units. With one unit not in operation, the flow of water to the pan may be shut off. A valve provided on the line which supplies water to the pan is provided for this purpose.)

b. Turn each water fountain

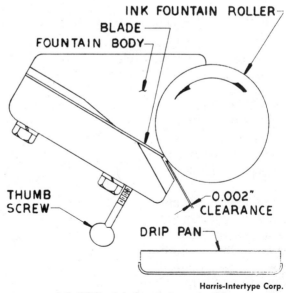

Harris-Intertype Corp.

16-109. *Ink fountain assembly.*

415

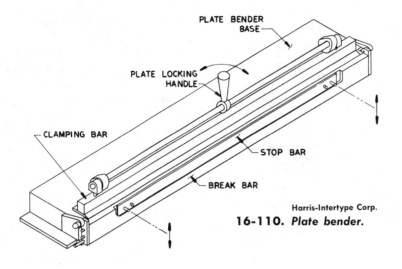

PLATE BENDER BASE

PLATE LOCKING HANDLE

CLAMPING BAR

STOP BAR

BREAK BAR

Harris-Intertype Corp.
16-110. *Plate bender.*

motor switch to the "on" position, and set the speed-control knob at a low setting.

c. Turn the water switch located on the master control panel to the "on" position.

d. Start the press. Run at slow speed with blanket cylinder (impression), ink, and water form roller throw-offs in the "off" position.

e. Allow the dampener rollers to run until they have picked up enough moisture to feel moist against the back of the hand.

PREPARING NEW PRESS PLATES FOR MOUNTING

If the edges of the plate are burred, remove the burrs with a file to prevent damage to form rollers, dampeners, and blankets. Careless handling of press plates can cause kinks and ruin the plate. Keep the plate dry. Don't remove the protective sheet of paper, if supplied.

Plates are received from the plate room after being exposed,

developed, and gummed. The plate-bending fixture, Fig. 16-110, is used to accurately make the leading- and trailing-edge bends. Fig. 16-111.

The steps to bend plates are as follows:

1. Make sure the plate bender's work surface is clean and dry.

2. Using the plate-locking handle, raise clamping bar.

3. Raise the stop bar until it locks in the "up" position.

4. Take the developed plate, placing it etched side down,

leading edge (bottom of page) first. Place it into the bender under the clamping bar until it locates against the stop bar.

5. Lock plate into position using the plate-locking handle, and lower the stop bar.

6. Swing break bar around, thus putting first bend on plate.

7. Release plate, and repeat above procedure for opposite edge of plate (top of page). Swing the break bar up enough to bend the plate so that the lip is vertical or the bend angle is approximately 116 degrees.

8. Raise stop bar and release plate.

9. Slide plate forward until second bend locates against the stop bar. Lock plate into position, and lower stop bar.

10. Swing break bar around, bending plate approximately at a 32-degree angle.

11. Unlock and carefully remove plate from bender. Plate is now ready for installation on printing unit. Handle plates carefully to prevent damage to the bends.

MOUNTING THE PRESS PLATES

The following steps are used to mount plates:

1. Place mode selector

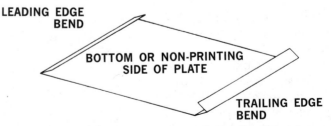

LEADING EDGE BEND

BOTTOM OR NON-PRINTING SIDE OF PLATE

TRAILING EDGE BEND

Harris-Intertype Corp.
16-111. *Leading-edge bend and trailing-edge bend of plate.*

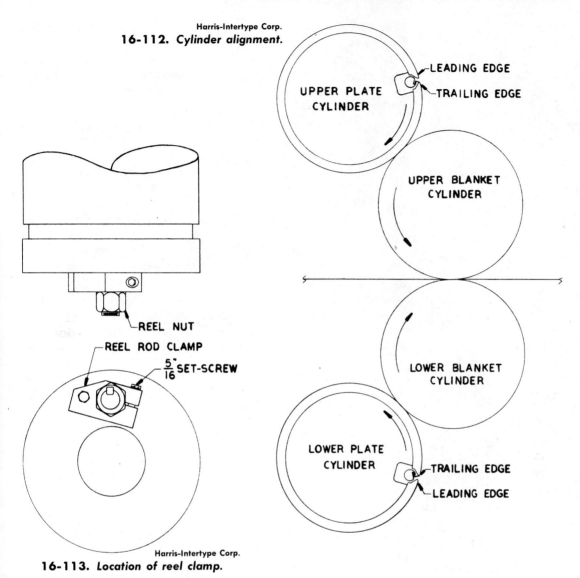

Harris-Intertype Corp.
16-112. *Cylinder alignment.*

Harris-Intertype Corp.
16-113. *Location of reel clamp.*

switch to "jog." Inch press over until the plate cylinder gap is directly in front of you. Fig. 16-112.

2. Put a 1 1/4" wrench on the reel rod extension. Fig. 16-113. Turn until the reel rod slot is centered in the plate cylinder gap. Put cylinder impression "on."

3. Inch the press until the plate cylinder gap is about 2" from the blanket cylinder. Put "safe" on.

4. Insert the leading edge of the plate into the plate-cylinder gap. Fig. 16-114. Hook bent leading-edge lip of the plate cylinder. On the top plate cylinder, the lip is on top, and the plate is

pressed up to seat it firmly. On the bottom plate cylinder, the press plate is pressed down to seat it over the lip. Be sure to center plate.

5. Continue to hold and slightly pull the tail end of the plate. Inch the press slowly for one complete revolution. When the plate-cylinder gap is again exposed directly in front of you, stop press and put "safe" back on.

6. Insert the bent tail end of

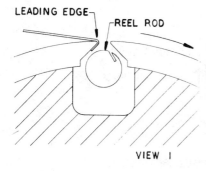

LEADING EDGE

REEL ROD

VIEW 1

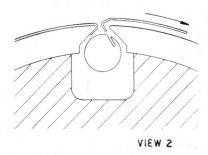

VIEW 2

the plate into the reel rod slot. Fig. 16-114. Two persons work together to press and hold the tail-end plate bend firmly into the reel rod slot. The person on the operator side of the press applies a 1 1/4" wrench to the reel rod extension and slightly tightens the plate.

7. Check to see that the ends of the plate align and seat properly in the groove.

8. Tighten the reel rod. Fig. 16-114.

9. Using a 5/16" allen "T" wrench, tighten the setscrews on the reel rod clamp, both work and gear sides.

10. Revolve the plate cylinders several revolutions with the impression "on." Recheck and

tighten the plate further if necessary.

MOUNTING THE BLANKET AND PACKING

The steps to make ready the blanket and packing are:

1. Make sure that the blanket cylinder is clean and dry.

2. Select packing sheet (s) of the proper thickness. The size of packing is 36" wide by 22 1/2" long. It may be cut on the cylinder if necessary. Fig. 16-115.

3. Apply a bead of glue to the leading edge of the cylinder, and affix the packing edge. Glue sprayed on is easier. Fig. 16-116.

4. Take the press off "safe." Inch the press over for one revolution.

VIEW 3

Harris-Intertype Corp.

16-114. *Plate lockup sequence.*

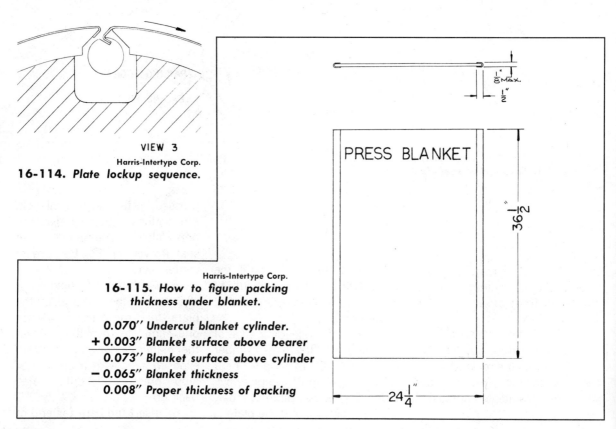

$\frac{1}{8}$ MAX.

$\frac{1}{2}''$

PRESS BLANKET

$36\frac{1}{2}''$

$24\frac{1}{4}''$

Harris-Intertype Corp.

16-115. *How to figure packing thickness under blanket.*

0.070" *Undercut blanket cylinder.*

+ 0.003" *Blanket surface above bearer*

0.073" *Blanket surface above cylinder*

− 0.065" *Blanket thickness*

0.008" *Proper thickness of packing*

Harris-Intertype Corp.
16-116. Packing installation.

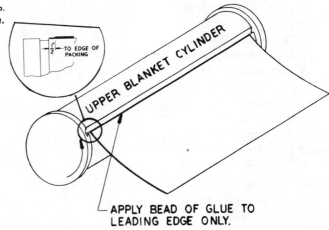

TO EDGE OF PACKING

UPPER BLANKET CYLINDER

APPLY BEAD OF GLUE TO LEADING EDGE ONLY.

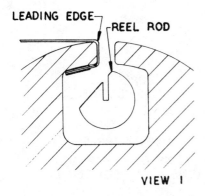

LEADING EDGE — REEL ROD

VIEW 1

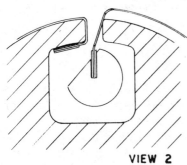

VIEW 2

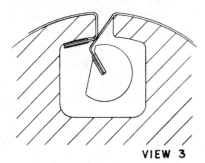

VIEW 3

Harris-Intertype Corp.
16-117. Blanket lockup sequence.

5. Return press to "safe." Cut the packing even with the gap on the trailing edge. *Do not* glue the trailing edge.

6. Insert the new blanket into the leading edge of the gap. Fig. 16-117, View 1. Hold the blanket in position by catching the metal edge with the flat on the reel rod. Check to see that the packing sheet is centered and parallel wlith the side edges of the blanket.

7. Take the press off "safe." Inch the cylinder over one revolution, holding the trailing edge. Return to "safe."

8. Apply grease to the blanket's trailing edge prior to tightening. The grease reduces friction between the rubber surface on the blanket and cylinder. The blanket will also conform better to the cylinder.

9. Insert the trailing-edge bar into the slot on the reel rod. Fig. 16-117, View 2. Check to see that the bar is square in the reel rod; also check to see that the leading edge is trapped in its proper position.

10. Begin to take up on the reel rod to draw the blanket tight around the cylinder. Fig. 16-117, View 3.

11. Replace the finger guard between the plate and blanket cylinder.

12. To iron the blankets out and properly seat them, the press is run with impression on for a short time.

13. Stop the press. Rotate the blanket cylinder so that the gap is facing you. Put press on "safe." Check the blanket and retighten the reel rod.

Also check the blanket for uniform tension. When thumped with the hand, the blanket should have the same sound across the width of the blanket.

14. If a gauge is available, check the blanket for the correct printing height. This should be about 0.003″ above bearers.

REGISTERING PRINTED IMPRESSIONS

The printing on one side of the web must be in correct position in relation to the printing on the other side. This is called back-up register. The margins, head, foot, and side must be uniform on both sides of the paper.

1. Check that the side margins are even and opposite each other on both sides of the web. Fig. 16-118. If the impressions of the upper printing cylinders (plates) are off center, adjust the upper plate cylinder using the special wrench provided to shift the position of the plate cylinder, and move the printed impression into proper register. Clockwise rotation will shift the impression toward the gear side of the printing unit, counterclockwise toward the work side.

2. If the lower plates are off center, adjust the lower plate cylinder as previously described.

3. Check that the leading and trailing margins are even and opposite each other on both sides of the web. If the impression on one side does not coincide with the impression on the other, determine which is not in register. Also determine by what amount it is out of register and in which direction. Fig. 16-118.

4. Take a gauge with a thickness equal to the amount which the register is out as determined in the first step. (*Example:* If the register between the two printing surfaces of the web is out 0.020", then use a 0.020" thick gauge.)

5. Loosen eccentric locking screw "A", Fig. 16-119.

6. Place the gauge between the yoke and eccentric on the appropriate side which will give the correction in the direction necessary.

7. Rotate the eccentric so as to close the gap between it and the gauge. Retighten locking screw "A". Remove the gauge. A gap will now exist of gauge thickness between the eccentric and the yoke.

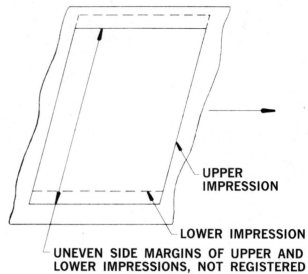

UPPER IMPRESSION

LOWER IMPRESSION

UNEVEN SIDE MARGINS OF UPPER AND LOWER IMPRESSIONS, NOT REGISTERED

Harris-Intertype Corp.

16-118. *Registration from one side of paper to opposite side.*

8. Loosen the three plate cylinder clamping bolts, noted as "B" in Fig. 16-119.

9. Rotate the plate cylinder to close the gauge thickness gap between the eccentric and yoke.

10. Retighten the three "B" bolts.

11. Start press and recheck circumferential register. If further adjustment is required, repeat Steps 1 through 10.

PRESS OPERATION

Safety features have been incorporated into the control system to protect the operator and prevent the press from being started at high speeds. The press can be stopped at any control panel by depressing the "stop" button switch. Before it can be started, the speed-control knob on the master control panel must be returned to "start." This insures starting at slow speed

and prevents damage. When the mode selector switch is in the "jog" position, the press can be operated at inch speed from any control panel; however, the start switch must be held "in." When the selector is in the "safe" position, the press cannot be started from any control panel. However, the ink and water fountain roll drive motors may be operated.

STARTING AND RUNNING THE PRESS

To start the press:

1. Turn the power on at the wall disconnect, and observe that the "power" indicator light glows.

2. Turn the speed-control knob on the master control panel to "start."

3. Set the power "on-off" switch at the master control to "on," and observe that the "press" indicator light glows.

4. Set the selector switch at the master control panel to "run."

5. Turn the master ink-water switch to "on" position.

6. Depress the "start" button at the master control panel.

7. Turn the water motor switch "on" at the unit control panel.

8. Place the water form roller throw-off handles at the units in the "on" position, and let the press run long enough for the moisture in the dampeners to dissolve the gum on the plates.

9. Turn the ink fountain motor switch "on" at the unit control panel.

10. Place the ink form roller throw-off handles in the "on" position, and watch the plate. If the image picks up ink and the plate stays clean in the non-image areas, raise the ink and water rollers. Shut off the ink and water motors.

11. Depress the "stop" button at master control panel or unit.

12. Engage the folder clutch. (Quarter-folder clutch, if necessary.) Take care to put the folder and units on timing marks.

13. Depress the impression throw-off handles.

14. Engage the ink and water form throw-off handles. Press should start to print.

15. Turn the ink and water motors on.

16. Check the web side lay at the former, and make adjustments (at paper roll stands) if necessary.

17. Set the ink and water motor-speed, variable-transformer controls on the press unit's control panel to desired speed. NOTE: If running color, check registration of color and adjust the compensator and/or register if necessary.

18. Turn the speed-control knob on the master control panel to the desired speed.

19. Check a printed copy, and make necessary adjustments to the ink and dampener flow by increasing or decreasing fountain roll speed. Adjust key settings for lateral ink coverage.

20. Check the brake adjustment. At running speed, the dancer roller should be approximately under the smooth idler roller.

SHUTTING DOWN THE PRESS

To shut down the press at the end of a run:

1. Turn the speed-control knob on the master control panel to a slow speed.

2. Turn the ink motor-speed controls on the press unit's control panel fully counterclockwise and set the ink motor-power "on-off" switch to "off."

3. Allow the press to run. This will remove excess ink from the inking system.

4. Disengage all ink form roller throw-off controls.

5. Turn the water motor-speed, variable-transformer controls on the press control's panel fully counterclockwise, and set the water motor-power "on-off" switch to "off."

6. Disengage water form roller throw-off controls.

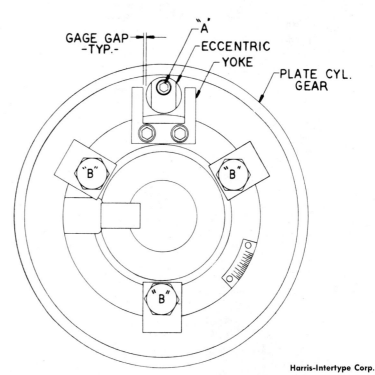

GAGE GAP
-TYP.-

"A"
ECCENTRIC
YOKE
PLATE CYL. GEAR

"B"   "B"

"B"

Harris-Intertype Corp.

16-119. *Circumferential register adjustment.*

7. Depress the "stop" push button on any control panel.

8. Move the impression throw-off control to the "off" position.

9. Set the mode selector switch on the master control panel to "jog."

10. Clean the press. Remove plates and wash blankets. CAUTION: Plates left on the cylinder for long periods (over a weekend) may cause rust accumulations in the lockup reel area.

11. Set the power "on-off" switch to "off," and observe that the "press" indicator light goes out.

12. Set mode selector switch on master control panel to "safe."

13. Turn off power at wall disconnect, and observe that the "power" indicator light goes out.

FOLDING TROUBLESHOOTING

PROBLEM	POSSIBLE CAUSE	REMEDY
Web not cutting at proper point.	Folder not timed to printing unit.	Time the folder.
Web will not adhere to cutting cylinder.	Pins broken or bent.	Replace pins.
Web being cut by nipper rollers.	Nipper rollers improperly adjusted.	Adjust nipper rollers.
Web not being cut cleanly by knife.	Knife blades improperly adjusted.	Adjust knife blades.
	Cutter rubber worn excessively.	Replace cutter rubber.
	Tabloid slitting-knife pressure incorrect.	Adjust slitting-knife pressure.
Quarter-folder not operating properly.	Quarter-folder not timed with other units.	Time the quarter-folder.
	Quarter-folder not engaged.	Engage quarter-folder.

REVIEW QUESTIONS

1. In a simple makeready, there is no need to clean the blanket. True or False?
2. Why is a press run begun with "waste sheets" instead of good paper?
3. The sheet sequence of a press refers to its sequence of operation. True or False?
4. A duplicator is a type of offset press. True or False?
5. Name the five basic systems of a duplicator.
6. A press that prints on both sides of the paper at the same time is called a perfecting press. True or False?
7. Printing on one side of the web must be in correct position in relation to the printing on the other side. What is this called?

Chapter 17 — Color

COLOR PERCEPTION

The colors we see are the reflection of visible areas of the electromagnetic spectrum. That is, the color of any object is the light that is reflected by the object.

Colors can be reproduced by adding together colored lights. Colors can also be reproduced by using materials that subtract colors from areas of the spectrum. The color of a printed reproduction is the remainder of light not subtracted (absorbed) by the ink, pigment, or paper. Printing is done with color-subtracting primaries (magenta, cyan, and yellow) to reproduce the colors desired.

Generally, we distinguish one color from another by its hue, saturation, and value. Hue refers to the property of color that gives it its name, such as red, blue, or green. Saturation is the purity of a color, or the relative amount of the hue. The more hue, the more saturated a color is. Value is the lightness (away from darkness) of a color. Any color can be described by combining the characteristics of hue, saturation, and value.

LIGHT

Light is a form of electromagnetic energy. The sun is the main source of natural light. Light is a small part of the total spectrum (range) of radiant energy. The spectrum is made up of a series of measurable wavelengths from very long radio waves to very short gamma rays. Fig. 17-1. The wave motion (frequency) and length (from wave crest to crest) combine to produce a constant speed of approximately 186,000 miles (300,000 kilometres) per second in vacuum for all forms of radiant energy. Fig. 17-2.

Light wavelengths vary from about 380 millimicrons (380 millionths of a millimetre) to about 770 mμ. (The symbol for millimicron is mμ.) The range of radiant energy between 380 mμ and 770 mμ is called the *visible spectrum*. The visible spectrum contains all the colors we can see. Looking at all the colors together in equal amounts, as in sunlight, we see white light. Any color of light other than white is only a part of the visible spectrum.

Light can come from many sources. These sources either generate light themselves (direct sources) or reflect light (indirect sources).

Direct sources emit light through heat excitation of atoms or molecules or as the result of energy absorption. Some solids and liquids, when heated to a high temperature, will incandesce (emit intense, bright light), generally in a continuous range of the visible spectrum. The filament of an ordinary light bulb emits light in this manner. Fig. 17-3. Certain gases or vapors, such as neon, mercury, or xenon, produce a discontinuous line, or band spectra, emission when their atoms or molecules are electrically excited. Fig. 17-4. Neon signs and pulsed xenon camera lights are examples of this kind of light emission.

Both the light bulb and the neon tube use heat to create light. Some materials emit light without the use of heat. These are cool, or luminescent, sources. Some of these materials can absorb radiant energy and immediately emit it as fluorescence (usually at longer waves). The television screen and the common fluorescent light utilize this principle. Phosphorescent materials dissipate stored energy slowly. They are used on watch dials and other objects to make them glow in the dark.

Most of the light we see comes from indirect sources. Light striking an object is called *incident light*. Fig. 17-5. This incident light is reflected, transmitted, or absorbed by the object, Fig. 17-6. We see the light that is reflected.

Some objects reflect part or most of the incident light. Objects usually reflect more light from some wavelengths than others. Any given object always

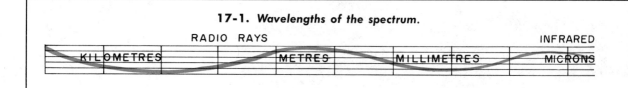

17-1. *Wavelengths of the spectrum.*

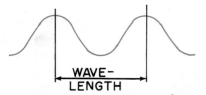

17-2. *The length of a wave is measured from crest to crest.*

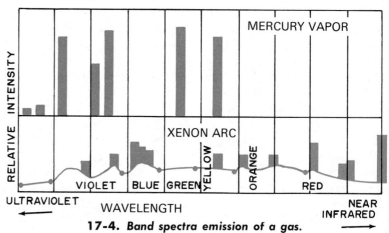

17-4. *Band spectra emission of a gas.*

reflects the same proportion of light of any particular wavelength. Because of these reasons, we tend to think of an object as possessing a color instead of thinking in terms of the changed condition of light from an indirect source.

Objects which transmit more or less of the incident light follow the same rules as for reflected light. The same proportion of a wavelength is always transmitted, and various amounts of wavelengths are selected along the visible spectrum.

Light which is absorbed by indirect sources is lost to our vision. However, the same rules apply for absorbed light as for reflected and transmitted light. Absorption of light by an object is always in proportion to any particular wavelength, while the amount is selective along the visible spectrum.

Achromatic (noncolor) indirect sources transmit and reflect about the same proportion of light from each wavelength. They are nonselective and are seen as white, black, gray, or neutral objects. Some objects will appear achromatic under selected indirect light.

Light Colors

Chromatic indirect sources transmit and reflect selectively the available wavelengths to extract and produce wavelengths we identify as a color (hue).

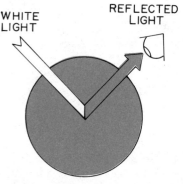

17-5. *Reflected light from an object.*

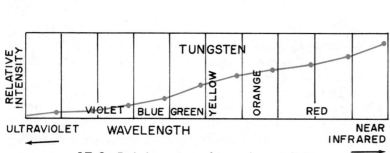

17-3. *Emission range of incandescent light.*

VISIBLE
LIGHT

| RAYS | ULTRAVIOLET | X-RAYS | GAMMA RAYS | COSMIC RAYS |

MILLIMICRONS   ANGSTROM UNITS   X-UNITS

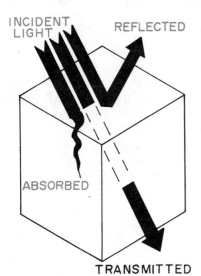

17-6. Reflected, transmitted, and absorbed light.

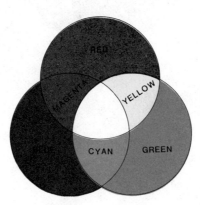

17-8. Additive primary light colors.

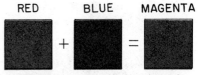

17-9. Magenta—the complement of green light.

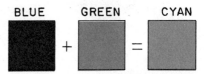

17-10. Cyan—the complement of red light.

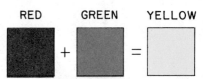

17-11. Yellow—the complement of blue light.

A beam of white light passing through a prism is bent. The shorter wavelengths are bent more than the longer wave-

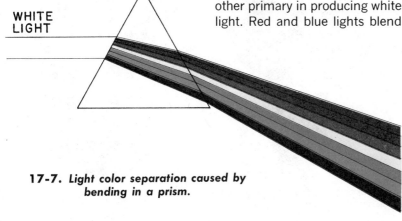

17-7. Light color separation caused by bending in a prism.

lengths. A visible spectrum is formed between 4,000 angstroms (measure of wavelength) and 7,000 angstroms. Fig. 17-7. The three primary light colors are seen as blue, green, and red. Added in equal amounts, these three produce white light. Fig. 17-8. Since all three must be added, any two primaries complement (make complete) the other primary in producing white light. Red and blue lights blend

to make magenta, which is the complement of green light. Fig. 17-9. Blue and green lights blend to make cyan, which is the complement of red light. Fig. 17-10. Green and red lights blend to make yellow, which is the complement of blue light. Fig. 17-11.

When the primary of any complementary light is added, white light is produced. For example, when the primary light blue is added to the complementary yellow, white light is produced.

425

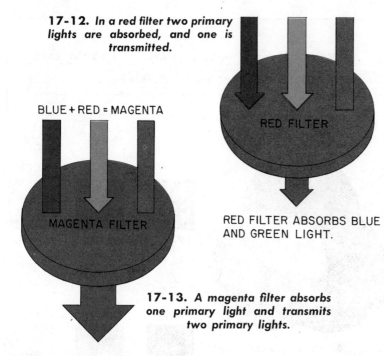

17-12. *In a red filter two primary lights are absorbed, and one is transmitted.*

BLUE + RED = MAGENTA

MAGENTA FILTER

RED FILTER

RED FILTER ABSORBS BLUE AND GREEN LIGHT.

17-13. *A magenta filter absorbs one primary light and transmits two primary lights.*

Subtracting Colors

Whenever a primary light color is subtracted (removed) from white light, its complementary color (the remaining two primaries) is seen. If any two primary light colors (a complementary color) are subtracted from white light, the primary complement is seen.

One method of subtracting primary colors in light is to use a filter of transparent dyed material. The dye absorbs all light except the filter color which is transmitted. A red filter, such as the Kodak Wratten filter No. 25 absorbs green and blue light, transmits red light. Fig. 17-12. A magenta filter transmits blue

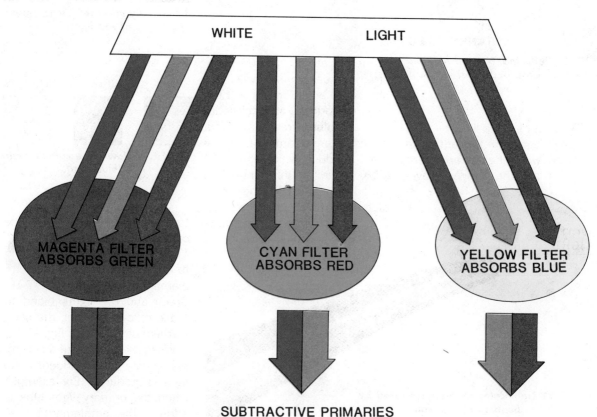

WHITE LIGHT

MAGENTA FILTER ABSORBS GREEN

CYAN FILTER ABSORBS RED

YELLOW FILTER ABSORBS BLUE

SUBTRACTIVE PRIMARIES

17-14. *Complementary light colors by filtration.*

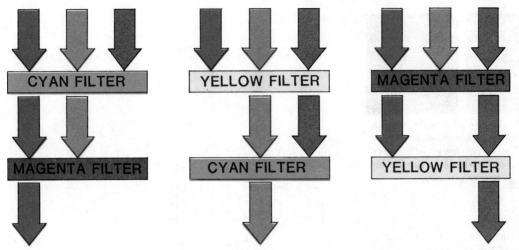

17-15. *The use of multiple subtractive primary filters to transmit remaining single primary light.*

and red, absorbs green. Fig. 17-13.

If two different primary filters are used to subtract colors, no light will be seen. Since each filter absorbs two-thirds of the spectrum, together they absorb the entire visible spectrum.

The complementary light colors (cyan, magenta, yellow) are called *subtractive primaries* because each is minus a primary light color. A subtractive primary color filter absorbs its complemented color. A magenta filter absorbs green, a cyan filter absorbs red, and a yellow filter absorbs blue. Fig. 17-14.

Two different subtractive primary filters absorb different primary colors and transmit the remaining primary color. Magenta and yellow filters absorb green and blue and transmit red. Yellow and cyan filters absorb blue and red, transmit green. Cyan and magenta filters absorb red and green, transmit blue. Fig. 17-15.

Opaque objects reflect the light which is not absorbed. The light reflected determines what color we sense the object possesses. A red object in white light would appear black in cyan-filtered light. Fig. 17-16.

LIGHT AND COLOR MEASUREMENT

Light intensity is measured in lumens per square foot. (One lumen per square foot equals one footcandle.) Various types of photometers are used to measure incident, transmitted, and reflected light. Modern meters are electronic and utilize photoelectric cells and filters to collect, compensate, and convert incoming light to direct-reading scales. A densitometer is a specialized form of light meter that measures optical density. *Optical density* is the negative logarithm of fractional transmission or reflection of light. The less light transmitted or reflected, the higher the density. A transmission of 50 percent of the light is equivalent to 0.3 density, while 25 percent transmission is equivalent to 0.6 density log units. Information

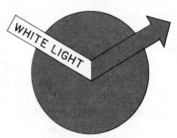

OBJECT APPEARS RED BECAUSE IT ABSORBS GREEN AND BLUE.

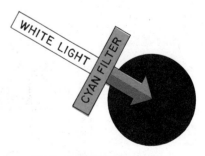

OBJECT APPEARS BLACK BECAUSE IT ABSORBS GREEN AND BLUE WHICH MAKE UP CYAN.

17-16. *The color of an object depends on the colors of incident light which strike it and the colors it reflects.*

427

17-17. *Under one light source, these colors will appear to match. Under another, they will differ. This is one drawback to comparing colors visually.*

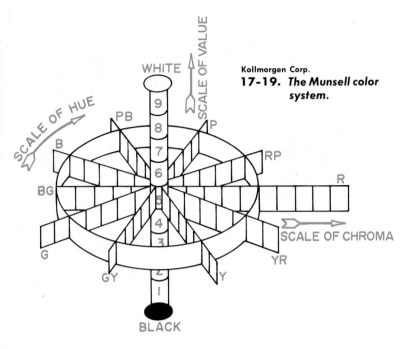

Kollmorgen Corp.

17-19. *The Munsell color system.*

concerning densitometric units is included in Chapter 11, "Halftone Photography."

There are three ways to measure color. Color can be visually compared with colored materials or lights. Fig. 17-17. Color can be determined by filtration, using three standard filters. Fig. 17-18. Color can be scientifically measured as to the amount of wavelengths by spectrophotometry.

THE MUNSELL SYSTEM

Many attempts have been made to incorporate the characteristics of reflected light into a logical color system. The general description of a color in terms of its name (hue), value (lightness), and saturation (purity) is insufficient when comparing it with a similar color. Albert H. Munsell, an American painter, evolved a system of color notation. He arranged colors on the basis of appearance. The hues are arranged in a circle. Fig. 17-19.

Beginning with red, samples of opaque pigments are hue numbered around the circle. In the center, perpendicular to the circle, a pole describes the value (lightness) of the hue in progressive steps from 1 through 9. Fig. 17-20. Step 1 is almost black and Step 9 is almost white. From the center pole, chroma (saturation)

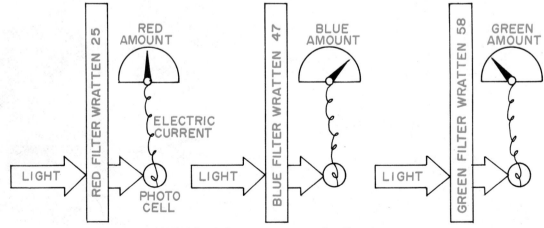

17-18. *Color measurement by filtration.*

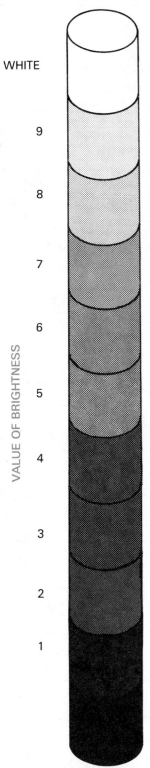

steps progressively range outward, as opaque samples for each value and hue. Fig. 17-21. This notation forms a three-dimensional globe. Each color has an identifying number. The Munsell notation 1.5R 5/6 refers to a red color. The 1.5R is the hue description. The 5 refers to the value level. The 6 means 6 steps from a neutral gray toward maximum saturation of available pigments. Generally, this color could be thought of as a bright medium red.

The Munsell book of colors has pigments. Generally, this color pages with all available values and chromas in order. The system is used to identify, compare, and describe colors by observation. The Ostwald color system and the Hunter color space use similar types of arrangements to describe colors.

THE MUNSELL-FOSS COLOR ORDER SYSTEM

The Munsell-Foss color order system is similar to the Munsell system. It is based on changes in value, hue, and saturation. Instead of a sphere, it is made as a cube. This design produces a relative color order determined by the yellow, magenta, and cyan colorants that produce all the colors in the cube. This design permits printers to produce their own color charts. These charts, printed with papers, inks, and equipment in the plant, represent the actual colors available for process color printings. The chart can be used as a production standard and for color selection by customers. The chart is produced from master films supplied by the Graphic Art Technical Foundation. Plates are made from the films and run with papers and inks regularly used for process color work. The resulting full-color chart is overprinted with eight tone levels of black to illustrate the composite four-color printings.

A numbering system printed with the chart is used to identify any color in the chart. This four-digit number represents in order the yellow, magenta, cyan, and black inks. Each color has a tone level from zero through eight.

17-20. *Value scale of the Munsell color system.*

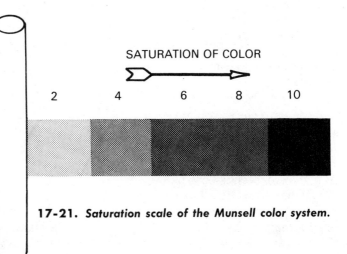

17-21. *Saturation scale of the Munsell color system.*

The tone levels have approximate halftone dot levels. These are: 0 = 0%, 1 = 4%, 2 = 13%, 3 = 23%, 4 = 33%, 5 = 53%, 6 = 74%, 7 = 87%, and 8 = 100%. The levels were selected to give the most practical visual range of difference between tones. A code of 5432 represents tone levels of 5 for yellow, 4 for magenta, 3 for cyan, and 2 for black.

The identifying number of each three-color patch on the chart is also determined by reference numbers printed on the chart. The trichromatic value is determined by one number which runs across the horizontal row of the chart and two numbers printed on the diagonal. The intersection between the horizontal and diagonal row makes a three-digit code for the trichromatic color. The color chart is overprinted in eight levels of black to illustrate four-color process printing. Levels 0–3 are located on Chart 1, while levels 4–7 are on Chart 2. The zero level has no black, while level 7 is a solid black. The chart is used for customer selection of colors that can be printed. The chart is also used to compare other printed samples with printed, notated colors on the chart.

FILTER DETERMINATION OF COLOR

The eye has three types of color receivers. Some are stimulated by green, others by red, and some by blue. Three filters, which correspond to the color areas of the eye receivers, can be used to determine color. The reflected light from an object is beamed through each of the filters and measured by a photoelectric cell. The three photocell measurements will specify color. The numbers do not, however, describe an actual color sensation to a person.

For the reproduction of color in printing, it is necessary to use filters that correspond to photographic film's light sensitivity or the photographic response to color. The Wratten series—Red 25, Blue 47, and Green 58—is broad-band filters commonly used in color separation. The measurement with such filters gives actinic (chemically active light) densities. The densities generally specify the appearance of a color. Actinic densities conform closely to the needs of photographic processes in reproducing color.

ICI CHROMATICITY DIAGRAMS

Chromaticity diagrams were developed by the International Commission on Illumination. The wavelengths of additive colors are plotted on a grid in angstrom units. Joined together, they form a tilted curve with an inclined

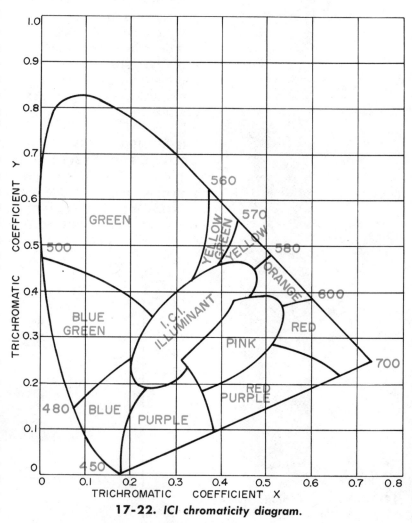

17-22. *ICI chromaticity diagram.*

base. Fig. 17-22. The illuminant C (daylight) used in graphic arts is located near the center of the figure. Very light colors are found near the illuminant. The chroma (saturation) of a color increases as it is located outward from the illuminant. The curve and base represent the chromaticities of monochromatic light (a source that emits a single wavelength) for each wavelength. The base line is a mixture of red and blue from opposite ends of the visible spectrum. These, of course, cannot be determined by monochromatic light.

The tristimulus values of a color are plotted on the grid. *Tristimulus* means the three light colors that stimulate the eye. These values—labeled X, Y, and Z—are measurements of the redness (X), the greenness (Y), and the blueness (Z) of a color.

Tristimulus values can be obtained by the filter method of color specification as previously described. The filters are made to closely resemble the way the eye sees color.

A spectrophotometer can be used to obtain tristimulus values. This instrument evaluates each wavelength of a color across the spectrum. These are plotted in intensity as a line across the wavelengths. From the spectrophotometric curve, the tristimulus values are calculated.

The filter method of obtaining tristimulus values is the simplest and most direct. The method is not as accurate as values from spectrophotometric curves. However, it does not require a great deal of instrumentation or lengthy calculations.

COLOR MEASUREMENT IN PRINTING

The two prime materials of printers, paper and ink, require color specification and measurement. The printer is often required to match the color of a paper or an ink or both. Measurements through color filters are used to determine the density of a color ink printing. Similar measurements are necessary for photographic color correction. Light sources and photographic materials are measured for their color emission and response.

REVIEW QUESTIONS

1. The color of an object is the light absorbed by that object. True or False?
2. Name the terms defined in the following:
   a. Light striking an object.
   b. The property of a color that gives it its name.
   c. The purity of a color.
   d. The lightness of a color.
3. The tristimulus values of a color are measurements of a color's relative intensity. True or False?

Chapter 18

Color Separation

The use of color in printed materials is increasing rapidly. Research and development are continuing to provide new materials and techniques for color reproduction. Those employed in the graphic reproduction industry should understand the theory of color. (See Chapter 17, "Color.") They should know how color is reproduced and be familiar with the characteristics of papers and inks. (Paper and ink are discussed in Chapters 25 and 26.)

This chapter will present methods for reproducing continuous tone color images, such as a color photograph or an oil painting.

CONTINUOUS TONE COLOR REPRODUCTION

Continuous tone color images are reproduced using the process color separation technique. *Color separation* is the division of a continuous tone multicolor original into several basic parts. The photographic process with color filters is used. Each filter separates one color in the original and allows it to be imposed on a negative. Four separations are needed: for yellow, cyan, magenta, and black. As explained in Chapter 17, yellow, cyan, and magenta are the primary printing colors. After color corrections are made, the separation nega-

tives are used to make printing plates. Each color has a separate plate. Fig. 18-1.

Each color is printed over the printed image of the other in perfect register. This overprinting of halftone dots, which relies on a blending of colors, reproduces the multicolor, continuous tone copy.

COLOR SEPARATION COPY

Continuous tone color copy has graduated variations in tone. An example is a color photograph. Continuous tone copy can be reflective or transmissive.

Reflective copy is any opaque copy that reflects light, such as photographs and oil paintings. *Transmissive* copy is transparent; it transmits light. Examples include slides and transparencies. These may be on reversal (positive) color film such as Kodachrome or on negative color film such as Kodacolor or Ektacolor. Fig. 18-2.

THEORY OF PROCESS COLOR SEPARATION

The three color printers are actually photographic records of the red, blue, and green light transmitted or reflected by the original copy. The term *printer*, in this case, refers to the negative used to make the plate for a particular color. The density in each of the separation negatives

represents the color of light on the original copy transmitted through the appropriate separation filter. The light that transmits through the clear portion of the separation negative is actually a record of the light that is absorbed by the original copy. The *cyan printer* is the "minus red" or "red light absorber," the *yellow printer* is the "minus blue" or "blue light absorber," and the *magenta printer* is the "minus green" or "green light absorber." Fig. 18-3. Black ink absorbs the red, blue, and green.

Figs. 18-4, 18-5, and 18-6 show how it is possible to produce the three *color* separation negatives. In each case, the *filter* used to expose the separation negative is the same color as the primary light color that is absorbed by the printing ink.

There are several basic methods for producing the *black* separation negative. Each varies with the method of separation, explained later in the chapter. *Halftone contact screens* and *panchromatic film* are used throughout the separation process to maintain the color balance and reduce the contrast control problems.

In studying the separation sequence, Figs. 18-4 through 18-6, notice that each separation negative is used to produce a plate that prints a positive image on

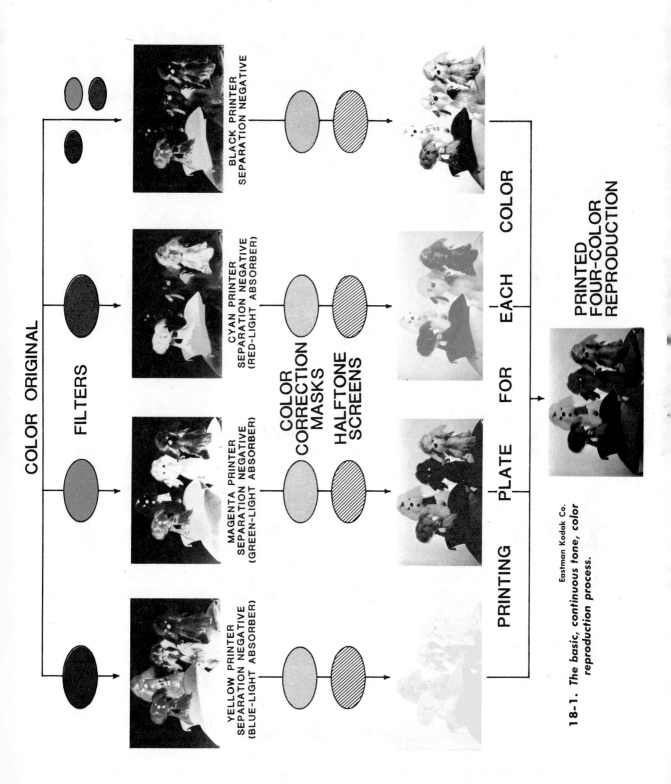

COLOR ORIGINAL

FILTERS

BLACK PRINTER
SEPARATION NEGATIVE

CYAN PRINTER
SEPARATION NEGATIVE
(RED-LIGHT ABSORBER)

MAGENTA PRINTER
SEPARATION NEGATIVE
(GREEN-LIGHT ABSORBER)

YELLOW PRINTER
SEPARATION NEGATIVE
(BLUE-LIGHT ABSORBER)

COLOR
CORRECTION
MASKS

HALFTONE
SCREENS

PRINTING   PLATE   FOR   EACH   COLOR

PRINTED
FOUR-COLOR
REPRODUCTION

Eastman Kodak Co.

18-1. The basic, continuous tone, color
reproduction process.

433

COLOR PHOTO
OR
PAINTING

POSITIVE REFLECTIVE
COPY

COLOR
TRANSPARENCY
OR
SLIDE

POSITIVE TRANSMISSIVE
COPY

ORANGE
KODACOLOR
OR
EKTACOLOR
NEGATIVE

NEGATIVE TRANSMISSIVE
COPY

18-2. *The types of continuous tone copy.*

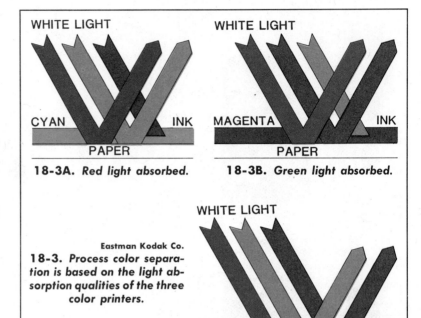

18-3A. *Red light absorbed.*

18-3B. *Green light absorbed.*

Eastman Kodak Co.
18-3. *Process color separation is based on the light absorption qualities of the three color printers.*

18-3C. *Blue light absorbed.*

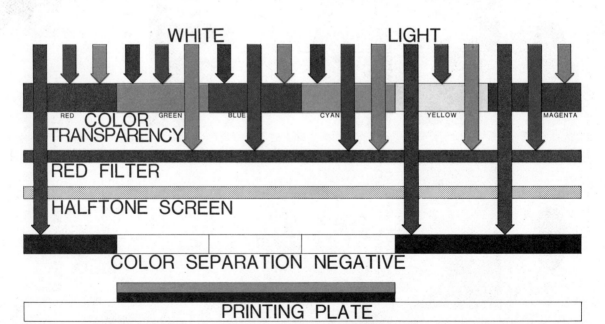

18-4. *The red filter lets red light reach the color separation negative, exposing these areas. The clear areas in the negative are the blues and greens. This negative produces the cyan printing plate.*

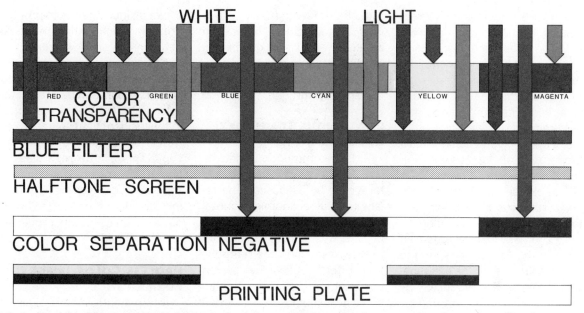

18-5. *The blue filter lets blue light reach the color separation negative, exposing these areas. The clear areas in the negative are the greens and reds. This negative produces the yellow printing plate.*

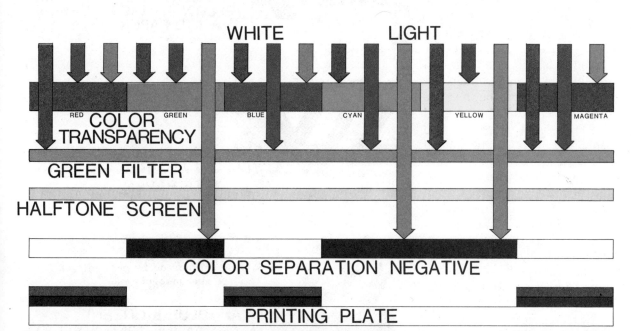

18-6. *The green filter lets the green light reach the color separation negative, exposing these areas. The clear areas in the negative are the blues and reds. This negative produces the magenta printing plate.*

435

the press sheet. This image represents light that was transmitted through each separation negative. The inks deposited by the printing plates represent the light colors that the original copy absorbed. The light colors emitted from the original copy are duplicated by the subtractive properties of undertone ink combinations.

This can be visualized by viewing continuous tone color copy through the three separation filters. The dark images produced through the filters correspond to the opaque portion of the separation negatives produced by that filter. The inks, printed by plates that were produced by use of filters, absorb the primary light colors that were absorbed by the original copy. The inks are transmitters of the remaining primary light colors.

To reproduce any primary light color by the process method, two primary pigment colors must be used. To reproduce red, both yellow and magenta ink must be used. Fig. 18-7. Since the yellow (minus blue) and magenta (minus green) inks contain colors other than red, they must be overprinted so the blue and green light are filtered out and only the red is transmitted through.

To reproduce green, both yellow and cyan ink must be used. Fig. 18-8. Since the yellow (minus blue) and cyan (minus red) inks contain colors other than green, they must be overprinted so the blue and red light are filtered out and only the green is transmitted through.

To reproduce a blue, both cyan and magenta ink must be used. Fig. 18-9. Since the cyan (minus

red) and magenta (minus green) inks contain colors other than blue, they must be overprinted so the green and red light are filtered out and only the blue is transmitted through.

CONTINUOUS TONE COPY CONSIDERATIONS

It is recommended that the size of the original continuous tone copy be as close to the finished job as economically possible. This assures image sharpness as well as color fidelity and reduces defects in the reproduction often caused by overenlargement. Copy containing scratches should be discarded. Copy that is too dense should be

avoided since it tends to produce printing which is flat and lacks detail in the shadow areas.

A major consideration is the light source used on the photographic separation devices. If the color potential is not contained in the incident light source, it can never be separated from the copy. This is true regardless of how much color is contained in the copy. Light sources emitting incident light in the 5,200 to 5,400 degrees kelvin range are recommended.

PROCESS COLOR IMAGE FORMATION

Intermediate image values on multiple-color copy can be repro-

WHITE LIGHT

18-7. *Red is produced by printing magenta ink over yellow ink.*

MAGENTA INK (RED & BLUE)
YELLOW INK (RED & GREEN)
WHITE PAPER

WHITE LIGHT

18-8. *Green is produced by printing cyan ink over yellow ink.*

CYAN INK (BLUE & GREEN)
YELLOW INK (RED & GREEN)
WHITE PAPER

WHITE LIGHT

18-9. *Blue is produced by printing cyan ink over magenta ink.*

CYAN (BLUE & GREEN)
MAGENTA INK (RED & BLUE)
WHITE PAPER

duced on a printing press only if they are converted into *halftone dots* or patterns. At a normal viewing distance these dots or patterns appear to have all the colors and image detail contained on the original, continuous tone image. To achieve this total color impression, a complex dot arrangement is required. The four ink-color dots are arranged into a rosette pattern. This pattern provides for a blending of all the color effects associated with each of the four colors. At a normal viewing distance the eye is unable to detect the presence of more than one color of dot within the field of view. Fig. 18-10.

A yellow dot printed side by side with a cyan dot produces a green, just as a complete overprinting of yellow over cyan would produce a green. Some properties of the yellow and cyan remain. It is these remaining properties that produce the range of colors other than the primary colors found in the original copy. If the cyan dot were made larger, the green would take on a blue cast. If the yellow dot were made larger, the green would be considerably lighter and look more like a chartreuse.

To avoid a moiré effect, different screen angles are assigned each of the printers. It is these separate angles that produce the rosette effect. Forty-five degrees is normally selected for the strongest color because 45 degrees is the least noticeable angle. The weakest color is placed midway between the next two strongest colors. A 30-degree difference between the angles of the strong colors is required to prevent a moiré pattern from forming. However, only a 15-

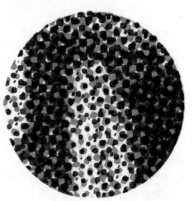

Rephotographed with permission from an illustration in a copyrighted Eastman Kodak Co. publication.

18-10. *A complete color image is produced by printing four colors, each on a separate plate. These produce all hues and shadings. The inks used are cyan (process blue), magenta (process red), yellow, and black. (If you hold this picture at a distance, you can see the rosette pattern.)*

degree difference is necessary between the weakest and any other color. The recommended screen angles are shown in Fig. 18-11.

When printing a continuous color job, the procedures established by the printing company determine which color is printed first. For example, some companies prefer to print yellow first. This can be followed by magenta, cyan, and black in that order.

The screen linage depends upon the paper used in printing. For example, offset newsprint is commonly 110 lines per inch, while quality work on coated stock is often 150 lines per inch.

COLOR SEPARATION METHODS

Color separations are prepared in a number of ways. The basic methods include (1) electronic

color scanning, (2) the direct screen method, and (3) the indirect screen method.

ELECTRONIC COLOR SCANNING

The electronic scanner examines the color original with a beam of light. Fig. 18-12. The scanner focuses a tiny spot of light on the surface of the original. The light moves across the surface in a line, scanning it from one end to the other.

After a line is scanned, either the original or the scanning lamp moves over and begins another line. Which part moves depends upon the manufacturer.

The light from these spots passes to three photocells equipped with color-separation filters. The light beam is separated into red, blue, and green

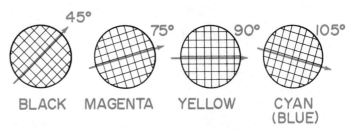

18-11. *The recommended screen angles for color printing plates.*

18-12. *The electronic scanning separation system.*

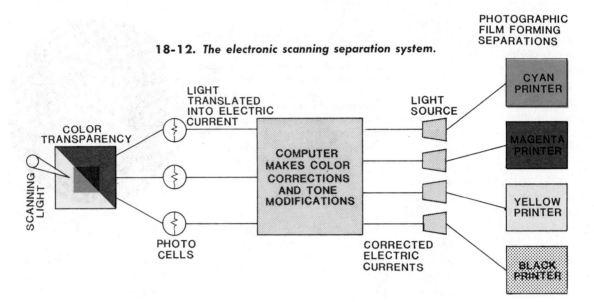

PHOTOGRAPHIC
FILM FORMING
SEPARATIONS

LIGHT
TRANSLATED
INTO ELECTRIC
CURRENT

LIGHT
SOURCE

COLOR
TRANSPARENCY

SCANNING LIGHT

PHOTO
CELLS

COMPUTER
MAKES COLOR
CORRECTIONS
AND TONE
MODIFICATIONS

CORRECTED
ELECTRIC
CURRENTS

CYAN
PRINTER

MAGENTA
PRINTER

YELLOW
PRINTER

BLACK
PRINTER

signals and fed into photocells. These translate the light received into electrical currents, which are fed into a computer. The computer evaluates the currents in terms of the paper on which the job will be printed, the inks used, and tonal qualities. It then corrects the currents so that the separations will represent the original colors. This color correction process makes adjustments for imperfections in paper and black and colored ink. The computer resolves by mathematical calculation for each color the tone value of that color at each point. If screened separations are being produced, the computer will convert these values to dot sizes.

The corrected currents are fed into a light source which exposes the photographic film. The light source varies in brightness in proportion to the corrected values of each color in the area scanned.

Scanners are either reciprocating or use a rotating drum. The reciprocating scanner can use rigid color originals, as a painting, or flexible copy, as a transparency. The drum scanner can use any original which can wrap around the drum. Some scanners will accept only color transparencies. Others accept only color separation negatives.

The output of scanners varies according to its purpose and

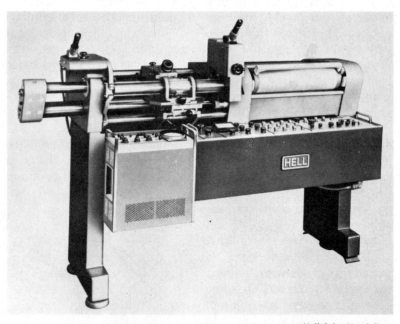

Hell-Color-Metal Corp.

18-13. *The scanner shown will accept transparent or reflection copy. It will produce same size or enlarged copy.*

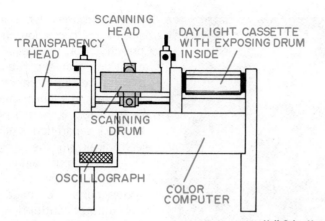

SCANNING
HEAD

TRANSPARENCY
HEAD

DAYLIGHT CASSETTE
WITH EXPOSING DRUM
INSIDE

SCANNING
DRUM

OSCILLOGRAPH

COLOR
COMPUTER

Hell-Color-Metal Corp.

18-14. *The "Vario-Chromograph" scanner equipped for 1 : 1 reproductions.*

manufacturer. Some produce continuous tone color separation negatives. Others produce relief printing plates or mechanically made halftone positives. Optical image formation systems produce halftone positives or negatives or color-correction masks. A *mask* is a device used to correct deficiencies in process inks by controlling the dot size on the separation film. The mask is discussed in detail later in this chapter. Relief printing plates are made by cutting the non-printing areas from the plate, dot by dot, with a vibrating stylus instead of a film exposure lamp.

Another scanning system uses optical image formation with a lens to project the image on the photographic film. The color original is scanned by the scanning lamp point by point. Part of the light is used to expose the film through a camera lens. Part of the same light is picked up by the photocells with filters to provide signals for the color-correction computer. The computer reads these signals and varies the brightness of the scanning

lamp. This serves as color correction. The detail of the picture is optically printed on the photographic film.

The output of the optical scanning system is either a contact print or a projection print.

A Scanning System

The "Vario-Chromagraph" scanner manufactured by the HCM Corporation, Fig. 18-13, scans transparent or reflection copy to produce color separations, either negative or positive. It will produce continuous tone or direct-screened copy the same size or enlarged. The maximum recording size for the same size copy is 335 mm × 450 mm (13 1/4" × 17 3/4"). Maximum enlargements are 270 mm × 440 mm (10 5/8" × 17 1/4"). All small transparencies up to 60 mm × 90 mm are suitable for enlargement. The unit can enlarge directly and continuously from 170 to 2,000 percent.

This scanning resolution becomes finer according to the enlargement. The color separations for enlargement are recorded in

the final printing size with either 100 or 200 lines per centimetre (250 to 500 to the inch) according to the printing process in use. This means a 20-times enlargement will have 2,000 lines per centimetre (10,000 lines per inch). In same-size recording, the scanning and exposing resolutions can be 200 or 400 lines per centimetre (500 or 1,000 lines per inch). The setup for scanning same-size and enlargement copy is shown in Figs. 18-14 and 18-15. The scanning drum is used for same size copy. A transparency holder replaces the drum for making enlargements.

For recording the same size, the transparency is mounted on a scanning drum. Fig. 18-16. It is driven at the same speed as the exposing drum by the same driving mechanism.

The recording side head is moved sideways by means of a mandrel (metal spindle) with a separate driving mechanism. The exposing head is connected to the scanning head by a rigid tube. This enables both to move along their drums at the same speed. The linear recording of

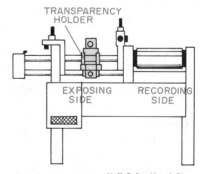

TRANSPARENCY
HOLDER

EXPOSING
SIDE

RECORDING
SIDE

Hell-Color-Metal Corp.

18-15. *The "Vario-Chromograph" scanner equipped for enlargement.*

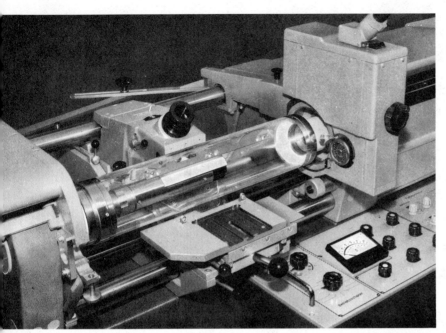

Hell-Color-Metal Corp.

18-16. *The transparency is mounted on a scanning drum.*

processed in the color computer, each in one correction channel. Correction for the yellow, magenta, and cyan separations occurs. In the fourth channel the signals from the fourth multiplier are used for unsharp masking. The black separation is achieved electronically in the computer, using the output values of the three main channels.

Corrections are made using the computer control panel. Fig. 18-18. The controls in the two left-hand panels are for the basic electronic adjustments. The central panel contains the color correction controls. The right-side panel controls adjustments for highlights, middletones, shadows, undercolor removal, and exposing density.

color separations occurs at the same time as linear scanning of the copy.

For enlargements the scanning drum on the exposing side is replaced by a transparency holder. Fig. 18-17. This holder is carried on a parallel guide in front of the scanning head and is moved up and down by a rotary tube. Small-size transparencies are held on a plexiglass plate, which is placed on the transparency holder by a vacuum.

The transparency is illuminated by a lamp. The light passing through the transparency is split into four beams in the optic head. Three of these go into photomultipliers and the fourth to a separate multiplier. The multipliers convert the varying brightnesses of light in electrical signals. These output signals of the three photomultipliers are

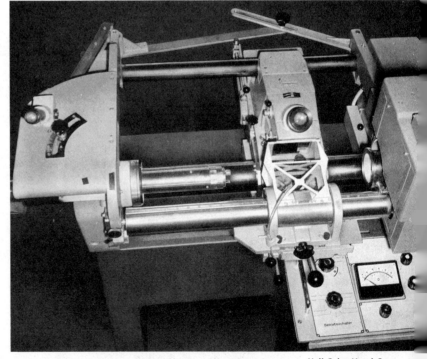

Hell-Color-Metal Corp.

18-17. *Enlargements are made by replacing the scanning drum with a transparency holder.*

ELECTRONIC
ADJUSTMENTS

COLOR
CORRECTION

CONTROLS FOR HIGHLIGHTS,
MIDDLETONES, SHADOWS,
DENSITY

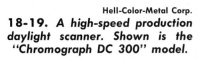

Hell-Color-Metal Corp.
18-18. *The computer control panel.*

There are many types of scanners that serve different purposes. One is designed for high-speed, daylight scanning of corrected color separations for all printing processes. Fig. 18-19. This machine will prepare color separations the same size as the original, 200 and 400 percent pre-enlargement. The color separations are re-enlarged or reduced to the required final size during screening.

Color transparencies or unmasked color negatives are most suitable as reproduction copy. An attachment provides the capability to scan flexible color-reflection copy.

The separations are recorded with 150 or 300 lines per centimetre. The maximum size for originals and separation films is 40 × 50 cm (16 × 20").

DIRECT SCREEN METHOD

Direct color separations are made by exposing the copy directly to a panchromatic lithographic type film. The exposure is made through the proper filters, masks, and a halftone screen. Fig. 18-20.

Two types of copy can be used in direct color separation, transmissive and reflective copy. With transmissive copy the light source penetrates the multicolor original. Fig. 18-21. The mask performs the color correction operation, and the filter separates the color. The screen forms the image into halftone dots which are recorded on film. This forms the separation negative.

With reflective copy the lights are in front of the multicolor image. Fig. 18-22. This is the same as with the black and white halftone photography. The reflected light has the colors separated by a filter. The remaining image is screened and has the color correction performed by a mask. The corrected, separated image is recorded on film. This forms the separation negative.

Hell-Color-Metal Corp.
18-19. *A high-speed production daylight scanner. Shown is the "Chromograph DC 300" model.*

The filters commonly used for masking direct color separations are shown in Chapter 17.

The screen angles are 105 degrees for cyan, 90 degrees for yellow, 75 degrees for magenta, and 45 degrees for the black separation.

Direct color separations can be made by three methods: contact, camera, and enlarger method.

Contact Method

The principal mask is made so that its emulsion side will be in contact with the base of the transparency. The base is the side opposite the emulsion side. Fig. 18-23. The finished mask is taped to the back of the transparency so the separation emulsion will contact the emulsion side of the transparency.

The separation filter for one color is placed under the light source. The mask, transparency contact screen, and film are exposed in a contact frame. This is repeated for each color, using the proper filter. A white light exposure can be used for the black separation instead of a filter.

With contact printing the separations made can only be the same size as the original transparency.

The method for making direct screen separation negatives uses the same principle as black and white negatives made by the contact method. Three exposures are used: no screen, or "bump;" main; and flash exposure.

The no-screen exposure, discussed in Chapter 11, increases highlight contrast on the printed illustration. The main exposure passes through a contact screen onto the film. The image from the color transparency is reproduced on the film. This exposure has little effect on the shadow areas of the separation negative. The flash exposure, made through the contact screen, transmits light evenly over the litho pan film. The flash exposure adds dots to the shadow areas which do not receive enough light from the copy to produce dots.

Following are the exposures used to make the four separation negatives.

	No Screen	Main	Flash
Cyan	x	x	x
Magenta		x	x
Yellow		x	x
Black		x	

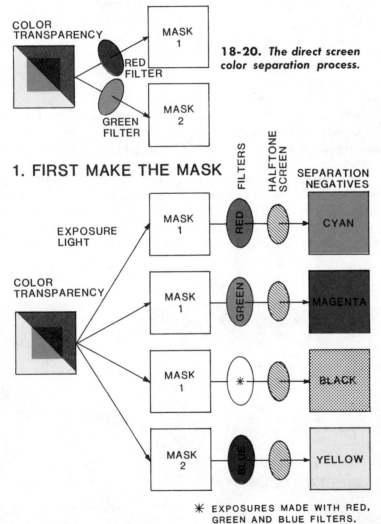

18-20. *The direct screen color separation process.*

1. FIRST MAKE THE MASK

2. THEN MAKE THE SEPARATION NEGATIVES USING THE MASKS

✳ EXPOSURES MADE WITH RED, GREEN AND BLUE FILTERS.

Camera Method Using Reflection Copy

To make a direct color separation using reflection copy, the camera operator must be thoroughly familiar with the techniques of halftone photography discussed in Chapter 11. Following is the procedure:

1. Place the multicolor reflection copy on the camera copyboard.

2. Set the lights on a 45-degree angle in front of the copyboard. Other angles can be used to produce different effects. The lights should be at a distance of at least twice the diagonal measure of the copy. Fig. 18-24.

3. Focus the camera.

4. Calculate the proper exposure. Use a light meter to measure the light falling on the copy. When filters are to be used, the amount of increased exposure must be determined. Enlarge-

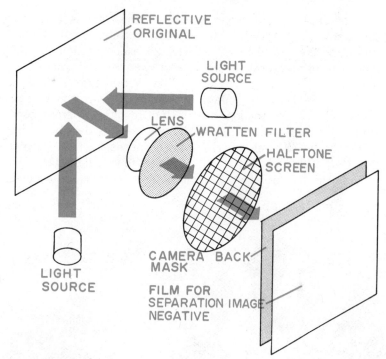

18-22. *The camera method of direct color separation using reflective copy.*

18-23. *The contact method of direct color separation.*

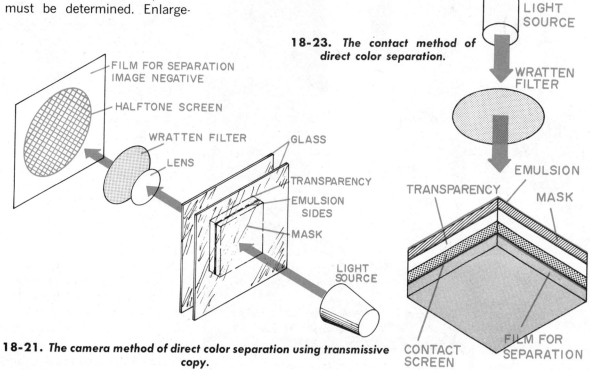

18-21. *The camera method of direct color separation using transmissive copy.*

ment or reduction of original copy changes the exposure. The final exposure calculation is made by using an exposure computer.

Film manufacturers' data sheets contain information on lighting, exposure time, and lens setting for the Wratten No. 25 filter (red filter for the cyan printer). Fig. 18-25. The expo-

sure for the other separations is found by multiplying the Wratten No. 25 exposure time by their recommended filter ratios.

The manufacturers' filter ratios will generally produce satisfactory results. Different conditions in various darkrooms may make it necessary for the camera operator to vary the ratios. Carefully kept records of exposure

data will help produce the ratios which work the best.

5. Place the proper filter in front of the camera lens. Fig. 18-26.

6. Set the timer for the proper exposure time.

7. Turn out the lights in the darkroom. Place a sheet of film in the camera back with the emulsion facing the lens. Place the contact screen on top of the film at the proper angle for the separation to be made. Fig. 18-27. Place the mask over the screen. Be certain the film and mask are in pin register. Close the back and make the exposure.

8. Develop the film following manufacturers' recommendations.

These steps produce one of the four separation negatives. The others are made the same way using different filters, screen angles, and exposure times.

If the separation negative needs hand-etching color correction, this is done before the plate is made. See the section in this chapter on color correction.

Camera Method Using Transmissive Copy

The principal mask is made with its emulsion side facing the emulsion side of the transparency. See Fig. 18-28. The principal mask and transparency are carefully registered and placed between two pieces of glass. This entire assembly is placed in the transparency holder on the camera copyboard. Fig. 18-29. The image should appear right-reading when viewed through the camera lens. The transparency should be between the lens and the mask.

18-24. The lights are set at a 45-degree angle in front of the copyboard.

KODALITH Pan Film 2568 (ESTAR Base)

ENGLISH

- Extremely high contrast, fast panchromatic film.
- Yields high-quality halftone direct color-separation negatives and positives by either projection or contact printing methods. Also suitable for linework.
- Dimensionally stable .004-inch (0.10mm) ESTAR Base.

Safelight: KODAK Safelight Filter No. 3 (dark green) in a suitable safelight lamp with a 15-watt bulb. Keep the film at least 4 feet (1.2 meters) from the safelight.

EXPOSURE • **Caution:** To prevent pinholes and spots, be sure the film and copyboard glass are clean and free of dust.

Meter Settings:

White-Flame Arc	Tungsten or Quartz-Iodine	Pulsed-Xenon Arc
ASA **40*** 17 DIN*	ASA **32*** 16 DIN*	ASA **40†** 17 DIN†

*Recommended for meters marked for ASA or DIN Speeds or Exposure Indexes and are for trial exposures in copying. They apply to *incident-light meters* directly and to *reflected-light meters* used with the KODAK Neutral Test Card (18% gray side) at the copyboard. A matte white card will serve, in which case expose for five times the calculated exposure time.
†This value indicates the relative speed of this material to pulsed-xenon illumination as measured by a light integrator.

Filter Factors for KODAK WRATTEN Filter No. 25: When a No. 25 Filter is used, multiply the amount of unfiltered exposure by the approximate filter factor given in the table below.

White-Flame Arc	Tungsten or Quartz-Iodine	Pulsed-Xenon Arc
5	3.2	5

Example of Exposure: For a same-size (1:1) line reproduction, with two 1500-watt pulsed-xenon arc lamps about 3 feet (0.9 m) from the copyboard, expose for about 10 seconds at *f*/22 through the KODAK WRATTEN Filter No. 25.

Screen Exposures: With KODAK Gray Contact Screens (Negative), the exposures through the WRATTEN Filter No. 25 will be 4 to 5 times longer than for linework. For glass crossline screens, the factor is much higher and varies with the method of use.

Filter Ratios Relative to the No. 25 Filter: To determine exposure times for other filters, multiply the exposure time for the KODAK WRATTEN Filter No. 25 by the filter ratios given below. Because lighting conditions vary, these ratios are approximate and are intended only as guides. The ratios are based on an exposure time of approximately 15 seconds with the No. 25 Filter.

Light Source	KODAK WRATTEN Filter					
	No. 8	No. 23A	No. 25	No. 47	No. 47B	No. 58
Pulsed-Xenon Arc	0.5	0.8	1.0	3.0	4.0	2.0
White-Flame Arc	0.5	0.8	1.0	2.5	3.0	3.0
Tungsten or Quartz-Iodine	0.6	0.8	1.0	10.0	12.0	4.0

Filter Factors: When colored copy must be photographed as black-and-white, use information published in these Kodak Publications: No. Q-44, *KODAK Filter Selector*, and No. Q-27, *Film and Filter Combinations for Photographing Colors as Black-and-White* (available through your graphic arts dealer).

Eastman Kodak Co.

18-25. A film manufacturer's data sheet.

18-26. The filter is inserted in front of the camera lens.

The camera is focused. The lights are placed behind the copyboard. The proper filter is placed in the lens barrel.

The screen is placed on the camera back at the proper angle.

The exposure must be ascertained.

Enlarger Method

A number of direct screen enlarger systems are commercially available, among them the Berkey "Graphic Master." Fig. 18-30. This system rapidly produces four-color separations through advanced automation of the direct screen process. In addition to producing continuous tone color separations, the system produces veloxes, mezzotints, continuous tone negatives and positives, color duplication, and continuous tone prints. A schematic of the system is shown in Fig. 18-31.

The enlarger head contains a xenon light source and a condenser or diffusing system. Adapter cones provide the optimum lamp position for even illumination of lenses of different focal lengths.

The film carrier contains register pins which lock the transparency, mask, and main stage

445

18-27. *The contact screen is placed at the proper angle.*

| GLASS |
| COLOR TRANSPARENCY |
| DIFFUSER |
| SENSITIVE MATERIAL-MASK |

18-28. *The principal mask is made with the emulsion side facing the emulsion side of the transparency.*

All exposure operations are automatically programmed and controlled from the four-channel programmer. It has four banks of timers. Each bank consists of a solid-state main exposure and flash timer for each color separation. The correct filter is automatically placed in front of the lens when the appropriate timing

18-29. *The mask and transparency are registered and placed in the transparency holder on the copyboard.*

in perfect register. This allows the masks to be changed while making a set of separations and still keeps the projected separations in perfect register.

Beneath the lens is a motorized, six-position filter wheel which is automatically controlled from the programmer. The enlarger head is motor-driven by pushbutton controls. A hand crank and digital counter provide additional focusing aids.

The register easel contains vacuum grooves and register pins for a variety of film sizes. The register pins are controlled by a pin programmer, which automatically raises the proper pair for a given film size. After the film is set on the pins and the vacuum is applied, the pins automatically retract. The luminescent flash panel is used to control the size of the shadow dot in negative halftones.

446

channel is started by push button.

Two push buttons provide constant, unfiltered illumination for sizing, focusing, and highlight measurement and for turning the power on and off. The cyan highlight, the controlling factor in color separation, is measured by a built-in aperture control meter. A ratio switch automatically multiplies the main exposure time by the proper factor for extreme enlargements.

The vacuum system is preprogrammed by the operator for a given film and screen size.

The unit is operated under darkroom conditions. It has a switch to control lighting in the darkroom. After programming, three controls are operated in the dark; main and flash exposures and a selector for film, screen, and overlay vacuum zones.

Separations from Color Negatives

Separations can be made from a color negative. The color negative has a full range of tones and colors. The tones are reversed and colors in the film are the

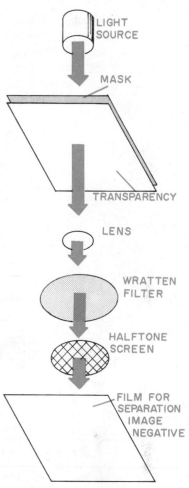

18-31. *A schematic of the Berkey enlarger process.*

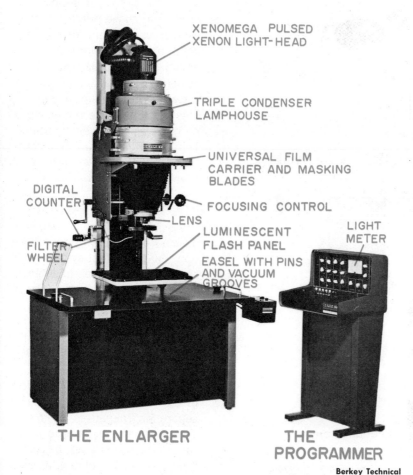

THE ENLARGER

THE PROGRAMMER

Berkey Technical

18-30. *The Berkey "Graphic Master" enlarger system.*

complements of the original colors. The negative has a color correcting mask built into it which gives it its orange color.

When the color negative is used for contact printing, it acts as a color filter. As the exposure light is passed through it, each area of the negative passes its components and absorbs its complementary color.

The color negative is exposed on Kodak "Resisto Rapid Pan Paper." It is designed for making black and white separations from color negatives. A tungsten light enlarger with a color corrected lens and a bulb is used. The separations are made by direct exposure using the proper filters. The prints can be masked or un- masked. Produced are separations for the magenta, cyan, and yellow printers. A black printer is generally not used. The basic steps are shown in Fig. 18-32.

Kodak "Pan Masking" film is used for masks. Two masks are used to increase or decrease color saturation. The "A" mask is made with a Wratten filter No. 29 (red) on the enlarger lens. The "B" mask is made with a Wratten filter No. 99 (green) on the lens. The "A" mask is used on the magenta separation. The "B" mask is used on the yellow separation. None is used on the cyan separation.

The orange-colored negative is placed in an enlarger. It is focused to the size wanted for the separation. Expose each separation print using the proper filter and masks. Black and white prints of each separation are produced. These prints are then used as copy on a process camera to make the color separation negatives. Fig. 18-32. The copy is screened at this time, producing screened separation negatives. This process is like producing a normal black and white halftone. The film manufacturer's recommendations for exposure and developing should be followed.

INDIRECT SCREEN METHOD

Indirect color separation produces a better quality reproduction than the direct system. The separations can be made in a camera, an enlarger, or a contact printing frame. Generally, three masks are made to correct the color for deficiencies in the ink.

Indirect separation differs from direct separation because four steps are needed. First the mask is made. Then the color separation negative is made. This is a continuous tone separation (no halftone dot pattern). Then the halftone photography is

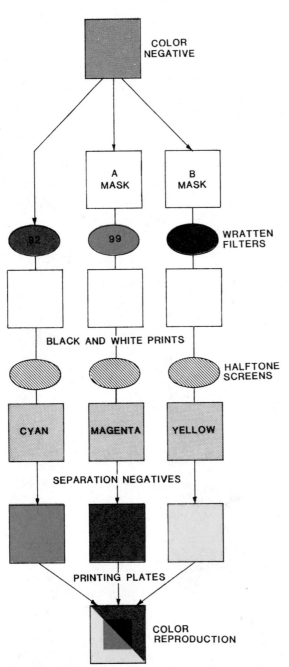

18-32. *Making separations from color negatives.*

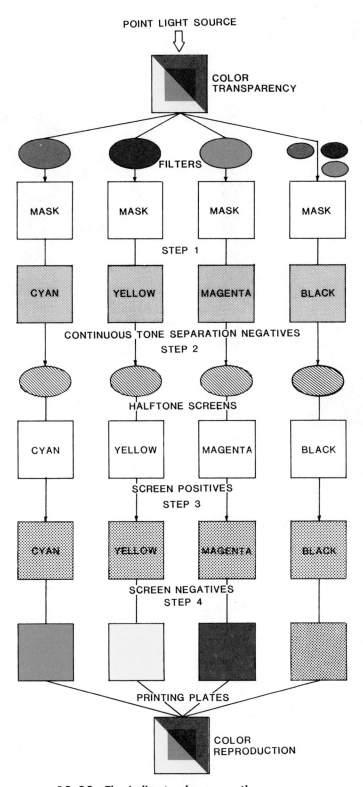

18-33. *The indirect color separation process.*

POINT LIGHT SOURCE

COLOR TRANSPARENCY

FILTERS

MASK MASK MASK MASK

STEP 1

CYAN YELLOW MAGENTA BLACK

CONTINUOUS TONE SEPARATION NEGATIVES
STEP 2

HALFTONE SCREENS

CYAN YELLOW MAGENTA BLACK

SCREEN POSITIVES
STEP 3

CYAN YELLOW MAGENTA BLACK

SCREEN NEGATIVES
STEP 4

PRINTING PLATES

COLOR REPRODUCTION

performed as a third step. A screen positive is made. Fourth, the screen positive is used to make a screen negative. Fig. 18-33.

The separation negatives are made by passing the exposure light through the transparency and mask and onto the separation negative film. As stated before, a red filter is used when making the cyan separation negative. A blue filter is used when making the yellow separation negative. A green filter is used when making the magenta separation negative. The black separation negative is often made by three exposures, one each with the red, green, and blue filter.

The transparency is mounted and held with narrow lithographer's tape in a jig sheet. Fig. 18-34.

A "Three-Point Transparency Guide" is mounted on the jig sheet. It is placed as close to the original as possible. Fig. 18-34. The patches marked A, M, B are three density aim points used for controlling the process. The A patch density is 0.40, the M is 1.30 and the B is 2.40. The color blocks marked C, M, and Y refer to cyan, magenta, and yellow. These reproduce on the waste portion of the separation and are used to identify them. For example, only the magenta block reproduces on the magenta separation as a mark to identify it. Fig. 18-34. For more information on the guide, see the last section of this chapter.

The transparency on the jig sheet is used to expose the mask. Fig. 18-35. After the mask is developed, it is evaluated by reading the A, M, and B patches

449

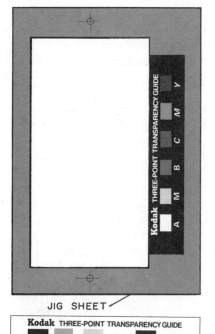

JIG SHEET

Kodak THREE-POINT TRANSPARENCY GUIDE

A	M	B	C	M	Y

THE GUIDE AFTER DEVELOPMENT. THIS WAS ON A MAGENTA SEPARATION.

Eastman Kodak Co.

18-34. *The transparency to be separated is mounted on a jig sheet. A "Three-Point Transparency Guide" is placed next to it.*

with a transmission densitometer. The densitometer measures different tones and expresses them in numbers. The A-B range and the mask number are measured. The A-B range is found by subtracting B density from A density. This is controlled by development. An increase in development time will increase the A-B range. A decrease in development time will decrease the A-B range. An increase in exposure time will increase the mask number. A decrease in exposure time will lower the mask number. After a change in development or exposure time is made, a new mask is made and tested. When

the mask is within the desired range, it is ready to use.

Next the mask is used to produce the continuous tone separation negative. Fig. 18-36. Each negative is made in this manner using the proper filter. Fig. 18-33. Each is developed according to the recommendations of the film manufacturer. Generally, the cyan negative is made first. It is developed and then evaluated with a densitometer. Adjustments are made in exposure and development times until a satisfactory cyan negative is made. These findings are used to produce the other negatives.

To achieve proper balance within the separation negatives, a Kodak color-separation calculator can be used. Fig. 18-37. The three aiming points on the negative are measured and used to determine if each negative is correctly exposed and developed. These control factors are the

EXPOSURE LIGHT

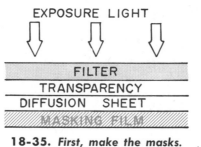

| FILTER |
| TRANSPARENCY |
| DIFFUSION SHEET |
| MASKING FILM |

18-35. *First, make the masks.*

EXPOSURE LIGHT

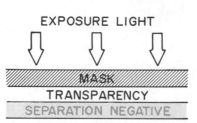

| MASK |
| TRANSPARENCY |
| SEPARATION NEGATIVE |

18-36. *Next, make the continuous tone separation negatives.*

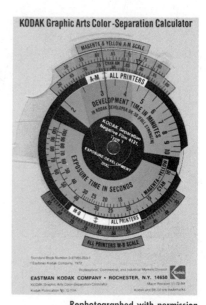

Rephotographed with permission from Eastman Kodak Co.

18-37. *The Kodak color calculator.*

density ranges from the A to M and M to B density patches. (For details in using the calculator read *Kodak Graphic Arts Color Calculator with the Kodak Three-Aim-Point Control-Method.*)

Much of the color film developing in industry is done with automatic processors. The technician must manipulate the exposure and development times to make corrections in the negatives.

After the continuous tone separation negatives are made, the next step is to make halftone screen positives. Any standard method for producing screened film positives may be used. This operation calls for skill and judgment by the technician. The masks and separation negatives are made by matching them to standard aim-point densities. All separations should be expected to meet the same standards. It is necessary to locate the areas of the transparency which are the highlights, middletones, and shadows. The location of highlight, middletone, and shadow dots must be controlled so they are in the places needed.

Separation negatives that are the same size as the desired finished reproduction can be made in a vacuum contact printing frame using a point-source light for exposure. If enlargement or reduction is needed, a process camera or an enlarger can be used. Fig. 18-38. The process includes setting the camera for the magnification wanted. Place a separation negative on the copyboard. Block off around its edges with black paper to lower the amount of flare. Set the copyboard lights behind the separation negative. A frosted glass is placed between the lights and the negative. Place the proper contact screen on the camera vacuum back. Remember that the suggested angles are 105° for cyan, 75° for magenta, 90° for yellow, and 45° for black. Make the cyan screen positive first. See if the exposure is correct. Then make the positives. They will be adjusted according to the exposure of the cyan negative.

The screen positives made are used to contact print the screen negatives. The printing plates are made with these screen negatives. Positive plates can be made using the screen positive directly.

METHODS OF COLOR CORRECTION

Basic color correction is designed to correct deficiencies in process inks by controlling (re-

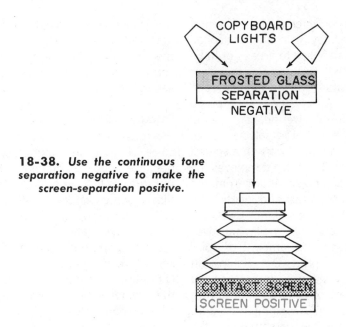

18-38. Use the continuous tone separation negative to make the screen-separation positive.

ducing) the amount of silver deposits (dot size) on the final separation film. The three methods are *electronic scanning, dot etching,* and *photographic masking.*

ELECTRONIC SCANNING

Electronic scanning color correction is achieved by modifying the exposure light when the separation negatives are exposed by the scanning process. First, the image light emitted from the copy is analyzed for its color value. Then, when the light is processed into modulated electrical currents, the currents are varied in intensity in direct proportion to impurities contained in the process inks. Fig. 18-12. Other factors such as paper, photographic material, and printing process are also considered. The corrected currents are converted back into corrected exposure light beams which are then used to expose the final separation negatives.

No local color correction is possible with the electronic scanning color correction process. Also, localized detail cannot be added to negatives by the scanning method. For more information, see the electronic color scanning section of this chapter.

DOT ETCHING

Dot etching color correction is achieved by reducing the size of the halftone dots on separation film with an etching solution. The dot etching process, which adjusts the dot sizes, is used after the film is completely processed. A specially formulated cyanide etch or Farmer's reducer are the two most common solutions used to remove the silver deposits from the processed film.

When all the dots on the film are to be reduced, it is submerged in an etching solution. When only a portion of the film is to be corrected (reduced), a protective staging lacquer or asphaltum is applied to areas not to be reduced. This protects the silver deposits from the etching solution. After the appropriate amount of silver deposits are removed from the selected area, the film is washed with a special solvent. The solvent removes the lacquer or asphaltum from the protected area and neutralizes the etching solution.

Dot etching on film positives *decreases* the amount of color that will print. Dot etching on film negatives *increases* the amount of color that will print.

The normal etching procedure calls for the person doing the etching to first evaluate the differences between colors on the original copy and colors produced by a proof of the uncorrected film. Then by using a color-analyzing device and experienced judgment, the appropriate dot size area for each film is determined. Then each film is corrected until the desired dot size is achieved. It takes considerable skill to develop a feeling for the correct dot size because the change in dot size is not directly proportional to the tone value on the original copy. Often a very small change in dot size may produce a large shift in color value. This is especially true for the middletone colors which correspond to those dot sizes within the 45 to 55 percent range. Dots can be reduced up to 10 percent of their original size by the etching process.

The dot etching process can be used to make local corrections and is often used in addition to the other methods of color correction. Because of the color and

image blending problems associated with dot etching, a loss of the photographic impression sometimes occurs in etched separation film.

PHOTOGRAPHIC MASKING

A mask is a weak image of the color original on photographic negative film (sometimes referred to as masking film). This film negative is used with the original color copy when making the color separation negatives.

Masking methods in use today serve three purposes. These are (1) to bring the density range of the original within the limits possible to reproduce on a press, (2) to correct for optical contamination in ink, and (3) to sharpen the detail of the printed color reproduction. Most masking systems perform all three functions at once. They must be given careful consideration by the technician as the masks are made.

The control of the density range is rather complex. The

problem is to try to reproduce the density range of the original color copy. It is not possible to duplicate the total density range of color transparencies. Even the best printing conditions cannot achieve this. It is possible to reproduce the density range of reflection copy.

Density range is controlled by the mask by compressing the tones into a narrower range. Printers use a gray scale with the original color copy. Fig. 18-34 shows a three-step gray scale. Steps are marked A, M, and B.

The density range of a transparency from highlight to shadow can approach 2.6. The density range of reflection copy approaches 2.0. Printing the three process inks on good coated stock can produce a density range of about 1.5. The use of the black printer increases this to about 2.0.

The mask is placed in register with the color original, and the separation film is exposed. This lowers the density range of the

DENSITY RANGE COMPRESSION

	Subtract
High original reading (shadow range of original)	2.40
Low density reading (highlight of original)	0.40
Density range of original	2.00
Negative highlight mask reading	1.10
Shadow mask reading	0.20
Density range of mask	0.90
Density range of original	2.00
Density range of mask	0.90
Density range of combination	1.10

18-39. How to find density range compression using the mask density range and the original density range.

MASK NUMBER FOR REFLECTION COPY

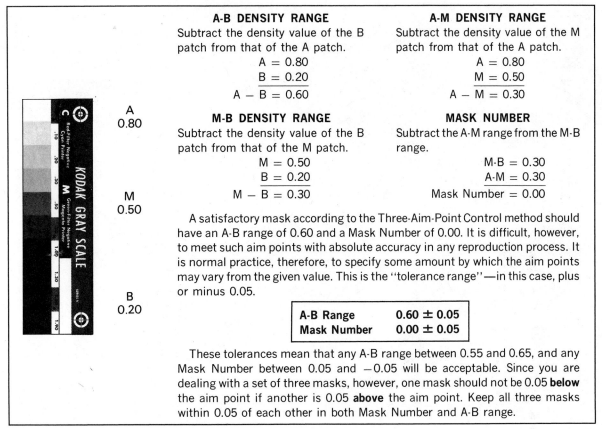

A-B DENSITY RANGE

Subtract the density value of the B patch from that of the A patch.

A = 0.80
B = 0.20
_____
A − B = 0.60

A-M DENSITY RANGE

Subtract the density value of the M patch from that of the A patch.

A = 0.80
M = 0.50
_____
A − M = 0.30

M-B DENSITY RANGE

Subtract the density value of the B patch from that of the M patch.

M = 0.50
B = 0.20
_____
M − B = 0.30

MASK NUMBER

Subtract the A-M range from the M-B range.

M-B = 0.30
A-M = 0.30
_____
Mask Number = 0.00

A = 0.80

M = 0.50

B = 0.20

A satisfactory mask according to the Three-Aim-Point Control method should have an A-B range of 0.60 and a Mask Number of 0.00. It is difficult, however, to meet such aim points with absolute accuracy in any reproduction process. It is normal practice, therefore, to specify some amount by which the aim points may vary from the given value. This is the "tolerance range"—in this case, plus or minus 0.05.

A-B Range	0.60 ± 0.05
Mask Number	0.00 ± 0.05

These tolerances mean that any A-B range between 0.55 and 0.65, and any Mask Number between 0.05 and −0.05 will be acceptable. Since you are dealing with a set of three masks, however, one mask should not be 0.05 **below** the aim point if another is 0.05 **above** the aim point. Keep all three masks within 0.05 of each other in both Mask Number and A-B range.

Eastman Kodak Co.

18-40. *How to find the mask number for reflection copy.*

original before the separation negatives are made.

One way to find out how much the density range of the original will be compressed is by finding the mask density range and the original density range and subtracting. Fig. 18-39.

Another method for checking the proper mask contrast is by finding the mask number. This number is the difference between the M minus B and A minus M density ranges of the mask. Figs. 18-40 and 18-41. Adjustment of the mask number permits the middletones to be

changed without radically changing the density range or highlight and shadow tone values.

By reading the log density values of the A, M, and B patches on the processed masks, the density range and mask number can be computed and adjusted to insure the mask is compensating for ink impurities, condensing copy range, controlling color tone, and providing for color balance as needed. A tolerance range has been computed into the control patch system. Fig. 18-42 illustrates the recommended tolerances for reflection

and transmissive copy. Fig. 18-43 indicates what corrective action is required when the processed mask exceeds the acceptable tolerance.

In processing, *mask number* is controlled by changes in *exposure*, while *density range* is controlled by changes in development. There is a minor correlation between the two activities inasmuch as mask numbers can be slightly affected by radical changes in development.

Sometimes *neutral density filters* are added to the three patches on the copy to compen-

MASK NUMBER FOR TRANSPARENCIES

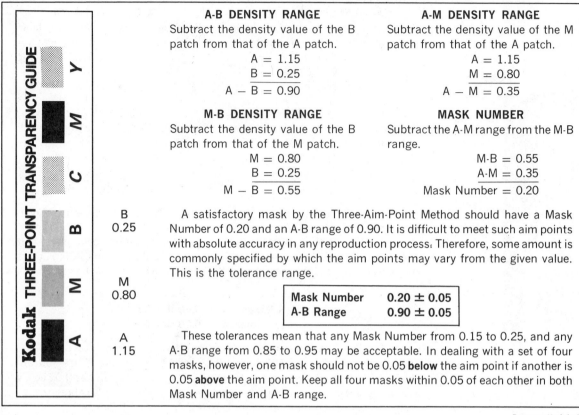

Kodak THREE-POINT TRANSPARENCY GUIDE

Y
M
C
B
M
A

B
0.25

M
0.80

A
1.15

A-B DENSITY RANGE

Subtract the density value of the B patch from that of the A patch.

A = 1.15
B = 0.25
A − B = 0.90

M-B DENSITY RANGE

Subtract the density value of the B patch from that of the M patch.

M = 0.80
B = 0.25
M − B = 0.55

A-M DENSITY RANGE

Subtract the density value of the M patch from that of the A patch.

A = 1.15
M = 0.80
A − M = 0.35

MASK NUMBER

Subtract the A-M range from the M-B range.

M-B = 0.55
A-M = 0.35
Mask Number = 0.20

A satisfactory mask by the Three-Aim-Point Method should have a Mask Number of 0.20 and an A-B range of 0.90. It is difficult to meet such aim points with absolute accuracy in any reproduction process. Therefore, some amount is commonly specified by which the aim points may vary from the given value. This is the tolerance range.

Mask Number	0.20 ± 0.05
A-B Range	0.90 ± 0.05

These tolerances mean that any Mask Number from 0.15 to 0.25, and any A-B range from 0.85 to 0.95 may be acceptable. In dealing with a set of four masks, however, one mask should not be 0.05 **below** the aim point if another is 0.05 **above** the aim point. Keep all four masks within 0.05 of each other in both Mask Number and A-B range.

Eastman Kodak Co.

18-41. *How to find the mask number for transparencies.*

sate for denser than normal copy. Neutral density filters absorb light equally throughout the visible spectrum. They are used to dim the amount of available light. This is done to keep the abnormally dense copy within the established tolerance range of the patches and thereby maintain the proper color tone and balance without adjusting established exposure times. (Neutral density filters are also discussed in Chapter 11.)

The recommended numerical values for range and mask number may not work for every production environment or type of press. For example, negative

mask numbers are often required when color separated images are to be printed on lithographic web-fed perfecting presses.

Direct screen silver masking recommendations are often different from the conventional recommendations. As discussed in earlier chapters, silver halide

MASK TOLERANCE

FOR REFLECTION COPY	1 Mask Number should fall between −0.05 and −0.15 2 A-to-B density ranges should fall between 0.55 and 0.65
FOR TRANSPARENT COPY	1 Mask Number should fall between 0.15 and 0.25 2 A-to-B density range should fall between 0.85 and 0.95

Eastman Kodak Co.

18-42. *Recommended mask tolerance ranges.*

MASK CORRECTIONS

IF MASK NUMBER IS	AND A-B RANGE IS	
LOW	LOW	**Increase development time to increase the A-B range.** If the Mask Number is only slightly low, no exposure change is needed. The increased development will also raise the Mask Number slightly. If the Mask Number is very low, the exposure should be increased slightly.
	CORRECT	**Increase the exposure to raise the Mask Number.** If a very large exposure increase is used, a slight decrease in development time may be needed to hold the A-B range constant.
	HIGH	**Increase the exposure to raise the Mask Number. Decrease development to decrease the A-B range.**
CORRECT	LOW	**Increase the development time to increase the A-B range.** This development increase will also tend to raise the Mask Number. Decrease the exposure slightly to hold the Mask Number constant.
	CORRECT	**No change necessary.**
	HIGH	**Decrease the development time to decrease the A-B range.** Since decreased development will tend to lower the Mask Number, a slight exposure increase may be necessary to hold the Mask Number constant.

MASK CORRECTIONS

IF MASK NUMBER IS	AND A-B RANGE IS	
HIGH	LOW	**Decrease exposure to lower the Mask Number. Increase the development time to increase the A-B range.**
	CORRECT	**Decrease the exposure to lower the Mask Number.** If a very large exposure decrease is used, a slight increase in development time may be necessary to hold the A-B range constant.
	HIGH	**Decrease the development time to decrease the A-B range.** If the Mask Number is only slightly high, this development decrease will also tend to correct the Mask Number. If the Mask Number is very high, a slight exposure decrease may also be needed.

18-43. Recommended correction to bring a mask within the acceptable tolerance range.

Eastman Kodak Co.

455

films develop density as the silver particles in their emulsion absorb and scatter the light hitting them. The film must be placed in an optical device which projects light from all directions through a diffuse system. If a condenser enlarger is used, much of the light projected will not reach the film because the enlarger projects directional light. If silver halide film is exposed in a condenser enlarger and measured with a standard transmission densitometer, it will not appear to have as much density as it did in the enlarger. Since the densitometer measures the diffuse density, the difference is caused by the use of two different optical systems. Always use the same system for exposing the film and measuring density.

The scattering of light by the silver particles in the silver halide film is called Callier's Q-factor. The Q-factor is the amount the density has to be multiplied to compensate for the change in density when using different types of optical systems.

Silver halide color-correcting masks scatter light. If used in a condenser enlarger, allowance must be made because they will appear to have a greater density range than is measured by a densitometer.

Color deficiencies in inks are another limiting factor. Process inks are designed to absorb about one-third of the visible spectrum and transmit two-thirds. Actually they absorb more and have a contaminated appearance. Cyan ink appears to be contaminated with a little magenta and yellow ink. Magenta ink appears to be contaminated

CORRECTIVE ACTION OF THE MASKS

Mask	Filter	Action	Inks Corrected by Mask
Magenta mask	Red	Reduces magenta ink printed in cyan areas and yellow areas.	Cyan
Yellow mask	Green	Reduces yellow ink printed in magenta areas.	Magenta
Cyan mask	Amber	Compresses the tone.	

18-44. *Use of masks will help compensate for optical impurities in ink.*

with yellow ink. Yellow ink appears free of contamination. These problems are due to the pigments available to the ink manufacturers.

Color correction for ink deficiencies is controlled by the mask. The process ink is transparent. The light passes through the ink and reflects from the paper. The ink absorbs certain parts of the spectrum. What we see as color is the remaining parts of the spectrum reflected from the paper. Since inks are not pure, they absorb a little of some colors they should not.

Since inks have optical impurities, there are problems when they are printed over each other. For example, when cyan and magenta are overprinted to make blue, the slight magenta and yellow in cyan will give the blue a pink cast. The magenta mask will reduce the magenta ink slightly wherever cyan prints, thus removing the pink cast. This mask is made with the red filter. Fig. 18-44.

As stated before, magenta ink appears to be contaminated with yellow ink. Since red is made by

printing magenta over yellow, the extra yellow makes the red appear orange. A mask is made with a green filter for the yellow printer. The mask will reduce the yellow in all areas where magenta is to be printed. Fig. 18-44.

The process inks have very little cyan contamination. The cyan mask is a tone compression mask. It uses an amber-colored filter. Fig. 18-44.

Remember that contamination in one color ink is corrected by filtering that color in one of the other color separation negatives. Contamination in magenta ink is corrected in the yellow separation, cyan ink is corrected in the magenta separation. Fig. 18-44.

The amount of color correction is given as *percent masking*. It is found by dividing the density range of the mask by the density range of the original.

Percent masking
$$= \frac{\text{Density range of mask}}{\text{Density range of original}}$$

Process inks are checked for color contamination using a reflection densitometer. The inks are printed on the stock to be used. Each is checked with the densitometer using a red, green, and blue filter. A typical set of readings is shown in Fig. 18-45.

Observe the cyan ink readings. The reading 1.39 is the desired reading. The green and blue light readings should be zero. Since they are not zero, this indicates some contamination of the cyan ink by these colors. These are undesired readings.

Magenta ink should have zero readings for red and blue light. Yellow ink should have zero readings for red and green light.

The density range of the mask is the difference between the density of the A and B patches on the mask. The density range of the original is found by examining it with a densitometer and recording the highest and lowest density reading, or A and B patches on the original could be used. The range is the difference between these readings.

Percent correction is found using the density readings made on the ink samples. The following examples refer to those reported in Fig. 18-45. Percent correction is found using the following formula:

Percent correction

$$= \frac{\text{Highest unwanted density}}{\text{Wanted density}}$$

When making these calculations, remember the following:

1. *Magenta ink* is evaluated to find the percent mask for *yellow* needed to correct the yellow contamination in magenta ink.

2. *Cyan ink* is evaluated to find the percent mask for *magenta* needed to correct the magenta contamination in cyan ink.

To find the percent mask for yellow:

Percent mask for yellow

$$= \frac{\text{(highest unwanted density)}}{\text{(wanted density)}}$$

$$= \frac{0.62}{1.32} = 47\%$$

When these formulas are applied to the data in Fig. 18-45, the following percentages are found:

Yellow mask—47%, or magenta ink has 47% contamination of yellow.

Magenta mask—21%, or cyan ink has 21% contamination of magenta.

A third function of a mask is to enrich the detail of the color reproduction. This is done by using an "unsharp" mask to make the separation negatives. An unsharp mask is made by placing a sheet of frosted acetate between the transparency and masking film when the exposure is made. This produces a separation in which the image edges between light and dark areas are exaggerated, increasing the contrast of the edge. When reproduced, it will give more detail.

Positive Masks

Positive masks are made from and used with *uncorrected intermediate separation negatives* as in the indirect separation system. Figs. 18-46 and 18-47 illustrate the cycle involved in making positive masks. Generally, only two positive masks are needed to correct deficiencies in uncorrected negatives and process inks.

The cyan separation negative is used to make the positive mask that is placed in register with the magenta negative. This is called mask "A." Fig. 18-48. The mask and negative are exposed to make the color-corrected magenta plate. This mask reduces the unwanted cyan influence contained in the magenta separation negative. The magenta ink impurities in the cyan ink are neutralized by masking the magenta printer in all areas where cyan ink also prints.

The *uncorrected magenta separation negative* is used to make the positive mask that is placed in register with the *yellow separation negative*. This is called the "B" mask, Fig. 18-48, and compensates for magenta ink impurities.

The size of the dots on the yellow printer is reduced in all places where magenta ink dots are also printing. This means magenta ink deficiencies are corrected by reducing the size of

AMOUNT OF LIGHT REFLECTED OFF PAPER

Ink	Red light	Green light	Blue light
Cyan ink	1.39	0.41	0.15
Magenta ink	0.09	1.32	0.62
Yellow ink	0.01	0.08	1.27

18-45. *Typical reflection densitometer readings of printed process ink samples.*

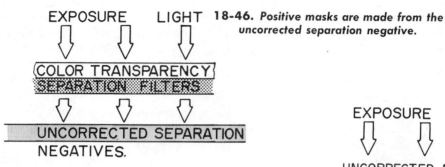

EXPOSURE   LIGHT   **18-46.** *Positive masks are made from the uncorrected separation negative.*

COLOR TRANSPARENCY
SEPARATION FILTERS

UNCORRECTED SEPARATION
NEGATIVES.

1 THE SEPARATION NEGATIVES ARE MADE WITH NO COLOR CORRECTION.

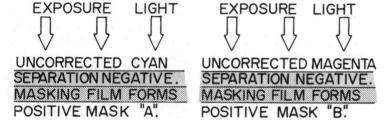

EXPOSURE   LIGHT   EXPOSURE   LIGHT

UNCORRECTED CYAN
SEPARATION NEGATIVE.
MASKING FILM FORMS
POSITIVE MASK "A".

UNCORRECTED MAGENTA
SEPARATION NEGATIVE.
MASKING FILM FORMS
POSITIVE MASK "B".

2 THEN THE UNCORRECTED SEPARATION NEGATIVES ARE USED TO MAKE POSITIVE MASKS—ONE FOR THE CYAN NEGATIVE(MASK "A") AND ONE FOR THE MAGENTA NEGATIVE(MASK "B").

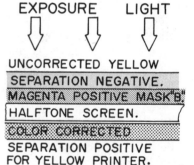

EXPOSURE   LIGHT

UNCORRECTED MAGENTA
SEPARATION NEGATIVE.
CYAN POSITIVE MASK "A"
HALFTONE SCREEN.
COLOR CORRECTED
SEPARATION POSITIVE
FOR MAGENTA PRINTER.

EXPOSURE   LIGHT

UNCORRECTED YELLOW
SEPARATION NEGATIVE.
MAGENTA POSITIVE MASK "B"
HALFTONE SCREEN.
COLOR CORRECTED
SEPARATION POSITIVE
FOR YELLOW PRINTER.

18-47. *Color-corrected separation positives are made using the positive mask and the uncorrected separation negative.*

the yellow dots. The overabundance of yellow effect in magenta ink is adjusted by reducing the amount of yellow ink in those areas where magenta ink also prints.

In summary, the first consideration of positive masking is that exposure light from the magenta separation negative is adjusted by a mask made from the cyan separation negative to reduce the magenta ink influence in areas where cyan ink is also printing. This light intrusion device ("A" mask) compensates for the major shortcoming of the cyan ink, which is its tendency to act as though it is contaminated with magenta ink. Exposure light

from the yellow separation negative is adjusted by a mask made from the magenta separation negative ("B" mask) to reduce the yellow ink influence in areas where magenta ink is also printing. This compensates for the major deficiency of magenta ink, which is its tendency to act like it is contaminated with yellow ink.

If a mask is used with the cyan separation negative, it is used to reduce the contrast because the other inks are not contaminated with cyan ink.

Negative Masks

Negative masks are normally made from and used with the actual color transparencies or

reflective copy. This requires that a slightly different method of exposure light control be used to expose and correct the final set of separation negatives. Negative masks correct for the same deficiencies that are corrected by positive masks.

The magenta printing plate should be made from a final separation film that is corrected by the addition of density to the cyan printing areas. The final yellow separation negative must

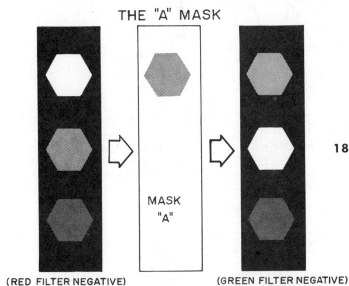

THE "A" MASK

MASK "A"

(RED FILTER NEGATIVE)
THE UNCORRECTED CYAN
SEPARATION NEGATIVE

IS USED TO
PRODUCE A
POSITIVE
MASK

(GREEN FILTER NEGATIVE)
WHICH IS USED WITH
THE UNCORRECTED
MAGENTA SEPARATION
NEGATIVE TO PRODUCE
A COLOR CORRECTED
MAGENTA SEPARATION
POSITIVE.

18-48. *Using the positive "A" and "B" masks.*

contain more density in those areas where magenta dots will also print. Either of the two negative masking systems shown in Fig. 18-49 will correct for the major color material and process ink deficiencies.

Negative masks tend to shorten copy range. This is especially beneficial when slides and transparencies are used as copy since they generally have extremely long range which greatly exceeds the range of contact halftone screens.

MASKING TECHNIQUES

Basic masking techniques used in color correction work employ negative masks. None of

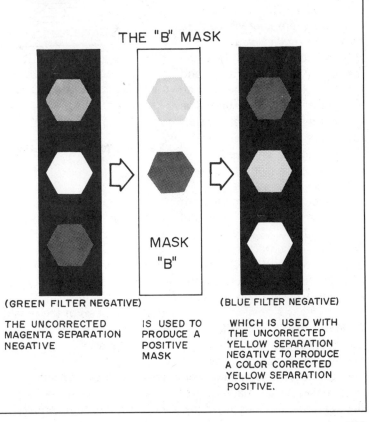

THE "B" MASK

MASK "B"

(GREEN FILTER NEGATIVE)
THE UNCORRECTED
MAGENTA SEPARATION
NEGATIVE

IS USED TO
PRODUCE A
POSITIVE
MASK

(BLUE FILTER NEGATIVE)
WHICH IS USED WITH
THE UNCORRECTED
YELLOW SEPARATION
NEGATIVE TO PRODUCE
A COLOR CORRECTED
YELLOW SEPARATION
POSITIVE.

I. MAKE THE MASK.

2. MAKE THE CORRECTED SEPARATION NEGATIVE.

18-49A. *Negative masking of transmissive copy.*

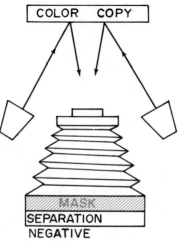

I. MAKING THE MASK.

2. MAKING THE SEPARATION NEGATIVE.

18-49B. *Negative masking of reflection copy.*

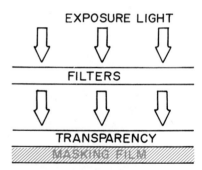

18-50. *Contact masks are made by placing the masking film in contact with the transparency for the exposure.*

the techniques are used with the scanning method of color separation. All may be used with either the direct or indirect separation methods. The basic masking techniques are *contact, camera back,* and *multilayer.*

It is recommended that the method of color separation and the masking technique be thought of as a single unit. The type of mask utilized determines, to a great extent, which separation method is employed.

CONTACT MASKS

Contact masks are made from positive transmissive copy and are considered negative masks. To make a contact mask, the unexposed masking film is placed in direct contact with the copy for exposure. Fig. 18-50.

CAMERA-BACK MASKS

Camera-back masks are negative masks, made as shown in Fig. 18-49. This technique permits masks to be made for reflective and transmissive copy.

The total separation system is shown in Fig. 18-51. Three color-correcting masks are made using a process camera. These are masks for the cyan, magenta, and yellow separation negatives. Two of the masks are used to make the black separation negative.

MULTILAYER MASKS

A multilayer mask is a color negative film that contains three layers: cyan, magenta, and yellow. The film is exposed to the color transparency. When it is developed, it forms a single mask. Since it has three layers, it serves as three masks. When the cyan separation is made, only the cyan layer is seen by the separation film through the red filter. The magenta separation film uses only the magenta layer when seen through the green filter. The yellow separation film uses only the yellow layer when seen through the blue filter.

Since all the layers are processed at the same time, a balanced set of masks is produced. The masks use a dye image which does not scatter light like a silver mask. Sometimes color correction requires one mask be given special attention. It is not possible to do this with the multilayer mask. Two commercially available multilayer masks are the Eastman Kodak "Trimask" and the AGFA-Gevaert "Multimask" film.

COLOR CORRECTION EVALUATION

Color control patches can be used to help evaluate the color

18-51. *The steps to produce a camera-back mask.*

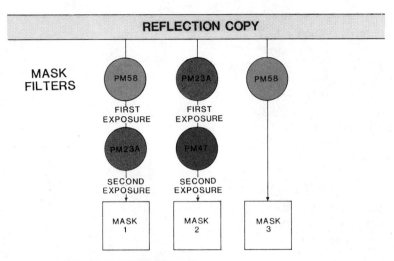

1. FIRST MAKE THE MASKS.

corrections of masks used with reflection copy. These patches should match the hue, value, and saturation of the inks used in printing. Commercial color control patches are shown in Fig. 18-52. These patches were selected as representative of the best average process ink colors. For average inks, the Kodak "Three-Aiming-Point" method produces proper color correction. The color control patches are used as a one-time adjustment in the mask making process. When proper color correction is achieved, the density range of the masks is recorded. This is used to modify the basic data for the "Three-Aiming-Point" control system.

PROCESS COLOR CONTROL SYSTEM

The contrast, detail, and color balance for process color printed images are determined by the density range and gamma curve

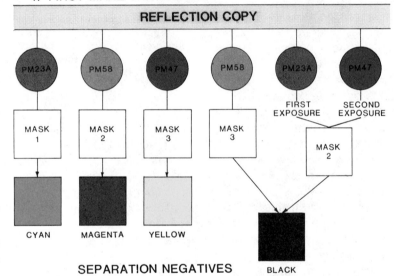

2. USE THE MASKS TO MAKE THE SEPARATIONS.

18-52. *Color control patches.*
Eastman Kodak Co.

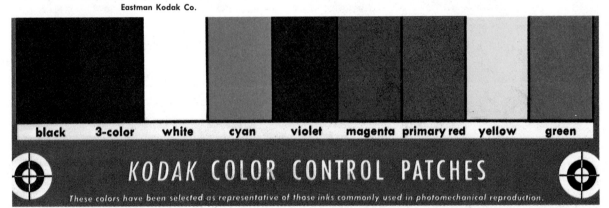

black 3-color white cyan violet magenta primary red yellow green

KODAK COLOR CONTROL PATCHES

These colors have been selected as representative of those inks commonly used in photomechanical reproduction.

shape for each of the four separation negatives. Fig. 18-53. These ranges and curves are the heart of the color separation control system. The object of any halftone control system is to coincide the density range of the copy with the basic density range of the halftone screen so that both fall within the detail reproduction parameters established by the printing press. The gamma curve shape controls the appearance aspects of the printed image within these parameters. In color reproduction this control and measurement concept is especially relevant. Extremely accurate control of the curve shape is required in color reproduction because the middletone dot size is as important as the dot sizes for the shadow and highlight areas. Fig. 18-54 illustrates that the variance in dot size for middletones can be extreme between two halftone separation negatives possessing equal density ranges and same-sized shadow and highlight dots. The color reproduction represented by curve Y will possess greater highlight contrast, darker middletones, and flatter shad-

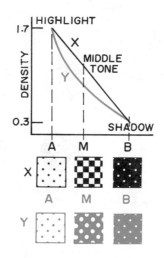

HALFTONE POSITIVES

Eastman Kodak Co.

18-54. *These gamma curves for two separation negatives have similar highlight and shadow dots but differ in the middletones.*

ows than the color reproduction represented by Curve X.

Eastman Kodak Company has developed a "Three-Aiming-Point" control system that uses the gamma curve and density range values to control color separation activities for process printing. The system provides controls to measure and predict the correct amount of silver deposits required in the highlight, middletone, and shadow areas of the masks and the separation negatives. The data derived from the three aiming points is used to produce balanced masks and correspondingly balanced separation negatives. The three control points are identified as the A, M, and B steps. The A step corresponds to the highlight area on the copy, the M step the middletone area, and the B step the shadow area. Fig. 18-54. Patches corresponding to a standard

density reading for each of the steps are added to the copy so that their images are transferred to the mask and separation negative during processing.

The control aspects of the system are founded on the relationship of the points on the curve to each other and not necessarily on the location of the curve to the scale. This means the relationship for the optimum printing densities must correspond to the curve shape and not the fixed scale since usable highlight, middletone, and shadow dots may be found almost anywhere on the scale, but are relatively fixed to the toe, middle and shoulder areas on the curve. Fig. 18-55 shows how two separation negatives can possess different density values with regard to the fixed scale but because their curve shapes are identical will

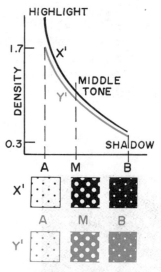

HALFTONE POSITIVES

Eastman Kodak Co.

18-55. *These two separation negatives have different density values, but their gamma curves are identical. They will produce the same A, M, and B results.*

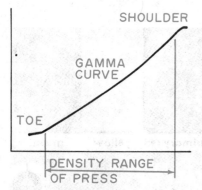

18-53. *The gamma curve and density range.*

produce the same A, M, and B results.

The two most important control characteristics of the gamma curve are the *density range* and the *curve shape*. Density range is the difference in density between any two specific points on the curve, normally A to M, M to B, or A to B. The A to B density is the range that corresponds to that which is printable in a typical printing press. It is also the range into which the copy must be compressed to provide detail producing dots in both the highlight and shadow ends of the scale. Curve shape indicates the contrast characteristics of the image represented by the curve —the steeper the curve, the greater the contrast.

Since it is difficult to measure the highlight, middletone, and shadow areas on many varieties of multiple-color copy, the three-aiming-point control patches are often used for measurement purposes. Those patches represent typical values for the three aspects of the copy. The patches are made sufficiently large to permit convenient measurement with visual or densitometric devices and probes. Control patches are especially helpful when slides are used as copy because they make it much easier to measure the highlight, middletone, and shadow areas on the small slide copy.

The patches are added to the copy so they receive the same exposure as the copy. In this fashion the patch images are transferred to the masks and film during exposure and as such are used to control the exposure and development of the masks and film.

REVIEW QUESTIONS

1. Name the terms defined by the following:
   a. The division of a continuous tone multicolor original into several basic parts.
   b. Opaque copy that reflects light.
   c. Transparent copy.
   d. The negative used to make a color plate.
2. Name the primary printing colors.
3. What colors of ink are used to produce primary red?
4. What colors of ink are used to produce primary blue?
5. To reproduce the range of colors found on original multicolor copy, the image must be converted to halftone dots. What sort of dot arrangement is used?
6. Name the three basic methods of color separation.
7. Name the three methods of basic color correction.

Plates for
Letterpress Printing

The plates used in letterpress printing can be divided into two basic groups: original plates and duplicate plates. *Original plates* are made from the original copy. *Photoengraving* is the process used to convert original images—such as drawings, photographs, and type images—into relief printing plates. The kinds of plates include line, halftone, and color process.

Photoengravings can be made from several different metals or plastics and by a number of different production methods. The materials and methods selected depend upon how the plates will be used. For example, the photoengraver should know if the plates are to be used on the press or for making duplicate plates. It is helpful to know the kind of press, paper, and ink to be used.

Duplicate plates are copies of the original plates. They include stereotypes, electrotypes, rubber plates, and plastic plates. These will be described later in this chapter.

ORIGINAL PLATES
PHOTOENGRAVING—
BASIC STEPS

A variety of processes and materials is available in photoengraving. The basic steps include photographing, stripping, exposing, etching, finishing, mounting,

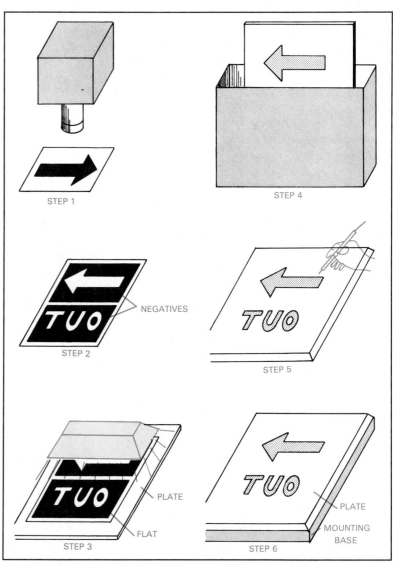

19-1. *The basic steps in photoengraving. (1) The original copy is photographed. (2) The negatives are assembled on a flat in the stripping operation. (3) The flat is exposed to the plate with a light source. (4) The plate is etched and inspected. (5) The plate is finished by beveling the edges and routing away the larger areas of unwanted metal. (6) The plate is mounted so it is type-high.*

and proofing. Fig. 19-1. The following is a general explanation of the process.

The original copy is photographed. It can be enlarged, reduced, or copied at its original size. The negative is a reverse of the original image. This reverse image is carried through the entire process, including making of the plate. When finished, everything on the plate will appear in reverse.

Since a number of negatives can be grouped together, the platemaking process can produce several jobs at one time. The various jobs on the finished plate can be cut apart and used as individual units. The negatives are mounted on a transparent, wax-coated, plastic sheet. This sheet serves as a temporary base during the exposure process. The process of mounting the negative is called stripping. See Chapter 13 for additional information.

The completed, stripped sheet is called a flat. If the flat contains the copy for a complete page, all the negatives must be placed so

that they read from right to left. This is because the negatives are in reverse, and the flat must be stripped so that the plate produced will print the copy reading from left to right.

The next step is to expose the flat to the metal plate. The metal plate has a light-sensitive coating called a *resist*. A number of different types of metal plates and resists are available. Each of these products uses about the same basic steps for exposure and development. Before using any of them, however, it is necessary to study the manufacturer's requirements.

The basic process includes placing the flat on top of the sensitized sheet and exposing it to a light source in a vacuum frame. The areas not covered by the dark parts of the negative are exposed to the light and are hardened. The length of exposure will vary, depending upon the type of sensitized plate and the light source.

After exposure, the plate is coated with a black etching ink.

The ink serves as an adhesive to hold the etching powder that will be applied later.

Next the plate is bathed in water. The water goes through the ink layer and washes the ink and the sensitized coating off the parts of the plate that were not exposed by the light source.

The washed plate is dried and then coated with an etching powder. The etching powder sticks to the parts of the plate with the ink coating. The powder is removed from the areas free of ink. The plate is heated, which causes the etching powder to melt. The powder forms an acid-proof coating on the image.

The next step is to etch the plate. There are a number of ways this is done. The process and chemicals used vary with the plate. In general, the plates are etched in an etching machine. It is essential that the process be carefully controlled. The chemical composition of the etching material, the temperature, and the system used to apply the etch to the material all influence the production of the plate.

The etching material not only removes metal from the unprotected areas, but will also eat into the sidewalls of the raised surface if the etch gets below the powder. To prevent this, the plate is etched, removed, and powdered again so the sidewalls are protected. It is then etched again. This is repeated until the proper depth of etch is reached. Fig. 19-2.

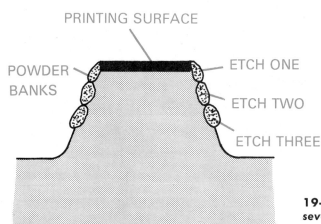

PRINTING SURFACE

POWDER BANKS

ETCH ONE

ETCH TWO

ETCH THREE

19-2. The plate is powdered several times during the etching process.

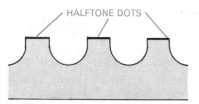

19-3A. *Proper etching produces clean, deeply etched areas.*

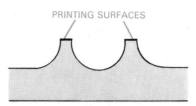

19-4A. *Clean etching.*

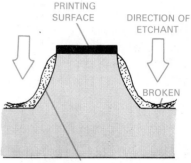

PROTECTIVE BANKING AGENT

19-6. *The Dow-Etching process protects the sides of the relief image.*

19-3B. *Ragged etched dots tend to trap ink and print unevenly.*

19-4B. *Improperly etched line cut permits ink to build on stepped surfaces and print.*

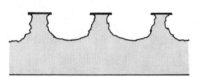

19-3C. *Undercut etched dots leave unsupported dot surfaces which tend to break off.*

It is very important that the etching process leave each dot clean and sharp. Fig. 19-3. If an etch is ragged, it tends to trap ink, and the dots print unevenly. If the dot is undercut, the overhang tends to break off. The overhang also makes it difficult to get duplicate plates to release from the mold.

A clean, line-cut etch is important. Fig. 19-4. A common problem is an etch with ragged edges. These ragged surfaces collect ink and will eventually print.

The depth of the etch is important. Shallow etching causes serious problems in printing and

producing duplicate plates. Recommended etching depths are shown in Fig. 19-5.

With Dow-Etching, a process developed by Dow Chemical Company, the etching and protection of the sides of the relief image occur at the same time. The etching solution contains chemicals which form a protective film on the surface of the plate. A special etching machine

splashes the etching chemical with great force against the non-image areas at an angle of about 90 degrees to the relief printing surface. This breaks the protective film, but since the force against the sidewalls is less, the film on them tends to resist the etch. Fig. 19-6. This process is used for both magnesium and zinc plates.

After the plate is etched, it is cleaned to remove the acid resist coating. The plate is inspected and finished. The finishing process includes hand engraving and

ETCHING DEPTHS IN THOUSANDTHS OF AN INCH

	Halftones for Newspaper Reproduction			Halftones for Magazine, Carton, Book, Catalog and Commercial Printers			
	55 & 65 Screen	65 Screen	85 Screen	100 Screen	110 Screen	120 Screen	133 Screen
Highlights	8	6.5	5	3.8	3.5	3.2	2.9
Middletones	5	4	3	2.6	2.4	2.2	2
Shadows	3	2.8	2.5	1.6	1.6	1.5	1.4

International Association of Electrotypers and Stereotypers, Inc.

19-5. *Recommended etching depths.*

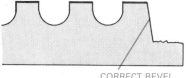

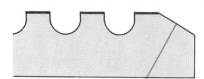

CORRECT BEVEL

IMPROPER BEVEL

International Association of Electrotypers and Stereotypers, Inc.

19-7. Bevels should be deep and as nearly vertical as possible.

International Association of Electrotypers and Stereotypers, Inc.

19-8. A photoengraving with all the dead metal possible left in to produce an electrotype.

additional local etching to improve the plate. Large areas of unwanted metal are removed by routing rather than etching. This is done by an electrically driven cutter, which cuts away the unwanted metal. The edges of the plate are beveled. Fig. 19-7.

If the plate will be used to make duplicate plates rather than for actual printing, the unwanted large metal areas (dead metal) are not routed away. They are needed when making the duplicate plates. Fig. 19-8.

The plate is then mounted on a base so it is type-high (0.918"). The base can be wood, metal, or plastic. If the plate will be used to make duplicate plates, it is not mounted.

After the plate is finished, a proof is taken. It is necessary to examine the quality of the photoengraving before it is used for printing. Proofs should be made with the same inks and papers that will be used for printing the job.

PHOTOENGRAVING—LINE PLATES

A line plate can be made from a copy of line drawings, type images, or any other copy that has no tonal features. Photographs are not used in line plate copies. Since the copy contains no tonal images, it is photographed directly. A negative is produced in which the copy appears transparent, and the rest of the negative is black. The image on the plate is formed by solid surfaces and therefore prints solid images. Fig. 19-9. (Line photography is explained in Chapter 10.)

PHOTOENGRAVING— HALFTONE PLATES

A halftone plate is used to print continuous tone illustrations, such as those found in a photograph. The process is the same as for line plates, except for the photographic process used when making the negatives.

A halftone reproduces the tone pattern shades, from white through black, of a continuous tone image. This is done by placing a film screen on top of the film and photographing the continuous tone image through the screen. The screen breaks the image up into dot patterns. The light tones have smaller dots. The darker tones have larger dots. See Chapter 11, "Halftone Photography." When the halftone is printed, it appears to the naked eye just like a continuous tone photograph. However, when examined through a magnifying glass, the thousands of small dots of various sizes can be seen.

PHOTOENGRAVING—COLOR PROCESS PLATES

Process plates are used to print four-color reproductions. This requires process plates to be made for each of the primary colors—magenta, yellow, and cyan—and one plate for black.

Negatives are made for each of these colors. These are called color separation negatives. As discussed in Chapter 18, color separation is done by photographing the original color image

THE ORIGINAL COPY

THE NEGATIVE

THE PLATE

THE PRINTED IMAGE

19-9. *How a line plate is produced by the photoengraving process.*

through color filters. The filter absorbs the colors of which it is composed and lets the single remaining color be recorded on the film. The separation negatives are rephotographed to produce positives. The positives are then photographed through a halftone screen. These screened nega-

tives are reproduced on the metal plates. The plate is etched, cleaned, and is ready for printing.

WRAPAROUND PLATES

A wraparound plate is a relief printing plate that is shallow etched and is a single unit. Many types are available. Some are made from a single metal sheet, while others use one type of metal for the printing surface and another for the base. Others have a plastic printing surface on a metal base or a plastic printing surface on a plastic base. Each type requires special equipment to make the plates.

The copy to be produced with the wraparound plates is photographed as explained for line and halftone relief plates. One difference is the stripping process. Since the wraparound plate is a single unit, all the copy must be assembled during the stripping to form the complete page. This is explained in Chapter 13, "Laying Out and Stripping the Flat." The stripped flat is then photographed, producing a negative of the page, which is used to process the plate.

PHOTOSENSITIVE PLASTIC LETTERPRESS PLATES

Photosensitive relief letterpress plates enable a printing firm to take advantage of cold composition, yet continue to use their existing letterpress printing equipment. Many companies, such as newspapers, have large investments in letterpress printing equipment and may be unable financially to change to offset presses. These plates make the continued use of these presses economically possible.

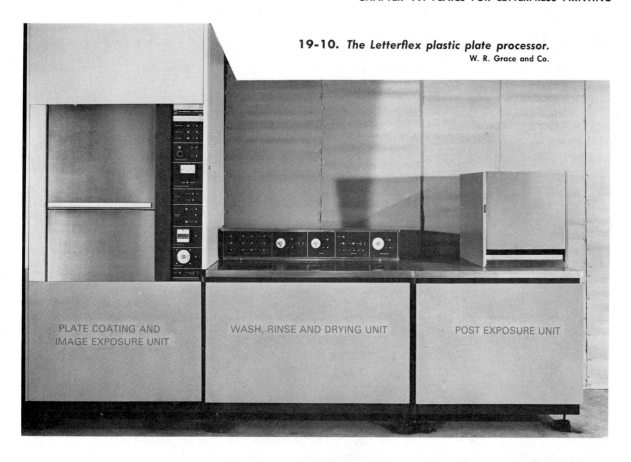

19-10. *The Letterflex plastic plate processor.*
W. R. Grace and Co.

PLATE COATING AND
IMAGE EXPOSURE UNIT

WASH, RINSE AND DRYING UNIT

POST EXPOSURE UNIT

There are several systems in use that produce lightweight plastic relief plates. Such systems are in the developmental stages and improvements are constantly being made. They are discussed in the following sections to illustrate technological developments in letterpress plate systems.

The Letterflex System

The Letterflex system produces a flexible, lightweight plastic relief plate directly from a photographic negative. (Letterflex is the trade name for the system developed by W. R. Grace and Co.) The original copy is generated with any cold composition system. This enables the printer to take advantage of the speed and savings of cold composition, but still utilize letterpress equipment.

The Letterflex plate is a resilient photopolymer material which forms the image bonded to a polyester film base. The depth of the relief image area is 0.020″. The thickness of the film base is 0.005″. The plate weighs less than one-half pound.

One processor available to produce these plates is shown in Fig. 19-10.

The basic steps to produce a Letterflex relief plate are shown in Fig. 19-11.

The film forming the plate is cut to size. It is then moved to the exposure tower. The negative of the original copy produced by the cold composition system is placed above the film and an exposure is made.

The exposed plastic plate is then placed in an exposure drawer for a back exposure. This hardens the surface and prevents the etching from going too deep.

The plastic plate is etched and washed in a water and detergent bath. Fig. 19-12.

The washed plate is dried and returned to the back exposure drawer for additional hardening. The plate is removed and is ready to be trimmed and mounted.

These plates can be mounted on a saddle or on a direct press

⊙ LETTERFLEX PLATEMAKING PROCESS

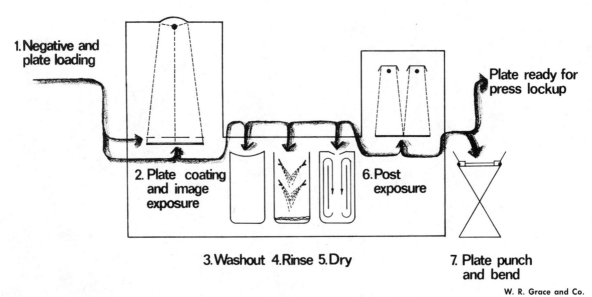

1. Negative and plate loading

2. Plate coating and image exposure

3. Washout 4. Rinse 5. Dry

6. Post exposure

Plate ready for press lockup

7. Plate punch and bend

W. R. Grace and Co.

19-11. *How to produce a Letterflex plastic relief plate.*

W. R. Grace and Co.
19-12. *The Letterflex plastic relief plate ready for the washout process.*

470

lockup, which has permanently mounted saddles needed to give the necessary cylinder buildup. A saddle is a cylinder which is mounted on the press plate cylinder. The plastic plate is mounted on the saddle. Fig. 19-13.

Although the major use of this plate is in newspaper production, other uses are being developed. Examples include business forms, telephone books, pocket books, and packaging.

The Dyna-Flex Printing System

The Dyna-Flex printing plate is a lightweight plastic relief printing plate that has an aluminum backing. (Dyna-Flex is the trade name for the system developed by the Dyna-Flex Corp.) The plastic layer is a photosensitive polymer about 1/100'' thick. The aluminum backing is about 1/200'' thick. The plate is precoated and delivered to the customer ready for exposure. It must be stored in a frozen condition.

The material to be printed is composed using normal cold composition equipment. See Chapter 6, "Cold Composition," for information on this process.

To produce a plate, the negative of the page to be printed is placed over the plate and exposed to an ultraviolet light source. The areas of the plate exposed to the light become insoluble in water. The plate is then developed in a plate processor.

The processor uses ordinary tap water to etch away the plastic areas not hardened by the ultraviolet light. The processor dries the plate, and it is ready to use.

W. R. Grace and Co.

19-13. The finished plastic relief plate is mounted on the press.

The Dyna-Flex plate can be used on curved cylinder as well as flatbed letterpresses. It is also used on large rotary letterpresses, such as those used in printing newspapers.

This plate is also used on offset printing presses. It enables the offset press to print without the use of water rollers and its water system. In effect, it permits printing by a dry offset process. The elimination of water from the process removes ink-drying problems.

Plates are produced rapidly. The first plate is complete in about four minutes. Additional plates can be produced every 45 seconds.

DUPLICATE PLATES

Duplicate plates permit increased production. Several copies of a job can be printed at the same time. For example, four duplicate plates could be made of a small job. They could be mounted on the press and print four copies instead of one for each impression. Duplicate plates made possible the development of high-speed rotary presses used for newspaper printing. A full page can be made as one semicylindrical plate. Advertisers can furnish printing firms with lightweight, inexpensive mats (described in the next section) and greatly reduce composition time. Fig. 19-14. The advertisement is composed once, and mats are made. The mats can be mailed to many different printing firms with no additional composition cost. Duplicate plates enable the original plates and type matter to be stored and thus protected from wear and damage.

There are four kinds of duplicate plates. These are (1) stereotypes, (2) electrotypes, (3) rubber plates, and (4) plastic plates.

THE STEREOTYPING PROCESS

Stereotype plates are used primarily in newspaper printing. They find some use in book and magazine printing.

Stereotyping involves two basic steps: (1) pressing a mold (called a mat), Fig. 19-14, and (2) casting the plate from molten metal. Fig. 19-15.

Mats are made from a single layer of a tough fibrous or plastic impregnated paper. It is specially prepared to resist heat. The metal typeform is placed on the flatbed of a roller-type press or hydraulic press. It is covered with a sheet of mat material and blanket of felt or cork. The bed moves under a heavy roller that presses the mat against the type. The surface of the metal type is embossed into the mat material.

Stereotype plates can be made flat or in a semicylindrical shape.

To cast a flat stereotype plate, the mats to make the page are taped together. The open areas

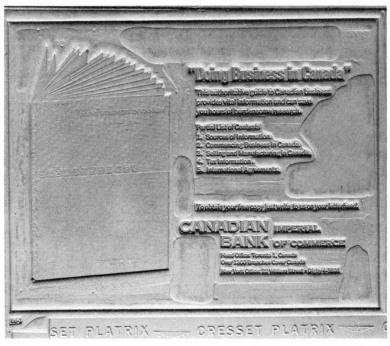

19-14. *A lightweight matrix used to produce duplicate plates.*

are backed with cardboard. The mats are then placed in a flat casting box. The box has two smooth iron plates. They are hinged together so that one can be dropped to a horizontal position. The mats are placed on the horizontal plate and held in position with three bars placed on three edges of the plate. The horizontal plate is raised to a vertical position against the other plate. The bars also serve to space apart the flat plates. The top is open. Molten stereotype metal is poured into the open end (at the top) until the mats are covered. When the metal has hardened, the plates are separated, and the stereotype plate is removed. It is cut and trimmed to the desired finished size. Fig. 19-16.

The thickness of the flat stereotype duplicate plate is varied by

19-15. *How to produce a stereotype.*

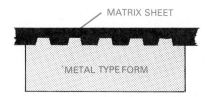

MATRIX SHEET

METAL TYPE FORM

19-16A. *Matrix sheet is pressed on the face of the metal typeform.*

19-16B. *The stereotype plate is formed by casting molten stereotype metal in the matrix.*

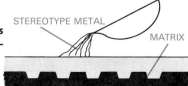

STEREOTYPE METAL

MATRIX

The exposure and washout take only a few minutes. Washout is accomplished with an aqueous washout solution of dilute caustic. Fig. 19-18.

The plate has a sharp image, which is necessary for the production of superior stereotype. Fig. 19-19. The plate is used for casting stereotypes in the conventional manner.

THE ELECTROTYPING PROCESS

An electrotype plate is made by electrolysis.

The steps for making an electrotype are shown in Fig. 19-20. The final preparation for a page when it is ready for printing is called lockup, when the metal type is locked in a form called a chase. (See Chapter 20 for details.)

The matrix is made by pressing a heated plastic sheet against the form in a molding press.

the width of the bars inserted between the plates. The thickness can range from type-high to a much thinner plate. Thin cast plates, called shell casts, are fastened to bases to make them type-high. To make a semicylindrical plate, first a flat plate must be made. This is used to form the mat for the semicylindrical plate.

The casting of semicylindrical plates is much like the casting of flat plates. The mat is backed with cardboard in the open spaces. Then the mat is placed in an oven, called a scorcher. This forms the mat into the desired curved shape. The curve must be the same as the press cylinder to which the plate is to be fastened. The curved mat is placed in an automatic casting machine. It casts the curved stereotype duplicate plate. When the metal has hardened, the curved plate must be trimmed to the proper size, so that it can be clamped to the cylinder of the press. Fig. 19-17.

Another pattern plate developed for use in the production of stereotype plates is the Dycril Type 40 photopolymer pattern plate. (Dycril Type 40 is the trade

name for the system developed by the DuPont Co.) The Dycril plate is 0.040″ thick with a 0.030″ relief image.

The plate permits the use of fast photocomposition equipment for generating the original image. A negative is made, and this is used to expose the plate. Dycril Type 40 plates are imaged by exposure to ultraviolet light.

19-17. *A curved stereotype duplicate plate.*

19-18. *The processed Dycril Type 40 photopolymer pattern plate after processing in a Dycril high-speed washout unit. This plate is designed as a fast access master from which stereotypes are made by conventional methods for letterpress printing.*

19-19. *A Dycril Type 40 photopolymer pattern plate after processing.*

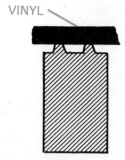

19-20A. *A preheated vinyl sheet is placed over the typeform.*

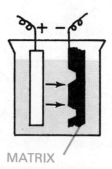

19-20D. *The matrix is electroplated with a thin layer of nickel.*

19-20G. *Lead or plastic is used to back up the shell.*

19-20B. *Vinyl sheet is pressed into the typeform on the molding press.*

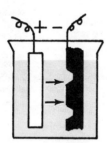

19-20E. *The matrix is electroplated in a copper solution.*

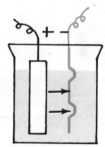

19-20H. *The shell is flash-plated with a thin layer of chrome.*

19-20C. *The inside of the matrix is sprayed with silver spray.*

19-20F. *The shell is stripped from the matrix.*

Figs. 19-20A and 19-20B. The matrix is then sprayed with a silver spray. Fig. 19-20C. This serves as a conductor of electricity. The matrix is electroplated with a thin layer of nickel. Fig. 19-20D. Then it is electroplated in copper electroplating solution. Fig. 19-20E. A copper shell about 12 to 15 mils thick is formed on the matrix. (A mil is a unit of length, equal to 1/1000".) When the proper thickness is obtained, the shell formed by the electroplating process is stripped from the matrix. Fig. 19-20F. It is backed with molten metal or plastic. Fig. 19-20G. This fills the cavities and brings the electrotype to the desired thickness. The shell is then flash-plated with chrome to improve the wearing qualities. Fig. 19-20H. The finished electrotype is leveled by hand operations.

When a typeform will be used to make the matrix for producing electrotypes, all open areas in the form should be filled with type-high dead metal. Fig. 19-21. The form should have type-high bearers at least 1/2" wide. If two or more jobs are locked in the same chase, 1/2" wide type-high separator barriers should be used for each job. The typeform should be carefully planned.

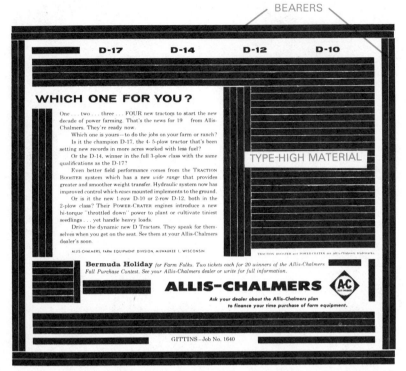

BEARERS

D-17   D-14   D-12   D-10

WHICH ONE FOR YOU?

One . . . two . . . three . . . FOUR new tractors to start the new decade of power farming. That's the news for 19— from Allis-Chalmers. They're ready now.

Which one is yours—to do the jobs on your farm or ranch?

Is it the champion D-17, the 4- 5-plow tractor that's been setting new records in more acres worked with less fuel?

Or the D-14, winner in the full 3-plow class with the same qualifications as the D-17?

Even better field performance comes from the TRACTION BOOSTER system which has a new *wide range* that provides greater and smoother weight transfer. Hydraulic system now has improved control which *eases* mounted implements to the ground.

Or is it the new 1-row D-10 or 2-row D-12, both in the 2-plow class? Their POWER-CRATER engines introduce a new hi-torque "throttled down" power to plant or cultivate tiniest seedlings . . . yet handle heavy loads.

Drive the dynamic new D Tractors. They speak for them-selves when you get on the seat. See them at your Allis-Chalmers dealer's soon.

ALLIS-CHALMERS, FARM EQUIPMENT DIVISION, MILWAUKEE 1, WISCONSIN

TRACTION BOOSTER and POWER-CRATER are Allis-Chalmers trademarks.

TYPE-HIGH MATERIAL

Bermuda Holiday *for Farm Folks. Two tickets each for 20 winners of the Allis-Chalmers Fall Purchase Contest. See your Allis-Chalmers dealer or write for full information.*

ALLIS-CHALMERS (AC)

Ask your dealer about the Allis-Chalmers plan
to finance your time purchase of farm equipment.

GITTINS—Job No. 1640

International Association of Electrotypers and Stereotypers, Inc.

19-21. *The open areas in a typeform to be used for producing electro-types should be filled with type-high dead metal.*

are also used for forms and other types of specialty printing. They are very durable and useful when printing on rough surfaces.

Molds for forming rubber plates are made by placing a sheet of thermosetting plastic matrix material over the metal typeform or engraving. The sheet is compressed under heat against the typeform. The form can contain metal type, electro-type plates, or photoengravings.

The rubber plate is formed in the mold by applying heat and pressure to the rubber material placed over the mold. The rubber plate is vulcanized in the proc-ess. Fig. 19-24. Next, the excess rubber is cut away. If the plate is a little too thick, it can be thinned by grinding on the back to a tolerance of $\pm.001$ inches. Thickness is checked with a rub-ber plate micrometer. Fig. 19-25.

If the electrotype is to be made from a photoengraving, it is nec-essary to rout the area next to the printing surface. Fig. 19-22. This routing should have a maxi-mum width of 1/8" around all live material. The routing is 0.035" deep. Dead materials are routed along their edge at a 45-degree angle. Fig. 19-23. This helps release the shell from the mold. A finished photoengraving is shown in Fig. 19-8.

RUBBER DUPLICATE PLATES

Printing with rubber plates is called flexographic printing.

Rubber plates are used in let-terpress printing for inexpensive paperbound books that are printed in large quantities. They

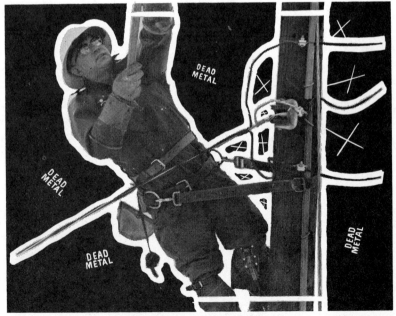

International Association of Electrotypers and Stereotypers, Inc.

19-22. *Rout the area next to the printing surface on photoengravings used for electrotypes.*

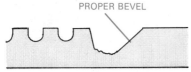

PROPER BEVEL

LIVE METAL   DEAD METAL

International Association of Electrotypers and
Stereotypers, Inc.

19-23. Dead materials are routed on an angle of 45 degrees.

Flexographic Technical Association, Inc.
19-25. The thickness of rubber plates is checked with a rubber plate micrometer.

Flexographic Technical Association, Inc.
19-26. The sticky-back plate is mounted on the press cylinder.

Flexographic Technical Association, Inc.
19-27. A brass-back rubber plate.

There are six types of mountings used with rubber plates: plain-back, sticky-back, pre-curved, brass-back, design rollers, and plate-mounted cylinders.

The plain-back rubber plate is mounted to the press plate cylinder with a sheet of adhesive backing material. This material is sticky on both sides. First, the adhesive backing material is applied to the press plate cylinder. Then the rubber plate is pressed onto the adhesive backing.

The sticky-back rubber plate is a plain-back rubber plate which has been pressed onto a sheet of adhesive backing material while still flat. The sticky-back plate is then mounted on the press cylinder. Fig. 19-26. After the plate is positioned on the cylinder, pieces of tape are wrapped around the edge of the adhesive material. This prevents solvents from getting under it.

The precurved rubber plate is molded to a permanent curve with approximately the same diameter as the plate cylinder. It is usually mounted in the same manner as the plain-back plate. It is used for jobs where accuracy is important.

The brass-back rubber plate is a rubber plate vulcanized to a sheet of spring brass. Fig. 19-27. It is precurved to the size of the press plate cylinder. A rubberized sheet of fabric is molded to the underside of the brass to prevent the plate from slipping on the cylinder.

Design rollers are made by vulcanizing rubber plates to a press plate cylinder. The major use is to print continuous patterns on roll stock. An example would be gift wrap.

Plate-mounted cylinders are just like design rollers, but are used to print noncontinuous designs. They can run at high speed and are used for long runs.

When the printing run is finished, the plate is cleaned with ink solvent. It is carefully wiped with a lint-free cloth. The plate is then lightly dusted with talc and stored in a paper folder to keep it out of direct contact with the air or sunlight.

PLASTIC DUPLICATE PLATES

One advantage of plastic duplicate plates is that they are light in weight. A plate weighing about one pound in plastic would weigh about 44 pounds if cast in metal. The printing quality of the plastic plate is equal to metal

The Monomelt Co., Inc.
19-24. A rubber plate cast in a matrix.

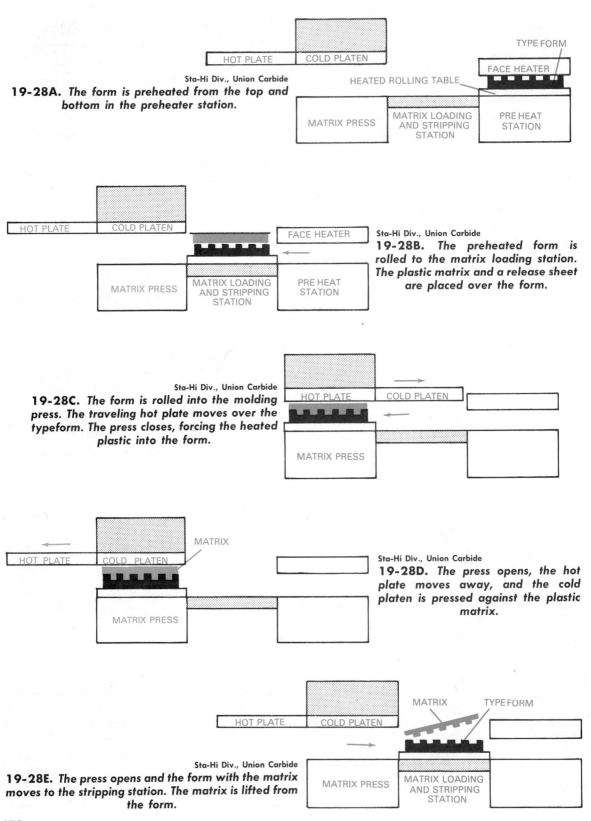

Sta-Hi Div., Union Carbide

19-28A. *The form is preheated from the top and bottom in the preheater station.*

Sta-Hi Div., Union Carbide

19-28B. *The preheated form is rolled to the matrix loading station. The plastic matrix and a release sheet are placed over the form.*

Sta-Hi Div., Union Carbide

19-28C. *The form is rolled into the molding press. The traveling hot plate moves over the typeform. The press closes, forcing the heated plastic into the form.*

Sta-Hi Div., Union Carbide

19-28D. *The press opens, the hot plate moves away, and the cold platen is pressed against the plastic matrix.*

Sta-Hi Div., Union Carbide

19-28E. *The press opens and the form with the matrix moves to the stripping station. The matrix is lifted from the form.*

duplicate plates. It takes about 4 minutes to produce the first plastic plate, while the first metal duplicate plate is made in about 10 minutes. The production cycle makes a plastic plate every 0.5 minute after the first is formed. Metal plates are produced every 0.3 minute after the first one is cast.

One printing plate system involves making a plastic matrix from the metal typeform and using it to form plastic duplicate plates. The following section describes the Hylox system, developed by the Sta-Hi Division of Union Carbide. Fig. 19-28.

1. The metal typeform is preheated at a preheat station. The form is placed on a heated rolling table. The face of the form is heated by a face heater. Fig. 19-28A.

2. The heated rolling table moves to the matrix loading and stripping station. Fig. 19-28B. Here the plastic matrix blank is placed on the form. Fig. 19-29. A release sheet is placed on the matrix. Fig. 19-30. The release sheet keeps the plastic from sticking to the matrix press platen. It is a Teflon-coated, fiberglass fabric.

3. The heated rolling table moves the form with the matrix blank to the matrix molding press. At the same time the hot plate moves over the matrix blank. The matrix molding press closes, forcing the plastic matrix blank into the metal typeform. Fig. 19-28C.

4. The matrix molding press opens. The hot plate moves off the formed matrix, while the cold platen moves over it. The molding press again closes, cooling the matrix. Fig. 19-28D.

Sta-Hi Div., Union Carbide

19-29. *The molding press operator places the plastic matrix blank on the preheated typeforms.*

Sta-Hi Div., Union Carbide

19-30. *The release sheet is placed over the plastic matrix blank.*

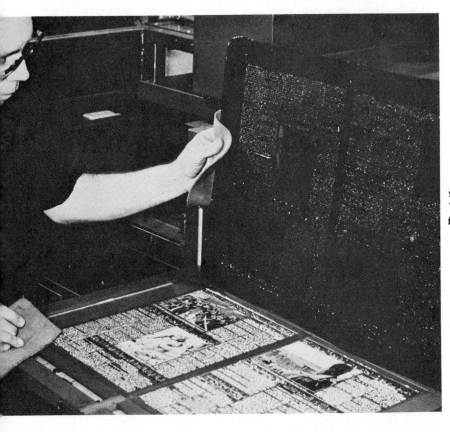

Sta-Hi Div., Union Carbide
19-31. *After the molding cycle, the finished matrix is lifted off the typeform.*

Sta-Hi Div., Union Carbide
19-32. *A shaver removes high spots on the finished matrix.*

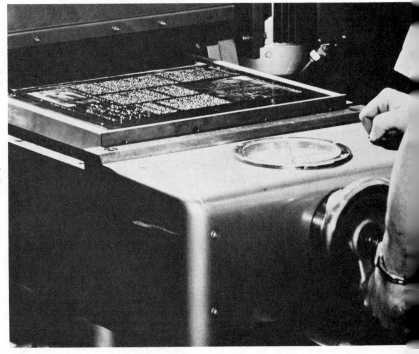

5. The molding press now opens and the heated rolling plate with the finished plastic matrix moves to the loading and stripping station. Fig. 19-28E. The matrix is lifted from the form. Fig. 19-31.

6. A shaver is used to remove the high spots resulting from spaces left around headline type, rules, and margins when the type page was locked up. Fig. 19-32. If the matrix is made from a photoengraving, no shaving is needed.

The production of duplicate plastic plates is shown in Fig. 19-33.

1. The plastic matrix is inserted in the platemaker press. Fig. 19-34.

2. A pad of hot plastic is deposited on the lower-half mold. Fig. 19-35. The plastic is formed from pellets and is heated to a molten state in the extruder. The extruder ejects the amount of molten plastic needed to make the plate.

3. The lower-half mold with the molten plastic moves to the platemaker. The platemaker closes, and the molten plastic is pressed into the matrix and rapidly cooled.

4. The platemaker opens, and the finished duplicate plate is automatically stripped from the matrix. The lower-half mold returns to its original position, and the finished duplicate plate is lifted from it. Fig. 19-36.

5. The cycle can be repeated to produce another duplicate plate. The process takes about 0.5 minute.

Duplicate plastic plates can be metal-plated to extend the number of impressions into the millions. The plate is treated first by

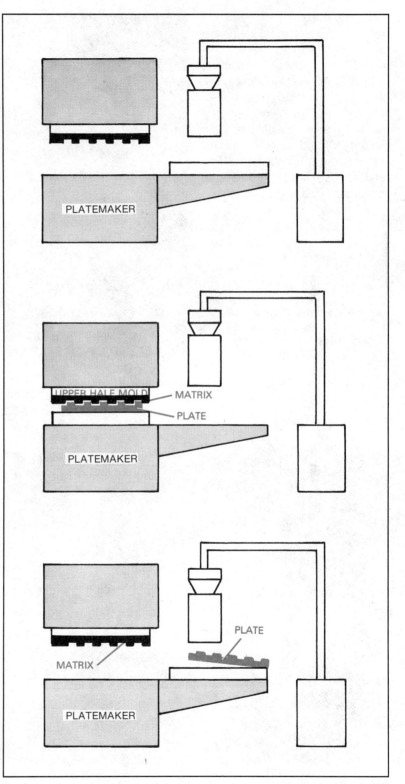

Sta-Hi Div., Union Carbide

19-33. *Production of a plastic duplicate plate.*

spraying it so that it conducts electricity. It is then nickel-plated in an electrolysis process to 1/10 mil. Next, 1/2 mil of nickel is added in an electroplating bath. The plate is flash-plated with chrome in the electroplating bath. The electroplating process is similar to that explained for the making of electrotypes. The plating is so thin that there is no noticeable image growth.

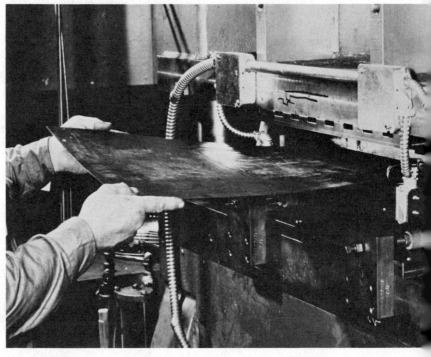

Sta-Hi Div., Union Carbide

19-34. The finished matrix is placed face down on the upper-half mold of the plate molding press.

Sta-Hi Div., Union Carbide

19-35. A slab of the molten plastic plate material is automatically metered on the lower-half mold.

Sta-Hi Div., Union Carbide

19-36. The finished plastic dupli-cate plate is lifted from the lower-half mold.

REVIEW QUESTIONS

1. Original images are converted to relief printing plates by what process?
2. On a letterpress plate, the images are in reverse. True or False?
3. Name the terms defined in the following:
    a. Process of chemically removing metal from portions of a plate.
    b. Relief printing plate that is shallow etched and is a single unit.
    c. A cylinder mounted on a press plate cylinder.
4. What are the four kinds of duplicate plates?
5. Printing with rubber plates is called flexographic printing. True or False?
6. What can be done to make plastic duplicate plates last longer?

Chapter 20

Imposition and Lockup

Imposition is the arrangement of pages in the proper order on the press sheet. A press sheet is a sheet printed on the press. The fundamental methods of imposition are the same for all forms of printing. A working knowledge of these methods is important since imposition is the basis for determining how work progresses in the stripping, lockup, pressroom, and bindery departments. It is the imposition plan that determines how a job will be printed, folded, assembled, and bound.

IMPOSITION TERMS AND MEANINGS

In order to understand the terms used to describe imposition, definitions are presented in three categories in the following sections.

CONTROL OF THE PRESS SHEET

The *gripper edge* of the press sheet enters the printing press first. It is held by the press gripping devices and placed against the front guide stops, as explained in the chapters on press operations. In all presses except the duplicator type press, one of the long sides of the sheet is usually chosen as the gripper edge. Fig. 20-1.

The *side guide edge* of the press sheet enters the press po-sitioned against the mechanical side guide. It is usually one of the short edges of the sheet. Fig. 20-1.

The *trail edge* of the sheet is opposite the gripper edge. Fig. 20-1.

The *non-guide edge* of the sheet is opposite the side guide edge. Fig. 20-1.

The *lead edge* of a printed press sheet enters a sheet-fed folder first. Fig. 20-1.

The *guide side edge* of a printed press sheet enters a sheet-fed folder positioned against the side guiding device on the folder. Fig. 20-1.

The *side frame edge* of a stack (lift) of paper is placed against the *side frame* of a paper cutter during cutting. Fig. 20-1. See Chapter 23, "Bindery and Finishing."

The *backgauge edge* of a stack (lift) of paper is placed against the *backgauge* of a paper cutter during cutting. Fig. 20-1.

The *lip (lap)* is the extension of one leg on a signature, explained in Chapter 23.

THE PRESS SHEET

The *image area* is the area on the surface of a press sheet that receives ink. It is measured in

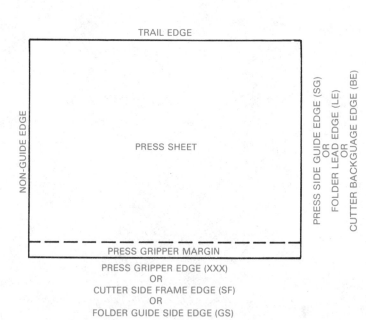

20-1. *The control edges of a press sheet.*

484

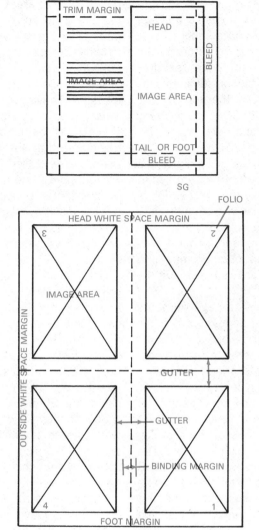

20-2. *Terms related to the press sheet.*

used for binding the paper together when booklets are made. Fig. 20-2.

GENERAL IMPOSITION TERMS

Face is the side of the sheet that is printed first. It is also called the *front* side of the sheet. Fig. 20-3A.

Back is the second or opposite side of the printed sheet.

Up is a term that refers to the number of times a particular printing form (page) appears on one side of a press sheet. Some common imposition expressions are one-up, two-up and so forth. Fig. 20-3A shows a one-up form; each form (page) appears only once on one side of the press sheet.

On (*out*) refers to how many finished copies of a job can be produced from one press sheet. Fig. 20-3A shows a one-on (out),

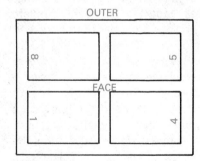

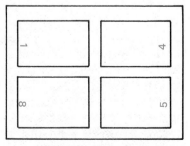

20-3A. *Sheet lay.*

picas, while the paper or press sheet is measured in inches. The upper part of the image area is called the *head,* and the lower part is called the *tail* or *foot.* Fig. 20-2.

Bleed occurs when the image "prints off" the edge of the sheet. Most bleeds are made by trimming the edge off the sheet after it is printed. Fig. 20-2.

Margins are of four types. The first type is created by the non-image area surrounding the image area. It is called *white space* or *gutter margin.* Fig. 20-2. The second type, *trim margin,* is the amount of paper that is trimmed from the press sheet. Fig. 20-2. The third type is the *gripper margin,* which is that portion of the press sheet that is set aside for the press grippers to grab. Fig. 20-1. The fourth type is the *binding margin.* This is the area of the press sheet that is

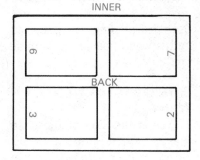

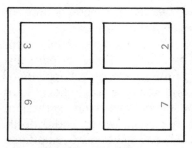

20-3B. *Stone lay.*

since only one finished eight-page booklet can be produced from one press sheet.

Signature refers to a printed sheet containing a number of pages arranged so that they will correctly fold and bind together as a part of or as a complete booklet. Most signatures are 4, 8, 16, or 32 pages. Fig. 20-3A shows a sheet that would produce one complete 8-page signature.

Outer form is the part of a press sheet, a signature, or a printing plate which contains the lowest page number. The face side shown in Fig. 20-3A is the outer form, since page one is on that side.

Inner form refers to the next lowest page number. The back side shown in Fig. 20-3A is the inner form.

Backing up is the act of printing the back side of a press sheet in correct register with the already printed front side.

486

Sheet lay refers to the arrangement of pages as they appear on the printed sheet.

Form (stone) lay refers to the arrangement of pages as they appear on the printing surface that transfers the ink to the paper. Fig. 20-3B is the form lay that produced the sheet lay shown in Fig. 20-3A.

A *dummy* is a miniaturized booklet folded and assembled in the same way the finished job is folded and assembled. A dummy is produced to show the size, shape, form, and general production plan of a printing job. Chapter 23 shows how a dummy is made.

Folio refers to page numbers printed on a page. Fig. 20-2.

Pagination refers to the page numbering scheme used to determine the location of pages on a signature-type press sheet.

Self-covered refers to a booklet that does not have a separate cover. Page one of the first signature is also the cover. The press sheet shown in Fig. 20-3 will produce a self-covered booklet, because page one of the first (and only) signature is also the cover.

Stripping is the process of correctly arranging film negative or positive image areas on a masking sheet to make a printing plate. The correct arrangement depends on the accuracy of the imposition plan, since the image areas on the plate cannot be moved (relative to each other) after the printing plate is made.

Lockup is the act of "locking" raised printing forms inside a metal frame, called a chase. As with stripping, the arrangement of the forms depends on the basic imposition plan.

Unit refers to a printing station on a roll (web-fed) press. Fig. 20-4.

Deck refers to the inking and printing system usually having one upper and one lower deck at each unit of a roll-fed printing press. Fig. 20-4.

Ganging refers to an imposition which combines several different sized jobs on one press sheet. Fig. 20-5.

Split fountain is when a press inking system is split to allow two or more colors to be printed at one time on the same press sheet from one ink fountain.

Imposition symbols are used on imposition layouts. These are shown and identified in Fig. 20-1.

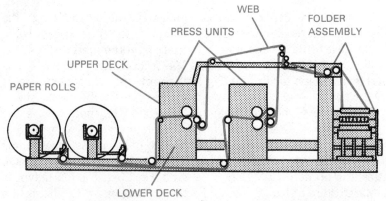

20-4. *The operator's side of a two-unit, web-fed offset press.*

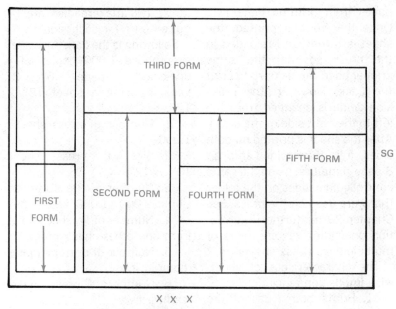

20-5. *A ganged sheet-lay imposition.*

wise, *work-and-turn, work-and-flop, center-row-change,* and *work-and-twirl* impositions. Each type of imposition possesses its own characteristics and advantages. These are explained in the following sections, using the basic imposition requirements necessary to produce one thousand copies of a saddle-stitched, 8-page, one-color, 6″ × 9″ booklet for each type of imposition. Each imposition will be considered one-up so that the comparisons can be more fully understood. In the interest of clarity, some of the imposition details, such as trim and gripper margins, are omitted from the illustrations.

For example the symbol XXX on the edge of the layout means that the edge is the press gripper edge. The symbol H refers to the head (top) of a page.

BASIC TYPES OF IMPOSITION

Basically, there are six major types of imposition. These include: *printed-one-side, sheet-*

PRINTED-ONE-SIDE (P1S) IMPOSITION

Letterheads, labels, business cards, and ledgers are typical examples of jobs that need to be printed on one side of the sheet only. P1S impositions, Fig. 20-6, are used to print one side of the sheet with one pass per color through the press. Each job or page has to be cut out of the press sheet. Ganging P1S impositions can become quite complicated if several different finished sizes are involved. Fig. 20-5.

Following is the data necessary to produce 1,000 copies of a one-up, one-color, 8-page, 6″ × 9″ booklet, using a sheet 24″ × 18″.

1. Number of press sheets: 1,000.

2. Size of press sheet: 24″ × 18″. (No trim).

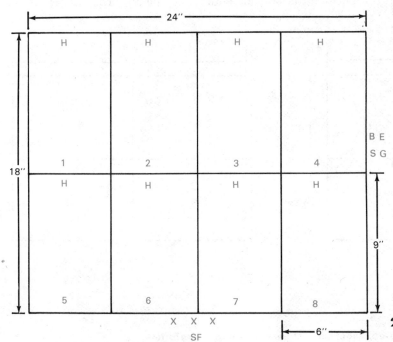

20-6. *A one-up, printed-one-side, sheet-lay, 8-page imposition.*

3. Number of press impressions: 1,000.

4. Number of finished copies from one press sheet: 1.

5. Number of printing plates required: 1.

6. Number of press make-readies: 1.

Printed-one-side impositions are impractical to use when making booklets because the back side of the sheet is not printed. Thus, paper would be wasted.

SHEETWISE IMPOSITION

Sheetwise imposition is often referred to by the terms *work and back, print and back,* and *front and back*. It requires two printing plates. One plate is used to print the *front* side of the press sheet, and the second plate is used to print the *back* side. A layout of an 8-page booklet is shown in Fig. 20-7. To print this booklet *sheetwise,* the *outer* four pages will print from printing plate one, and the *inner* four

pages from printing plate two. Once the front is printed, the sheet is turned and reloaded in the press so that the same gripper edge can be used to print the back. However, the press side guide is changed from the left to the right side of the press. After the sheet is printed on both sides, it is then folded into an 8-page signature, using the same control guide edges on the folder that were used on the press. See Chapter 23 for further information on folding requirements of multiple-page press sheets.

The characteristics of sheetwise impositions include:

1. Prints both sides of the press sheet.

2. Changes printing plate for the back side.

3. One-up press sheet is the same size as the signature.

4. Produces only one copy per one-up press sheet.

5. Maintains the same side guide and gripper edge.

6. Sheet turns end for end.

7. Two makereadies are required (one for each side).

Following is the data necessary to produce 1,000 copies of a one-color, 8-page, 6″ × 9″ booklet, using a sheet 18″ × 12″.

1. Number of press sheets: 1,000.

2. Size of press sheet: 18″ × 12″.

3. Number of press impressions: 2,000 (1,000 each side).

4. Number of finished copies from one press sheet: one.

5. Number of printing plates required: two.

6. Number of press make-readies: two.

WORK-AND-TURN (PRINT-AND-TURN) IMPOSITION

Work-and-turn imposition is sometimes called print-and-turn. In a one-up *work-and-turn* imposition, all the pages of a signature are combined in one printing plate. The *outer* form

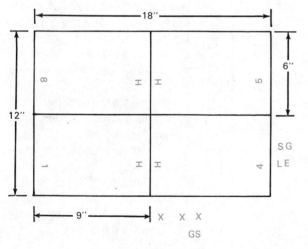
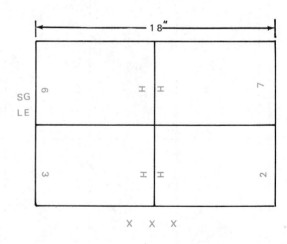

PRINTED FROM PLATE ONE
(OUTER PLATE)
FRONT (FACE)

PRINTED FROM PLATE TWO
(INNER PLATE)
BACK

20-7. A one-up, sheetwise, sheet-lay, 8-page imposition.

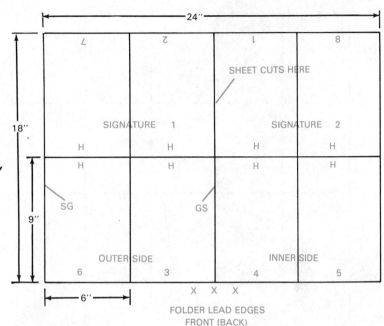

20-8. *A one-up, work-and-turn, sheet-lay, 8-page imposition.*

occupies one-half of the plate, and the *inner* form the other half. Fig. 20-8. The inner *and* the outer image areas are printed on the first (front) side of the press sheet from the combined printing plate. The sheet is then turned, and the same inner and outer printing plate is used to print the second (back) side. The difference is that the inner form printed on the back side "backs up" the outer form printed on the front side and so forth.

Two completed copies per one-up press sheet are eventually produced. The same edges of the sheet are generally used as the control guide edges in printing both sides. To accomplish this, the side guide device on the press is switched from one side of the press to the other side. When this is done, the same edge of the paper can be used as the side guide edge for the printing of the second side after the

sheet is turned. The gripper edge remains the same throughout the entire printing procedure.

After both sides are printed, the sheet is cut in half, producing two identical signatures from one press sheet. Fig. 20-8. Note how the press sheet is imposed by splitting the sheet into an inner and outer arrangement at *right angles* to the gripper edge. Note also how the press side guide edge eventually becomes the folder side guide edge for one sheet after the press sheet is cut in two pieces. The press gripper becomes the folder lead edge for the other half of the press sheet. The second half has a raw edge but no guide edge. To establish a guide edge, the second sheet is given a light cut on a paper cutter. This establishes the new side guide for the folder.

An examination of Fig. 20-9 will show that if a work-and-turn imposition were a four-up ar-

rangement, an eight-out condition would be produced, and the press sheet would have to be eight times larger than the finished booklet.

Fig. 20-9 shows a four-up imposition; each page appears four times on one side of the press sheet. Page one could have been imposed in several different positions on the press sheet. However, it is generally imposed so that the folder guide side for each signature corresponds to where the sheet will be cut. Then the folder settings will be the same for each signature.

The characteristics of work-and-turn impositions include:

1. Prints an inner and outer image area on both sides of a one-up press sheet.

2. Does not change printing plates.

3. One-up press sheet must be twice as large as the finished-sized signature.

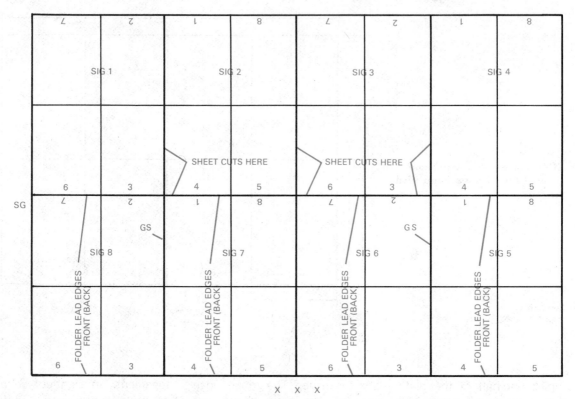

20-9. *A four-up, work-and-turn, sheet-lay, 8-page imposition.*

4. Produces two completed copies per one-up press sheet.

5. Sheet cuts before folding.

6. Maintains the same sheet-control guide edges.

7. Saves press impressions.

8. Saves makeready time.

9. Saves stripping or lockup time.

10. Sheet turns end for end at right angles to the press gripper.

Following is the data necessary to produce 1,000 copies of a one-color, 8-page, 6″ × 9″ booklet, using a sheet 24″ × 18″.

1. Number of press sheets: 500.

2. Size of press sheets: 24″ × 18″.

3. Number of press impressions: 1,000 (500 for side one and 500 for side two).

4. Number of finished copies from one press sheet: two.

5. Number of printing plates required: one.

6. Number of press makereadies: one.

The work-and-turn imposition is the most widely used imposition for book production.

WORK-AND-FLOP IMPOSITION

Work-and-flop imposition is sometimes referred to by the terms work-and-roll or *work-and-tumble*. All pages for *work-and-flop* impositions are combined into one plate. Both *inner* and *outer* image areas are printed on one side of a press sheet at the same time. A work-and-flop imposition is split into an outer and inner arrangement *parallel* to the gripper edges. Fig. 20-10 shows that in a work-and-flop imposition, one edge of the sheet is always used as the side guide edge, but two different edges are used as the press gripper edges.

Work-and-flop impositions are considered troublesome by most printers because any variation in stock size from gripper edge to gripper edge causes trouble in the backup register. For this reason, all stock to be run work-

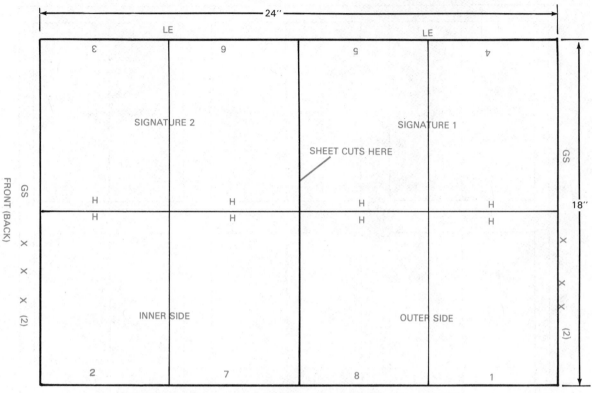

20-10. *A one-up, work-and-flop, sheet-lay, 8-page imposition.*

and-flop must be squared before going to press.

The characteristics of work-and-flop impositions include:

1. Prints an inner and outer image area on both sides of a one-up press sheet.

2. Does not change printing plate.

3. One-up sheet must be twice as large as the finished-size signature.

4. Produces two completed copies per one-up press sheet.

5. Sheet cuts before folding.

6. The paper must be cut squarely.

7. Saves press impressions.

8. Less time required for makeready.

9. Saves stripping or lockup time.

10. Sheet flops edge for edge, parallel to the press gripper.

11. Saves on plate costs.

The data necessary to produce 1,000 copies of a one-color, 8-page, 6″ × 9″ booklet are the same as that for a work-and-turn imposition.

CENTER-ROW-CHANGE IMPOSITION

Sometimes in printing small folders and flat jobs, it is possible to gang several jobs on one press sheet in order to save impressions in the pressroom. When the maximum size sheet allowable on a press is too small for imposing a full work-and-turn arrangement, a center-row-change layout can often be used. In a center-row-change imposition, all the pages except the center row are imposed to run work-and-turn, and the center row is laid out to run sheetwise.

In planographic (lithographic) printing, after the sheet is printed on one side, the first plate is taken off, and the changed backup plate is put on. In relief (letterpress) printing, only a transposition of the center forms is necessary. The image areas are imposed so that six 4-page folders can be produced from one press sheet. Fig. 20-11.

One disadvantage in running a

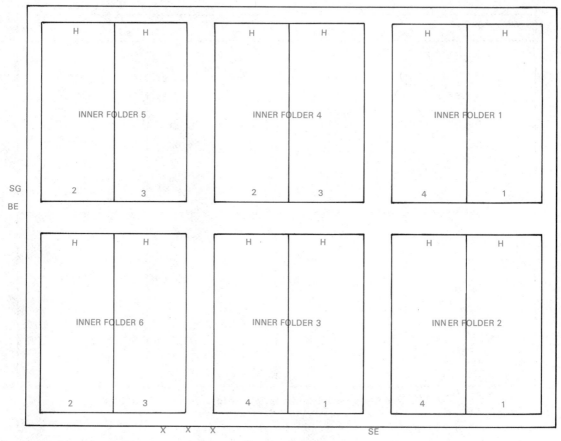

20-11. *A three-up, center-row-change, sheet-lay imposition.*

job in this manner is the additional makeready on the second side after the center plates are changed. Also, this imposition is not useful for book publication.

The characteristics of center-row impositions include:

1. Prints both sides of the press sheet.

2. Press sheet size is based on press limitations.

3. Produces at least three completed copies per press sheet.

4. Cuts at least in thirds for folding.

5. Maintains same side guide and gripper edges.

6. Saves on press impressions.

7. Allows for modified work-and-turn arrangements on smaller sized presses.

It is extremely impractical to print an 8-page booklet using a center-row-change imposition.

WORK-AND-TWIRL IMPOSITION

Work-and-twirl imposition is sometimes called *work-and-twist*. This type of imposition is used to print two exactly alike image areas on one side of a press sheet. It is used when a plain P1S imposition cannot be used conveniently. The back side of a work-and-twist press sheet is never printed. Two different parts of the same form are im-

posed in such a fashion that each part prints side by side on a double-sized sheet. Fig. 20-12. After the sheet is printed the first time, it is twirled end for end and printed again. Work-and-twist impositions are often used to print letterpress blank rule forms so that rules at right angles to each other need not be pieced into one form. Study Fig. 20-12 to see how this imposition can save time at the makeup frame.

The characteristics of work-and-twirl impositions include:

1. Prints one side of press sheet only.

2. Does not change form.

3. Sheet twice as large as finished size.

4. Produces at least two completed copies exactly alike.

5. Paper cuts in half.

6. Changes both guide and gripper edge.

7. Must have paper cut and squared.

8. Saves on press impressions, but must have two impressions to complete one side.

9. Turns sheet edge for edge and end for end in a twisting fashion, but does not reverse side of sheet.

10. Saves on makeready.

11. Passes through the press twice for each color.

12. Saves makeup time at the composition frame.

It is extremely impractical to print an 8-page booklet using a work-and-twirl imposition.

SELECTING THE TYPE OF IMPOSITION

An evaluation of each imposition's characteristics and advantages must be made to determine the most efficient type of imposition for a job. Generally three steps are involved: initial decision regarding the best imposition to use, making a dummy, and finalizing the imposition plan.

MAKING THE INITIAL DECISION

All factors which are involved in a job must be considered when deciding what imposition to use. The advantages and characteristics of the imposition must be considered. In addition, the impositor must consider the job size, volume, and use of color in relation to the size of the presses and bindery equipment available. The object is to use the maximum available size of all equipment in the easiest and fastest way possible. Large volume, small size jobs are usually printed in multiples, as two-up or four-up. Work-and-turn is usually used for short runs but not for multiple color on one side of a job. The first step, therefore, requires an initial production plan based on these production considerations.

MAKING THE DUMMY

The dummy is used to develop the imposition plan. It is folded,

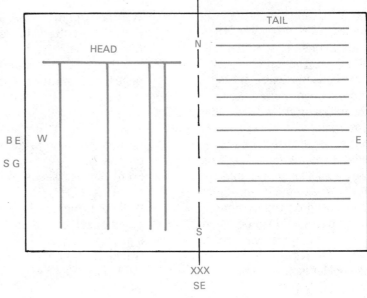

AFTER FIRST PRINTING

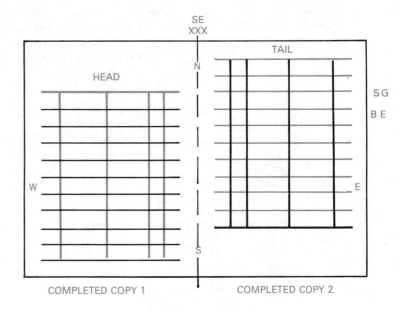

AFTER SECOND PRINTING

20-12. *A one-up, work-and-twirl, sheet-lay imposition.*

assembled, and bound in accordance with the production considerations of the initial and final plans. The dummy helps the impositor visualize the specific production requirements.

The following steps will explain how to make a dummy for a 16-page, 6″ × 9″, separate-cover booklet. Remember, all the plans for any booklet's guides, folding, imposition, assembly, and binding are based on the dummy.

Develop a list of the production requirements and operations. Information regarding the 16-page booklet is as follows:

Booklet:
1. Will be saddle stitched.
2. Will be assembled by hand and consist of two elements, a cover and a signature.

3. Will be trimmed on a guillotine cutter to a 6″ × 9″ size.
4. Will have 16 numbered pages not counting the cover.

Cover:
1. Was assumed to be printed 2-up and printed on one side.
2. Front cover bleeds on four sides.
3. Will be trimmed out of press sheet before folding.
4. Will be folded on a table-top buckle folder prior to assembly.
5. Will have a 1/4″ lip.

See Fig. 20-13 for a sheet layout of the cover press sheet.

Inside pages:
1. Printed one-up sheetwise

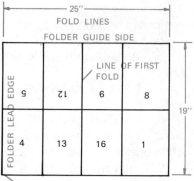

SIGNATURE DUMMY SHEET BEFORE
FOLDING INTO 16 PAGES

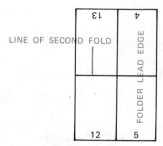

FIRST FOLD OF SIGNATURE
DUMMY SHEET

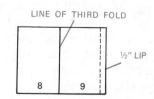

SECOND FOLD OF SIGNATURE
DUMMY SHEET

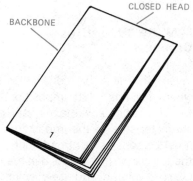

THE THIRD FOLD FORMS THE DUMMY
SIGNATURE FOLDED INTO 16 PAGES

20-14. *How to fold the signature dummy.*

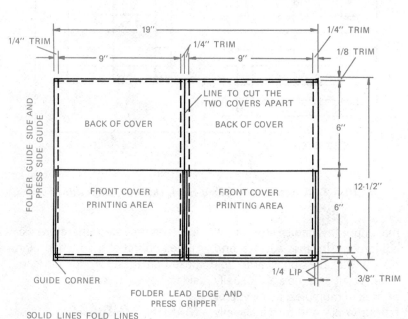

20-13. *This cover sheet lay diagram will print two covers per sheet.*

1/4" LIP

FOLD LINE

COVER DUMMY SHEET
BEFORE FOLDING

COVER
FRONT

COVER LIP

COVER DUMMY SHEET
AFTER FOLDING

20-15. *Folding the cover dummy.*

explained in the folding section of this chapter.

Now fold the cover dummy. Fig. 20-15. It has a 1/4" lip on

CLOSED HEAD AT TOP

BACKBONE

COVER
FRONT

SIGNATURE

LIPS TO FRONT

20-16. *To assemble the dummy booklet, keep the closed head to the top and the lip on the front leg.*

the front and a single fold. The lip on the cover must be less than that on the signature so that the folding machine will open the booklet in the center.

Hand-assemble the dummy's inside page sheet into the dummy cover. Keep the backbone to the left, and the closed heads to the top when assembling. Fig. 20-16. Plan for, but do not staple, the dummy since it will have to be unfolded later on.

Write the page numbers on the dummy. Fig. 20-14. In separate cover work, the cover is not usually counted or numbered. Therefore, the first page of the signature will be numbered page 1 in the book.

Cut a V-notch in all sides of the dummy requiring trim and a square notch in the edge requiring a lip. Fig. 20-17.

Unfold the dummy, and use it to determine how all prebinding work should be laid out. It will show where the trim and lip al-

as a 16-page signature. See Fig. 20-14 for the press sheet forming the inside pages.

2. Will be folded on a jobber buckle folder prior to assembly.

3. Will have 1/2" lip.

Hand-fold a cover and a signature dummy sheet the same way the folder will.

Mark the signature folder's lead edge and guide side to identify the folder-guide corner. Fig. 20-14. The folder-guide corner can then be used to determine the press-guide corner. Make the first fold to allow for 1/2" lip. Make the rest of the folds. This is

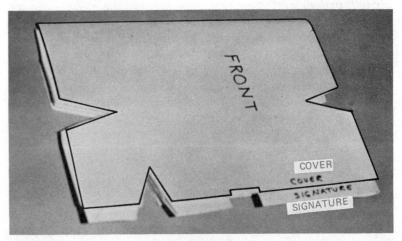

20-17. *By cutting identifying notches, the lip and trim locations can be easily determined after the dummy is opened.*

lowance must be made on the press sheet. Fig. 20-18. It also shows how the folder guide corner can be used to determine the press guide corner, as well as the basic imposition plan.

It is advisable that the dummy remain with the job while it is processed through the shop.

FINALIZING THE IMPOSITION PLAN

If the initial imposition selection seems feasible, six production requirements must be met.

Requirement 1—Control of Press Sheet

The major factors to consider in controlling the press sheet are the placement of the *lip* and the *control* edges. The control edges are the *press gripper edge, the press side guide edge, the folder lead edge, the folder guide side edge, the cutter side frame edge, and the cutter backgauge edge.* Fig. 20-1.

The following example is for sheet-fed presses. Roll-fed press considerations are presented later in the chapter.

Controlling nonfolding and printed one side (P1S) press sheets. For simple P1S jobs or jobs printed on two sides not requiring folding, no lip is required. Therefore only the selection of the control edges need be determined. The gripper and side guide edges are selected by considering the number of trims needed and the location of the image. They must be chosen so that they correspond to one or both of the cutter's side frame and/or backgauge edges to maintain registration between the printing press and the paper cutter.

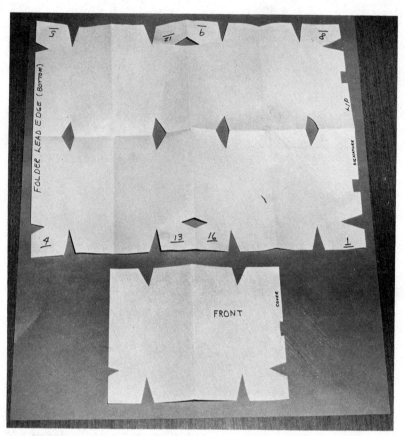

20-18. *The finished dummy sheet. Notice the page numbers.*

When the press and cutter control edges correspond, the distance from the guide edges of the sheet to the place where the paper is cut will match with the distance to the printing, regardless of how much variance there is in the size of the press sheet. In other words, if the same edges of the press sheet are used as controlling guides for both the cutting and the printing operations, proper registration between both will occur.

Another nonfolding imposition factor to consider is whether the press sheet can be cut on a flat cutter after it is printed. Straight cuts should go through the press sheet without cutting through

any of the elements. This is especially important when different size elements are ganged onto one press sheet. Fig. 20-5.

Controlling press sheets requiring folding. Press sheets for folded jobs that will be saddle-bound generally require a lip to insure that the folded paper opens in the proper place when it is processed in the bindery. (Bindings are discussed under Requirement 2.) The size of the lip margin is based on the requirements of the machine that will process the folded paper. The lip is often taken off the folder-tail end of the press sheet to conserve on paper. See Chapter 23 for an explanation of how the lip is developed. Folded jobs that are not saddle-bound do not require a lip.

The control edges for folded jobs are planned so that the press control edges correspond to the folding machine control edges as well as the cutting machine control edges. This is done to maintain registration between the press, the folder, and the cutter. Generally, the press side guide edge of the sheet is the same as the folder lead edge, and the press gripper edge is the same as the folder guide side edge. This is done to maintain the press-folder registration. The long side, generally the gripper edge, of the press sheet is positioned against the guide side device on the folder for greater control when the sheet is folded. Cutting control edges are determined as previously explained.

20-19. *Methods of assembling paper.*

Requirement 2—
The Assembling Specifics

Imposition considerations regarding how a job will be assembled are closely related to how that job will be bound. Chapter 23 explains this relationship in depth. However, an overview of the assembling requirements will be presented here to show how these factors directly relate to the imposition plan. A printed job can be assembled in any or all of three different ways: *side*, *saddle*, and/or *looseleaf*. Fig. 20-19.

Looseleaf assembling is simply the placing of loose, unfolded printed press sheets on top of one another. The imposition planning required for looseleaf assembling is limited to insuring that the image area for each page is correctly placed on the

press sheet. This placement is based on the required binding margin. Fig. 20-20. The page number on the *back* side is generally one more than the page number on the *front* side of the sheet.

Signatures, or folded press sheets, can be assembled either by placing them side by side or by inserting them one inside the other. The first type is called *side assembling* (gathering), and the latter is called *saddle assembling* (gathering).

For example, if a 32-page job consisting of two self-covered, 16-page signatures were *side-gathered,* the first signature would contain pages 1 through 16. The second signature, which is assembled behind the first

signature, would contain pages 17 through 32.

If, however, the signatures for that same 32-page booklet were saddle-gathered, the first half (leg) of the outside signature (outsert) would contain pages 1 through 8, and the second half (leg) of that same signature would contain pages 25 through 32. The first half of the inside signature (insert) would contain pages 9 through 16, and the second half would contain pages 17 through 24.

The location of pages on a press sheet (pagination) can become very complicated when signatures are involved. Impositions determine the location of pages on press sheets, based on the binding margin requirements

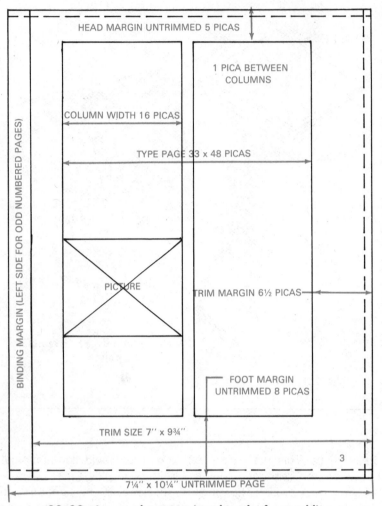

HEAD MARGIN UNTRIMMED 5 PICAS

1 PICA BETWEEN COLUMNS

COLUMN WIDTH 16 PICAS

TYPE PAGE 33 x 48 PICAS

BINDING MARGIN (LEFT SIDE FOR ODD NUMBERED PAGES)

PICTURE

TRIM MARGIN 6½ PICAS

FOOT MARGIN UNTRIMMED 8 PICAS

TRIM SIZE 7″ x 9¾″

3

7¼″ x 10¼″ UNTRIMMED PAGE

20-20. *Image placement in a looseleaf assembling.*

and on how these press sheets are folded and assembled. The location of each page on a folded press sheet depends on how each sheet is folded. In addition, the total number of pages per signature is based on how the press sheets are folded.

Requirement 3—The Binding Specifics

Although there are six major methods of binding booklets explained in Chapter 23, there are only two major binding consider-ations that relate to development of the basic imposition plan. These are the *binding margin requirement* and the *shingling requirement.*

The binding margin require-ment refers to the amount of paper that must be taken out of the binding margin to bind the pages and/or signatures to-gether. There are two types of binding: *side* and *saddle.*

Side binding is used when pages or signatures are looseleaf or side-assembled. It is the bind-ing of paper through the side. Side binding requires that the impositor allocate extra paper to the binding margin to allow for the binding. The amount of extra space allotted depends on the type of binding material and the location of the binder.

Booklets which are side-bound require large binding margins, can have many pages, and re-quire no lip or shingling margin allocations. They will not open flat.

Saddle binding, used only when signatures are saddle-assembled, is the binding of paper through the very backbone edge. The *backbone* is the edge formed where the signature is folded and secured to the cover. Saddle-bound booklets do not require extra margin space for the binding devices, but they generally require additional mar-gin space for the lip and shin-gling requirements. The number of pages in saddle-bound books is limited. Booklets that are sad-dle-bound will open flat.

Shingling refers to the in-crease in the backbone margins of the outside signatures used in making saddle-bound books. This increase in margin space is required to compensate for the "creep" or "push out" effect caused by the thickness of the inner signatures. Naturally, this creeping effect increases with each thickness of paper and number of signatures. The best method to determine how much creep will occur for each job is to make a dummy out of the actual stock planned for the job, and pierce a straight pin through the side of the dummy. Fig. 20-21. The dummy can then be un-folded, and the distances from

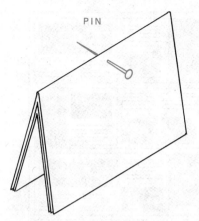

PIN

20-21. *The dummy booklet is pierced with a straight pin.*

the backbones to the holes for each page can be measured. Fig. 20-22. The variance in hole distances determined by the measuring can then be compensated for during the stripping or lockup operations.

Requirement 4—The Paper Specifics

The impositor selects the most economical type and size of paper to use for a particular job. An impositor will sometimes recommend that the size of a booklet be modified so that the required press sheet will cut more economically out of a common size paper.

For example, a four-to-sixteen page, 6″ × 9″ booklet signature will cut very economically from the basic size of *book* paper (25″ × 38″). The wrap-around cover for that same booklet will cut very economically from the basic size of *cover* paper (20″ × 26″). However, if the job were 6 1/2″ × 9 1/2″, neither the signature nor the cover would cut economically from the basic-sized stock. When normal

trims are added to the larger booklet, the stock will be too small to accommodate the booklet. An impositor must develop the basic imposition plan to conform to the size of the selected paper.

Requirement 5—The Printing Press Specifics

The major imposition considerations regarding *sheet-fed* printing presses are the *specifications* and the *image* requirements.

The two major specification considerations are the *size of press sheet* and the *amount of gripper bite* required for the press. There are other considerations with regard to press specifications, but the size of sheet and the gripper bite are the major ones. The maximum-size sheet that can be printed on the press will determine the type of imposition and the amount of

pages and signatures that can be printed on a press sheet at one time. The impositor selects the imposition and the press which will give the most economical results. For example, running a booklet two-up *work-and-turn* (produces four-out) on a larger-sized press instead of a one-up *sheetwise* (produces one-out) on a smaller-sized press will considerably reduce the number of press impressions, the number of plates, and the number of press makereadies.

Press *gripper margin* is the other major specification that should be considered by impositors. Generally, no printing is possible within the gripper margin. This restriction, however, does not cause a problem since most jobs are imposed so that trims and other nonprinting areas are placed within the gripper margin. If bleeds are involved, however, the imposition

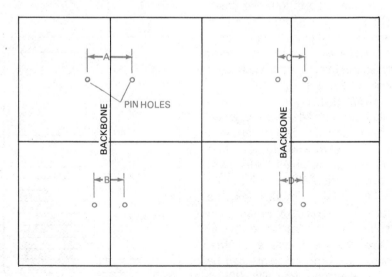

NOTE: DISTANCE BETWEEN PINHOLES EXAGGERATED TO EMPHASIZE ILLUSTRATION.

20-22. *How to measure the distance from the backbones to the pinholes on the outside signature.*

must be planned so that bleed areas print away from the gripper.

Printing image requirements include three major considerations: *roller stripping, solids in line with low ink image areas,* and *color.*

Roller stripping occurs when too much ink must be distributed to the printing plate from the form rollers. That is, the rollers run out of ink before the entire plate is covered with ink. This generally occurs on plates that are so long that the front part of the plate takes too much ink off the inking rollers before they reach the back part of the plate. Impositors often impose large press sheets in a manner that will distribute the solid areas across the entire sheet. Fig. 20-23.

The imposition plan must also insure that light ink coverage areas, such as fine line or screen areas, are not imposed in line with heavy, solid areas (reverses, for example) on the press sheet. Otherwise, the fine lines or screens will "plug" as a result of the extra ink applied to the form rollers to insure good coverage of the solid areas. Fig. 20-24.

Color is the third imposition planning consideration. Lighter-colored and nontransparent inks should be imposed to print first on the press sheet. This third consideration also requires that split-fountain impositions be used whenever it is practical. A split-fountain imposition can save considerable press time, since two or more colors can be printed at one time. Fig. 20-25. Split-fountain work is imposed so that all alike colors are kept to respective areas of the sheet.

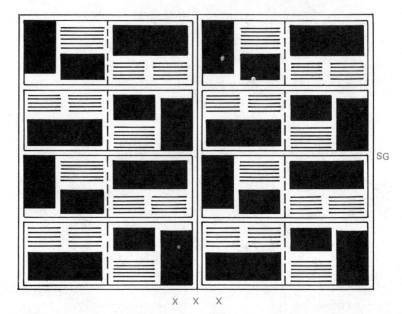

20-23. *Image areas should be imposed on a press sheet so that the solid areas are distributed across the entire sheet.*

Imposition planning for roll-fed (web) presses is based on three major factors. These are the *width of web,* the *length of cutoff,* and the *number and type of printing units.*

The *width of the web* is the distance across a roll of paper. Fig. 20-26. This distance determines the maximum size that can be printed from the web. Whether this maximum size is

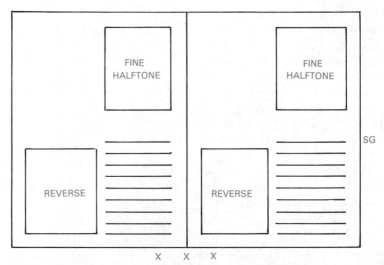

20-24. *Press sheets should be imposed so that the fine halftone is not in line with the solid reverse. The reverse requires extra ink, which could clog the halftones.*

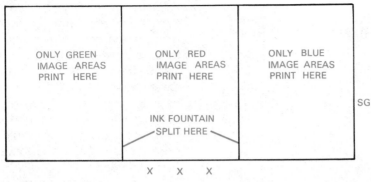

ONLY GREEN IMAGE AREAS PRINT HERE

ONLY RED IMAGE AREAS PRINT HERE

ONLY BLUE IMAGE AREAS PRINT HERE

SG

INK FOUNTAIN SPLIT HERE

X   X   X

20-25. *A split fountain can be used to save press time. The imposition is made so that all jobs with the same color are kept to one area of the press sheet.*

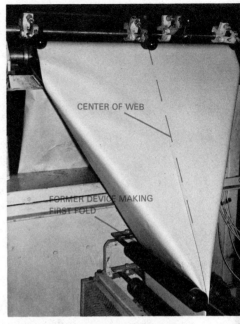

CENTER OF WEB

FORMER DEVICE MAKING FIRST FOLD

20-28. *Making the first fold.*

the width or depth of the finished booklet is determined by how many times the web sheet is folded by the folder attached to the press. If quarter-folded, the width will be the maximum size; if eighth-folded, the depth will be the maximum size.

The *length of cutoff* is a constant factor determined by the circumference of the cylinder that cuts the web into sheets. The cutting cylinder makes the first right-angle fold and determines the maximum size of a booklet in the dimension not already determined by the web width. See Figs. 20-27 through 20-29 to visualize how a typical web folder works.

The number and type of *printing units* determine the number and type of pages that can be

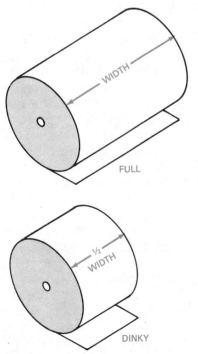

WIDTH

FULL

½ WIDTH

DINKY

20-26. *A full roll (web) and a dinky roll (web) of paper.*

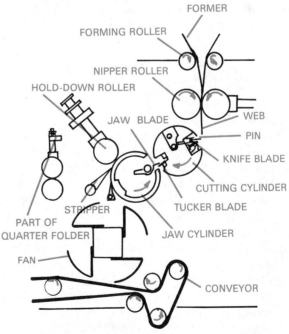

FORMER

FORMING ROLLER

NIPPER ROLLER

HOLD-DOWN ROLLER

JAW BLADE

WEB

PIN

KNIFE BLADE

CUTTING CYLINDER

TUCKER BLADE

JAW CYLINDER

STRIPPER

PART OF QUARTER FOLDER

FAN

CONVEYOR

20-27. *Major parts of a typical web folder.*

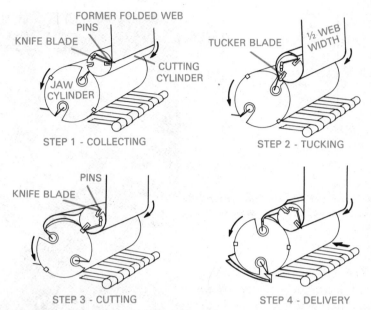

STEP 1 - COLLECTING

STEP 2 - TUCKING

STEP 3 - CUTTING

STEP 4 - DELIVERY

20-29. *Sheeting the web and making the second and succeeding folds. In this operation, the cutting cylinder tucks and cuts the former-folded web into the jaw cylinder to make the second fold at right angles to the fold produced by the former. The lead edge of the web is first grabbed by pins on the rotating cutting cylinder, Step 1. Then a tucker blade, opposite the knife blade in the cutting cylinder, inserts the web into the jaw cylinder, traveling in the opposite direction of the cutting cylinder, Step 2. The unsheeted web is then grabbed by pins and cut away from the fold, Step 3. The element that was cut away is then delivered to the fan or the quarter folder, depending on how the stripper device is set, Step 4. The end still attached to the web is grabbed by the pins to begin the tucking and sheeting process again. The quarter fold is made at a right angle to the tucked fold.*

printed with one pass through a web press. For example, each unit of a *perfecting* web press will produce four broadside (full-sized newspaper) pages, 8 tabloid (half the size of ordinary newspaper) pages, 16 book-type pages, or 32 book-type pages. Sixteen book-type pages can be printed if the web is quarter-folded, and 32 pages if the web is eighth-folded.

Regardless of how many or what type of pages are imposed to print at each unit on a perfecting press, half of the pages are usually printed onto the web from the top deck and half from the bottom deck. Each unit is capable of printing a full-width web or a half-width web, called a dinky. Fig. 20-26. Dinkies produce only one-half the number of pages possible from a full web.

If color is involved, the impositor must plan for the web to go through a separate unit for each color to be printed on one side of the web. An exception to this is the "S" wrap arrangement, which permits two colors to be printed on one side of a web by transferring ink from the lower-deck plate and the upper-deck blanket. Fig. 20-30. Also, the first color to be printed on most web presses is usually printed in the unit farthest away from the folder.

To repeat, the imposition for web-fed presses is based on the type of folder and the number and type of printing units on the press. The dimensions of a booklet to be printed on a web press are determined by the width of the web sheet, the length of the cutoff, and the number of times the web is folded. The maximum number of pages or colors that can be printed on each page on a web press is determined by the capability of the web folder and the number of units to be used.

Requirement 6—The Folder Specifics

In sheet-fed folding, the imposition and page number sequence are based on the overall folding plan. Generally, the method of folding is determined when the dummy is developed.

The possible combinations of folds which will produce multiple-page signatures are quite extensive. Fig. 20-31. However, once the combination of folds is decided, only the type and size of folder need to be determined before the imposition plan can be finalized. A complete discussion of folding machines is presented in Chapter 23. Impositors need only be concerned with the capabilities of the four major types:

quad, *double-16, jobber,* and *web.*

Quad folders are used exclusively for book work. They fold all press sheets relatively the same way. The imposition requirements are basically predetermined when press sheets are imposed for this type of folder. A press sheet entering the quad folder is eventually divided into four separate, standardized (16-page) signatures, each of which is folded in the same fashion. Quad folders can gather the folded 16-page signatures either in a side or a saddle fashion to produce two 32-page booklets or four 16-page booklets. Since the size ranges of the quad folder are fixed, they will always produce a specific number of pages within a given booklet size range. Because of the standardized way quad folders fold and gather signatures, impositors must insure that each page is correctly imposed in a particular place on the press sheet, based on how the signatures are gathered.

Double-16 folders are similar to quad folders. The major difference is that double-16 folders divide standard-sized press sheets into just two 16-page signatures. The imposition for this folder is also based on how the machine folds and gathers press sheets. The number and size of pages that can be produced on a double-16 folder is standardized to the extent that they fold and gather 16-page signatures either in a side fashion or a saddle fashion. This machine can produce standardized outsert-insert or separate signature arrangements.

Jobber folders are very versa-

tile. Unlike the quad and double-16 folders, each jobber folder can produce many different folding combinations. The jobber folder is comprised of separate folding sections. Each folding section provides at least one parallel "up fold" and/or one parallel "down fold," with most having a "2-up" and "2-down" folding potential. Each time a section is added, the folding potential is increased in direct proportion to the number of folding plates in the added section. The added sections can be arranged to provide either right-angle or parallel folds.

The imposition for jobs on jobber folders is based on the size of the folder and the folding plan. The dummy used to develop the imposition plan for jobber folders must be folded the same way the press sheet will be folded. For example, the placement of pages on the press sheet depends on which folding plates and how many sections are to be used on the folder. As with any other folder, the size of the finished

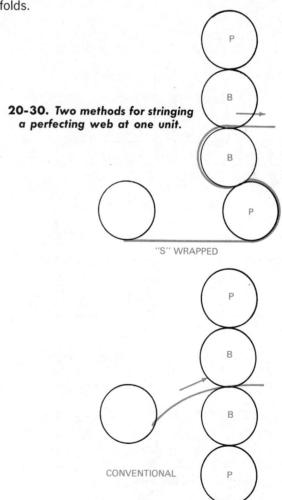

20-30. *Two methods for stringing a perfecting web at one unit.*

"S" WRAPPED

CONVENTIONAL

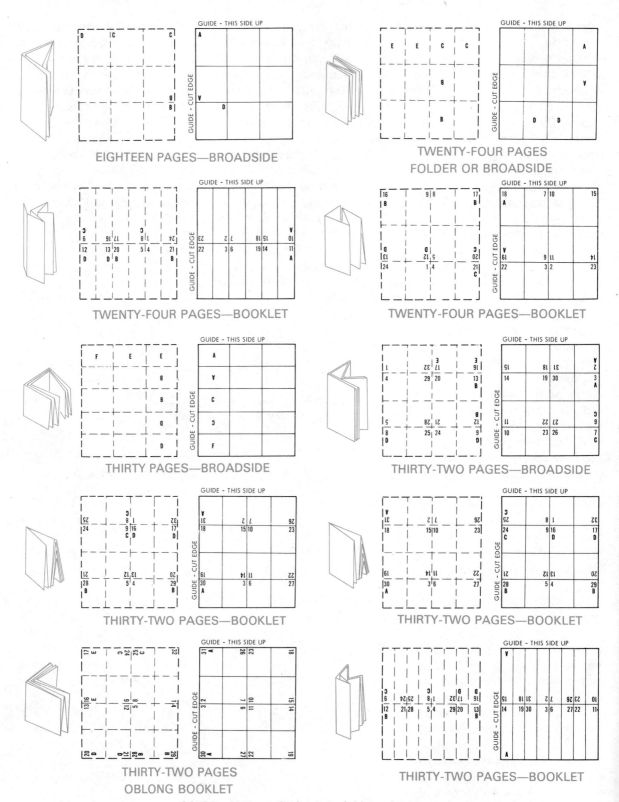

EIGHTEEN PAGES—BROADSIDE

TWENTY-FOUR PAGES
FOLDER OR BROADSIDE

TWENTY-FOUR PAGES—BOOKLET

TWENTY-FOUR PAGES—BOOKLET

THIRTY PAGES—BROADSIDE

THIRTY-TWO PAGES—BROADSIDE

THIRTY-TWO PAGES—BOOKLET

THIRTY-TWO PAGES—BOOKLET

THIRTY-TWO PAGES
OBLONG BOOKLET

THIRTY-TWO PAGES—BOOKLET

20-31. *Some multiple-page fold combinations.*

page is limited by the maximum size of press sheet that can be folded.

Normally, the open legs of a signature folded on a jobber folder are the first pages of the signature. (A leg is a folded page.) This should be kept in mind when developing the imposition plan.

A full discussion of *web folders* is beyond the scope of this text. However, a brief explanation of the basic web imposition theory will be given, using a typical web folder equipped with a quarter folder. The major parts of this folder are shown in Fig. 20-27.

The former is the device that makes the first fold in the center of the web. Fig. 20-28. The cutting cylinder cuts the once-folded web and makes the second fold at right angles to the first fold by cutting and tucking the web into the jaw cylinder. Fig. 20-29. If the stripper is engaged, the quarter-fold device then makes the third fold at right angles to the second fold. If the stripper is not engaged, the web is delivered in tabloid form without any further folding. However, if an eighth-folder were available, it would make another fold at right angles to the quarter fold.

Several characteristics of web folders should be emphasized. For example, the size of the web cutoff, as previously indicated, is always a fixed value for each press, which means the size of the *image area* for one dimension of a booklet can vary, but the size of the *paper* for that dimension will be constant. In other words, the image area size can vary from nothing to the maximum size at the option of the impositor. Conversely, the

size of the image area of a booklet not already determined by the cutoff is based on the width of the web that will fit the press. However, the size of the paper, unlike the cutoff, is not fixed, but based on the width of the web. The image area for either dimension of a booklet printed on a web press can be smaller than the maximum size, but the size of the sheet will be fixed and in direct relationship to the circumference of the cutoff cylinder and the web width.

Impositors should know that when more than one web is strung on a web press, all webs are folded together, which is unlike sheet-fed folding. In sheet-fed folding, each sheet is individually folded, then side or saddle gathered. In web folding, each web is placed on top of the other at the former, and all are "sheeted" and folded together. This also includes dinky webs, which are generally strung on the press so that the pages printed on them end up tucked inside the folded, full-sized webs.

A dummy should be used in imposition planning for web presses to insure that all image areas will print in the correct position on the press sheet.

The web impositor must determine: *the number of units needed, the method of stringing the webs, the amount and location of the lip, the page locations, the location of the heads, and the placement and value of all trims.*

DEVELOPING THE IMPOSITION PLAN

Although imposition planning is based on many considerations, it is really not as complicated as the previous discussion

might suggest. Planning must include those elements necessary to produce the job in the most economical manner. Three basics to consider are the *number of parts* for the job, *processing particulars,* and *selection of processing equipment.*

The impositor should keep in mind that all parts of the job must have corresponding trims once assembled and bound; that all control guides must correspond; that all processing, trim, and binding margins must be correct; and whether the job can be economically processed using the selected type of imposition and bindery equipment.

DEVELOPING THE SHEET-FED IMPOSITION PLAN

Assume the imposition plan to be developed is for a job requiring 500 copies of a 16-page, saddle-stitched, separate-covered, one-color, 6″ by 9″ booklet. Although many acceptable imposition plans are possible, the one presented in the following example is typical of the way an average printer might actually develop the plan.

Number of parts. Assume only two parts are required to produce this booklet, a four-page cover and a 16-page signature. The four pages of the cover are not numbered or counted in the booklet.

Processing particulars. It is recommended that the material presented here be compared with the material presented in Chapter 23 and with the chapters on press operation and paper for a more complete understanding of why the following imposition plan was developed. Observe that no spoilage is computed.

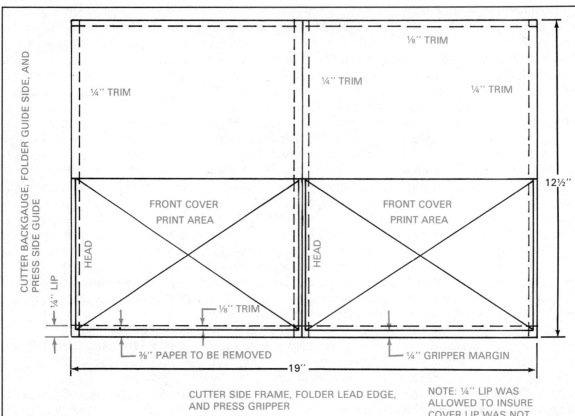

20-32. *The cover sheet lay.*

CUTTER SIDE FRAME, FOLDER LEAD EDGE, AND PRESS GRIPPER

NOTE: ¼" LIP WAS ALLOWED TO INSURE COVER LIP WAS NOT LARGER THAN SIGNATURE LIP.

Cover particular. Fig. 20-32.

1. Stock

   Press Stock:

Number of Sheets Needed	250
Size of Sheet	19" × 12 1/2"
Direction of Grain	Long
Produces	2 Finished Copies

   Parent Stock:

Number of Sheets Needed	125
Size of Sheet	20" × 26"
Direction of Grain	Short
Basic Weight	80 lb.
Produces	2 Press Sheets
Type of Stock	Cover

2. Margins

Lip Margin	1/4"
Binding Margin	None Required for Saddle Binding
Trim Margin	1/4" Head, 1/4" Foot, 1/8" Front

   (Note how these conform to the trims for the signatures.)

Gripper Margin . . . . 1/4"

3. Control Guide. Fig. 20-32. Observe that the cutter, folder, and press guides correspond.

4. Imposition. The head lo-

cations are shown in Fig. 20-32. Note that only the first page of the cover will be printed.

Type of Imposition . . . . Printed One Side
(Requiring Folding)

Number Up 2
Number Out 2
Number of Printing Plates 1
Number of Press Impressions 250
Number of Press Makereadies 1

(This information was developed through the use of a dummy. See Chapter 23 for a more detailed explanation of how the dummy for this particular job was produced.)

5. Press Selection. Chief 20 which will handle sheets 14" × 20".

6. Folder Selection. Tabletop which will handle sheets 14" × 20".

Signature particulars. Fig. 20-33.

1. Stock
   Press Stock:
   Number of Sheets Needed 500
   Size of Sheet . . . . 25" × 19"
   Direction of Grain . . . . Short (Parallel
   to Backbone)
   Produces . . . . One Finished
   Copy
   Parent Stock:
   Number of Sheets Needed 250
   Size of Sheet . . . . 25" × 28"
   Direction of Grain . . . . Long
   Basic Weight . . . . 60 lbs.
   Produces . . . . 2 Press Sheets
   Type of Stock . . . . Book

The example shown in Chapter 23 shows the signature parent stock to be 19" × 25". The 25" × 38" sheet was used here to show the relationship of grains between press-sized sheets and parent-sized sheets.

(*Signature particulars* continued on page 508.)

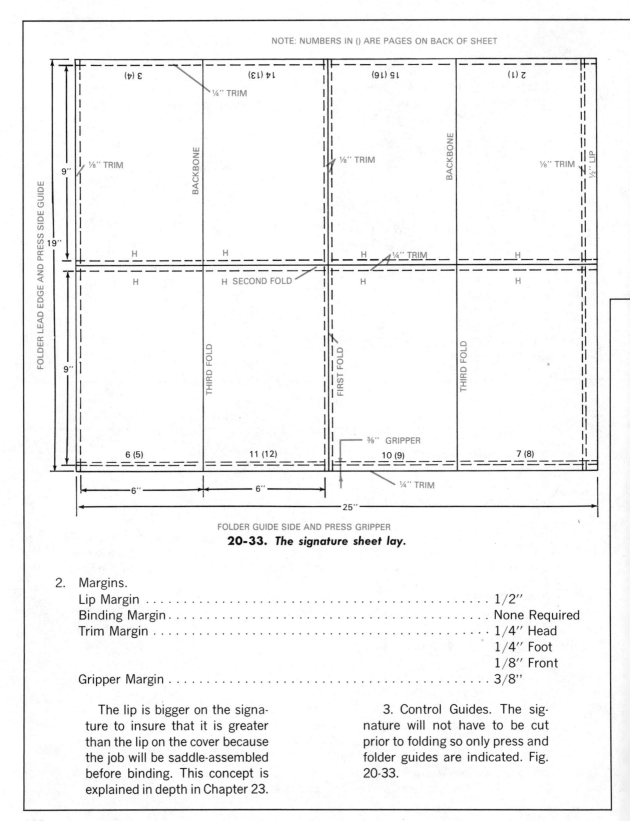

NOTE: NUMBERS IN () ARE PAGES ON BACK OF SHEET

20-33. *The signature sheet lay.*

2. Margins.
    Lip Margin . . . . 1/2″
    Binding Margin. . . . . None Required
    Trim Margin . . . . 1/4″ Head
                                                                                1/4″ Foot
                                                                                1/8″ Front
    Gripper Margin . . . . 3/8″

The lip is bigger on the signature to insure that it is greater than the lip on the cover because the job will be saddle-assembled before binding. This concept is explained in depth in Chapter 23.

3. Control Guides. The signature will not have to be cut prior to folding so only press and folder guides are indicated. Fig. 20-33.

4. Imposition. The head locations and pagination layout are shown in Fig. 20-33. Note how the numbers of the pages which share the same backbone (companion pages) add up to one more than the total number of pages in the signature. For example, 6 + 11 = 17, 12 + 5 = 17, and so forth.

Type of Imposition. . . . . Sheetwise (Requiring Folder)
Number Up. 1
Number Out. 1
Number of Printing Plates 2
Number of Press Impressions . . . . 1,000 (500 per side)
Number of Press Makereadies . . . . 2 (one for each plate)

5. Press Selection. Harris LTN, 22″ × 34″.

6. Folder Selection. Jobber folder, 20″ × 26″.

DEVELOPING THE WEB IMPOSITION PLAN

The steps necessary to develop an imposition plan for jobs to be printed on web-fed presses are similar to those that have already been discussed in the text. The major difference is how the dummy is made. The *web dummy* is used to simplify the planning effort by helping the impositor to determine visually the production requirements *unique to the web press.*

Making the Web Dummy

Assume that an impositor must develop the web imposition plan to produce a 6″ × 9″, saddle-stitched, 40-page self-covered booklet. The booklet is to be printed with two colors of ink (black and one color) on pages 1, 10, 31, 9, 32, 22, and 29. The steps required to produce a web-press dummy for this job are as follows:

1. Gather the web dummy sheets in the order they will print and fold. Keep the dinky on the bottom and to the operator's side. Fig. 20-34. The number of sheets is based on the number of pages and colors. See Fig. 20-38 to understand why the dummy sheets were placed in the order indicated by Fig. 20-34.

2. Identify the lead edge, the print side, and the placement order of each web dummy sheet by placing appropriate marks. Fig. 20-34.

3. Fold all dummy sheets together the same way the web folder will fold the web sheets. The closed-page legs of the dummy will be the front half of the dummy booklet after it is folded. Fig. 20-35. Note that the web is quarter-folded.

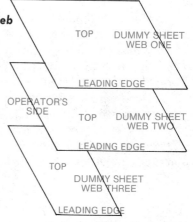

20-34. *Gathering the web dummy sheets.*

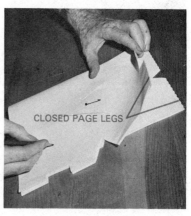

20-35. *The folded dummy.*

4. Cut lip and trim identifying notches. Fig. 20-36. The "V" notches are made in all areas that are to be trimmed, and the rectangular notch is made in the lip edge.

5. Number the pages. Underline the bottom of each page number to help determine the location of the heads.

6. Unfold the dummy sheets, and use the identifying marks and notches to help figure the pagination, lip, and trim values. Fig. 20-37.

Developing the Web Processing Particulars

Assume the specifications of the perfecting roll-fed press to be used call for a 22 3/4" cutoff and a maximum full-web width of 36" with a minimum full-web width of 29". Also assume the bindery equipment requires a 1/2" lip. A typical imposition plan would be as follows:

1. Determine the number of printing units. For the example, four units will be required (one unit to print the color and three units to print all the black). Two

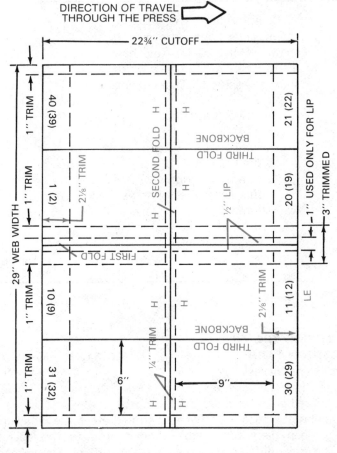

20-37. *Pagination and margin values for each web. These are the top views. The page numbers in parentheses are printed from the lower deck. The others are printed from the upper deck at each unit. Fig. 20-37A: Web one. Press units three and four.*

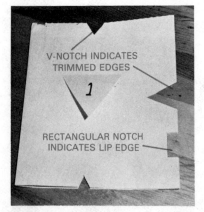

20-36. *Cutting the identifying notches.*

full web units producing 16 pages each and one dinky unit producing 8 pages will be needed to print the black on 40 pages. One separate unit will be needed to print the color on the pages requiring color.

2. Determine the method of stringing the web. Two full 29" webs and one 14 1/2" dinky web will be required. The dinky will run as the bottom web on the operator's side. Fig. 20-38. The color for the color pages will be printed on web one in unit four,

and the black for the same pages will be printed in unit three. Units one and two will print the remaining black ink pages not already printed in unit three.

3. Determine the amount and location of the lip. Fig. 20-37. The lip is developed by offsetting the quarter folds. Note that equal lip margins are allocated to each side of the first fold because the lip must be taken out of the middle of the sheet.

4. Determine the page locations. Fig. 20-37.

5. Determine the head locations. These are shown by the "H" symbol. Fig. 20-37.

6. Determine the value for all trims. The trims are computed by allowing for the lip, and then by subtracting the dimensions of the finished booklet from the dimensions of the folded web. Remember, the web dimensions are based on the web width and cutoff dimensions. Fig. 20-37.

LOCKING UP TYPEFORMS

Typeforms (used in relief printing) are locked up on an imposing table. The person doing the work is called a *stoneman.*

When a job is to be locked up, the stoneman needs the job

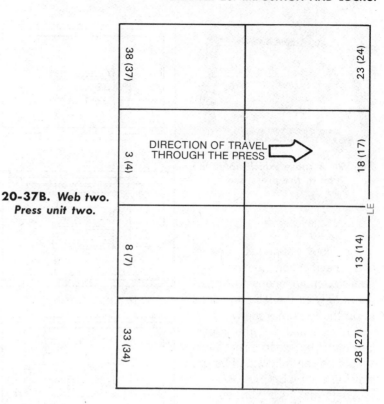

20-37B. *Web two. Press unit two.*

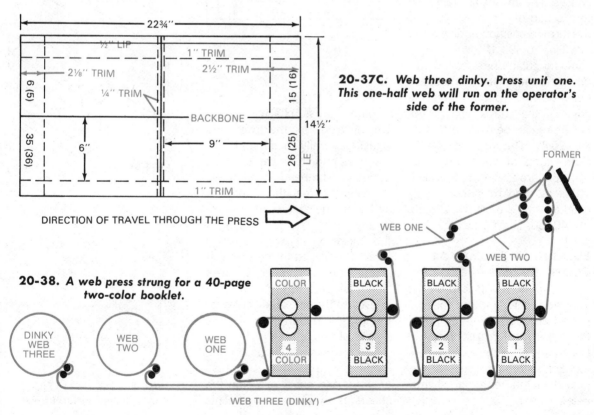

20-37C. *Web three dinky. Press unit one. This one-half web will run on the operator's side of the former.*

20-38. *A web press strung for a 40-page two-color booklet.*

20-39. *A chase which holds the type to the press bed.*

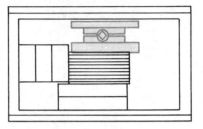

STEP ONE

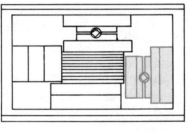

STEP TWO

STEP THREE

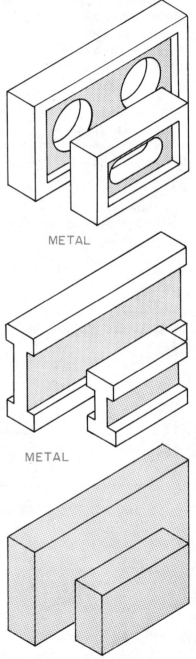

METAL

METAL

WOOD AND PLASTIC
20-41. *Typical furniture.*

order, copy, approved proofs, and specification for printing. The stoneman needs to understand fully all the job conditions to do the lockup properly.

It is essential that the imposing table be clean. The table should be carefully wiped before starting each job.

Typeforms are locked in chases. The chases are fastened to the bed of the press to hold the form in position during printing. Fig. 20-39.

Rectangular units, called *furniture,* are used to fill the space between the typeform and the edge of the chase. Fig. 20-40. Furniture can be wood or metal. Fig. 20-41. The most commonly used widths of wood and metal furniture are 2, 3, 4, 5, 6, 8, and 10 picas. The most commonly used lengths are 10, 15, 20, 25, 30, 40, 50, and 60 picas.

LOCKING UP FORMS FOR PLATEN PRESSES

The typeform is placed on the imposing table, and the chase is placed around it. For the hand-fed press the form is placed in the center or slightly above center. For automatic presses it is placed in the center or slightly below center.

Platen press chases usually are beveled on the two long sides. Generally these sides are identical, and either can serve as the head. The head of the chase is placed nearest the stoneman as he or she stands at the imposing table. This is the side of the chase which will be down when it is placed in the press. It is the bottom guide edge. The side guide is always on the left. Therefore the side guide edge for the form is the left side as it lies on the stone.

The form should be positioned in the chase so that the press operator can easily examine the sheets as they are printed. This

512

20-42. *The head of the form is placed facing the head of the chase.*

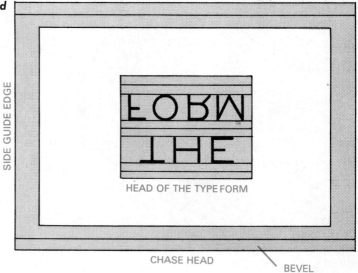

SIDE GUIDE EDGE

HEAD OF THE TYPE FORM

CHASE HEAD

BEVEL

helps the operator detect any problems that may cause poor image reproduction. The head of the form should be facing the head of the chase or the side guide edge. Fig. 20-42.

Preparing the Form

The form is placed on the imposing table with the head in the proper direction. The chase is placed over the form and positioned so that the form is near the center. Now place the furniture around the sides of the form. Fig. 20-40. First, place furniture solid at the head and left sides of the form. Next place a piece of furniture on the top side next to the form. Insert the quoins (discussed in the next section) and fill in the space to

the chase. Then repeat this for the right side of the form. The furniture should be arranged so that it will not bind when the quoins are tightened. Before the furniture is tightened, remove

the string from around the form. Be certain the furniture is in place on all four sides before the string is removed.

There are several ways to arrange the furniture around the form for a lockup. Choose the one which will use the fewest lengths of furniture and the least number of pieces. These arrangements are shown in Figs. 20-43 and 20-44.

Inserting the Quoins

Quoins are used to apply the pressure needed to lock the form and furniture to the chase. There are several different kinds available. Fig. 20-45.

The number of quoins to use depends upon the size of the typeform. Critical to a successful lockup is placement of the quoins for uniform pressure on

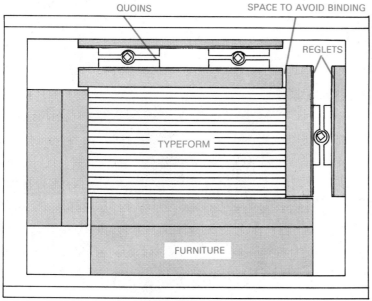

QUOINS

SPACE TO AVOID BINDING

REGLETS

TYPEFORM

FURNITURE

HEAD OF CHASE

20-43. *The chaser method for arranging furniture.*

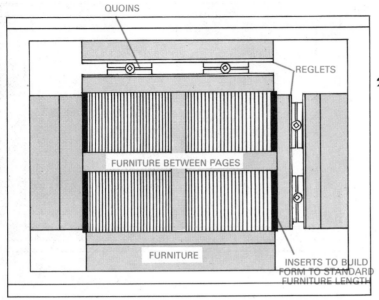

QUOINS

REGLETS

FURNITURE BETWEEN PAGES

FURNITURE

INSERTS TO BUILD FORM TO STANDARD FURNITURE LENGTH

HEAD OF CHASE

20-44. *The squared method for arranging furniture.*

It is a common practice to place strips of reglets on both sides of the quoins. Fig. 20-46. *Reglets* are wood strips that are the same height as the furniture. They are available in 6-, 12-, and 18-point thicknesses. They keep the quoins from damaging the edges of the furniture. If metal furniture is used, reglets also prevent the quoins from slipping while the form is in the press. If there is no space for a reglet, use strips of tagboard (a tough, firm cardboard).

After the quoins are in place, fill the space remaining to the chase with furniture. Then tighten the quoins slightly, but not fully. Fig. 20-47 shows a form

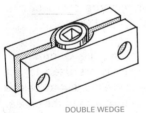

HIGH SPEED

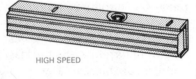

DOUBLE WEDGE

all parts of the typeform. A very small job may require only one set of quoins on each side. Most jobs require two sets on each side. Very large forms may require extra sets of quoins.

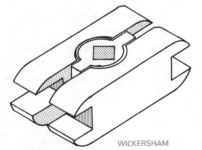

WICKERSHAM

20-45. *Typical quoins.*

20-46. *Reglets are placed between the quoins and the furniture.*

REGLETS

514

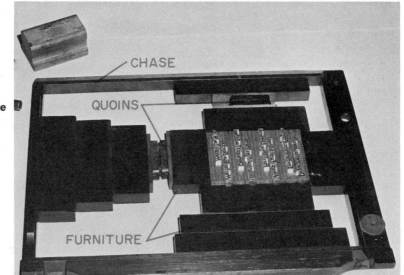

20-47. *A form with all furniture and quoins in place.*

with the furniture and quoins in place.

Locking Up the Form

After all materials are in place for the lockup, make certain the form is square and the furniture will not bind. Then begin to lock the form.

To lock the form, insert the key in the pair of quoins on the long side of the chase nearest the solid side. Tighten slightly. Then lightly tighten the next pair of quoins. Now lightly tighten the quoins on the side. Fig. 20-48. Inspect the form to see that all the parts are together properly. Check special things such as rules and borders.

If the lockup appears satisfactory, slowly loosen the quoins in the same sequence that they were tightened. Now tighten them with your fingers until they are firm. The form is now ready to be planed.

20-48. *Tightening the quoins with a quoin key.*

QUOIN KEY

PLANER

TYPEFORM

20-49. *Planing a typeform.*

To plane the form, place the planer on top of it. Lightly tap with a mallet or quoin key. Fig. 20-49. Work the planer over the face of the entire form. Check to see that all the parts of the form are flush. If a part sticking up will not move down easily, see if something is below it on the imposing table. Do not attempt to pound pieces flush. They are easily damaged. To move the form to check below, it is necessary to lock the quoins with the key before it can be lifted.

After the form is planed, the quoins are locked tightly. Do not completely tighten each one the first time. Apply some pressure with each, and then go back and tighten a little more. Only enough pressure is needed to hold the form in the chase. Excess pressure will cause the form to buckle.

To test the form for tightness, lift the edge of the chase and place something, such as the quoin key, under it. Then press all over the surface of the form with your fingers. Fig. 20-50. If it does not move down, the form is ready for the pressroom. If an area is loose, the form must be placed back on the imposing table, unlocked, and the cause found and corrected. Common problems include furniture binding, quoins improperly placed, warped or bent furniture, or an improperly justified typeform.

LOCKING UP FORMS FOR THE CYLINDER PRESS

The principles of lockup for platen presses apply to cylinder press lockup. There are some differences in the procedures used for cylinder press lockup.

Cylinder press chases are not

beveled but have square edges. Most have a top and bottom side. The top side is marked on the chase and should be placed up on the imposing table. Larger

20-50. *Testing the form for tightness.*

chases have solid or removable crossbars. They keep the forms from sagging and help distribute the pressure of quoins evenly over the form. Fig. 20-51.

Most cylinder press chases have the head marked on the chase. The head of the form should be placed at the head of the chase.

Preparing the Form

Two major factors to be considered in positioning the form in the chase are (1) the guide edge of the sheet on which the form is to be printed must strike the guides at a suitable place under the press grippers, and (2) the typeform must be back where it will clear the press grippers. Study Chapter 22, "Cylinder Press Op-

eration," for information on cylinder press feeding systems.

Most cylinder presses have a line across the gripper end of the press bed. The typeform should not come past this line. Since this distance varies on different presses, the stoneman must know which press to use to print the job.

If a form is to be locked in a full-size chase, the stoneman must position the form very accurately to allow the proper press gripper margins. If the press operator cannot get the proper gripper margins, the job will have to be moved in the chase and relocked.

If the job is small, a smaller chase is used. In this case, the press operator can move it

by shifting the chase on the press bed.

Inserting the Quoins

The positioning of quoins is the same as the platen press lockup. For large forms, the quoins should be placed at least every six inches.

Locking the Form

The cylinder press form is locked up in the same manner as for platen press lockup. Since the forms are usually larger, it takes very careful work to get the proper position of each part. In some cases the cylinder press form is planed after it is on the bed of the press rather than on the imposing table.

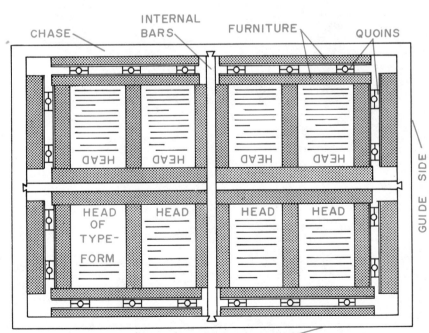

20-51. A lockup for eight-pages-up of a sixteen-page signature. Notice the use of internal bars to keep the forms from sagging.

REVIEW QUESTIONS

1. Name the terms defined by the following:
   a. The arrangement of pages on the press sheet.
   b. The edge of the press sheet that enters the printing press first.
   c. Area on the surface of the press sheet that receives ink.
   d. The side of the sheet that is printed first.
   e. A printed sheet containing a number of pages that will be folded to form part of a book or a whole booklet.
   f. A miniature booklet folded and assembled the same way the finished job will be.
2. How many printing plates are required for each press sheet when using sheetwise imposition?
3. How many plates are required for work-and-turn imposition?
4. Work-and-flop imposition prints inner and outer image areas on one side of a press sheet. True or False?
5. What is another name for work-and-twirl imposition?
6. One way to assemble signatures is to insert them one inside the other. What is this method called?
7. What is roller stripping?
8. One disadvantage of jobber folders is that they are not very versatile. True or False?
9. Name the terms defined in the following:
   a. Rectangular units used to fill the space between typeform and edge of chase.
   b. Used to apply pressure to lock form and furniture to the chase.

Chapter 21

Platen Press Operation

Platen presses are part of the letterpress group. Cylinder and rotary presses are also of the letterpress group.

While the following discussion is centered around the Original Heidelberg automatic platen press, the principles shown can be applied to presses manufactured by other companies. Fig. 21-1. The specific controls and adjustments will vary, but the operating principles are the same.

HOW THE PRESS OPERATES

The press, Fig. 21-2, is inked from the *ink fountain*. The ink is moved to the typeform by a series of distributing and form rollers.

The *typeform* is locked in a *chase,* which is then locked to the *bed* of the press.

The stock to be printed is

placed on the *feed table.* The top sheets of the stock pile on the feed table are separated by a blast of air. The top sheet is lifted away from the pile with vacuum suckers. An arm, called the *gripper,* grasps the edge of the sheet as it is released by the suckers. The gripper places it on the platen. The *platen* is the surface that holds the sheet as it is printed. The platen closes up against the typeform. The ink on the form is pressed against the paper, making an impression.

Next the gripper moves the printed sheet to the delivery pile. While this is being done, the ink rollers are inking the form once more, and the suckers are lifting another sheet. The process is continuous.

The speed is controlled by the press operator. The operator must make certain the typeform prints on the sheet in the place desired. Adjustments must be made so that the impression printed is clear and even. The operator must regulate the flow of ink so that the form does not get too much or too little. Carefully made adjustments are essential.

THE FEEDING SYSTEM

The preparation of the feeding system on an automatic platen press requires careful adjust-

Heidelberg

21-1. The Original Heidelberg platen press.

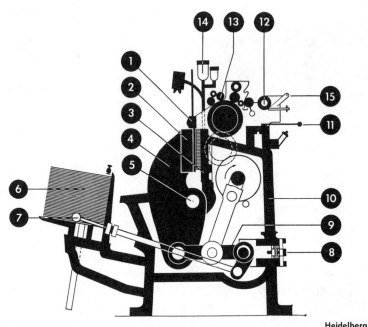

Heidelberg

21-2. The major parts of the Original Heidelberg platen press: (1) Paper fed by rotating grippers. (2) Platen printing surface. (3) Type bed. (4) Printing platen. (5) Platen journals. (6) Feed and delivery piles. (7) Impression adjustment. (8) Safety device to prevent excessive printing pressure. (9) Toggle lever applies 40 to 60 tons printing pressure. (10) Machine base. (11) Single-lever, central-lubrication control. (12) Fountain roller. (13) Form rollers. (14) Wet or dry spray. (15) Ink fountain.

For commercial register, positioning is easiest if the form is centered with the center mark on the chase. The center mark on the chase coincides with the center of the front feed table.

To position stock under these conditions:

1. Place one sheet of stock to be used on the feed table.

2. Run the feed table to the top position.

3. Center the sheet on the center mark.

4. Set the side standard to one side of the sheet.

5. Print a proof on the sheet. Measure to make certain it is printing in the position wanted. Adjust the side standard until the proper location is obtained.

6. Set the side standard on the other side of the sheet.

7. Lower the table. It is now ready to be loaded.

Some jobs are printed using the guides to provide hairline

ments. The operations required are listed here.

1. Lower the feed table. The feed table is raised and lowered by pressing down on the checking-pawl lever with one hand and turning the crank handle. Fig. 21-3. Disengage the delivery table before adjusting the feed table.

2. Position the side standards on the feed table.

3. Load the stock on the feed table.

4. Position the sheet steadiers.

5. Adjust the sucker bar.

6. Adjust the air blast and tripping springs.

7. Adjust pile height control.

8. Adjust feed table lift control.

9. Adjust automatic stop control.

POSITIONING STOCK ON THE FEED TABLE

Two methods are used to determine location of the print on the sheet. *Commercial* register is used with printings that do not require exact location of the print on the sheet. *Hairline* register, or register with guides, is available for printing that requires exact location of the print on the sheet. For example, multicolor printings, where the colors are superimposed, require this method of registration.

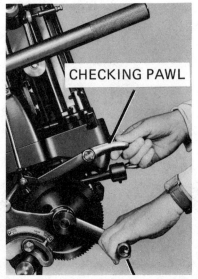

CHECKING PAWL

CRANK HANDLE

Heidelberg

21-3. Adjusting the feed table.

register. The adjustment of the guides will be covered in the section on impression.

(The following section deals with the feeding system, Figs. 21-4 through 21-17; the delivery system, Figs. 21-18 through 21- 23; and the inking system, Figs. 21-24 through 21-32.) (Pages 521–529.)

THE FEEDING SYSTEM

21-4. *To load stock, lower the feed table to the lowest position. Fan the paper as it is placed on the table.*

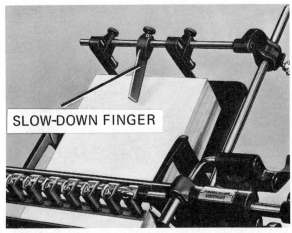

21-6. *A slow-down finger can be used to prevent the lower sheets from being dragged forward as the top sheet is fed into the press.*

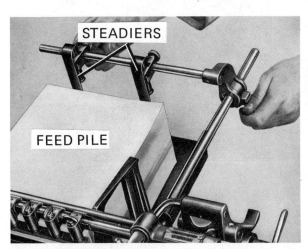

21-5. *After the stock is on the feed table, install sheet steadiers. They are pressed lightly against the pile and tightened.*

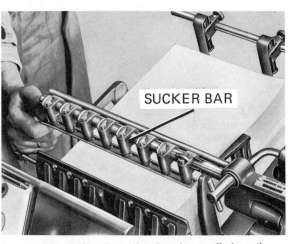

21-7. *The sucker bar lifts the sheet off the pile so that the gripper can grasp it. The gripper moves the sheet to the platen. Various papers require different amounts of suction. Thin stock requires less suction than heavy stock. The press operator should install the sucker bar that best suits the paper to be printed.*

21-8. *Suction can be reduced by adjusting the sucker bar clip.*

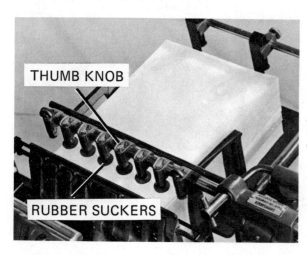

21-9. *Rubber sucker discs can be used instead of a sucker bar for very heavy stock. As many discs can be used as are needed. Each disc can be individually shut off. A thumb knob at the top of each sucker does this. The suckers should be centered on the pile.*

21-10. *While the press is running, the angle of the sucker bar can be adjusted. A scale shows the direction the adjustment is being made. The degree of tilt is determined by the amount of air blast needed to separate the sheets. Heavy, stiff papers require a strong blast for separation. They require little or no sucker tilt. Lightweight papers require little air blast for separation. They use a greater degree of sucker tilt.*

21-11. *The sucker bar vacuum control starts and stops the suction from reaching the suckers. When the control is off, the press will run but not pick up paper.*

21-13. *Tripping springs extend over the front edge of the pile. They can also be used on the right and left sides of the pile. They are adjusted with thumbscrews.*

21-12. *The amount of the air blast is controlled by a valve. Heavier stock requires a stronger blast. The operator makes this adjustment until the paper on the feed table separates properly.*

21-14. *The height of the air blast is controlled by the feed blower. The control handle is set in the top position for light and medium weight stock. For heavy stock it is in the lower position.*

21-15. The pile-height control has a scale showing settings for various weights of stock. Adjust it until the stock feeds properly. Lightweight papers feed best from a low pile height. Heavier stocks require a higher pile height.

PILE HEIGHT CONTROL

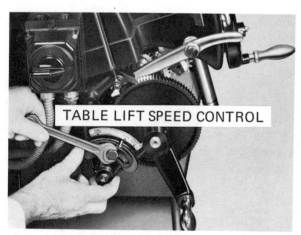

TABLE LIFT SPEED CONTROL

21-16. The table lift speed control adjusts the rate the feed table rises. For most work it is set on normal. Heavier stock requires that it rise faster. Set the adjustment toward the "cardboard" marks for a faster rate of rise.

21-17. The automatic stop control can be set to shut off the press if the suckers fail to pick up a sheet.

AUTOMATIC STOP CONTROL

THE DELIVERY SYSTEM

21-18. *The delivery table is disengaged by loosening the handwheel. Hold the table in one hand and lower it. It can be pulled up by hand without loosening the handwheel.*

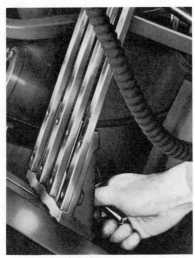

21-20. *After setting the delivery standards, loosen the clamping lever on the rear delivery standard. Slide the standard until the gripper edge of the sheet is 1/2" from the front edge of the delivery table. Tighten the clamping lever.*

21-21. *Adjust the air blast while the press is running. See Fig. 21-12.*

21-19. *After the sheet is positioned to the form on the feed table, run one sheet through the printing process. Stop the press with the sheet still in the gripper on the delivery side. Set the right and left delivery standards to the edges of the sheet. Set one at the rear edge of the sheet.*

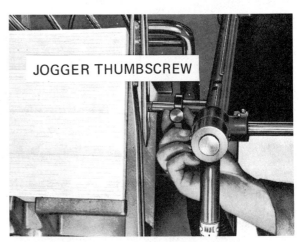

21-22. *Adjust the jogger. It shakes the delivery pile and helps the sheets stack evenly. To set the jogger, loosen the thumbscrew and slide it against the edge of the pile. Tighten the thumbscrew.*

21-23. *The jogger is pneumatic and operates only when the feeder is picking up sheets. The jogger is started by turning the jogger switch to a vertical position.*

JOGGER SWITCH

THE INKING SYSTEM

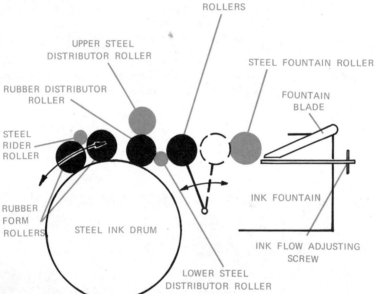

RUBBER DUCTOR ROLLER OSCILLATES BETWEEN DISTRIBUTOR AND FOUNTAIN ROLLERS

UPPER STEEL DISTRIBUTOR ROLLER

STEEL FOUNTAIN ROLLER

RUBBER DISTRIBUTOR ROLLER

FOUNTAIN BLADE

STEEL RIDER ROLLER

INK FOUNTAIN

RUBBER FORM ROLLERS

STEEL INK DRUM

INK FLOW ADJUSTING SCREW

LOWER STEEL DISTRIBUTOR ROLLER

21-24. *The ink is placed in the fountain. The fountain roller rotates in the ink. The flow of ink on the fountain roll is controlled by a fountain blade. The blade is adjusted by a row of screws set on the back of the fountain. The ink is transferred from the steel fountain roller to the rubber ductor roller. The ductor roller moves back and forth between the fountain roller and the lower steel distributor roller. The lower steel distributor roller transfers the ink to the rubber distributor roller. The ink is smoothed by the upper steel distributor roller.*

The rubber distributor roller applies ink to the large steel ink drum. The form rollers run on bearers between the typeform and the ink drum. They rotate on the ink drum, pick up a layer of ink, move over to the typeform and roll a layer of ink over it. The form rollers then move back to the ink drum and repeat this cycle for each sheet printed.

21-25. *This lever controls the distance the fountain roller turns with each impression. The greater the turn, the more ink is transferred.*

ROLLER TENSION SCREW

21-27. *The rubber distributor roller sets itself when it is placed in the machine. The tension between the rubber distributor roller, the ink drum, and the lower steel distributor roller is regulated with tension screws. The tension should be very light. The tension can be checked by pulling a strip of tissue between the rollers when the spring-loaded locks are in place.*

21-26. *Rubber and steel distributor rollers. The rubber distributing roller can be set in place or removed by lifting the spring-loaded locks and swinging the locks out of the way. The steel distributor roller can then be raised.*

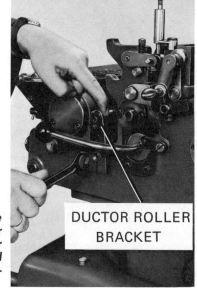

DUCTOR ROLLER BRACKET

21-28. *The ductor roller must be parallel with the fountain roller and the lower steel distributor roller. It is placed in a parallel condition by loosening and adjusting the ductor roller bracket.*

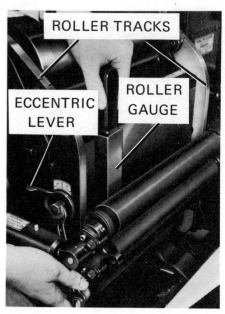

21-29. *The form rollers have roller tracks. They are used to adjust the pressure of the form rollers against the typeform. This pressure is adjusted using the eccentric lever.*

21-30. *This lever raises the form-roller extension tracks. In a raised condition the press can be run to regulate the ink flow, but the form roller will not touch the inking drum. The typeform will not be loaded with ink.*

21-31. *When the press impression is off, the ink supply automatically stops. Ink can be run up with the fountain. "Running up" refers to getting the ink into the system so that its flow can be adjusted.*
To run up the ink, press down on the fountain trip lever and lock it with the lever catch. This will enable the ductor roller to transfer ink with the press running "off impression." It is also necessary to pull the "pull to trip suction" lever and raise the extension tracks of the form rollers.

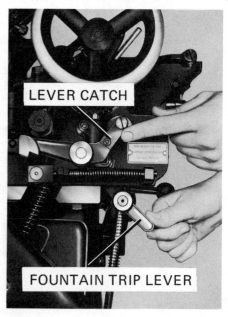

RIDER ROLLER

21-32. *The rider roller is mounted above and between the form rollers. It provides an extra supply of ink to the form rollers.*

INKING HINTS

When printing halftones it is especially important to use a good quality ink. Cheap "jobbing black" ink will not give good results. Inferior ink will give prints that appear grey and mottled on the paper. Platen inks are rich in pigment and are stiff. They should flow smoothly. Special inks are made for printing halftones on platen presses. These can usually be used straight from the can. If a halftone has a lot of lighter tonal ranges, a few drops of thin varnish should be added to the ink. This helps keep the screen highlights open. Halftones having a lot of darker tones may require the addition of a little reducer. Sometimes a few drops of varnish will help improve the quality of the print.

Surface driers can be added to the ink to increase the rate of drying. For single-color halftones, liquid cobalt surface drier is used. Usually one to three percent solution of drier is added.

When printing process-color jobs, better results can be obtained by using the proper color sequence. The two recom-

mended sequences are magenta, yellow, cyan, and black; or black, yellow, magenta, and cyan. If black is not a dominant color, the black, yellow, magenta, and cyan sequence is used. In all other cases, start by printing the magenta color. Additional information on process color printing is given in Chapter 17, "Color."

Use standard process inks for process-color printing. These can be used directly from the can. Inks are made for use on the various makes of presses. Purchase the process ink designed for the press and paper on which the color job is to be printed.

It is important to keep the temperature and humidity constant. The best conditions are a temperature of 70° F. (21 °C) and a humidity of 60 to 70 percent. If these vary between the printing of colors, the paper changes size. Then it will be difficult to get the colors to register.

An anti-offset spray can be used. It is sprayed over each sheet after it is printed. This spray keeps the sheet from offsetting ink onto the sheet above

it. Reduce the spray until it can barely be seen.

Special inks are available for printing large, solid areas on platen presses. These are made thicker and have a rich pigment concentration. They can be thinned if necessary. This helps keep the paper from sticking to the typeform.

Care must be taken to prevent the printed sheets from sticking together. To help reduce this, the delivery pile should be removed after 500 to 600 sheets are printed.

The printed sheets must be examined for ink slur. *Ink slur* occurs when the letters and halftone screens fill in with ink. This is usually caused by too thin an ink, too heavy an ink feed, or form rollers slipping on the form.

Picking is another inking problem. *Picking* happens when the paper sticks to the typeform. When it is removed, part of the paper surface is pulled off. This is usually caused by inks used at a low temperature. Inks that are too thick also cause this because they tend to become sticky. The ink can be thinned with additives.

Sometimes picking is caused by the paper. The sizing or coating may be unsatisfactory.

Mottling occurs when the ink film prints unevenly on the paper. This may be caused by the pigment separating from the binder (varnish). Too much packing can cause mottling. It causes the paper to be squeezed too hard against the typeform.

Another cause is ink that is too thin. It can be thickened with additives or proper ink can be ordered for the job.

(The following section deals with printing with guides, Figs. 21-33 through 21-42; operating the press, Figs. 21-43 through 21-47; and locking the form, Fig. 21-48.) (Pages 530–534.)

PRINTING WITH GUIDES

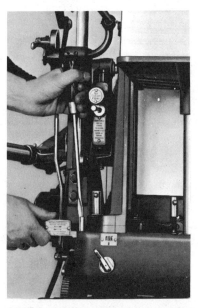

21-33. One adjustment to be made when printing with guides is to move the left-hand feed table standard to the left against its stop.

21-35. A third adjustment is to turn the knurled handle so it drops and its pin engages with the hole in the lever below. This lever engages and disengages the movement of the guides. Guides can be engaged or disengaged only when the press is stopped.

21-34. A second adjustment needed when printing with guides is to remove the extended screw. Then move the cam forward against the stop. Tighten the screw. The cam then causes the gripper to open, permitting the sheet to drop onto the bottom guides to register the sheet.

21-36. Guides are used to position the paper on the press so that the impression is printed in the desired location. Two types of guides are used: brass and nickel. Brass guides are used on jobs requiring the lower margin on the stock to be 14 points or more. Nickel guides are used on jobs requiring margins of 1 1/2 to 13 points.

530

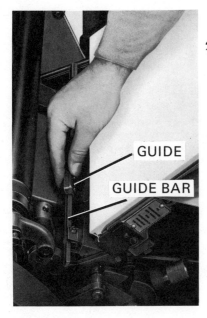

21-37. *Guides on the right side of the press are installed on the guide bar.*

GUIDE

GUIDE BAR

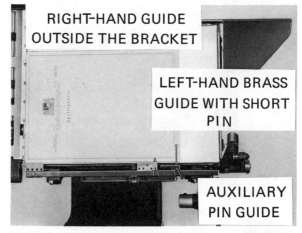

RIGHT-HAND GUIDE OUTSIDE THE BRACKET

LEFT-HAND BRASS GUIDE WITH SHORT PIN

AUXILIARY PIN GUIDE

21-38. *The right-hand guide always is positioned near the end of the guide bar. It is on the outside of the bracket holding the bar to the machine.*

RIGHT-HAND GUIDE

LEFT BRASS GUIDE WITH LONG PIN

21-39. *The left-hand guide is moved along the guide bar to suit the size of the stock to be printed. It should be between the left end and the middle of the stock. Pins can be used with guides to keep the stock from sliding over the guides.*

21-40. *The guide bar has a microadjustment that permits it to be moved up or down four points at either bracket.*

21-41. *A slide spring is used with nickel guides. It is on a special bar below the guide bar. It helps guide the stock onto the nickel guide. It should be mounted next to the left-hand movable nickel guide.*

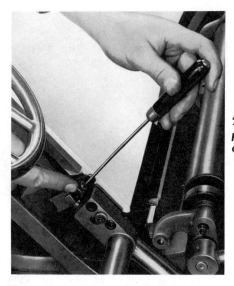

21-42. *Side guides are used to position the stock for printing. They can be adjusted to move up to four points.*

OPERATING THE PRESS

21-43. *To start the press, turn the front guard down. The press will not start with the guard up. Turn on the motor. Push the clutch lever to the left. To stop the press, turn the handle of the clutch lever clockwise. The motor will continue to run, but the platen and rollers will stop. The press can be stopped immediately by turning up the front guard.*

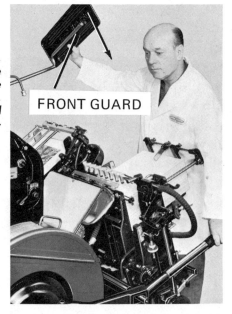

FRONT GUARD

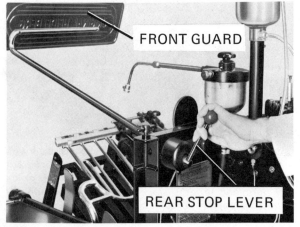

FRONT GUARD

REAR STOP LEVER

21-44. *Behind the press is another stop lever.*

21-45. *The speed of the press is regulated by the speed control. One revolution changes the speed 200 impressions per hour.*

21-46. *The impression throw-off lever will immediately stop the press from printing an image. Impression pressure is adjusted with the knurled adjusting rings. To increase impression, turn the lower ring clockwise. To decrease, turn it counterclockwise. The upper ring locks the lower ring and keeps it from turning.*

21-47. *If the impression is set so it exceeds the maximum desired, a shear collar will break.*

LOCKING THE FORM

BEVELED EDGE

21-48. *The chase has a bevel on one edge. The form must be locked in the chase so the bevel is toward the gripper edge. If the margin is to be more than 18 points, additional furniture should be placed between the form and the side of the chase.*

LOCKING THE TYPEFORM TO PRINT WITHOUT GUIDES

The beveled side of the Heidelberg chase is always the gripper edge. It has a center mark which corresponds to the middle of the paper. To print a job without guides, center the paper on the center mark on the chase. Locate the form in the chase so that it will print in the proper position on the centered paper. The stock must extend over the beveled edge of the chase by the amount of the gripper margin, which is 18 picas. With this procedure the form is not necessarily in the center of the chase. It is located to print where desired on the sheet, when the sheet is centered.

LOCKING THE TYPEFORM TO PRINT WITH GUIDES

When printing with guides the form is locked in the lower right corner of the chase. The gripper margin is the same as when printing without guides.

The upper mark shows the position of the nickel guides. The minimum paper margin is 1 1/2 points, if the form is locked at the very bottom of the chase. The lower mark shows the position of the brass guides. Type locked at the bottom of the chase will have a paper margin of 14 points. If more margin is needed, the type has to be moved away from the bottom of the chase.

(The following section deals with preparing the platen, Figs. 21-49 through 21-54.)

PREPARING THE PLATEN

21-49. *The platen is covered with a tympan. A tympan is a heavy, oiled paper sheet. It cushions the paper being printed. Packing is placed beneath the tympan.*

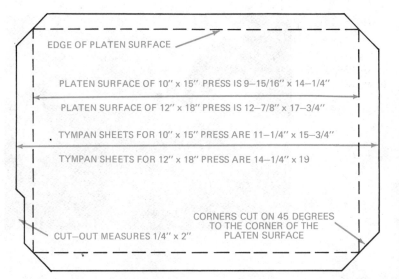

EDGE OF PLATEN SURFACE

PLATEN SURFACE OF 10" x 15" PRESS IS 9—15/16" x 14—1/4"

PLATEN SURFACE OF 12" x 18" PRESS IS 12—7/8" x 17—3/4"

TYMPAN SHEETS FOR 10" x 15" PRESS ARE 11—1/4" x 15—3/4"

TYMPAN SHEETS FOR 12" x 18" PRESS ARE 14—1/4" x 19

CORNERS CUT ON 45 DEGREES TO THE CORNER OF THE PLATEN SURFACE

CUT—OUT MEASURES 1/4" x 2"

21-50. *The tympan is cut 1" longer and wider than the platen. Corners are cut on 45°.*

SIDE TYMPAN BAR

21-52. *The left side of the tympan is held with a tympan bar. The right side is held with clamps. See Fig. 21-49.*

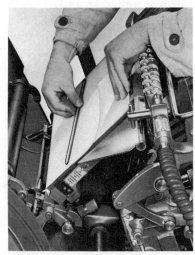

21-51. *The bottom edge of the tympan is folded. It is placed over the edge of the platen and held in place with the tympan bar. The tympan is then pulled to the top of the platen. The top edge is folded and held in place with a tympan bar.*

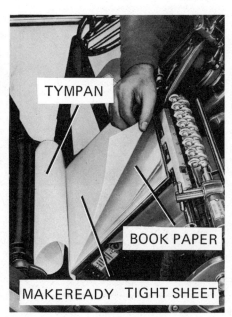

TYMPAN

BOOK PAPER

MAKEREADY TIGHT SHEET

21-53. *Packing for job work consists of layers of paper placed below the tympan. It is adjusted in thickness until all parts of the job print with equal impression. Packing consists of three to five sheets book paper cut the same size as the platen, a makeready tight sheet which is book paper cut large enough to be caught in the tympan bars, one to two sheets of pressboard and the tympan sheet. Packing for printing halftones is the same as for job work except a thin rubber blanket is pasted to the tight sheet in the halftone area.*

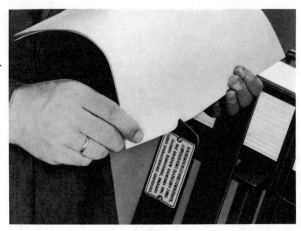

21-54. *This gauge is used to measure packing thickness. It usually is 1/25" thick.*

PREPARING OVERLAY SHEETS— SPOT-UP TECHNIQUE

If a job prints unevenly, an overlay sheet is made. It consists of a printed sheet with tissue glued to it in the areas where the printed image is poor. Fig 21-55 shows a sheet marked and ready for spotting up (adding tissue). The letters on the sheet refer to what is to be done to that area. "T" means add tissue. A second "T" means add a second layer of tissue. "F" means add a layer of folio paper. Folio paper is 0.002" thick. "B" means add a layer of book paper. It is 0.003" thick. "S" means scrape the surface to reduce thickness. "X" means cut out the tissue overlay.

To prepare the overlay sheet, first print an impression on 50-pound super paper. (Super paper is one of the classes of paper.) Study the impression from the back. If the form has punched into the paper, the form needs to be relocked. See Chapter 20, "Imposition and Lockup." If the entire impression is too heavy, remove a sheet from the packing. If the form prints heavy at the bottom but not at the top, remove a sheet of packing and increase the impression. If it prints heavy at the top but not at the bottom, add a sheet to the packing and decrease the impression.

If the printed sheet has weak areas, they must be marked and spotted up. To mark them, turn the sheet with the printed side up. Place a sheet of carbon paper under the sheet with the carbon side up. Draw a line around each area which needs attention.

Place a sheet of paper the thickness desired on the area to be spotted. Cut around the line drawn with a knife. Paste the piece cut to the overlay sheet. Do the small areas first.

The finished overlay sheet must be placed in position in the packing. Lay the overlay sheet printed side up on the tympan and against the guides. Using a sharp knife, cut L-shaped stab marks in two corners. Fig. 21-56. Cut through the tympan sheet. Remove one sheet of packing,

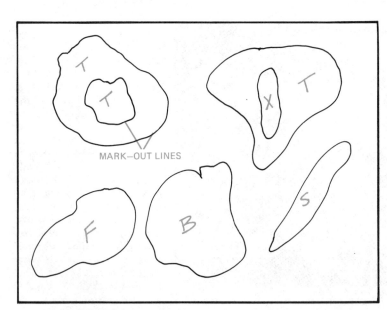

MARK—OUT LINES

21-55. *A sheet marked out and ready for spotting up.*

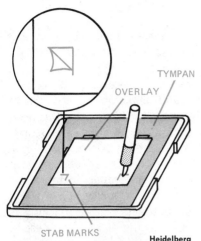

21-56. The position of the overlay sheet is marked with L-shaped cuts.

STAB MARKS

TYMPAN

OVERLAY

Heidelberg

replacing it with the overlay sheet. Match up the stab marks. Put a few drops of paste under the bottom edge of the tight sheet.

Print another impression to see if the overlay is adequate. If it is too light in some area, add to the overlay in that area.

PREPARING AN UNDERLAY

An underlay is material placed under a plate or engraving to make it type-high. Before a form is locked in the chase, all parts must be type-high. This is not usually a problem with areas of type. Halftones do cause problems. They are mounted on wood or metal bases. The total thickness of the halftone plate plus the base must be type-high (0.918''). This is measured with a micrometer or type-high gauge.

The height is increased by gluing sheets of paper to the bottom of wood bases. If the plate is mounted on a metal patent base, the paper is inserted between the plate and the base.

If wood bases are too high, they must be sanded until the proper thickness is obtained.

Paper is seldom placed under type. The only exception is occasional use under large display type.

Once the form is type-high, the overlay sheet can be prepared.

3M MAKEREADY OVERLAY SYSTEM

Halftone plates have highlights, middletones, and shadow tones. Fig. 21-57. *Highlights* are those areas of the plate that are almost entirely etched away. This lightens the printing dots. *Middletones* include a range of tones heavier than highlights but lighter than shadow tones. Shadow tones are almost a solid area. They have a very small dot pattern. Each of these areas needs special attention during makeready. Normally, middle-

tones require one or two layers of tissue. Shadow areas require two or three layers of tissue. Highlights require no makeready.

The 3M Company has a makeready overlay system that uses 3M overlay material and a 3M makeready exposure unit. Fig. 21-58. The overlay material has a thermoplastic, heat-activated layer on one side. The overlay material is available in thicknesses from 0.007'' to 0.010''. When processed in the exposure unit, it expands. The 0.007'' material expands to 0.011''. The 0.010'' material expands to 0.0165''.

To make the overlay, first pack the press to produce a good print. A sheet of this overlay material is then placed in the press, and an impression is printed on it. Any good halftone ink can be used. Black is preferred but colors can be used. If colored ink is

MIDDLE TONES

DARK TONES

HIGHLIGHT

21-57. A halftone can have highlights, middletones, and shadow tones.

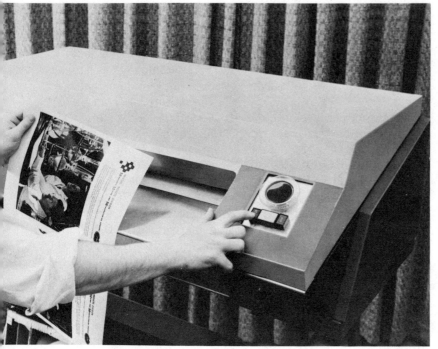

21-58. *A makeready exposure unit.*

3M Company

the places having the largest surface area to be printed. Remember, the dark areas need more pressure to print properly than the middletone or highlight areas. The thickness of this overlay sheet varies with the density of area to be printed.

This overlay sheet is placed under the tympan in the same manner as explained for spotting up overlays. Normal packing is used on the platen. It is recommended that packing for the 3M overlay be reduced by the thickness of the 3M sheet. The elastic nature of the thermoplastic layer will absorb minor irregularities. If necessary, adjustment of packing can be aided by the addition of two or three sheets of tissue.

ADJUSTING FRISKET FINGERS

Frisket fingers are narrow metal bars used to hold the sheet flat. Fig. 21-59. They should be kept clear of the area to be printed. Frisket fingers are held on a bar with a screw. Fig. 21-60.

(The following section shows other press adjustments, Figs. 21-61 through 21-66.)

used, it must be converted to black. This is done by coating the sheet with a special black 3M makeready powder. Excess powder is removed. Rub the powder over the colored areas with cotton. When a dull sheen appears, it is ready to use. Make certain all areas of the impression are printing solidly on the 3M sheet.

The overlay sheet is fed into the 3M exposure unit. It has an infrared radiant heating bar. The sheet is fed automatically past the heater bar and reappears at the delivery slot. The thermoplastic layer swells in proportion to the heat absorbed by the ink. The areas of the sheet with

dense ink images absorb more heat than those with a less dense ink image. The heat causes the dense parts to swell more than the lighter parts. This gives an overlay sheet that is thicker in

FRISKET FINGERS

Heidelberg

21-59. *Frisket fingers hold the sheet flat during the impression cycle.*

Heidelberg

21-60. *How to insert the bar that holds the frisket fingers.*

FRISKET FINGER BAR

OTHER PRESS ADJUSTMENTS

SPRAY ADJUSTMENT

POWDER CONTAINER

21-61. *As the sheets are printed they are stacked on the delivery table. Sometimes the ink on a sheet makes a smear on the back of the sheet on top of it. This is called offset. Offset is prevented by spraying each sheet with a fine offset powder. The valve to adjust the amount of spray is on the side of the spray powder container.*

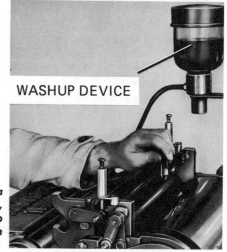

WASHUP DEVICE

21-62. *The automatic washup device contains a washup fluid that dissolves ink. To clean the press, start it up. Stand behind the press. Let the washup fluid flow over half the length of the steel fountain roller.*

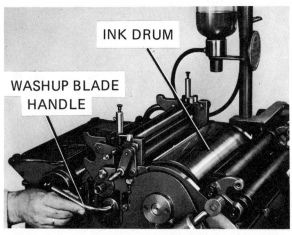

21-63. *Place the washup blade against the ink drum. This cleans away the ink into a sludge basin. Apply washup fluid several times. Wipe the washup blade with a clean cloth. Remove ink from the fountain with an ink knife.*

21-65. *Remove the sludge basin and clean it.*

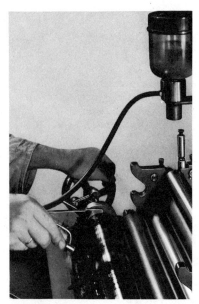

21-64. *Run washup fluid in the fountain.*

21-66. *After washing up at the end of the day, take the tension off the distributing rollers.*

EMBOSSING

Embossing is the process of pressing a design into paper to raise it above the surface of the sheet. Fig. 21-67 shows the procedure called spot embossing.

A *die* is needed for embossing. The die is a metal form. It has cut into it the shape of the figure to be embossed. Fig. 21-67. It is fastened in a chase just like a typeform. The chase is mounted on the press bed. The rollers are removed from the press.

A soft, plastic makeready plate is placed on the platen. The press is closed by hand. The plastic material is forced into the die. It takes the shape of the die cavity. It must then dry into a hardened mass. This is called the *counter.* The edges of the

21-67. *A die used in embossing.*

counter must be trimmed to remove excess material.

The sheets of paper to be embossed are fed between the die and counter. When the press closes, the counter forces the paper into the die. The paper is stretched and keeps the shape of the die cavity.

There are several ways to make counters. One way is to use strawboard, which is like a cardboard sheet. The strawboard is soaked with a paste until it is soft and wet. It is then placed on the platen. A thin, oiled sheet is placed over it. The die is locked on the press bed. The platen is closed against the die. The strawboard is forced into the die cavity. It remains closed until the strawboard is dry. After it is dry, the press is opened. The counter is removed from the die. The oiled sheet is removed. Unneeded edges are trimmed away.

Paper that is to be embossed should be conditioned before embossing. It is stored in a cabinet with high humidity to soften the paper a little. This prevents cracking of the surface as it is

stretched between the counter and the die.

Large and deep embossings require a heated dye. A heating element with dye attached is locked into a special chase. The temperature is adjusted to produce a sharply embossed edge. Heat dye and stamping require specialized equipment and procedures.

DIE CUTTING AND CREASING

Die cutting is the process of cutting shapes from paper or cardboard on a press. The die has knifelike edges. Instead of printing on paper, it cuts through it. Examples of die-cut jobs are envelopes and cardboard boxes.

Dies can be made from steel cutting rule. It is much like rule used to print lines. However, it is of a tough steel and has a cutting edge.

Dies are also used for scoring and creasing. Fig. 21-68. A *cutting die* cuts all the way through. A *scoring die* cuts about halfway through. A *creasing die* makes a crease in the paper or cardboard.

Corrugated boxes are good examples. They are cut to shape with a cutting rule. The same die will have creasing rules. In one operation a box is cut and creased.

Very simple rectangular dies can be made by cutting steel cutting rule to length and forming it into a rectangle. This is the same as when setting rule. Wood or metal furniture is used to block in the form. It is locked in a chase just like a typeform.

Do not use the lead cutter on cutting rule. It is too hard and will damage the machine. An easy way to cut it is to place the cutting rule in a vise. With a triangular file make a V-notch in the side of rule where it is to be cut. Then bend the rule. It will snap along the V-notch. If the

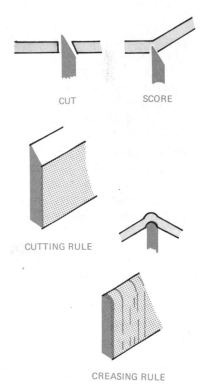

CUT   SCORE

CUTTING RULE

CREASING RULE

21-68. *Steel rules are used for cutting, scoring, and creasing.*

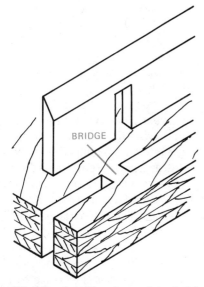

21-69. *A bridge is used to hold the sections of the die-cutting board together.*

21-70. *Rubber blocks are used to free the paper after it is die cut.*

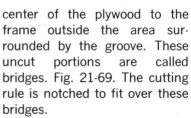

edges are rough, they can be filed. If bent slightly, straighten by tapping with a hammer against a flat metal surface.

After the rule is cut to length and locked in a chase, it is ready to go on the press. The steps for the die cutting are:

1. Remove the rollers from the press. The knife edges of the rule would cut them deeply. Store the rollers in a vertical position. They should not touch anything.

2. Put two layers of tympan on the platen. Glue these together.

3. Put a sheet of 20-gauge brass, hard aluminum, or stainless steel beneath the double tympan. The die will cut through the double tympan to the metal. Glue the metal to the bottom tympan. This will keep the tympan's center section, cut free by the die, from falling out.

4. Set the gauge pins the same way as for a printing job.

5. Run the press and feed one sheet at a time. Sometimes the pieces that are cut loose tend to fall into the press. If this is a problem, file two small V-notches in the cutting rule edge. This will keep the pieces being cut out from falling loose. They can be pushed out later by breaking the little connecting paper links left by the V-notches.

Dies for mass production made with cutting rule have a plywood base. The shape of the object is cut into the plywood all the way through the board. This is called the *die board*. The steel cutting rule is placed in the slot. It must be formed carefully to the curves and angles desired.

As the slot is cut in the cutting board, it is stopped at points along its path. This uncut part of the groove serves to hold the center of the plywood to the frame outside the area surrounded by the groove. These uncut portions are called bridges. Fig. 21-69. The cutting rule is notched to fit over these bridges.

After cutting, scoring and creasing rule is inserted in the die board. Rubber or cork blocks are glued to the board. They are

American Numbering Machine Co.

21-71. *A numbering machine.*

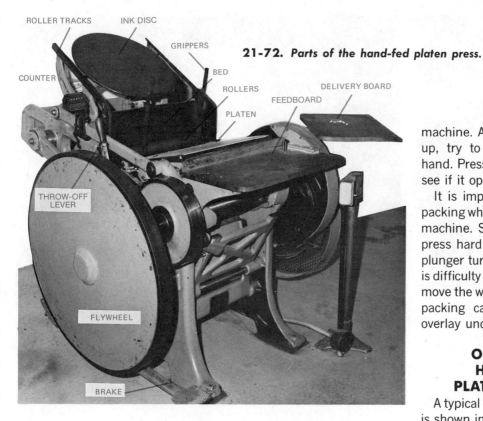

21-72. *Parts of the hand-fed platen press.*

ROLLER TRACKS · INK DISC · GRIPPERS · BED · COUNTER · ROLLERS · DELIVERY BOARD · FEEDBOARD · PLATEN · THROW-OFF LEVER · FLYWHEEL · BRAKE

machine. After the job is locked up, try to turn the wheels by hand. Press the plunger down to see if it operates easily.

It is important to use a hard packing when using a numbering machine. Soft packing may not press hard enough to make the plunger turn the wheels. If there is difficulty getting the plunger to move the wheels, additional hard packing can be added as an overlay under the tympan.

OPERATING HAND-FED PLATEN PRESSES

A typical hand-fed platen press is shown in Fig. 21-72. They are found in a few small job shops and are used by hobbyists. While they do not have all the features of the automatic platen, their operation is much the same.

The basic steps to operate this press include:

1. Put on the tympan. Add several sheets of packing.
2. Ink the press.
3. Put typeform in the press.
4. Set the guides on the tympan.
5. Position the grippers.
6. Print a trial impression.
7. Adjust the packing so the job prints evenly. Prepare a makeready sheet if needed.
8. Print the job.
9. Clean the press.

(The following section deals with operating the hand-fed platen press, Figs. 21-73 through 21-87.) (Pages 544–547.)

soft enough to compress easily. When the die cuts the paper, they compress. When the press opens, they expand. This pushes the paper off the die. Fig. 21-70.

The die board is locked in the press in the same manner as a typeform.

NUMBERING

Some jobs, as tickets and receipt books, are printed with consecutive numbers. This is done with a typographic numbering machine. Fig. 21-71.

The machines are type-high. They have five or more wheels. On the edge of each wheel is a series of numbers. For printing consecutive numbers, each wheel would have a series run from 0 through 9. Machines are

available that will print in odd numbers, as 1, 3, 5, 7.

The numbering machine is locked in the typeform with the type. The wheels have ratchets on their sides. They are connected to a plunger at the end of the shaft. When the press prints an impression, the plunger is pressed down. When the press opens, the plunger snaps up. This spring action turns the wheels to the next number.

The surface of the plunger commonly has the abbreviation *No.* on it. This prints as it is forced down.

Care must be exercised when locking a numbering machine in a form. If it is locked too tight, the machine may jam. It is better to use metal furniture next to the

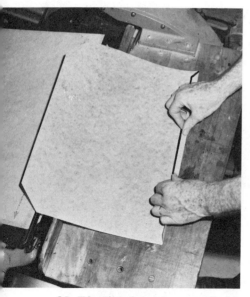

21-73. *The platen is covered with a sheet of oiled tympan. Cut to size using the old tympan as a guide. Fold about 1" of the bottom edge.*

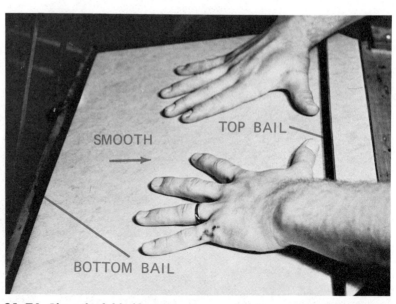

SMOOTH

TOP BAIL

BOTTOM BAIL

21-74. *Place the folded bottom edge over the lower edge of the platen. Close the bail to hold the tympan in place. Smooth the tympan to the top of the platen. Fold it over the top edge and close the top bail. The press packing is the same as described for the automatic platen press. See Figs. 21-53 and 21-54.*

21-75. *To ink the press, turn the flywheel by hand until the rollers are off the ink disk. Wipe it clean with a cloth. Be certain the typeform is not in the press.*

21-76. *Place some ink on the side of the disk.*

21-77. Run the motor and engage the throw-off lever. This will start the rollers moving up and down the ink disk. Run at a moderate speed until the ink is spread evenly over the rollers and disk.

21-79. After sliding the chase against the press bed, lift the spring clamp and lower it over the top edge of the chase. The form is now ready for the printing process.

21-78. To install the chase with the typeform, first rest it on the side of the press. The edge to go down in the press should rest on the side of the press.

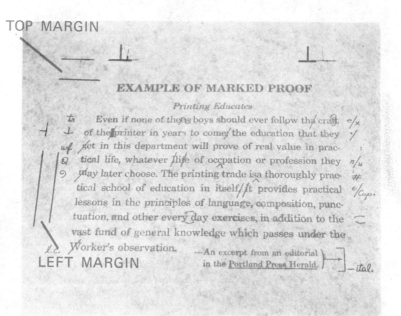

21-80. The first step in setting the guides is to print an impression of the typeform on the tympan. Examine the job layout to find the width of the top margin. Measure and mark this distance from the top row of type printed on the tympan. Do this in two places near the right and left edges of the printed image. Now find the size of the left margin. Measure and mark it from the left side of the print form.

21-81. *Insert the gauge pins at each mark. The pointed tail of the gauge pin should pierce the tympan about 1/4" below the margin mark. Push the pin into the tympan until its pointed front feet rest on the margin mark.*

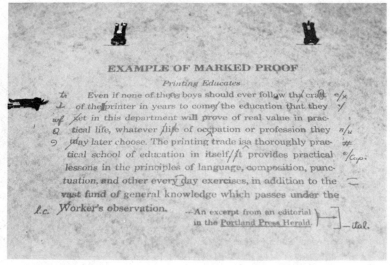

21-82. *Set the gauge pins at each margin mark.*

21-83. *When all gauge pins are in place, put a sheet of paper against the pins and print an impression on the sheet. Measure the margins. Adjust the gauge pins, and print another trial impression. Repeat this until the impression is printing in the exact place desired. Then push the pointed front legs of the gauge pins into the tympan.*

21-84. *Grippers may be used if needed. They are flat metal arms which help hold the sheet flat against the tympan when the sheet is being printed. Grippers should be set to touch the sheet in the margins. They must be clear of the printed area.*

21-85. *To feed the press, place the paper on the feedboard. Fan the sheets so it is easy to grasp them one at a time. Start the press with the throw-off lever in the "off" position. The rollers will move over the ink disk and type, but the platen will not close tight on the type.*

21-86. *Use your right hand to pick a sheet of paper off the feed pile.*

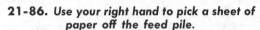
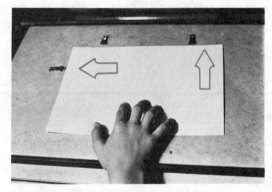

21-87. *When the platen opens, place the sheet against the bottom gauge pins and slide against the left gauge pin. Push the throw-off lever to the "on" position. The press will close and print. When the platen opens, remove the printed sheet with the left hand and place it on the delivery board. At the same time, take a fresh sheet with the right hand and place it on the platen. With practice, it is possible to keep feeding and removing sheets without touching the throw-off lever.*

***Danger.** Remember to feed the press only when the platen is open. If a sheet does not go in correctly or falls, let it go. Then move the throw-off lever to the "off" position.*

Examine the sheets as they are printed to see if the impression is good. If not, stop the press and make corrections.

CLEANUP

After the job is run, the chase is removed from the press. It is cleaned, and the form is distributed to the type case. Cleaning and distributing hand-set type is discussed in Chapter 7.

To clean the press:

1. Make certain the power is off.

2. Move the rollers below the ink disk. Move them by turning the flywheel by hand. (On some hand-fed platen presses it is possible to drop the disk for cleaning.)

3. Wipe the ink from the disk. Use a clean cloth dampened with press wash.

4. Now start wiping the rollers. Use a soft, clean cloth dampened with press wash. As the rollers are wiped, move them onto the disk. Move the flywheel

by hand to do this. Keep wiping them as they move up the disk. Wipe the rollers gently, as the surface is easily damaged.

5. Clean the rollers until they are at the top of the disk. Then clean the disk below the rollers. Some of the ink not removed from the rollers will get on the disk.

6. Slowly move the rollers down the disk. Carefully wipe each one again. Continue until they are clean.

7. Rollers should not be left on the disk. This will cause them to develop a flat side. Roll them down by hand until they are over the press bed. Since there is no chase on the press, the rollers are not pressing against anything. The tension springs on the rollers can be released at this point.

After the press and rollers are clean, remove any ink or oil that may be on other parts of the press.

PRESSROOM SAFETY

The equipment in the pressroom is expensive but not dangerous if operated according to the manufacturers' instructions. Following are some general safety suggestions:

1. Keep the pressroom clear of obstructions such as paper skids or trucks.

2. Do not operate a press until you are certain you know how to control it.

3. Never work in the pressroom alone. A second person must always be present to assist in case of accident.

4. Know the location of switches and emergency electrical cutoffs.

5. Only one person should operate the press. Those observing should stand clear.

6. Do not remove or shut off safety devices.

7. Shut off electrical power before attempting repairs.

8. Keep all soiled rags in fireproof containers.

9. Remove all loose clothing and jewelry before operating a press. Roll up long sleeves.

10. Wipe up lubricants and cleaners spilled on the floor.

11. Keep the floor clear of waste paper.

12. Wear rubber gloves if pressroom chemicals irritate the skin.

13. All chemicals should be stored in properly labeled containers.

14. Do not lean against running machinery. Keep hands away from moving parts.

REVIEW QUESTIONS

1. Name the parts of the platen press described by the following:
   a. The typeform and chase are locked to this.
   b. Stock to be printed is placed here.
   c. These lift sheets of paper from the pile.
   d. The surface that holds the press sheet as it is printed.
2. When printing with guides, the form is locked in the center of the chase. True or False?
3. If a job prints unevenly, an overlay sheet may be used. What is an overlay sheet made of?
4. For what purpose is an underlay used?
5. What is embossing?
6. After cleanup, why should the rollers *not* be left on the disk?

Cylinder Press Operation

Chapter 22

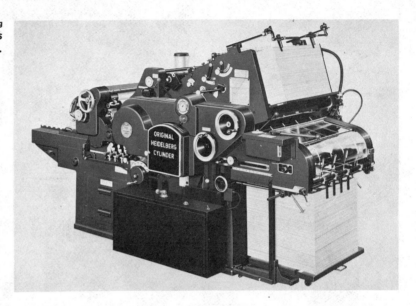

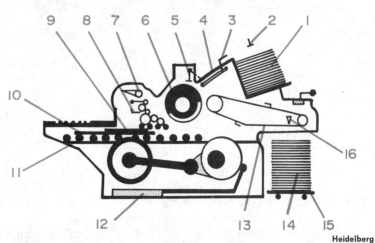

Heidelberg

22-1. Single-color cylinder press viewed from the operator's side.

Cylinder presses are part of the letterpress group. Fig. 22-1. Platen and rotary presses are also of the letterpress group.

The following discussion is centered around the single-color Original Heidelberg cylinder press. The principles shown can be applied to presses manufactured by other companies. The specific controls and adjustments will vary, but the operating principles are the same.

In this chapter the terms *operator's side* and *drive side* are used. The operator's side is the side of the machine where the press operator stands to control the press. The drive side is the other side of the press.

HOW THE PRESS OPERATES

Following is a brief, generalized statement telling how the single-color Heidelberg cylinder press operates. The major parts are shown in Fig. 22-2.

The press is inked by the *ink fountain* and a series of rollers. The fountain stores the ink and regulates the flow to the rollers. The typeform is inked by the form rollers.

The typeform is locked in a

Heidelberg

22-2. Major parts of the single-color cylinder press. (1) Paper feed stack. (2) Sucker bar. (3) Mechanical feed grippers. (4) Feedboard. (5) Swinging transfer grippers. (6) Impression cylinder. (7) Inking system. (8) Roller washup. (9) Typeform in a chase. (10) Type bed. (11) Bed rollers. (12) Moving gear rack. (13) Paper delivery chain. (14) Paper delivery stack. (15) Delivery board on casters. (16) Anti-offset spray.

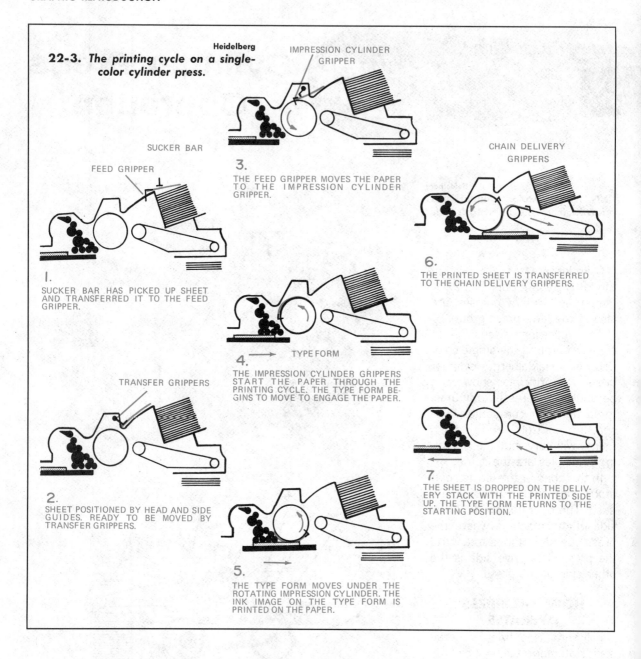

22-3. *The printing cycle on a single-color cylinder press.*

Heidelberg

IMPRESSION CYLINDER GRIPPER

SUCKER BAR

FEED GRIPPER

3. THE FEED GRIPPER MOVES THE PAPER TO THE IMPRESSION CYLINDER GRIPPER.

CHAIN DELIVERY GRIPPERS

6. THE PRINTED SHEET IS TRANSFERRED TO THE CHAIN DELIVERY GRIPPERS.

1. SUCKER BAR HAS PICKED UP SHEET AND TRANSFERRED IT TO THE FEED GRIPPER.

TYPE FORM

4. THE IMPRESSION CYLINDER GRIPPERS START THE PAPER THROUGH THE PRINTING CYCLE. THE TYPE FORM BEGINS TO MOVE TO ENGAGE THE PAPER.

TRANSFER GRIPPERS

7. THE SHEET IS DROPPED ON THE DELIVERY STACK WITH THE PRINTED SIDE UP. THE TYPE FORM RETURNS TO THE STARTING POSITION.

2. SHEET POSITIONED BY HEAD AND SIDE GUIDES. READY TO BE MOVED BY TRANSFER GRIPPERS.

5. THE TYPE FORM MOVES UNDER THE ROTATING IMPRESSION CYLINDER. THE INK IMAGE ON THE TYPE FORM IS PRINTED ON THE PAPER.

chase. The chase is locked to the *bed* of the press. The major steps of operation are shown in Fig. 22-3.

1. The stock to be printed is placed on the *feed table.*

2. Each sheet is lifted off the pile by the *sucker bar.* It uses a vacuum to lift each sheet. The sucker bar moves the sheet to the *feedboard gripper.*

3. The feedboard grippers move the sheet to the front guides where it is positioned by the front and side guides.

4. The swing arm grippers transfer the sheet to the grippers on the impression cylinder.

5. The *impression cylinder grippers* hold the paper on the cylinder, and it begins to rotate through the printing cycle.

6. At this time the *press bed* with the typeform moves to engage the paper. The typeform moves under the *inking rollers.* As the form moves under the

Heidelberg

22-4. The electrical box. Arrow points to main electrical switch.

rotating impression cylinder, the ink image is printed on the paper.

7. After the image is printed, the sheet is transferred to the *chain delivery grippers*.

8. The chain delivery drops the sheet on the *delivery board*. The printed side is up.

9. The type bed and typeform move back to the starting position.

10. Another sheet is picked up from the feed table, and the cycle is repeated.

Each press operator has a favorite order of steps for setting up a cylinder press. Following is a suggested sequence:

1. Be certain the press is clean. Wash if necessary.

2. Perform required lubrication.

3. Be certain the proper rollers are in place.

4. Pack the impression cylinder.

5. Clean the typeform and position it on the press bed.

6. Unlock the form and clamp the chase to the press bed.

7. Check the cuts to be certain they are type-high. Make any needed height changes.

8. Plane and lock the form.

9. Set sheet standards on feed table.

10. Load stock.

11. Adjust sheet separation: (1) air blast and (2) vacuum.

12. Set the side guides.

13. Adjust the holddowns.

14. Adjust the head stops.

15. Adjust the automatic stop.

16. Set up the delivery system.

17. Ink the press.

18. Print one sheet. Check for quality of the printed impression.

19. Make an overlay if needed.

20. Check registration.

21. Make final adjustments of the inking unit.

22. Run the job.

OPERATING CONTROLS

The main electrical switch is on top of the control box. Fig. 22-4. A red pilot light located on top of this box is on when the power is on.

There is a single-lever control for stop, run, paper, and impression. Fig. 22-5. The main electrical switch must be "on" before this control will function. The press is started by moving this lever to "run." In this condition it is not feeding paper or ink. When the lever is moved to "paper" the feeder starts operating. This is done when the suckers start their descent to the pile. The sheets of paper start through the press but are not printed. When the lever is moved from "paper" to "impression," the inking system operates and the actual printing begins. The lever is moved to "impression" when the feed grippers, holding a sheet, are halfway down the feed table.

If the press stops, the single-lever control must be returned to

Heidelberg

22-5. The single-lever control for stop, run, paper, and impression.

the "stop" position before the press can be operated again.

A second stopping lever is located in the top of the cylinder's side frame. Fig. 22-6. It must be

Heidelberg

22-6. A second stopping lever is located in the top portion of the cylinder's side frame.

22-7. *A third stop lever is located near the fluorescent delivery light on the operator's side of the press.*

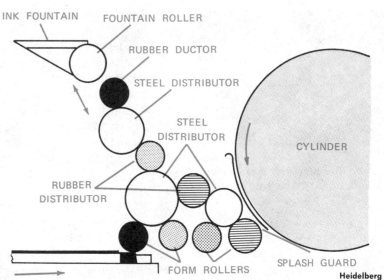

INK FOUNTAIN — FOUNTAIN ROLLER

RUBBER DUCTOR

STEEL DISTRIBUTOR

STEEL DISTRIBUTOR

CYLINDER

RUBBER DISTRIBUTOR

SPLASH GUARD

FORM ROLLERS

22-8. *The ink is transferred from the fountain roller to the other rollers by the ductor roller. The ductor moves back and forth between the fountain roller and the first steel distributor cylinder. The other rollers move the ink to the form rollers. The form rollers ink the typeform.*

raised and held up until the press stops.

A third stopping lever is on the operator's side. Fig. 22-7. When it is pulled to the rear, the valve on the air pump is opened. This causes the impression to be tripped automatically.

In addition to the three operator-controlled stops, the press has automatic trips. One is located on the swing arm and trips the impression when not blocked by a fed sheet. Another trip is on the rear delivery pad. A jammed sheet between the gripper bar and pads will cause it to trip. A third automatic trip at the bottom of the delivery frame trips the press when the delivery table reaches its lowest point. When the cover over the bed of the press is raised, the control lever is locked and the press cannot be started. If the delivery guard is raised, the press will be

tripped. All stops and trips must be in operating position before the press will go on impression.

THE INKING SYSTEM

Ink is placed in the *fountain*. The *fountain roller* rotates in the

ink. The ink flow is controlled by the *fountain blade* and the amount of rotation of the fountain roller. The fountain blade is regulated by a series of keys on the back of the fountain. Figs. 22-8—22-22 (Pages 552–556) describe the inking system.

22-9. *The ductor roller is removed by opening the sliding bearing on the operator's side and pushing the roller journal into it. This permits the drive side of the roller to come free of its socket. To install the ductor roller, place the journal of the roller into the open sliding bearing. Then slide the other end into the socket on the drive side. Remember to lock the open bearing.*

Heidelberg

22-10. *Tension springs press the ductor roller against the fountain roller. Tension is regulated with two adjusting screws. To do this, position the ductor roller against the fountain roller. Turn the screws until the ductor roller lightly touches the distributor roller. Lock each screw with its locknut. To check the adjustment, place a strip of paper between the rollers on each end. If the paper can be pulled out slowly without tearing, the pressure is right.*

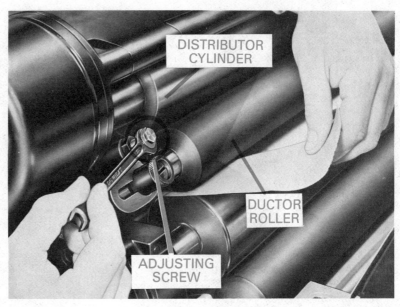

Heidelberg

22-11. *The distributor roller has a needle-bearing sleeve on each end. This fits into the guide block. Once installed, secure the safety latch. To remove the roller, the needle-bearing sleeve on the operator's side must be removed. Do not change the settings of the adjustment screws in the needle bearings while the rollers are out. This will change the alignment of the rollers.*

Heidelberg

22-12. *Each distributor roller must touch two steel distributor cylinders. To adjust the distributor roller, release the safety latch on each side. Then loosen the adjustment screw on each needle-bearing sleeve. Press the distributor roller lightly against the two steel distributor cylinders. Check the pressure with paper strips at each end. Tighten the screws and put the safety latches in position.*

ROLLER GAUGE
STANDING TYPE-HIGH

Heidelberg

22-13. *The form rollers must lightly touch the steel distributing cylinders and be type-high above the press bed. Make the type-high adjustment first. To make this adjustment, ink the form roller. Slide the roller gauge under the form roller. Remove it and observe the ink strip on the gauge. It should be about 1/16" wide.*

Heidelberg

22-15. *To adjust the form roller against the steel distributing cylinders, use the hexagon nuts on the journal boxes. First loosen the hexagon nuts on both sides of the press. Then push the form rollers against the steel distributing cylinders and tighten the hexagon nuts.*

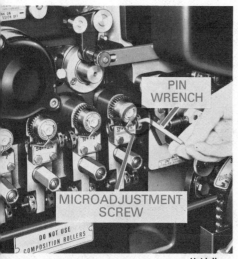

PIN
WRENCH

MICROADJUSTMENT
SCREW

DO NOT USE
COMPOSITION ROLLERS

Heidelberg

22-14. *The form roller type-high adjustment is made with the microadjustment screw. Above the screw is a scale which shows the center position of the roller and whether it is raised or lowered.*

ADJUSTING
KEYS

Heidelberg

22-16. *The fountain blade is regulated with adjusting keys. They control the ink flow to the press.*

Heidelberg

22-17. *The fountain roller has an adjustable ink feed. The press operator should try to adjust the ink with this control before trying to reset the adjusting keys.*

Heidelberg

22-18. *The fountain trip lever will permit the operator to run the press and ink the rollers while the press is "off impression." This lever will also trip the ink supply and permit the press to run "on impression."*

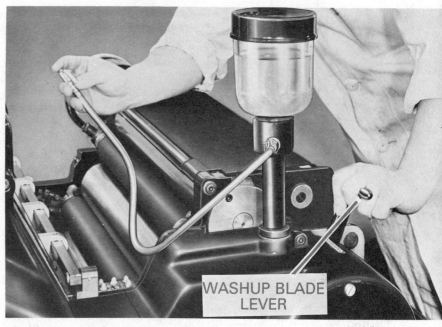

Heidelberg

22-20. *To clean the press, first insert the sludge basin. Then set the single-lever control at the "run" position. Engage the washup blade. It removes the ink sludge from the steel distributing roller.*

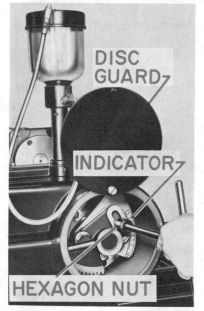

Heidelberg

22-19. *The three steel distributor cylinders move back and forth horizontally in opposite directions. The amount of movement is controlled by the indicator. Most jobs require movement of 3/4" to 1". Solids and reverses often require the maximum movement allowed.*

Heidelberg

22-21. *Next flow cleaning fluid from the roller washing device over the rollers. Do one-half of the rollers from one side. Then clean the other half. Continue to wash the rollers until they are clean. Remove the sludge basin and clean it. Wipe the washup blade with a cloth.*

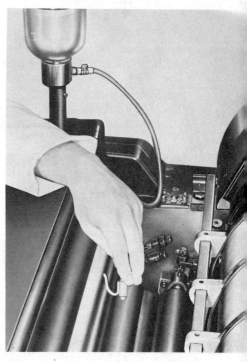

Heidelberg

22-22. *Remove ink from the fountain with an ink knife. Open the fountain and wash with cleaning fluid and a cloth. Clean the splash guard which is over the impression cylinder.*

LOCKING THE CHASE ON THE BED

Place the chase with the type on the press bed. Loosen all the quoins in the form and raise the two chase locks which secure the chase to the bed. Fig. 22-23.

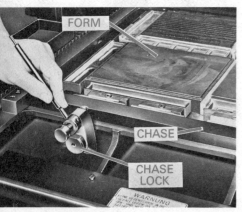

Heidelberg

22-23. *The chase locks secure the chase to the bed.*

Screw the round-headed screws in the chase until they contact the bearers on the side of the bed. Fig. 22-24. This locates the chase and permits it to be removed and replaced without losing register. Now plane the form and retighten the quoins.

PREPARING THE IMPRESSION CYLINDER

Opinions vary on the makeup of the impression cylinder packing. No set rule for packing can apply for all jobs and for all cylinder presses. Under actual working conditions, the hard packing without a rubber blanket has proved most valuable for line and type forms. A medium hard packing is best for mixed forms of type matter and plates and for heavy forms.

All sheets of the packing should have a 90-degree fold of about 1″ at the head. The folded part is inserted into the clamping bracket, which holds the packing on the cylinder. No loose sheets should be inserted in the packing.

Packing is made of two sections, permanent and temporary. The permanent packing is placed next to the cylinder. Fig. 22-25. It remains on the cylinder through many uses. The temporary packing is placed over the permanent packing. It is adjusted for thickness and receives makeready. It is usually replaced after each job is run.

The recommended maximum packing thickness is 0.047″. This

Heidelberg

22-24. *The side bars of the chase have two screws which help keep it in register.*

includes the thickness of the stock to be printed. The most common thickness for printed stock is 0.002″ or 0.003″. The following packing is listed in the order in which the sheets are placed on the cylinder. The first sheets are placed next to the cylinder. They are held on the

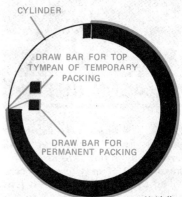

CYLINDER

DRAW BAR FOR TOP TYMPAN OF TEMPORARY PACKING

DRAW BAR FOR PERMANENT PACKING

Heidelberg

22-25. *How the packing is placed on the cylinder.*

22-26. *The clamp with the cylinder grippers is opened with a single handwheel.*

cylinder with clamps and drawbars.

Permanent Section	Thickness
Two pressboards about 0.008″ each, one end loose	0.016″
Temporary Section	
One tympan sheet (This sheet wraps around the lower drawbar)	0.006″

PACKING PINS

22-27. *Packing pins pierce the packing.*

	Thickness
Five to seven machine-finish sheets about 0.002″ each, one end loose	0.010″
One tympan sheet, one end loose	0.006″
One tympan top sheet, pulled tight by the top drawbar	0.006″
Total thickness of packing	0.044″
Thickness of stock to be printed	0.003″
Total thickness	0.047″

To clamp the packing, raise the cylinder guard. Fig. 22-26. Open the clamp with the handwheel. Insert the folded cylinder packing in the clamp. Tighten the clamps with the handwheel. The front edge has four packing pins which hold the packing. The pins pierce the packing. Fig. 22-27. After the packing is in place, the tympan is installed. Fig. 22-28. Turn the cylinder until the two drawbars are visible. The tympan on the permanent packing is wrapped around the lower drawbar. Draw it tight with the pawl and pin wrench. Drawbars are released by pulling the release bolt.

Very little makeready is usually needed to prepare the impression cylinder. If it is, study the makeready section in Chapter 21, "Platen Press Operation."

PREPARING THE FEEDING SYSTEM

The feeding system includes the tripping and separator springs, feed table, air blast, sucker bar, feedboard, and guides. Figs. 22-29 through 22-56 (Pages 557–563) describe the feeding system.

22-28. *The blanket is wrapped around the first drawbar. The tympan is wrapped around the top drawbar.*

22-29. *A series of tripping springs is set into the front edge of the pile. The springs help separate the sheets as they are lifted by the sucker bar. All springs must be set the same height. Normally this is 3/8″ below the top of the blower tubes.*

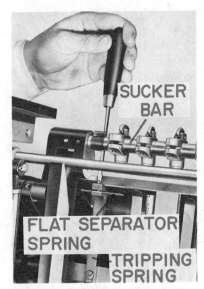

SUCKER BAR

FLAT SEPARATOR SPRING

TRIPPING SPRING

Heidelberg

22-30. Flat separator springs are used when printing on cardboard or stock that is curled up at the corners.

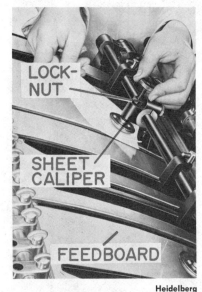

LOCK-NUT

SHEET CALIPER

FEEDBOARD

Heidelberg

22-31. Sheet calipers are located on the feedboard. They prevent more than one sheet at a time from being fed in the press. To adjust the caliper, place two sheets of paper beneath it. Tighten the caliper until it is difficult to pull the paper loose. Tighten the locknut.

558

Heidelberg

22-32. The feed table is lowered using the handwheel on the operator's side. The white ball handle must be set on "off." This disengages the automatic feed.

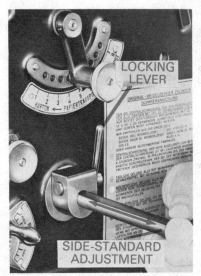

LOCKING LEVER

SIDE-STANDARD ADJUSTMENT

Heidelberg

22-33. The side standards of the feed table are vertical bars which fit on each side of the paper stack. They are adjusted by moving the side-standard adjustment control. Be certain to lock it when positioned.

Heidelberg

22-34. The paper to be printed is centered on the feedboard. A scale is on the feed table. The same scale is on the chase, side guide bar, and delivery. The sheet is fed from the feed table to the feedboard in a forward movement and slightly sideways toward the drive side.

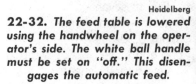

WHITE BALL HANDLE

FEED TABLE HANDWHEEL

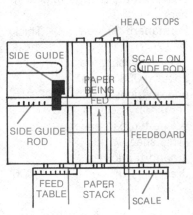

HEAD STOPS

SIDE GUIDE

SCALE ON GUIDE ROD

PAPER BEING FED

SIDE GUIDE ROD

FEEDBOARD

FEED TABLE

PAPER STACK

SCALE

1. THE PAPER IS FED TO THE HEAD STOPS ON THE FEEDBOARD. IT DOES NOT TOUCH THE SIDE GUIDE.

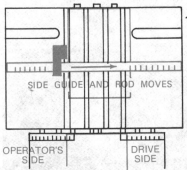

SIDE GUIDE AND ROD MOVES

OPERATOR'S SIDE

DRIVE SIDE

THE HEAD STOPS PUSH THE PAPER BACK SLIGHTLY. THE SIDE GUIDE MOVES OVER AND PUSHES THE PAPER IN POSITION SO IT IS IN REGISTER.

Heidelberg

22-35. *Before loading the feed table, the sheets should be fanned out to prevent their sticking together.*

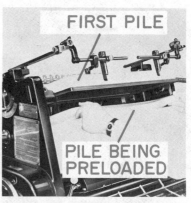

FIRST PILE

PILE BEING PRELOADED

Heidelberg

22-37. *While the press is operating, a second pile of paper can be loaded. When the first pile is gone, remove the empty table, position the new pile, and continue printing.*

Heidelberg

22-36. *After the feed table is loaded, raise it until the top sheet reaches the approximate feeding position. Then use the height control. The feeding position for printing board is to have the top sheet touch the sucker bar. With thick sheets the top sheet should clear the bar 3/16". Light sheets should clear the bar 3/8". Turn off all suckers beyond the edge of the sheet.*

Heidelberg

22-38. *The feed table can be loaded to print two-up. Two piles of sheets are placed side by side on the feedboard. A center divider is placed between the bars of the feed standard.*

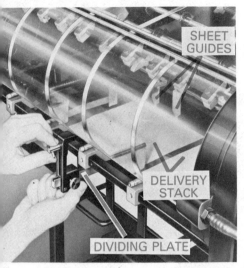

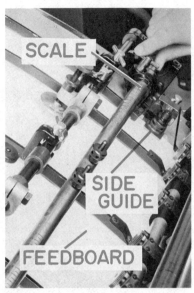

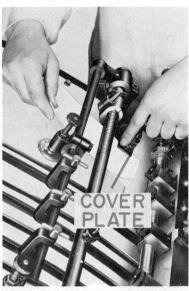

Heidelberg

22-39. The delivery of the press must be arranged to receive sheets printed two-up. A dividing plate is placed on the center of the square bar, which has movable sheet guides. The sheet guides are set so that each sheet touches them as it drops on the paper stock.

Heidelberg

22-41. Guides are used to position the paper while it is transferred by the feeding system to the impression cylinder. The typeform is locked in a chase. The scale on the chase is used to locate the form on the feed table. Review Fig. 22-34. This position is used to set the side guide.

Heidelberg

22-42. The side guide has a cover plate. The plate is adjusted to three times the thickness of the stock to be printed. The plate prevents the sheet from rolling up at the side guide. As the feed grippers move the sheet off the feedboard, the cover plate rises to avoid contact with the sheet. The sheet is registered from one side only. Slide the side guide not being used out of the way. For most printing the side guide on the operator's side is used.

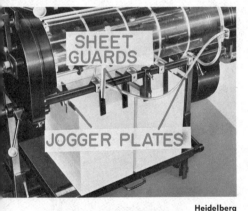

Heidelberg

22-40. Sheet guards are used to help the paper stack neatly on the delivery pile. Two guards are used on each pile. The jogger plates vibrate the sheets as they are delivered to the pile. This helps keep the edges even as the pile gets larger.

Heidelberg

22-43. The side guide has a microadjustment that permits hairline register of a printed job. To make the adjustment, loosen the thumbscrew and adjust the setting with the knurled screw. A scale to assist in the adjustment is on the guide.

Heidelberg

22-44. *As the sheet is fed to the guides on the feedboard, a slight side movement places it against the side guide. A lever controls the direction of this side movement. If the lever is down, the movement is toward the drive side. If it is up, the movement is toward the operator's side. When printing on both sides, the side guides are changed. For example, if the first side was printed with the guide on the operator's side, the reverse side will be printed with the side guide on the drive side.*

Heidelberg

22-46. *Six permanently located front guides adjust the margin on the front edge of the sheet so the feed grippers can grasp it. This margin is 3/8''. The micrometer screw permits adjustments up to 5/16''. During registration the front guides move up, pushing the sheet backwards up the feeder table as the side guide pushes the sheet sideways. Only two front guides are normally used. They are located about one-fourth of the sheet width from each edge. They must be matched pairs, measured from the center of the press. The front guides not used are lowered out of the way.*

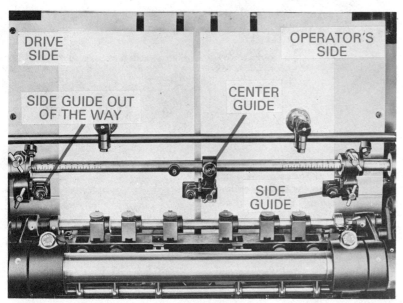

Heidelberg

22-45. *This shows how to set the guides to print two-up. Sheet movement is toward the operator's side. To register the second sheet, a guide is placed in the center of the bar. If the sheets are printed on the back, the guides are reversed.*

561

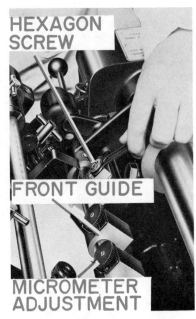

HEXAGON SCREW

FRONT GUIDE

MICROMETER ADJUSTMENT

Heidelberg

22-47. *The height of the front guides above the paper must be adjusted. This adjustment is made with the hexagon screw on the front guide bar. A scale shows the direction the adjustment is being made.*

Heidelberg

22-50. *The sheets are lifted from the feed table with a sucker bar and moved to the feedboard. Here, the feed gripper moves the sheet across the feedboard. Review Fig. 22-3. The top sheet on the feed table is separated from the pile by a blast of air. Air-blast pressure controls are located on the air pump itself and on the operator's side. Blower height is adjusted by the control located next to the air-blast pressure control. For normal paper it is set at the center of the scale. It is set higher for light papers and lower for heavier papers.*

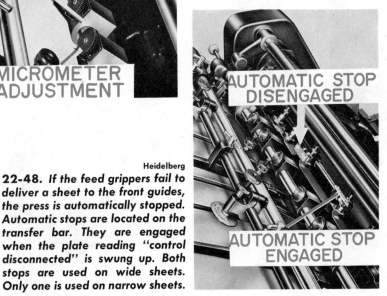

AUTOMATIC STOP DISENGAGED

AUTOMATIC STOP ENGAGED

Heidelberg

22-48. *If the feed grippers fail to deliver a sheet to the front guides, the press is automatically stopped. Automatic stops are located on the transfer bar. They are engaged when the plate reading "control disconnected" is swung up. Both stops are used on wide sheets. Only one is used on narrow sheets.*

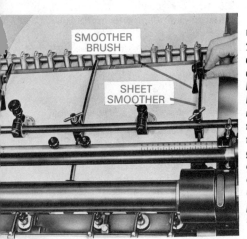

SMOOTHER BRUSH

SHEET SMOOTHER

Heidelberg

22-49. *Short sheet smoothers are used to keep the sheet from rolling up when moving down the feedboard. Sheet smoothers with steel bands act as sheet brakes. They retard the forward movement of the sheet when it is released by the feed grippers to enter the front guides. Sheet smoother brushes act as a brake when the sheet travels down the feedboard. They are used with all papers intended for printing at high speeds. Brushes should always be used in pairs and evenly spaced on the sheet.*

Heidelberg

22-51. *The tilt at which the sucker bar meets the paper must be adjusted. This is done with a lever on the feeder on the operator's side. The thinner the paper, the more tilt is required. A scale is provided to show tilt. Cardboard requires a "1" setting. Thin papers require a "5" setting.*

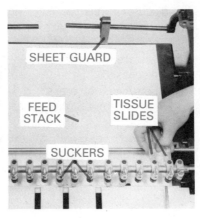

Heidelberg

22-52. *When printing on thin paper, tissue slides are put on the suckers. They enable the suckers to pick up the sheets closer to the front edge. This reduces the possibility of picking up two sheets. All suckers not used should be closed.*

Heidelberg

22-55. *The impression cylinder has a brush which holds the sheet against the cylinder. As the press is running, the brush automatically moves away from the cylinder to allow the grippers to pass.*

Heidelberg

22-53. *When feeding heavy papers and cardboard, rubber sucker disks are snapped over each sucker. All suckers not used should be closed.*

Heidelberg

22-54. *When printing a second color on a multicolor job, the height-control bar could smear the freshly printed areas each time it touched it. To prevent this, two rubber sleeves are placed on the bar. They are set to touch in the margin.*

Heidelberg

22-56. *The impression cylinder's brush pressure is controlled by a handle. It has three settings: "brush off," "brush on medium," and "brush on full." If there is danger of smearing the ink, reduce the brush pressure.*

PREPARING THE DELIVERY SYSTEM

The delivery system includes the delivery table, jogger, mis-delivery tripping device, chain delivery, delivery grippers, air blast, powder spray, and sheet brakes. Review Fig. 22-3.

Figs. 22-57 through 22-68 describe the delivery system.

THE VERTICAL CYLINDER PRESS

Another type of cylinder press is the vertical press. The follow-ing discussion centers on the Miehle vertical cylinder press. Fig. 22-69. The basic systems of this press are much the same as those discussed for the Original Heidelberg cylinder press.

A unique feature of the vertical press is that the bed and cylinder each perform one-half of the printing stroke. The press bed is in a vertical position and moves

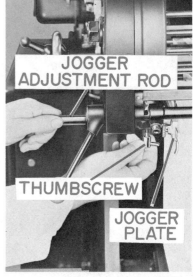

Heidelberg

22-59. *The jogger plates on the delivery pile are adjusted with the jogger adjustment rod. It is used when running light paper or jobs where the vibrations will not smear the freshly printed sheets.*

Heidelberg

22-57. *The delivery table is raised with a handwheel. If the control lever is on the "paper" or "impression" position, the white handle below the handwheel must be lifted. When the table reaches its highest position, release the white handle. As the press runs, the delivery table automatically lowers. When the delivery table reaches its lowest level, the press automatically stops.*

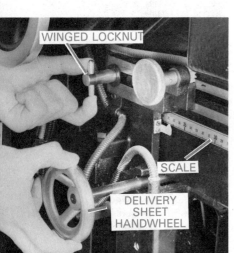

Heidelberg

22-58. *The front of the delivery table has four stops. The printed sheet touches these as it reaches the delivery table. The stops are adjusted according to the sheet size. This adjustment is made with the delivery sheet handwheel. It is locked in its setting with the winged locknut.*

Heidelberg

22-60. *The jogger is disengaged by raising the rear stop or by the jogger control knob.*

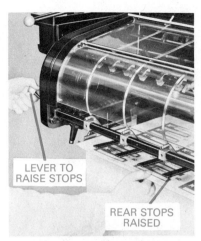

Heidelberg

22-61. *The rear delivery stops do not need to be changed for various sheet sizes. They can be swung up while the press is running so that sample sheets can be removed for inspection.*

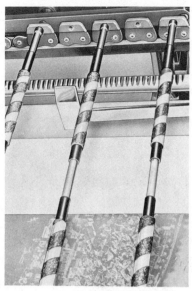

Heidelberg

22-64. *Sandpaper sleeves can replace star wheels when running lightweight papers.*

WHITE WHEEL

METAL DISC

Heidelberg

22-62. *The misdelivery tripping device stops the press if sheets to the delivery table pass above the fingers of the front stops. To start the press, first remove the paper jam. Then lift the metal disk until it latches in place. The white handle resets the disk mechanism.*

WINGED NUT

KNURLED WHEEL

Heidelberg

22-65. *The sheet is carried by the chain-delivery mechanism to the front paper stops. The delivery gripper must open at exactly the proper time to release the sheet to the delivery table. This adjustment is made by a knurled wheel on the operator's side. Generally, the heavier the paper, the sooner the grippers should open. This adjustment is made while the press is running.*

SPRING-LOADED END OF SPRING

$\frac{3}{16}$" ROLLER

STAR WHEEL

SPINDLE

Heidelberg

22-63. *After the sheet is printed, it is transferred from the impression cylinder grippers to the chain-delivery grippers. Before reaching the delivery table, the sheet is turned so the printed side is up. It is supported by a series of star wheels. The star wheels are adjusted to run in areas in which there is no printing.*

Heidelberg

22-66. *Air-blast jets are located below the front stop bar. They create an air cushion between the top of the delivery pile and the sheet being delivered. This keeps the sheet from dragging on the top of the pile.*

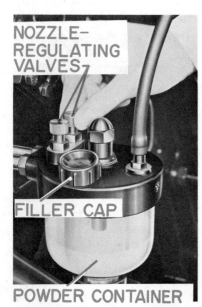

Heidelberg

22-67. *The powder-spraying device delivers a fine powder mist over the printed sheets as they arrive at the delivery board. The powder helps prevent the fresh ink from marking the bottom of the sheet above it.*

up and down in a vertical plane. The impression cylinder also moves in a vertical plane as it rotates.

The basic steps in the two-cycle printing process are shown in Figs. 22-70 and 22-71.

1. To begin the printing cycle, the bed is up and the cylinder down. The cylinder stops for a moment. A sheet is fed from the feed pile to the transfer table when the cylinder starts down. The transfer table moves the sheet to the cylinder. Here it is grasped by the cylinder grippers.

2. At the same time the bed starts to move down and the cylinder up, the cylinder begins to

Heidelberg

22-68. *The powder-spraying device's air supply is regulated by a valve on the pump.*

Miehle Div., MGD Graphic Systems, Rockwell International Corp.

22-69. *The feeder end of the Miehle vertical cylinder press.*

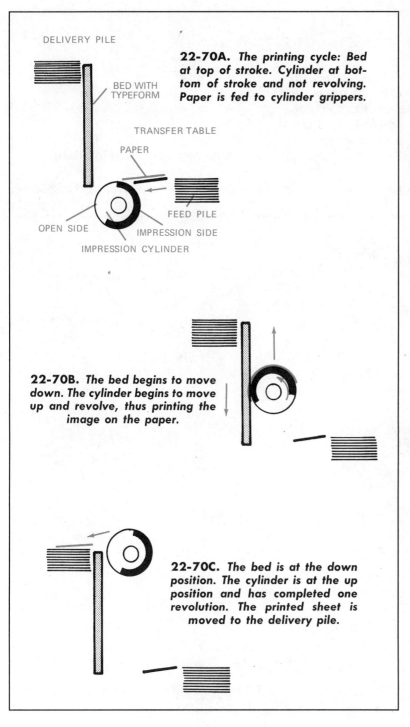

22-70A. *The printing cycle: Bed at top of stroke. Cylinder at bottom of stroke and not revolving. Paper is fed to cylinder grippers.*

DELIVERY PILE

BED WITH TYPEFORM

TRANSFER TABLE

PAPER

FEED PILE

OPEN SIDE

IMPRESSION SIDE

IMPRESSION CYLINDER

22-70B. *The bed begins to move down. The cylinder begins to move up and revolve, thus printing the image on the paper.*

22-70C. *The bed is at the down position. The cylinder is at the up position and has completed one revolution. The printed sheet is moved to the delivery pile.*

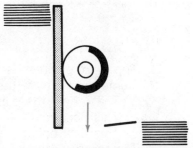

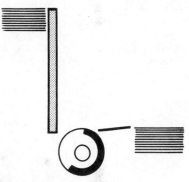

22-71A. *The nonprinting cycle: The bed starts moving up. The cylinder starts moving down but does not revolve. The open side of the cylinder clears the typeform.*

22-71B. *The press is now returned to begin cycle one and print another sheet.*

rotate. This rolls the sheet against the typeform, and the image is printed on the sheet.

3. The bed reaches its lowest position. The cylinder reaches its top position. The delivery grippers take the sheet from the cylinder grippers and move it to the delivery table.

4. The bed now starts to move up and the cylinder down. The cylinder does not rotate. The open side of the cylinder is opposite the typeform, providing clearance. The sheet is registered to the cylinder grippers on the down stroke of the cylinder.

5. The bed reaches its top position and the cylinder its lowest position. Another sheet is fed to the cylinder. The two cycles repeat, thus printing another sheet.

REVIEW QUESTIONS

1. The cylinder press is a type of offset press. True or False?
2. Name the parts of the cylinder press described in the following:
   a. These hold the paper on the cylinder.
   b. This part holds the typeform and chase.
   c. This part holds the printed sheets.
3. Temporary packing on the impression cylinder is replaced after each job is run. True or False?
4. On a vertical cylinder press, both the bed and the cylinder move. True or False?

Bindery and Finishing

Bindery operations include any preparatory or finishing work performed on paper to get that paper ready for the reader. Bindery operations include finishing activities, such as paper drilling, folding, cutting, stitching, and padding.

BINDERY OPERATIONS

Bindery operations have two main branches, soft-cover and hard-cover. A *soft-cover operation* involves a printed piece with a soft cover, such as a booklet or magazine or paperback book. *Hard-cover operations* include printed pieces having a hard cover.

Bindery operations are further divided into four areas: edition, job, pamphlet, and library bindery work.

Edition bindery work is any type of finishing work involving medium to large runs of edition-type publications, such as encyclopedias. Normally, the machinery installed in edition binderies is fully automatic and produces a high volume of work. Edition bindery work includes both hard-cover and soft-cover work. The machine shown in Fig. 23-1 is an example of edition finishing equipment.

Job bindery work includes medium to large volume work and is usually performed in a trade bindery. The type of equipment in a job bindery is not as fully automated as the edition bindery equipment and is slightly more versatile. Fig. 23-2. Some non-machine finishing work is performed. Most job bindery work involves standardized soft-cover or hard-cover book work.

Pamphlet bindery work involves a wide variety of work, ranging from simple padding jobs to the production of complicated booklets. Conventional print shops usually perform this type of work. Periodical publications, such as monthly magazines, are produced in pamphlet binderies. Generally, pamphlet bindery equipment is very versa-

COLLATOR   STITCHER   TRIMMER

McCain Manufacturing Co.

23-1. *Typical edition-type bindery equipment designed for high-speed production. Note that this machine has a built-in booklet trimmer.*

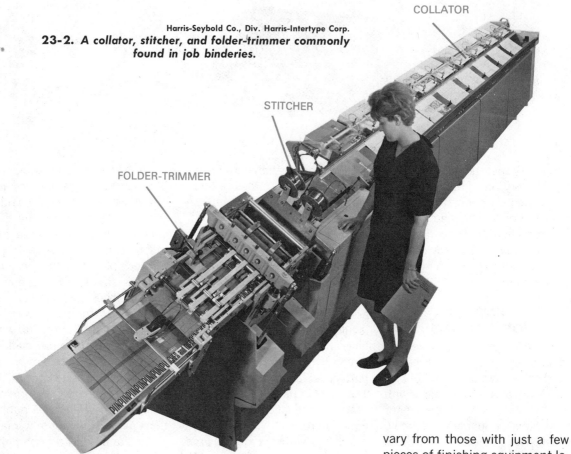

23-2. A collator, stitcher, and folder-trimmer commonly found in job binderies.

COLLATOR

STITCHER

FOLDER-TRIMMER

tile and is limited to soft-cover work. Fig. 23-3.

Library bindery work is a very specialized type of finishing work. It is heavily oriented toward handcrafting and varies from fine book hand-binding to book rebinding or repair. The unit cost for library bindery work is normally the highest of all bindery work.

Modern bindery installations vary from those with just a few pieces of finishing equipment located in a duplicating department to a fully equipped bindery facility installed in a comprehensive print shop. Some installations, known as trade binderies, specialize in finishing printings produced in other plants.

The complexity of bindery work can vary from the simple stapling of a two-sheet report to the in-line construction of a textbook. *In-line* means that the work is automatically processed from one operation to the next without a stop in the production process. Often in-line equipment is set up in line with a web press. The continuous production of business forms and pocket books is a typical example of in-line work. The equipment pictured in Fig.

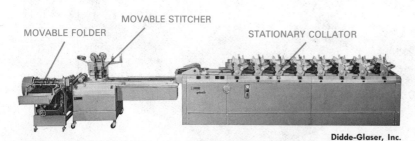

MOVABLE STITCHER

MOVABLE FOLDER

STATIONARY COLLATOR

23-3. A pamphlet bindery machine. It has a trimmer, stitcher, and collator. It could stand alone or hook up with any number of multipurpose devices.

23-4 is an example of roll-to-roll in-line equipment. Roll-to-roll means that the paper starts as a roll at one end of the machine and ends up as a roll on the other end. Both the printing and bindery work occur during the process.

SAFETY IN THE BINDERY

The bindery is the most dangerous area in the print shop. A bindery worker must develop safe work habits from the very beginning to prevent accidents.

Any electrically operated piece of bindery equipment can cause severe electrical shock and can be dangerous even with the electrical power turned off. Operators must never put their hands or fingers into a machine without turning off the power and locking down moving parts not protected by safety devices. All electrically powered equipment should be properly grounded, safety coded, and set up in a well-lighted area.

Operations which may cause eye injury should not be performed unless the operator uses safety glasses or a face shield.

An example of such an operation is changing the wire on a stitcher. Ear plugs are useful when operating equipment, such as a folder, that has a high noise level.

Paper can be a very hazardous material in the bindery. Paper cuts can be especially bothersome. Paper scattered on the floor can become dangerously slippery. Lifting a heavy carton can cause back injuries. Stacking paper cartons too high is a dangerous practice.

PLANNING IN THE BINDERY

Bindery work, usually performed last, is often referred to as finishing work. However, bindery work must be one of the first production *planning* considerations. Before the job is printed, the plans for the bindery operations must be made. Review Chapter 20, "Imposition and Lockup," to see how bindery operations are involved in planning.

There are two basic types of planning involved in bindery work: *standing operating planning* (SOP) and *specific planning* (SP).

Standing operating planning includes those bindery procedures that are the same for every job. Once the plans are set, the operators do the same thing every time. *Specific operating planning* includes those bindery procedures which relate specifically to one particular job. They have to be worked out for each job separately.

STANDING OPERATING PLANNING (SOP)

Following are recommended standing operating planning procedures for a bindery.

1. Establish a uniform procedure and sequence of finishing operations. This plan should provide for the flow of work through the bindery in an established route, utilizing labor-saving and time-saving techniques wherever possible. For example, SOP planning could require that a two-up job be folded and stitched two-up before trimming apart. The information necessary to process a job through the bindery is on a *bindery job ticket*. Fig. 23-5.

2. Standardize trim requirements, folding methods, and sheet guides in relation to imposition and presswork. Standard operations, measurements, and methods make job planning easier throughout the plant.

3. Schedule bindery operations and load the machines to provide the greatest productivity while meeting delivery dates.

4. Establish a plan for cutting paper. This information is recorded on a *paper-cutting slip*. Fig. 23-6. An effective plan reduces waste, provides for inven-

23-4. A fully automatic in-line assembling device for business forms. This particular model is a roll-to-roll machine that prints and does finishing work.

TYPICAL BINDERY JOB TICKET

Description

Customer _____ Ph. _____

Bldg. _____ Rm. No. _____ Copy Due _____

Del. Date _____

Final Size _____ Quant. _____ No. Impress. _____

Description _____

_____

Body _____ Pps. _____ Cover _____ Pps. _____

Other _____

Stock

Stock _____ Size _____ Brand _____ Sub. _____

Color _____ Press Size _____ Shts. _____

Tot. Shts. _____ Fin. _____ Location _____ From _____

Stock _____ Size _____ Brand _____ Sub. _____

Color _____ Press Size _____ Shts. _____

Tot. Shts. _____ Fin. _____ Location _____ From _____

Imposition

Type Pg. Size _____ Pagination _____

Margin: Top _____ Bot. _____ Gutter _____ Margin _____

Trim _____ Lip _____ Bleed _____

Press Sht. Size _____ No. Up _____ No. Sigs. _____

No. Pps. _____ W. & Turn _____ Sheetwise _____ W. & Tumble _____

W. & Twist _____ Other _____

Bindery

Instructions _____

_____

Hand Operations: Gather _____ Count _____ Collate _____

Machine: Cut _____ Fold _____ Stitch _____ Other _____

Drill _____ Rd. Cr. _____ Slot _____ Collate _____ Bind _____

Trim: Margins: Top _____ RS _____ LS _____ Bot. _____

Wrap _____ Shrink _____ Pad _____ No. _____ Band _____ Other _____

Del. to _____

Address _____

23-5. A bindery job ticket has the information needed for processing a job through the bindery.

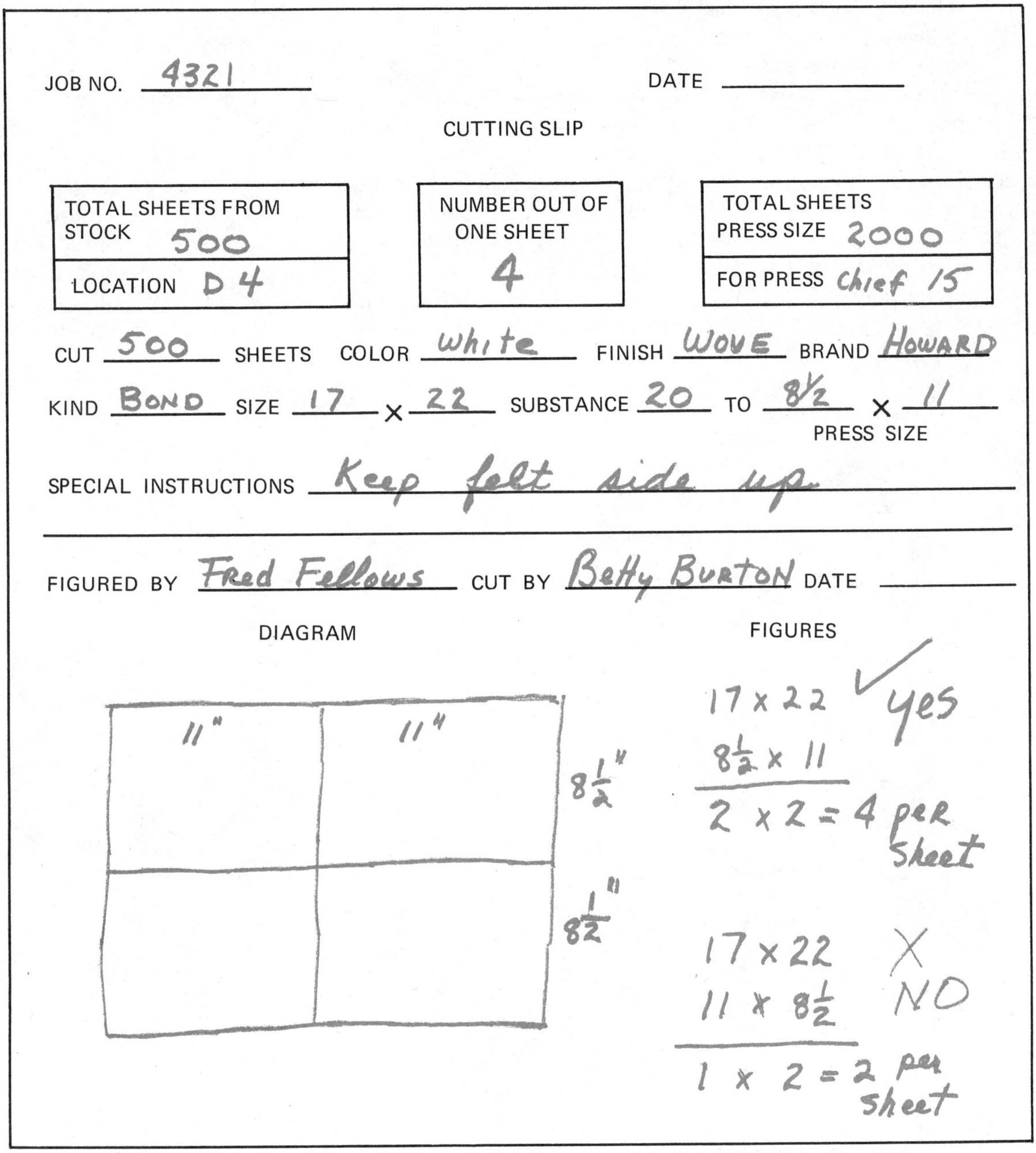

JOB NO. __4321__   DATE _____

CUTTING SLIP

| TOTAL SHEETS FROM STOCK 500 | NUMBER OUT OF ONE SHEET 4 | TOTAL SHEETS PRESS SIZE 2000 |
| LOCATION D 4 | | FOR PRESS chief 15 |

CUT __500__ SHEETS   COLOR __white__   FINISH __WOVE__ BRAND __HOWARD__

KIND __BOND__ SIZE __17__ x __22__ SUBSTANCE __20__ TO __8½__ x __11__
                                                              PRESS SIZE

SPECIAL INSTRUCTIONS __Keep felt side up.__

FIGURED BY __Fred Fellows__   CUT BY __Betty Burton__ DATE _____

DIAGRAM   FIGURES

11"   11"

8½"

8½"

17×22 ✓ yes

$8\frac{1}{2} \times 11$

$2 \times 2 = 4$ per sheet

17×22 ✗ NO

$11 \times 8\frac{1}{2}$

$1 \times 2 = 2$ per sheet

23-6. Paper-cutting slips give the bindery worker a cutting plan to follow.

tory control, and reduces cutting room confusion.

5. When planning the bindery operations for a job, use a bindery checklist. It contains a listing of all items to be considered when planning. A few examples include finishing operations, number of pages in a signature, location of the lip, and special things such as bleeds, inserts, and split pages.

SPECIFIC PLANNING (SP)

As stated before, each job has specific requirements that must be performed. For example, with sheet-fed work, the first specific finishing operation is the placement and relationship of the press, folder, and cutter guides. Consideration must be given to the placement of the press side guide and press gripper with regard to the edge of the press sheet. Specific planning will determine which sheet edge should be the press side guide edge and which sheet edge should be the press gripper edge so the folding and cutting guide edges can be located. Review Chapter 20 for other details.

Determining the Guide

Whenever a press sheet has to be folded or cut, the press guide edges are selected, and the bindery work is performed using these *same guide edges*. This maintains the registration in the finished job. The printing, folding, or cutting distance from the guide edge *will not vary* if that same edge of the paper is used as the guide for both printing and bindery operations.

Often when work requires folding, it is laid out with the press side guide edge corresponding to the folder lead edge, and the press gripper edge corresponding to the folder guide side edge. This will allow the guide corners of the press sheet

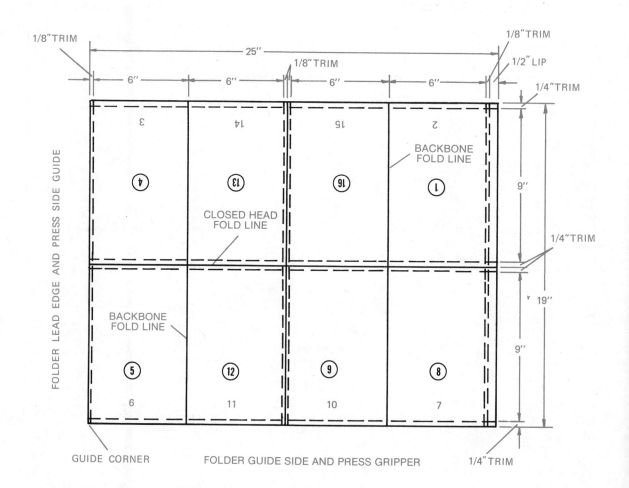

DASH LINE IS TRIM LINE.
SOLID LINE IS FOLD LINE.
THE NUMBER IN THE CIRCLES IS THE NUMBER OF
THE PAGE ON THE BACK OF THE SHEET.

23-7. The top side of a signature sheet layout for a 16-page booklet. Notice the numbers indicated for the pages on the back of the sheet.

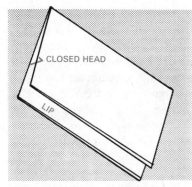

23-8. *The lip is an extension of one leg of the signature.*

and folder to correspond. (The press sheet's guide corner is the intersection of the side guide and gripper edges. The folder's guide corner is the intersection of the edges of the guide side and lead edges.) When this procedure is followed, the fold and printing distances from the guide edges will correspond.

If the guide edge is damaged and cannot be used, a new guide can be made. Anytime a sheet is cut or folded using the original guide edge, a new guide edge is created. The new guide edge is the edge on either side of the cut or fold. These new guides are used to make additional folds or cuts.

Fig. 23-7 shows the relationship between the press and bindery guide edges. Note the guide corner of the press sheet corresponds to the guide corner for the folder.

Planning for the Lip

Another specific consideration is the need for a signature assembling extender. The extender is known in the trade as a *lip* or a *lap*. It is an extension of one side

of a signature. Fig. 23-8. Notice the lip indicated in Fig. 23-7. The lip is used to help open signatures in the center for assembling or saddle-binding. A lip is usually not required for a side-binding.

A 1/2" lip is usually used for automatic assembling and binding machines, and a 1/4" lip is used for hand assembly. Fig. 23-9 shows how automatic assembling and stitching machines utilize this lip to open signatures. Machines which utilize suction devices may not require a lip.

When all elements of a booklet are assembled for hand-fed stitching, the lip on the center-most signature should extend beyond all other signature lips to insure that the assembled booklet will open correctly at the center.

The Bindery Dummy

A *dummy* refers to a paper model of the job folded and assembled in the same way the finished job will be folded and

assembled. It shows the size, shape, form, and general plan of the printed job. Making the dummy is a very important specific planning step. The dummy is a production work plan that shows how a job should be processed. The dummy helps the planner visualize the complete product. On it are shown the order of assembly and the relationship of bleeds, folds, trims, imposition, and guides needed for the job.

The steps required to construct a dummy are simple, but the planning skill required is extensive. All the printing and finishing requirements have to be visualized by the planner before developing the dummy. Some of the factors that must be considered are the number and size of pages, number of signatures, number and type of inserts, and information regarding the cover. In addition, the basic imposition plan, the folding requirements, and the basic assembly and binding plan must be consid-

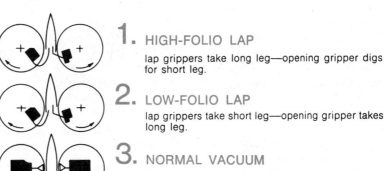

1. HIGH-FOLIO LAP
lap grippers take long leg—opening gripper digs for short leg.

2. LOW-FOLIO LAP
lap grippers take short leg—opening gripper takes long leg.

3. NORMAL VACUUM
front sucker takes front leg—rear sucker takes rear leg.

4. PARALLEL FOLD/NO-LAP
center sucker takes closed edge—opening gripper takes open edge.

McCain Manufacturing Co.

23-9. *The lip is used to open the signature in the center.*

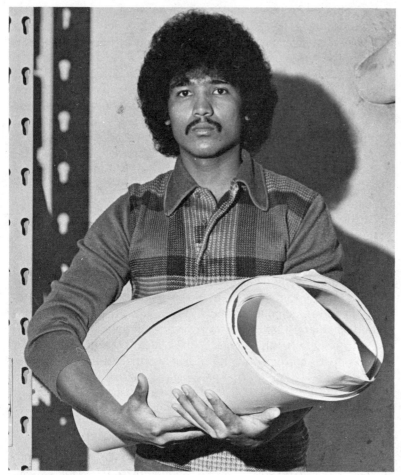

23-10. *Paper is folded to protect the edges and makes the lift easier to handle.*

acteristics of paper are whether the paper's weight, size, and grain are proper for the equipment and method chosen to process it, or whether the paper will have to be scored prior to folding. Some typical paper *cutting considerations* are whether a paper will absorb ink in time to permit cutting without undue delay, whether a paper's fiber structure will require a special bevel on the cutter knife, or whether a paper's surface characteristics will cause the paper to cut crooked on the cutter.

PAPER HANDLING

A bindery worker must know the proper method of placing and lifting paper. Paper should be placed as close to the finishing machine as possible. This will make it easier for the operator to transfer the paper to the machine.

A bindery worker should learn how to handle and carry paper. If the sheet size is too big to allow a lift to be picked up by the edges, then two sides of the lift should be folded over to make it easier to handle. (A *lift* is the greatest number of sheets that can be properly handled at one time.) Fig. 23-10 illustrates the correct method of carrying a folded lift of paper.

Those handling paper should use the flap system when opening paper packages. The flap system keeps the unused paper in the package clean, keeps the package label intact and easy to read, and makes it easier to remove any paper left in the package. Fig. 23-11 shows how the slits made along the two short sides, the bottom, and part of the top sides of the label end of a

ered. Since this is a complex operation, a planning checklist should be consulted before making the dummy. The construction of a dummy is explained in Chapter 20.

PAPER IN THE BINDERY
SELECTING THE PROPER PAPER

Production difficulties in the bindery often result from the improper selection of paper. There are too many factors involved to set up a foolproof guide for the proper selection of paper. No manufacturer can produce a paper that combines all essential processing qualities for all machines found in the bindery. The proper methods of handling paper and an understanding of the various cutting and folding properties of paper must be known by the person ordering paper and by the bindery worker. A review of Chapter 25, "Paper," should prove very helpful in this regard.

Some typical factors to consider regarding the *folding char-*

23-11. *A paper package flap in the raised position to illustrate where the slits should be made.*

23-12A. *To hand-jog paper, first stand the paper on edge and bend it.*

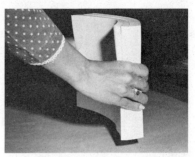

23-12D. *Raise the stock, and drop it on the table.*

paper package form the flap. The flap should be folded and closed after the paper needed is removed.

PAPER JOGGING AND WINDING

Jogging is the vibration of a stack of paper so that all the sheets line up evenly along the edges. On printed stock, jogging is done to help maintain proper registration in the event the press sheets vary in size. On unprinted stock, jogging is done to insure that all stock will be cut square.

Jogging can be done by hand or by machine and is considerably easier to do if air is allowed to get between each sheet. The air acts as a separator between the sheets of paper. The action of getting air between the sheets of paper is called *winding* the stock.

The proper way to hand-jog stock is shown in Fig. 23-12. Two machine joggers are shown in Fig. 23-13.

Remember, when jogging press sheets in preparation for cutting, the paper should be jogged to both guide edges. The guide corner of the press sheets should go into the corner of the

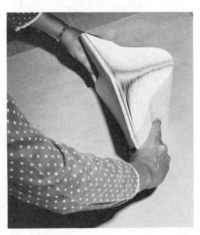

23-12B. *Then squeeze the ends, and bend the stock back to a flat condition.*

23-12C. *Release the edges, and tap the stock on the ends.*

machine jogger to insure that both guide edges of all printed stock line up evenly.

Certain types of paper require special handling procedures for jogging and winding. Pressure-sensitive papers require special handling because of their sensitive coatings. Pressure-sensitive paper should not be squeezed together during jogging because the pressure created by the

GUIDE CORNER

23-13. *Two of the many types of vibrating-table paper joggers available today. The paper is placed on top of the machines. As a result of the vibrating action of the table, the stock is jogged to the edges that were placed against the side of table.*

577

squeezing can cause the coatings to discolor or mark.

HANDLING GUMMED PAPER

Gummed-surface paper requires special handling in the bindery. This paper must be kept completely dry, and it should not be squeezed because the squeezing action can cause it to stick together. Gummed-surface paper should be kept tightly packaged until it is ready for processing. Scraps that are to be saved should be rewrapped immediately because the gummed coatings tend to absorb moisture from the air. Heat-set gummed-surface paper should be kept cool and away from direct sunlight.

PAPER CUTTING

A great variety of flat-sheet paper-cutting equipment is used in binderies today. The most common type of flat-sheet paper cutter is the guillotine cutter. It uses a shearing action. Fig. 23-14. Modern guillotine cutters are manufactured in many different styles and sizes, ranging from simple hand-operated devices to automated machines. Each has its own capabilities and applications. Size is specified by the size of the throat opening. For example, a 42″ cutter will cut stock up to 42″ wide.

Some of the more sophisticated flat-sheet, paper-cutting machines are tape controlled and are referred to in the industry as *programmed cutters*. If a machine is tape controlled, it means that various back gauge settings can be programmed into a memory system, which will automatically move the back gauge after a cut is made. This saves

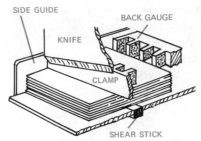

23-14. A guillotine cutter uses a shearing action.

the operator from handling the lift or manually changing the measure each time a cut is made, and as a result, greatly decreases the cutting time on most jobs. Fig. 23-15.

Many different devices and materials are available to help move the heavier lifts across the table on the bigger cutters. One is an air film device built into the bed. Fig. 23-16. The use of wax, talcum powder, Teflon fluorocarbon resin spray, or silicone spray on the cutter table have proven effective for moving stock across the table on smaller cutters.

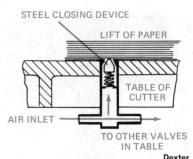

23-16. An air film valve diagram. The paper is partially supported by the air escaping from these valves. The weight of the paper depresses the spring-loaded device, which allows escaping air to create an upward pressure.

Paper Cutter Components

Several components on flat-sheet cutters—such as the shear stick, the clamp, and the knife—require special attention. Shear sticks (cutting blocks) are made from wood, fiber, or plastic. The cutting action of the knife produces a groove in the shear stick. When the groove becomes too deep or worn, the stick should be reversed or re-

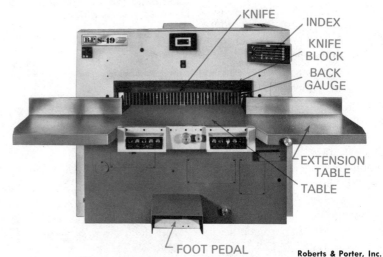

23-15. A programmed paper cutter with a tape memory system that automatically moves the back gauge.

23-17. *Removing the shear stick.*

placed. Fig. 23-17. Be certain the power to the clamp and knife is off before removing the stick.

The knife should be adjusted to firmly touch the shear stick when making a cut. If adjustment is difficult, makeready paper can be placed under the stick to compensate for a wavy or improperly sharpened blade. Fig. 23-18. The stick should be level with or slightly lower than the table of the cutter.

Paper-cutter clamps can be mechanically or hydraulically operated, depending on the type and cost of the paper cutter. Fig.

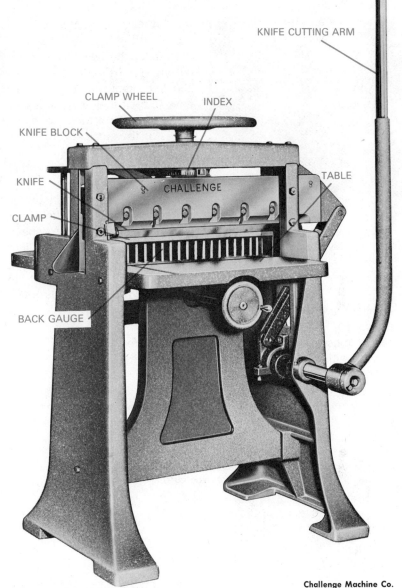

KNIFE CUTTING ARM

CLAMP WHEEL

INDEX

KNIFE BLOCK

KNIFE

CLAMP

BACK GAUGE

TABLE

CHALLENGE

Challenge Machine Co.

23-19. *A hand-operated, lever-type cutter equipped with a mechanical clamp device.*

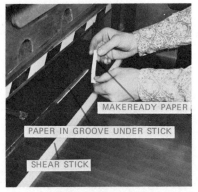

MAKEREADY PAPER

PAPER IN GROOVE UNDER STICK

SHEAR STICK

23-18. *Makeready paper is used to build up a low section of the stick.*

23-19 shows a cutter equipped with a mechanical clamp. The purpose of the clamp is to keep the paper from moving away from the back gauge while the paper is being cut. Quality cutters have levers or valves that allow an operator to adjust the pressure of the clamp on the paper. Most clamps are equipped with a boot which is used to provide a smooth surface for the bottom of a relieved clamp. Fig. 23-20. (A relieved clamp has a part of the front surface removed.) When the boot is removed, the back gauge can be brought forward into the relieved portions of the clamp. It is used when making narrow cuts

579

23-20. *A back gauge meshed into a relieved clamp that has the false clamp or boot removed.*

the bevels recommended for paper-cutting knives. Notice how the angle (the bevel) differs for cutting various materials. Knives should be kept sharp. Dull knives have to fight their way through a lift of stock and often weld the edges of the stock together and cause it to cut crooked. A dull knife makes a thud at the end of each cut.

The bite adjustment should be set so the knife cuts the paper cleanly across the entire sheet. Generally, this will leave a slight score mark on the shear stick. The basic steps required to change a knife are shown in Fig. 23-22.

Cutter Safety

1. Handle paper cutter knives (on and off the machine) very carefully.

2. Be certain the paper cut-

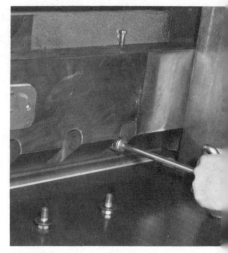

23-22A. *Lower the knife to its lowest position, and turn off the power to the clamp and the knife. Remove the knife-holding bolts.*

smaller than the thickness of the clamp. Fig. 23-20 shows a back gauge meshed into a relieved clamp, with the boot removed.

The knife is probably the most important component on a flat-sheet cutter. Fig. 23-21 shows

ter has two controls that must be pushed before the cutter operates. The two controls require the operator to use both hands to make a cut, insuring that the hands are clear of the table.

3. Keep the cutter table clear of scrap stock.

4. Work alone at the cutter. This prevents a second person from accidentally starting the machine.

5. Watch for accidental double cycling of the cutter blade. Do

SINGLE-BEVEL
KNIVES

DOUBLE-BEVEL
KNIVES

23-21. *Recommended bevel angles of paper knives for cutting common materials.*

SINGLE-BEVEL KNIVES

Material	A
Standard Bevel	24 1/2°
Hard Paper	30°
Medium Hard Paper	26°
Soft Paper	23°
Abrasive Paper and Cloth	22°

DOUBLE-BEVEL KNIVES

Material	A	B	C
Foil	30°	26°	1/16″
Glassine and Cellophane	30°	24°	3/16″
Rubber Materials	26°	18°	1/8″
Hard Fiberboard	30°	26°	3/16″

23-22B. *Restore the knifeless knife block to its normal position. Note how the blade is held in place by a slide built into the frame.*

23-22C. *Attach the carrying handles, and remove the dull blade.*

23-22E. *Place the new blade into the cutter. Remove the carrying handle. Lower the knife block to its lowest position, and install the knife-holding bolts. The bolts should be tightened just enough to make them snug, to permit adjustment of the blade's position.*

not reach for the cut stock or scraps until the blade has stopped.

Figuring Paper Cuts for the Press

Before cutting paper for the press, verify the information contained on the paper-cutting slip. Check how many units can be cut from one sheet, and how many sheets have to be cut. Once the number of units possible from one sheet is known, the total number of sheets needed can be determined by dividing

23-22F. *After reversing or replacing the stick and with the power off, tighten the blade-adjusting bolts until kraft paper placed beneath it bows up, as shown.*

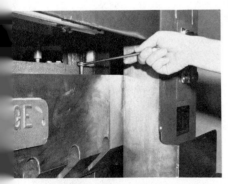

23-22D. *Back off the blade-adjusting bolts located in the top of the knife block, in case the new blade is deeper than the old one. Remove all makeready paper under the cutting stick.*

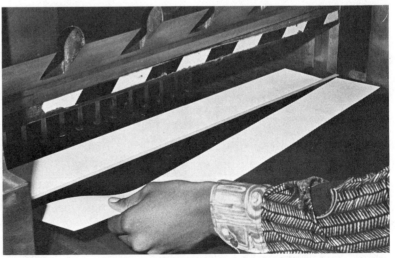

23-22G. *Test cut a sheet of kraft paper until the paper is cut cleanly across the entire sheet. If additional adjustments are necessary, repeat the adjusting process until satisfactory results are achieved.*

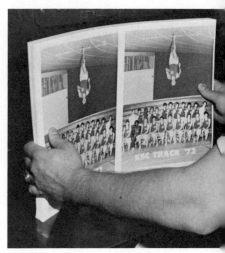

23-25. *Jog the press sheets to their guide sides to maintain the register. The cutter table is a good surface for jogging.*

23-23. *Paper to be cut should be placed at cutter-table height. The lift truck should be locked in place, and the carton should be carefully supported on a skid.*

the number cut out of one sheet into the total number needed. Study Chapter 25 for information on how to figure paper cuts for the press.

The cover was printed two-up on the press sheets, which means the press sheet will have to be cut in two before folding the individual covers.

23-26. *Insert the jogged lifts into the cutter. The lift is placed into the left side of the cutter with the jogged press sheet's guide edges against the side frame and the back gauge.*

Cutting Paper

Place the stock as close to the paper cutter as possible. Fig. 23-23 shows how a lift truck can be used to raise the stock to cutter-table height. Open only those cartons necessary to cut the job. Once a carton is opened, the remaining paper is exposed to edge and moisture damage.

Arrange for a place to put the cut units as they are removed from the cutter. Now set up a paper-cutting machine, and cut the paper. One procedure for cutting paper is explained in Figs. 23-24 through 23-30. It uses a cover for a 6″ × 9″, 16-page, saddle-stitched booklet.

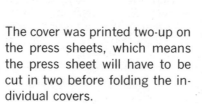

23-24. *Set the cutter to cut 9 1/2″ from the back gauge to the knife. Lock the back gauge. Transfer the paper to the table in even number lifts, preferably in reams.*

23-27. *Using both hands, jog the lift against the side frame and back gauge. This step may have to be repeated several times before the paper lines up squarely into the cutter.*

23-28. *Bring the clamp down on the stock to see if the pressure will set off the ink. If the pressure is proper, bring the clamp and blade down with the foot pedal. The blade will cut the paper and automatically return to a raised position.*

STACKING CUT PAPER FOR THE PRESSROOM

The cut paper is stacked printing side up. Check that the coated side on pressure-sensitive stock and felt side on uncoated stock are stacked face up. Conventionally coated stock should be stacked coated side up, and the watermarks on bond stock should be stacked so that they can be read from the top of the stack. Tag or mark the guide edges for the press operator.

Special Paper-Cutting Techniques

Fig. 23-31 shows how a split back gauge setting will permit two different-sized cuttings with one back gauge setting. A typical application of this technique would involve cutting 8 1/2″ × 11″ letterheads out of 17″ × 22″ bond. For example, after the 8 1/2″ side was cut using the combined center and left side of the gauge, the 11″ side could be cut using the split right side of the gauge without changing the cutter setting. Fig. 23-32 shows how an angle-cutting device can be used to assist an operator to make angle cuts.

Cutting Specialty Papers

Certain papers, such as pressure-sensitive papers, can be easily damaged by the blade or the clamp during the cutting process. The damage is not always immediately visible but shows up after several days.

To cut pressure-sensitive paper, reduce the normal clamp pressure and lower the clamp

23-30. *Place the other half of the two-up lift into the cutter. Cut it to the 9 1/2″ width. Remove it from the cutter.*

23-31. *Top view of a back gauge with the right unit split.*

23-29. *Wait until the blade returns to the top of its stroke before removing scrap or the cut unit. Place the cut unit on the wing of the table.*

23-32. *An angle-cutting device attached to the back gauge.*

slowly. Block off the clamp pressure with a separate stack of paper. Fig. 23-33. The pressure can be cushioned with a cutting pad. Fig. 23-34. A sheet of chipboard could be placed on the top and bottom of the stack prior to cutting. Pressure can be distributed by cutting more than one lift of the same height at a time.

When cutting thin stock, such as manifold or onionskin, reduce the clamp pressure and underlay the stock with chipboard. Talcum powder on the fingers keeps them from sticking to gummed stock.

Solutions to Paper-Cutting Problems

The following are some possible solutions for paper-cutting problems.

23-33. *The blocking-off method of cutting pressure-sensitive paper. Make the height of the blocking stack slightly less than the height of the pressure-sensitive paper.*

23-34. *Clamp-cushion method of cutting pressure-sensitive paper. Sponge rubber can be used if cutting pads are not available.*

TROUBLE	CAUSE	SOLUTION
Stock drawing (top sheets too long) after cutting.	Insufficient clamp pressure.	Increase pressure.
	Dull knife.	Sharpen knife.
	Too large a lift.	Make smaller lifts.
	Slippery stock.	Make smaller lifts.
Knob being formed along edge of stock after cutting.	Nick in blade.	Change and regrind blade.
Paper wider in middle after cutting.	Knife not firmly seated.	Tighten knife bolts and adjusting screws.
	Too soft paper.	Make smaller lifts.
	Burrs on knife.	Hone the blade.
	Knife too thick.	Regrind or replace blade.
Edges wavy or not square after cutting.	Too much clamp pressure.	Reduce clamp pressure.
	Back gauge out of square.	Square back gauge.
Burred edges after cutting.	Dull knife.	Sharpen blade.
	Trying to trim too little.	Allow for larger trims.
Bad bottom sheet after cutting.	Loose shear stick.	Replace stick.
	Cutting slot too deep.	Replace stick.
	Blade bite adjusted too low.	Decrease blade bite.
Entire sheet not being cut.	Bow in blade.	Regrind blade or add makeready paper.
	Blade bite adjusted too high.	Increase blade bite.

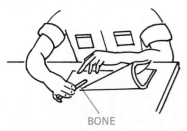

23-35. *Hand-folding with a bone. Note how the worker registers and holds the edges of a sheet while making the fold.*

Paper to be Folded

Paper to be folded should be cut square and no bigger than the folding equipment used. The grain direction on paper to be folded should run parallel to the backbone if it is to be folded into signatures. If paper is to be folded, scored, or perforated on a buckle folder (described in the next section), the grain on the paper should run parallel to the folding rollers. Press operators should avoid creating a high water imbalance on the offset press, because paper that has absorbed too much moisture from the press will easily develop wrinkles on the folder.

FOLDING IN THE BINDERY

The folder is a finishing machine. In addition to folding stock it can trim, glue, slit, score, and perforate.

Paper can be folded by hand or by either of two basic types of folding machines: buckle or knife.

Fig. 23-35 shows how to hand-fold paper. The edges of the sheets are registered and held with one hand. The fold is made by creasing the paper with a *bone*. A bone is made from bone or plastic.

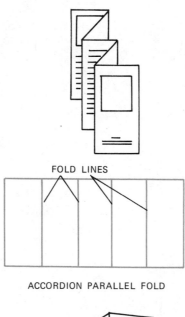

FOLD LINES

ACCORDION PARALLEL FOLD

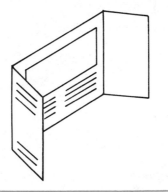

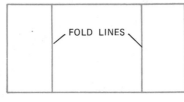

FOLD LINES

GATE PARALLEL FOLD

23-36. *Gate and accordion parallel folds.*

KINDS OF FOLDS

A complete listing of all kinds and uses of folds would likely fill several chapters in a book of this nature. However, the subject of folding is greatly simplified if it is understood that all possible folds are actually modifications of two

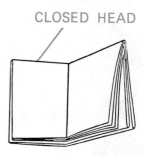

CLOSED HEAD

BOOKLET RIGHT ANGLE FOLD

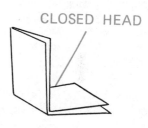

CLOSED HEAD

FRENCH RIGHT — ANGLE FOLD

23-37. *French and booklet right-angle folds.*

basic folds. These two basic folds are known as parallel and right-angle folds. *Parallel folds* are characterized by all folds being made parallel to each other. In *right-angle folds*, each fold is made at a right angle to each preceding fold.

Parallel folds work best when made with the grain of the paper. Fig. 23-36 shows two typical applications of parallel folds.

Right-angle folds are usually used on jobs having wide pages. Every other fold in a right-angle folded signature is made against the grain. This type of fold develops closed heads in signatures, which tend to trap air. A closed head is a fold wrapped around the top part of a signature. Fig. 23-37. This trapped air makes it difficult to make square folds.

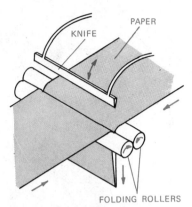

23-38. *In knife-type folders, a descending knife blade creases the paper and forces it between the folding rollers.*

Therefore, the closed heads on the sheet are usually perforated when they are made on the folder to allow some of the trapped air to escape. Fig. 23-37 shows two typical right-angle folds.

MACHINE FOLDING

Machine folding is performed so quickly that it is difficult for beginning bindery workers to

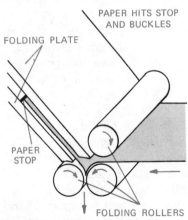

23-39. *In buckle folders, the paper hits a stop and buckles into the folding rollers.*

586

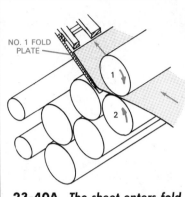

23-40A. *The sheet enters fold plate one.*

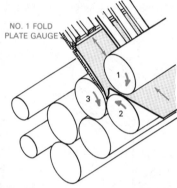

23-40B. *The sheet buckles and receives the first fold.*

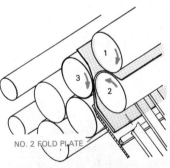

23-40C. *The once-folded sheet enters fold plate two.*

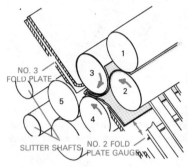

23-40D. *The sheet receives the second fold.*

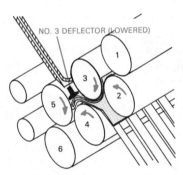

23-40E. *The twice-folded sheet bypasses fold plate three.*

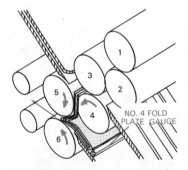

23-40F. *The sheet receives the third fold using the fourth fold plate.*

MGD Graphic Systems

23-40. *A four-plate, buckle-folder diagram. Roller two is the stationary roller.*

fully understand how the folds are actually made. Fig. 23-38 shows how knife-type folders work, and Fig. 23-39 shows how buckle-type folders work. In knife-type folders, the folds are not actually made by the knife, but by the folding rollers. The knife pushes the paper into the rollers, which form the fold by rolling the paper between them. Although knife-type folders are slower operating, they are used almost exclusively for booklet work because they are the most accurate for making right-angle folds.

Fig. 23-39 illustrates the principles behind buckle-type folding machines. Elements of the buckle folder, such as the folding plate, the paper stop, and the folding rollers, all work together to force the paper to be folded. The folding plate will allow a sheet to slide in or out without puckering the sheet. The plate, along with the paper stop, permits the folding rollers to catch the sheet and buckle it in a predetermined place. This predetermined place can be changed by simply adjusting the distance from the paper stop to the place where the buckle occurs.

Many varieties of folds are possible with buckle folders. Fig. 23-40. This variety is possible on a buckle folder because the press sheet can be driven into any or all folding plates with just one pass through the machine. Thus, buckle folders are more versatile than knife-type folders, which usually fold paper only once at each station. Buckle folds should be made with the grain. Buckle folders are less accurate on right-angle folds than knife folders and cannot handle as thin or as large a sheet as knife-type folders.

Machine folders are manufactured in many different styles, ranging in size from simple tabletop models to large machines that will handle sheets as large as 74". These modern folders come equipped with any of three basic types of feeders: friction stream, continuous stream, or pile. Figs. 23-41 through 23-45.

CLASSIFICATION OF FOLDERS

The three classifications of folders are tabletop, jobber, and trade bindery folders, such as

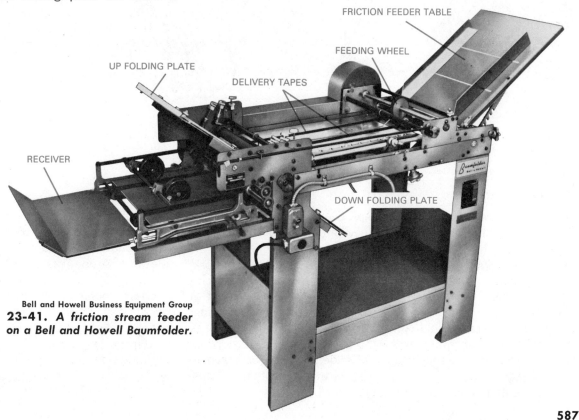

FRICTION FEEDER TABLE

FEEDING WHEEL

UP FOLDING PLATE

DELIVERY TAPES

RECEIVER

DOWN FOLDING PLATE

Bell and Howell Business Equipment Group
23-41. A friction stream feeder on a Bell and Howell Baumfolder.

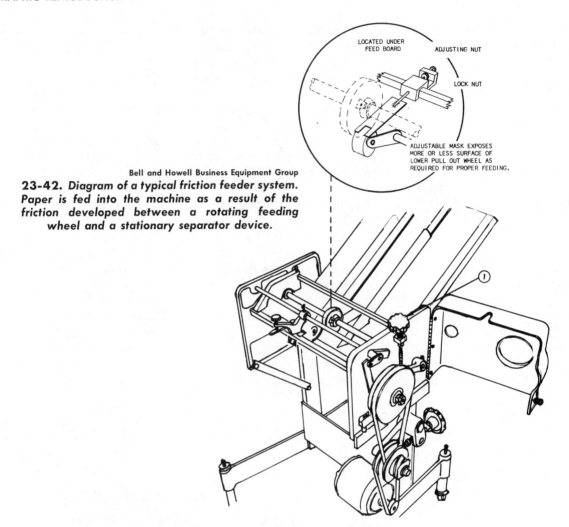

LOCATED UNDER
FEED BOARD

ADJUSTING NUT

LOCK NUT

ADJUSTABLE MASK EXPOSES
MORE OR LESS SURFACE OF
LOWER PULL OUT WHEEL AS
REQUIRED FOR PROPER FEEDING.

Bell and Howell Business Equipment Group
23-42. *Diagram of a typical friction feeder system. Paper is fed into the machine as a result of the friction developed between a rotating feeding wheel and a stationary separator device.*

the double-16 and quad. They are sheet-fed folders. Web printing equipment has a web folder in-line. Web folders are specialized, single-purpose folders and are beyond the scope of this text. Fig. 23-46.

Tabletop folders will fold only parallel folds with one pass through the machine. They usually are equipped with friction stream feeders and no more than two parallel folding plates. They rarely fold a sheet bigger than 12″ × 18″. Fig. 23-47.

Jobber folders are the workhorses of pamphlet binderies and perform a great variety of work, such as scoring, gluing, trimming, and slitting, as well as intricate folding. Fig. 23-43. Jobber folders can be arranged to make many parallel folds. Fig. 23-48.

Trade bindery folders are used for edition work. Double-16 folders produce two 16-page signatures from one press sheet. These signatures can be either inserts or outserts. An *outsert* would be a 16-page signature that can stand alone. An *insert* is a 16-page signature that is stuffed inside the outsert, often by the action of the folder. See Fig. 23-49 to visualize how 32-

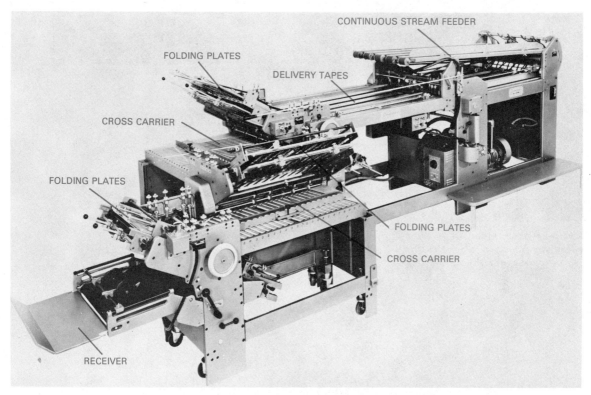

CONTINUOUS STREAM FEEDER

FOLDING PLATES

DELIVERY TAPES

CROSS CARRIER

FOLDING PLATES

FOLDING PLATES

CROSS CARRIER

RECEIVER

Bell and Howell Business Equipment Group

23-43. *A continuous stream feeder attached to a Baumfolder. This type of feeder permits the machine to run continuously while the feeder is being loaded.*

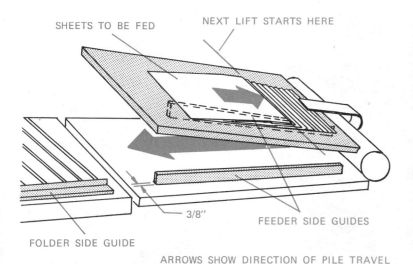

SHEETS TO BE FED

NEXT LIFT STARTS HERE

3/8"

FEEDER SIDE GUIDES

FOLDER SIDE GUIDE

ARROWS SHOW DIRECTION OF PILE TRAVEL

23-44. *A continuous stream feeder.*

23-45. *A pile-fed folder. The stock is loaded onto the feeder in a vertical stack, or pile fashion.*

23-46. *A web folder. In addition to folding paper, it also cuts the paper into sheets.*

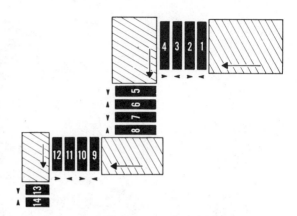

STANDARD ARRANGEMENT FOR CONVENTIONAL FOLDING

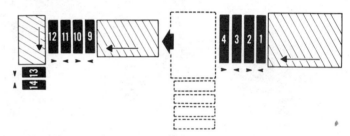

ARRANGEMENT FOR MULTIPLE PARALLEL FOLDS

23-48. *Jobber folders can be arranged to make many parallel folds.*

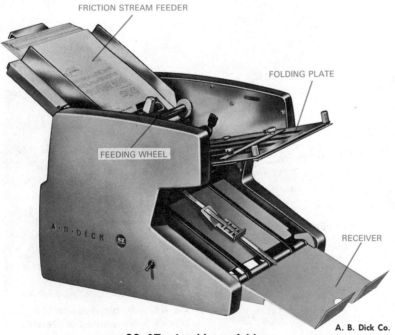

FRICTION STREAM FEEDER

FOLDING PLATE

FEEDING WHEEL

A·B·DICK

RECEIVER

A. B. Dick Co.

23-47. *A tabletop folder.*

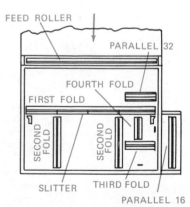

FEED ROLLER

PARALLEL 32

FOURTH FOLD

FIRST FOLD

SECOND FOLD

SECOND FOLD

SLITTER

THIRD FOLD

PARALLEL 16

23-49. *A double-16 folder diagram. The sheet is slit in half by a slitter at the first fold. Each half is then folded by a continuing series of folding stations to make inserts or outserts.*

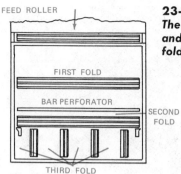

FEED ROLLER

FIRST FOLD

BAR PERFORATOR

SECOND FOLD

THIRD FOLD

23-50. *A quad-folder diagram. The large press sheet is perforated and slit into four parts by the folder. Each part is then folded into a signature.*

page signatures can be made on double-16 folders.

The quad folder, as its name implies, can produce four 16-page (or two 32-page) signatures from one press sheet. Insert and outsert arrangements are also possible with quad folders. Fig. 23-50.

SETTING UP A FOLDER

Before attempting to set up a folder, study the instructions contained in the operator's manual accompanying the machine. In general, the following steps are necessary to set up a folder properly.

1. Set up the major components of the machine for the particular job.

2. If the folder is equipped with a pile-type feeder, load the stock. This is an important step, since improperly loaded folders will not feed correctly. The stock should be loaded very evenly and level. It should also be well winded and have a very slight upward curl on the lead edge. Stock is loaded last on friction-fed folders.

3. Rough out the folding settings by hand since any fine adjustments now would change when stock is run under power.

4. Under power, fine-adjust the feeder and determine the best overall machine speed. (Each added section should run slightly faster than the preceding section to allow leading sheets to get out of the way of following sheets.)

5. Make final adjustments of folds under power.

6. Adjust the paper receiver.

7. Engage special devices

after all fold settings are finalized.

8. Tighten adjusting mechanisms and recheck all settings.

9. Engage the counter. It tells how many sheets have been folded.

10. Start and run the machine.

11. Offload the paper from the receiver as finished units pile up. All folded units should be checked for bad folds by squaring each offloaded lift to see if the ends of any units protrude beyond normal. Those protruding are improperly folded and should be discarded.

OPERATING A TABLETOP FOLDER

Tabletop folders are set up much the same way as any other folder having a friction feeder. The main difference is the size and weight of stock that can be folded. Figs. 23-51 through 23-58.

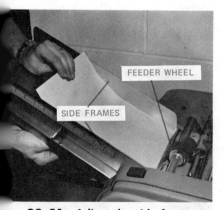

FEEDER WHEEL

SIDE FRAMES

23-51. *Adjust the side frames to center the stock on the feeder wheel without restricting the flow of stock into the machine.*

23-52. *Adjust the feeder wheel bite until the paper is pulled into the folder under resistance. Wheel bite is the force used to pull the paper into the machine.*

23-53. Adjust the stone wheel's exposed surface for a space of about 1/8″ to help separate the infeeding sheets. The stone wheel is the wheel directly beneath the feeder wheel.

FEEDER WHEEL

METAL FLANGE

STONE WHEEL

23-57. Load the feeder. The stock must be fanned and loaded in a cascaded fashion, with the printing side down.

UPPER FOLDING PLATE ADJUSTMENT

23-54. Adjust the folding plate for proper length.

OPERATING A BUCKLE FOLDER

To set up a pile-fed buckle folder for signatures requires considerable skill, which can only be acquired by practice and understanding the information contained in the operator's manual. Fig. 23-59. The major steps required to fold a 16-page signature are shown in Figs. 23-60 through 23-77 (Pages 593–596).

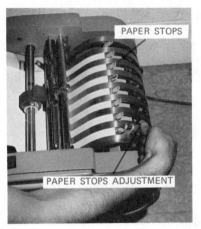

PAPER STOPS

PAPER STOPS ADJUSTMENT

23-55. Adjust the paper stops to even the folds.

23-56. Adjust the receiving system to keep the folded units from buckling up.

23-58. Offload folded units and check for incorrectly folded units.

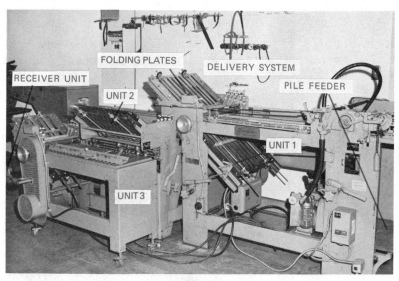

23-59. *The feeder, folder, and delivery unit of a buckle folder.*

23-61. *Center the feeder wheel on the stock.*

23-62. *Adjust the top rails.*

23-60. *Wind and load the stock on the pile feeder. Page one should be toward the rear of the machine and facing down.*

23-63. *Adjust the paper stops.*

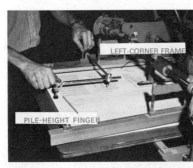

23-66. Set the pile-height finger to rest on the center of the back edge of the pile. Adjust the pile height.

23-64. Adjust the side frames. The left-corner frame should be in line with the feeder-guide device on the feeder table.

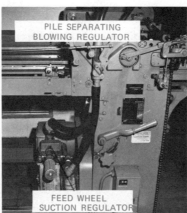

23-67. Adjust the air-blowing and suction force by regulating the valve opening.

23-69. Adjust the feeder guide. The guide should be in use with the feeder corner side frame.

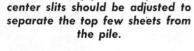

23-65. Adjust the air slits. They should be adjusted so the outer slits blow deeply into the pile. The center slits should be adjusted to separate the top few sheets from the pile.

23-68. Adjust the double-sheet detector, and center it on the feeder wheel. The detector will stop the folder if more than one sheet is fed. Add the holddown devices.

23-70. The feeder guide should feed the sheet square with feeder roll number one.

594

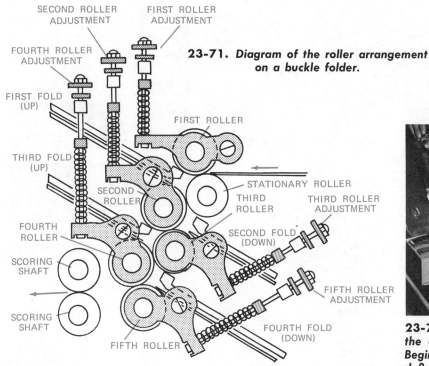

SECOND ROLLER ADJUSTMENT

FIRST ROLLER ADJUSTMENT

FOURTH ROLLER ADJUSTMENT

FIRST FOLD (UP)

FIRST ROLLER

THIRD FOLD (UP)

STATIONARY ROLLER

SECOND ROLLER

THIRD ROLLER

THIRD ROLLER ADJUSTMENT

FOURTH ROLLER

SECOND FOLD (DOWN)

SCORING SHAFT

FIFTH ROLLER ADJUSTMENT

SCORING SHAFT

FOURTH FOLD (DOWN)

FIFTH ROLLER

23-71. *Diagram of the roller arrangement on a buckle folder.*

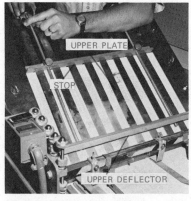

UPPER PLATE

STOP

UPPER DEFLECTOR

23-74. *Adjust the stops, and set the deflector blades to be used. Begin with the first fold. Raise the deflector on the first plate so the sheet feeds to it. Then set the stop to buckle the sheet in the correct location for the first fold. Run a few sheets through to check this setting. Repeat this procedure for all other folds. Lower the deflector on all plates that will not be used.*

FOLDING ROLLERS

23-72. *View of folding rollers with the top folding plates removed. This permits easy access to rollers and adjusting devices.*

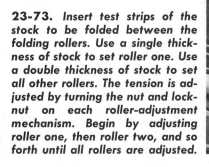

23-73. *Insert test strips of the stock to be folded between the folding rollers. Use a single thickness of stock to set roller one. Use a double thickness of stock to set all other rollers. The tension is adjusted by turning the nut and locknut on each roller-adjustment mechanism. Begin by adjusting roller one, then roller two, and so forth until all rollers are adjusted.*

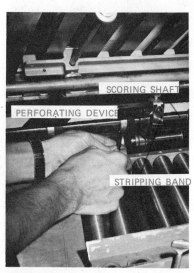

SCORING SHAFT

PERFORATING DEVICE

STRIPPING BAND

23-75. *Adjust the scoring shaft's wheels.*

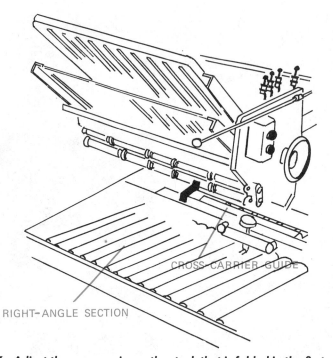

RIGHT-ANGLE SECTION

CROSS-CARRIER GUIDE

HOLDDOWN DEVICE

STACKING WHEELS

23-77. *Add a holddown finger on the receiving unit to keep the folded signature from popping open. Adjust the stacking wheels to keep the signatures in order as they flow out of the folder.*

23-76. *Adjust the cross carrier so the stock that is folded in the first units hits the cross carrier properly after leaving the rollers.*

FOLDING HINTS

The following are some trouble-saving hints regarding folders:

* Any closed head made on a folder should be perforated to allow air trapped in the head to escape.

* Paper should be protected from moisture since it creates control problems on the folder.

* Hydro-lining devices can be used on a folder to help make difficult folds. This device puts a stream of liquid along a fold line to reduce the paper's resistance to folding at that point.

* A single layer of tape wrapped around the folding rollers in a spiral fashion will help keep thin sheets from buckling and creasing.

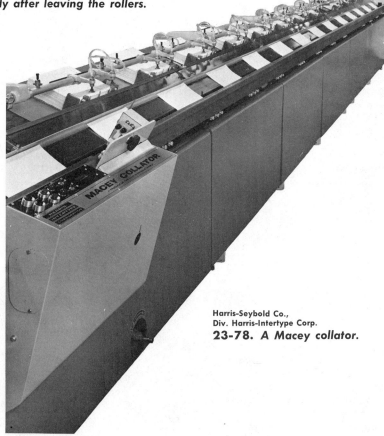

Harris-Seybold Co.,
Div. Harris-Intertype Corp.
23-78. *A Macey collator.*

Didde-Glaser, Inc.

23-80. A flat-sheet collator.

A. B. Dick Co.

23-79. A foot-powered, hand-operated collator. The operator loads the sheets for the pages in the bins. Once the bin is loaded, the operator steps down on the foot pedal. When the pedal is released, one sheet from every loaded bin is pushed forward to be hand-gathered.

ASSEMBLING IN THE BINDERY

Assembling, often called collating or gathering, refers to the actions required to get all the various parts of a printed piece together in the correct order.

Assembling can be done by hand or by machine. Hand-assembling can be accomplished in many ways, such as picking up sheets from piles sequentially laid out around a large table.

Fig. 23-78 shows one version of a machine-gathering device known as a collator. Collators are manufactured in many different styles and models. Some machine collators can gather only flat sheets. Figs. 23-79 and 23-80. Others can gather flat sheets

or signatures. Fig. 23-81. Still other assembling machines gather flat sheets, stitch them, and then fold them into signatures. Fig. 23-82.

HAND-ASSEMBLING BOOKLETS

Following are the steps required to assemble by hand a booklet comprised of a cover and one signature. A more efficient method would involve a collating machine that would assemble

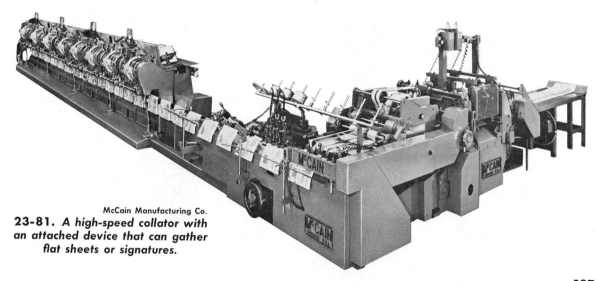

McCain Manufacturing Co.

23-81. A high-speed collator with an attached device that can gather flat sheets or signatures.

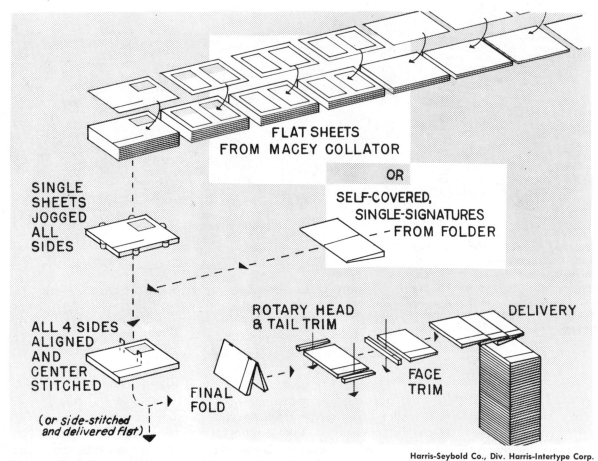

Harris-Seybold Co., Div. Harris-Intertype Corp.

23-82. *This collating system gathers flat sheets, stitches them, and then folds them into signatures. The sheet must be accurately trimmed and jogged before the assembly operation begins.*

and bind the booklet on a single run through the machine.

1. Lay the covers and signatures out on a table with the signatures to the right. Fig. 23-83.

2. Assemble the signatures into the covers by using the lip to flip the cover open. You can use glycerin to make your fingers sticky. Insert the signatures into the cover from right to left.

3. For ease of operation, jog books to the head in groups of ten. Fig. 23-84. The head is usually the guide edge on book work.

4. Stack the stuffed units in preparation for binding.

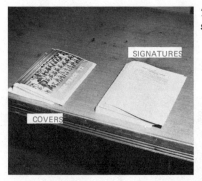

23-83. *Covers and signatures are slightly cascaded to expose each lip for easy opening.*

23-84. *Signatures are assembled into the cover. Then the assembled booklets are jogged to the head.*

CASE BINDING

A case-bound book is a hard-cover book. The cover is made separately, and the sewn signatures are inserted and fastened to the cover. Fig. 23-85 shows the major parts of a book. The bindery worker should be able to rec-

23-86. *Signatures about to be side-gathered into a square.*

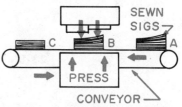

23-87. *An automatic smashing machine. Signatures are stacked at A, smashed at B, and delivered at C with the air squeezed out.*

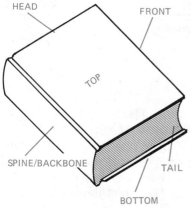

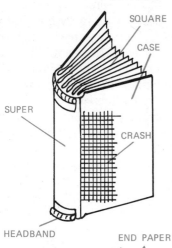

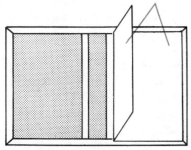

23-85. *Parts of a book.*

ognize the case, jacket, super or crash, spine or backbone, head, front, end paper, top, bottom, tail, and headband of a book.

A case-bound book is assembled in three main operations. These are identified as the inner-page assembly operation, the forwarding operation, and the casing-in operation.

The inner-page assembly operation involves four major steps: (1) gathering of the flat sheets, signatures, inserts, and tip-ons; (2) binding; (3) nipping; and (4) trimming. To assemble a case-bound book:

1. *Gathering* involves the collation or gathering of all elements into one "square." An element can be a signature, a flat sheet, or an insert. A square is that part of a book that has been gathered, bound, nipped, and trimmed. Fig. 23-86 shows signatures in a side-gathering position.

2. *Binding* is usually done with thread. The major types of sewing are explained later in the text.

3. *Nipping,* or smashing, involves squeezing the air out of the signatures to make the square thinner. This step is also known as *bundling.* Fig. 23-87.

4. *Trimming* involves cutting all sides of the gathered, bound, and nipped square except the spine side.

The *forwarding operation* involves four major steps: rounding, backing, crashing, and headbanding. Forwarding is performed on the square after it is assembled.

1. *Rounding* makes the backbone convex. Fig. 23-88. Rounding helps the book to open and stay open.

2. *Backing* is often done with a heavy, concave piece of iron. Fig. 23-89. Backing tends to make the rounding permanent and provides a hinge joint for the cover.

3. *Crashing* involves adding along the backbone a supporting fabric called *crash* and a strong paper called *super.* Fig. 23-90.

4. *Headbanding* is the process of adding cloth strips on the ends of the backbone. This is

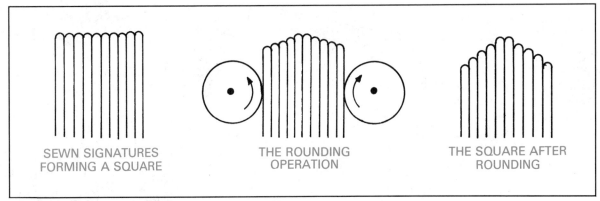

23-88. A "square" before, during, and after rounding.

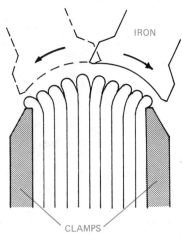

23-89. A rounded "square" being backed by a jointing iron.

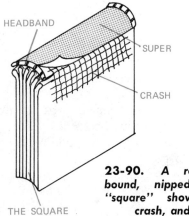

23-90. A rounded, backed, bound, nipped, and trimmed "square" showing the super, crash, and headbands.

done for decoration only, since headbands no longer serve a functional purpose. Fig. 23-90. A typical machine process for adding crash, super, and headbands is shown in Figs. 23-91 and 23-92.

The *casing-in operation* is the action required to attach the forwarded square to the case. The case refers to the hard book covers. The case is made first, then the square is attached to it with *end papers*. End papers are the outside sheets used to bind the square to the case. This attachment is called tipping. Two major steps are involved:

1. *Casemaking* involves the placement of cover material over two stiff boards. Fig. 23-93.

2. *Tipping* is the operation that assembles the case to the square by gluing the end papers to both the case and the backbone of the square.

FASTENING IN THE BINDERY
BINDING MATERIALS

There are many different paper binding materials available. *Wire* is used for wire stitching. Fig. 23-94 through 23-96.

Stitching wire is available in spools. It is normally bought by the pound in either a flat or round style. The flat style is usually chosen whenever additional strength or penetrating power is required. Although stitching wire is basically made of steel, it is often alloyed with bronze, tin, aluminum, or stainless steel. In addition, stitching wire is available with a lacquered or non-lacquered finish. Lacquer-finished wire has a special coating which resists tarnishing and is used whenever rust or moisture are significant factors in binding a job.

Stitcher operators should follow closely the instruction manual supplied with the machine. Figs. 23-94 and 23-97.

Glue is another fastening material. Hot glue is used in perfect-binding machines. Cold glue is used when pasting is automat-

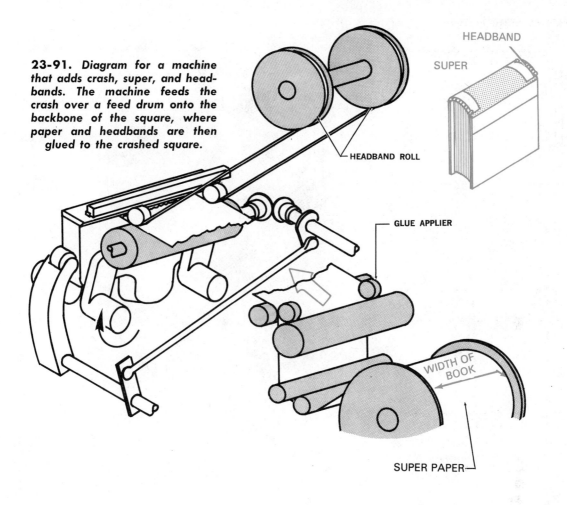

23-91. *Diagram for a machine that adds crash, super, and headbands. The machine feeds the crash over a feed drum onto the backbone of the square, where paper and headbands are then glued to the crashed square.*

HEADBAND

SUPER

HEADBAND ROLL

GLUE APPLIER

WIDTH OF BOOK

SUPER PAPER

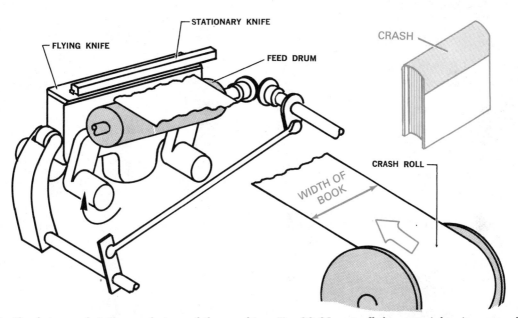

STATIONARY KNIFE

FLYING KNIFE

FEED DRUM

CRASH

CRASH ROLL

WIDTH OF BOOK

23-92. *The flying and stationary knives of the machine, Fig. 23-91, cut off the material to its proper length.*

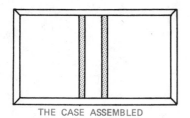

THE CASE ASSEMBLED

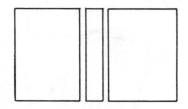

COVER MATERIAL

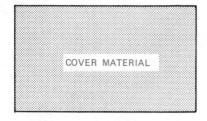

PARTS OF THE CASE

23-93. *The case is made of binder boards and the book-cover material.*

SPOOLS OF WIRE

Harris-Seybold Co., Div. Harris-Intertype Corp.

23-94. *A stitching and folding device using two spools of stitching wire.*

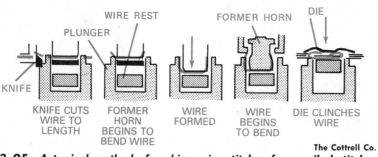

WIRE REST

PLUNGER

FORMER HORN

DIE

KNIFE

KNIFE CUTS WIRE TO LENGTH

FORMER HORN BEGINS TO BEND WIRE

WIRE FORMED

WIRE BEGINS TO BEND

DIE CLINCHES WIRE

The Cottrell Co.

23-95. *A typical method of making wire stitches from coiled stitcher wire. Note how a knife cuts the wire from the spool.*

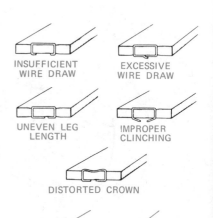

INSUFFICIENT WIRE DRAW

EXCESSIVE WIRE DRAW

UNEVEN LEG LENGTH

IMPROPER CLINCHING

DISTORTED CROWN

23-96. *A perfect stitch and some common stitching problems.*

A PERFECT STITCH

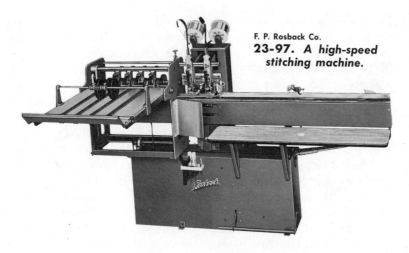

F. P. Rosback Co.

23-97. A high-speed stitching machine.

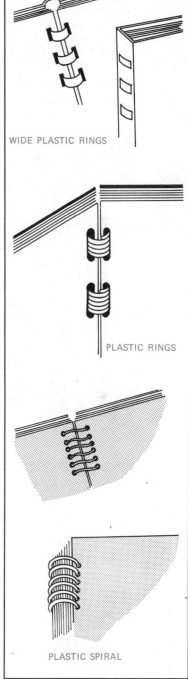

WIDE PLASTIC RINGS

PLASTIC RINGS

PLASTIC SPIRAL

23-99. Plastic binders.

ically done as part of a folder or a press operation. Fig. 23-98.

Another binding material is the *thermoplastic capsule*. These capsules are embedded in paper. Through the application of infrared, electrical high frequency, vibrating heat energy, the thermoplastic capsules are turned into a gluelike substance, causing the folded paper to bind together along the folded edge.

Thread and *Holland tape* are also used for binding paper. Thread is normally used to sew paper together. Holland tape is generally used to improve the appearance of printed pieces by covering other unsightly binding materials, such as staples or mechanical binding devices. When a job is to have Holland tape applied to the backbone, the tape is cut oversize so the edges of the tape will be neat and even after the backbone is trimmed.

There are also a number of mechanical binding devices available. These include plastic binders, wire spiral binders, ring-type binders, screw post binders, and spring-back binders. Figs. 23-99 through 23-103.

PASTE CONTAINER

PASTE-SPREADING WHEEL

23-98. A pasting device mounted on a jobber folder.

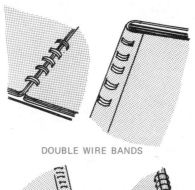

DOUBLE WIRE BANDS

WIRE SPIRAL

23-100. Wire binders.

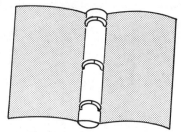

23-101. *A ring binder.*

ASSEMBLED BOOKLET

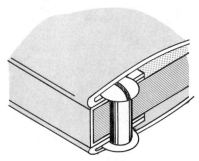

SECTION THROUGH SCREW POST
23-102. *A post binder.*

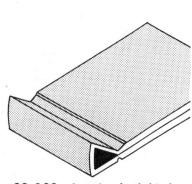

23-103. *A spring-back binder.*

They are available in a wide range of styles and sizes.

METHODS OF BINDING

There are six basic methods of binding: *side binding, saddle binding, perfect binding, paste binding, thread binding,* and *loose-leaf binding.*

In *side binding* with wire, the sheets or signatures are gathered side by side. Fig. 23-104. Side binding requires that extra paper be allotted to the backbone just for the binding. Books bound in this fashion have less sheet area available for printing and never open flat. Side binding is normally done with wire or thread.

Saddle binding is so called because the signatures to be saddle bound straddle the binding device in much the same manner as a saddle is placed on a horse. Saddle binding is normally done with wire. Fig. 23-105. Saddle-bound signatures normally require a lip because they are placed inside each other instead

of side by side. Saddle-bound books will open relatively flat, but their thickness will be limited. Little backbone space is needed for saddle binding. An increase in margin of the printed page is needed for the outside signatures on the thicker saddle-bound books because of the "creep" or "push out" effect caused by the thickness of the inner signature backbones.

Perfect binding uses an adhesive binding material. In perfect binding, the flat sheets or signatures are first gathered side by side. Extra space is then allotted to the backbone of the flat sheets or signatures to compensate for the backbone paper, which will be cut off by a rotating *skiving* knife during a milling operation. This milling operation involves the removal of paper from the backbone in order to expose glue to each sheet in the book. After the backbone is skived, a hot glue is rolled onto the *milled* backbone and sometimes crash is added to the glued area for

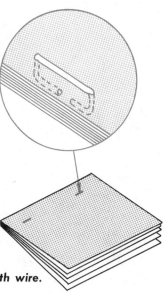

23-104. *Side binding with wire.*

23-105. *Saddle binding with wire.*

23-106. A perfect-binding machine.

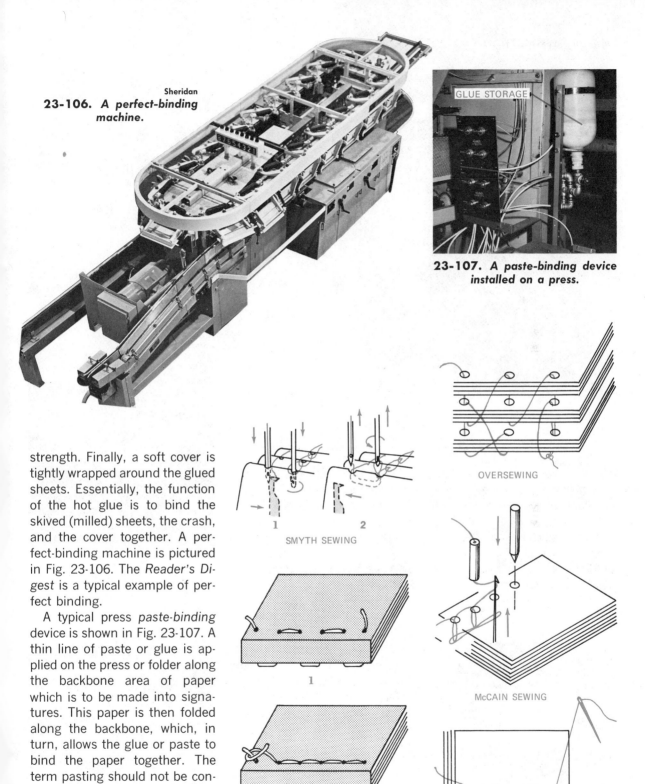

23-107. A paste-binding device installed on a press.

GLUE STORAGE

OVERSEWING

SMYTH SEWING

McCAIN SEWING

UP—AND—DOWN SEWING

SADDLE STITCHING

23-108. Methods of sewing used in thread binding.

strength. Finally, a soft cover is tightly wrapped around the glued sheets. Essentially, the function of the hot glue is to bind the skived (milled) sheets, the crash, and the cover together. A perfect-binding machine is pictured in Fig. 23-106. The *Reader's Digest* is a typical example of perfect binding.

A typical press *paste-binding* device is shown in Fig. 23-107. A thin line of paste or glue is applied on the press or folder along the backbone area of paper which is to be made into signatures. This paper is then folded along the backbone, which, in turn, allows the glue or paste to bind the paper together. The term pasting should not be confused with tipping, which is a technique used in case-binding operations.

Fig. 23-108 illustrates different methods of sewing used in

McCain Manufacturing Co.
23-109. *A side-sewing machine.*

NOTICE THE WIRE STITCHES ARE STAGGERED

KSC TRACK '72

23-111. *The stitches on every other booklet are offset. This is done so the backbones will flatten prior to trimming.*

23-112. *Stacked booklets ready for stitching.*

thread binding. These include Smyth sewing, hand sidesewing, saddle up-and-down sewing, and oversewing. Sewing is usually done by machines of the type pictured in Fig. 23-109. Thread binding is generally used on case-bound books.

Loose-leaf binding is the process required to bind loose or flat sheets of paper. Loose-leaf binding utilizes mechanical binding devices.

SADDLE WIRE BINDING PROCEDURES

To saddle wire bind a soft-covered booklet using a semiautomatic stitching machine:

1. Determine the actual placement of the wire stitching on the booklet by adjusting the location of the stitching heads on the stitching machine. Fig. 23-110. Many stitching heads make their stitches alternately. Fig. 23-111. Several booklets should be test-stitched to check the stitch placement.

2. Load the assembled cover and signature on the feeder table. Fig. 23-112. Open the booklet at the center, and place

23-110. *Adjust the positions of the stitching heads using a booklet as a guide.*

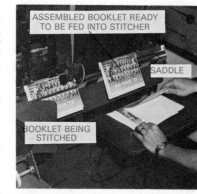

ASSEMBLED BOOKLET READY TO BE FED INTO STITCHER

SADDLE

BOOKLET BEING STITCHED

23-113. *Assembled booklets being hand-fed onto the saddle of the stitcher.*

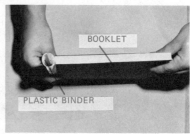

23-116. *Assemble the materials to be bound. Select a plastic binder about 20 percent greater than the thickness of the booklet.*

23-114. *Two persons can feed the stitcher. One feeds the signatures from the front. Another person in the back places the covers over them.*

front of the stitcher and the covers from the back. Fig. 23-114. Still another way is to work from the front, placing the signature on the saddle first and then the cover. Fig. 23-115.

Other assembling machines have a collator that assembles the cover and signatures and then automatically feeds them to the stitcher.

it on the stitcher saddle. Fig. 23-113. Keep the lip to the front of the machine so the guide is kept to the head of the job. The stitcher will move the unit along

the saddle to the stitcher head. The stitched units will be off-loaded on a conveyor.

Another way to do this job is to feed the signatures from the

PLASTIC BINDING PROCEDURES

The steps required to bind a booklet with a mechanical plastic binder are shown in Figs. 23-116 through 23-120. The two major items of equipment necessary to bind a booklet with plastic are a punch and a comb assembly.

TRIMMING IN THE BINDERY

Trimming is the removal of unwanted portions of paper through the use of paper-cutting and trimming machines. There are two major types of trimming operations, the trimming of flat sheets and folded sheets.

TYPES OF TRIMMERS

Book trimmers are manufactured in many different styles.

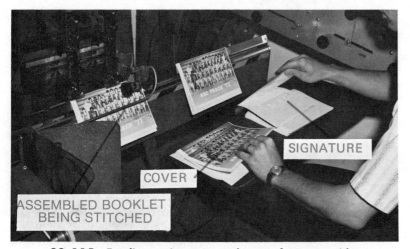

23-115. *Feeding a signature and cover from one side.*

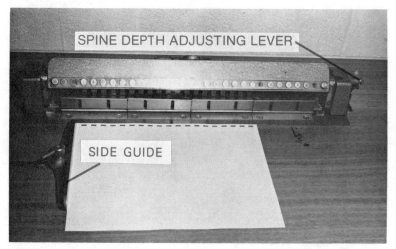

23-118. *Insert the booklet into the punch and against the side guide, and punch the holes.*

23-117. *Position the side guide for the punch so the holes are punched in the proper location. Adjust the spine depth with the adjusting lever. Generally, the thicker the booklet, the narrower the spine depth.*

Figs. 23-121 and 23-122. Some trim only one booklet at a time, while others trim entire stacks of books at one time. *Single-knife book trimmers* use one knife to trim all three sides of a booklet in three separate cuts. *Multiple-knife book* trimmers use separate blades for trimming each side of a book in one cut. Fig. 23-123 illustrates the principles involved in three-knife trimmers. Other, more complicated four- and five-knife trimmers are used to trim books that are imposed in a multiple-on fashion. A *multiple-on job* is one having more than one finished copy on a press sheet. The two extra blades on the five-knife trimmers are used to trim the additional books out of the folded press sheet.

TRIMMING MULTIPLE-ON JOBS ON A NONPROGRAMMED CUTTER

To *trim out* a properly prepared job on a manually oper-

ated paper cutter, only one cutter setting should be required.

To process a *flat press sheet* job involving chipboard insertion, padding, and trimming on a manually operated guillotine cutter:

1. Jog the press sheets to the guide edges. Fig. 23-124.

2. Trim the jogged sheets by setting up the cutter back gauge to the width desired. Fig. 23-125. Place stock against the guide and back gauge, and press the two start buttons. The cutter will automatically lower the clamp and complete the cut.

TRIMMING FLAT SHEET JOBS TO BE FOLDED

When making the final trims on jobs that are to be folded, the location of the trims should be based on the distance from the fold to the trims and not necessarily on the overall dimensions of the finished piece. The ends of the sheet to be folded must meet

23-119. *Insert the plastic binder into the comb assembly with the open side up. Adjust the comb so the binder is opened properly for assembly.*

23-120. *Assemble the pages face down onto the teeth of the binder. Close the binder, and remove the booklet.*

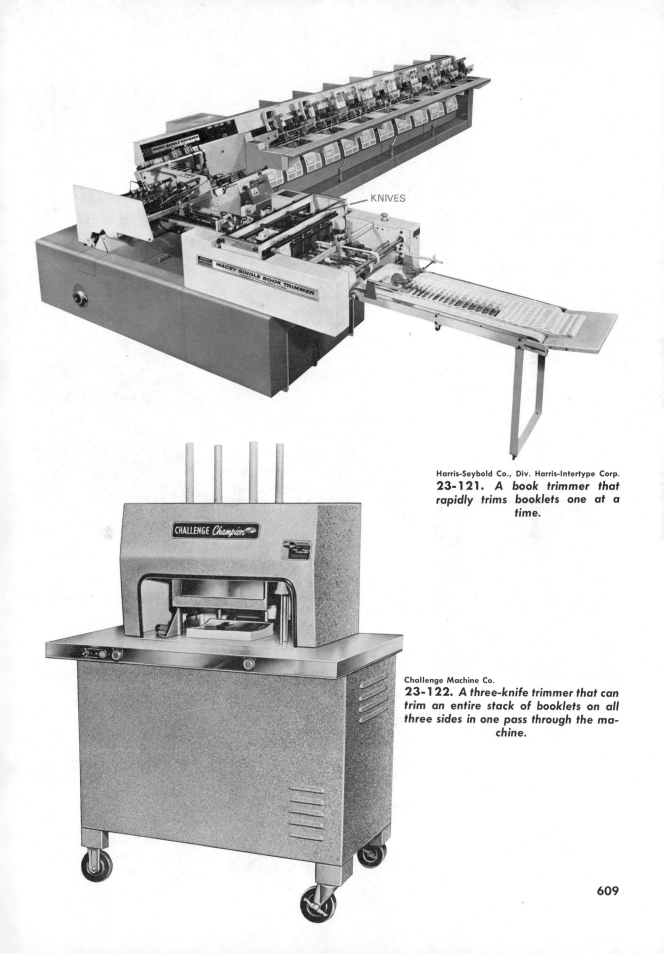

KNIVES

23-121. *A book trimmer that rapidly trims booklets one at a time.*

23-122. *A three-knife trimmer that can trim an entire stack of booklets on all three sides in one pass through the machine.*

609

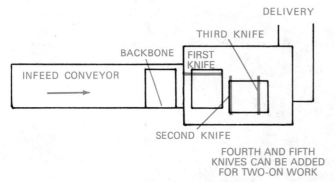

DELIVERY

THIRD KNIFE

BACKBONE

FIRST KNIFE

INFEED CONVEYOR

SECOND KNIFE

FOURTH AND FIFTH
KNIVES CAN BE ADDED
FOR TWO-ON WORK

23-123. *Diagram of an in-line, three-knife, trimming operation.*

23-126. *Mark the trim lines on the assembled and bound booklet.*

evenly after the sheet is trimmed and folded. It is advisable that jobs that are to be trimmed and folded be test-cut and test-folded before the entire job is trimmed. This is especially true for jobs that will have more than one fold or jobs having fold lines that must be on a specific place on the press sheet.

BOOK TRIMMING ON A FLAT SHEET CUTTER

The procedures for trimming a soft-cover booklet on a guillotine cutter with a split back gauge are shown in Figs. 23-126 through 23-136.

23-127. *Set the center section of the back gauge for a measure equal to the book width. Cut off the front edge on a test booklet.*

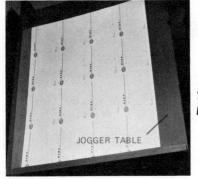

JOGGER TABLE

23-124. *Jog the chipboard and press sheets to the guide edges.*

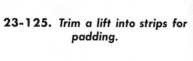

23-125. *Trim a lift into strips for padding.*

SIDE GUIDE

LEFT SECTION OF BACK GAUGE

BOOKLET

23-128. *Split the left section of the back gauge.*

23-129. *Trim the tail off the test booklet at a back gauge setting determined by the distance from the untrimmed head to the trimmed foot.*

23-130. *Split and adjust the right section of the back gauge. Trim off the head of the booklet at a cutter setting that is determined by the distance from the trimmed foot to the trimmed head. The trimmed foot of the booklet is inserted into the machine on the right side, and the head is cut off.*

23-132. *Test-cut a full stack of booklets and examine accuracy. The accuracy determines the number of booklets that can be trimmed at one time. Jog a stack of booklets to the backbone. Crush the backbones with the clamp.*

23-134. *Flip one-half the booklets to be cut over to make the stack even on both edges. Do not flip end for end.*

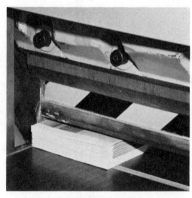

23-135. *Trim off the tail.*

FINGER

CENTER BACK GAUGE

23-131. *Attach holddown fingers to the center back gauge to keep the stacked booklets from drawing away from the gauge when they are cut.*

23-133. *Cut the front edge off.*

23-136. *Trim off the head. Stack the booklets for counting and banding.*

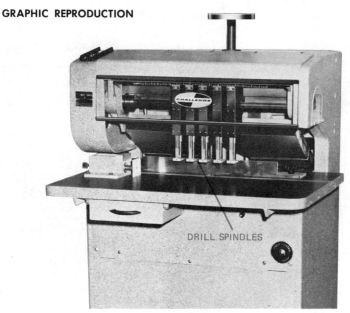

Challenge Machine Co.

23-137. *A multiple-spindle drill.*

DRILL SPINDLES

OTHER BINDERY OPERATIONS

There are many other finishing operations that bindery workers should be able to perform. The most common of these are drilling, slotting, cornering, padding, and packaging. There are also several less common operations such as labeling, tasseling, stuffing, tipping, addressing, and mailing. Another group of finishing operations is customarily performed in the pressroom instead of the bindery. These are identified as leafing, perforating, scoring, die cutting, bronzing, flocking, varnishing, laminating, and embossing operations.

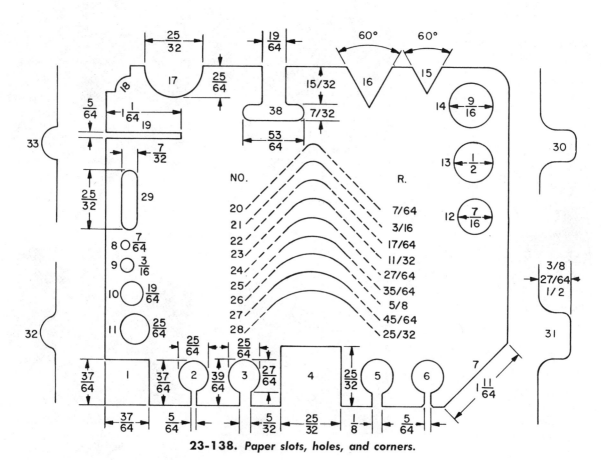

23-138. *Paper slots, holes, and corners.*

23-139. A universal paper punch.

performed on the corners of paper. Fig. 23-138 shows common drilling, slotting, and cornering operations. Holes, slots, and cornering operations are also performed by punching machines. Fig. 23-139. Paper-drilling machines use a hollow drill. Fig. 23-140. Drilling bits can be fluted on the inside, beveled on the outside, or specially hardened on the tip. Fluting compresses the paper and permits it to travel up the barrel of the bit more freely. Outside bevels are designed for drilling cloth and plastic as well as paper. Diamondized tips are especially hardened to provide for longer drill life. Drill life can also be extended by the use of sharpening devices. Fig. 23-141.

Drilling Paper

To drill paper on a single-spindled paper drill:

1. Mark the proper location of the holes on the test sheet.

PAPER DRILLING, SLOTTING, AND CORNERING

Paper drilling makes round holes in paper. It is usually performed on a machine called a paper drill. Paper-drilling machines range from single-spindled, hand-powered devices to fully automatic, multiple-spindled, hand-production models. Fig. 23-137. Some paper-drilling machines can also slot and corner paper. *Slotting* is making holes that are not round, and *cornering* is any operation

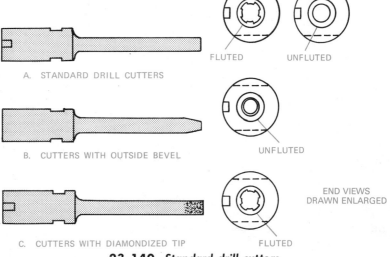

A. STANDARD DRILL CUTTERS

FLUTED   UNFLUTED

B. CUTTERS WITH OUTSIDE BEVEL

UNFLUTED

C. CUTTERS WITH DIAMONDIZED TIP

FLUTED

END VIEWS
DRAWN ENLARGED

23-140. Standard drill cutters.

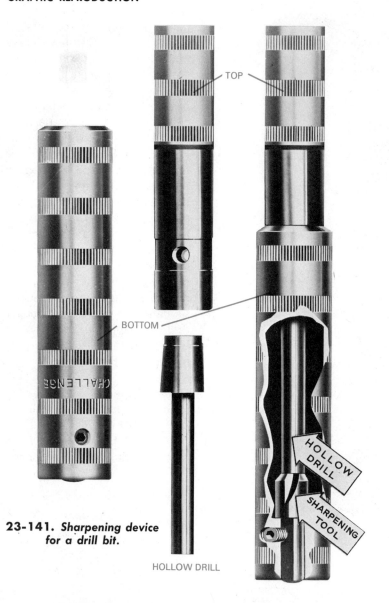

TOP

BOTTOM

CHALLENGE

23-141. *Sharpening device for a drill bit.*

HOLLOW DRILL

HOLLOW DRILL

SHARPENING TOOL

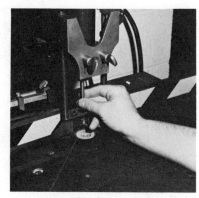

23-142. *Insert the bit.*

23-143. *Align the hole location marks with the bit. Once aligned, the side and back gauge settings can be finalized.*

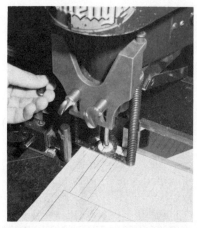

23-144. *Adjust the side gauge using a wrench to tighten the guide-stop adjusting bolts.*

2. Select and sharpen the drill bit. Fig. 23-141.

3. Insert the bit into the machine with a firm upward stroke. Fig. 23-142.

4. Align the bit with hole location marks on the paper, and apply holding pressure with the bit and the paper holddown device to keep the test paper from moving. Fig. 23-143. Place the edge of the paper guide against the test paper, and align the guide with the guide stop. Tighten the guide-stop device. Fig. 23-144.

5. Repeat Step 4 for every hole location desired.

6. Set the back gauge. The back gauge locates the distance the hole is drilled from the edge of the paper. Fig. 23-145. The

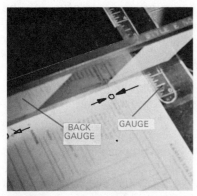

23-145. *Once the paper is aligned with the gauge, the back gauge should fit snugly against the paper. The back gauge's locking thumbscrews (not shown), located under the table, are then tightened to lock the back gauge into its position.*

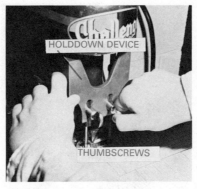

23-148. *Adjust the paper holddown device.*

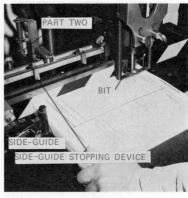

23-149. *Drill the paper.*

23-146. *Adjust the bit pressure.*

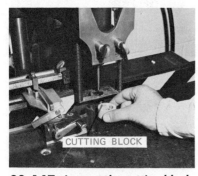

23-147. *Inspect the cutting block.*

gauge markings are the distance from the center of the hole to the back gauge.

7. Adjust the bit pressure. Use only enough pressure to drill cleanly through all paper while the foot pedal is at the lowest comfortable position. Fig. 23-146.

8. Change the cutting block if it is worn out. Fig. 23-147.

9. Adjust the holddown device to touch the top of the stock. It helps prevent paper from slipping away from the guides while the paper is being drilled. Fig. 23-148.

10. To drill the paper, insert the lift of paper securely against both guides. Lower the rotating bit with the foot pedal. Fig. 23-149.

Making Round Corners on Paper

Round corners can be made with a small hand-operated device, Fig. 23-150, or on a paper-drilling machine. Fig. 23-151 shows a paper-drilling machine set up to corner paper. Basically, the paper is cornered on the machine with a device that replaces

23-150. *A hand-operated device to make round corners.*

23-151. *Paper drill modified to make round corners on paper.*

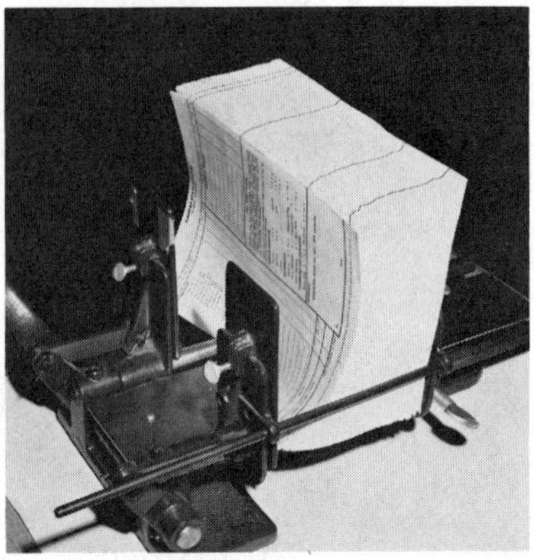

23-152. ***Load the paper into the banding device.***

the drilling bit and paper hold-down device. Two corner guide rails are added to the drill table to guide the paper accurately under the cornering device. To corner paper, an operator sets up the machine, makes all final adjustments, and makes the corners by lowering the cornering blade through the lift of paper.

Packaging Paper

Paper can be packaged in several different ways using a variety of materials. For instance, paper can be wrapped in kraft paper, bound with string, bound with gummed paper tape, and/or banded into bundles. Paper can also be boxed, enveloped, skidded, banded, or wrapped in a plastic shrink wrap. Regardless of the method selected, bindery workers generally have to package each job that is processed through the bindery.

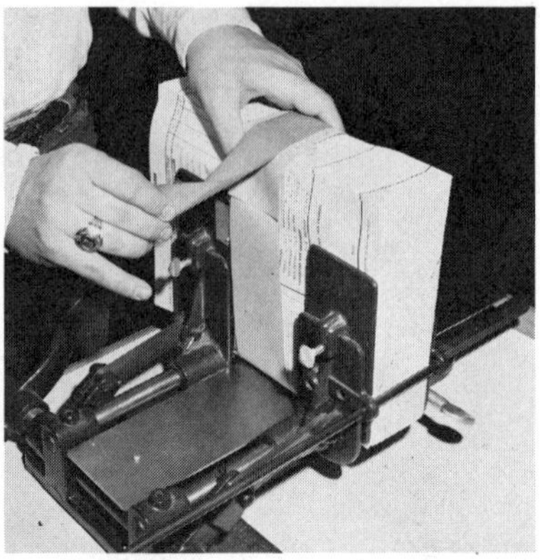

23-154. ***Wrap the paper band around the paper.***

Paper can be banded using the banding device shown in Fig. 23-152. The steps to band paper are shown in Figs. 23-153 through 23-155.

Plastic shrink wrapping is widely used. Since the plastic wrap is usually transparent, the contents can be easily identified. Shrink wrapping is generally faster, cheaper, and stronger than other types of wrapping. The following is an explanation of a simplified shrink wrapping method.

1. Count and stack the paper to be wrapped into even sized stacks.
2. Adjust the wrapping table to the height of a stack. The adjustment should be made so the stack is centered vertically on the cutting-arm wire when the arm is in the cutting position. Fig. 23-156.
3. Insert the paper into the plastic wrap, and pull both the paper and the wrap into the packaging position on the wrapping table. Fig. 23-157.
4. Lower the cutting arm. The plastic should be approximately 1/2″ bigger than the paper on all sides. Cutting fuses the plastic. Do not raise the cutter arm until the package is completely sealed. Fig. 23-158.
5. Place the package into the heat tunnel. A small hole should be made in the plastic packaging material before it is inserted into

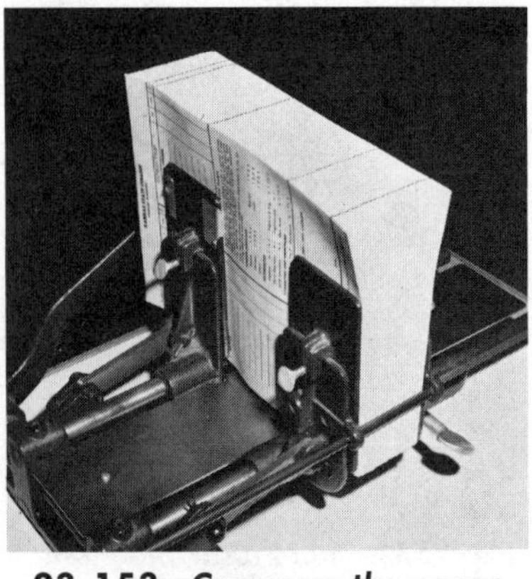

23-153. ***Compress the paper.***

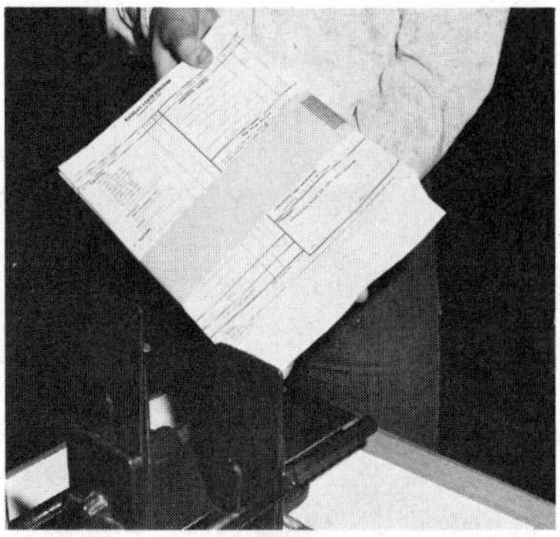

23-155. ***A banded package of paper.***

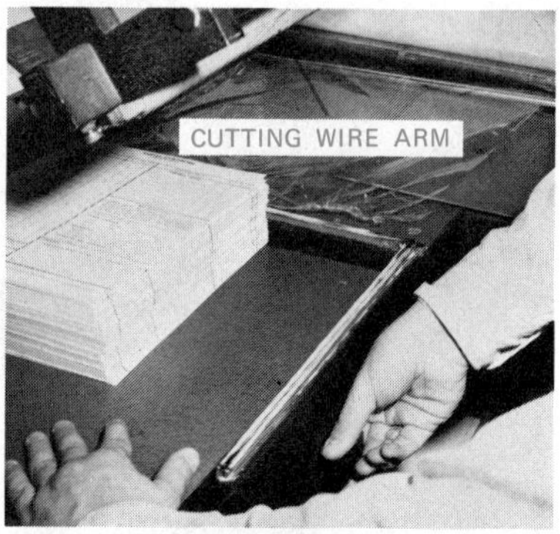

23-156. ***Adjusting the height of the wrapping table.***

23-157. *Place the package into the wrapping position.*

the heat tunnel. The heat shrinks the plastic tightly to the paper.

PAPER PADDING

There are two basic methods of padding paper (binding paper into pad form). The difference is the adhesive used. The conventional method of padding paper uses a water-soluble compound that will adhere to any type of paper. The other method uses a compound that works only on pressure-sensitive paper. Pressure-sensitive paper is used for making duplicates without carbon paper.

The conventional compound is soluble in water only until it

23-158. *Seal the package.*

dries. The steps for conventional padding are:

1. Tip the padding device. Fig. 23-159. Make sure the swinging back is tightly closed. If a device is not available, any flat surface, such as a counter top, would be satisfactory as long as weights can be placed on top of the paper to be padded. Fig. 23-160.

2. Load the jogged paper into the guide edge of the padding device first. Continue to load until the device is full. Fig. 23-161.

3. Apply holding pressure to the paper stack, straighten the padding device, and open the swinging gate. Fig. 23-162.

23-159. *A padding device. Tipping it permits the force of gravity to help hold the paper during loading.*

23-160. *A counter top or any flat surface can be used to pad paper.*

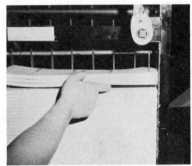

23-161. *Material is loaded into the padding device.*

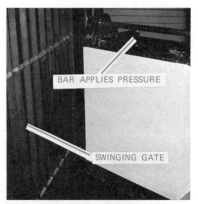

23-162. *Notice how the opened gate exposes the padding edge, thereby simplifying the padding operation.*

23-163. *Apply the padding compound. Use one heavy coat or two thin coats, and cover evenly the entire area to be padded.*

23-164. *Separate the padded strips with a padding knife. The pads can also be laid flat for this operation.*

23-166. *Load the pressure-sensitive paper onto the padding press.*

4. With a brush, apply the padding compound evenly across the entire area to be padded. Let the compound dry as specified by the manufacturer. Fig. 23-163.

5. Remove the padded paper from the padding device, and split each strip apart with a padding knife. Fig. 23-164.

Padding compound for pressure-sensitive paper uses a preferential absorption principle on the two types of pressure-sensitive coatings. The compound is designed to turn both types of coatings into an adhesive without affecting the noncoated area. In other words, when properly collated sets are padded and fanned, a break apart will occur wherever there is a combination of two uncoated surfaces.

The following is a typical method of padding a pressure-sensitive, multiple-part form:

1. Collate the printed parts into sets with the CB paper on top, the CFB paper in the middle and the CF paper on the bottom. (CB is coated on the back. CF is coated on the front. CFB is coated on front and back.)

2. Jog the collated sets to the guide side. Note that the guide edge is opposite the padding edge. Fig. 23-165.

3. Trim off the padding edges to expose fresh coatings.

4. Load collated sets into the tipped padding device with the padding edge first. Fig. 23-166.

5. Apply just enough hold-down pressure to keep the sets from slipping.

6. Straighten the padding device, open the swinging gate, and apply the padding compound with horizontal strokes. Do not use a brush that has been used to pad paper conventionally. Allow to dry as specified by the manufacturer of the compound. Fig. 23-167.

7. Remove the padded material from the padding device, and break it into sets by fanning the edges.

23-165. *Jog the collated sets to the guide edges in a machine jogger.*

23-167. *Apply padding compound.*

REVIEW QUESTIONS

1. Job bindery work deals only with soft-cover books. True or False?
2. What is meant by "in-line" construction of a book?
3. Bindery work is planned after a job has been printed. True or False?
4. One side of a signature may extend past the other for easier opening. What is this extender called?
5. Name the terms defined in the following:
   a. Greatest number of sheets of paper that can be properly handled at one time.
   b. Vibrating a stack of paper to make edges line up.
   c. Getting air between sheets of paper to make it easier to handle.
6. It is best to make parallel folds at right angles to the grain of the paper. True or False?
7. What is the difference between an insert and an outsert signature?
8. What is another word for assembling?
9. Name the types of binding described in the following:
   a. Signatures are side-gathered, skived, then glued.
   b. Signatures are placed inside one another; they straddle the binding device.
   c. Glue is applied to paper before paper is folded into signatures.
   d. Uses sewing methods to bind books.

Chapter 24

Screen Process Printing

Screen process printing is used to reproduce designs and for decoration. Posters, display materials, wrapping paper, and special designs on fabrics are often printed by the screen process. The process is used to print on glass, metal, and plastics, as well as paper. For example, plastic bottles, such as those used for suntan oil, are printed with the screen process. Screen process printing can be used to print halftones and full-color work. Fig. 24-1.

While the process adapts well to the large letters used for display and advertising purposes, it is not suitable for reproduction of large areas of reading material found in books and magazines.

The image carrier in the screen process is a frame with a porous material, such as silk, stretched tightly over it. The design to be printed is cut into a stencil. The areas to be printed are removed, leaving openings in the stencil. The stencil is then fastened to the screen. The screen is placed on the surface to receive the ink image. Ink is placed on the screen and moved across it with a squeegee. The squeegee is a tool with a rubber blade used to remove surface

General Research, Inc.

24-1. Advertising posters printed with the screen process.

ink. The ink is forced through the openings in the screen and the open areas on the stencil. The ink is thus deposited on the printing surface. The screen frame is raised, leaving the ink image on the surface.

TYPES OF SCREENS

Of the many types of screens used, the most common are silk, multifilament polyester, monofilament polyester, nylon, and wire cloth. The common wire cloths in use are stainless steel and copper.

Silk, the original screen fabric, is still widely used. All hand-cut stencils and transfer photostencils will adhere to it.

Multifilament polyesters (Dacron, Terital, and Polylast) are stronger and have a more uniform weave than silk. They are especially useful for textile printing.

Monofilament polyester, nylon, and wire cloth provide a very uniform weave and permit freer ink passage than silk or the multifilament polyester fabric. The major disadvantage is that film stencils adhere poorly to it. Nylon tends to stretch with use and should be stretched on the frame while wet.

Stainless steel wire cloth is preferred for detailed, accurate work. Stainless steel will kink and deform easily, and must be handled carefully. If deformed, it will not recover as well as fabrics. Wire cloth has the advantage of long life and is used for long-run commercial jobs. It should be stretched with mechanical stretchers as it is fastened to the frame.

The size of mesh is indicated by a number. The larger the number, the finer the mesh is. For example, an 8XX mesh has larger openings than a 16XX mesh. The XX means the fabric is "double extra." Double extra fabrics should be used for screen process printing. Common mesh sizes are shown in Fig. 24-2. This chart shows the number of openings per square inch, the size of the openings, and the percent of open area the mesh provides.

The mesh to use depends upon the desired effect wanted on the finished job. The finer meshes give a more uniform ink image. Usually screens above

STENCIL FABRIC COMPARISON CHART

Mesh Counts*					Mesh Openings—Inches*					Percent Open Area*				
XX	A	B	C	D	E	A	B	C	D	E	A	B	C	D	E
6XX	74	74	70	74	70	0.0094	0.0089	0.0094	0.0077	0.0106	47	43	45	34	55
8XX	86	86	90	92	88	0.0077	0.0068	0.0071	0.0071	0.0079	45	34	42	42	48
10XX	109	109	108	110	105	0.0057	0.0049	0.0059	0.0057	0.0065	40	30	43	39	47
12XX	125	125	120	125	120	0.0045	0.0042	0.0055	0.0045	0.0057	32	28	45	30	47
14XX	139	139	138	139	135	0.0038	0.0037	0.0049	0.0043	0.0051	30	26	47	35	47
16XX	157	157	157	157	145	0.0035	0.0032	0.0041	0.0035	0.0047	31	25	41	24	46
18XX	166	170	166	175	165	0.0031	0.0033	0.0037	0.0034	0.0042	31	31	38	34	47
20XX	173	178	185	...	180	0.0030	0.0031	0.0035	...	0.0041	28	29	43	...	47
25XX	200	198	196	200	200	0.0025	0.0027	0.0033	0.0029	0.0034	23	26	44	32	46
...	...	...	230	225	230	...	...	0.0028	0.0022	0.0029	...	...	42	42	46
...	...	...	240	245	250	...	...	0.0026	0.0026	0.0024	...	...	39	38	36
...	...	...	260	260	270	...	...	0.0023	0.0023	0.0021	...	...	36	35	32
...	...	...	283	280	...	...	...	0.0022	0.0021	...	...	...	37	34	...
...	...	...	306	300	...	...	...	0.0019	0.0018	...	...	...	34	29	...
...	...	...	330	330	325	...	...	0.0017	0.0016	0.0017	...	...	30	27	30
...	...	...	380	390	400	...	...	0.0012	0.0011	0.0015	...	...	22	18	36

*FABRIC CODE
XX—Silk & multifilament polyester
A—Silk
B—Multifilament polyester
C—Nylon
D—Monofilament polyester
E—Stainless steel

Atlas Silk Screen Supply Co.

24-2. *Common mesh sizes.*

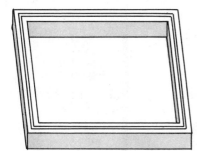

24-3. *A wood screen process frame.*

12XX are used only for fine detail work and the reproduction of halftones.

PREPARATION OF THE FRAME

A rigid, strong screen frame can be made of metal or wood. Fig. 24-3.

The screen material is stretched tightly over the frame. It can be attached by wedging it into the groove on the frame with a screen process cord. The screen may also be stapled or tacked to frames not having grooves.

The size of the frame to use varies with the size of the job to be printed. Since the screen also holds the ink supply, it should extend 2″ to 4″ beyond all sides of the stencil. Fig. 24-4. If the squeegee is to be moved from

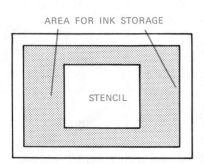

24-4. *The frame should be large enough to allow for ink storage.*

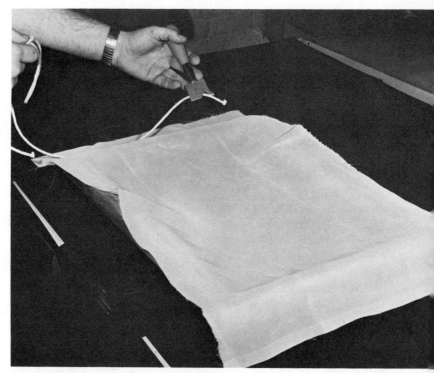

24-5. *The screen is cut several inches larger than the frame. The screen is laid over the frame. The cord is placed in the cord tool.*

24-6. *The cord is pressed into the groove as the screen is pulled tight.*

24-7. *The excess screen is cut off after the screen is secured to the frame. The bottom side of the frame is shown here.*

24-8. *The edge between the frame and the screen is sealed with gummed paper tape. Notice how the tape is notched to form the corner. The top side of the screen is shown here.*

side to side, there must be more area on the sides.

To fasten the screen to the frame:

1. The screen should be 2″ to 4″ larger than the frame. Place the frame on a table, and lay the screen over it. Put the cord in the cord tool. Fig. 24-5.

2. Start fastening the screen to the frame on one of the long sides. The leg on the tool pushes the cord and screen into the groove in the frame. Fig. 24-6.

3. Work the cord in all around the frame. Fig. 24-7.

4. The screen should be free of all wrinkles or looseness, with no slack. Cut off any excess screen. Fig. 24-7.

Lacquer is applied over the edge of the frame where the screen touches it. This helps join the screen to the frame.

Turn the frame over, and place folded, gummed paper tape around the edge. Fig. 24-8. Glue half the strip to the screen and half to the frame. Give a coat of lacquer to the paper strips to preserve them. The screen is now ready to have the stencil adhered to it.

A special tool that looks like pliers can be used for stretching the screen. Fig. 24-9. Another device clamps along the edge of

24-9. *A tool that resembles pliers is used to stretch the screen as it is fastened to the frame.*

the screen and pulls tight an entire edge. Metal frames are available that have built-in screen-stretching devices.

Most new screens made of fabric have some kind of sizing or wax deposit that must be removed before the screen is used. Wet the screen with hot water, and sprinkle a little kitchen cleanser powder on it. Rub lightly with a rag, using a circular motion. Rinse and rub the surface of the screen with your hand to remove all particles of the cleanser. Rinse thoroughly with clear water, and let the screen dry.

If the screen is one that has been used, be certain all traces of ink and the stencil have been dissolved and removed with solvents. Then wash as mentioned for new screens.

MAKING THE STENCIL

The stencil is a sheet of material on which the image to be printed is recorded. There are many different types of stencils, such as knife-cut stencils and presensitized photographic stencils. As stated before, the areas to be printed are removed, leaving openings through which the ink is forced.

KNIFE-CUT STENCILS

The film used is made of two layers. The top layer is a colored transparent film. The bottom layer is a clear plastic sheet. Fig. 24-10. The top layer forms the actual stencil. The bottom layer provides support for the stencil until it is adhered to the screen. The bottom layer is then peeled away, leaving the stencil on the screen.

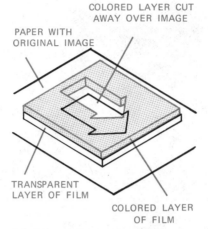

24-10. *Knife-cut stencil film has two layers. The colored layer forms the stencil. The transparent layer is the backing.*

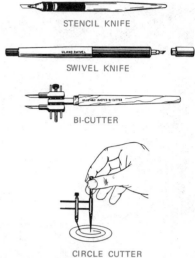

24-11. *Common stencil-cutting tools.*

The original artwork for a knife-cut stencil can be in any form. It can be a pencil, ink, or painted drawing.

Some of the stencil-cutting tools are shown in Fig. 24-11. The basic tool is the stencil knife. There are several kinds available. One type has a swivel blade. Another, the bi-cutter, has two blades. The distance between the blades is adjustable. The bi-cutter is used to cut parallel lines. One type of circle cutter is shown in Fig. 24-11.

To make the stencil, the two-layer film is placed over the artwork. The areas to be removed are outlined with a very sharp knife. The knife must cut through the colored layer but not the clear layer. Practically no pressure is required. After cutting, the areas to be removed are peeled off the clear back sheet. A knife or tweezers can be used. Protect the film from perspiration or grease from the hands. Cover the areas likely to be touched with a plastic sheet.

The stencil is now ready to adhere to the screen. Be certain the colored film is clean. One suggestion is to pick up any particles of loose film and dust with a piece of adhesive tape which has had some of the stickiness reduced. The screen must also be absolutely clean.

The two-layer stencil is placed on the bottom side of the screen with the colored side next to the screen. When you look through the top of the screen, you can see the stencil below. The film must be flat against the screen. It is helpful if the stencil is placed on a piece of glass, which will provide a firm, smooth, flat base. Fig. 24-12.

An adhering liquid is applied to the top of the screen with a soft rag or absorbent cotton. Be certain to use the adhering thinner recommended for the brand of film being used. Gently moisten the entire surface of the film through the screen. Do not press or rub the screen. Make each stroke in the same direction. Fig. 24-13.

Begin the adhering process in the upper left-hand corner of the stencil. Apply adhering liquid in strokes of about 10". Once an area about 10" square has been moistened, dry it. Then proceed down to the next 10-inch-square area, as shown in Fig. 24-14. (NOTE: As a beginner you may find it easier to work in areas 3 or 4 inches square.)

Continue until the entire stencil is adhered. Then quickly wipe off the adhering liquid with a dry rag. The wiping action should be gentle. It is important to use a fan to blow a large volume of air over the screen while adhering. The faster the adhering liquid is removed after applying, the sharper the film edge will be. If the adhering liquid is left on too long, it will burn the edges of the image.

Before peeling off the plastic backing, check to see if the film is dry and adhered properly. If there are irregularities, repeat

RIGHT WRONG

Ulano
24-13. *Gently moisten the film with strokes from left to right. Do not press or rub on the screen.*

the adhering operation after one minute of drying time. Dry the stencil from the top side of the screen with a fan for a few minutes. After it is completely dry, peel off the plastic backing. If it does not come off easily, the film is not completely dry. Fig. 24-15.

After printing, the stencil can be removed from the screen with lacquer thinner. Place the frame with the stencil on top of some newsprint. Wet the top of the screen with lacquer thinner. Fig. 24-16. After the screen has soaked for a few minutes, rub gently with a shop towel and pull away the newsprint. Most of the stencil will be on the paper. Add fresh newsprint and repeat until the entire stencil is dissolved. Then clean the screen with rags and the proper cleaner until the meshes are all open. (The cleaner to use depends on the paint or ink that was used.)

PRESENSITIZED PHOTOGRAPHIC STENCILS

A number of presensitized photographic films are available. These films have the photosensitive coating applied in the factory. When received by the printer, they are ready to use. Basic data for the products of one manufacturer are shown in Fig. 24-17.

Presensitized photographic stencils require finished artwork. The film records all the details of the image to be printed. Therefore the original copy must be

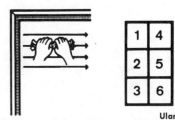

24-14. *Apply adhering liquid in 10" squares, starting at the upper left-hand corner.*

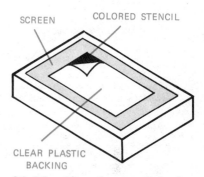

24-15. *After the stencil is dry, peel off the plastic backing.*

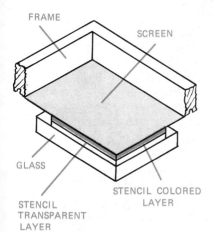

24-12. *When adhering the stencil to the screen, place the stencil on a hard, flat surface, and place the screen on top of it.*

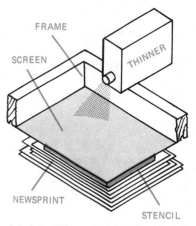

24-16. *When cleaning the stencil, place it on a pile of newsprint. Pour the lacquer thinner on the top side of the screen.*

CHECK CHART "P" ULANO PRESENSITIZED SCREEN PRINTING FOTOFILMS

NAME OF FILM / COLOR OF FILM	RX200 RX300 / RED	XPM2 XPM3 / BLUE	BLUE POLY 2 & 3 / BLUE	SUPER PREP / GREEN	HI-FI GREEN / GREEN	HI-FI RED / RED
2 Mil polyester support	√	√	√	√		
3 Mil polyester support	√	√	√			
5 Mil Vinyl support					√	√
Top-coated to prevent sticking during humid conditions	√	√	√	√	Not needed	Not needed
Sharpest printing	√	√				
Finest details and best half-tone dots	√	√	√			
Best resistance to aggressive inks, solvents and abrasion	√	√				√ *
Long machine runs	√	√				√
Ability to hide tape marks and dirt particles, minimum touch-up				√	√	
Best visibility through finished screen for register setting	√			√	√	√
For permanently flexible screens that must be stored for long periods						√
Resistance to water based inks						With special treatment
Printing on highly polished or slightly tacky surfaces					√	√
For printed circuits, instrument dials, name plates and industrial printing	√	√				√
Adhesion to silk, wire, nylon and polyester	√	√	√	√	√	Best on silk and wire
For poor positives, rough handling and poor housekeeping			√	√	√	

*Not recommended for ketone based inks

24-17. Examples of presensitized, screen-printing films.

exactly the way the printed job is to appear.

The basic steps to make a presensitized photographic stencil are (1) exposing, (2) developing, (3) washing out, and (4) adhering. Fig. 24-18. The following discussion is related to the Ulano presensitized photographic film. When using another brand of film, follow the manufacturer's instructions.

First, a photographic positive copy is made of the original artwork. This positive is then exposed to the presensitized film, which later becomes the stencil. On the developed presensitized film, the dark areas of the artwork wash away, leaving open the spaces needed for the stencil.

Using Ulano Bluepoly-2 and Bluepoly-3 Presensitized Screen Process Films

These are general-purpose polyester-backed films. They are available with a 2- or 3-mil base.

1. Expose the Ulano screen-process film and the photographic positive with a carbon arc light source. Generally, a 35-ampere arc at 30" will make a good film in 1 1/2 minutes. The longer the exposure, the thicker the film is. Try some test exposures to see what length of time gives the best results.

2. The film is developed using special chemicals labeled "A" and "B". Mix one ounce (28 grams) of "A" and 1 1/4 ounces (35 grams) of "B" in one pint (0.5 liter) of water. Shake until chemicals are completely dissolved. Pour this developer in a developing tray. When not in use,

protect the developer from strong light. One tray will last one day. Discard remaining developer every day. It produces a strong gas and should not be stored.

3. Immerse the exposed film in the developer with the film side up for 1 1/2 minutes.

4. Remove the film from the developer, and wash in warm water (92–96° F., or 33–36 °C) until the design is clean. Then wash in cold water.

5. Place the developed film, with the plastic base down, on a flat, hard surface, such as a piece of glass. The glass must be smaller than the inside opening of the screen process frame.

6. Place the screen frame on top of the film, and press the screen lightly against the film. Now cover with a piece of news-

HYDROGEN PEROXIDE MIX

Hydrogen Peroxide Strengths	Mixes For 1 1/2%	
	Water	Hydrogen Peroxide
3%	1 part	1 part
6%	3 parts	1 part
30%	19 parts	1 part
35%	22 parts	1 part

Ulano

24-19. Making a 1 1/2 percent hydrogen peroxide mixture from different strengths.

print, and blot the moisture. Use enough newsprint to remove the water. Allow the film to dry. While it is drying, block out the screen area around the stencil.

7. After the film is dry, peel off the plastic backing sheet. Then wash off any adhesive remaining on the film with benzine or toluol.

8. To remove the film from nylon, polyester, or wire screen, use full-strength laundry bleach. Then rinse the screen with water. The film is removed from a silk screen with water. If any haze is left, apply a small amount of enzymes. Then wash with vinegar to kill the action of the enzymes.

Using Ulanocron RX-200 Presensitized Photostencil Film

A red film with highest resolution, this Ulano film has a wide exposure latitude. It gives excellent results on stainless steel mesh for close tolerance printing as required for printed circuits and dials.

1. Place the artwork next to the plastic support sheet.

2. Expose for 3 minutes at 3,000 footcandles. Generally, good results are achieved using a 35-ampere arc at 30″ for 3 min-

utes, or 110-ampere arc at 48″ for 2 minutes.

3. Develop in 1 1/2 percent hydrogen peroxide for 90 seconds. You can also use Ulano developers "A" and "B", as explained for Bluepoly film. Fig. 24-19 gives directions for making the 1 1/2 percent hydrogen peroxide mix from different strengths of hydrogen peroxide.

4. Wash in warm water (95° F., or 35 °C) and rinse in cold water when the image is clean.

5. Fasten to the screen and dry, as explained for Bluepoly film. Remove traces of adhesive remaining on the film, using toluene or xylene as the solvent.

Using Ulano XPM-2 and XPM-3 Presensitized Film

This film adheres well to all fabrics.

1. Place the artwork next to the plastic support sheet.

2. Expose for 4 minutes at 3,000 footcandles. Generally, good results are obtained using a 35-ampere arc at 30″ for 4 minutes, or 115-ampere arc at 48″ for 2 1/2 minutes.

3. Develop in 1 1/2 percent hydrogen peroxide for 90 seconds.

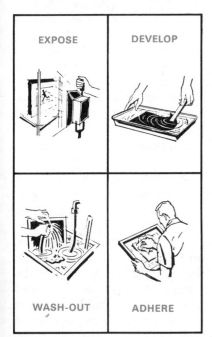

EXPOSE DEVELOP

WASH-OUT ADHERE

Ulano

24-18. How to make a stencil with presensitized film.

4. Wash in warm water (95° F., or 35 °C) and rinse in cold water when clean.

5. Lay the film emulsion side up in an alcohol bath. Make this mixture of one part water to one part alcohol. It is recommended that methyl alcohol be used, but isopropyl or ethyl alcohol will work. Immerse in this bath for 60 seconds, if adhering to wire, and 10 to 15 seconds for nylon, polyester, or silk.

6. Fasten to the screen and dry, as explained for Bluepoly film. Remove traces of adhesive remaining on the film, using toluene or xylene as the solvent.

MASKING THE NONPRINTING AREAS

After the stencil is attached to the screen, the area between the stencil and the frame must be blocked out. The two most com-

STENCIL
SCREEN
STENCIL ON SCREEN

TAPE
PAPER MASK
PAPER MASK IN PLACE

24-20. *A paper mask is taped over the open screen area.*

mon ways of doing this are with a paper mask or a liquid masking material.

Paper masking is satisfactory when a small number of copies are to be printed. The ink will eventually penetrate the paper mask and spot the finished prints. A mask can be made of a heavy bond or kraft paper. It can be applied to the top or bottom of the screen.

To make a mask, cut the paper slightly smaller than the inside of the frame. Place the paper on top of the stencil, and outline the stencil area, which must be open. Make the opening large enough to allow for a layer of tape around the edge of the stencil. Cut the opening in the mask. Position it over the stencil, and secure in place with 3/4″ masking or gummed tape. Fig. 24-20. Be certain all edges are carefully taped so that no ink can penetrate the edges of the mask.

Liquid masking is available with a lacquer base or a water base. If a water-base ink is to be used, the lacquer-base masking liquid is necessary. If a lacquer-base ink is to be used, the water-base masking liquid is necessary. Both are applied in the same manner. They can be brushed on or spread with a cardboard squeegee. It is best to lean the frame against a support so it is on an angle. Fig. 24-21. The masking liquid should be applied to the back, or bottom, of the screen. Two thin coats are usually enough. Allow to dry between coats. Examine the finished job for pinholes, and brush additional masking liquid over any that appear. Permit the mask to dry thoroughly before printing.

LIQUID MASK

24-21. *Place the frame at an angle when you apply a liquid mask.*

PRINTING A SCREEN PROCESS JOB

A screen printing press has a flat printing surface, register guides, a screen frame, a means of feeding stock, inking, and working the paint through the stencil to the material to be printed. The following discussion is related to a hand-operated, screen process press. Mechanical presses are discussed later in this chapter.

REGISTRATION

The screen frame to be used is fastened to the flat printing surface. The frame is hinged so that it can be lifted. It can be removed from the table by pulling the hinge pins. Fig. 24-22. The clamp is adjustable to hold frames up to 3″ thick. Usually it is advantageous to place some type of spacing material on the bottom side of the frame opposite the hinges. This material will

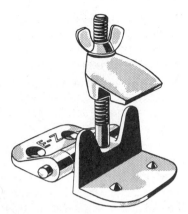

24-22. *Hinge for a screen process frame.*

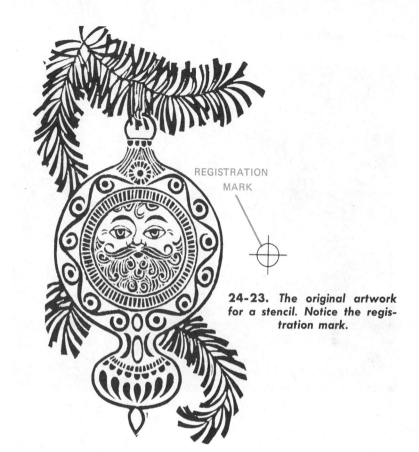

REGISTRATION MARK

24-23. *The original artwork for a stencil. Notice the registration mark.*

hold the screen slightly above the surface of the paper upon which it is to print, and thus help keep the screen from sticking to the paper and spoiling the print.

The original artwork usually has registration marks in each corner. These are small crosses. Fig. 24-23. The artwork is placed on the table beneath the screen in the position in which the job is to be printed. A clear plastic sheet can be placed over the artwork to protect it. This material is taped to the table so it will not move.

SETTING THE GUIDES

The guides now are set. The guides position each sheet so the image is printed on the paper in the same position as on the original artwork. For most work three guides are used. Two are placed on the front edge of the sheet and one on the side. Fig. 24-24. On wood tables the guides are usually glued to it. Guides can be heavy cardboard, plastic, or metal strips. If the press uses a vacuum table to hold the sheets, the guides are glued to the top of the table.

24-24. *The paper upon which the image is to be printed is positioned beneath the screen. Paper guides are used to position each sheet for printing.*

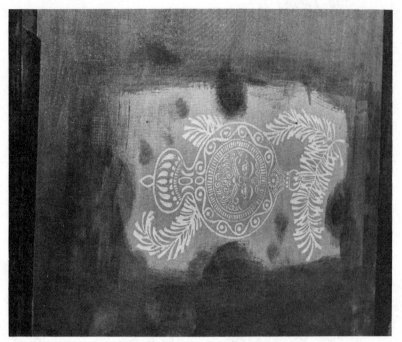

24-25. *The screen areas around the stencil are sealed to keep the ink from going through them.*

moves the squeegee across the screen. Fig. 24-26. While this requires little pressure, it takes practice to learn to do it properly. Now the screen is lifted by a spring. Fig. 24-27.

The second person, the racker, removes the sheet and places it on the drying rack or in a mechanical dryer. While this is being done, the operator of the squeegee is placing another sheet on the table, and the cycle repeats.

The squeegee operator only passes the squeegee across the stencil once. If the print was made with a pass from left to right, the next pass is made from right to left.

A quantity of paint is placed on the screen. The squeegee operator must control the paint and keep it a uniform thickness. The

ADHERING THE STENCIL

Next the stencil is positioned over the artwork. It is carefully registered, and the screen lowered on it. The stencil is then adhered to the back of the screen. All nonprinting areas in the screen are blocked with lacquer. Fig. 24-25. Generally, the register marks on the stencil are not blocked with lacquer until a few proof sheets are run. If the proofs are correct, the register marks are closed with lacquer, and the press is ready to print the job.

INKING AND PRINTING

The press is usually operated by two people. One, the person who operates the squeegee, places a sheet of stock on the table against the guides. The screen is lowered, and he or she

24-26. *Lower the screen on the paper, and squeegee a layer of ink across the stencil.*

24-27. After the ink is passed over the stencil, lift the frame and remove the printed sheet.

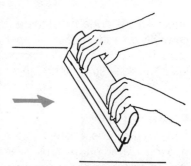

24-29. The two-handed squeegee is also slanted in the direction of the stroke.

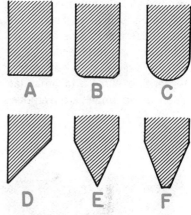

A—SQUARE EDGE
B—SQUARE EDGE WITH ROUNDED CORNERS
C—ROUND EDGE
D—SINGLE—SIDED BEVEL EDGE
E—DOUBLE—SIDED BEVEL EDGE
F—DOUBLE—SIDED BEVEL EDGE, FLAT POINT

24-30. The most commonly used shapes for squeegee blades.

number of sheets that can be printed depends upon coverage required by the stencil openings.

One-hand and two-hand squeegees are shown in Figs. 24-28 and 24-29. The squeegee is slanted slightly in the direction of the stroke.

There are several types of rubber edges for squeegees. Fig. 24-30. The square edge is used for printing on flat stock. The square edge with slightly rounded corners is used when a heavier deposit of ink is needed. It is also used to print light colors on dark backgrounds and to print with fluorescent inks. The single bevel is used to print on glass. The double-sided bevel edge is used to print on round or uneven surfaces. It is also used to print delicate textile designs. The round edge is used for textile printing where a heavy deposit of ink is wanted. The double-sided bevel with a flat point is used to print on ceramic objects.

When the rubber edge shows signs of wear, it must be sharp-

24-28. The one-handed squeegee is slanted in the direction it is pushed.

631

ened. This is done by rubbing it carefully on a sheet of sandpaper on a flat surface. Be certain to keep the edge straight and in its original shape.

CLEANUP

When the job is finished, waste paper is placed on the table. The ink left on the screen is removed by scraping it with cardboard strips. Next, the screen is cleaned with soft rags and a proper cleaner. The cleaner to use depends upon the paint used. An explosion-proof screen washer is shown in Fig. 24-31.

Oil base paints, poster paints, enamels, and fluorescent paints can be removed with kerosene or turpentine. Vinyl and other lacquer compounds are removed with lacquer thinners. Tempera water-base paints are removed with water.

The screen can be stored with the stencil left on it if the job will be rerun at some future time. The stencil can be removed from the screen by using the proper solvents, discussed earlier in the section on making stencils.

MULTIPLE-COLOR SCREEN PROCESS

The processes covered so far in this chapter have been for one-color work. A stencil is made, adhered to a screen, and is ready to print. Many screen process jobs require the use of two or more colors. The basic process is just the same as previously discussed, except a separate screen is made for each color. The major problem is to get the screens in proper register for printing the colors.

Following is a suggested plan for preparing screens for multi-color work.

1. Draw register marks on the original artwork. As stated before, these are small crosses located in each corner of the sheet. Fig. 24-23.

2. Decide in which order the colors are to be printed. This decision requires some experience and judgment. Basic things to remember are:

* The basic paints are opaque and transparent. Opaque paint will cover any color below it. Transparent paints will not cover other colors, but tend to change their color. A transparent yellow over a transparent blue will give a green area.
* When using opaque paints, print the background and largest areas first.
* Print lighter opaque colors before the darker. Remember, however, a light, opaque area can be printed on a dark background when necessary.

3. Prepare the stencil for the first color. Details vary with the type of stencil. The basic types were explained earlier in this chapter. Be certain to number the screen, and identify the color it is to print. For example, if the first screen to be printed is to use a blue color, it is numbered #1-blue.

Often colors on a design meet. It is a common printing practice to allow the darker color to overlap the lighter color. To do this, the stencil for the lighter color is

24-31. A screen-washing unit.

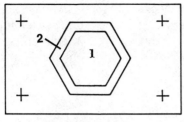

ORIGINAL DESIGN

NO. 1 COLOR   NO. 2 BLACK

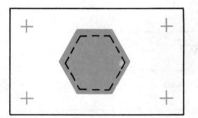

STENCIL FOR NO. 1 COLOR
SHOWING EXTRA FOR OVERLAP

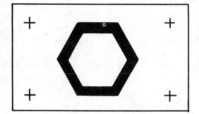

STENCIL FOR NO. 2 COLOR
EXACT SIZE

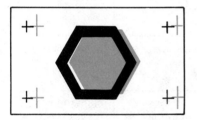

THIS HAPPENS WHEN PRINTED
OFF—REGISTER

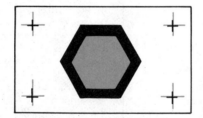

FINISHED JOB PRINTED IN
GOOD REGISTER

24-32. *Each color in a multicolor job requires a separate stencil. It is important to accurately register all the stencils.*

made slightly larger than the area wanted. Usually 1/16″ is enough. The lighter area is printed first. The stencil for the darker area is made true size. It is printed next. It will overlap the light color and give a clean edge between them. Fig. 24-32.

4. Place the stencil on the screen-printing table. Position it with the register marks on the table. Lower the screen on the stencil, and adhere it to the screen.

5. Finish preparing the screen, and then print the first color. Let it dry.

6. Prepare another screen for the second color. Follow the steps just mentioned. Of critical importance is the positioning of the second stencil on the print-

ing table so it matches the register marks used for the first stencil.

Any number of colors can be printed. Each will print in the intended place if the register marks are carefully located before adhering the stencil to the screen.

Remember that an additional color should not be printed until the color printed before it is dry. Drying time varies with the type of paint used.

PAINTS, LACQUERS, INKS, AND OTHER PRINTING COMPOUNDS

The compounds used in screen process printing are made of two basic parts, the pigment and the vehicle. The *pigment* is a finely ground coloring matter. There are many different pigments. The one selected depends upon the type of compound. Fillers are often added with the pigments. They do not add color but are used to extend the volume of the ink.

The *vehicle* is the liquid part of the printing compound. It consists of a volatile solvent and some type of binder. The volatile solvent varies with the type of printing compound. It provides the compound with the capability of flow necessary for printing. The solvent evaporates after the job is printed. The binder (usually an oil, resin, or gum substance) remains with the pigment on the printed surface. It forms a film around the pigment particles, keeping them adhered to the surface of the material.

Following are general characteristics of some commonly used

633

printing compounds. Details concerning drying time, thinners, washup fluids, and types of stencils to use are given in Fig. 24-33. These are only examples. Each manufacturer has specific recommendations, and they should be followed.

Exterior enamels and screen process enamels are used for interior and exterior applications on metal, masonite, wood, and

COMMONLY USED SCREEN PROCESS PRINTING COMPOUNDS

	Drying Time	Thinner	Washup	Stencil
Exterior Enamels and Screen Process Enamels	Air-dry 4 to 6 hours, or oven-dry 150° F. for 30 minutes	Mineral spirits	Mineral spirits	Any type
Screening Lacquer	Air-dry 20 to 40 minutes	As recommended by manufacturer	Lacquer thinner	Photographic or lacquerproof
Transparent Process Enamels	Air-dry 6 hours	Mineral spirits	Mineral spirits	Any type
Gloss Acrylic Colors	Air-dry 1 hour; can heat-dry up to 150° F.	As recommended by manufacturer	As recommended by manufacturer	Water soluble
Screen Process Ink	Air-dry 30 minutes or apply forced heat a few seconds	Mineral spirits or special manufacturer's thinner	Mineral spirits or special manufacturer's thinner	Any type
Vinyl Ink	Air-dry 20 to 40 minutes	Vinyl thinner	Vinyl thinner or vinyl screen wash	Photographic or water-soluble film
Mylar Inks	Air-dry 20 minutes to 2 hours, or use forced air up to 150° F.	As recommended by manufacturer	As recommended by manufacturer	Photographic or hand-cut, water-soluble film
Baking Enamel	Varies with temperature: 500° F.—1 minute 450° F.—1 1/2 minutes 360° F.—6 minutes 325° F.—12 minutes 275° F.—30 minutes	As recommended by manufacturer	As recommended by manufacturer	Any direct-emulsion film or film that is lacquerproof
Glass Ink	Heat-cured	As recommended by manufacturer	As recommended by manufacturer	Any type
Textile Inks	Air-dry 30 minutes, or heat-dry 275° F. 5 minutes	As recommended by manufacturer	Mineral spirits or as recommended by manufacturer	Any type
Nylon Inks	Heat-dry 300° F. 3 minutes, or air-dry 15 minutes	As recommended by manufacturer	Mineral spirits	Recommend direct photo stencil

24-33. *General characteristics of screen process printing compounds.*

other rigid and semirigid materials. They print well on glass, cardboard, and plastics. They dry to a hard, glossy finish.

There are several *screening lacquers* available. Some are designed for use on fabrics, leather, wood, and paper. Others work well on plastics, metal, glass, and paper.

Transparent process enamels are used on materials such as foil, metallic paper, metalized plastic, and metal. The colors, due to their transparency, appear rich and vibrant when printed on transparent plastic or glass. Unusual effects can be created by printing one color over another.

Gloss acrylic colors are designed to print on acrylics, polystyrene, butyrates, rigid vinyls, and heat-cured plastics. They are available in opaque and transparent colors.

Screen process ink is used to print indoor displays on paper or cardboard. It can also be used on fabrics and wallboard. These inks are widely used for posters, streamers, and banners. They will permit a job to be die-cut and folded after printing. They are available in flat and gloss finish.

Vinyl inks are designed for printing on vinyl film and other vinyl finishes. They are available in flat and gloss. The gloss vinyl color can be printed on flat stock that is to be vacuum-formed after printing.

Mylar inks are designed to print on untreated mylar and other polyester films. They can be overprinted with other types of inks. Be certain to wash up immediately after running the job because mylar inks are difficult to remove from the screen after they have dried. They are available in opaque and transparent color. These inks print in good detail; fine lines and halftones will be of good quality.

Baking enamel is used on appliances, automotive trim, metal signs, and other applications requiring a tough, chemical-resistant film. Enamel must be baked to dry completely. It will permit parts to be screen printed flat and then formed to their final shape.

Glass inks are made with an epoxy base. They are designed for printing on glass that is subject to moisture, high humidity, or immersion in water. They offer resistance to acids, alkalies, solvents, abrasion, salt spray, and thermal shock. They are prepared by mixing a precise amount of catalyst into the color one-half hour before use. The amount of catalyst is prescribed by the manufacturer.

Textile inks adhere to any fabic. When dry, they leave the material flexible. They are colorfast to washing after they are heat-treated. The colors may be overprinted to obtain different secondary colors. Since the colors are transparent, they work best over white or light-colored fabrics.

Special heavily pigmented paints are available for printing on heavy materials, such as pennants. Since they are opaque, the light colors print over dark materials.

Nylon inks are designed to print on nylon, taffeta, rayon, and acetate fabrics. They are colorfast to washing after they are heat-treated. They do not stiffen the fabric. Nylon inks are opaque and can be used over dark-colored fabrics.

There are many other special compounds available for screen process printing. Special resists are used for printed circuits in the electronics industry. They resist the acid used to etch printed circuits. There are ceramic printing vehicles for use on china and pottery. A silver ink is available for printing areas needing to conduct electricity. The areas can be soldered. Adhesives are available that can be screen printed for jobs that require flocking. Fluorescent inks absorb the ultraviolet energy of sunlight and artificial light. They tend to glow as if they had a light source behind them. Metallic inks dry with a smooth surface. They retain their metallic luster for a long time.

MECHANICAL PRESSES AND EQUIPMENT

The basic procedures for screen process printing on mechanical flatbed and cylinder presses are much the same as those described for the hand-operated press. They do offer considerable accuracy and require very accurate setup of the screen and guides.

Fig. 24-34 shows a flatbed press designed to print on 48" × 84" steel sheets. The sheets are hand-fed at the right end of the machine. The press automatically registers, prints, and ejects the sheet. A conveyor can be installed to carry away the sheets. This particular press prints sheets that will then be formed into 30- and 55-gallon steel drums.

24-34. *This screen printing machine prints on 48" × 84" steel sheets. They are then formed into 30-gallon and 55-gallon drums. The sheets are hand-fed into the machine.*

A high-speed, cylinder screen process press is shown in Fig. 24-35. It is designed to print packages, signs, and displays. This press is made in a variety of sizes. The smallest handles work up to 11" × 12". The largest will print sheets up to 44" × 64". They will print heavy solid areas, do fine line work, and print halftones. They will print on rigid and semirigid paper, cover stock, sheet plastics, and lightweight cardboard.

The method of operation is shown in Fig. 24-36. The revolving cylinder is perforated and has a vacuum. The vacuum holds and moves the sheet as it contacts the perforations. The squeegee is stationary during the printing cycle. The screen and cylinder are reciprocal in action so that the stock is moved forward at the same speed as the screen. The stock and the stencil touch only on a straight line be-

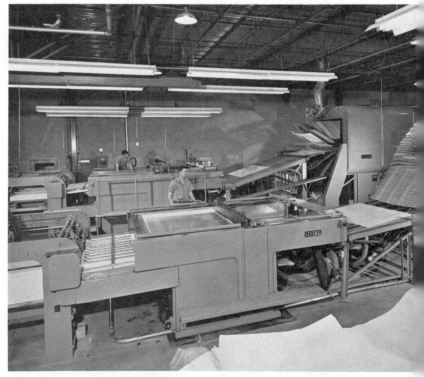

24-35. *A high-speed, cylinder screen process printing press. It is used to print packages, signs, and displays. On the right end it feeds into a dryer. See Fig. 24-37 for a photo of the dryer.*

636

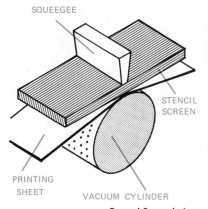

SQUEEGEE

STENCIL
SCREEN

PRINTING
SHEET

VACUUM CYLINDER

General Research, Inc.

24-36. *The cylinder-type, screen process printing cycle.*

General Research, Inc.

24-37. *An enclosed-chamber wicket dryer. It speeds the production of screen process printing.*

neath the squeegee. After each impression, the squeegee lifts up, and the screen moves back to the starting position.

This press has a split-fountain printing feature. Several colors can be run at the same time in one screen. The color splits can be run as close as 1/2″ apart.

A screen process wicket dryer, Fig. 24-37, can be connected in-line with the press shown in Fig. 24-35. It can use room-temperature, high-volume forced air or a carefully controlled higher temperature. This type of dryer permits the printed sheet to recapture the normal moisture in the pressroom. This minimizes warping, shrinking, curling, and registration problems.

Another type is a high-velocity, air jet dryer, which pulls 100 percent fresh air into the dryer and expels all the evaporated solvents out of the machine. Fig. 24-38. The sheets are fed flat

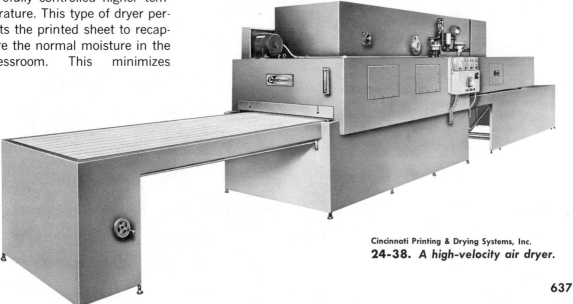

Cincinnati Printing & Drying Systems, Inc.

24-38. *A high-velocity air dryer.*

on a conveyor into the drying cabinet.

A continuous textile screen printer will print 1,500 yards per hour with a repetitive pattern 72″ long. Fig. 24-39.

There are many other types of screen process presses. One is designed to print on cylindrical objects. Fig. 24-40. The screen always remains horizontal. It will print on objects up to 8″ in diameter and 12″ long. It can be adjusted to print on objects as small as a pencil.

The object to be printed rests on rollers. It is raised until it almost touches the screen. The squeegee is stationary and touches the screen directly above the high point on the cylindrical object. To print, the squeegee is pushed down slightly. The screen is moved from one side to the other, and prints the image on the revolving cylindrical object.

Precision Screen Machines, Inc.

24-39. *The in-feed end of a continuous textile screen printer. It will print 1,500 yards per hour, repeating a design 72″ long. It will print 200 yards per hour, repeating a design 120″ long.*

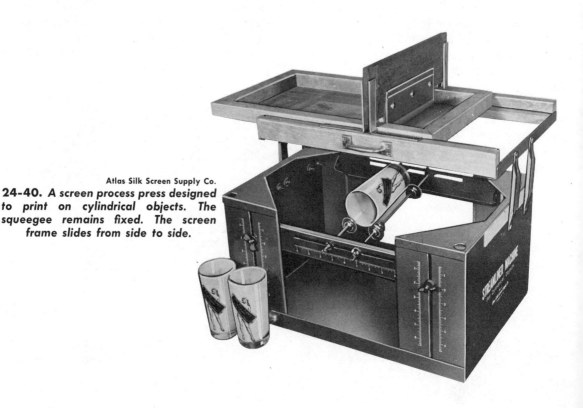

Atlas Silk Screen Supply Co.

24-40. *A screen process press designed to print on cylindrical objects. The squeegee remains fixed. The screen frame slides from side to side.*

REVIEW QUESTIONS

1. What fabric was used originally for screen printing?
2. A 12XX mesh has smaller openings than a 20XX mesh. True or False?
3. When making knife-cut stencils, the knife must cut through both layers of the film. True or False?
4. Presensitized photographic stencils require finished artwork. True or False?
5. Using a paper mask is one way to block out the area between the stencil and the frame. Name another.
6. When screen printing, pass the squeegee across the stencil four times, once from each side. True or False?
7. Name the types of ink described in the following:
   a. Will adhere to any fabric; colors are transparent.
   b. Used for indoor displays; permits a job to be die-cut and folded.
   c. Made with an epoxy base; resistant to acids and alkalies.

Chapter 25 — Paper

HOW PAPER IS MADE

The manufacture of paper involves two major processes: (1) producing the pulp and (2) manufacturing the paper. The pulp-producing process includes debarking, chipping, pulping, bleaching, beating, refining, adding nonfibrous ingredients, and cleaning the pulp. The manufacturing of paper includes forming the paper, producing watermarks, removing water, drying, and finishing the paper.

While there are many materials which go into the making of paper, wood is the basic raw material. It takes years for trees to grow large enough to be used for pulp. To maintain a continual supply, the paper companies operate tree farms. They plant seedlings and care for them through the years. When the trees are large enough, they are cut and shipped to the pulp mill. Fig. 25-1.

In addition to wood, paper-making companies use large amounts of sulfur, magnesium, quick lime, salt cake, caustic soda, chlorine, and starch. A mill uses a lot of electrical power and heat and requires a large fresh-water supply.

RECYCLED PAPER

Recycled paper is waste paper that has been reclaimed and used to produce new products. The federal government has issued the following statement about recycled paper. "The various paper stocks shall contain minimum specified percentages, by weight, of fibers reclaimed from solid waste or waste collected as a result of a manufacturing process but shall not include those materials generated from and reused within a plant as part of the papermaking process."

High-grade waste paper is recycled into the manufacture of fine printing papers. Low-grade waste paper is recycled into corrugated board and building board. Old newspapers can be

The Mead Corp.

25-1. Typical scene at a paper mill's wood yard.

recycled into the production of newsprint.

PRODUCTION OF PULP

The manufacture of paper depends upon an adequate supply of pulp. Pulp fibers are obtained from wood, woody fibrous materials, and reclaimed from products made of these materials.

The nonwoody materials used include cotton, flax, hemp, jute, sugar cane (bagasse), esparto (long, coarse grass), and various straws. The wood pulp sources are divided between *softwoods* (coniferous) and *hardwoods* (deciduous). The hardwood trees include poplar, gum, beech, maple, birch, and chestnut. Softwood trees include pine, fir, spruce, and hemlock. Reclaimed pulp fibers come from rags and recycled paper.

All paper fibers are made of a compound called *cellulose* $(C_6H_{10}O_5)$. This compound makes up the general structural framework of plants and wood. Cellulose is found in varying amounts in different materials. Cotton is about 90 percent cellulose, wood 60 percent, and straw 30 percent. Manufacture is economically possible only when the fiber is low in cost, in large supply, and available year around. The fiber must have proper length, and the plant must render sufficient fiber for the bulk used.

Wood is the principal source of paper fibers. Besides cellulose, wood contains lignin and small amounts of minerals, resins, and oils. Lignin serves as a binder and support for the cellulose fibers of woody plants. Wood usually contains 53 to 64 percent

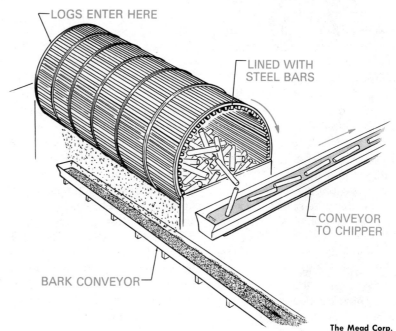

25-2. *Debarking drum. Bark is burned for fuel.*

The Mead Corp.

cellulose and 18 to 30 percent lignin.

DEBARKING

The logs are taken from the storage areas at the mill to the debarking area. Usually they are moved on a conveyor or in a water trough. The bark is removed by rotating in a drum, or by hydraulic water pressure. A debarking drum unit is shown in Fig. 25-2. It is lined with steel bars which rub the logs clean. Any logs which are not cleanly debarked are put through the drum a second time.

In a hydraulic debarker the log is turned, and high-pressure jets of water strip off the bark. Pressure is in the range of 1,500 to 2,000 pounds per square inch.

CHIPPING AND GRINDING

Logs are ground when used for mechanical pulping and chipped when used for chemical pulping

processes. Grinding the log produces pulp directly. Fig. 25-3. Chipping reduces the log to a size that can be chemically processed to make pulp.

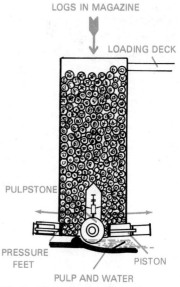

25-3. *Magazine grinder for mechanical pulping.*

When preparing wood for chemical pulping, the debarked logs are carried by conveyor to the chipper. A chipper is a machine which cuts up the log into chips about one inch long. It has a large disk which has knives fastened to it. The log drops into a trough which feeds it against the disk at a 45-degree angle. It takes just a few seconds to cut up a five-foot log.

The chips are passed over several screens which sort out oversize chips. These are sent to a rechipper. Sawdust and undersize chips are moved to furnaces to be used as fuel. The proper size chips are moved to a storage area for chemical pulping.

PULPING

There are three general pulping methods: mechanical, chemical, and mechanical-chemical combinations. The pulping process reduces the chips to their fibers. It is the fibers which are used to make paper.

Mechanical Pulping

The mechanical pulping process uses a grinder to reduce logs to fibers. Fig. 25-4. The logs leave the debarker, are cut to length, and flow to the grinder. The logs are held to the grindstone by hydraulic pressure. The grindstone tears the fibers from the logs. The fibers mix with water spray, which is played on the grindstone.

Coarse stones make a coarse pulp, while finer grit stones produce fine pulp. The fibers are made up of fiber bundles, single fibers, and *fines,* which are broken or shattered fibers. Fines provide filler between the fiber bundles and help make a uniform sheet. Since lignin is part of the ground fibers, papers made from this pulp are very opaque.

The grinding process forms pulp *slurry.* The slurry is passed over a series of screens. Pieces of wood and slivers are removed and the good pulp is sent to a cleaning unit. This pulp is called groundwood pulp. The process uses about 90 to 95 percent of the log. Considerable electrical power is needed to operate a groundwood mill. These mills are economical only where there is low-cost electrical power. However, this process is less expensive than chemical pulping.

Chemical Pulping

There are several chemical pulping methods in use. Basically, they all have one common goal: to separate chemically the chips into fibers and remove the lignin. A flow diagram for a typical chemical pulp mill is shown in Fig. 25-5.

Chemical pulping uses the chips produced in the chipping process. It dissolves the lignin which binds the fibers together, thus separating them. This is done in a digester. Here the chips are placed with chemicals, such as caustic soda and sodium sulfite, to remove the lignin. These form the cooking liquor. The mixture is heated by adding live steam directly into the digester. Another way to add heat is to pump the liquor through a heat exchanger.

When the chips are cooked, the pressure in the digester is released. The pulped chips are moved to a blow tank. From the blow tank the pulp is washed and screened. This removes the cooking chemicals and the dissolved noncellulose materials. During the cooking process, turpentine and other volatile substances are distilled. These are sometimes recovered as a by-product.

The unbleached pulps are brown in color. They are used for wrapping paper and bags. Bleached chemical pulps have an almost unlimited use in production of paper of many qualities.

Mechanical-Chemical Pulping

The combination of chemical and mechanical pulping treats the wood chips under pressure before pulping. The chips are soaked in a sodium sulfite solu-

FEED PISTON
PRESSURE FOOT
PULPSTONE
CYLINDER
WOOD HOPPER
PULP AND WATER

25-4. Hydraulic piston in continuous-feed grinder.

CHIPS FROM CHIPPER

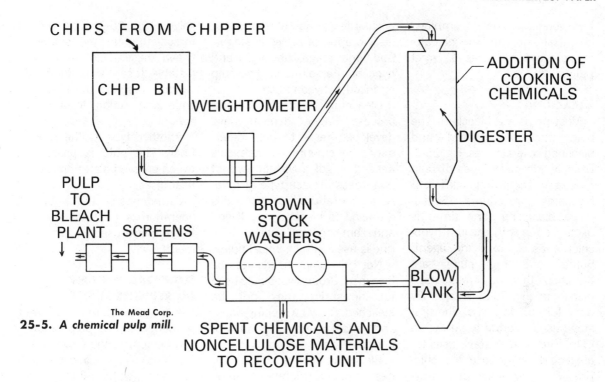

CHIP BIN

WEIGHTOMETER

ADDITION OF
COOKING
CHEMICALS

DIGESTER

PULP
TO
BLEACH
PLANT

SCREENS

BROWN
STOCK
WASHERS

BLOW
TANK

The Mead Corp.
25-5. *A chemical pulp mill.*

SPENT CHEMICALS AND
NONCELLULOSE MATERIALS
TO RECOVERY UNIT

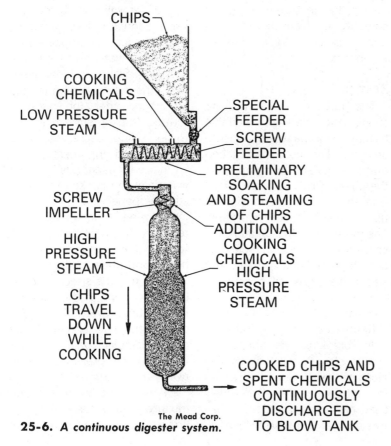

CHIPS

COOKING
CHEMICALS
LOW PRESSURE
STEAM

SPECIAL
FEEDER
SCREW
FEEDER
PRELIMINARY
SOAKING
AND STEAMING
OF CHIPS

SCREW
IMPELLER

HIGH
PRESSURE
STEAM

ADDITIONAL
COOKING
CHEMICALS
HIGH
PRESSURE
STEAM

CHIPS
TRAVEL
DOWN
WHILE
COOKING

COOKED CHIPS AND
SPENT CHEMICALS
CONTINUOUSLY
DISCHARGED
TO BLOW TANK

The Mead Corp.
25-6. *A continuous digester system.*

tion in containers under pressure. Fig. 25-6. This softens the chips and makes them easier to press and grate into pulp. This is especially helpful with hardwoods. Hardwoods are difficult to pulp mechanically.

A similar process called chemi-ground soaks the log in a strong soda solution to soften it.

The semichemical process is another way to reduce chips. The chips are pressure cooked in any of the cooking liquors to remove some of the lignin. The partially digested chips are sent through a rotary grater, called an attrition mill. It separates the chips into fiber bundles.

In all of these methods, the chemical and mechanical pulping processes have been combined. This produces longer, stronger fibers than the mechanical groundwood process. It also makes it easier to pulp hardwoods. The combined chemical and mechanical pulping process produces a larger pulp yield.

BLEACHING

Most pulps are bleached. The pulp may be washed and bleached several times. Fig. 25-7. Each of the main types of pulp requires somewhat different bleaching procedures. Single-stage bleaching (one time) is usually done with calcium hypochlorite as an oxidizing agent. Sulfite and rag pulps are bleached this way. Multistage bleaching, Fig. 25-8, is generally done for sulfate pulps. The first stage uses chlorine to purify the pulp. The second stage uses an alkaline to neutralize the chlorine. The third stage uses a hy-

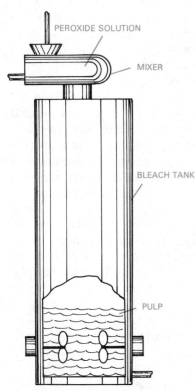

25-7. A bleach tank.

pochlorite solution to remove the discoloration of previous stages. Additional stages are alkali and hypochlorite solutions. The pulp is rinsed between stages.

Bleaching is a highly technical process. Paper chemists have developed tests to help determine the amount of chemicals needed to get a certain level of brightness in each type of pulp. As a general practice, peroxides are used to bleach groundwood and semichemical pulps. Chlorine is used with chemical pulps.

Not all pulp needs to be bleached. Groundwood pulp used for newsprint may not be bleached. Brown wrapping paper and paperboard pulp is not bleached.

Bleaching changes the brightness of paper. Brightness can be tested by instruments which compare the reflection from a paper or pulp to established standards.

BEATING

The purpose of beating is to change the fibers to a suitable formation for the type of paper to be made. The mechanical action of the beater shortens and splits the fibers. Tiny fibers are raised from the surface and ends of the fiber. This is called *hydration.* The more the pulp is beaten, the shorter the fibers will become and the more dense, hard, and strong the paper will become.

REFINING

Refiners cut and hydrate the pulp, breaking the fibers into smaller strands called fibrils. The stock passes through the refiner in a continuous flow. One widely used refiner is a jordan. It has two conical elements which re-

volve. Fig. 25-9. The pulp is forced through the space between these. This space is adjustable. It can be set to produce various results, from a light, squeezing action to a cutting action.

Another type is the disk refiner. The pulp is passed between grooved plates on two vertical disks.

Sometimes the beating operation is omitted, and only the refiner is used for fiber treatment.

NONFIBROUS PAPER INGREDIENTS

A number of materials must be added to the pulp before it can be sent to the papermaking machine. Since cellulose is a hydrophilic (water-uniting) material, paper will absorb moisture like a sponge unless something stops the action. Compounds like rosin repel water and are known as *sizing.* Sizing is added either when the pulp is beaten (engine sizing) or after the paper is formed (tub or surface sizing). Rosin sizing decreases paper strength and brightness.

Unsized paper is termed waterleaf and is used for things such as paper towels. Light sizing, termed *slack,* is used in letterpress paper. Heavy sizing is termed *hard* and is used in bonds and offset papers.

Paper may be sized internally by mixing rosin in the pulp during beating. External sizing is done in the dryer end of the machine. Sizing is rolled on the surface in a size press located between the drying rollers.

Fillers are added to the pulp mixture (called furnish) to improve the texture and plug

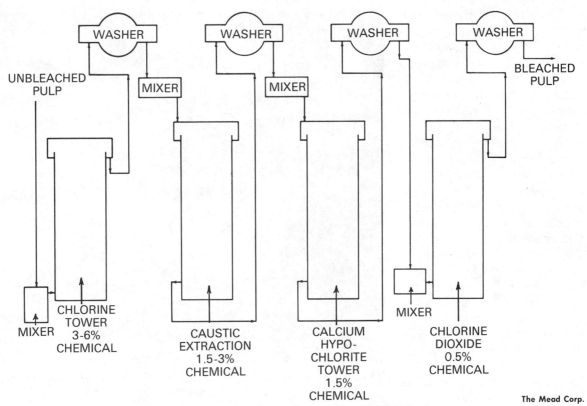

UNBLEACHED
PULP

WASHER   WASHER   WASHER   WASHER

BLEACHED
PULP

MIXER   MIXER

MIXER

CHLORINE
TOWER
3-6%
CHEMICAL

CAUSTIC
EXTRACTION
1.5-3%
CHEMICAL

CALCIUM
HYPO-
CHLORITE
TOWER
1.5%
CHEMICAL

MIXER

CHLORINE
DIOXIDE
0.5%
CHEMICAL

The Mead Corp.

25-8. *Flow diagram for typical multistage bleach plant.*

25-9. *A jordan engine, or refiner.*

spaces between the fibers. Clay, calcium carbonate, and titanium dioxide are commonly used fillers. These are "loaded" into the pulp, to about 30 percent of the total volume. These pigments help achieve maximum paper smoothness, increase opacity, and reduce "strike through" of the ink.

Coloring is added to the furnish in the form of acid and direct dyes of mineral or synthetic pigments. Acid dyes show a preference for groundwood pulp and dislike bleached pulp. Direct dyes prefer pure cellulose and tend to dye most where they first come in contact with the pulp. Mineral pigments are low in dyeing ability and seldom used.

Most of the other substances

placed in the furnish are called additives. These could include fluorescent dyes and tinting colors to aid in brightness, and binders in the form of corn and potato starches. *Binders* are adhesives used to fasten pulp and furnish together.

After the mechanical or chemical pulp has been bleached, beaten, and furnished with sizing, fillers, and coloring, it is placed in a large tank, call a *stuff chest*. The solution, or *stock,* is further diluted with water and sent through a jordan headbox refiner. This engine shortens and hydrates the paper fibers. Additional water is added to reduce the solid content to about four percent. From the jordan the stock is sent to the papermaking machine headbox. Fig. 25-10. At this point the fibers account for about one-half of one percent of the solution. The stock is poured on the revolving wire through a gate, called a *slice.* The amount of solution matches the wire speed to maintain even paper formation.

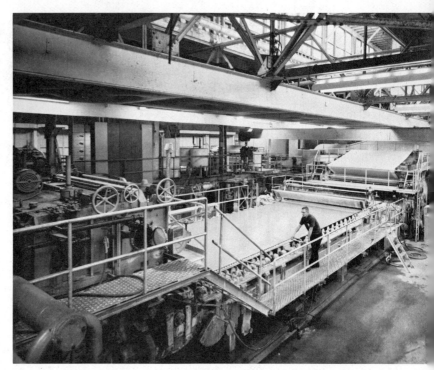

25-10. *The headbox is on the left-hand side of this papermaking machine.*

CLEANING

Before the pulp is fed to the paper machine, it is cleaned. It can be screened or cleaned with a pressure drop cleaner. The screen is a mechanical method of removing fiber clumps, undercooked wood chips, and other foreign matter. The pressure drop cleaner rotates the pulp at high speed. The unwanted lumps and materials are heavier than the fibers. The pulp enters near the top. The swirling pulp moves down to the bottom of the cleaner. The inner spiraling column moves toward the top and is removed. The lumps and un-

wanted material are too heavy to move to the top and are removed at the bottom.

A continuous metering system that carries the pulp from the refiners to the machine chest supplying the paper machine is shown in Fig. 25-11.

MANUFACTURING THE PAPER

Modern paper machines are very large. They require huge buildings and extensive power and utility facilities. See Fig. 25-12, which shows paper being formed on a fourdrinier paper machine.

FORMING THE PAPER

After the pulp is properly processed and all additives have been blended, it is stored in the *ma-*

chine chest where it is further diluted. Fig. 25-11. This diluted pulp is pumped to a *machine regulating box* that controls the flow to the machine. The pulp is again diluted with water which has some paper solids in it. The pulp is then passed through screens to remove lumps. This screened pulp enters the headbox on the fourdrinier machine. Fig. 25-12. This is called the wet end of the paper machine. The headbox agitates the pulp and spreads it on the *wire,* an endless belt of woven wire. The pulp is spread on this wire belt, forming the paper layer. The water drains and is sucked through the wire belt, leaving the fibers and additives on top of the wire.

The paper on the wire passes under a dandy roller, a cylinder

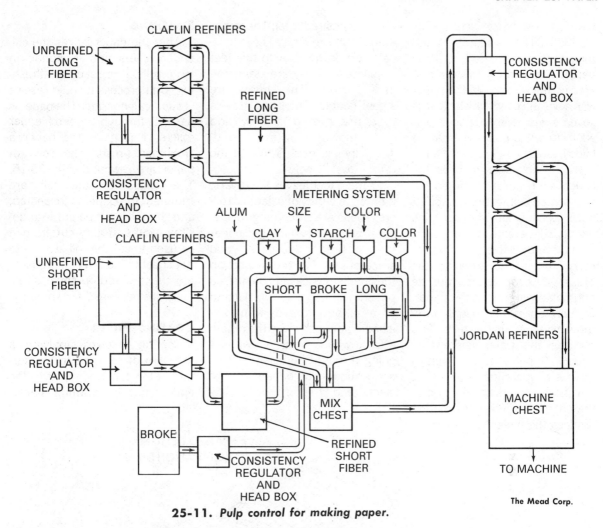

UNREFINED LONG FIBER

CLAFLIN REFINERS

CONSISTENCY REGULATOR AND HEAD BOX

REFINED LONG FIBER

METERING SYSTEM

ALUM   **SIZE**   **COLOR**

CLAY   **STARCH**   **COLOR**

UNREFINED SHORT FIBER

CLAFLIN REFINERS

CONSISTENCY REGULATOR AND HEAD BOX

SHORT   **BROKE**   **LONG**

BROKE

CONSISTENCY REGULATOR AND HEAD BOX

MIX CHEST

REFINED SHORT FIBER

CONSISTENCY REGULATOR AND HEAD BOX

JORDAN REFINERS

MACHINE CHEST

TO MACHINE

The Mead Corp.

25-11. *Pulp control for making paper.*

Champion Paper Co.

25-12. *The headbox, fourdrinier section, and dryer section. This machine complex is 912 feet in overall length, and can be operated at speeds up to 2,200 feet per minute to produce 275 tons of fine printing papers per day.*

covered with wire gauze. Fig. 25-13. This levels the fibers and makes the watermark on the paper. If the dandy roller is covered with a wire mesh, the paper will have a woven finish. If it is covered with evenly spaced parallel wires, the paper will have a laid finish.

When the paper reaches the couch roll (a roller at the end of the screen), it cannot support itself because it still contains about 80 percent water. It is supported by woolen felts, which carry the paper through the presses. The presses squeeze additional water from the paper. Suction boxes are used to remove water from the felts. This reduces the water content to about 70 percent. The web is now self-supporting.

The web enters the dry end of the paper machine. This section reduces the moisture content to

the final desired level. The paper enters the dryers. They have cast-iron drums four to five feet in diameter. They are staggered in two rows. The drums are steam heated. The paper travels over the heated drums, and more moisture is evaporated. The paper is held tightly to the drums by felt belts.

As the paper leaves the dryers, it enters a series of calender rollers. These are smoothing rollers. Fig. 25-14. They give the paper the desired thickness and smoothness. Paper finished on these rollers is called *calendered* paper. The paper is now wound on a roll and is ready to be finished. Paper can leave the dryers and be wound on a reel without going through the calender rollers. Antique-type papers are not calendered.

FINISHING

After the paper leaves the calender rollers and is wound in large rolls, it is ready for finishing. One process it could receive is *supercalendering*. The paper is passed through supercalender rollers. This gives the paper a smoother finish. The rolls of paper are rewound. Fig. 25-15. The edges of the roll are trimmed, the paper is inspected, and the rolls can be cut into desired widths. Rotary cutters can be used to cut the roll stock into flat sheets. The large, flat sheets are cut to standard sheet sizes. They are packaged for shipping.

COATING PAPER

Coating involves applying a thin film of pigment to the surface of the paper. It improves the appearance and printing charac-

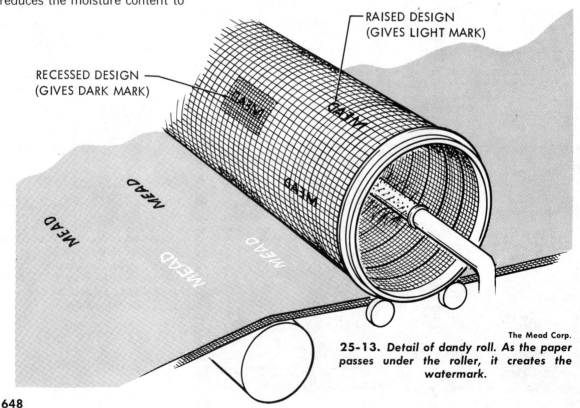

RAISED DESIGN
(GIVES LIGHT MARK)

RECESSED DESIGN
(GIVES DARK MARK)

The Mead Corp.

25-13. Detail of dandy roll. As the paper passes under the roller, it creates the watermark.

teristics of the paper. It provides a smoother surface, higher opacity, better whiteness, and a range of gloss from dull to glossy.

The paper, before coating, is made as a machine-finished raw stock. The coating is actually a printing process applied to the surface of the paper. Coatings are made up of pigments and adhesive to fix the pigment to the paper surface.

The composition of coatings varies. All coating materials are suspended in water. The water evaporates and the solid materials remain, forming the coating. Typical adhesives include casein, plant protein, starches, animal glue, polyvinyl alcohol, water-soluble resins, and methyl cellulose.

Pigments used for coating are listed in Fig. 25-16 in order of their increasing opacity. *Clay* from Georgia is bleached white and widely used. It is inexpensive and chemically inert. *Calcium carbonate* (chalk) is precipitated by sodium hydroxide and is a byproduct of cooking liquors. It requires more adhesive than clay, but is a good absorber and ink trapper. *Satin white* is a pigment that comes from lime and alum. *Blanc fixe* is barium sulfate. It is very opaque but expensive. The most opaque and expensive pigment is *titanium oxide*. It is seldom used alone, but is added to other mineral pigments to increase the opacity of the coating.

Coated stock is made both on the papermaking machine and separately, or off-machine. Depending on the use, coatings may be made for any of the major printing processes. The most common division is be-

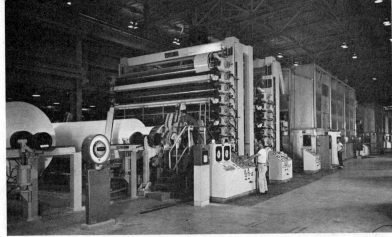

Champion Paper Co.

25-14. *The dry end of a paper machine. The web of paper is being wound onto a reel at the left, after having passed through the two calender stacks shown in the center of the picture.*

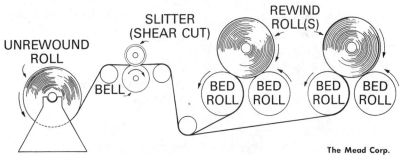

The Mead Corp.

25-15. *Surface friction rewinder, multiple shafts.*

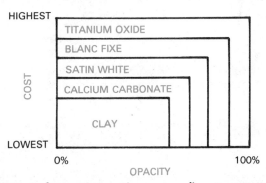

25-16. *Pigments for paper coatings, according to cost and opacity.*

tween letterpress and offset coatings. Paper may be coated one side (C1S), both sides (C2S), or even double coated for a smoother surface.

There is a variety of automatic coating methods. These include blade, roll, pressure, and cast coaters. The *blade coater* uses a roller to apply the coating material to the paper web. Fig. 25-17.

The liquid coating filters into the surface of the paper. A revolving wiping rod removes any of the coating which is still liquid. Two-sided coating is done on two

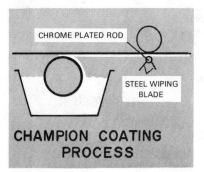

Champion Paper Co.

25-17. A blade coater.

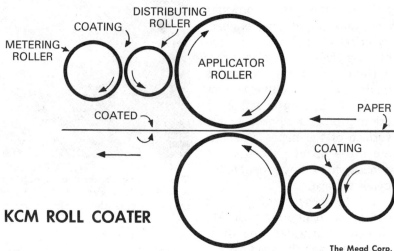

KCM ROLL COATER

The Mead Corp.

25-19. Roll coating two sides of the paper.

separate coaters. Usually the paper is passed over drying drums before entering the second coater.

Another type of knife coater is the trailing blade. Fig. 25-18. The coating is applied to the moving web, giving it an excess coating. The excess is removed by a flexible steel blade. This system is used to coat publication-grade papers on the paper machine.

Another blade-type coater is the air knife blade coater. The web runs over a roller in the coating material. At a second roller, the coated web is exposed to the air knife. The air knife does not touch the paper. It produces a jet of air which removes the excess coating.

Roll coating passes the web between two large rollers. The large rollers have a coating applied to their surface by smaller rollers. Fig. 25-19. This system can coat both sides of the web at the same time.

Another type of roll coating is pressure or gravure coating. Fig. 25-20. This coater uses an intaglio metering roll which transfers the coating to a rubber-covered application roller. The doctor blade removes the excess coating from the application roller. This roller transfers the coating to the paper. Both sides are coated at the same time.

Cast-coated papers are the highest quality available. The process is slow and expensive. However, the paper surface is unexcelled in gloss and smoothness.

The paper is coated on one side of the web. This side with the wet coating is pressed against the surface of a heated metal drum. The drum surface is chromium plated and polished. It produces a coating with mirror-like quality.

Two other coating systems are shown in Fig. 25-21. The spread shaft coater uses rollers to

25-18. An off-machine trailing blade coater. Base stock is coated on both sides at speeds up to 2,500 feet per minute, or up to 300 tons per day of fine printing grades.

Champion Paper Co.

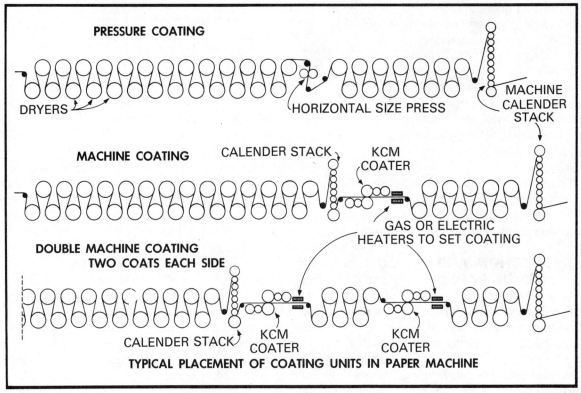

PRESSURE COATING

DRYERS

HORIZONTAL SIZE PRESS

MACHINE CALENDER STACK

MACHINE COATING

CALENDER STACK

KCM COATER

GAS OR ELECTRIC HEATERS TO SET COATING

DOUBLE MACHINE COATING
TWO COATS EACH SIDE

CALENDER STACK

KCM COATER

KCM COATER

TYPICAL PLACEMENT OF COATING UNITS IN PAPER MACHINE

The Mead Corp.

25-20. *Methods of coating paper.*

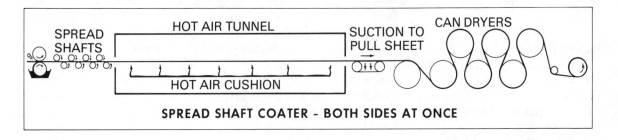

SPREAD SHAFTS

HOT AIR TUNNEL

SUCTION TO PULL SHEET

CAN DRYERS

HOT AIR CUSHION

SPREAD SHAFT COATER - BOTH SIDES AT ONCE

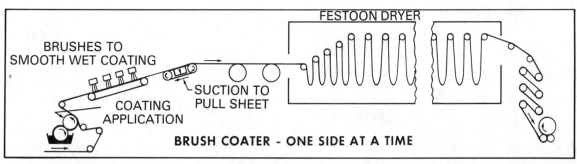

FESTOON DRYER

BRUSHES TO SMOOTH WET COATING

SUCTION TO PULL SHEET

COATING APPLICATION

BRUSH COATER - ONE SIDE AT A TIME

The Mead Corp.

25-21. *Two other ways of coating paper.*

smooth and distribute the coating before it enters the drying tunnel. The brush coater applies the coating with a roller. Brushes are used to smooth the coating. The web then goes through a festoon dryer. A festoon dryer moves the paper over sticks in an air tunnel. This system is finding less use in the paper industry.

Coated papers must be dried after coating. Generally, this is done by high-velocity air dryers or dryers using radiant heat.

SELECTION AND USE OF PAPER

PAPER FAMILIES

Papers are made to be used for either industrial and manufacturing purposes or for writing and printing. Industrial stocks are called coarse paper. Printing and writing stocks are known as fine paper. Fine papers are divided into families. These include book, cover, print, thin, business, bristol, and blanks. Fig. 25-22.

BOOK PAPERS

Book papers make up the largest family of fine papers. This family includes almost all papers used for publication purposes. Fig. 25-23. Book papers available range from those used for the most economical printing to the highest quality publication. Dif-

FINE PAPER FAMILIES	BOOK
	COVER
	PRINT
	THIN
	BUSINESS
	BRISTOL
	BLANKS

25-22. Paper families.

UNCOATED	COATED
VELLUM	CAST
ANTIQUE	DULL
MACHINE	COATED TWO SIDES
ENGLISH	COATED ONE SIDE
SUPERCALENDERED	FILM

25-23. Book paper finishes.

ferent finishes and degrees of smoothness are available. The heaviest print to the finest halftone dot can be reproduced as necessary.

The book family has two main branches. These are uncoated and coated book papers.

Uncoated Book Paper Finishes

The *uncoated* branch of the book family has members who are identified according to their finish. The finishes are listed in order from the roughest to the smoothest. *Vellum* is the roughest finish. This paper is usually made from soda pulp which has fluffy fibers, making a soft, bulky sheet. A slightly smoother finish, *antique,* is created while the paper is still on the papermaking machine.

When paper is run through a calendering stack on the dryer end of the papermaking machine, the resulting surface is called a *machine finish.* This finish has a uniform, smooth surface. An even smoother surface, called *English finish,* is made by running short-fibered paper slowly through the calendering stack. *Supercalendered* papers are the smoothest of all uncoated book papers. As stated before, this finish is made from a special set of additional calendering rollers. These rollers, running at different speeds, polish

and iron the paper to a supercalendered finish. The smoother the finish of the paper, the more nearly perfect will be the reproduction of the printed image.

Coated Book Paper

Coated book paper was originally developed to aid in reproducing halftones for letterpress. Later the offset process began to use coated stock. Many specialized coatings have since developed.

Paper coated on both sides is generally used for high quality work, particularly halftones and multicolor. The lower grades are used in general publication work.

Paper coated on one side is primarily used for label printing or for posters and paper to be pasted on a backing.

Dull-coated paper is produced either by using nonglossy pigment or by altering the calendering so that the coating does not receive a high polish. This coating is used where soft or mellow reproductions are desired, or where the absence of glare is a requirement.

Cast-coated papers are produced by drum-drying the coating, which results in a high gloss. They are used principally in prestige work and advertising.

Film-coated paper is produced by applying a thin layer of coating on the paper in the dryer end of the machine. It is used for book work where a lightweight paper is desirable.

Book paper may also be divided between paper made for letterpress and paper made for offset. In general, offset papers are more heavily surface sized and are always *internally* or *engine sized.* The offset sheet must be highly *stable, resist picking,* and be *hydrated* longer to produce a harder sheet. Offset papers that are coated generally have a more uniform surface than coated letterpress papers.

BUSINESS PAPERS

Business papers make up the second family of papers. Fig. 25-24. They are used primarily to carry correspondence and related business activities. Prominent members of the business family are the bond, ledger, safety, and writing papers.

There are two types of bond papers: those which have cotton content and the chemical wood bonds. The cotton content papers are made either of 100 percent cotton rags and linters or a percentage of cotton with chemical wood pulp. The chemical wood fibers are obtained from both hard- and softwoods.

Bond papers are well beaten during manufacture. Extensive beating produces a short fiber of good strength, resulting in a sheet which has good "feel"; that is, it will snap or rattle when handled. All bonds are internally and/or externally sized. Hard sizing is added for two purposes: to resist the absorption of writing fluids and to add to the body or stiffness of the sheet.

There are five grades of cotton-content bond papers which are ranked according to the percentage of cotton in the sheet. These are usually 25, 50, 75, 100 percent and super 100 percent

cotton content. Further subdivisions among the five grades depend on the qualities of the cotton and chemical wood fiber, the speed at which the paper is made, and the manner in which it is dried. Chemical wood bonds (called sulphite) are graded from number 1, the highest, through number 5, the lowest.

These papers are made as *woven or laid stock.* The finishes are regular, *light cockle,* and *heavy cockle.* Other manufactured finishes include plate, super plate, antique, ripple, vellum, linen, and handmade. The cockle finishes, which appear wrinkled or puckered, are produced during air drying. Other finishes are embossed or plated, that is, pressed between smooth metal sheets.

Writing papers are similar to bonds, but as a rule are made softer with a surface tooth (roughness) for writing and erasing. Grades range from extra fine to tablet. The most common finishes are English, embossed, or laid.

Ledger papers are used for business records. They are made similar to bonds but are heavier, stronger, more rigid, and usually more durable. They have a nonglare finish suitable for typing and writing. The heavier weights will stand erect for filing.

Safety papers are designed to provide protection against changes or erasures on the surface and to give internal identification against counterfeiting. Three common methods are used to produce safety paper. One method uses chemicals added to the beater or to the paper surface. If ink eradicators are used, the paper turns brown.

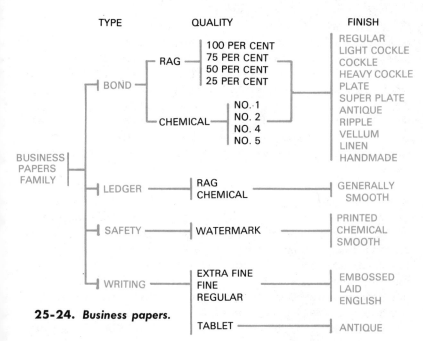

25-24. Business papers.

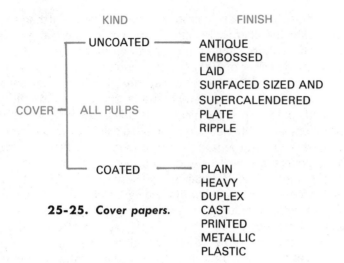

KIND   FINISH

COVER — ALL PULPS

UNCOATED —
- ANTIQUE
- EMBOSSED
- LAID
- SURFACED SIZED AND
- SUPERCALENDERED
- PLATE
- RIPPLE

COATED —
- PLAIN
- HEAVY
- DUPLEX
- CAST
- PRINTED
- METALLIC
- PLASTIC

25-25. *Cover papers.*

Another method uses a two-sided chemical background on the surface. Erasures expose the white stock underneath and change the background color.

Many of the safety papers have watermarks for the customer and flexographic printing for identification and proof against erasure. Safety papers are used for checks, drafts, licenses, certificates, and all types of legal and business transactions where alterations need to be detected. These papers are smoothly finished and made in the same manner as bond and ledger papers.

COVER PAPERS

Cover papers as a family are among the most colorful and decorative of all papers. Like the book papers, the cover papers are divided between coated and uncoated stocks. Fig. 25-25.

The pulp used to make cover stock varies from mechanical and chemical pulps to include sulphate, sulphite, cotton, and soda. The antique finish predominates in uncoated cover.

Embossed, laid, watermark, and deckle edges are common. Deckle is a ragged edge patterned after the edges of handmade paper. Covers are made in a great array of colors designed to attract attention and give prestige to the material between the covers. Uncoated covers are designed to show off bold solids and line work.

Sized and supercalendered (S & SC) covers are made for economical halftone work where prestige and durability are not as important. Other uncoated finishes are plate and ripple. The ripple finish is polished and wrinkled. Uncoated covers may be purchased in double or triple weight for stiffness and wearing qualities.

The *coated covers* are the fancy members of the cover family. Some, called plain-coated cover, are made like machine-coated book, only heavier. Heavy-coated cover is off-machine coated to a high finish and used for advertising halftone printings. Duplex covers are coated in different colors and

finishes on each side and are used in advertising where both sides are seen. Cast-coated cover is made from supercalendered and machine-coated base stock, then coated with a plastic composition, and dried against a chromium-plated drum.

Some covers are metallic coated with powders made from copper, aluminum, or bronze. Several, with a coating adhesive of pyroxylin lacquer, require special inks that dry by oxidation alone. Metallic foil covers are heavy papers glued to aluminum and other metal foils. Plastic-coated or acetate foil covers are produced for rugged use and water resistance.

These examples of uncoated and coated covers indicate the wide diversity of kinds, colors, and surfaces of the cover family. Often richly colored, covers are made to imitate many other materials such as wood, leather, and metal by texture, feel, weight, and sight.

BRISTOL PAPERS

Bristol papers are a fourth family of fine papers. Fig. 25-26. Originating in Bristol, England, this family of card stock is widely used in printing. The two important branches are the printing and writing bristols.

The writing bristols have two important members, index and wedding bristols. *Index* is finished with a slight tooth for business uses. It is used for many types of printed forms, cards, and records. *Wedding* bristols are papers of smooth or slight tooth finish designed for formal use. A less known member of the writing bristols is the cream postcard. This card imitates the government postal card in color and finish.

The *printing* bristols are not designed for writing. They are used in advertising and display printings. The finish is made in antique and plate for line and halftone work. Another member of the printing bristols is the bogus (false) bristol. These may have reclaimed liners or fillers. They may be used as tickets which expose the dyed liner when the ticket is torn.

Folding bristols are printing bristols that are more flexible. They are made with longer fibers that give additional strength in folding operations.

Printing bristols are stiffer than index bristols. They do not have the strength characteristics, uniformity, or appearance of the index bristols. Usage is mainly in areas where short life is expected. Bristols may be coated, pasted, or laminated. The coating can be applied on one side or two sides by excess coating or cast-coating.

BLANKS AND PAPERBOARDS

Paperboards and *blanks* as a family are similar in manufacture and use. They are heavy, thick, and made of layers of paper. Most have a thick, nonprintable inside layer. Outside layers are suitable for coating and printing. *Posterboard* is a blank that is lined on one side for printing. The back side is not. *Railroad board* is a lined blank. It is used extensively for ticket stock. *Thick china* is the name of a thin (0.011″) coated blank.

Mill blanks have a middle of printed news. Patent coated board, which is not coated, uses a white outside liner. Do not confuse these fine papers with binder or builder boards, which are coarse papers. The term cardboard is not used. It has a double meaning and may even be used to identify corrugated board.

THIN PAPERS

The *thin papers* are a loosely knit group of papers. They are really members of the book and business paper families. Some types are Bible, manifold, and onionskin. Thin papers save weight and space. *Bible paper,* actually a book paper, is a thin paper used in large volumes, since thin paper reduces the thickness of the book. *Manifold papers* belong to the business paper family. They are used mainly for copies of original business communications. Because they are thin, several copies can be produced by strike-on procedures. They save postage and filing space. Manifold papers are made in a similar manner to bond paper. *Onionskin* is a manifold that is translucent. This paper may have a glazed finish.

PRINT PAPERS

Print papers are another family of fine paper. *Newsprint* is the outstanding member of this family. It is made of at least 75 percent groundwood. The remainder is chemical pulp, usually sulphate pulp. It is designed for relief printing and is highly absorbent. This paper is not durable. Newsprint is used almost entirely for the printing of newspapers. It is made in a soft, smooth finish.

Offset newsprint is made with internal and external sizing. This gives better fiber bonding and less lint and fuzz. In general, the web offset process demands greater strength in paper than the letterpress web process.

Rotogravure newsprint differs chiefly in the whiteness and smoothness required for this process. This paper is made with a machine finish and is surface sized.

PAPER MEASUREMENT

Paper, like other materials, uses a system of measurement which grew out of its different uses. Cloth is measured by the yard. Wood is measured by the board foot. *Paper is measured by the pounds per 1,000 sheets.*

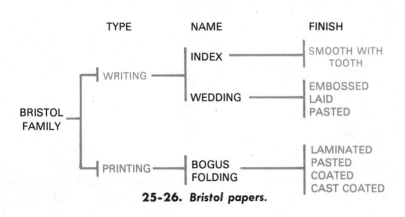

25-26. Bristol papers.

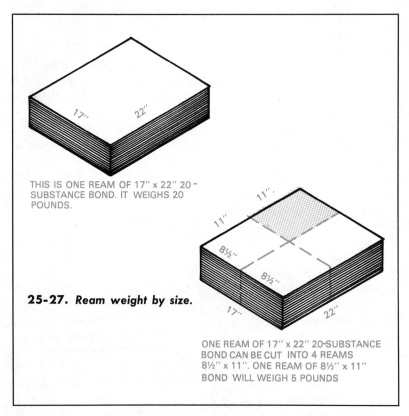

THIS IS ONE REAM OF 17″ x 22″ 20-SUBSTANCE BOND. IT WEIGHS 20 POUNDS.

25-27. Ream weight by size.

ONE REAM OF 17″ x 22″ 20-SUBSTANCE BOND CAN BE CUT INTO 4 REAMS 8½″ x 11″. ONE REAM OF 8½″ x 11″ BOND WILL WEIGH 5 POUNDS

Different kinds and sizes of paper were gradually developed to fit certain needs. The business papers settled on a general size of 17″ × 22″. This is an economical size to print or fold into four 8 1/2″ × 11″ sheets. Paper is wrapped and sold in 500-sheet lots called *reams*. The weight of 500 sheets in the 17″ × 22″ size became the basis by which printers could identify and purchase business paper. Using the 17″ × 22″ size as basic, the ream weight of larger and smaller sheets of the same substance would be determined. The terms *basis weight* and *substance* became synonymous. *The substance or basis weight is the weight of one ream of the paper in the basic size.* A 20-substance bond, for example, is a ream of paper in the basic size (17″ × 22″) that weighs 20 pounds. Four reams, size 8 1/2″ × 11″, cut from the 17″ × 22″, would each weigh 5 pounds. Fig. 25-27.

Each family of paper, such as book or cover, has its own basic size. The following sizes are based on the U.S. customary measuring system:

Bond—17″ × 22″
Book—25″ × 38″
Cover—20″ × 26″
Index bristol—
    25 1/2″ × 30 1/2″
Newsprint—24″ × 36″
Blanks—22″ × 28″

Every kind of paper has its own substance numbers, based on the different sizes of each paper. Each family has commonly used sheet thicknesses. Paper thickness is called *caliper*. Board thickness is referred to as *points*. These different thicknesses and sizes influence the basis weight. This increases the difficulty of comparing papers of different families by either substance number or through the basic size.

The *basis weight* is the weight per unit area. To find the weight per unit area of papers in different paper families, an equivalent weight chart is used. Fig. 25-28. This chart lists the common substances of a paper in one family. It shows equivalent substances of papers in other families.

The letter M stands for 1,000. The 1,000-sheet weight, or *M number,* is easy to use in determining the cost per pound and weight of any size and amount of paper for a particular substance. Fig. 25-29.

UNIVERSAL BASIC SIZE (THE MM SYSTEM)

For a number of years printers and papermakers have proposed to substitute a universal basic size for the awkward basis weight practice. A universal size of 25″ × 40″ (*1,000 square inches*) would become the standard for weighing 1,000 sheets. The weight of 1 M (1,000) sheets in the universal size, 1 M square inches, would be used as an identifying number for each type of paper. It would also be a simple method of calculating any amount and size of paper of that number. It could also be a means of comparing different kinds of paper by weight. Fig. 25-30.

In the MM system, the first M represents 1,000 square inches.

EQUIVALENT WEIGHTS OF VARIOUS
PAPERS IN REAMS OF 500 SHEETS

	Book 25 × 38	Bond and Ledger 17 × 22	Cover 20 × 26	Printing Bristol 22 1/2 × 28 1/2	Index 25 1/2 × 30 1/2	Tag 24 × 36
Book	**30**	12	16	20	25	27
(Basis Weights	**40**	16	22	27	33	36
in Bold)	**45**	18	25	30	37	41
	50	20	27	34	41	45
	60	24	33	40	49	55
	70	28	38	47	57	64
	80	31	44	54	65	73
	90	35	49	60	74	82
	100	39	55	67	82	91
	120	47	66	80	98	109
Bond and	33	**13**	18	22	27	30
Ledger	41	**16**	22	27	33	37
(Basis Weights	51	**20**	28	34	42	46
in Bold)	61	**24**	33	41	50	56
	71	**28**	39	48	58	64
	81	**32**	45	55	67	74
	91	**36**	50	62	75	83
	102	**40**	56	69	83	93
Cover	91	36	**50**	62	75	82
(Basis Weights	110	43	**60**	74	90	100
in Bold)	119	47	**65**	80	97	108
	146	58	**80**	99	120	134
	164	65	**90**	111	135	149
	183	72	**100**	124	150	166
	201	79	**110**	136	165	183
	219	86	**120**	148	179	199
Printing	100	39	54	**67**	81	91
Bristol	120	47	65	**80**	98	109
(Basis Weights	148	58	81	**100**	121	135
in Bold)	176	70	97	**120**	146	162
	207	82	114	**140**	170	189
	237	93	130	**160**	194	216
Index	110	43	60	74	**90**	100
(Basis Weights	135	53	74	91	**110**	122
in Bold)	170	67	93	115	**140**	156
	208	82	114	140	**170**	189
Tag	110	43	60	74	90	**100**
(Basis Weights	137	54	75	93	113	**125**
in Bold)	165	65	90	111	135	**150**
	192	76	105	130	158	**175**
	220	87	120	148	180	**200**
	275	109	151	186	225	**250**

S. D. Warren Company, Div. Scott Paper Company

25-28. Equivalent weights chart.

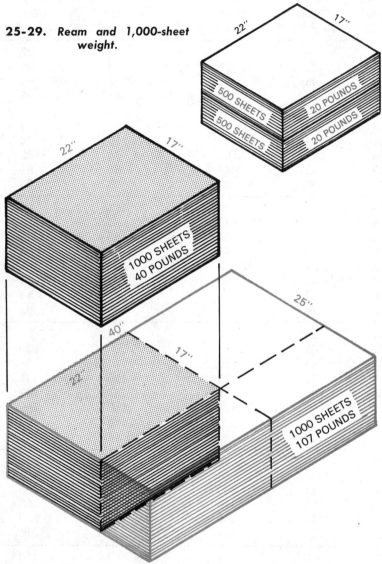

500 SHEETS 17" x 22" 20 SUBSTANCE
BOND WEIGHS 20 POUNDS.
1000 SHEETS WEIGHS 40 POUNDS

25-29. *Ream and 1,000-sheet weight.*

500 SHEETS
500 SHEETS
20 POUNDS
20 POUNDS

22"   17"

1000 SHEETS
40 POUNDS

40"   17"   25"   22"

1000 SHEETS
107 POUNDS

25-30. *The M weight of basic size bond compared to MM weight of bond.* •

The second M represents the 1,000-sheet weight.

To obtain the MM weight of paper, use the following formula:

$$\frac{\text{Width} \times \text{length} \times 1,000}{\text{Universal size} \times 1,000} = \frac{\text{M sheet weight}}{\text{MM weight}}$$

For example, 20-substance bond paper, 17" × 22", has a 1,000-sheet weight of 40 pounds. (One ream of the bond weighs 20 pounds. Therefore, two reams—1,000 sheets—weigh 40 pounds.) To find the MM weight:

$$\frac{17 \times 22 \times 1,000}{25 \times 40 \times 1,000} = \frac{40 \text{ lbs.}}{\text{MM weight}}$$

374 MM weight = 40,000 lbs.
MM weight = 107 lbs. (approx.)

A universal sheet, 25" × 40", of 20-substance bond has an MM weight of 107 pounds for 1,000 sheets. The MM weight can be used to determine the thousand-sheet weight of any paper size in the same MM basis. First move the decimal point in the MM number three places to the left. Then multiply this number by the sheet area of the paper. Round off the product to the nearest pound.

For example, cover paper, ream basis, 20" by 26", substance 65, has an MM weight of 250. Fig. 25-31. To find the 1,000-sheet weight of another size of this cover paper, say 23" by 35", the sheet area is multiplied by the MM factor as follows:

Area × MM factor = 1 M sheet weight

23" × 35" × .250 = 201.250 lbs.

1 M sheets, 23" × 25", will weigh 201 pounds.

The Equivalent Weight Chart, Fig. 25-31, can be rearranged to position the MM factors in numerical sequence. The result, the MM Sequence Chart, Fig. 25-32, is used to identify paper substance and family simultaneously.

The chart may be used to compare different papers in weight relationship. For example, the chart shows that an M weight of 211 identifies 100-substance book. This paper is similar in

EQUIVALENT WEIGHT FOR MM BASIS

Substance	Family	Basis Size	MM Weight
9	Bond	17 X 22	48
13	Bond	17 X 22	70
16	Bond	17 X 22	86
20	Bond	17 X 22	107
24	Bond	17 X 22	128
35	Book	25 X 38	74
40	Book	25 X 38	84
45	Book	25 X 38	95
50	Book	25 X 38	105
60	Book	25 X 38	126
70	Book	25 X 38	147
80	Book	25 X 38	168
90	Book	25 X 38	189
100	Book	25 X 38	211
82	Bristol	22 1/4 X 35	208
100	Bristol	22 1/4 X 35	254
120	Bristol	22 1/4 X 35	305
140	Bristol	22 1/4 X 35	356
160	Bristol	22 1/4 X 35	406
82 1/2	Bristol	22 1/2 X 28 1/2	257
90	Bristol	22 1/2 X 28 1/2	281
100	Bristol	22 1/2 X 28 1/2	312
120	Bristol	22 1/2 X 28 1/2	374
140	Bristol	22 1/2 X 28 1/2	437
248	Cardboard	28 X 44	403
288	Cardboard	28 X 44	468
341	Cardboard	28 X 44	554
50	Cover	20 X 26	192
65	Cover	20 X 26	250
80	Cover	20 X 26	308
100	Cover	20 X 26	385
90	Index Bristol	25 1/2 X 30 1/2	231
110	Index Bristol	25 1/2 X 30 1/2	283
140	Index Bristol	25 1/2 X 30 1/2	360
170	Index Bristol	25 1/2 X 35 1/2	437

Substance	Family	Basis Size	MM Weight
24	Ledger	17 X 22	128
28	Ledger	17 X 22	150
32	Ledger	17 X 22	171
36	Ledger	17 X 22	193
40	Ledger	17 X 22	214
50	Manila	24 X 36	116
60	Manila	24 X 36	139
70	Manila	24 X 36	162
100	Manila	24 X 36	231
150	Manila	24 X 36	347
32	Newsprint	24 X 36	74
35	Newsprint	24 X 36	81
40	Newsprint	24 X 36	93
50	Offset Book	25 X 38	105
60	Offset Book	25 X 38	126
70	Offset Book	25 X 38	147
80	Offset Book	25 X 38	168
100	Offset Book	25 X 38	211
200	Postcard	28 1/2 X 45	312
240	Postcard	28 1/2 X 45	374
280	Postcard	28 1/2 X 45	437
300	Postcard	28 1/2 X 45	468
80	Tag	24 X 36	185
100	Tag	24 X 36	232
150	Tag	24 X 36	347
175	Tag	24 X 36	405
200	Tag	24 X 36	463

25-31. Equivalent weight chart for MM measurement.

weight to an 82-substance bristol, as seen by the preceding figure (208) in the MM weight column. It is also similar to 40-substance ledger, as shown by the next MM figure (214) in the MM weight column. The MM weights in closest proximity on the chart are also nearest for ream substance comparison.

The MM chart is a way to use a common index to specify and identify paper. At the core of indexing and listing systems is the establishment of a relationship of the weight, area, and thickness of a paper in convenient size and quantity. Practical problems in paper estimation and consumption can be solved by use of MM weight numbers.

METRIC PAPER SIZES*

The metric linear measure unit used to indicate paper sizes is the millimetre (mm). Following are the metric paper sizes specified by the International Organization for Standardization (ISO), the world body which writes engineering and product standards. In the United States, standards are set by the American National Standards Institute (ANSI). It is possible that the ANSI will accept the ISO standards.

There are three ISO paper series in use. These are the A, B, and C series. The A series is for general printed matter. The B series is for charts, posters, and maps. The C series is for envelopes and folders designed to hold paper from the A series.

---

*John R. Lindbeck, *Metrics in Career Education*, Peoria, Illinois: Chas. A. Bennett Co., Inc., 1975, pp. 74–78.

MM SEQUENCE CHART

MM Weight	Kind	Basis	Substance
39	thin	17 × 22	7.25
42	book	25 × 38	20
43	thin	17 × 22	8
46	manilas	24 × 36	20
48	bond	17 × 22	9
56	thin	17 × 22	10.5
58	manilas	24 × 36	25
59	thin	17 × 22	11
63	book	25 × 38	30
69	manilas	24 × 36	30
70	bond	17 × 22	13
74	book	25 × 38	35
74	newsprint	24 × 36	32
79	newsprint	24 × 36	34
81	manilas	24 × 36	35
84	book	25 × 38	40
86	bond	17 × 22	16
93	manilas	24 × 36	40
93	newsprint	24 × 36	40
95	book	25 × 38	45
105	book	25 × 38	50
107	bond	17 × 22	20
116	manilas	24 × 36	50
126	book	25 × 38	60
128	bond	17 × 22	24
128	ledger	17 × 22	24
139	manilas	24 × 36	60
147	book	25 × 38	70
150	kraft	24 × 36	65
150	ledger	17 × 22	28
162	manilas	24 × 36	70
168	book	25 × 38	80
171	kraft	24 × 36	74
171	ledger	17 × 22	32
185	manilas	24 × 36	80
185	tag	24 × 36	80
192	cover	20 × 26	50
192	kraft	24 × 36	83
193	ledger	17 × 22	36
208	bristol	22 1/2 × 35	82
211	book	24 × 38	100
214	ledger	17 × 22	40
231	index bristol	25 1/2 × 30 1/2	90
231	manilas	24 × 36	100
232	tag	24 × 36	100
235	ledger	17 × 22	44
250	cover	20 × 26	65
253	book	25 × 38	120
254	bristol	22 1/2 × 35	100

25-32. A sequence chart for MM weight.

MM SEQUENCE CHART (Continued)

MM Weight	Kind	Basis	Substance
257	bristol	22 1/2 × 28 1/2	82 1/2
281	bristol	22 1/2 × 28 1/2	90
283	index bristol	25 1/2 × 30 1/2	110
289	manilas	24 × 36	125
289	tag	24 × 36	125
305	bristol	22 1/2 × 35	120
308	cover	20 × 26	80
312	bristol	22 1/2 × 28 1/2	100
312	post card	28 1/2 × 45	200
347	manilas	24 × 36	150
347	tag	24 × 36	150
351	blotting	19 × 24	80
356	bristol	22 1/2 × 35	140
360	index bristol	25 1/2 × 30 1/2	140
374	bristol	22 1/2 × 28 1/2	120
374	post card	28 1/2 × 45	240
385	cover	20 × 26	100
403	cardboard—2 ply	28 × 44	248
405	post card	28 1/2 × 45	260
406	bristol	22 1/2 × 35	160
437	index bristol	25 1/2 × 30 1/2	170
437	bristol	22 1/2 × 28 1/2	140
437	post card	28 1/2 × 45	280
439	blotting	19 × 24	100
457	bristol	22 1/2 × 35	180
463	tag	24 × 36	200
463	manilas	24 × 36	200
468	cardboard—3 ply	28 × 44	288
468	post card	28 1/2 × 45	300
499	bristol	22 1/2 × 28 1/2	160
500	cover	20 × 26	130
526	blotting	19 × 24	120
554	cardboard—4 ply	28 × 44	341
561	bristol	22 1/2 × 28 1/2	180
601	cardboard—5 ply	28 × 44	370
614	blotting	19 × 24	140
695	cardboard—6 ply	28 × 44	428

25-32. A sequence chart for MM weight.

The sizes in the A series are shown in Fig. 25-33. The largest size, A0, will have an area of one square metre. The ratio of the sides is based on the proportion $1:\sqrt{2}$. The A0 size is 841 mm × 1189 mm, which equals 1m². The smaller sheet sizes are found by dividing the *longer sides* by two. Fig. 25-34. For example, the A1 sheet is half the size of the A0 sheet. The A4 sheet is nearest to the popular 8 1/2″ × 11″ sheet.

Fig. 25-33 shows the ISO sizes for envelopes. They are designed to hold the A-series sheets unfolded or folded. For example, an A1 sheet will fit unfolded into a C1 envelope. If it is folded in half, it will fit a C2 envelope.

The sizes of the B-series paper are shown in Fig. 25-35. These sizes are midway between the sizes of the A series.

Paper using the U.S. customary system of measurement is presently sold by the pound-weight per ream. The international paper sizes relate all basic weights to the A0 sheet size.

The ISO system expresses the basic weights in grams per square metre (g/m²). A rough conversion of U.S. customary weights to ISO metric for basic book weights can be made by multiplying the weight in pounds by 1.5. For example, a 50-pound book paper is about the same as 75 g/m².

NONPAPER MATERIALS

Printing is done on other materials besides paper. Printing can be found on glass bottles, metal cans, leather, wood, fabric, plastic, and foil. Most of these items require highly specialized processes. Often the printing is done on the completed product. Due to the diversity of these materials, only two—foils and plastic films—will be considered. These materials are made in sheet or roll form. They can be printed by most of the major processes.

Aluminum foil is widely used. It is supplied with a paper back, and it is usually printed by rotogravure. The foil is bright or satin finished. It is made in thick-

A AND C SERIES

A-Series Paper-Trimmed Sizes			C-Series Envelopes		
Size	Millimetres	Inches*	Size	Millimetres	Inches*
A0	841 × 1189	33 1/8 × 46 3/4	C0	917 × 1297	36 1/8 × 51
A1	594 × 841	23 3/8 × 33 1/8	C1	648 × 917	25 1/2 × 36 1/8
A2	420 × 594	16 1/2 × 23 3/8	C2	458 × 648	18 × 25 1/2
A3	297 × 420	11 3/4 × 16 1/2	C3	324 × 458	12 3/4 × 18
A4	210 × 297	8 1/4 × 11 3/4	C4	229 × 324	9 × 12 3/4
A5	148 × 210	5 7/8 × 8 1/4	C5	162 × 229	6 3/8 × 9
A6	105 × 148	4 1/8 × 5 7/8	C6	114 × 162	4 1/2 × 6 3/8
			**DL	110 × 220	4 5/16 × 8 5/8
A7	74 × 105	2 7/8 × 4 1/8	C7	81 × 114	3 1/4 × 4 1/2
A8	52 × 74	2 × 2 7/8	C8	57 × 81	2 1/4 × 3 1/4
A9	37 × 52	1 1/2 × 2			
A10	26 × 37	1 × 1 1/2			

*To nearest 1/8 inch.
**Standard commercial envelope, takes size A4 sheet.

25-33. A-series paper sizes are listed on the left, C-series on the right.

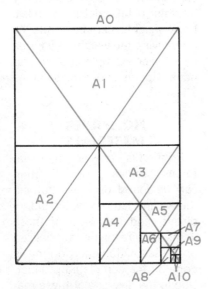

25-34. A-series paper divisions. All sheets have the same proportions whether the shorter side is doubled or the longer side halved. For sheet sizes larger than AO, the number precedes the letter. For example, size 2A is twice as large as AO.

B-SERIES PAPER— TRIMMED SIZES

Size	Millimetres	Inches*
B0	1000 × 1414	39 3/8 × 55 5/8
B1	707 × 1000	27 7/8 × 39 3/8
B2	500 × 707	19 5/8 × 27 7/8
B3	353 × 500	13 7/8 × 19 5/8
B4	250 × 353	9 7/8 × 13 7/8
B5	176 × 250	6 7/8 × 13 7/8
B6	125 × 176	4 7/8 × 6 7/8
B7	88 × 125	3 1/2 × 4 7/8
B8	62 × 88	2 1/2 × 3 1/2
B9	44 × 62	1 3/4 × 2 1/2
B10	31 × 44	1 1/4 × 1 3/4

25-35. B-series paper sizes with inch equivalents.

*To nearest 1/8 inch.

nesses from 0.003″ to 0.006″. Aluminum foil can be coated to accept regular or colored ink. Often the foil is embossed during processing.

Plastic films differ from coatings, since they are unsupported by any backing material. Thicker plastics are called sheetings.

Plastic films range from 0.0002″ to 0.050″ in thickness. The films are made by extrusion or casting. The chemical composition of a film determines its use. A great variety of films are made. Most are printed by the flexographic and rotogravure processes. Films are divided between stretch and nonstretch films. In the packaging industry, films are grouped by usage, porosity, and heat-shrink or boilproof properties, depending on use requirements. Most plastic sheets and films require inks designed for the chemical composition of the plastic.

PROPERTIES OF PAPER

Learning about paper properties develops an understanding of how paper reacts when it is processed or used for a specific purpose. Paper properties, the nature of the materials that make up paper, aid in identification and comparison. The properties of paper are classified into groups. These groups are: optical, structural, strength, physical, surface, and chemical.

Examples of optical properties are: color, brightness, opacity (the opposite of light transmission), and gloss (glare). Fig. 25-36. A small amount of blue dye is often added to white paper. This bluish tint makes the paper appear whiter.

Structural properties are part of paper construction. These include: *formation* (manner in which fibers are matted), *thickness* (width of the sheet from side to side), and *porosity* (the amount of space between fibers). Paper towels are purposely made porous. There is space between the fibers to absorb large amounts of water.

Strength properties include tensile (pull apart) and tearing (ripping) strength. Sulphate pulp is added to groundwood pulp in making newsprint. Sulphate fibers are much stronger and add to the strength of the paper.

Physical properties include: moisture content (amount of water in paper), dimensional stability (resistance to change in size), and degree of sizing (resistance to moisture). Bond papers are hard sized. Fluid writing inks will not "feather" (spread out) as ink is applied to the surface.

Surface properties include smoothness and fuzziness. A halftone, printed by letterpress on newsprint, is rarely above a 75-line screen. The paper surface is not smooth enough to reproduce accurately a halftone screen finer than 75 lines.

Chemical properties include the acidity or alkaline activity, tinting tendency, and others. A paper which has a heavy concentration of acidity will prevent ink from drying through chemical interaction.

The properties of paper determine how it can be used because they indicate how well paper will print and run on the press, and the quality of reproduction. Some paper properties are easily identified, such as grain direction. Others, such as *runability* (the ease with which paper will mechanically travel through the press), are made up of many properties and are difficult to identify by a single characteristic. The paper manufacturer develops many of the characteristics that a particular paper

exhibits. This includes selection of the fibers and other materials. The paper manufacturer determines the pulping, beating, pressing, drying, calendering, and coating conditions. All of these paper materials and manufacturing processes and their variables establish and determine paper properties. Because of the complexity of these variables, papermaking is an art as well as a science.

COMMON PAPER PROPERTIES

Most papers used in printing have some properties in common. These can be used as a general guide to determine the adequacy of the paper being used. Good characteristics are as follows:

1. Paper should be dimensionally stable. There should be little expansion or elongation when the paper is processed. The moisture expansion of the paper should not cause registration problems when the grain is parallel to the cylinder.

2. Color should be uniform to the eye and match from lot to lot.

3. The sheet should have sufficient strength for the use intended. Usually this can only be determined by testing a sample under actual conditions in which the paper will be used.

4. The paper should be clean. The surface should be free of dust or lint. Viewing against a light should show the sheet to be clear of impurities in the body.

5. Paper should have sufficient opacity. A black object be-

25-36. *Gloss meter checking of a machine-width strip to determine whether gloss of paper is within specifications.*

neath the paper should not show through the paper. Paper must have opacity suitable for the intended use, such as printing on both sides.

6. The grain should run the length of the sheet for most operations. The grain normally should not be visible.

7. The uncoated paper surface should be treated by calendering or sizing. This adds smoothness and improves ink application. However, excessive sizing reduces absorption and printing quality.

8. The sheet should have enough filler to provide bulk and body and increase absorbency and opacity. Filler may be as much as 10 to 12 percent of a coated sheet. Excessive filler slows ink drying and lowers the "cushion" properties of the sheet.

9. Minerals and chemicals in the paper should not be chemically active. They must not react with materials in contact with the paper, such as ink pigment, metals, or fountain solution.

Moisture in Paper

Several paper properties are affected by temperature and moisture. Moisture in the form of water vapor in the air is called *humidity*. *Relative humidity* is the percentage of moisture in the air in relation to the total amount (absolute humidity) the air could hold at a particular temperature. If the air temperature is reduced, the amount of vapor it can hold is reduced. Thus, as air temperature is lowered, the relative humidity increases until the cooled air is saturated (100 percent relative humidity). This is called the dew point. Further cooling

squeezes out moisture in the form of condensation. As the air temperature varies, so does the relative humidity.

As stated before, paper fibers are primarily cellulose, and they easily unite with water. Many of the problems in using paper are directly related to the changes that occur in paper due to the *hygroscopic* (moisture take-up) nature of cellulose. Ninety percent of the millions of hollow fibers that make up an uncoated paper will change in less than ten minutes following a change in relative humidity.

As the moisture content of the air changes, the size of the paper changes, mostly across the grain. The paper fibers change little in length but swell or shrink in circumference. This causes the paper to expand or shrink noticeably in a cross-grain direction. A 35" uncoated offset sheet will expand across the grain about 1/25" for each 10 percent

increase in relative humidity. (This ratio is true only when the relative humidity varies from 35 to 65 percent.) Fig. 25-37.

A condition of high relative humidity or low relative humidity can cause paper to curl around the grain direction. This is caused by the difference and amount of fibers on the wire and felt sides. The larger, more uniform fibers are deposited on the screen (wire side). The size and density of these fibers cause this side to accept and lose moisture faster. When a sheet of paper gains moisture, the wire side "grows" faster, making the paper curl to the felt side. If the paper loses moisture, the wire side shrinks faster, causing the paper to curl to the wire side.

When paper is stacked,

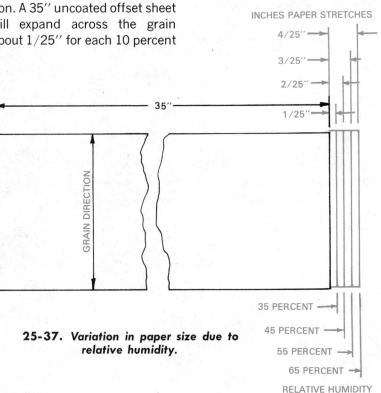

25-37. Variation in paper size due to relative humidity.

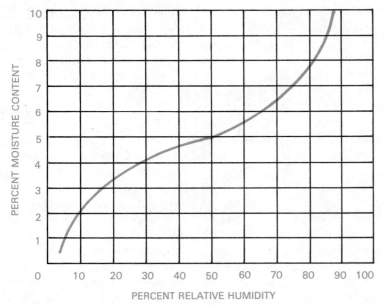

25-38. *Rate of change in paper's moisture content in relation to relative humidity.*

All paper should be stored wrapped and sealed. High stacking without support is dangerous and compresses paper at the bottom. Sufficient space should be left between stacks for air movement. Stacks should be on skids or pallets for easy movement. Every attempt should be made to keep out dust and dirt and to avoid excessive temperatures or moisture. Partial packages should be resealed after use. Paper should never be stored on end. Careful handling will avoid tearing or gouging wrappers. Never pick up more paper than you can lift with one hand. Large sheets are rolled in thirds when carried loose. Avoid bending corners and nicking edges when handling or jogging paper. These defects will cause misfeed and jams on the press.

PAPER SELECTION BY PROPERTIES

A particular paper is selected for a printing job because it best satisfies the requirements of the printer. The buyer chooses paper with several objectives in mind. Foremost is the ability of the sheet to perform satisfactorily for the intended use. The paper must compare favorably with similar papers as to quality, print rendition, and economy. To evaluate, the buyer must classify the paper and identify, measure, or compare the properties and characteristics of the paper.

Buyers can compare papers from sample sheets furnished by paper companies. The paper is identified by family, substance, finish, and traditional usage. While investigating properties of the sheet, the buyer is interested in how these properties affect

changes in relative humidity affect the edges of the paper first. If the edges lose moisture, they shrink. The result is paper with "tight" edges and a "belly" in the sheet. When the edges gain moisture, they expand across the grain. This condition creates wavy-edged paper.

Any of the above conditions causes trouble in processing and registering the sheet. Paper manufacturers try to minimize such problems by:

1. Making paper with 5 to 6 percent moisture content. This percentage of moisture will produce a paper with a relative humidity balance of 40–50 percent at a temperature of 75 degrees F.

2. Wrapping and sealing the paper in water-resistant packaging to preserve the moisture content.

Most paper dimensional problems occur because the paper is not in balance with the relative humidity when it is used. Paper is most stable dimensionally when it is used in a room where the relative humidity ranges between 40 to 50 percent at a temperature of 75 degrees F. Fig. 25-38 illustrates that the least changes in moisture content of paper occur in a range of 30 to 60 percent relative humidity.

PAPER STORAGE

Paper must be handled gently and stored carefully. Large plants are air-conditioned and humidity controlled. The paper they receive remains in its original wrapper until the entire package slowly adjusts to the inside temperature and humidity.

Paper should be stored in the same atmosphere as the pressroom. All stacks should be properly labeled, indicating: date of arrival, brand, kind, finish, size, M weight, grain direction, and number of sheets per package.

the processing (printability) of the paper. Processing methods such as letterpress, offset, or stencil require different paper properties. Not all papers meet the requirements for a particular process.

For the evaluation of paper, the characteristics exhibited are separated into three areas: usage, processing, and print properties.

1. *Usage properties* of the sheet are shown by characteristics such as grain direction, formation, weight, caliper, coating, strength, and bulking.

2. *Processing properties* are those which enhance or inhibit the ability of the sheet to be processed. Some of the characteristics are curl, pick, dimensional stability, tinting tendency, and acidity of the coating.

3. *Print properties* are those which affect the quality of the print. Some of the characteristics are: color, opacity, smoothness of surface, blocking tendency, and brightness of the paper.

End Use Properties

Looking at a sample, a buyer can examine several of the *use properties* of the paper. Among the characteristics seen is the visible extent and direction of the grain. Examination of both sides of the paper determines if one is different from the other. The top or felt side may be more absorbent and have a closer structure. This side may produce better printing than the wire side. The buyer can see and determine opacity and formation of the sheet. Paper with dark and light areas having large clumps of fibers irregularly spaced throughout the paper would have poor or wild formation.

The paper's rate of absorption of oil and water is important to production. This is particularly important if the paper is to be used for gluing or packaging. The buyer is interested in the dimensional stability and would like to know if the sheet has uniform weight and is calipered evenly. A careful examination of the surface paper is made, noting the finish, the sizing, and the properties of the coating.

Processing Properties

To evaluate the characteristics of a paper for printing processes, it is important to be aware of the condition of the paper. The condition of the paper as it is being processed will most affect the printability of the sheet. *Printability* is the ability of the paper to accept the ink image and to travel through the press.

Poor printability may be the result of handling, deterioration, or manufacture. Printability is directly affected by temperature, humidity, and treatment by processing equipment.

A common problem while running paper is the rupture of the surface or coating of the paper. This may be causd by excessive tack of the ink or by a lack of strength in the surface or coating of the paper. A pick test can be made of the paper prior to printing to aid in determining the rupture characteristics of the stock's surface.

Curling of stock is often a problem during processing. A wet-curl test prior to printing may expose structural curl of the paper. In a similar manner, a tinting test can aid in determining the relationship of the acidity of the paper to the fountain solution. These tests of paper may be made before it is used for printing.

Print Properties

The reliability and quality of the print may be directly affected by the properties of the paper. A blue ink test or a K & N ink test can be used to examine absorption and the smoothness of the paper. The brightness and gloss of the paper can be measured by a reflectance meter to evaluate their effect on the print. Visual inspection can be used to recognize interference in the quality of the print by surface trash (spray, dirt, and dried ink). Careful vis-

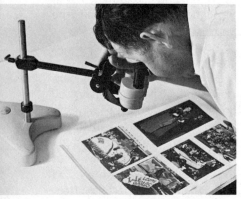

25-39. Checking for defects in print with a twenty-power binocular viewer.

ual inspection will reveal poor coating or formation of the paper, which can lead to loss of print quality. Fig. 25-39.

Some problems show up after printing: dryer migration, blocking of the sheets, tendency to ghosting, setoff, and chalking. These problems are examined in Chapter 26, "Ink." While many of these problems can be traced directly to the equipment or the ink, several are directly related to the characteristics of the sheet.

PAPER EVALUATION
COMPARISON TESTING

A number of simple, practical tests are available to examine paper characteristics. These are *comparison tests* designed to be used within the shop. The results of the tests are not normally transferable from one plant to another. Such tests are not scientific in nature. They are only significant at the time of the test. Such tests have no relationship to previous or later results when using the same testing materials. However, these tests are valuable to the printer because they form a basis of comparison between papers undergoing the same conditions of process and usage. Using a series of practical tests to determine the end use characteristics of paper, a printer can select paper according to usage. These tests give a printer a view of the physical condition of the paper prior to printing.

Printability tests aid in detecting problems and conditions while the printing is in progress. These tests help predict the reliability of the printing and the amount of spoilage. A number of tests can also be applied to the

printed sheet. They examine the quality of the print and aid in solving future printing problems.

The success of practical testing methods depends on three factors: the paper used, the environmental conditions, and the relationship of the paper properties. Practical paper testing does not, as a rule, examine individual characteristics, many of which are related. The tests should be selected to give the specific information required for a particular sheet. There are close relationships between the paper, the printing equipment, and the ink. Any attempt to consider paper as an isolated material whose characteristics and qualities can be determined without regard to printing process or ink is false and misleading.

ESTIMATING

Estimating is done to determine the amount of paper needed to complete a printing job. This includes the number of copies, the number and size of the pages, and the spoilage. *Spoilage* is determined by the number of operations the paper

will go through before the work is completed and the volume of the job. The amount of spoilage differs with the various processes of printing as well as the quality of the work. Offset web press spoilage is generally higher than sheet-fed offset. Sheet-fed offset spoilage may be higher than letterpress. A high spoilage percentage is usual for short runs.

Each additional processing of the paper, as in multicolor printing and finishing operations, increases the percentage of spoilage. Spoilage percentage can be used for the following example: A job with a press run of 6,000 sheets requires 3 percent spoilage for the first run. This requires an additional 180 sheets. If these sheets were folded in the bindery, an additional 2 1/2 percent of spoilage, or 150 sheets, may be required. A total of 6,330 sheets would need to be delivered to the press.

PAPER DIAGRAMS

Paper diagrams are visual layouts showing where the paper is to be cut.

To determine the number of pieces of a certain size that can be cut from a full sheet, a diagram is drawn of the cutting procedure. A simple diagram shows the cutting of 8 1/2" × 11" pieces from a sheet sized 17 1/2" × 22 1/2". Fig. 25-40. The letters indicate the sequence of cuts.

This can be shown also by simple arithmetic:

Basic sheet size:	17 1/2" × 22 1/2"
Size to be cut:	8 1/2" × 11"
2	× 2 = 4 pieces

The 8 1/2 goes into 17 1/2 two times; 11 goes into 22 1/2 two times. (Disregard remainders.) 2 × 2 = 4 sheets.

Diagramming the full sheet is especially useful if a combination cut is necessary. If 8 1/2" by 11" pieces are cut from a whole sheet sized 20" × 26", the diagram would show the stock must be cut lengthwise first to get the maximum number of pieces. Fig. 25-41.

This is shown as a combined cutting by the figures:

Basic sheet size:
     20″ × 26″
Size to be cut:
     11″ × 8 1/2″
     ————————————
     1 × 3 = 3 pieces
Remaining size:
     9″ × 26″
     8 1/2″ × 11″
     ————————————
     1 × 2 = 2 pieces
Total = 5 pieces from 20″ × 26″ sheet

A general rule can be used to determine if the maximum number of pieces is being cut from a full sheet. Figure the square inches of waste paper. If this sum is larger than the sum of square inches of the cut piece, further attempts should be made to cut out more pieces. If the 20″ × 26″ sheet was figured as a straight cutting, the diagram would show excessive waste.

In Fig. 25-42, total waste is figured by multiplying the length by the width of both waste strips: 17″ × 4″ = 68 sq. in. and 26″ × 3″ = 78 sq. in. This makes a total of 146 sq. in. of waste and is greater than the area of the cut piece (8 1/2″ × 11″ = 93.5 sq. in.). This rule does not apply for square pieces, unusual sizes, or when two or three pieces can be cut from a full sheet.

Combination cuts, or "Dutch cuts," occur when the full sheet size is not directly proportional to the size of the piece being cut. Some of the more common Dutch cuts are:

25-40. *Standard method of cutting.*

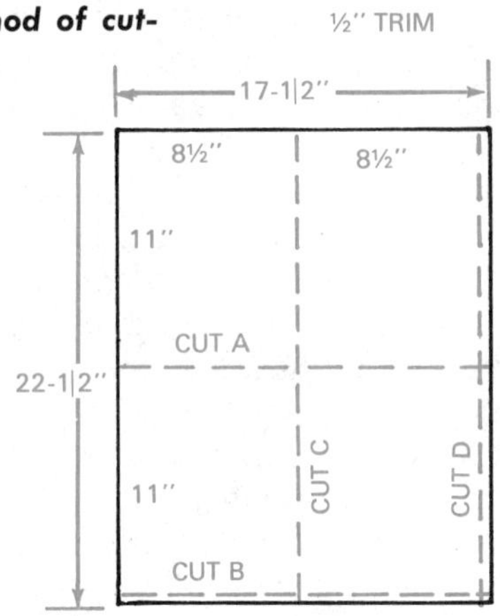

½″ TRIM

DOTTED LINES SHOW STOCK CUTS. CUT IN ALPHABETICAL ORDER.

The amount of waste may be compared for different sized full sheets. This will show which size is most economical to use. The percentage of waste for each size can easily be determined by dividing sheet area by waste area.

Example: Which is a greater saving when cutting 5″ × 8″ pieces of index: the use of 22 1/2″ × 28 1/2″ sheets or 25 1/2″ × 30 1/2″ sheets?

Full Sheet	Piece Size	Number Out
22″ × 34″	7 1/2″ × 10 1/2″	9
20″ × 26″	8 1/2″ × 11″	5
28″ × 34″	8 1/2″ × 11″	10
25 1/2″ × 30 1/2″	8 1/2″ × 11″	8
22″ × 28″	9″ × 12″	5

22 1/2″ × 28 1/2″
5″ × 8″
————————————
4 × 3 = 12
Sheet area = 641.25 sq. in.
Waste area = 161.25 sq. in.

Percentage waste = $\dfrac{161.25}{641.25} \times 100$

Percentage waste = 25.15

25 1/2″ × 30 1/2″
8″ × 5″
————————————
3 × 6 = 18
Sheet area = 777.75 sq. in.
Waste area = 57.75 sq. in.

Percentage waste = $\dfrac{57.75}{777.75} \times 100$

Percentage waste = 7.43

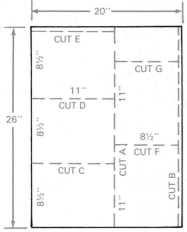

25-41. Combination cutting.

DOTTED LINES SHOW STOCK CUTS. CUT IN ALPHABETICAL ORDER.

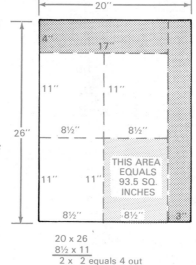

25-42. Figuring square inches of waste.

20 x 26
8½ x 11
2 x 2 equals 4 out

WASTE
4 x 17 equals 68 SQ. INCHES
3 x 26 equals 78 SQ. INCHES
TOTAL 146 SQ. INCHES

pressroom and bindery can process. The processing size is determined by: the size of the untrimmed page, the number of pages in a signature, size of press, and method of folding. Usually the grain direction of the sheet is parallel to the binding so the pages will be flat. Sometimes it is more important in offset work to have the sheet grain long, regardless of the binding.

To determine the amount and size of paper to cut for a publication, the following method is used.

Example:
5,000 booklets
Page size = 6″ × 9″
Trim 1/4″
96 pages, self-covered
Signature = 32 pages

The paper to be used is a 25″ × 38″ size book, 60 substance. A diagram of the 6″ × 9″ pieces and trim is drawn to determine the process size. Fig. 25-43.

Four ranks of four pages are imposed in the following manner. The dotted lines indicate trim area when the signature is folded. Since each signature contains 32 pages, each booklet of 96 pages will require three processing size sheets, or 15 M processing size sheets for the 5 M booklets. An additional 6 percent, or 900 sheets, is added for spoilage, for a total of 15,900 25″ × 38″ sheets. Bindery spoilage would be an additional amount. Each thousand sheets of this size weighs 120 pounds. The total weight required is then 120 pounds × 15.9, or 1,908 pounds.

An estimating chart, Fig. 25-44, can be used to determine the number and size of sheets re-

The total sheet area in each size is divided into the waste area for each size. This figure is multiplied by 100 to give the percent of waste. The lower waste percentage determines the most economical cut. This is true regardless of the number of pieces that can be cut from any size.

Often a number of sheets are needed to produce the finished product, such as a booklet. The maximum size of sheets to be used is limited by the largest sheet size the equipment in the

ALL TRIM 1|4″

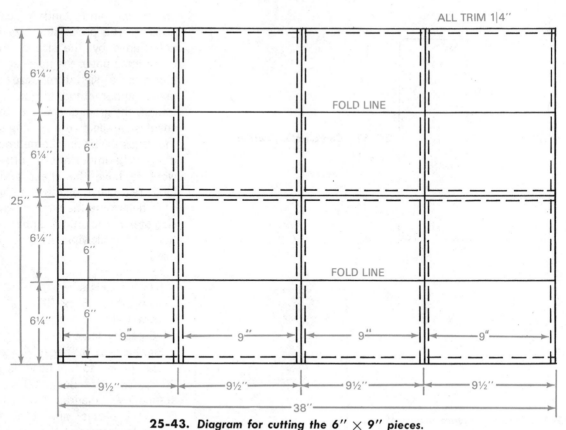

25-43. *Diagram for cutting the 6″ × 9″ pieces.*

quired for the number of pages and size of booklet desired.

A cutting chart, Fig. 25-45, simplifies the method for determining the number of sheets required for cutting into smaller pieces. Spoilage should be determined before using the chart.

HANDLING PAPER

Handling paper involves selecting, moving, and determin-

ing amounts needed. The number of sheets in a package or carton is usually indicated on the wrapper. Larger amounts of paper may be skid-wrapped, and the reams marked (flagged) by slips of paper. Fig. 25-46. When paper is removed from a container, the sheets should be marked on the container.

Counting loose paper takes clean hands and a quick eye.

With the left palm up, take about 1″ of paper at the edge away from you and roll the paper over your hand, allowing the parallel edge to flare and separate. Count the flared sheets in convenient groups of four or five sheets. Fig. 25-47. As you count, use the right thumb to group the sheets and the first finger to guard the successive groups counted.

PAPER ESTIMATING CHART

Page Size	Number Pages	Number out of Sheet	Standard Sheet Size
3 1/2 × 6 1/4	4	24	28 × 44
	8	12	28 × 44
	12	8	28 × 44
	16	6	28 × 44
	24	4	28 × 44
4 × 9	4	12	25 × 38
	8	12	38 × 50
	12	4	25 × 38
	16	6	38 × 50
	24	2	25 × 38
4 1/4 × 5 3/8	4	32	35 × 45
	8	16	35 × 45
	16	8	35 × 45
	32	4	35 × 45
4 1/2 × 6	4	16	25 × 38
	8	8	25 × 38
	16	4	25 × 38
	32	2	25 × 38
5 1/4 × 7 5/8	4	16	32 × 44
	8	8	32 × 44
	16	4	32 × 44
	32	2	32 × 44
5 1/2 × 8 1/2	4	16	35 × 45
	8	8	35 × 45
	16	4	35 × 45
	32	2	35 × 45
6 × 9	4	8	25 × 38
	8	4	25 × 38
	16	2	25 × 38
	32	2	38 × 50
7 × 5 1/2 Oblong	4	8	23 × 29
	8	4	23 × 29
	16	2	23 × 29
7 3/4 × 10 5/8	4	8	32 × 44
	8	4	32 × 44
	16	2	32 × 44
8 1/2 × 11	4	4	23 × 35
	8	2	23 × 35
	16	2	35 × 45
8 3/4 × 11 1/2	4	8	36 × 48
	8	4	36 × 48
	16	2	36 × 48
9 × 12	4	4	25 × 38
	8	2	25 × 38
	16	2	38 × 50

25-44. *This chart can be used to figure the size and number of sheets required for a job.*

DETERMINING NUMBER OF
FULL SHEETS NEEDED

Explanation. Find the number of pieces that cut out of the sheet size selected. Find that number in the left-hand column—follow across to the figure in the column designating the quantity required (quantity shown at the head of each column). For instance, a job cuts 16 out of a sheet; the order is for 3,500 pieces—see figure 16 in left-hand column and follow across to the 3000 column. The figure is 188. Then add 1/2 of the amount in the 1000 column for the extra 500, making a total of 220 sheets. Make allowance for waste, as required.

	100	250	1000	2000	3000	4000	5000
1	100	250	1000	2000	3000	4000	5000
2	50	125	500	1000	1500	2000	2500
3	34	84	334	667	1000	1334	1667
4	25	63	250	500	750	1000	1250
5	20	50	200	400	600	800	1000
6	17	42	167	334	500	667	834
7	15	36	143	286	429	572	715
8	13	32	125	250	375	500	625
9	12	28	112	223	334	445	556
10	10	25	100	200	300	400	500
11	10	23	91	182	273	364	455
12	9	21	84	167	250	334	416
13	8	20	77	154	231	308	385
14	8	18	72	143	215	286	358
15	7	17	67	134	200	267	334
16	7	16	63	125	188	250	313
17	6	15	59	118	177	236	295
18	6	14	56	112	167	223	279
19	5	14	53	106	158	211	264
20	5	13	50	100	150	200	250
21	5	12	48	96	143	191	239
22	5	12	46	91	137	182	228
23	5	11	44	87	131	174	218
24	5	11	42	84	125	167	209
25	4	10	40	80	120	160	200
26	4	10	39	77	116	154	193
27	4	10	38	75	112	149	186
28	4	9	36	72	108	143	179
29	4	9	35	69	104	138	173
30	4	9	34	67	100	134	167
31	4	9	33	65	97	130	162
32	4	8	32	63	94	125	157
33	4	8	31	61	91	122	152
34	3	8	30	59	89	118	148
35	3	8	29	58	86	115	143
36	3	7	28	56	84	112	139
37	3	7	28	55	82	109	136
38	3	7	27	53	79	106	132
39	3	7	26	52	77	103	129
40	3	7	25	50	75	100	125

25-45. *A chart to determine number of full sheets required for paper to be cut to size.*

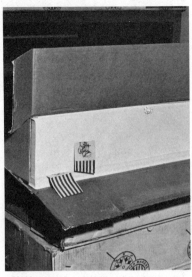

25-46. *"Flagged" reams.*

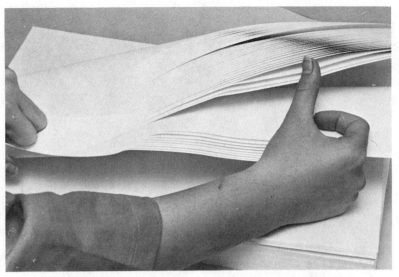

25-47. *Proper method of counting paper by hand.*

REVIEW QUESTIONS

1. Paper fibers are made of what compound?
2. Rotating the logs in a drum is one method of removing bark. Name another.
3. All pulp must be bleached before it can be made into paper. True or False?
4. Name the paper ingredients described in the following:
   a. Improve paper's texture and plug spaces between fibers.
   b. Makes paper less water-absorbent.
   c. Adhesives used to help hold the pulp mixture together.
5. Before paper enters the "dry end" of the paper machine, what is its moisture content (percentage)?
6. What is the name of the roller which makes the watermark on paper?
7. Coating must be done on the papermaking machine. True or False?
8. Name the types of paper described in the following:
   a. General name for printing and writing stocks.
   b. Paper used for publication purposes.
   c. Paper designed so that changes or erasures can be easily detected.
   d. Thin, translucent paper.
9. Define the term *basis weight*.
10. What is the size of the metric AO paper?
11. Name the paper properties described in the following:
    a. The way the fibers are matted.
    b. The amount of space between fibers.
    c. Amount of water in paper.
    d. Ease with which paper will travel through the press.

Ink is a mixture of coloring matter and fluids. The coloring matter is *pigment* or *dye*. The fluids are the *vehicle* part of the ink.

The colorant (pigment or dye) serves to block or filter light reflecting from the paper's surface. An image printed on paper changes the amount and kind of light reflected from any area where ink is applied. The black inked letters on this white paper provide large differences in light reflection. The difference is called contrast. Contrast makes the letters easy to see.

In printing, the ink must be permanently attached to the paper. The ink must dry in such a way that the pigment cannot be smeared or wiped off. The vehicle in ink dries and fastens the pigment to paper.

INK MANUFACTURE

Ink is made by mixing pigments and vehicles together. The dry pigments are first wetted down by the vehicle in a paddle-type mixer. Fig. 26-1.

The mixed ink is too coarse for printing. It must be put into grinders that reduce the pigment particles in size and mix them throughout the vehicle. A three-roll mill, Fig. 26-2, is used to grind inks for letterpress and offset presses. This grinder has three rollers almost touching each other. The middle roller is driven at a different speed than the two outside rollers. The ink is ground between the rollers. The rollers force the pigment or dye to completely mix (disperse) into the vehicle. Other types of grinders, such as ball mills and sand grinders, are used for thinner inks.

The manufacture of ink today requires many ingredients. These ingredients specialize ink for a particular purpose, printing process, and paper. Each kind of ink is made from a specific formula. Many thousands of new formulas are made each year. New inks are necessary as new

26-1. *A high-speed mixer of this type is generally used to disperse fluid inks or to predisperse pigment before milling.*

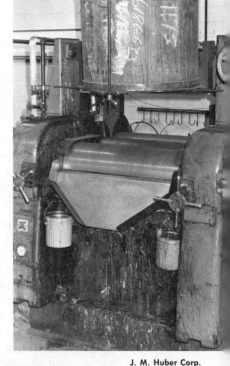

26-2. *A three-roll mill. This mill is the final processing step before packaging most medium-bodied inks. Adjustments for dispersion are made by the controls on the front and rear of the mill.*

26-3. Ink fountain and rollers of a duplicator.

materials, processes, and techniques become part of the printing industry.

VEHICLES

Vehicles are a combination of oils, resins, dryers, and special compounds. Vehicles are used in ink to carry the pigment from the ink fountain across the rollers onto the image carrier. Fig. 26-3. The image carrier retains the ink until a print is made on paper.

Vehicles require several kinds of ingredients to work properly.

The vehicle must fasten the pigment to paper. These fasteners are varnishes, resins, and drying oils. They form a dry coating or film to adhere the pigments.

Evaporative, or volatile, materials can be used. They temporarily keep certain film-forming materials like resins in a fluid state. These volatile materials may be thinners or solvents. Alcohols or petroleum solvents are in common use.

Special compounds (additives) are used to control the way in which the ink works under different conditions. Only small amounts are added to the ink. Dryers, waxes, retardants, dis-

persing agents, and soap belong in this category.

TERMS

You will need to know certain terms to understand the nature of vehicles. For example, linseed oil is made into litho varnish (a common vehicle) by cooking to a certain thickness, or *viscosity.* Viscosity generally is a measure of the consistency of plastic flow. The speed of the flow is used as the measurement of viscosity.

Plastic flow means that a sticky kind of heavy liquid requires a push before it will flow. Many vehicles tend to thicken when at rest but thin out when stirred. This condition is called *thixotropy.*

The science of flow is *rheology.* It deals with *Newtonian liquids*—those which flow (like water) in proportion to force applied. This science also deals with *non-Newtonian* fluids. These fluids, like ink vehicles, do not respond directly or in proportion to force applied. Stickiness of ink is called *tack.*

VARNISHES

As linseed oil is cooked, it gains in "*body*" or *consistency.* *Consistency* is a word used for several properties that are considered as one. Consistency is collectively the word for viscosity, thixotropy, surface tension, cohesion, adhesion, and flow-affecting forces. The consistency of an ink varies because of changes in temperature, age, and degree of ink agitation. Litho varnish is made in various consistencies. The thinnest varnish is numbered 00000. Thicker varnishes are numbered from 0000 to 0. Then numbers from 1 to 0. Then numbers from 1

through 9 are used. Number nine, a very thick varnish, is called a *body gum,* while those in the zero series are called *reducers.*

Litho varnishes have natural drying properties that form a film. Drying is speeded by adding salts of certain metals. Most widely used are cobalt, lead, and manganese salts.

SYNTHETIC OILS

Modern inks use litho varnishes and other film-forming materials. In general, litho varnishes are too soft and dry too slowly for modern presses. The development of synthetic drying oils has improved the drying time of modern ink. Among these oils are dehydrated castor oil, epoxy oil, and alkyd oils.

RESINS

Other vehicle improvements have been produced by adding resins to litho varnish. Many of the resins (natural or synthetic) require an added solvent to remain liquid at normal temperature. Combinations of drying oils and resins are known as oleo-resinous varnishes. The resin provides ink durability and gloss. The varnish provides drying and flexibility of ink.

Natural resins are gums or sap from trees. *Synthetic resins* include epoxy, phenolic, maleic, urea, and melamine. The advantages of synthetic products are their uniformity, abundance, and ability to be tailor-made for use.

Lacquers are used in fast-drying inks as vehicles. Lacquers dry by evaporation of their volatile solvents. Many of the lacquers are made of vinyl, nitrocellulose, and ethyl cellulose.

Solvents

Solvents are fluids which dissolve solids. They reduce the viscosity or consistency of solids and liquids. In inks, vehicle solvents keep film-forming resins and celluloses liquid. The film formers are held in liquid state until the ink is applied to the *substrate* (paper, plastic, and so forth). The solvent is then removed, and the ink dries.

Solvents are grouped by their boiling points. Low boilers have boiling points below 100 °C (212° F.). Medium boilers are between 100 °C and 150 °C (212–302° F.). High boilers are between 150 °C and 225 °C (302–438° F.). At or above the boiling point, solvents evaporate. Most solvents are flammable. Some are toxic and can cause disease, disabilities, and even death.

Acetone is an example of one of the low-boiling solvents. It boils at 56 °C (132° F.). It dissolves cellulose, resins, and oils. Highly flammable, it is used only for very fast drying inks.

Many solvents are derived from coal tar and petroleum. As a group, they are known as *hydrocarbons*. Benzol, toluol, naphtha, benzene, hexane, and kerosene are hydrocarbon solvents. They are widely used in inks which have synthetic resins.

Methyl (wood) and ethyl (grain, ethanol, or spirit) alcohols dissolve gums, such as rosin and shellac. They have been widely used in flexographic printing and for spirit varnishes. Higher-boiling alcohols, such as octanol alcohol (185 °C, or 366° F.) are used in heat-set inks.

Many solvents are made for exacting uses. Because of the great variety of solvents, they are named by the group to which they belong. Some of the solvent groups used in printing are the nitroparaffins, terpenes, alcohol-ethers, esters, and chlorinated compounds.

The kind of vehicle used for an ink is determined by the purpose of the ink, the printing process, the kind of paper, and the method of ink drying. Typical examples of drying are shown in Fig. 26-4.

VEHICLE DRYING

Vehicles can be grouped by the way that they dry. These groups are: nondrying oil, drying oil, solvent and resin, glycol and resin, resin oil, and resin wax.

ABSORPTION DRYING

The *nondrying* oils are used with absorbent paper. They "dry" by penetration into the paper. These oils carry some of the pigment into the paper. Some pigment may remain on the surface and can be rubbed off. Newsprint and mimeo papers are made to absorb nondrying oils. Commonly used oils are rosin and petroleum oils. When dyes are used in place of pigments, they may become part of the vehicle. Dyes seldom remain on the surface.

Absorption drying requires a thin ink with high color strength. This kind of ink is not used for quality printing. The absorbing oils travel along the paper fibers and create a fuzzy image. Nonabsorbent paper cannot be used with this ink.

OXIDATION AND POLYMERIZATION

Most of the inks used in letterpress and offset printing dry by *oxidation*. The vehicle absorbs oxygen and becomes solid.

Metallic salts added to the ink as dryers speed drying time. Lead, cobalt, and manganese salts act as *catalysts* to dry the vehicle. (A catalyst is a substance that causes a chemical change, but is not part of the change.)

Some inks dry by combining small molecules into large molecules. This process is called polymerization. This causes the large molecules to become solid. A chemical change starting with

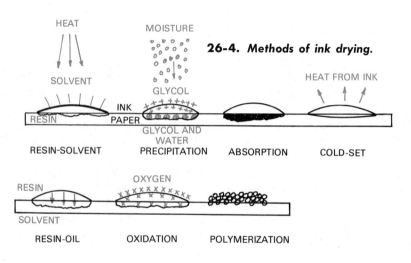

26-4. *Methods of ink drying.*

oxygen thickens the oils to a rubbery mass called a *gel.* Gelled ink is considered "set" (can be handled carefully) and continues to dry until the ink is hard. Some oils that dry by polymerization are linseed (flax), tung, perilla, and castor oil. Linseed oil that has been cooked dries by oxidation. Fig. 26-5 shows a cooker for producing varnishes.

RESIN-SOLVENT DRYING

The solvent and resin method of drying is used in gravure, flexography, and other processes requiring high-speed drying. A resin such as epoxy or vinyl is dissolved in a suitable solvent. The resin-solvent vehicle dries by evaporation of the solvent, leaving the solid resin behind as a dry film. Fig. 26-4. Different processes and materials require different combinations of resins and solvents. Flexographic inks use alcohol and lacquer solvents. Gravure inks use hydrocarbon solvents. Offset and letterpress inks use petroleum solvents. Additional speed in evaporation is obtained by heating the printed ink. Heat-set inks are used in high-speed offset and letterpress web presses.

MOISTURE-SET DRYING

Resins are also used in *moisture-set* or precipitation drying. This method commonly uses resin dissolved in glycol. Glycols seek water. When the glycol-resin solution as a vehicle is printed on paper, it is sprayed with water or steam. The glycol combines with the water and is absorbed into the paper. The resin which loses the glycol returns (precipitates) to a solid film. Fig. 26-4. This action occurs rapidly, causing

J. M. Huber Corp.

26-5. A varnish kettle. Shown here is the upper portion of a 1,000-gallon varnish reactor. From here, the unit is charged with its ingredients prior to manufacture. The size of batches ranges from 6,000 to 10,000 pounds.

the ink to dry instantly. Moisture-set inks are widely used in letterpress printing of food packaging material.

RESIN-OIL DRYING

The *resin-oil* group of vehicles dry by absorption and oxidation. Inks made with this vehicle are called quick-set. The drying is faster because it is a combination of resin solidification and oxidation of the oil. When the ink is printed, some of the resin's solvent is absorbed into the paper. The solid resin makes a thin, dry shell over the ink surface. Fig. 26-4. This surface can be handled immediately after printing.

The oil portion of the ink below this surface dries more slowly by oxidation. If handled roughly too soon after printing, the surface will be broken. The ink will then smear. Additions to this ink can easily upset the balance of the resin and oil drying sequence. These inks are used where short-run work requires immediate handling.

COLD-SET DRYING

The *cold-set* inks use vehicles which must be heated to become liquid. The vehicle is a combination of wax and resin. Applied hot to the paper, these inks dry by cooling to room temperature. The hot liquid becomes solid when cooled. These inks are used with specialized, heated letterpress equipment. Fig. 26-4.

PIGMENTS

Most of the coloring of an ink is created by the pigment. It is important to understand that ink

26-6A. *Reflected colors of light due to different ink colors.*

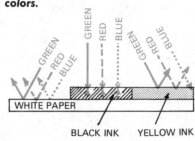

WHITE LIGHT

WHITE PAPER

BLACK INK   YELLOW INK

in general is used to block or filter the light from the surface printed. Dull, black, opaque ink on white paper reflects little light. The ink is seen by contrast with the light reflected from the white surface surrounding it. Transparent inks act as filters, screening some of the light reflected from the printed surface. Fig. 26-6A.

Pigments are of two general types. Some are obtained from *inorganic* materials, such as metals and minerals. Mineral pigments are characterized by large particle size and heavy weight. They dry well in drying oils and are generally insoluble. Others are made from *organic* materials, such as coal tar.

Most pigments used today are manufactured. The manufactured organic pigments are dyes made from byproducts of coal tar and solvents. Pure dyes are called *toners*. The dyes are precipitated in water. The water is filtered out to produce *dry* colors. *Flushed* colors are made by separating the color from the water by adding oils. Some pigment dyes contain minerals and are called *lakes*.

Natural and Synthetic Organic Pigments

Pigments made from natural or artificial dyestuffs are known as natural organic or synthetic organic pigments. The natural organic pigments are produced from organisms which were once alive. Synthetic organic pigments are produced by processing chemicals to make dyes. Both natural and synthetic organic pigments are derived from compounds of carbon.

Natural dyestuffs are from sources such as the indigo root (deep blue) and cochineal insects (carmine).

Synthetic dyestuffs were developed in 1856. Almost all organic pigments used in inks today are synthetic.

Coal tar is the basic material from which synthetic pigments are made. The coal tar is distilled, producing light, medium, and heavy oils called crudes. The light oils contain benzol and toluol. Medium oils contain phenol (carbolic acid) and naphthalene. Heavy oils (creosote oils) contain anthracene.

These materials from the crudes are treated with various acids and other chemicals to produce *intermediates*. The intermediates are chemically treated to develop dyestuffs. One chemical process, called *diazotization*, is the interaction of an intermediate with chemicals to produce a *diazonium compound*. This compound will react with other intermediates to form azo colors. Most azo colors are toners, insoluble in water. These are dried and used directly as pigments. Other azo colors are water soluble. They are true dyestuffs and must be precipitated onto a material to be used as a *lake* pigment. The word *lake* means the dyestuff has been deposited on an inert base and has become insoluble in water. These bases include barium chloride, calcium chloride, alumina hydrate, and gloss white. Fig. 26-6B demonstrates the chemical breakdown of coal tar by distillation and chemical treatment to produce toners and lakes.

The manufacture of organic pigments is highly specialized. Rigid controls, complex procedures, and exacting standards are observed by the laboratories. Precipitation vats and solution tanks are used to produce toners and lakes. Filter presses squeeze water from the precipitated colorant. The pressed colors (filter cakes) are oven-dried and pulverized. The dry pigments are often blended prior to packaging.

Black pigments are in greatest use. Practically all of the black pigments are a form of carbon. *Lampblack* is a pigment made by collecting the soot from poorly burned creosote oils. The pigment *carbon black* is made by burning natural gas in limited air. The carbon is deposited on iron sheets, called channels, in a continuous production process. *Furnace blacks* are made by burning oil or gas in limited air inside horizontal furnaces. The fine, dense black is collected by filter bags or water spray. *Bone blacks* are made by charring animal bones, mainly from sheep.

The colored pigments are manufactured products. Most of the reds are synthetic dyestuffs. Para-reds, toluidine reds, and lithol reds are toners. These reds vary in color from orange to maroon. Their final color depends on the addition of other materials and the method of manufacture.

The orange and yellow pigments have in the past been associated with metals. The chrome yellows contain lead. Other metals used for orange pigments include cadmium, zinc, and molybdenum. Synthetic pigment dyestuffs include the Hansa yellows, the benzidine yellows and oranges, Persian orange, and tartrazine yellow.

Blue pigments of organic nature are the Peacock blue (a lake) and phthalocyanine blue. Inorganic blues include the iron blues and ultramarine blues.

Many of the green pigments are made from combinations of yellow and blue pigments. Brilliant green, malachite green, and Victorian green are toners. Toners are precipitated by an acid process into pigments.

The white pigments are used as colorants when they are naturally opaque. Transparent white pigments are used to extend inks. Titanium dioxide is the most widely used white opaque pigment. It is often combined with barium sulfate and zinc oxide.

The most transparent pigment in use is alumina hydrate. Another transparent is gloss white, a mixture of alumina hydrate and barium sulfate. Other transparents include blanc fixe, (precipitated barium sulfate), calcium carbonate, magnesium carbonate, and silica aerogel.

The transparent whites are used to extend colored inks, to make tints, and to provide working properties to inks. Most transparent white inks use a combination of pigments. These combinations help achieve balance in use and cost of inks.

DAYLIGHT FLUORESCENT PIGMENTS

Brilliant colors are created in modern fluorescent inks. Dyestuffs from the fluorescein family are made into pigments by chemical interaction with synthetic resins. These pigments absorb ultraviolet light. The color intensity appears greater due to the emitted light combined with the normally reflected light.

Inks made from these pigments give greater brilliance when applied as a thick film (0.001″ to 0.002″). Thinner films reduce brilliance. Silk screen, gravure, and letterpress processes produce good results. Some recent developments may produce satisfactory ink for the offset process.

PERMANENCY OF PIGMENTS

Both natural and synthetic pigments have different degrees of resistance to chemicals and surfaces. Offset inks, for example, are highly resistant to bleeding in water. Inks used for medical labels must be resistant to

26-6B. The preparation of toners and lakes from coal tar through distillation and chemical treatment.

alcohol bleeding. A table of the permanency and resistance of various ink pigments is shown in Fig. 26-7.

INK COMPOUNDS AND ADDITIVES

Many inks require additional ingredients in order to work and dry properly. Most additives are mixed into the ink during manufacture. A few compounds can be added by the press operator. Only small amounts can be added without causing serious problems in the ink.

Greases, such as tallow, wool grease, and lanolin, aid in ink setting and lubrication. Wool grease is also used with beeswax to prevent crystallization of waxes in ink. Lubrication is necessary in some inks to aid in transfer and distribution.

Thin oils and *solvents* may be added to reduce tack. They are useful for rapid penetration and quick setting.

Wetting agents are chemicals which help the vehicle to cover the pigment particles. This improves pigment dispersion and renders a more uniform ink.

Antioxidants are additives that slow down surface drying. The function of this additive is to use up oxygen. This slows the oxygen reaction of the drying oils but does not prevent polymerization.

Deodorants are added to eliminate the odors of oil and dryers. Perfumes may be included to impart a fragrance to the ink.

PRINTING WITH INK

Ink is transferred from a supply to produce a print. The ink must meet the requirements of the process (press) image, paper,

and end use of the print. In Chapter 25, "Paper," the uses of various kinds of paper were discussed. The paper surface determines the kind of ink to be used.

Very absorbent paper can use ink that dries by absorption. Newsprint, rotogravure paper, and mimeo paper have the characteristics for absorption-drying inks. These inks are thin, free flowing, and have little tack. Letterpress news ink may be printed and dried at high speeds. Drying may leave some loose pigment on the surface. Some smudging is likely. Newspapers are short-lived, and permanence of print is not important. Speed, economy, and reliability of news ink are important.

Some papers are sized to resist moisture. These papers are not highly absorptive. Inks to match these papers dry by oxidation. Coated papers have the smoothest surface. Generally, the smoother the paper, the finer the reproduction can be made. Inks to match these surfaces are finely ground. They may have high gloss, rub resistance, and quick-drying characteristics.

Nonabsorbent materials, such as foils, glass, and some plastics require inks that grip the surface. These smooth surfaces must be treated before the inks can adhere.

Only two very general characteristics of papers, absorption and smoothness, have been considered. Other paper characteristics also affect the ink and how it is used.

INK AND PRESS

Inks are made to match the method of printing. Letterpress, litho, gravure, and screen inks

differ because of the method of transferring the image. Each process requires a certain general type of ink. The press speed and kind of paper determine the method of drying. The nature of the image is a factor in the formulation of the ink. Halftone inks, for example, are finely ground, with blue added for tone.

RELIEF PROCESS

Letterpress ink is applied only to the raised portion of the type or cuts. The ink must have the ability to cling to the metal. It must cover the entire surface but not run over the edges. It must readily transfer through the roller train to the image carrier and then to the paper. It must retain its shape during the press impression so that the print is an accurate reproduction.

Letterpress inks are generally classified into *job, flatbed, cylinder, rotary* and *web, news,* and *special inks.*

Job inks are general-purpose inks. They are made for open platen presses. The body is thick (high viscosity). The vehicle is short. Drying is usually by oxidation.

Flatbed and cylinder inks cover a wide range of specialized inks. Many are made for particular brands of presses. All cylinder inks are generally of medium body and flow well. The pigment is finely ground and nonabrasive. The vehicle is usually drying oil and synthetic resin. Drying is by oxidation and polymerization. Faster presses use inks with thinner body and longer vehicles. Dryers are normally a mixture of cobalt and paste. Since offset is a problem with some papers, some reducers are added to set

PERMANENCY AND RESISTANCE OF INK PIGMENTS

	Permanency	Alkali Resistance	Resistance to Alcohol Bleeding	Resistance to Water Bleeding	Paraffin Bleeding	Baking Resistance	Trans. or Opaque
Chrome Yellow	Very Good	Poor	Excellent	Excellent	Excellent	Very Good	Opaque
Cadmium Yellow	Excellent	Excellent	Excellent	Excellent	Excellent	Excellent	Opaque
Hansa Yellow	Very Good	Very Good	Poor	Excellent	Poor	Good	Semi-Trans.
Benzidine Yellow	Fair	Good	Good	Excellent	Good	Excellent	Semi-Trans.
Yellow Lake	Poor	Poor	Fair	Poor	Excellent	Excellent	Trans.
Molybdate Orange	Very Good	Fair	Excellent	Excellent	Excellent	Very Good	Opaque
Orange Lake	Poor	Poor	Poor	Poor	Excellent	Excellent	Trans.
Chrome Green	Very Good	Poor	Excellent	Excellent	Excellent	Very Good	Opaque
Phthalocyanine Green	Excellent	Excellent	Excellent	Excellent	Excellent	Excellent	Trans.
Tungstated Green	Good	Good	Poor	Excellent	Excellent	Excellent	Trans.
Milori Blue	Excellent	Fair	Excellent	Excellent	Excellent	Excellent	Trans.
Phthalocyanine Blue	Excellent	Excellent	Excellent	Excellent	Excellent	Excellent	Trans.
Peacock Blue	Poor	Poor	Poor	Poor	Excellent	Poor	Trans.
Tungstated Blue	Good	Fair	Poor	Excellent	Excellent	Very Good	Trans.
Tungstated Violet	Good	Fair	Poor	Excellent	Very Good	Very Good	Trans.
Toluidine Red	Very Good	Excellent	Poor	Good	Poor	Very Good	Opaque
Red Lake C	Good	Fair	Fair	Good	Excellent	Good	Trans.
Lithol Red (Sodium)	Fair	Fair	Fair	Fair	Excellent	Poor	Semi-Trans.
Lithol Red (Barium)	Good	Fair	Fair	Excellent	Excellent	Good	Semi-Trans.
Lithol Red (Calcium)	Good	Fair	Fair	Excellent	Excellent	Excellent	Semi-Trans.
Rubine Red	Good	Fair	Very Good	Excellent	Excellent	Very Good	Semi-Trans.
Para Red	Very Good	Very Good	Poor	Fair	Poor	Poor	Opaque
Phloxine Red	Poor	Good	Poor	Poor	Excellent	Good	Trans.
Naphthol Red	Very Good	Excellent	Good	Excellent	Poor	Good	Trans.

26-7. This table lists various ink pigments and their permanency and resistance.

the ink quickly. Waxes may be added to prevent offset and scuffing. (An example of offset is shown in Fig. 26-14.)

Rotary and web press inks must dry fast. These inks have thinner body and longer vehicles than flatbed inks. Heat-set inks are widely used in publication work. Generally the softer papers use slower drying inks with more nondrying oils. As stated before, the halftone inks contain finely ground pigments.

Slow, flatbed newspaper web presses and fast rotary presses use about the same kind of ink. These inks dry by absorption of the mineral oils. Thinness and tack depend on speed and paper surface. R.O.P. (run of paper) color inks are similar to other web inks. Since these inks do not harden, ink storage and drying are not problems. Misting, the fine spraying out of ink, is a problem on high-speed webs.

Special inks are designed both for image carriers and for the surface printed. Cartons printed from rubber plates require inks that will not harm the rubber. Other relief plates, such as plastic, nylon, photopolymer, and steel, require special formulations of ink. *Hot carbonizing, engraved* printing, and *magnetic* check printing are letterpress processes which require special inks.

Fig. 26-8 shows the relationship of paper and ink to the kind of form that is used in letterpress. It must wipe clean from the face of the plate before printing.

Magnetic inks use pigments such as iron oxide black. This pigment can magnetically store information after printing. The ink film thickness, the amount of pigment, and print quality are critical and require careful work.

Flexographic inks, used with flexible rubber plates, are highly fluid. The fluidity of the ink and drying speed require few rollers. Ink is fed from an engraved roller in a pan. The amount fed is determined by the depth of engraving in the roller. This rotary method prints flexible materials especially well. It is used for printing on films, foils, paper, and carton stocks.

Originally, flexographic inks were made of soluble dyes derived from analine, but modern inks contain insoluble pigments. The ink has a high percentage of solvents to make it fluid and dry rapidly. Alcohol is a common solvent. A film former, such as shellac or resin, is used to bind the pigment to the stock printed. Drying is by evaporation. Heat may be used to speed drying. Pigmented inks are more opaque and expensive than dye inks.

Much of the printing is for packaging materials. Generally, the printing is *roll to roll.* The printed web is rewound immediately after it is printed. Drying is accelerated by hot air or heat lamps. The paper or film web is then cooled by running it over water-chilled rollers. Additives to the ink are added for press stability and drying speed. Plasticizers and glycol-ethers extend drying time. Some oils are used to extend working properties.

The flexographic process has printing problems which usually involve ink. Many of the problems, such as *feathering* (ragged edges), *mottle* (patterns), and *fill in* of type or halftones, are related to drying speed. Other problems are contamination of the ink by water or moisture.

Some flexographic inks use water as a solvent. These are *water-based* inks. Pigments and film formers are soluble in water. These inks dry mainly by evaporation.

Letterpress Ink Coverage

The amount of ink required to cover the print varies with the paper and ink pigment. The chart in Fig. 26-9 shows the average coverage according to paper and pigment.

Offset Ink

Offset presses print by indirect lithography. As discussed earlier, ink is rolled on a grease-receptive plate, and the image is transferred to paper. This method requires ink that works well with water. The components of the ink must prefer a greasy surface. The pigments cannot be soluble in water (bleed). The *tinctorial strength* (intensity of color) must be great. The ink film transferred is thinner and requires a higher concentration of color than letterpress inks. Offset inks are formulated fairly tacky. As the press is run, the ink picks up water from the dampened plate. This *water-in-ink emulsion* reduces ink tack. The ink must resist the acidic nature of the water-dampening solution. To meet these and other requirements, offset inks are specially formulated for press, paper, drying, and end use.

Sheet-fed offset inks usually have litho oils and resins as vehicles. They dry by oxidation and polymerization. For high gloss, fast drying, and rub resistance, synthetic varnishes are used.

PAPER, INK, AND FORM RELATIONSHIP CHART FOR LETTERPRESS

Stock	Ink	Form
Antique Book	Bond or Job	Type, Line, HT* up to 85-Line
Bible	Bond (Hard drying)	Type, Line, HT up to 65-Line
Blotting (Wove finish)	Job	Type, Line, HT up to 65-Line
Blotting, Coated	HT (Suited to press)	Type, Line, and HT up to 150-Line
Bristol Index	Job (run gray)	Type, Line, and HT up to 100-Line
Cast Coated	Special (for best results)	Type, Line, HT up to 133-Line
Coated Blanks	HT	Type, Line, and HT up to 150-Line
Coated Book	HT (suited to press)	Type, Line, and HT up to 150-Line
Cockletone, Rippletone, and Linen Finishes	Bond or Job	Type, Line, and HT up to 85-Line
Cover, coated	HT or Gloss	Type, Line, HT up to 133-Line
Cover, uncoated	Cover	Type, Line
Dull coated	HT (suited to press)	Type, Line, HT up to 133-Line
Eggshell	Bond or Job	Type, Line, HT up to 85-Line
Enamel	HT or Gloss	Type, Line, HT up to 133-Line
Envelopes	Bond or Job	Type, Line, HT up to 85-Line
Featherweight	Job (hard drying)	Type, Line, HT up to 85-Line
Flint	Metallic (special)	Type, Line, HT up to 133-Line
Glassine	Special (Varnish)	Type, Line, HT up to 65-Line
Gummed	Job (for type and line) HT (for solids and HT)	Type, Line, HT up to 133-Line
Laid Finish	Bond	Type, Line, HT up to 65-Line
Laid Text	Bond	Type, Line, HT up to 85-Line
Ledger	Bond or Job mixture (run gray)	Type, Line, HT up to 65-Line
Litho, coated	HT	Type, Line, HT up to 120-Line
Manifold	Job	Type, Line
Metallic	Metallic or Overprint	Type, Line, HT up to 110-Line
Mimeo and Mimeo Bond	Job or News	Type, Line, HT up to 65-Line
Newsprint	News, HT or HT/Job mixture	Type, Line, HT up to 85-Line
Offset, regular	Job	Type, Line, HT
Parchment	Bond or Cover	Type, Line
Plate	Job (run gray)	Type, Line, HT up to 100-Line
Post Card	Job	Type, Line, HT up to 85-Line
Rag Content Bond	Bond	Type, Line, HT up to 85-Line
Safety (used for checks)	Bond (run gray)	Type, Line, HT up to 85-Line
Thin Papers (Onionskin)	Bond (hard drying)	Type, Line
Uncoated Book	HT or Soft Book	Type, Line, HT up to 120-Line
Vellum Cards	Bond or Job	Type, Line
Wove Finish	Job	Type, Line, HT up to 65-Line

* Halftone

26-8. Paper stock, ink, and form relationship for letterpress printing.

LETTERPRESS INK ESTIMATING CHART

	No. 1 Enamel	No. 2 Enamel	Litho Coated	S & SC* High Finish	S & SC Low Finish	MF Book	Dull Coat	Print Paper	Antique Book	Offset Stock	Bond Stock	Cover Stock
Blacks	250	200	200	225	175	160	150	150	110	125	110	100
Blue Lake	200	160	160	180	140	130	120	100	90	100	90	80
Bronze Blue	185	150	150	165	130	125	110	95	85	95	85	75
Cover Blue										70	65	55
Peacock Blue	190	150	150	170	130	120	115	95	95	95	95	75
Process Blue	190	150	150	150	170	130	120	115				
Bismark Brown	185	150	150	165	130	125	110	95	85	95	85	75
Photo Brown	200	160	160	180	140	130	120	100	90		90	
Chrome Green	120	95	95	100	85	75	70	60	55	60	55	50
Green Lake	200	160	160	180	140	130	120	100	90	100	90	80
Orange										70	70	60
Persian Orange	180	145	145	160	130	115	110	90	80	90	80	50
Purple Lake	200	160	160	180	140	130	120	100	90	100	90	50
Cover Red										60	60	50
Opaque Red	125	100	100	110	85	80	75	60	55	60	55	50
Process Red	190	150	150	170	130	120						
Transparent Red	200	160	160	180	140	130	120	100	90	100		
Cover White										60	55	50
Mixing White	120	95	95	110	85	80	70	60	55	60	55	50
Tint Base	270	215	215	240	190	175	150	120	135			
Transparent White	200	160	160	180	140	130	120	100	90	100	90	
Cover Yellow										70	70	60
Yellow Lake	185	150	150	165	130	125	110					
Process Yellow	125	100	100	110	85	80	75					
Aluminum Ink	135	130	130	130								
Gold Ink	60	55	55	55								
Overprint Varnish	300	250	250	270	210							

Figures above indicate the number of thousand square inches to the pound of ink.

No allowance for waste or washup has been made in the above figures.

For typeforms, figure on the basic of 15% of the above figures.

For solid forms which are the full size of the press bed, figure an additional 15% for excess color.

When one color is printed over another, the second impression will take 40% less than that required for the first impression.

26-9. This table shows the average letterpress ink coverage for various types of paper.

*Sized and supercalendered

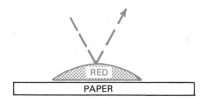

26-10. Mass tone light reflectance.

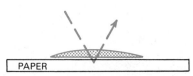

26-11. Undertone light reflectance.

Web press inks are made for high-speed equipment. Newspaper (publication) presses use nondrying oils that "dry" by penetration into absorbent stocks. Commercial web presses use inks that dry by evaporation. Heat is applied in ovens (dryers) that boil away solvents from resins and oils. All web inks require less tack than regular sheetfed inks.

Offset Ink Problems

Some ink problems are peculiar to the offset press. These are related to water, chemicals, transfer, and the nature of the paper printed. The process requires the ink film on the plate image to be split twice. The film is split when the image is transferred from the plate to the blanket. The film is split again as the blanket image is transferred to the paper. A thin coverage results.

From the fountain to the sheet, the ink is subjected to considerable abuse. It is worked by and drives friction rollers that spread it to a film. The film surface is subjected to heat by friction. The dampening system adds 5 to 25 percent water to this film, as water-in-oil emulsification. Tack is reduced. Transfer must only be to the ink-sensitive areas of the plate. Double image transfer to the paper is expected of an ink that must have an affinity for grease, rubber, and paper. It is subjected to fountain acids and paper surface chemicals. Yet it must make a print that is smooth, dense, and sharp. To do this offset inks are characterized by their *body, drying ability,* and *color.*

The body of the ink is identified by tack, length, and thixotropic condition. Tack is measured by the resistance to splitting. Length is the distance ink will stretch from an ink knife without dripping. As mentioned earlier, thixotropic condition is the nature of ink to gel when at rest and break down, or become less viscous, when worked.

Ink drying requires an ink that will not offset in the pile. It must dry despite higher humidity and presence of some acid. Yet it must not dry on the press or leave loose pigment on the paper surface. Many inks are supplied to the printer with the proper amount of dryer added.

The color of a thick body of ink is known as the *mass tone.* It is the color of light reflected from the ink body. Fig. 26-10. When an ink is spread into a thin transparent film on a paper, a color called the undertone is seen. The *undertone* is the color of light reflected from the paper through the ink. Fig. 26-11. Usually the print is a combination of mass tone and undertone. Ink color is also determined by the intensity of pigment coloration. The ability of the pigment to hold color when white ink is added is called the tinting strength. Mass tone, undertone, tinctorial strength, and paper color combine to determine ink color.

A common ink problem is *picking* on coated papers. Fig. 26-12. Picking means that the ink tears away part of the coating as the paper is printed. (This may be caused by excessive ink tack.)

Chalking is loose pigment on the paper surface. It is caused by excessive absorption of the vehicle by the stock. Insufficient vehicle is left on the surface to bind

26-12. Picking.

the pigment. Adding heavy varnish or using less absorptive paper can correct this problem.

Piling is a buildup of ink on rollers, plate, and blanket. It is sometimes called caking. This problem is caused by vehicle contamination. Usually, excessive water is transferred into the ink, reducing the vehicle's ability to transfer ink. Paper dust or linting can contaminate the vehicle, causing caking.

When ink is transferred into the dampening solution, it is known as an oil-in-water emulsion. This can cause a problem called *tinting*. A light, overall ink tint is transferred from the dampening system to the plate.

The surface of the paper printed can cause a chemical action in the ink, making the pigment "bleed" into the dampening solution. Changing stocks or ink usually remedies this problem.

Scumming is caused by ink transferred to desensitized (water-receptive) areas of the plate. Fig. 26-13. Excessive ink, soft ink, and improper fountain solution are causes of scumming. When the fountain solution is highly acidic, the plates may be etched. The plate loses the protective gum coating in nonimage areas of the plate. Loss of gum or wetting of the plate causes scumming in nonimage areas.

Printing *sharp* is a gradual loss of ink transfer to the paper. The print becomes weaker. Excess acid in the dampening system can be the cause. The acid may be attacking the plate image, making it more water-receptive and less ink-receptive. A high-tack ink may transfer poorly or

destroy the image surface. Ink that dries too fast may dry on rollers. The rollers can then lose their ability to transfer ink.

As mentioned in earlier chapters, ink is sometimes transferred from the face of one sheet to the back side of the sheet above in the delivery pile. This condition is called *offset*. Fig. 26-14. The sheets often stick together, ruining the printing. Offset occurs when the ink does not match the paper and press. Rough, absorbent papers are seldom affected by offset. Smooth and coated papers are offset when the ink fails to set before another sheet touches the ink print. Additives to the ink can reduce or eliminate offset. Fast-setting or *antioffset* compounds change the setting speed of ink. Reducing varnish thins and allows ink to penetrate fast. The ink vehicle can be shortened to speed up ink setting. Waxes and greases can be used in small amounts. These materials form a film over the ink print. The slick film adds rub resistance and re-

26-13. Scumming.

duces offset. Mechanical separation of the sheets with offset sprays reduces offset. Granular materials, such as starch, can be added in small amounts to the ink. These provide a gritty suface on the print, reducing offset. Offset can be reduced by: running a thinner ink film, racking sheets, eliminating static, and careful attention to solids while printing.

Ink Drying Problems

The setting of an ink produces a gel condition which later dries to a hard film. The *drying time* of ink should not exceed 24 hours. The drying time of ink is extended by: *excessive amounts of moisture, lack of oxygen,* and *cold.* Excessive moisture may come from a high relative humidity in the pressroom or in the paper. Acid from the dampening solution or in the paper also retards ink drying. A solution with a pH of 4.0 or less will retard or prevent ink drying. Printing papers seldom have a pH below 5.0. Higher pH (alkaline) paper speeds drying. Excessive alkalinity in a paper, however, can destroy or neutralize the acidity of the dampening solution.

Drying time is lengthy for inks that have little or no metallic dryers. The use of large amounts of weak or diluted dryers will prevent ink from drying. The amount of dryers in the ink must be adjusted to the surface of the stock, the vehicles in the ink, and the desired speed of drying. Conventional dryers for inks combine paste and cobalt. An ounce per pound of ink is considered maximum usage.

Oxygen for drying is available between and within the sheets of

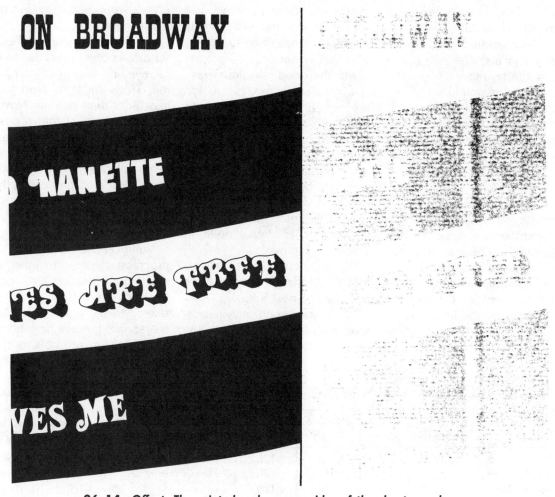

26-14. *Offset. The printed and reverse sides of the sheet are shown.*

paper in the delivery pile. Printing large solids requires abundant oxygen for proper drying. "Winding" sheets, racking sheets, and running ink concentrated and spare all aid in obtaining proper drying. Rough porous papers have fewer drying problems than smooth nonporous papers.

The room temperature, ink temperature, and delivery pile temperature affect the rate of drying. Drying time is shortened from the normal rate about 25 percent for each 10-degree Fahrenheit rise in temperature. Oxidation during drying creates heat. This in turn speeds up drying, creating more heat. Excessive heat by flame or in the pile can cause blistering and pigment blush, which is a loss of color in inks. Iron blues and chrome greens easily change color with excessive heat.

Ink manufacturers select pigments according to the customers' needs as well as pigment performance. The chart in Fig. 26-7 shows common pigments and their ability to withstand chemicals and printing conditions.

The actual drying time of an ink depends on the following conditions:

1. Humidity—amount in the air, paper, and moisture in the ink.

2. Temperature of ink in delivery pile.

3. Paper porosity relative to ink absorption and air movement.

4. Acidity of paper and dampening solution.

5. Ink film thickness. Generally, the heavier the inking, the longer the drying.

6. Amount and kinds of dryers used. Cobalt dryers are said to dry from the top of the ink film down to the paper. Paste dryers are said to dry from the paper surface up to the ink film surface.

7. The nature of the ink. Some pigments, due to their metallic composition, aid in the drying process. The blends of oils and varnishes that make up the ink vehicle affect the drying rate. When a second print is made on top of a print, the ink *traps* on the first ink. Failure to trap means the second ink will not adhere to the first ink. Usually the first ink has dried to the extent that nondrying oils are on top of the dried ink film. These oils, greases, or waxes are too slippery (insufficient tack) to hold the second ink. The first ink is said to have crystallized.

In wet multicolor or dry multicolor printings, trapping problems can be reduced by the following methods.

1. Do not use waxes, greases, or additional dryer in the first ink-down.

2. Do not permit the previous ink to thoroughly dry before printing the next ink.

3. Make certain each successive ink is less tacky than the previous ink used. (Consult with the ink maker.)

4. The ink amount necessary for proper coverage is due to the relative tinctorial strength of the ink. Thick ink films tend to be less tacky than thin ink films in the same kind of ink. (Consult ink maker for proper sequence.)

5. The drying effect seems to be cumulative on inks printed in succession on top of each other. The dryers in the previous inks tend to shorten the drying time of the later inks.

Multiple-color runs must be progressively closer together with single-color presses. Ink problems on web offset presses are related to the type of ink used. Newspaper presses have no dryers. They use absorption-drying inks. Commercial web offset presses with dryers generally use heat-set inks. Both have common ink problems related to the offset process. The heat-set inks also have problems with the solvents and resins. Problems of heat-set inks drying are related to the press dryer and chill rollers.

Drying with heat-set inks depends on the following:

1. Evaporation temperature of the solvent.

2. Temperature and length of press dryer.

3. Speed of web.

4. Moisture in ink and paper.

5. Ink temperature on leaving chill rollers.

The dryer cannot be heated above a temperature that would char or blister the paper. (*Blisters* are bubbles caused by liquid in the paper turning to vapor.) The press dryer is affected by the moisture content of the paper, ink evaporation, and ink cover-

OFFSET INK ESTIMATING CHART

Kind of Paper	Enamel	Label	Machine Finish	Antique	Offset
Blacks	350	240	180	135	135
Purple	300	240	170	120	115
Bronze Blue	325	240	180	130	140
Milori Blue	315	220	160	95	110
Trans. Green	310	235	180	120	110
Opaque Green	190	130	105	95	85
Yellow Lake	250	190	140	115	135
Lemon Yellow	225	160	120	85	80
Persian Orange	275	185	130	100	100
Opaque Orange	225	165	125	95	85
Semi-trans. Red	300	200	130	95	100
Opaque Red	225	170	120	95	95
Tint Base	375	240	180	125	120
White	200	120	100	80	80
Brown	300	210	140	100	110

The figures above are the number of thousand square inches that one pound of ink will cover. Measure with a ruler the amount of square inches of solid coverage on the copy. Multiply this figure by the number of impressions to be printed. Determine the amount of thousand square inches to be obtained from the shade to be printed from one pound of ink as shown on the chart. Divide this number into impressions × square inches covered.

26-15. *This table shows the average offset ink coverage for various types of paper.*

age. The ink will not dry if the boiling point of the ink solvent is above temperature limits in the dryer. The dry resin remaining after solvent evaporation can be tacky unless the paper is cooled by chill rollers.

Offset Ink Coverage

The amount of ink necessary to run a job depends on: length of run, kind of paper and surface, amount of coverage, kind of ink, and thickness of film. The paper surface's absorbency and the ink pigment are the greatest determiners of ink coverage. Fig. 26-15 shows sheet-fed coverage according to these factors.

RECENT DEVELOPMENTS IN INK DRYING

Newer methods of ink drying are being used. Most of these methods are linked to pollution abatement and the need for faster drying with less adverse effects on paper and inks. Some of these methods in use or under study are ultraviolet, microwave, chemical, and coating.

ULTRAVIOLET DRYING

Ultraviolet energy from a light source is used to agitate molecules in the ink film and cause them to cross-link. The molecules are monomers whose atoms vibrate and heat up when exposed to ultraviolet light. The heating causes the monomers to join together, cross-linking to "cure" the ink. This system is used largely with web presses and requires special inks. The ink dries in milliseconds, without effluents. Fig. 26-16 shows the various energy areas of the electromagnetic spectrum. This

26-16. *The electromagnetic wavelength spectrum.*

shows that the longer the wavelength and the lower the frequency, the less energy the wave carries.

MICROWAVE DRYING

Lower energy microwaves tend to generate heat in most of the ink vehicle but not the paper. While microwave drying is used in many industrial applications,

the cost and health hazard have limited its use in printing.

Drying occurs when heat causes resins or monomers to form into solids. Microwave drying requires expensive equipment and is used mainly on web presses.

CHEMICAL DRYING

In a sense, all inks change chemically when drying. Chemical drying refers to the deliberate attempt to cause a change through an *activator* or catalyst.

The activator triggers monomers to cross-link and form a chain (a polymer), thus becoming a solid. The activator itself is usually set free to change monomers by applying heat. The polymers most in use are epoxy resins and unsaturated polyesters. Common terms for the catalytic inks are solventless and solid-state inks.

OVERCOATING DRYING

Overcoating and heated drying have been in use for some time. The newer method is to coat wet ink with resins mixed in an emulsion with alcohol and water. The system is used on web presses, and drying is by solvent loss, causing the resin to harden. The coating is referred to as an *alcohol-soluble propinate* and is valuable because of the reduction in stock effluents and the speed of drying. The coater is usually positioned between the press units and the folder. The coating is 10 to 45 percent solids with a mixture of 75 percent isopropyl alcohol and 25 percent water. When a heavy coat is applied, a high gloss results. Thin coatings just to dry ink may not be economically practical.

689

LETTERPRESS
INK PROBLEMS

An ink correctly formulated will seldom present problems to the press operator. Information must be given to the ink maker for proper formulation. This information includes: type of printing equipment, complete information on paper, description and position of the image, use of ink in relation to other inks and varnishes, and the drying needs.

Many letterpress ink problems start with the misuse of general-purpose job inks. They are misused for specialized papers, presses, and drying conditions. Other problems begin with excessive use of additives to the ink. Adding less than enough is better than adding too much.

Ink problems—such as picking, chalking, piling, offset, trapping, drying, and others—are common to letterpress and offset. These problems were discussed under "Offset Ink Problems" in this chapter. Other letterpress ink problems are: backing away in the fountain, poor distribution, misting, thick or thin ink, dull gloss, slurring, strike-through, and mottling.

Some problems can be determined by testing the ink. Read the section on ink tests, later in this chapter.

Backing away means the ink does not flow to the fountain roller. Thus ink is not available to be spread by the fountain blade. Fig. 26-17. Printing will become lighter during the run as less ink is taken from the fountain. The ink may be too thick for the blade gap. The ink may be too "short" and need a "longer" varnish (binding varnish) added. An ink

J. M. Huber Corp.

26-17. Ink backing away from the fountain. The ink shown on the left is not following the fountain as it should. This condition is generally caused by a very short-bodied ink.

is called "short" if, when it is permitted to run off an ink knife, it falls in large drops. It is called "long" if it flows off the knife in a continuous, unbroken stream.

Improper ink flow may also be caused by the fountain and ink being clogged with paper fibers, dried ink, and dirt. Ink may have dried in a heavy film on the fountain roller. The ink may be "livered." An ink is referred to as livered when the vehicle has partially evaporated and the ink is in a gelled state.

The ink may also have excessive pigmentation or simply gel easily. Mechanical or hand agitation aids ink flow, preventing thixotropic gelling. Another reason for poor ink flow may be that the ink is simply too cold to flow.

Poor distribution may be a mechanical problem, an ink problem, or both. Improper roller settings and flat, swelled, or badly worn rollers cause poor and uneven distribution of ink. Slick rollers, the result of dried varnish and pigment filling the pores, impairs distribution of ink.

The ink may be too "short" to transfer. Heavily pigmented ink may not have enough vehicle to carry the pigment. The pigment can be too coarse or poorly mixed to transfer. The vehicle can be drawn away from the pigment while running.

Poor distribution causes piling on inking surfaces. Parts of rollers and the print may be without ink. The print will be uneven. Increasing the ink flow usually increases the problem.

Some inks are not compatible with plastic or synthetic rubber rollers. The ink maker can solve this problem. Before changing or "doping" the ink, proper roller settings and roller conditions must be determined. For ink that is too "short," add "long" varnish. For heavy ink, use reducing varnish. Poorly ground or poorly mixed inks should not be used.

Poor ink distribution can also be caused by any of the conditions related to ink backing away in the fountain. Linty stocks build up fibers on the rollers and in the fountain, causing poor distribution.

Misting refers to a fine spray of ink thrown from the rollers. It settles on the printing, the press, and surrounding area. Misting is a health and fire hazard.

Misting can be caused by thin inks on high-speed rollers. Ink is thrown outward by the centrifugal force of the roller. The ink should be "shortened" and made more viscous (sticky) with binding varnish. Slower press speeds reduce misting.

Thick or thin inks cause problems. Ink that is *thin* can cause problems other than misting. It is the source of mottled prints, skidding rollers, slurs, showthrough, and uneven printing. Where these conditions are general or severe, it is wiser to replace the ink.

Thick ink, like thin ink, is relative to the job for which the ink was designed. In *thin* inks, the vehicle-to-pigment ratios are too high. In *thick* ink, the reverse is true. Thick ink fails in the fountain and causes poor distribution.

Thick ink may be too tacky. It will pick the paper, fail to trap, and can heat and destroy rollers. Unless thick ink has "livered"

with age, a reducer can be added. A compound can lower the ink tack. It is easier to reduce an ink than to "body up," or thicken, an ink.

Loss of gloss detracts from the full appearance of a print. Ink gloss is determined by the gloss of paper and amount of ink varnish on the surface. When the ink is thin or the paper highly absorbent, the varnish is drawn into the paper. This action can be slowed by adding heavy (gloss) varnish. Faster drying by adding cobalt dryer helps. Changing ink to a resin type vehicle helps. A typical example is the use of halftone ink on a cast-coated sheet. The glossy, highly absorptive coating dulls conventional enamel halftone ink.

A *slur* is a blurred print. It is caused by rollers sliding on the form. Rollers slip because of roller conditions, improper settings, oily tracks, or thin ink. After correcting mechanical and roller conditions (out-of-round, swelled, slick, and so forth), the ink can be thickened with binding varnish or dry pigment.

A *mottle* is a speckled print. The mottled print has small patches of light and dark color.

Strike-through is the pattern of inky oil showing through the paper. It is seldom a problem of varnish vehicles. It can be a problem of nondrying oils in penetration-drying inks. News ink and mimeo inks can show strike-through. Like the dull gloss problem, it must be corrected by: thickening the inks, shortening the drying time, or using a less absorptive paper surface. Reducing the amount of ink used can reduce strike-through.

INK TESTS

The testing of inks is routine among ink manufacturers. Tests are made to determine the purity and quality of the materials used. Tests made during manufacture are concerned with accuracy of measurements and reliability of processing. Tests are also made on the finished product to control quality and determine usefulness of the ink for specific applications.

Almost all the ink used in small and moderate-sized printing plants is prepared in final form by the ink manufacturer or distributor. Large amounts are tailor-made for certain papers, presses, and usage. The final and most authoritative testing of any ink is the press and the print. The distributor and manufacturer of ink have the experience of thousands of inks and their performance in regard to the specific needs of press, paper, and print. They select pigments, vehicles, and additives which have a history of good performance.

The printer or press operator must determine the adequacy of a particular ink as it will actually be used. New inks can be compared with suitable inks already on hand. An ink log or record of the behavior of the ink is filed. By comparing inks before and after use, the press operator can evaluate new inks and known inks for specific work. Comparative ink testing is used to determine *running characteristics* and reliability of inks.

Running characteristics are ink properties required to easily print good work. Tests for running ink can be divided between those that examine the ease of

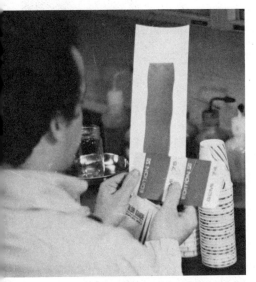

J. M. Huber Corp.

26-18. Color matching. *One of the most important functions of an ink maker is determining the relative color of an ink. This is generally accomplished by visual comparison of a print to the standard color.*

printing and those that consider the quality of the print. Figs. 26-18 through 26-21 show common laboratory tests to examine running characteristics of inks. Figs. 26-22 and 26-23 show two common ink problems that can occur during a press run.

End-use tests judge the ability of the print to withstand the ravages of weather, chemicals, and physical stress. Fig. 26-24 shows an instrument used to rub off ink from the surface of the sheet to determine handling and abrasion characteristics.

Running-ink testing deals with inking the image and making the print. A good running ink prints well with little or no attention by the press operator. Good ink is worked on the press. Poor ink works the press operator. A good running ink should be easy to

work. It should maintain body and print continuously without change. It should function without frequent supervision. In short, its performance must be reliable and predictable.

The press is the best testing device for ink. All other testing methods are designed to give information that *suggests* how the ink will run on the press. They are important because these tests can aid in determining working qualities of an ink before the job is printed.

ORDERING INKS

Since the ink is related to the paper, the process, and the skill of the operator, it is essential that the ink be ordered to balance the needs and requirements of the shop and the job. When ordering ink, the following

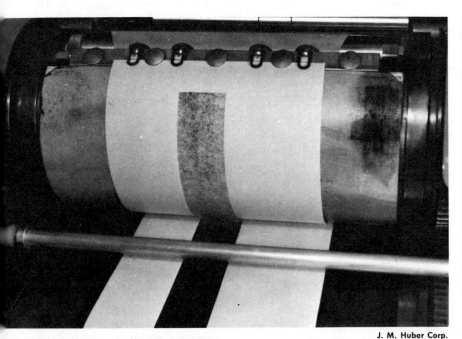

J. M. Huber Corp.

26-19. Ink offset test. *Offset is generally determined by running a print through a laboratory proofing press. The print comes in contact with a second sheet of paper that picks up any ink that is not "set" into the stock.*

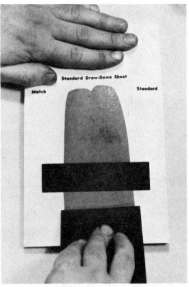

J. M. Huber Corp.

26-20. Draw-down test. *The draw-down is the basic tool of the ink industry to determine top tone, mass tone, and undertone of production batches versus a standard ink.*

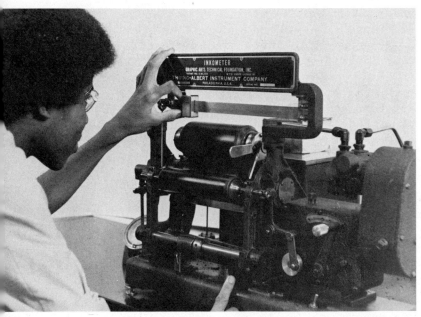

J. M. Huber Corp.

26-21. *Tack testing. Tack is measured on the Thwing-Albert inkometer. A volume of 1.3 cm³ of ink is evenly distributed on the inkometer and run at 1200 RPM with a roller temperature of 90 °F (32 °C).*

J. M. Huber Corp.

26-23. *"Ghosting"—the appearance of a faint image in an area that should be printing solid. This is attributed to improper setting of form rollers on the press.*

information should be sent to the supplier.

1. Printing process, the kind of plates, rollers, and press on which the job is to be printed.

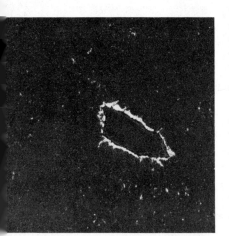

J. M. Huber Corp.

26-22. *"Hickey." The common cause of this phenomenon is an excess of paper fiber or clusters of fibers which build up on a plate.*

2. The kind of paper or surface on which the job is to be run, submitting a sufficient sample for proofing.

3. Nature of form, approximate coverage. Indicate solids, reverses.

4. Type of ink required (gloss, regular, heat-set, opaque, transparent, and so forth).

5. The sequence in which the colors are to be run, if one or more colors are to overprint others, and the time interval between colors.

6. Speed of drying required.

7. If the job is to be printed both sides, what is the time interval between printing the first and second side?

8. What kind of spray is used, if any?

9. What kind of press heaters are used, if any? What temperature?

J. M. Huber Corp.

26-24. *Rub test. The Sutherland ink rub tester is used to determine the rub qualities of an ink. This device uses a two-pound or four-pound weight with a rub strip attached. The number of rubs may be varied to increase or decrease the severity of the test.*

10. What degree of light-fastness is required?

11. What is the end use of the printed job?

Ink should be purchased in economical sizes and amounts. Most modern inks do not store for extended periods and should not be purchased for several years' usage. When buying for inventory, standard colors or mixes should be obtained only for those most commonly used. New orders received should be checked to determine color and consistency.

INK CARE

Inks are highly complex chemical combinations. They must be stored and preserved with care. All inks generally should be kept in an enclosed, fire-resistant metal cabinet, away from excessive temperatures and light.

All inks need to be covered to prevent drying or adulteration. All cans must be clearly labeled and have the date of purchase clearly marked. Special job inks should be identified with the job and kept apart from regular inks. The outside surfaces of cans and tubes should be free from ink spills. Ink cabinet shelves should be arranged by color, with ink grouped according to usage. Older inks should be moved to the front of the shelf, to be used first. Lids of small cans must be wiped clean and coated with oil on the inner side to facilitate removal at a later date. The practice of putting oil or water on top of ink to prevent drying causes adulteration and does not, in most instances, retard drying. Less ink is lost by drying if the ink is stored in small cans. Plastic caps, which are placed on top of ink, are used in place of lids and slow down oxygen-related drying.

When removing ink from the can, try to keep the surface level. Digging out ink leaves exposed holes in the ink. The walls of these holes dry. It is difficult to remove (skim) the dried film.

Cans must be opened carefully. The portion of label covering the lid sides is cut away, and a clean ink knife is placed against the lip of the lid. The lid is forced off by tapping the butt of the knife on a surface. Avoid damaging the lid during removal. It must fit tightly when put back on the can.

REVIEW QUESTIONS

1. What is the fluid part of ink called?
2. Ink must have ingredients which "fasten" the pigment to the paper. Varnish is one such ingredient. Name two others.
3. The purpose of solvents in ink is to keep film-forming materials liquid. True or False?
4. How do inks made with nondrying oils dry?
5. Drying by oxidation means that the vehicle absorbs oxygen and becomes solid. True or False?
6. In moisture-set drying, the ink is sprayed with glycol. True or False?
7. What is the coloring matter in ink called?
8. What is the function of wetting agents in ink?
9. Letterpress ink must be able to cling to metal and be attracted to grease. True or False?
10. Name the ink problems described in the following:
    a. Ink tears away part of the coating from the paper.
    b. Loose pigment on the paper surface.
    c. Ink transfers to water-receptive areas of plate.
    d. Buildup of ink on rollers, plate, and blanket.
    e. Transfer of ink from the face of one sheet to the back of another.

ANSWER KEY

Chapter 1

1. Copying and printing
2. Too slow, too expensive
3. Development of an original image; conversion of original image to printing-image carriers; inking of printing image; transfer of inked image
4. Spirit duplication; mimeograph; offset; letterpress; gravure; screen
5. False
6. True
7. True
8. True
9. False

Chapter 2

1. False
2. No
3. (Any four) Press operator, compositor, platemaker, bookbinder, stripper, proofreader
4. True
5. True
6. False
7. Press assistants
8. Offset

Chapter 3

1. The art department
2. Ready to be photographed
3. The metre
4. 1000
5. The kilogram
6. 6
7. 12
8. To measure the thickness of metal plates
9. 40
10. The length of a complete set of lowercase letters in one typeface
11. U.S. Secret Service
12. For the life of the author plus 50 years

Chapter 4

1. True
2. Use an editing terminal
3. Should be: Offset lithography is one of the most widely used of the printing processes.
4. Lower case, boldface, transpose
5. Cross-ing

Chapter 5

1. Serifs
2. True
3. False
4. Mechanical
5. True
6. False
7. Using the actual center would make the layout appear too low.
8. 32 × 43 picas
9. False
10. False
11. True
12. No
13. True
14. True
15. Fixative

Chapter 6

1. Yes
2. Composing lines that are exactly the same length
3. True
4. True
5. True
6. Optical character recognition
7. True
8. Video display terminal
9. (Any one) From a series of dots; from a series of line segments (vector generation); from a series of horizontal or vertical strokes
10. False

Chapter 7

1. False
2. A metal frame which holds the type in the press during printing
3. One
4. Type is upside down or from the wrong font.
5. False
6. True
7. Separating one line of type from another
8. Set without leads
9. True
10. Live matter

Chapter 8

1. A solid bar of metal with typefaces on top
2. Ludlow Typograph and Linotype
3. False
4. In a galley
5. They are melted, cast into bars (pigs), and reused.
6. Elektron
7. True

Chapter 9

1. False
2. Paste-up
3. Line, continuous tone, color
4. Line copy
5. Continuous tone copy
6. Reduction minimizes small imperfections.
7. Surprint
8. Other copy is printed in the blank area (mortise).
9. The image is photographed through a halftone screen.
10. 7 1/2"
11. 100%
12. True
13. True
14. A page number
15. False

Chapter 10

1. a. Copyboard
   b. Carriage
   c. Bellows
   d. Ground glass
   e. Lens
2. True
3. True
4. True
5. Enlarge
6. Exposure time

Chapter 11

1. False
2. Film
3. Magenta and gray
4. Use a densitometer.
5. The highlight
6. The shadow
7. Main, flash, and bump exposures

Chapter 12

1. False
2. Developer, stop bath, fixer (hypo)
3. To remove chemicals
4. To stop development during the inspection

5. False
6. True
7. True
8. True
9. True

Chapter 13

1. True
2. Separate flats used to expose the same plate
3. Separate flats used to expose separate plates
4. True
5. Underside (bottom)
6. a. Press sheet lines
   b. Gripper line
   c. Plate bend-over line
   d. Trim lines
   e. Image placement lines
7. Removing stripping base from image areas of film
8. True

Chapter 14

1. Yellow
2. True
3. True
4. False
5. During development
6. False
7. True
8. Small, rainbowlike circles between the film on a flat and the glass on a vacuum frame. They indicate good contact.
9. (Any one) Projection system, transfer system, direct-image system.

Chapter 15

1. Duplicators, sheet-fed offset, and web offset presses
2. a. Feeder system
   b. Delivery system
   c. Printing system
3. Single sheet and stream
4. Plate, blanket, and impression
5. Makeready
6. False
7. Packing affects cylinder diameters, and, consequently, their speeds. If the units of the press are not running at uniform speed, the plate life, printing quality, and the functioning of the press will be adversely affected.

Chapter 16

1. False
2. Fine adjustments of press settings will probably have to be made before the best results are obtained. It is more economical to use waste sheets during this time.
3. True
4. True
5. Inking, dampening, cylinder, plate, paper
6. True
7. Back-up register

Chapter 17

1. False
2. a. Incident light
   b. Hue
   c. Saturation
   d. Value
3. False

Chapter 18

1. a. Color separation
   b. Reflective copy
   c. Transmissive copy
   d. Printer
2. Cyan, magenta, and yellow
3. Yellow and magenta
4. Cyan and magenta
5. Rosette pattern
6. Electronic color scanning, direct screen method, indirect screen method
7. Electronic scanning, dot etching, photographic masking

Chapter 19

1. Photoengraving
2. True
3. a. Etching
   b. Wraparound plate
   c. Saddle
4. Stereotypes, electrotypes, rubber plates, and plastic plates
5. True
6. They can be plated with metal.

Chapter 20

1. a. Imposition
   b. Gripper edge
   c. Image area
   d. Face (or front)
   e. Signature
   f. Dummy
2. Two

3. One
4. True
5. Work-and-twist
6. Saddle assembling (or saddle gathering)
7. Rollers run out of ink before entire plate is covered.
8. False
9. a. Furniture
   b. Quoins

Chapter 21

1. a. Bed
   b. Feed table
   c. Vacuum suckers
   d. Platen
2. False
3. A printed sheet with tissue glued to areas where printed image is poor
4. To make a plate or engraving type-high
5. Pressing a design into paper to raise it above the surface of the sheet
6. They will develop a flat side.

Chapter 22

1. False
2. a. Impression cylinder grippers
   b. Bed
   c. Delivery board
3. True
4. True

Chapter 23

1. False
2. Work goes automatically from one operation to the next without stops.
3. False
4. Lip (or lap)
5. a. Lift
   b. Jogging
   c. Winding
6. False
7. Outsert can stand alone; insert is placed inside an outsert.
8. Collating (or gathering)
9. a. Perfect binding
   b. Saddle binding
   c. Paste binding
   d. Thread binding

Chapter 24

1. Silk
2. False

3. False
4. True
5. Liquid masking material
6. False
7. a. Textile ink
   b. Screen process ink
   c. Glass ink

Chapter 25

1. Cellulose
2. Hydraulic water pressure
3. False
4. a. Fillers
   b. Sizing
   c. Binders
5. 70%

6. Dandy roller
7. False
8. a. Fine paper
   b. Book paper
   c. Safety paper
   d. Onionskin
9. The weight of one ream of paper in the basic size
10. One square metre
11. a. Formation
    b. Porosity
    c. Moisture content
    d. Runability

Chapter 26

1. Vehicle

2. Resins and drying oils
3. True
4. By absorption into the paper
5. True
6. False
7. Pigments
8. They help the vehicle cover the pigment particles.
9. False
10. a. Picking
    b. Chalking
    c. Scumming
    d. Piling (or caking)
    e. Offset

INDEX